CW01658577

Chartered Institute of Housing

Help with Housing Costs: 2025-26

Universal credit, housing benefit, state pension credit, support for mortgage interest and council tax rebates

All the rules in a single volume

Sam Lister, Roger Thwaits
and Martin Ward

SHELTER

Guide to Housing Benefit and related titles
Peter McGurk and Nick Raynsford, 1982-88
Martin Ward and John Zebedee, 1988-93
John Zebedee and Martin Ward, 1993-2003
John Zebedee, Martin Ward and Sam Lister, 2003-12
Sam Lister and Martin Ward, 2012-14

Help with Housing costs: Guide to Housing Benefit
Sam Lister and Martin Ward, 2014-23
Sam Lister and Martin Ward and Roger Thwaits, 2023-24

Help with Housing costs: Universal Credit and Council Tax Rebates
Sam Lister and Martin Ward, 2014-23
Sam Lister and Martin Ward and Roger Thwaits, 2023-24

Help with Housing Costs: All the rules in a single volume
Sam Lister, Roger Thwaits and Martin Ward, 2024-26

Sam Lister is policy and practice officer at the Chartered Institute of Housing (email: *sam.lister@cih.org*) and a founding director of Citizens Advice Worcester and Citizens Advice Herefordshire. He has specialised in housing benefit and social security since 1993.

Roger Thwaits studies and writes about HB, CTR and UC. He has been involved with these schemes since they began in 1982, 1990 and 2013. At present he is focusing on supported accommodation and how vulnerable people's housing costs are met.

Martin Ward is an independent consultant and trainer on housing and benefit related matters (e-mail: *mward@knowledgeflow.org.uk*). He has provided consultancy services and training for several national organisations as well as many local authorities and large and small housing providers across the UK since 1982.

ISBN 978-1-7395388-1-1

Edited and typeset by Davies Communications
(www.daviescomms.com)

Printed by MBA Group Ltd

Chartered Institute of Housing

CIH is a registered charity and not-for-profit organisation. This means that the money we make is put back into the organisation and funds the activities we carry out to support the housing sector.

We have a diverse membership of people who work in both the public and private sectors in 20 countries on five continents across the world. We were granted a Royal Charter in 1984, and our work is governed by our Royal Charter and Byelaws, overseen by the Privy Council. We are also a registered charity, with education at the core of our charitable status.

Registered charity in England and Wales (244067) and Scotland (SC040324).

Chartered Institute of Housing
Suites 5 and 6
First Floor, Rowan House
Westwood Way
Coventry
CV4 8HS

Telephone: 024 7685 1700

E-mail: *customer.services@cih.org*

Website: *www.cih.org*

Shelter

Shelter exists to defend the right to a safe home and fight the devastating impact the housing emergency has on people and society. We do this with campaigns, advice and support – and we never give up. We believe that home is everything.

88 Old Street
London
EC1V 9HU

Telephone: 0300 330 1234

Website: *shelter.org.uk*

For online housing advice and access to our emergency helpline, visit *shelter.org.uk/housing_advice*

Registered charity in England & Wales (263710) and Scotland (SC002327).

Preface

This new guide explains how you can get help towards your rent, service charges, mortgage interest and council tax. It includes universal credit, housing benefit, state pension credit, support for mortgage interest and council tax rebates. It gives the rules that apply from 6 April 2025, using information available on that date.

We welcome comments and criticisms on the contents of our guide and make every effort to ensure it is accurate. However, the only statement of the law is found in the relevant Acts, regulations, orders and rules (chapter 1).

We are grateful for the help and encouragement of many people who have been essential to the writing and production of this guide. This year we would like to thank Julia Service at UC Notes and Susan Habermass at Metropolitan Thames Valley Housing.

Special thanks go to Richard Stanier for his invaluable comments and help throughout each year, John Zebedee for the original material, Linda Davies and Peter Singer for editing and production.

Sam Lister, Roger Thwaits and Martin Ward

April 2025

Contents

Chapter 1 **Introduction**

- Summary: paras 1.1-3
- The benefits you can get: paras 1.4-12
- Law and guidance: paras 1.13-16
- Monthly and weekly figures: paras 1.17-25

Welcome

1.1 This new guide explains how to get help with your rent, mortgage interest, service charges and council tax. It gives the rules from 6 April 2025 about universal credit (UC), state pension credit (SPC), housing benefit (HB), support for mortgage interest (SMI) and council tax rebates (CTR).

1.2 The guide is used throughout Great Britain by people claiming benefits, advisers, social and private landlords, benefit administrators and appeal tribunals.

1.3 The tables in this chapter:

(a) summarise which benefit or benefits you can claim (table 1.1)

(b) explain the main terms we have used (table 1.2)

(c) give recent statistics about households on benefits (table 1.3)

(d) show the main changes in benefit law since April 2024 (table 1.4).

Table 1.1 **What you can claim**

	Working age claims	**Pension age claims**
Renters		
Rent and service charge payments	UC	HB
But in supported or temporary accommodation	HB	HB
Owners		
Mortgage interest payments	SMI	SMI
Service charge payments	UC	SPC
Shared owners		
Rent and service charge payments	UC	HB
Mortgage interest payments	SMI	SMI
All		
Living costs	UC	SPC
Council tax	CTR	CTR

Table 1.2 **Terminology used in this guide**

Working age benefits

You can get UC or other working age benefits if you are under pension age, or you are in a couple and at least one of you is under pension age.

Pension age benefits

You can get SPC or other pension age benefits if you are over pension age, or you are in a couple and both of you are over pension age.

Pension age

Pension age is 66 for everyone. It is expected to start increasing to 67 in 2026.

Claimant

A claimant is someone who is making a claim for benefit or someone who is getting benefit.

Joint claimant

If you are in a couple, you usually have to make a joint claim for UC. For SPC, HB and CTR, one of you claims on behalf of you both and you are referred to as 'claimant' and 'partner'.

Benefit unit

Your benefit unit means you (both of you if you are in a couple) and any children and young persons you are responsible for.

Extended benefit unit

Your extended benefit unit means your benefit unit and any non-dependants who live in your household.

Single person

You are a single person if you aren't in a couple. You are called a single person whether or not you have children or young persons.

Couple

You are a couple if you are two people who are married, in a civil partnership, or living together as a couple. You are called a couple whether or not you have children or young persons.

Child

A child is someone under 16.

Young person

A young person is someone aged 16 to 19 who is in secondary education or has just left it.

Non-dependant

A non-dependant is an adult son, daughter, relative or friend who lives with you on a non-commercial basis.

Supported or temporary accommodation

This means accommodation where you receive support or where you were placed because you were homeless, but only if it meets one of the definitions in table 13.1.

General accommodation

This means any other kind of rented accommodation.

Renter, tenant and tenancy

Renter, tenant and tenancy refer to any kind of rent-payer (for example a licensee).

Landlord and agent

Your landlord is the person with the right to let your home. Your landlord may manage your tenancy and collect your rent, or may have an agent who does this.

Social renter rules

If you rent from the council or a registered housing association, your housing costs are usually calculated using the social renter rules.

Private renter rules

If you rent from a private landlord or a company, firm or similar, your housing costs are usually calculated using the private renter rules.

Local housing allowances

LHAs are the main way of calculating eligible rent under private renter rules.

Assessment periods in UC

UC is assessed on a monthly basis. Your first assessment period begins on the day you claim UC and the following ones start on the same date each month.

Benefit weeks in SPC or HB

SPC and HB are calculated on a weekly basis. In SPC, your benefit weeks can start on any day of the week. In HB, they always start on a Monday.

Housing costs element in UC

Your housing costs element (HCE) is the full amount of rent and service charges that UC can meet.

Eligible rent in HB

Your eligible rent is the full amount of rent and service charges that HB can meet.

Housing cost contributions/non-dependant deductions

If you have one or more non-dependants, they may be expected to contribute towards your rent. These are called housing cost contributions in UC or non-dependant deductions in HB.

Capital

Capital means savings, investments etc. In a couple, both partners' capital is included. If you/your partner have capital over £16,000 (apart from disregarded capital), you can't get UC or HB.

Income

Income means earnings, benefits etc. In a couple, both partners' income is included. If you/your partner have income (apart from disregarded income), your UC, SPC or HB are reduced.

The benefits you can get

Benefits if you have a working age claim

1.4 You have a working age claim if you are single and under pension age (currently 66), or you are in a couple and at least one of you is under pension age.

1.5 Working age claimants can get:

(a) UC towards your living costs
(b) UC towards your rent and service charges in general accommodation
(c) HB towards your rent and service charges in supported or temporary accommodation
(d) SMI towards your mortgage interest payments
(e) UC towards your service charges if you are an owner
(f) CTR towards your council tax.

But you continue to get HB in general accommodation if you have been getting HB since before 12 December 2018 (or, in some postcodes, since before an earlier date) and haven't yet transferred to UC.

Benefits if you have a pension age claim

1.6 You have a pension age claim if you are single and over pension age (currently 66), or you are in a couple and both of you are over pension age.

1.7 Pension age claimants can get:

(a) SPC towards your living costs
(b) HB towards your rent and service charges in general accommodation (para 1.11)
(c) HB towards your rent and service charges in supported or temporary accommodation
(d) SMI towards your mortgage interest payments
(e) SPC towards your service charges if you are an owner
(f) CTR towards your council tax.

Claims for benefit

1.8 You get UC and SPC by claiming them from the DWP, and you can get SMI as part of that claim. You get HB and CTR by claiming them from your local council. It is easy to claim any of these benefits online. You need to have your national insurance number and details of your capital and income. For SPC you can alternatively claim by telephoning 0800 991234.

1.4 WRA 4(1)(b), SPCA 1(2)(b), 4(1A); UC 3(2)(a); UCTP 6A(4)

1.5 WRA 8(2); WRWA 18; LGFA 13A(1), 80(1),(2); UCTP 6A(2); UC sch 1 paras 3, 3A, 3B; LMI 3

1.6 Pensions Act 1995, sch 4 para 1(6); SPCA 1(2)(b), 4(1A); UCTP 6A(4); HBP 5

1.7 SPCA 2(3); SSCBA 130(1); WRWA 18; LGFA 13A(1), 80(1),(2); PC 6; UCTP 6A(4); HBP 5, 12(1); LMI 3

1.8 SSAA 1(1A)-(1C),(4)(za),(ab),(b); UC(C&P) 8; SS(C&P) 4ZC(2)(k), 4D(6A), sch 9ZC; HBW 83A sch 11; HBP 64A sch 10

Payments of benefit

1.9 The following are the main rules:

(a) UC is based on assessment periods of one month. You are usually paid at the end of these, or your landlord can be paid part of your UC.

(b) SPC is based on benefit weeks. You are usually paid fortnightly or four weekly, or your landlord can be paid part of your SPC.

(c) HB is based on benefit weeks. You are usually paid four weekly. If you are a council renter your HB goes straight to your rent account. In other cases, your landlord can be paid your HB.

(d) SMI is based on monthly periods. You are usually paid at the end of these and the payments go straight to your mortgage lender. SMI is a long-term loan towards your mortgage interest or similar payments.

(e) CTR is based on benefit weeks and goes straight to your council tax account.

Legacy benefits that are being replaced

1.10 UC has largely replaced the 'legacy benefits', and the transfer to UC should be completed by April 2026 at the latest. The legacy benefits are:

(a) HB for working age claimants, unless you live in supported or temporary accommodation

(b) JSA(IB) – income-based jobseeker's allowance

(c) ESA(IR) – income-related employment and support allowance

(d) IS (income support)

(e) child tax credit and working tax credit.

All tax credit cases ended or migrated to UC on or before 5 April 2025.

1.11 From 2026, SPC is expected to start replacing HB for pension age claimants, unless you live in supported or temporary accommodation.

Other benefits

1.12 The following benefits continue alongside UC and SPC:

(a) HB if you live in supported or temporary accommodation

(b) (until 2028) HB for pension age claimants

(c) DHPs (discretionary housing payments)

(d) benefits towards disability costs (e.g. PIP, DLA etc)

(e) new style JSA (previously called JSA(C))

(f) new style ESA (previously called ESA(C))

(g) benefits for carers, child benefit and all other state benefits.

1.9 WRA 7; SSAA 134; UC 21; UC(C&P) 47; PC 1(1) – 'benefit week', 6; SS(C&P) 26B, 26BA; HBW 2(1) – 'benefit week', 92; HBP 2(1), 73

1.10 WRA 33, sch 6; UCTP 5(1), 6A

1.11 WRA 34, sch 4

1.12 UCTP 2(1) – 'new-style ESA', 'new-style JSA'; 6A(2),(4); DFA 1(2) – 'relevant award of universal credit', 2(1)

Examples: Help with housing costs

1. A single tenant under 66

Priti is a single person under 66 who rents her home. She meets the conditions for getting benefit (chapter 2), so she can get:

- UC towards her living needs and her rent
- CTR towards her council tax.

2. A single tenant over 66

Len is a single person over 66 who rents his home. He meets the conditions for getting benefit, so he can get:

- SPC towards his living needs
- HB towards his rent
- CTR towards his council tax.

3. A shared owner couple both under 66

Jane and Olu are a couple both under 66 who are shared owners (part renting and part buying their home). They meet the conditions for getting benefit, so they can get:

- UC towards their living needs and rent
- SMI towards their mortgage interest
- CTR towards their council tax.

4. A home owner couple both over 66

David and Katerina are a couple both over 66 who are buying their home on a mortgage. They meet the conditions for getting benefit, so they can get:

- SPC towards their living needs
- SMI towards their mortgage interest
- CTR towards their council tax.

5. A single person living in supported accommodation

Aaron is a single person under 66 who lives in supported accommodation. He meets the conditions for getting benefit, so he can get:

- UC towards his living needs
- HB towards his rent.

Law and guidance

Statute law and case law

1.13 Statute law means acts, regulations and orders passed by the government. Case law means judgments made by the Upper Tribunal, the High Court, the Court of Appeal, the Sheriff's Court, the Court of Session and the Supreme Court. Statute law and case law are binding on decision makers such as the DWP and local councils.

1.14 Statute law is given in the footnotes and in appendix 1. Case law is given in the text. Statute law and case law are available online as shown in the footnote to this paragraph.

Government guidance

1.15 Government guidance advises decision makers about how to interpret the law, but isn't binding on them. Guidance is given in the text. It is available online as shown in the footnote to this paragraph.

Abbreviations

1.16 Appendix 4 gives a list of abbreviations used in the text, and a key to the abbreviations used in the footnotes.

Monthly and weekly figures

1.17 This section gives the rules that result from UC being a monthly benefit and SPC and HB being weekly.

Time limits

1.18 When we give combined time limits (e.g. 'three months/13 weeks'), the monthly one applies to monthly benefits and the weekly one to weekly benefits.

Converting unearned income or housing costs to a monthly figure for UC

1.19 To convert unearned income, rent or other housing costs to a monthly figure for UC:

(a) multiply weekly payments by 52 then divide by 12

(b) multiply two-weekly payments by 26 then divide by 12

(c) multiply four-weekly payments by 13 then divide by 12

(d) multiply three-monthly payments by 4 then divide by 12

(e) divide annual payments by 12.

If your unearned income fluctuates, the monthly amount is calculated over any identifiable cycle, or if there isn't one, over three months or whatever period would give a more accurate result. For earned income see paras 22.8 and 23.13.

1.14 Legislation: www.legislation.gov.uk
Courts England and Wales: https://caselaw.nationalarchives.gov.uk/
Older court cases: www.bailii.org
Upper Tribunal from 2016: www.gov.uk/administrative-appeals-tribunal-decisions
Older Upper tribunal: https://administrativeappeals.decisions.tribunals.gov.uk/Aspx/default.aspx

1.15 UC-DWP ADM: www.gov.uk/government/publications/advice-for-decision-making-staff-guide
UC Operational Guidance (OG): https://depositedpapers.parliament.uk/depositedpaper/2286620/details
SPC-DWP DMG: www.gov.uk/government/collections/decision-makers-guide-staff-guide
HBGM: www.gov.uk/government/collections/housing-benefit-and-council-tax-benefit-manual
HB circulars: www.gov.uk/government/collections/housing-benefit-for-local-authorities-circulars

1.19 UC 73(2),(3), sch 4 para 7(2)

Monthly housing costs for UC if you have rent-free periods

1.20 If you are a renter and have rent-free periods, you can get UC towards your rent even during the rent-free periods, because all your annual payments are averaged over a full year. First calculate the annual figure as follows:

(a) if your payments are weekly, subtract the number of rent-free weeks from 52, and multiply your weekly payment by the result

(b) if your payments are two-weekly, subtract the number of rent-free two-weeks from 26, and multiply your two-weekly payment by the result

(c) if your payments are four-weekly, subtract the number of rent-free four-weeks from 13, and multiply your four-weekly payment by the result

(d) in any other case, add together all the payments you are liable to make over a 12 month period.

Then divide the result by 12.

Converting income to a weekly figure for SPC or HB

1.21 To convert any kind of income to a weekly figure for SPC or HB:

(a) if it is for a multiple of weeks, divide by the number of weeks it covers

(b) if it is for a calendar month, multiply by 12 then divide by 52

(c) if it is for a year and you have a pension age claim, divide the annual amount by 52

(d) if it is for a year and you have a working age claim, divide the annual amount by 365 or 366 then multiply by seven

(e) if it is for any other period longer than a week, divide the amount by the number of days it covers, then multiply by seven

(f) if it is for a period less than a week, that is the weekly amount.

Converting housing costs to a weekly figure for SPC

1.22 To convert owner service charges or other housing costs to a weekly figure for SPC:

(a) add together all the payments for a year

(b) then divide the result by 52.

Converting housing costs to a weekly figure for HB

1.23 To convert rent or other housing costs to a weekly figure for HB:

(a) if it is due in multiples of weeks, divide by the number of weeks it covers

(b) if it is due calendar monthly, multiply by 12 then divide by 52

(c) if it is due daily, multiply by seven to find the weekly figure.

1.20 UC sch 4 para 7(3),(3A),(4)

1.21 PC 17(1); HBW 33; HBP 33(1)

1.22 PC sch 2 para 13(3)

1.23 HBW 80(2); HBP 61(2)

Weekly rent for HB if you have rent-free periods

1.24 If you are a renter and have rent-free periods, you can only get HB during the periods when rent is due, not during the rent-free periods. During those periods, the calculation factors (your applicable amount, income and any non-dependant deductions) are adjusted as follows:

(a) if your rent is a weekly amount, multiply the calculation factors by 52 or 53, then divide by the number of weeks when rent is due in that year;

(b) in any other case, multiply the calculation factors by 365 or 366, then divide by the number of days when rent is due in that year.

Converting the benefit cap to weekly or monthly figures

1.25 The benefit cap is an annual figure and is converted as follows:

(a) divide by 52 to give a weekly figure or

(b) divide by 12 to give a monthly figure.

Table 1.3 **Households getting help with rent**

Working age households receiving help with rent	
(a) On UC renting from a social landlord	2,157,397
(b) On HB renting from a social landlord	729,464
(c) On UC renting from a private landlord	1,611,189
(d) On HB renting from a private landlord	150,660
Pension age households receiving help with rent	
(e) On HB renting from a social landlord	889,504
(f) On HB renting from a private landlord	214,629

Note: Source DWP Stat-Xplore, figures for November 2024

1.24 HBW 81; HBP 62

1.25 UC 80A(1); PC sch 2 para 13(3); HBW 75CA(1)

Table 1.4 **Summary of UC and HB changes from April 2024**

6 Apr 2024 SI 2024/11	LHA rates restored to the 30th percentile rent based on the rent officer's list of rents for the year ending 30 September 2023, subject to the national limits (para 12.18). National limits raised by 18.6% for the four-bedroom rate and by between 12.1% and 12.8% for the other sizes of accommodation.
13 May 2024 SI 2024/536	The administrative earnings threshold is raised to the monthly equivalent of working 18 hours per week at the national living wage or a single person and to 29 hours per week for a couple (para 4.13).
8 Jun 2024 SI 2024/604 SI 2024/611	Various new forms of transitional protection are introduced for working-age couples, mixed-aged couples, and pension age claimants who receive a tax credits closure notice and go through managed migration. These ensure the claimants' new UC/SPC award is no less than their legacy benefits or SPC and tax credits immediately before they migrated.
10 Oct 2024 SI 2024/964	Certain payments from the estate of a deceased infected person that were derived from an approved blood scheme for people infected by NHS blood products are disregarded as capital in HB and SPC.
21 Oct 2024 SI 2024/919	Consequential changes arising from the introduction of pension age disability payment (PADP) in Scotland which replaces attendance allowance.
29 Nov 2024 SI 2024/1092	Annual changes to the HB subsidy rules.
27 Jan 2025 SI 2025/3	Further consequential changes as a result of the introduction of PADP and final closure of tax credit awards.
28 Feb 2025 SI 2025/44	Minor changes to capital disregards for disasters, emergencies, etc (para 21.43).
21 Mar 2025 SI 2025/227	Consequential changes arising from the introduction of adult disability allowance in Scotland which replaces DWP's DLA.
5 Apr 2025 SI 2024/611	Final closure of remaining CTC and WTC awards as part of phase one managed migration.
31 Jan 2025 06 Apr 2025 SI 2025/5	LHA rates frozen during 2025-26 at their April 2024 cash level.
1/6 Apr 2025 SI 2025/295	Benefits up-rating based on September 2024 consumer prices index of 1.7 percent and July 2024 average earnings of 4.1 percent for SPC.

Planned changes

Sep 2024 - 2026	Second phase of managed migration to UC. Remaining ESA(IR) awards without tax credits migrate to UC. Full roll out of UC expected to be completed by April 2026 (Autumn Budget 2024, HC 295, para 4.113).
2025 or 2026	Changes to the rules for HB in supported accommodation (table 13.1 to improve the quality and value for money and in England to underpin the licensing requirements being introduced under the Supported Housing (Regulatory Oversight) Act 2023 (para 13.2). (Supported Housing regulation: consultation, MLCLG/DWP 20 February 2025.)
2025 or 2026	Reform of the work capability assessment (WCA) so that the activities and descriptors are based on how PIP is assessed. Changes start on a new-claims only basis (Work Capability Assessment, DWP 2023, CP 930; Autumn Statement 2023, CP 977, para 3.34 and Autumn Budget 2024, HC 295, para 3.45).
2026 onwards	Start of the merger of pension age HB with SPC on a new-claims only basis at first. The merger will create a new 'housing credit' element of SPC. At some point yet to be determined existing pension age HB caseload will undergo managed migration to SPC. (Hansard, House of Commons Debates, Vol 752, 29 July 2024, Col 1038; Autumn Budget 2024, HC 295, para 4.111; Welfare Reform Act 2012, s33, schedule 4).
Apr 2026 – Mar 2028	State pension age is gradually rising from 66 to 67 (Pensions Act 1995, s126, sch 4 para 1(7)-(8)).

Chapter 2 **Who can get benefit**

- Universal credit: paras 2.5-9
- State pension credit: paras 2.10-15
- Housing benefit: paras 2.16-19
- Council tax rebates: paras 2.20-23
- Support for mortgage interest: paras 2.24-25
- Financial conditions: paras 2.26
- Housing costs conditions: paras 2.27-32
- Couple cases in more detail: paras 2.33-42

Summary

2.1 This chapter explains who can get universal credit (UC), state pension credit (SPC), housing benefit (HB), council tax rebates (CTR) and support for mortgage interest (SMI).

The conditions for getting benefit

2.2 For each of the benefits:

(a) you must make a claim (chapter 32)

(b) you must meet the basic conditions (paras 2.5-25)

(c) you must meet the financial conditions (para 2.26) and

(d) to get help with housing costs you must meet the housing costs conditions (paras 2.27-32).

Working age and pension age claims

2.3 Benefits can be for working age claims, pension age claims, or both age groups:

(a) you can make a working age benefit claim if:

- you are single and under pension age or
- you are in a couple and at least one of you is under pension age

(b) you can make a pension age benefit claim if:

- you are single and over pension age or
- you are in a couple and both of you are over pension age.

2.2 WRA 3, 11; SPCA 1-3, SSAA 1(1); SSCBA 130(1),(3); LGFA 13A, 80, sch 1A para 2, sch 1B paras 3, 4

2.3 WRA 3, 4(1)(b),(4); SPCA 1(2)(b),(6), 4(1A); UCTP 6A(1),(2),(4),(5); HBW 5; HBP 5; CTRE(PR) 3, 14, 15; CTRW(PR) 3, 22-25; CTRSW 3; CTRSP 12

Pension age

2.4 Pension age is currently 66, and in this guide we use 'over 66' to mean aged 66 or more. Pension age is expected to increase to 67 during 2026-28.

Universal credit

Who can get UC

2.5 UC is for both living costs and housing costs:

(a) to get UC, you must meet the conditions in table 2.1

(b) to get UC towards housing costs you must also meet the housing costs conditions (para 2.28).

And in all cases, you must make a claim and meet the financial conditions (para 2.26).

Housing costs UC can meet

2.6 UC helps with rent and service charges for working age renters and shared owners, and service charges for working age owners.

Table 2.1 **Basic conditions for UC**

Conditions

(a) You must be under pension age (under 66)

(b) You must be over 16

(c) You must not be an excluded 16 or 17 year old

(d) You must not be an excluded student

(e) You must not be an excluded migrant

(f) You must not be a prisoner or member of a religious order

(g) You must in most cases be in the UK

(h) You must accept a claimant commitment if required to do so

Notes:

- Conditions (c)-(h) are explained in chapters 3 and 4
- Single people must meet all the conditions
- In a couple, at least one must be under pension age and meet the other conditions

---

2.4 Pensions Act 1995, sch 4 para 1(6)-(8); WRA 4(4); SPCA 1(6); HBW 2(1) – 'qualifying age for state pension credit' HBP 2(1); CTRE(PR) 2(1); CTRW(PR) 2(1); CTRSW 4(1) – 'pensionable age'; CTRSP 2(1)

2.5 WRA 1(3), 3, 4(1), 5, 11(1)-(3); SSAA 1(1),(4)(za)

2.6 WRA 11(1)-(3); UC 25(1),(2)(a),(c), 26(2)-(4)

T2.1 WRA 4, 6(1)(a); UC 8, 9, 11, 14, 19; IAA 115(1),(3)

UC if you are single

2.7 If you are a single person, you must meet all the basic conditions to get UC. You make the UC claim, you get the single rate of UC, and your own income and capital is taken into account.

UC if you are claiming as a joint claim couple

2.8 You get UC as a joint claim couple if:

(a) you both meet all the basic conditions or

(b) you both meet all those conditions except that (only) one of you is:

- over 66 or
- an excluded student.

You jointly make the UC claim, you get the couple rate of UC, and both you and your partner's income and capital is taken into account.

UC if you are in a couple but claiming as a single person

2.9 You get UC as a single person (although you are in a couple) if:

(a) you (the claimant) meet all the basic conditions and

(b) your partner is:

- an excluded 16 or 17 year old
- an excluded migrant
- a prisoner or member of a religious order or
- absent from the UK.

You make the UC claim, you get the single rate of UC, but both you and your partner's income and capital is taken into account.

Example: UC in a couple but claiming as a single person

Vicky and Dave are a couple in their 40s. Vicky meets all the basic conditions for UC. Dave meets all those conditions except that he is in prison on a sentence of three months.

- Vicky can make a claim for UC
- She qualifies for the single rate of UC (not the couple rate)
- But both Vicky and Dave's income and capital is included in the UC claim.

2.7 WRA 3(1), 5(1)

2.8 WRA 3(2), 5(2)

2.9 WRA 4(2); UC 3, 18(2), 22(3)

State pension credit

Who can get SPC

2.10 SPC is for both living costs and housing costs:

(a) to get SPC, you must meet the conditions in table 2.2

(b) to get SPC towards housing costs you must also meet the housing costs conditions (para 2.28).

And in all cases, you must make a claim and meet the financial conditions.

2.11 There are two kinds of SPC:

(a) the guarantee credit of SPC is the only kind you can get if you are making a current claim

(b) the savings credit of SPC was abolished on 6 April 2016 unless you reached pension age before that date.

In this guide, 'SPC' always means the guarantee credit unless we state otherwise.

Housing costs SPC can meet

2.12 SPC helps with service charges for pension age owners, rent paid by Crown tenants and certain other payments that aren't included in HB (table 17.2 and paras 17.15-18).

Table 2.2 **Basic conditions for SPC**

Conditions

(a) You must be over pension age (over 66)

(b) You must not be an excluded migrant

(c) You must not be a prisoner or member of a religious order

(d) You must in most cases be in the UK

Notes:

- Conditions (b)-(d) are explained in chapter 3
- Single people must meet all the conditions
- In a couple, both must be over pension age and at least one must meet the other conditions

2.10 SPCA 1(2),(3), 2(1),(3); SSAA 1(1),(4)(ab); PC 6(1),(6)(c)

2.11 SPCA 1(3), 3(1)

2.12 SPCA 2(3); PC 6(6)(c), sch 2 paras 1(1)(b), 13(1)

T2.2 SPCA 1(2), 2(3),(9); IAA 115(1),(3); PC 6(2),(3)

SPC if you are single

2.13 If you are a single person, you must meet all the basic conditions to get SPC. You make the SPC claim, you get the single rate of SPC, and your own income and capital is taken into account.

SPC if you are claiming as a couple

2.14 You get SPC as a couple if

(a) you are both over pension age and

(b) you both meet the other basic conditions.

One of you makes the SPC claim on behalf of you both, and you are called 'claimant' and 'partner'. You get the couple rate of SPC, and both you and your partner's income and capital is taken into account.

SPC if you are in a couple but claiming as a single person

2.15 You get SPC as a single person (although you are in a couple) if:

(a) you are both over pension age

(b) you (the claimant) meet all the basic conditions and

(c) your partner is:

- an excluded migrant
- a prisoner or member of a religious order or
- absent from the UK.

You make the SPC claim, you get the single rate of SPC, but both you and your partner's income and capital is taken into account.

Example: Claiming SPC as a couple

Phil and Liz are a couple in their 70s. They meet all the basic conditions for SPC.

- Phil and Liz can make a claim for SPC
- They qualify for the couple rate of SPC
- And both Phil and Liz's income and capital is included in the SPC claim.

2.13 SPCA 1(3), 2(1)-(3),(5)(b); PC 6(1)(b),(6), 14

2.14 SPCA 1(2),(3), 2(1)-(3),(5)(a), 4(1A), 5; PC 5(1)(a)-(h), 6(1)(a),(6), 14

2.15 PC 5(1)(c),(d),(f),(h), 14

Housing benefit

Who can get HB

2.16 HB is for housing costs (not living costs). To get HB:

(a) you must meet the conditions in table 2.3

(b) you must also meet the housing costs conditions (para 2.28).

And you must make a claim and meet the financial conditions (para 2.26).

Housing costs HB can meet

2.17 Pension age HB helps with rent and service charges for renters and shared owners. Working age HB does the same but only if:

(a) you live in supported or temporary accommodation (tables 13.1 and 13.2) or

(b) you have been getting HB in general accommodation since before 12 December 2018 (or, in some postcodes, since before an earlier date) and haven't transferred to UC since then.

Table 2.3 **Basic conditions for HB**

Conditions

(a) If you live in general accommodation, you must be over pension age (over 66)

(b) If you live in supported or temporary accommodation (STA), you can be any age

(c) You must not be an excluded 16 or 17 year old (para 3.6)

(d) You must not be an excluded student (para 3.14)

(e) You must not be an excluded migrant (para 40.2)

(f) You must not be a prisoner or member of a religious order (paras 3.23, 3.26)

(g) You must in most cases be in the UK (para 8.30)

Notes:

- Conditions (c)-(g) are explained in chapter 3
- Single people must meet all the conditions
- Some people under pension age remain on HB in general accommodation because they haven't yet transferred to UC (para 2.17)

2.16 SSCBA 130(1),(3), 134(1); SSAA 1(1),(4)(b)

2.17 WRA 33(1)(d), 36, sch 6; SSCBA 130(1)(a),(2); UCTP 6A(2),(4); HBW 12(1)(a),(e); HBP 12(1)(a),(e)

T2.3 SSCBA 130(1), 134(1), 137(2)(a),(f),(h)-(k); IAA 115(1)(j); CLCA 6(1)-(4); UCTP 6A(1),(2),(4); HBW 7(13),(13D), 9(1)(j), 10, 56(1); HBP 7(13),(13D), 9(1)(j), 10

HB if you are single

2.18 If you are a single person, you must meet all the basic conditions to get HB. You make the HB claim, you get the single rate of HB, and your own income and capital is taken into account.

HB if you are in a couple

2.19 You get HB as a couple if:

(a) you (the claimant) meet all the basic conditions and

(b) your partner meets all those conditions, or meets them all except for being:

- an excluded migrant
- a prisoner or member of a religious order or
- absent from the UK.

You make the HB claim on behalf of you both, and you are called 'claimant' and 'partner'. You get the couple rate of HB, and both you and your partner's income and capital is taken into account.

Example: Claiming HB as a single person

Sean is a single man in his 20s getting UC. He moves from a relative's home to a hostel which counts as supported accommodation (table 13.1).

- Sean can make a claim for HB
- He qualifies for the single rate of HB
- Sean's income and capital are disregarded in his HB claim because he is on UC .

2.18 SSCBA 130(1); HBW 22(1), 25; HBP 22(1), 25

2.19 SSCBA 130(1), 136(1), 136A; HBW 2(1) – 'couple', 8(1)(b),(e), 23, 82(1); HPB 2(1) – 'couple', 8(1)(b),(e), 23, 63(1)

Council tax rebates

Who can get CTR

2.20 You can get CTR if you are liable for council tax as a resident. Chapter 28 explains who is liable and who is a resident. You must also make a claim and meet the financial conditions.

2.21 There are two kinds of CTR:

(a) national CTR – this applies in England to pension age claims, and in Scotland and Wales to all claims

(b) local CTR – this applies in England to working age claims.

In this section we only give the rules for national CTR. Local CTR varies depending on where you live (para 29.13).

CTR if you are single

2.22 You can get CTR as a single person if you are liable for council tax as a resident. You make the CTR claim, you get the single rate of CTR, and your own income and capital is taken into account.

CTR if you are in a couple

2.23 You can get CTR as a couple if you (the claimant) are liable for council tax as a resident. You make the CTR claim on behalf of you both, and you are called 'claimant' (or 'applicant') and 'partner'. You get the couple rate of CTR, and both you and your partner's income and capital is taken into account.

Support for mortgage interest

2.24 You can get SMI if:

(a) you are liable for mortgage interest or other loan secured on your home (para 27.2)

(b) you are on UC, SPC, JSA(IB), ESA(IR) or IS or have claimed one of them but do not qualify because your income is too high and

(c) except where you have claimed SPC, you have completed the three-month waiting period.

2.25 If you are single, you make your own claim for SMI. If you are in a couple, you make a joint claim. SMI is a loan rather than a benefit, and you don't normally have to repay it until you stop qualifying for benefit or you sell your home.

2.20 LGFA 13A, 80, sch 1A para 2, sch 1B paras 3-5; CTRE(PR) 11-13, sch 1 paras 2-4; CTRW(PR) 22-25, 28-31; CTRSW 13, 14, 16, 19, 20; CTRSP 14, 14A, 16, 18, 19

2.21 LGFA 13A(1),(2),(4), 80, sch 1A para 2, sch 1B paras 3-5; CTRSW 13, 14; CTRSP 14, 14A

2.22 CTRE(PR) sch 1 paras 2-4, 6(1), 11, sch 8 para 4(1); CTRW(PR) 22-25, sch 1 paras 1(1), 5, sch 6 paras 1(1), 7, sch 13 para 1(1); CTRSW 13(3), 22, 35, 36; CTRSP 14(3), 20, 21(1), 61

2.23 CTRE(PR) sch 1 paras 2-4, 6(1), 11, sch 8 para 4(1); CTRW(PR) 22-25, sch 1 paras 1(1), 5, sch 6 paras 1(1), 7, sch 13 para 1(1); CTRSW 13(3), 22, 35, 36; CTRSP 14(3), 20, 21(1), 61

2.24 WRWA 18; LMI 2(1) – 'claimant', 'single claimant', 3, 8(1)(b), sch 1

2.25 LMI 4, 9, 16

Financial conditions

2.26 To get UC, HB or CTR your capital (apart from disregarded capital) mustn't be over £16,000. And to get UC, SPC, HB or CTR your income mustn't be too high for you to qualify. The detailed rules are in chapters 21-24.

Housing costs conditions

2.27 You can get help with the following kinds of housing costs:

(a) rent
(b) mortgage interest
(c) service charges
(d) council tax.

2.28 To get help with rent, mortgage interest or service charges, you must meet:

(a) the payment condition – this says which housing costs can be met (chapter 10)
(b) the liability condition – this says you must have a legal obligation to make payments (chapter 9)
(c) the occupation condition – this says you must occupy the accommodation as your home (chapters 7-8) and
(d) if you have non-dependants, the amount they are assumed to contribute towards your housing costs must not be too high for you to qualify (para 6.17).

Similar rules apply to CTR (para 30.7). In all cases, you must also meet the basic and financial conditions for benefit described earlier in this chapter.

Your actual costs

2.29 Your 'actual' rent, service charges, mortgage interest or council tax means the amount you are liable to pay on your home.

Your eligible costs/housing costs element

2.30 Your 'eligible' rent, service charges, mortgage interest or council tax means the (often lower) amount used in calculating your benefit (chapters 10-13). In UC, your eligible rent and service charges make up your 'housing costs element' (para 16.32).

2.26 WRA 5, 8; SPCA 1(2)(c), 2, 15; SSCBA 130(3), 134(1); LGFA 80(2),(5), sch 1A para 2(2); sch 1B para 3(7); UC 18, 22; PC 6, 15; HBW 43, 71; HBP 43, 51; CTRE(PR) 11(2), sch 1 paras 2-4, 7, 10; CTRW(PR) 22-25, 30, sch 1 paras 2, 4, sch 6 paras 4, 6; CTRSW 13(6), 66, 79; CTRSP 14(5), 40, 47

2.27 WRA 11; SSCBA 130(1)(a),(2); WRWA 18; LGFA 13A(1), 80(1),(2); UC 25(2)(a),(c), sch 1 paras 2, 7, 8; PC 6(6)(c), sch 2 paras 1(1), 13(1); HBW 12(1); HBP 12(1); LMI 3(2), sch 1

2.28 WRA 11(1),(3); SSCBA 130(1),(2), 137(2)(h)-(j); WRWA 18(1),(8), 19(2); LGFA 13A(1), 80, sch 1A para 2, sch 1B paras 3-6; UC 25(1), sch 1-3, sch 4 para 13; PC sch 2 paras 1(1), 3, 4, 13(1), 14; HBW 7-12, 70; HBP 7-12, 50; LMI 3(2), sch 1-3; CTRE(PR) sch 1 paras 2-4, 8; CTRW(PR) 22-25, sch 1 para 3, sch 6 para 5; CTRSW 13(3)(a), 90; CTRSP 14(3)(a), 48

2.30 UC 26(2), sch 4 paras 22, 31, 32, 33; PC sch 2 para 13(2); HBW 2(1), – 'eligible rent', 11(1); HBP 2(1), 11(1)

Social and private renters

2.31 Renters are divided into two kinds:

(a) you are a 'social renter' if you rent from a social landlord. This means a local council or registered housing association

(b) you are a 'private renter' if you rent from a private landlord. This means anyone else, for example, a private individual, a lettings agency, a company, a registered charity, or a not-for-profit organisation.

These affect how much of your rent you can get help with (chapters 11-12).

Supported, temporary and general accommodation

2.32 Rented accommodation is divided into two kinds:

(a) 'supported or temporary accommodation' (STA) means any of the kinds of rented accommodation in tables 13.1 and 13.2

(b) 'general accommodation' means any other rented accommodation such as a house, flat, houseboat, mobile home, etc.

This affects whether you get help with rent and service charges from UC or HB (para 12.4-5).

Couple cases in more detail

Couples

2.33 Table 2.4 gives more detail about claims by couples for UC and SPC. It explains which benefit you can get and whether you get benefit as a couple or as a single person.

Polygamous marriages

2.34 You are in a 'polygamous marriage' if you or your husband or wife are married to more than one person under the laws of a country which permits polygamy.

2.35 The members of the polygamous marriage who live in your household can get benefit as follows:

(a) if all of you are over pension age you can claim SPC as a polygamous marriage

(b) if one or more of you are under pension age:

- the two of you who were married earliest can claim benefit as a couple
- each other person in the marriage can claim benefit as a single person and
- which benefit each of you can get is decided by the normal rules for couples and single people.

2.31 UC sch 4 paras 1(4), 2 – 'provider of social housing', 20, 30; HBW A13(1), 13C(5)(a), 14(1),(2)(b), sch 2 para 3; HBP 13C(5)(a), 14(1),(2)(b), sch 2 para 3

2.32 UC sch 1 paras 2, 3, 3A, 3B, 7; UCTP 6A(1),(2),(4)

2.34 SPCA 12(1); UC 3(5); HBW 2(1) – 'polygamous marriage', HBP 2(1); CTRE(PR) 5(1); CTRW(PR) 5(1); CTRSW 5(3); CTRSP 2(1) – 'polygamous marriage'

2.35 UC 3(4); UCTP 5(1); PC 5(3)-(6), 8, sch 3 para 1(5); HBW 23, 25(2); HBP 23(2), sch 3 para 1(4),(5)

Table 2.4 Claims by couples for UC and SPC

Your circumstances	What you can claim
Both of you are under 66	
(a) Neither of you is in any excluded group	You can jointly claim UC as a couple
(b) One of you is an excluded student	You can jointly claim UC as a couple
(c) One of you is an excluded migrant, absentee from the UK, prisoner, or member of a religious order	The other can claim UC as a single claimant
Both of you are over 66	
(d) Neither of you is in any excluded group	Either of you can claim SPC as a couple
(e) One of you is an excluded migrant, absentee from the UK, prisoner, or member of a religious order	The other can claim SPC as a single claimant

Notes:

- In cases (c) and (e), claiming HB may affect an excluded migrant's immigration status (para 40.11).
- For mixed age couples see paras 2.37-42 and DWP circulars A3/2019 and A9/2019.

2.36 But if you are in a mixed age polygamous marriage and were getting HB or SPC as a polygamous marriage before 15 May 2019, you can continue to do so for as long as you remain on either of those benefits and remain in a polygamous marriage.

Mixed age couples

2.37 You are a 'mixed age' couple if one of you is aged 66 or over and one aged under 66.

General rule for mixed age couples

2.38 If you are a mixed age couple, you can only make working age claims. In other words:

(a) you can claim UC and

(b) you can claim working age HB in supported or temporary accommodation, but not in general accommodation.

T2.4 SPCA 1(2), 2(1), 4(1A); UC 3(2),(3); PC 5(1)(c),(d),(f),(h)

2.36 SI 2019/37 art 4

2.37 SPCA 4(1A); SI 2019/37 art 2(2); UCTP 6A(5); UC 3(2)(a); HBW 5; HBP 5

2.38 SPCA 4(1A); WRA 3(2), 4(1)(b); UCTP 5(1)(d), 6A(2),(4); UC 3(2)(a); HBW 5; HBP 5

If you become a mixed age couple while on HB

2.39 You become a mixed age couple if:

(a) you are a single person under 66, and become a couple with someone over 66

(b) you are a single person over 66, and become a couple with someone under 66 or

(c) you are a couple both under 66, and the older partner reaches 66.

2.40 If you become a mixed age couple while you are on SPC or HB or both, your SPC and HB end. You can then claim UC as described in para 2.38.

Exception if you claimed SPC or pension age HB before 15 May 2019

2.41 You can make a claim for SPC or pension age HB as a mixed age couple if you (the claimant) have been:

(a) in a mixed age couple since before 14 May 2019 and

(b) on SPC or pension age HB (or UC to which you transferred from tax credits) since before that date.

Exception if your partner(s) can't get UC

2.42 You can make a claim for pension age HB as if you were a single person if:

(a) you (the claimant) are in a mixed age couple and

(b) your partner(s) can't get UC because of being an excluded 16/17 year old, migrant, absentee from the UK, prisoner, or member of a religious order (chapter 3).

Examples: Mixed age couples

1. Becoming a mixed age couple while on HB

Linda is aged 67 and has been getting pension age HB (but not since before 15 May 2019). Elsa is aged 62 and moves in with her as her partner.

- Linda's HB ends, and Linda and Elsa can make a claim for UC as a couple (para 2.40).

2. On SPC since before 15 May 2019

Haoyu and Beatha are a mixed age couple (one over 66 and one under). They have been on SPC since before 15 May 2019 and are now moving from a relative's home to a rented home.

- They can claim pension age HB as a couple at their new home (para 2.41).

2.39 SPCA 4(1A); WRA 4(1)(b),(2); UCTP 7(1); UC 3(2)(a); HBW 5; HBP 5

2.40 SPCA 4(1A); WRA 4(1)(b),(2); UCTP 7(2)-(4); UC 3(2)(a); HBW 5, 79(1); HBP 5, 59(1)

2.41 SI 2019/37 art 4; UCTP 6A(5)

2.42 SI 2019/37 art 7

Chapter 3 **Exclusions from benefit**

- General rules: paras 3.1-5
- 16/17-year-olds: paras 3.6-13
- Students: paras 3.14-22
- Prisoners and members of a religious order: paras 3.23-26

General rules

3.1 This chapter explains who is excluded from UC, SPC, pension age HB, and HB in supported or temporary accommodation. (You can't claim working age HB in general accommodation.) The rules about SMI and CTR are in chapters 27 and 29.

The excluded groups

3.2 You may be excluded from UC, SPC or HB if you are:

(a) a 16/17-year-old (UC and HB only) (para 3.6)

(b) a student (UC and HB only) (para 3.14)

(c) a prisoner (para 3.23)

(d) a member of a religious order (para 3.26)

(e) absent from the UK (chapter 8) or

(f) a migrant (chapter 40).

We refer to these as 'excluded groups'.

Single people and couples

3.3 You can't get benefit if you are:

(a) a single person in an excluded group or

(b) a couple, both in an excluded group.

Couples with only one in an excluded group

3.4 You can get benefit if your partner is in an excluded group and you aren't. The benefit calculation uses your joint income and capital (para 21.4) unless your partner isn't included in your benefit unit (para 5.28).

3.2-3 WRA 4(1)(a)-(d), 6(1)(a); SPCA 1(2)(a),(5), 2(1),(3),(4); SSCBA 137(2)(a),(b),(f),(h),(i),(l); IAA 115(1),(3); CLCA 6; UC 8, 9-11, 12-14, 19; PC 2, 3; HBW 7, 10, 56; HBP 7, 10

3.4 WRA 4(2), 6(1)(a); SPCA 1(2)(a),(5); SSCBA 130(1); IAA 115(1),(3); UC 3(1)-(3), 19(1)-(3); PC 5(1)(a)-(d),(f),(h); HBW 2(1) – 'couple', 'partner', 8(1)(e), 21(1),(2), 25(1), 82(1); HBP 2(1), 8(1)(e), 21(1),(2), 23(1), 63(1)

Other exclusions from benefit

3.5 You also can't get:

(a) UC, SPC or HB if you don't meet the financial conditions (para 2.26)

(b) UC, SPC or HB for your housing costs if you don't meet the housing costs conditions (para 2.27)

(c) HB if you have a working age claim and live in general accommodation (table 2.3).

16/17-year-olds

3.6 This section applies if you are aged 16 or 17. There are different rules depending on whether you are a care leaver (para 3.12).

16/17-year-old care leavers

3.7 If you are a care leaver aged 16 or 17, you can only get UC towards your living costs if:

(a) you have a child or young person in your benefit unit or

(b) you have limited capability for work or for work and work-related activity or are waiting for a work capability assessment and have a doctor's note.

3.8 But you can't get benefit towards your housing costs. In other words, you can't get UC on general accommodation or HB on supported or temporary accommodation.

Other 16/17-year-olds

3.9 If you are aged 16 or 17 and aren't a care leaver, you can get UC towards your living and housing costs if you are in one of the following eligible groups:

(a) you have a child or young person in your benefit unit

(b) you have limited capability for work or for work and work-related activity or are waiting for a work capability assessment and have a doctor's note

(c) you are without parental support (para 3.13)

(d) you are pregnant and within 11 weeks before your expected date of birth

(e) you are within 15 weeks after giving birth (including a still-birth after 24 weeks of pregnancy) or

(f) you meet the conditions for a UC carer element (para 16.20).

3.10 You can also get:

(a) UC towards your housing costs if you are in one of the eligible groups or

(b) HB towards your housing costs if you live in supported or temporary accommodation (whether or not you are in an eligible group).

3.5 WRA 5, 11(1),(3); SPCA 2(1),(3); SSCBA 130(1)(a),(3)(b), 134(1); UC 18, 25; PC sch 2 paras 1(1), 3, 4, 13; UCTP 6A(1),(2),(4)

3.7 WRA 4(1)(a),(3); UC 8(1)(a),(b),(d),(e),(2)

3.8 WRA 11(5)(a); UC sch 4 paras 1(3), 4; CLCA 6(1)

3.9 WRA 4(3); UC 8(1)(a)-(g), 8(4) – 'confinement'

3.10 WRA 11(1); UCTP 6A(2)

Couples

3.11 If you are in a couple, you can get UC if at least one of you is in an eligible group or aged 18 or over (table 2.4).

Who is a care leaver

3.12 You are a 'care leaver' for these purposes if you were in care for at least 13 weeks/three months between the ages of 14 and 16 (in England and Wales) or between the date of your children's hearing and the age of 16 (Scotland). The 13 weeks/three months doesn't include periods of up to a month in respite care. But in England and Wales it does include periods in hospital or a youth offender institution if you would otherwise have been in care.

Who is without parental support

3.13 You are 'without parental support' if you aren't in care but:

(a) you have no parent or guardian or

(b) you can't live with them because you're estranged from them or

(c) living with them would seriously risk harm to you or risk your physical or mental health or

(d) they can't support you financially because they have a physical or mental impairment, or are detained in custody, or are prohibited from entering or re-entering the UK.

Examples: 16/17-year-olds

1. A 16-year-old with a baby

Tama is aged 16 and has a baby. She lives in a rented bedsit and is estranged from her parents.

- She can get UC towards her living costs and her rent because she is without parental support. Or if the bedsit is supported accommodation, she can get UC towards her living costs and HB towards her rent.

2. A 17-year-old receiving parental support

Wesley is aged 17. He lives in a rented bedsit and his parents help him out financially. He doesn't meet any of the conditions in para 3.9.

- He can't get UC or HB towards his living costs or rent.

3.11 WRA 4(2); UC 3(3)(a)

3.12 UC 8(4); CLCA 6(2)-(4); CLC(E) 3, 4; CLC(W) 3, 4; CLC(S) 2

3.13 UC 8(3), (4) – 'parent'

Students

3.14 This section applies if you are a student. It only affects you if you are claiming UC or working age HB. If you are claiming SPC or pension age HB, all students can claim benefit.

UC and HB for students

3.15 If you are a student, you have to be in an eligible group to get UC towards your living costs. The UC eligible groups are in table 3.1.

3.16 You can also get:

(a) UC towards your housing costs if you are in one of the UC eligible groups or

(b) HB towards your housing costs if you live in supported or temporary accommodation and are on UC or in one of the HB eligible groups.

The HB eligible groups are in table 3.2.

Who is a student

3.17 You are a 'student' for these purposes if you are undertaking:

(a) full-time advanced education

(b) full-time non-advanced education

(c) any other education that is incompatible with your UC work-related requirements.

In UC, this includes government-sponsored work-preparation courses for under 25-year-olds but not courses provided by your employer.

Advanced education

3.18 Advanced education means education above level 3 (e.g. a degree). It counts as full time if you get a student loan or grant. Or if you don't get a loan or grant, this is usually decided by the educational establishment's description of the course rather than the amount of time the student devotes to the course (FO v SSWP, ADM H6067).

Non-advanced education

3.19 Non-advanced education means education up to level 3 (e.g. A levels). In UC, it always counts as full time if it includes more than 12 hours per week of guided learning during term time. In HB the time limit is usually 16 hours.

The period you count as a student

3.20 You count as a student from the day you start your course to the day it ends, or you abandon it or are dismissed from it. This includes all term-times and vacations within that period.

3.14 WRA 4(1)(d),(6); UC 12, 13; SSCBA 137(2)(i); HBW 56(1)

3.15 WRA 4(1)(d),(6)(b); UC 14

3.16 WRA 11(1); SSCBA 137(2)(i); UCTP 6A(2); HBW 56(2)(a)-(i)

3.17 WRA 4(6); UC 5(1)-(4), 12(1A),(1B),(2),(4), 14(1)(a); HBW 53(1) – 'full-time student', 'full-time course of study', 56(2)(h)

3.18-19 UC 12(3); HBW 53(1) – 'full-time student', 'full-time course of study', 'higher education', 56(4)
FO v SSWP (UC) [2022] UKUT 73 (AAC)

3.20 UC 13(1); HBW 53(2)

3.21 For UC only, you also count as a student until the 31 August after:

(a) your 16th birthday, in all cases and

(b) your 19th birthday if you began non-advanced education before that birthday.

Couples

3.22 If you are in a couple you can get UC and HB if at least one of you is in an eligible group or isn't a student (table 2.4).

Table 3.1 **UC eligible groups for students**

(a) You have a child or young person in your benefit unit

(b) You have a foster child placed with you

(c) You are in non-advanced education (para 3.19) without parental support (para 3.13) and are aged under 21 (or aged 21 and reached that age while on your course)

(d) You are taking time out of your course with the consent of your educational establishment because you are (or have been) ill or caring for someone and you aren't eligible for a student loan or grant

(e) Your course isn't full-time (paras 3.17-19)

(f) You are on PIP or ADP, DLA, SADLA or CDP, attendance allowance, or an equivalent benefit (para 21.18) and

- have limited capability for work or for work and work-related activity and
- were assessed as having this (in a claim for UC or ESA) before you started receiving education (Kays v SSWP)

(g) You are a couple and one of you has reached pension age

(h) You transferred to UC as part of managed migration (para 25.22) – but this way of qualifying only applies until:

- you end your course or change it
- you become a single person or couple (or a couple with a different partner)
- your earnings were at or above the administrative threshold (para 4.11) but reduce below it
- your UC stops for over three months due to an increase in your earned or unearned income or
- your UC stops (for any length of time) for any other reason.

3.21 UC 5(1)

3.22 WRA 4(2); CBA 130(1); UC 3(2)(b); HBW 8(1)(e), 82(1)

T3.1 WRA 4(6); UCTP 60; UC 12(2), 13(4), 14(1)(a)-(f)
Kays v SSWP [2022] EWCA Civ 1593

Table 3.2 **HB eligible groups for students**

(a) You have a pension age HB claim (para 3.14)

(b) You are on UC and live in supported or temporary accommodation (tables 13.1 and 13.2)

(c) You have a child or young person in your benefit unit

(d) You have a foster child placed with you

(e) You are in non-advanced education and are aged under 21 (or aged 21 and reached that age while on your course)

(f) You are taking time out of your course with the consent of your educational establishment because you are (or have been) ill or caring for someone and you aren't eligible for a student loan or grant

(g) Your course isn't full-time (paras 3.17-19)

(h) You qualify for a severe disability premium or disability premium (paras 18.20, 18.26)

(i) You have been accepted for ESA purposes as having limited capacity for work for at least 28 weeks (ignoring gaps of up to 12 weeks) or

(j) You have a UK grant that includes an amount for deafness

Examples: Students

1. A student with a child

Richie is a 35-year-old student at university. He is renting a flat from a private landlord and lives there with his eight-year-old son.

- He can get UC towards his living costs and his rent because he has a child in his benefit unit.

2. A student with no children

Shahina is a 19-year-old student at university. She is renting a flat from a private landlord and lives there alone. She doesn't meet any of the conditions in table 3.2.

- She can't get UC or HB towards her living costs or rent.

T3.2 HBW 56(2)(a)-(j),(2A),(6)

Prisoners

3.23 You are a prisoner if you are in custody, whether you are:

(a) detained serving a sentence or

(b) detained on remand (pending trial or pending sentencing) or

(c) detained in hospital or

(d) on temporary release.

But you don't count as a prisoner if you are detained for a non-criminal matter (e.g. for contempt of court or a debt) (JC v SSWP).

3.24 If you are a prisoner:

(a) you can't get UC or SPC towards your living costs but

(b) you may be able to get UC, SPC or HB towards your housing costs for a limited amount of time in some cases (para 8.25).

3.25 If you are in a couple and your partner is a prisoner, you can get UC, SPC or HB as a couple while your partner is included in your benefit unit (para 5.28) and then as a single person.

Religious orders

3.26 You can't get UC, SPC or HB if you are a member of a religious order and are fully maintained by them. This typically applies to monks and nuns whose order provides their food and other needs. The exclusion doesn't apply to members of religious communities, whose members often do paid work or keep their own possessions (ADM E3010-11, DMG 78680-83, HBGM A3.255-57).

3.23 UC 2 – 'prisoner', 19(1)(c),(4); PC 1(2) – 'prisoner', 5(1)(c), sch 3 para 2; HBW 7(14),(15),(16A); HBP 7(14),(15),(16A)
JC v SSWP (ESA) [2024] UKUT 13 (AAC)

3.24 WRA 6(1)(a); CBA 130(1); SPCA 2(3),(9); UC 19(1)-(3); PC 6(2),(3); HBW 7(13),(16)(c)(i),(16A),(17); HBP 7(13),(16)(c)(i),(16A),(17)

3.25 UC 3(3)(c); PC 5(1)(c), sch 2 para 3(b); HBW 2(1) – 'couple', 'partner', 8(1)(c), 21(2); HBP 2(1), 8(1)(c), 21(2)

3.26 WRA 6(1)(a); SPCA 2(3),(9); CBA 130(1)(a), 137(2)(i); UC 19(1)(a); PC 6(2)(b),(3); HBW 9(1)(j); HBP 9(1)(j)

Chapter 4 **The claimant commitment**

- What is a claimant commitment: paras 4.1-7
- Earnings thresholds: paras 4.8-14
- Limited capability for work: paras 4.15-20
- People with children: paras 4.21-23
- Sanctions and hardship payments: paras 4.24-31

What is a claimant commitment

4.1 Claimant commitments only apply to UC. They are a record of:

(a) your work-related requirements

(b) the sanctions that can apply if you don't meet these requirements and

(c) your duty to notify changes.

Agreeing to a claimant commitment

4.2 You need to accept a claimant commitment when you claim UC and when your circumstances change. If you are in a couple, you both need to do this. You can view and update your commitment online and you should be able to discuss and update it with your work coach.

4.3 If you don't agree to a claimant commitment, you can't get UC. Or if you fail to accept a change during your award of UC, you could be subject to a sanction.

Exceptions to the claimant commitment

4.4 You don't have to agree to a claimant commitment if:

(a) you lack the capacity to do so or

(b) exceptional circumstances make it unreasonable to expect you to do so (FO v SSWP) or

(c) you are terminally ill (para 16.18).

4.1 WRA 4(1)(e), 14; UC 15

4.2 WRA 4(1)(e), 14; UC 15(4)

4.3 WRA 4(1)(e), 14, 26, 27; UC 15(4), 100

4.4 WRA 4(2); UC 16; FO v SSWP (UC) [2022] UKUT 56 (AAC)

Table 4.1 **No work search or availability requirements**

If you are in any of these groups, you don't have to meet the UC work search or availability requirements (para 4.6). But in some cases you have to meet the work-focused interview or work preparation requirements.

Employed earners, self-employed, work capability, temporary inability to work	(a) Your employed earnings are above the administrative threshold (para 4.11). (b) You are gainfully self-employed and the minimum income floor (MIF) applies to you (para 4.14). (c) You have limited capability for work (LCW), or for work and work-related activity (LCWRA) (para 4.15). (d) You are unable to work due to illness (usually no more than 14 days) or you are undertaking agreed work preparation.
Children, fostering, adoption, pregnancy *If you are in a couple, (e), (f) and usually (g) can only apply to one of you: you jointly choose which of you this is*	(e) You are responsible for a child under three years old; or (for up to 12 months) for a child under 16 whose parents can't care for them and who would otherwise be likely to go into local authority care. (f) You are the foster parent of a child under 16 years old. (g) You have adopted a child under 16 years old and it is within 12 months of the date of adoption (or the date 14 days before the expected date of placement if you request the 12 months to begin then), but this does not apply if you are the child's close relative (para 9.30) or foster parent. (h) You are pregnant and it is no more than 11 weeks before your expected date of delivery, or you were pregnant and it is no more than 15 weeks after your baby's birth (including a still-birth after 24 weeks of pregnancy).
Pension age, carers, students, domestic violence	(i) You have reached pension age. (j) You meet the conditions for a UC carer element, or would do so except that you share your caring responsibilities with someone who gets the carer element instead of you (para 16.21), or you do not do so but the DWP agrees you have similar caring responsibilities.

T4.1 (a) UC 90(1),(2), 99(1),(6)
(b) UC 90(5); NIUC 89(5)
(c) WRA 19(2)(a), 21(1)(a)
(d) UC 99(4),(4ZA),(4ZB),(5)(a),(c)
(e) WRA 19(2)(c),(6), 20(1)(a), 21(1)(aa); UC 86, 91(2)(e),(3);
(f) UC 2, 85, 86, 89(1)(f), 91(2)(a)-(d)
(g) UC 89(1)(d),(3)
(h) UC 89(1)(c)
(i) UC 89(1)(a)
(j) WRA 19(2)(b); UC 30, 89(1)(b),(2)

	(k) You are a student and you fall within eligible group (d) in table 3.1, or you have a student loan or grant (other than a part-time postgraduate master's degree loan) and fall within any of the groups in that table. (l) You have been a victim of actual or threatened domestic violence within the past six months from a partner, former partner, or family member you are not (or no longer) living with. A 'family member' includes any close relative (para 9.30). It also includes a grandparent, grandchild, step-brother/sister or brother/sister-in-law or, if any of them are in a couple, their partner. This applies for 13 weeks from when you notify the DWP about it, but only if it has not applied to you during the previous 12 months. It can apply for a further 13 weeks if you are responsible for a child.
Treatment abroad, drug/alcohol programmes, emergencies etc, death in the family	(m) You are temporarily absent from the UK in connection with treatment, convalescence or care for you, your partner or a child or young person, and you meet the conditions in para 8.37. (n) You are in an alcohol or drug dependency treatment programme and have been for no more than six months. (o) You temporarily have new or increased child care responsibilities (including when a child is affected by death or violence) or are dealing with a domestic emergency, funeral arrangements etc, and the DWP agrees. (p) Your partner, or a child or young person you or your partner are responsible for, or a child of yours (even if not included in your benefit unit) has died within the past six months.
Prisoners, court proceedings, police protection, public duties	(q) You are a prisoner claiming UC for housing costs. (r) You are attending a court or tribunal as a party to proceedings or witness. (s) You are receiving police protection and have been for no more than six months. (t) You are engaged in activities which the DWP agrees amount to a public duty.
Note: There are no work-related requirements for claimants who fall under items (g) to (k) and during the first 13 weeks of (l).	

T4.1 (k) UC 68(7), 89(1)(da),(e)
(l) UC 98
(m) UC 99(3)(c)
(n) UC 99(3)(e)
(o) UC 99(4A)-(4C),(5)(b),(5A)
(p) UC 99(3)(d)
(q) UC 99(3)(b)
(r) UC 99(3)(a)
(s) UC 99(3)(f)
(t) UC 99(3)(g)

4.5 Or your work coach can suspend work-related requirements when it is unreasonable to expect you to carry them out. The DWP calls this a 'discretionary easement' (ADM paras J3250-3262). It could apply if you are homeless, living in supported or temporary accommodation, or at risk of homelessness (OG file 82).

Work-related requirements

4.6 Your work-related activities can include:

(a) looking for work (the work search requirement)

(b) being available for work (the work availability requirement)

(c) attending an interview with your UC coach (the work-focused interview requirement)

(d) carrying out preparation for work (the work preparation requirement).

4.7 This chapter gives the main rules about which of these requirements apply to you. Table 4.1 summarises the groups of people who aren't expected to carry out activities (a) or (b).

Example: Accepting a claimant commitment

Sarah is a single person with children aged two and five. She loses her job and claims UC.

- Sarah needs to agree to a claimant commitment in order to get UC
- She is only expected to carry out work-focused interview and work preparation activities
- But when her younger child reaches three, she will also be expected to carry out work search and work availability activities (para 4.22).

Earnings thresholds

Employed earners

4.8 There are two earnings thresholds for employed earners:

(a) the conditionality threshold and

(b) the administrative threshold.

These affect which work-related requirements you have to carry out in order to get UC.

The conditionality threshold

4.9 If your earnings are at or above the conditionality threshold, you aren't expected to carry out any work-related requirements to get UC. This threshold is also called the 'individual threshold'.

4.5 WRA 17(4), 18(3); UC 99(2A),(5),(5A),(5B)

4.6 WRA 13; UC 93-97

4.7 WRA 17, 18, 19; UC 97, 98, 99

4.8 WRA 19(3),(4); UC 90, 99(1),(6)

4.9 WRA 19(3),(4); UC 90(1)

4.10 The threshold is in table 4.2. This equals what you would earn in a month if you were working the following number of hours a week at your rate of the national minimum wage:

(a) if you have a child under three, 16 hours a week

(b) if you don't have a child under three, 35 hours a week, or 30 hours per week if you are an apprentice.

For a couple (including a couple claiming as a single person), it is this amount for each of you. For both single people and couples, the DWP can agree a lower number of hours if you have a disability, ill health or caring responsibilities for a child or adult.

The administrative threshold

4.11 If your earnings are below the conditionality threshold but at or above the administrative threshold, you are only expected to carry out work-focused and work preparation activities.

4.12 If your earnings are below the administrative threshold, you are expected to carry out all work-focused activities.

4.13 The threshold is in table 4.2. For a single person, it is what you would earn for working 18 hours per week at the 21+ rate of the national minimum wage (even if you are under 21). For a couple it is what you would earn if one of you was working 29 hours per week at the 21+ rate, or between you, if you were working 29 hours per week at that rate.

Table 4.2 **Earnings thresholds from April 2025**

	(a) Minimum wage	(b) Conditionality threshold	
		If you have a child under 3	Other cases
■ Aged 21 or over	£12.21	£846	£1851
■ Aged 18 to 20	£10.00	£693	£1516
■ Aged 16 or 17	£7.55	£523	£1145
■ Apprentices	£7.55	–	£981
		(c) Administrative threshold	
■ Single person		£952	
■ Couple		£1534	

Notes: Minimum wage figures are hourly. Threshold figures are monthly and are rounded. The minimum wage rate for a person aged 21 or over is also called the national living wage.

4.10 UC 88(1), 90(2)-(4)

4.11 WRA 21; UC 99(1),(2)

4.12 WRA 22

4.13 UC 99(6)

T4.2 UC 6(1A), 88(1), 90(2)-(4), 99(6); SI 2015/621, regs 4, 4A; SI 2016/68 reg 3

Self-employed earners

4.14 Self-employed earners don't have to meet any of the work-related requirements. But if your profit is low, you can be treated as having earnings equal to the minimum income floor (MIF) (paras 23.21-25). The MIF is usually the same as the conditionality threshold.

Limited capability for work

Who qualifies as having LCW or LCWRA

4.15 This section explains who has limited capability for work (LCW) or limited capability for work and work-related activity (LCWRA), and how these affect your UC.

4.16 The DWP decides whether you qualify as having LCW or LCWRA or neither (paras 16.9-16). You usually have to provide a doctor's certificate or other medical evidence and then take part in a work capability assessment (WCA).

Work capability assessments

4.17 The assessment is points-based and looks at whether you can carry out a fixed list of activities. It is usually carried out by phone, but if appropriate the DWP can ask you attend a medical assessment. The Government is planning to reform the WCA activities (and how they are described) to ones based on the PIP assessment. It is expected to publish its plans in early 2025 but the changes are only likely to affect new claims from 2026 onwards (Autumn Budget 2024, para 3.45) (table 1.4).

Exceptions to WCAs

4.18 You qualify as having LCW or LCWRA without a work capability assessment if:

(a) you have one of the medical conditions in table 4.3 or

(b) you had LCW/LCWRA when you were last on UC, and have now reclaimed UC within six months of it ending or

(c) you transferred to UC while you were on main phase ESA or were getting national insurance credits instead of it or

(d) you transferred to UC from SDA when you were aged 65 (i.e. in the year before you reached pension age) and at the time of transferring you were in receipt of PIP, an equivalent rate of DLA, or constant attendance allowance with an industrial injury or war disablement pension.

4.14 UC 62, 90(5)

4.15 WRA 12(2), 37; UC 38

4.16 WRA 37; UC 39, 40

4.17 UC 39(3),(4), 40(2),(3), 43, 44

4.18 UC 21(3C), 39(1),(6); UC(C&P) 26(5); UCTP 19, 21, 24

How LCW affects your UC

4.19 If you have LCW:

(a) you are only expected to carry out work-focused and work preparation activities in order to get UC and

(b) you qualify for a UC work allowance in the assessment of your earnings (table 22.3)

(c) but you don't normally qualify for an LCW element in your UC (para 16.9) and

(d) you aren't excluded from the benefit cap (table 20.3).

How LCWRA affects your UC

4.20 If you have LCWRA:

(a) you aren't expected to carry out any UC work-related activities

(b) you qualify for a UC work allowance (table 22.3)

(c) you qualify for an LCWRA element in your UC (para 16.9) and

(d) you are excluded from the benefit cap (table 20.3).

People with children

4.21 Having one or more children in your benefit unit affects which activities you have to carry out in order to get UC.

4.22 If your youngest child is:

(a) aged under one, you aren't expected to carry out any UC work-related activities

(b) aged one or two, you are only expected to carry out work-focused and work preparation activities

(c) aged three or over, you are expected to carry out all work-related activities.

Similar rules apply if you are an adopter or foster parent (table 4.1).

4.23 These rules apply to single people and couples. But if you are in a couple, they apply to the partner who is the lead carer (you can select who this is), and the other partner is expected to carry out all work-related activities.

4.19 WRA 21

4.20 WRA 19(1),(2)(a)

4.21 WRA 20, 21

4.22 WRA 20, 21, 22; UC 89(1)(d),(f), 91(2)

4.23 WRA 19(6)

Table 4.3 **Work capability: medical conditions**

You don't have to have a work capability assessment when these apply.

Limited capability for work (LCW)

(a) You are receiving, or recovering from, treatment for haemodialysis, plasmapheresis or total parietal nutrition.

(b) You are receiving, or recovering from, in-patient treatment in hospital or similar institution.

(c) You are prevented from working by law, for reasons relating to possible infection or contamination.

(d) You have a condition that is life threatening or could cause substantial physical or mental health risk to others.

(e) You are a joint claim couple, and one of you is over pension age and is entitled to PIP, DLA, SADLA, ADP or CDP.

Limited capability for work and work-related activity (LCWRA)

(f) You are terminally ill (para 16.18).

(g) You are pregnant and there is a serious risk of damage to you or your baby's health.

(h) You are receiving chemotherapy or radiotherapy for cancer, or likely to receive it within six months, or recovering from it.

(i) You are a joint claim couple, and one of you is over pension age and is entitled to:

- the daily living component of PIP or ADP,
- the highest rate of the care component of DLA, SADLA, or CDP,
- attendance allowance or PADP,
- armed forces independence payment.

Sanctions and hardship payments

Who gets a sanction

4.24 The DWP can impose a sanction that reduces your UC if:

(a) you don't apply for a vacancy, don't take up a work offer, or don't meet your work-related requirements; or

(b) you lose work or pay voluntarily or for no good reason; or

(c) a sanction is transferred from your JSA or ESA to your UC.

But you can't be sanctioned if you have limited capability for work and work-related activity (LCWRA).

T4.3 UC 39(6),(7), 40(5),(6), sch 8, sch 9

4.24 WRA 26, 27; UC 113(3), 112, sch 11

The amount of your sanction

4.25 Your sanction equals:

(a) the whole of your UC standard allowance (table 16.1) if you are aged 18 or over; but

(b) 40% of your standard allowance if you are aged 16 or 17, or don't have any work-related requirements, or only have to attend a work-focused interview.

There are detailed rules about the length of your sanction (ADM K3011-34, K4010-20, K5020-50).

Who gets a hardship payment

4.26 The DWP must award you a hardship payment if:

(a) your sanction equals the whole of your standard allowance

(b) you make an application for each hardship period

(c) you have met your work-related requirements during the past seven days and

(d) the DWP agrees that you are 'in hardship'.

Meaning of hardship

4.27 You are 'in hardship' only if:

(a) your sanction means that you can't meet your and your benefit unit's 'most basic and essential needs' for accommodation, heating, food and/or hygiene and

(b) you have made 'every effort' to access alternative support, and to stop incurring other expenditure.

The hardship period

4.28 Each hardship payment covers a hardship period that runs from the day you applied (or if later, the day you provided information and evidence) to the day before your next normal monthly payment of UC is due (or if that is seven days or less, to the day before the next but one payment is due).

The amount of the hardship payment

4.29 Your hardship payment equals 60% of the UC you lost (as a result of the sanction) in the last assessment period but one. It is converted on a daily basis to cover the number of days in your hardship period.

4.25 UC 101-105

4.26 WRA 28(1); UC 116(1)

4.27 UC 116(2),(3)

4.28 UC 117

4.29 UC 118

Repaying hardship payments

4.30 Hardship payments are recoverable, but you can ask the DWP not to recover them, and the DWP has the discretion to waive recovery (BORG 5.83-85). In practice, the DWP usually recovers them at the 15% rate used for overpayments (table 37.1(a)). This means you are expected to repay them by receiving less UC in the future.

4.31 But you don't have to repay hardship payments during any assessment period in which your earnings (including your partner's if you are claiming UC as a couple) are at least equal to the conditionality earnings threshold (para 4.9). And once you have had this level of earnings for 26 weeks since a sanction last applied to you, they stop being recoverable altogether.

4.30 WRA 28(2)(f); SSAA 71ZH; UC 119(1)

4.31 UC 119(2),(3)

Chapter 5 **Your benefit unit**

5.1 This chapter is about the people in your home. It explains when a partner, child or young person is included in your claim for benefit.

Who is in your benefit unit

5.2 Your benefit unit means:

(a) you

(b) your partner if you have one and

(c) your children and young persons if you have them.

Your benefit unit doesn't include non-dependants (chapter 6) or other people in your home.

Terminology: benefit unit and family

5.3 You, your partner and your children/young persons are treated as a unit for all the benefits in this guide. In the law, UC uses the term 'benefit unit', HB and CTR use 'family', and SPC doesn't have a specific term. In this guide we use 'benefit unit' for all the benefits.

Examples: Your benefit unit

1. A single person with children

Remington is a single person with children aged 13 and 17. Her mother lives in her home with them.

- Remington's benefit unit is made up of herself and her two children. Her mother is not part of it, but instead is a non-dependant (chapter 6).

2. A couple with a lodger

Avery and Lucas are a couple. They have a lodger who lives in the spare bedroom in their home.

- Avery and Lucas's benefit unit is just the two of them. Their lodger is not part of it, but instead is a source of income (para 21.29).

5.2 UC 3-5, PC 4A, 5, 6(1),(6)(d), sch 2A; HBW 19-21; HBP 19-21; CTRE(PR) 7(1); 8(1); CTRW(PR) 7(1), 8(1); CTRSW 12; CTRSP 10(1), 11(1)

5.3 SSCBA 137(1) – 'family'; UC 3; CTRE(PR) 6; CTRW(PR) 6; CTRSW 4(1) – 'family'; CTRSP 2(1) – 'family

Single people and couples

Single people

5.4 You are a 'single person' if you aren't in a couple. Your benefit unit is:

(a) you and

(b) any children or young persons you are responsible for.

Couples

5.5 You are a 'couple' if you are two people who are members of the same household and are:

(a) a married couple or

(b) civil partners or

(c) living together as a married couple or civil partners.

If you are in a polygamous marriage see paras 2.34-36.

UC couples: joint claims and claiming as a single person

5.6 UC has two rules about couples:

(a) if you can get UC as a joint claim couple (para 2.8), your benefit unit is:
- both of you and
- any children or young persons either (or both) of you are responsible for;

(b) if you are in a couple but can only get UC as a single person (para 2.9), your benefit unit is:
- you and
- any children or young persons you are responsible for.

SPC, HB and CTR couples

5.7 If you are a couple claiming SPC, HB or CTR, your benefit unit is (in all cases):

(a) both of you and

(b) any children or young persons either (or both) of you are responsible for.

Members of the same household

5.8 You only count as a couple if you are members of the same household. This applies to married couples and civil partners as well as couples who are living together (JP v SSWP; Broxtowe BC v CS).

5.4 WRA 10; SSCBA 137(1) – 'family'; SPCA 2(3),(5); UC 4(1),(2); PC 6(6)(d), sch 2A para 1; HBW 19(1), 20(1); HBP 19(1), 20(1)

5.5 WRA 39(1) – 'couple'; SSCBA 137(1) – 'couple'; SPCA 17(1) – 'couple'; CTRE(PR) 4; CTRW(PR) 4; CTRSW 5(1); CTRSP 2(1) – 'couple'

5.6 WRA 2, 3(2); UC 3(1)-(3), 4(1)

5.7 SPCA 2(5); PC 6(1),(6)(d), sch 2A paras 1, 2; SSCBA 137(1) – 'family'; HBW 20(1); HBP 20(1); CTRE(PR) 4, 6

5.8 WRA 39(1) – 'couple'; SSCBA 137(1) – 'couple'; SPCA 17(1) – 'couple'; CTRE(PR) 4; CTRW(PR)
JP v SSWP (IS) [2014] UKUT 17 (AAC); Broxtowe BC v CS (HB) [2014] UKUT 186 (AAC)

5.9 'Household' has its ordinary English meaning. It generally means a domestic arrangement involving two or more people who live together as a unit (R(IS) 1/99), even when they have a reasonable level of independence and self-sufficiency (R(SB) 8/85). It requires a settled course of daily living rather than visits from time to time (R(F) 2/81). So if you keep your eating, cooking, food storage, finances (including paying your housing costs), living space and family life separate you are unlikely to be members of the same household.

5.10 You aren't a couple if you:

(a) live in different dwellings and maintain them as separate homes (R(SB) 4/83) or

(b) live in the same dwelling but lead separate lives rather than living as one household (CIS/072/1994).

And you can't be a member of two (or more) households at the same time (R(SB) 8/85).

Living together

5.11 If you aren't married or in a civil partnership, you are only a couple for benefit purposes if you are living together as though you were. This means considering:

(a) your purpose in living together (Crake and Butterworth v SBC) and

(b) if your purpose is unclear, your relationship and living arrangements.

5.12 The following factors are relevant (Crake, PP v Basildon DC):

(a) whether you share the same household

(b) the stability of your relationship

(c) your financial arrangement

(d) whether you have a sexual relationship

(e) whether you share responsibility for a child

(f) whether you publicly acknowledge you are a couple

(g) the emotional element of your relationship.

The decision should be based on the totality of the evidence, and none of the factors is conclusive in itself (DK v SSWP) unless you don't share a household.

5.13 Two people who live in the same home aren't necessarily a couple, even if they live together for reasons of 'care, companionship and mutual convenience' (R(SB) 35/85). For example, they may be a couple, or house sharers, or one may be renting from the other.

Ending a relationship

5.14 If you were a couple but your relationship has ended, your shared understanding that it has ended and your actual living arrangement are more important than any shared responsibilities and financial arrangements you still have (CIS/72/1994). But if you remain married or in a civil partnership, a shared understanding may not be enough by itself to show you are no longer a couple (CIS/2900/1998).

5.11 Crake and Butterworth v SBC [1982] All ER 498 (QBD)

5.12 PP v Basildon DC (HB) [2013] UKUT 505 (AAC);
DK v SSWP [2016] CSIH 84 reported as [2017] AACR 10

Councils adopting DWP decisions

5.15 If you are getting UC or SPC, and also claiming HB or CTR, the council is likely to adopt the DWP's decision about whether you are a couple. But:

(a) if the DWP decided you are in a couple, the council must make its own decision about this if you say the DWP is wrong (R(H) 9/04);

(b) if the DWP awarded you a passport benefit on the basis that you aren't in a couple, the council should accept this unless it has evidence of fraud which the DWP is unaware of and hasn't considered (CH/4014/2007).

Temporary absence of your partner

5.16 You continue to count as a couple if your partner is temporarily absent (paras 5.28-30).

Children and young persons

5.17 Your benefit unit includes the children and young persons that you are responsible for.

5.18 A 'child' means someone under the age of 16.

5.19 A 'young person' means someone aged 16 or more but under 20 (other than your partner) who:

(a) is in non-advanced education (para 3.19) and

(b) isn't getting UC, HB or ESA in their own right.

Someone normally counts as a young person if you get child benefit for them (table 5.1).

Responsibility for a child or young person

5.20 For benefit purposes you are responsible for a child or young person if they normally live with you. This is a question of fact and is usually straightforward. For example, they could be your son or daughter, adopted by you, a step-child, a grandchild or any other child or young person (whether related to you or not), so long as they normally live with you.

5.21 A child or young person can only be the responsibility of one single person or couple at any one time. If they normally live with two or more single persons or couples, they are the responsibility of the single person or couple with the main responsibility. This can be difficult when care is shared equally. It is decided taking account of all the circumstances, not just who receives the child benefit or the amount of time spent at each address (MC v SSWP). The courts have decided that not allowing a child to be part of both households doesn't amount to unlawful discrimination (Humphreys v HMRC; TD v SSWP and LB Richmond; R (Cotton) v SSWP).

5.16 UC 3(6); PC 5(1)(a); HBW 21(1),(2); HBP 21(1),(2); CTRE(PR) 8(1); CTRW(PR) 8(1); CTRSW 12; CTRSP 11(1)

5.17 SSCBA 137(1) – 'family'; UC 4(1); PC 6(6)(d), sch 2A para 1; CTRE(PR) 6(1); CTRW(PR) 6(1); CTRSW 10(1); CTRSP 7(1)

5.18 WRA 40 – 'child'; SSCBA 137(1) – 'child'; PC sch 2A para 2(1); CTRE(PR) 2(1) – 'child' CTRW(PR) – 'child'; CTRSW 4(1) – 'child'; CTRSP 2(1) – 'child'

5.19 UC 5; PC 4A; HBW 19; HBP 19; CTRE(PR) 2(1) – 'young person'; CTRW(PR) – 'young person'; CTRSW 6; CTRSP 4

5.20 UC 4(2); PC sch 2A para 3(1); HBW 20(1); HBP 20(1); CTRE(PR) 7(1); CTRW(PR) 7(1); CTRWS 7(2); CTRSP 10(1)

5.21 UC 4(4); PC sch 2A para 3(3); HBW 20(2),(3); HBP 20(2),(3); CTRE(PR) 7(2),(3); CTRW(PR) 7(2),(3); CTRWS 7(4),(5); CTRSP 10(2),(3)
MC v SSWP (UC) [2018] UKUT 44 (AAC); Humphreys v HMRC [2012] UKSC 18;
TD v SSWP and LB Richmond [2013] UKUT 642 (AAC); R (Cotton) v SSWP [2014] EWHC 3437 (Admin)

Choosing who has responsibility

5.22 When two separated parents (or other caregivers) choose which of you has the main responsibility for a child or young person, the DWP or council usually accepts this unless your choice doesn't reflect the arrangements between you. In UC and SPC this is called 'nominating' who has responsibility.

Examples: Responsibility for children

1. Shared custody

When Bill and June divorced, they shared the care of their children. In practice the children live with June on weekdays and with Bill at weekends. In school holidays the children frequently go back and forth. June makes most practical arrangements relating to schooling and other matters.

- The children are likely to be included in June's benefit unit, not Bill's (para 5.21).

2. Adoption

Ruby and Eric are on UC. They adopted a daughter Hester when she was aged eight and Hester has lived with them ever since.

- Hester wasn't included in Ruby and Eric's benefit unit when she was first placed with them (para 5.24), but was included as soon as she was adopted by them (paras 5.20, 5.24).

3. Fostering

Karen and Rodney fostered a son Kia when he was a baby and Kia has lived with them ever since. Kia will soon leave school and take up work. At that point Karen and Rodney have been advised to charge him a commercial rent for his room.

- Kia isn't included in Karen and Rodney's benefit unit while he remains a foster son (para 5.24). When Karen and Rodney charge him rent, he should be able to claim UC towards it because he doesn't fall within any of the exclusions in table 9.2.

Councils adopting HMRC decisions

5.23 For HB or CTR if a child spends equal amounts of time in different households the council may treat the child as normally living with the household that gets child benefit for them (as decided by HMRC) or in Scotland, based on the DWP's decision about UC.

Fostering (kinship care) and adoption

5.24 When a child or young person:

(a) is placed with you as a foster child, they aren't included in your benefit unit

(b) has been adopted by you, they are included in your benefit unit

(c) is placed with you prior to adoption, they are included in UC and SPC but not HB.

5.22 UC 4(5); PC sch 2A para 3(4); HBW 20(2)(b),(3); HBP 20(2)(b),(3); CTRE(PR) 7(2)(b),(3); CTRW(PR) 7(2)(b),(3); CTRWS 7(5); CTRSP 10(2)(b)

5.23 HBW 20(2)(a); HBP 20(2)(a); CTRE(PR) 7(2)(a); CTRW(PR) 7(2)(a); CTRWS 7(6); CTRSP 10(2)(a)

5.24 UC 4(4), 4A(1); PC sch 2A para 4(3); HBW 21(3); HBP 21(3)

Children in local authority care

5.25 A child or young person isn't included in your benefit unit if they are in local authority care, unless this is a planned short-term break to give you time off from caring for them, or one of a series of such breaks.

Children who normally live elsewhere

5.26 A child or young person isn't included in your benefit unit if they spend some time with you but don't normally live with you (TD v SSWP, JB v SSWP). For example, if you often look after a child who normally lives with their parent, the child is included in their parent's benefit unit, not yours.

Temporary absence of children

5.27 A child or young person continues to be included in your benefit unit while they are temporarily absent (paras 5.28-30).

Table 5.1 **Who is a young person**

Someone aged 16 or more but under 20 is a 'young person' (para 5.19) during any or all of the following periods (the periods in which child benefit can be paid for them):

(a) Until the 31st August following their 16th birthday (in all cases, whether or not they are in education, training or work)

(b) While they are undertaking a course of education which:

- is not above GCE A level or equivalent (national standard level 3) [www] and
- takes up more than 12 hours per week on average during term-time of tuition, practical work, supervised study or taking examinations and
- they began before their 19th birthday

(c) While they are between two courses which meet the above conditions. But this only applies if they are enrolled on and actually start the second course

(d) While they are undertaking approved training which is not provided under an employment contract. This includes many kinds of employment preparation course etc [www]

Table continued ➤

5.25 UC 4(6)(b), 4A(1); PC sch 2A paras 4(3), 5; HBW 21(1); HBP 21(1); CTRE(PR) 8(1); CTRW(PR) 8(1); CTRWS 7(7),(8); CTRSP 11(1)

5.26 UC 4(4); PC sch 2A para 3(3); HBW 20(2)(b),(3); HBP 20(2)(b); CTRE(PR) 7(2)(b); CTRW(PR) 7(2)(b); CTRWS 7(4); CTRSP 10(2)(b)
TD v SSWP and LB Richmond (HB) [2013] UKUT 642 (AAC); JB v SSWP and Basingstoke and Deane BC [2014] UKUT 223 (AAC)

5.27 UC 4(7); PC sch 2A para 6; HBW 21(1); HBP 21(1); CTRE(PR) 8(1); CTRW(PR) 8(1); CTRWS 12; CTRSP 11(1)

T5.1 UC 5; PC 4A; HBW 19; HBP 19; CTRE(PR) 2(1) – 'young person'; CTRW(PR) 2(1) – 'young person'; CTRSW 6; CTRSP 4
www.gov.uk/what-different-qualification-levels-mean
www.hmrc.gov.uk/manuals/ccmmanual/ccm18035.htm

(e) From when they leave the above education or training until the last day of August, November, February or May, whichever comes first. This is called the 'child benefit terminal date'.

(f) If they are aged 16 or 17, from when they leave the above education or training until the end of the 20th whole week after that. This is called the 'child benefit extension period'. But it only applies if:

- they are not in remunerative work and
- they are registered for work, education or training with the Careers Service or Connexions Service and
- an application is made, within three months of the end of the education or training, for child benefit to continue during this period.

Absences of your partner, child or young person

Absences in the UK

5.28 You continue to count as a couple while one of you is temporarily absent within the UK (para 8.2), or in many cases while you both are (para 8.11). And (except as described in paras 5.24-26) a child or young person continues to be included in your benefit unit while they are temporarily absent. However, a partner, child or young person stops counting as a member of your benefit unit if their absence is likely to exceed 52 weeks (or in exceptional circumstances, to substantially exceed that).

Absences abroad

5.29 A partner, child or young person who is absent abroad (para 8.2), continues to be included in your benefit unit so long as their absence:

(a) is unlikely to exceed the time limit (or to 'substantially' exceed it in SPC/HB cases if your circumstances are exceptional) and

(b) hasn't yet reached the time limit.

5.30 The time limit is:

(a) two months (UC) or eight weeks (SPC/HB) if their absence is in connection with a death in the family (para 8.34)

(b) six months (UC) or 26 weeks (SPC/HB) if their absence is to receive medical treatment (para 8.36) or

(c) one month (UC) or four weeks (SPC/HB) for other absences abroad.

For absences that are partly in the UK and partly abroad, the rules are the same as in para 8.40.

5.28 UC 3(6); PC 5(1)(a); HBW 21(1),(2); HBP 21(1),(2)

5.29 UC 11(1)(a),(b)(i); PC 5(1)(f); HBW 7(13C),(13D),(16)(d)(iii); HBP 7(13C),(13D),(16)(d)(iii)

5.30 UC 11(1)(b)(ii),(2),(3); PC 5(1A),(1B),(1C); HBW 7(13D),(13E),(16)(d)(ii); HBP 7(13C),(13D)(16)(d)(iii)

Chapter 6 **Non-dependants**

- Who is a non-dependant: paras 6.1-16
- How much are non-dependants expected to contribute: paras 6.17-31

Who is a non-dependant

6.1 A 'non-dependant' is an adult son, daughter, other relative or friend who:

(a) normally lives with you

(b) isn't part of your benefit unit (para 5.2) and

(c) doesn't have a tenancy or other commercial arrangement.

6.2 Typically, a child who lives at home becomes a young person at the age of 16, and then becomes a non-dependant after leaving non-advanced education (table 5.1).

People who aren't non-dependants

6.3 The following are not non-dependants:

(a) your partner (even if you are in a couple but claiming UC as a single person)

(b) children and young persons in your benefit unit

(c) foster children and other children and young persons who aren't included in your benefit unit (paras 5.24-26)

(d) a joint renter with you

(e) a lodger of yours

(f) a resident landlord

(g) a separate tenant of your landlord's

(h) household members of anyone in (d)-(g).

Terminology: extended benefit unit

6.4 Your 'extended benefit unit' means your benefit unit (you, your partner, children and young persons) plus any non-dependants you have. (In the law, this term is used for UC but not SPC, HB or CTR.)

6.2 UC sch 4 para 9(2); PC sch 2 para 1(4); HBW 3(1); HBP 3(1); CTRE(PR) 9(1); CTRW(PR) 9(1); CTRSW 8(1); CTRSP 3(1)

6.3 UC sch 4 para 9(2); PC sch 2 para 1(5)-(7); HBW 3(2); HBP 3(2); CTRE(PR) 9(2); CTRW(PR) 9(2); CTRSW 8(2); CTRSP 3(2)

6.4 UC sch 4 para 9(1)

Normally living in the accommodation with you

6.5 To count as a non-dependant a person must live in the accommodation with you. It is enough if they share a living room or kitchen with you (CPC/1446/2008), even if you each have your own bedroom (CH/542/2006, CH/3656/2005) and might be enough even if they can't make use of the shared areas due to disability (CPC/3379/2008). But it isn't enough if they share just a bathroom or toilet, or communal areas. such as halls, corridors and stairways.

6.6 The person must also 'normally' live with you. This includes someone who is temporarily absent, so long as they intend to return (for UC, within six months). But it doesn't include:

(a) someone who is actually living away from you, even if they may eventually return

(b) a short-term or regular visitor whose normal home is elsewhere (JP v Bournemouth BC) or

(c) someone you take in temporarily because they have nowhere else to go (CH/4004/2004), though this may change as time goes by (CH/3935/2007).

6.7 When a student leaves home in stages, the question of where they normally live is decided on its merits and not solely on the amount of time they spend in each location (RR v SSWP). If they live in university halls during term, return during vacations and remain registered with your local doctor etc, their normal residence is usually with you. But if they rent privately, return home less frequently and are registered with a local doctor at university, that usually counts as their normal residence.

Non-dependants who are a couple

6.8 If your non-dependant has a partner, the partner is also your non-dependant. They are expected to contribute:

(a) one amount each towards your housing costs in UC but

(b) one amount between them in SPC, HB and CTR.

Non-dependants with children

6.9 If your non-dependant has children or young persons, they are included in either the non-dependant's benefit unit or yours, depending on who is responsible for them. For example, if your daughter is your non-dependant and has a son of her own, the son may be included in either the daughter's benefit unit if she is responsible for him, or yours if you are.

Non-dependants with non-dependants

6.10 If your non-dependant has non-dependants, they usually count as your own non-dependants. For example, if your uncle is your non-dependant and his adult daughters also live with you, both the uncle and the adult daughters are your non-dependants.

6.5-6 UC sch 4 para 9(2); PC sch 2 para 1(4); HBW 3(1); HBP 3(1); CTRE(PR) 9(1); CTRW(PR) 9(1); CTRSW 8(1); CTRSP 3(1)
JP v Bournemouth BC (HB) [2018] UKUT 75 (AAC) reported as [2018] AACR 30

6.7 RR v SSWP (UC) [2024] UKUT 261 (AAC)

6.8 UC sch 4 para 13(1); PC sch 2 para 14(3); HBW 74(3); HBP 55(3); CTRE(PR) sch 1 para 8(3);
CTRW(PR) sch 1 para 3(3), sch 6 para 5(3); CTRSW 90(3); CTRSP 48(3)

6.9 UC sch 4 para 9(1)(a),(2)(a); PC sch 2 para 1(4); HBW 3(1); HBP 3(1); CTRE(PR) 9(1); CTRW(PR) 9(1); CTRSW 8(1); CTRSP 3(1)

6.10 UC sch 4 para 9(2); PC sch 2 para 1(4),(5)(a); HBW 3(1); HBP 3(1); CTRE(PR) 9(1); CTRW(PR) 9(1); CTRSW 8(1); CTRSP 3(1)

Joint renters

6.11 If you jointly rent your home, your joint renters are not your non-dependants. Each joint renter makes a separate claim for benefit that includes any members of their benefit unit (partner, children and young persons).

Joint renters with non-dependants

6.12 But if you jointly rent your home and there is also a non-dependant living there, the following applies:

(a) if the non-dependant normally lives with only one of the joint renters, the non-dependant is included in the claim of only that joint renter

(b) if the non-dependant normally lives with more than one of the joint renters:

- in UC, the non-dependant is included in the claim of only one joint renter (usually the joint renter who makes the earliest UC claim)
- in SPC, HB and CTR, the non-dependant amount (para 6.17) is shared between the joint renters using similar rules to those in para 10.14.

Lodgers

6.13 If you have a lodger, your lodger is not your non-dependant. Nor is anyone who is a member of your lodger's household but not yours.

Who is a lodger

6.14 A lodger is someone who pays you rent on a commercial basis. (We use 'lodger' because benefit law doesn't have a convenient term.) But you count as a non-dependant rather than a lodger if:

(a) you don't have a tenancy (or similar) agreement – even if you have exclusive occupation of your own room (KC v SSWP) or

(b) you have an excluded liability (table 9.2).

Resident landlords

6.15 If you have a resident landlord, your landlord is not your non-dependant. Nor is anyone who is a member of your landlord's household but not yours.

Separate tenants

6.16 If your dwelling is rented out to separate tenants (for example a house in multiple occupation), a separate tenant isn't your non-dependant. Nor is anyone who is a member of the tenant's household but not yours.

6.11 UC sch 4 para 9(1)(a),(2)(a); PC sch 2 para 1(7); HBW 3(2)(d); HBP 3(2)(d); CTRE(PR) 9(2)(d); CTRW(PR) 9(2)(d); CTRSW 8(2)(c); CTRSP 3(2)(d)

6.12 UC sch 4 para 9(2)(f); PC sch 2 paras 1(4), 14(5); HBW 3(1), 74(5); HBP 3(1), 55(5); CTRE(PR) 9(1), sch 1 para 8(5); CTRW(PR) 9(1), sch 1 para 3(5), sch 6 para 5(5); CTRSW 8(1), 90(5); CTRSP 3(1), 48(5)

6.13 UC sch 4 para 9(2)(d); PC sch 2 para 1(6)(a); HBW 3(2)(e)(i); HBP 3(2)(e)(i); CTRE(PR) 9(2)(e); CTRW(PR) 9(2)(e); CTRSW 8(2)(d); CTRSP 3(2)(e)

6.14 KC v SSWP [2012] UKUT 114 (AAC)

6.15 UC sch 4 para 9(2)(e); HBW 3(2)(e)(ii),(iii); HBP 3(2)(e)(ii),(iii)

6.16 UC sch 4 para 9(1)(a),(2)(a); PC sch 2 para 1(7),(8); HBW 3(1),(4); HBP 3(1),(4)

Non-dependant amounts

6.17 The benefit rules assume that your non-dependants will contribute towards your housing costs unless one of the exceptions applies. This is called:

(a) a housing cost contribution in UC – this is deducted from your housing costs element (para 16.33)

(b) a non-dependant deduction in SPC, HB or CTR – this is deducted from your housing costs addition (para 17.15), your eligible rent (para 18.2) or your eligible council tax (para 30.7).

Tables 6.1-3 give the amounts and exceptions.

Single non-dependants

6.18 Whether you are claiming UC, SPC, HB or CTR, one housing cost contribution or non-dependant deduction applies for a single non-dependant unless the exceptions apply.

Non-dependant couples: UC

6.19 If you are claiming UC, two housing cost contributions apply for a non-dependant couple (one each), but:

(a) if the exceptions apply to one of them, there is only one contribution (from the other) or

(b) if the exceptions apply to both of them, there is no contribution.

Non-dependant couples: SPC, HB and CTR

6.20 If you are claiming SPC, HB or CTR, one non-dependant deduction applies for a non-dependant couple calculated as follows:

(a) if the exceptions in table 6.2 apply to both, there is no contribution

(b) if the exceptions apply to one only, based on the gross income of the other partner

(c) in any other case, based on their combined gross income.

Exceptions based on the non-dependant's circumstances

6.21 A non-dependant is not expected to contribute towards your housing costs if he or she is in the categories in tables 6.1-3.

6.17 UC sch 4 para 13(3); PC sch 2 para 14; HBW 74; HBP 55; CTRE(PR) sch 1 para 8; CTRW(PR) sch 1 para 3, sch 6 para 5; CTRSW 90; CTRSP 48

6.18 UC sch 4 para 13(1); PC sch 2 para 14; HBW 74; HBP 55; CTRE(PR) sch 1 para 8; CTRW(PR) sch 1 para 3, sch 6 para 5; CTRSW 90; CTRSP 48

6.19 UC sch 4 para 13(1),(2)

6.20 PC sch 2 para 14(3),(4); HBW 74(3),(4); HBP 55(3),(4); CTRE(PR) sch 1 para 8(3),(4); CTRW(PR) sch 1 para 3(3),(4), sch 6 para 5(3),(4); CTRSW 90(3),(4); CTRSP 48(3),(4)

6.21 UC sch 4 para 16; PC sch 2 para 14(7); HBW 74(7),(8),(10); HBP 55(7)-(9); CTRE(PR) sch 1 para 8(7),(8); CTRW(PR) sch 1 para 3(7),(8), sch 6 para 5(7),(8); CTRSW 90(7),(8); CTRSP 48(7),(8)

Exceptions based on your circumstances

6.22 Non-dependants are not expected to contribute to your housing costs if you or your partner:

(a) are on one of the following disability benefits:
- the daily living component of PIP or ADP
- the middle or highest rate of the care component of DLA, SADLA or CDP
- attendance allowance or PADP or an equivalent benefit (para 21.18)

(b) are entitled to one of those disability benefits but not getting it because of being in hospital (this only applies if you are claiming UC or CTR)

(c) are certified as severely sight-impaired or blind by an ophthalmologist or

(d) have regained your sight in the last 28 weeks.

In these cases, there are no housing cost contributions in UC and no non-dependant deductions in SPC, HB and CTR. This is the case for all your non-dependants, whatever their circumstances.

Exceptions if you are on SPC as well as HB or SMI

6.23 Non-dependants aren't expected to make the same contribution twice. So if a deduction is made from your HB, the same deduction isn't made from SPC. Or if a deduction is made from your SMI, only the balance is deducted from SPC.

Delayed non-dependant deductions in SPC, HB and CTR

6.24 This rule applies if:

(a) you are over 66 (and so is your partner if you are in a couple)

(b) you are getting SPC, HB or (except in Wales) CTR and

(c) a change occurs that causes a non-dependant deduction to start or increase.

In these cases the start or increase in the deduction is delayed until 26 weeks after the change actually occurs. But the non-dependant is taken into account straight away for other purposes such as the rules about the size of your home (chapter 14).

6.22 UC 2 – 'blind', sch 4 para 15; PC sch 2 para 14(7); HBW 74(6),(10); HBP 55(6), sch 3 para 6(4),(5); CTRE(PR) sch 1 para 8(6),(11),(12); CTRW(PR) sch 1 para 3(6), sch 6 para 5(6); CTRSW 2(1) – 'blind', 90(6); CTRSP 48(6)

6.23 PC sch 2 para 14(2A),(7)(dd)

6.24 SS(D&A) 7(12F),(12G); HBP 59(10)-(13); CTRE(PR) sch 1 para 46(10)-(13); CTRSP 59(10)-(13)

Non-dependant's gross income in SPC, HB and CTR

6.25 When your non-dependant's 'gross income' is used (tables 6.2-3), it includes:

(a) employed earnings (before tax, national insurance, etc are deducted)

(b) self-employed net profit (after the deduction of reasonable expenses but before tax, national insurance, etc are deducted)

(c) social security benefits, pensions and credits (except as in para 6.26)

(d) state, occupational and private pensions

(e) rental income

(f) maintenance

(g) charitable and voluntary income and

(h) interest on savings.

Because the 'normal' amount of gross weekly income is taken into account, short-term variations are likely to be ignored, but longer-term changes are taken into account.

6.26 The following are wholly disregarded:

(a) PIP or ADP

(b) DLA, SADLA or CDP

(c) attendance allowance or PADP

(d) constant attendance allowance paid with an industrial injury or war disablement pension

(e) armed forces independence payment

(f) payments from the government-sponsored trust funds in para 21.43.

Working at least 16 hours per week

6.27 You count as working at least 16 hours per week (tables 16.2-3) if:

(a) you are employed or self-employed in work for which payment is made or expected and

(b) you work at least 16 hours per week on average.

The law calls this 'remunerative work'.

6.28 If your hours vary, they are averaged as follows:

(a) if there is no recognisable cycle to your work, over five weeks or whatever period would give a more accurate figure

(b) if your work has a recognisable cycle (for example you work a regular pattern of shifts), over the whole of that cycle. In this case, the averaging includes periods you don't work.

6.25 PC sch 2 para 14(2); HBW 74(2); HBP 55(2); CTRE(PR) sch 1 para 8(2); CTRW(PR) sch 1 para 3(2), sch 6 para 5(2); CTRSW 90(2); CTRSP 48(2)

6.26 PC sch 2 para 14(8),(9); HBW 74(9),(11); HBP 55(10),(11); CTRE(PR) sch 1 para 8(9),(10); CTRW(PR) sch 1 para 3(9), sch 6 para 5(9); CTRSW 90(9); CTRSP 48(9)

6.27 PC sch 2 para 2(1); HBW 2(1) – 'remunerative work', 6(1); HBP 2(1), 6(1); CTRE(PR) 10(1); CTRW(PR) 10(1); CTRSW 10(1); CTRSP 6(1)

6.28 PC sch 2 para 2(2),(4); HBW 6(2),(4); HBP 6(2),(4); CTRE(PR) 10(2),(4); CTRW(PR) 10(2),(4); CTRSW 10(2),(4); CTRSPR 6(2),(4)

6.29 And if your work has a recognisable cycle of a year, the result of (b) applies throughout the year. For example, if you work at a school for at least 16 hours every week in term-times, you count as working at least 16 hours per week throughout the year (even if you don't work during holidays).

6.30 You continue to count as working at least 16 hours per week:

(a) while you are on holiday or

(b) while you are absent from work 'without good cause' or

(c) for the purposes of the HB childcare disregard (table 22.5) only:

- for up to 28 weeks on sick leave – so long as you are getting statutory sick pay, ESA, income support because of incapacity for work, or national insurance credits instead of these
- for up to 39 weeks on parental leave – so long as you are getting statutory maternity, paternity, shared parental or adoption pay, or maternity allowance, or income support because of paternity leave.

6.31 But you don't count as working at least 16 hours per week:

(a) if you are doing unpaid work

(b) if your only income is from a Sports Council award (para 21.31)

(c) while you are absent from work 'with good cause' (for example you are laid off)

(d) in any benefit week in which you are on JSA(IB), ESA(IR) or income support for more than three days or

(e) while you are on sick or parental leave, except as described in para 6.30.

6.29 PC sch 2 para 2(3); HBW 6(3); HBP 6(3); CTRE(PR) 10(3); CTRW(PR) 10(3); CTRSW 10(3); CTRSP 6(3)

6.30 PC sch 2 para 2(5); HBW para 6(5), 28(2)-(4),(14); HBP 6(5), 31(2)-(4),(14),(15); CTRE(PR) 10(5), sch 1 para 25(2)-(4),(14),(15); CTRW(PR) 10(5), sch 1 para 19(2)-(4),(15),(16), sch 6 para 21(2)-(4),(15),(16); CTRSW 10(5), 77(3)-(5),(16),(17); CTRSP 6(5), 29(2)-(4),(15),(16)

6.31 PC sch 2 para 2(1),(5)-(8); HBW 6(1),(5)-(8); HBP 6(1),(5)-(8); CTRE(PR) 10(1),(5)-(8); CTRW(PR) 10(1),(5)-(8); CTRSW 10(1),(5)-(8); CTRSP 6(1),(5)-(8)

Table 6.1 **Housing cost contributions in UC: 2025-26**

In UC housing cost contributions are a monthly amount which the DWP deducts from your housing costs element (para 6.17).

Amount of housing cost contribution

The contribution is always £93.02 per month (per assessment period) for each of your non-dependants. If your non-dependants are in a couple, there is one contribution for each of them.

When there is no housing cost contribution

There is no housing cost contribution in UC for a non-dependant who is in any of the following categories

(a) Under 21

(b) On SPC

(c) Responsible for a child under five years old

(d) On carer's allowance or carer support payment

(e) A member of the armed forces who is away on operations if they are your son, daughter, step-son or step-daughter (but only if they lived with you before leaving and plan to return when the operations end)

(f) A prisoner (para 3.23)

(g) On one of the following disability benefits:

- the daily living component of PIP or ADP
- the middle or highest rate of the care component of DLA, SADLA or CDP
- attendance allowance or PADP or an equivalent benefit (para 21.18) or

(h) Entitled to one of those disability benefits but not getting it because of being in hospital.

Note: There are no housing cost contributions at all if you (the claimant) or your partner are disabled as described in para 6.22.

T6.1 UC sch 4 paras 14(1), 16; SI 2025/295 reg 32(3)

Examples: Monthly housing cost contributions in UC

No-one in these examples (except the younger son in example 2) is in any of the groups for whom there are no deductions (table 6.1). In each case the housing costs element is used in the calculation of UC (para 16.32).

1. One non-dependant

Ewan's eligible rent is £600.00 per month. He has one non-dependant, his daughter aged 30.

- Eligible rent £600.00
- One housing cost contribution – £93.02
- Housing costs element £506.98 per month

2. Two non-dependants

Rosie's eligible rent is £950.00 per month. She has two non-dependants, her sons aged 20 and 24.

- Eligible rent £950.00
- One housing cost contribution (older son only) – £93.02
- Housing costs element £856.98 per month

3. Two non-dependants who are a couple

Hazel's eligible rent is £700.00 per month. She has two non-dependants, her son and daughter-in-law.

- Eligible rent £700.00
- Two housing cost contributions (para 6.18) – £186.04
- Housing costs element £513.96 per month

Table 6.2 **Non-dependant deductions in SPC/HB: 2025-26**

In SPC and HB, non-dependant deductions are a weekly amount which the DWP deducts from your eligible housing costs or the council deducts from your eligible rent (para 6.17). If your non-dependants are in a couple see para 6.20.

Non-dependants working at least 16 hours pw	**SPC or HB**
Gross weekly income	**Weekly deduction**
■ at least £577	£126.65
■ at least £463 but under £577	£115.45
■ at least £348 but under £463	£101.35
■ at least £266 but under £348	£62.00
■ at least £183 but under £266	£45.15
■ under £183	£19.65
Other non-dependants	£19.65

When there is no non-dependant deduction

There is no non-dependant deduction in SPC or HB for a single non-dependant in any of the following categories:

(a) Under 18
(b) A youth trainee getting a training allowance
(c) A member of the armed forces who is away on operations
(d) Under 25 and on UC without any earned income
(e) On SPC
(f) Under 25 and on JSA(IB) or IS
(g) A full-time student if you are on pension age HB or are a mixed age couple
(h) A full-time student (but not during the summer vacation if the student works 16+ hours)
(i) A prisoner or
(j) A live-in carer looking after you or your partner, who was provided by a charitable or voluntary organisation that makes a charge for this.

Notes:

- See paras 6.25-31 for how a non-dependant's hours and income are assessed.
- If you are claiming both SPC and HB, or SPC and SMI see para 6.23.
- There are no non-dependant deductions at all if you (the claimant) or your partner are disabled as described in para 6.22.

T6.2 PC sch 2 para 14(1),(2),(7); HBW 3(2)(f), 74(1),(2),(7),(8); HBP 3(2)(f), 55(1),(2),(7)-(9); SI 2025/295 regs 23(3), 24(3), 29(4)

Examples: Weekly non-dependant deductions in HB

No-one in these examples (except the younger son in example 2) is in any of the groups for whom there are no deductions (table 6.2). In each case the maximum HB is used in the calculation of HB (para 18.2).

1. One non-dependant

Nathan's eligible rent is £150 per week. He has one non-dependant, his daughter aged 30. She works full time and has a gross income of £300.00 per week.

- Eligible rent £150.00
- One non-dependant deduction – £62.00
- Maximum HB £88.00 per week

2. Two non-dependants

Lily's eligible rent is £230.00 per week. She has two non-dependants, her sons aged 20 and 24. The older son works full-time and has a gross income of £200.00 per week. The younger son is on UC and has no earned income.

- Eligible rent £230.00
- One non-dependant deduction (older son only) – £45.15
- Maximum HB £184.85 per week

3. Two non-dependants who are a couple

Wayne's eligible rent is £200.00 per week. He has two non-dependants, his son and daughter-in-law. They work full-time and have a joint gross income of £600.00 per week.

- Eligible rent £200.00
- One non-dependant deduction (para 6.19) – £126.65
- Maximum HB £73.35 per week

Table 6.3 **Non-dependant deductions in CTR: 2025-26**

In CTR, non-dependant deductions are a weekly amount which the council deducts from your eligible council tax (para 6.17).

Amount of housing cost contribution

The deduction depends on whether your non-dependant works at least 16 hours per week and then on their gross income (para 6.25). If your non-dependants are in a couple, there is one deduction between them. If one or both work at least 16 hours per week, the deduction uses their combined gross income.

Non-dependants working at least 16 hours per week

England		**Scotland**		**Wales**	
Income	*Deduction*	*Income*	*Deduction*	*Income*	*Deduction*
At least £579.00	£15.35	At least £586.00	£15.95	At least £577.00	£18.70
At least £463.00	£12.80	At least £474.00	£13.40	At least £463.00	£15.65
At least £266.00	£10.20	At least £273.00	£10.55	At least £266.00	£12.45
Under £266.00	£5.00	Under £273.00	£5.35	Under £266.00	£6.25

Other non-dependants

England	£5.00	**Scotland**	£5.35	**Wales**	£6.25

When there is no non-dependant deduction

There is no non-dependant deduction in CTR for a single non-dependant who is:

(a) in England and Wales and in Scotland for pension age CTR, in any of the categories in table 6.2

(b) in Scotland for working age CTR, in any of the categories (a)-(e) in table 6.2, on ESA(IR), IS or JSA(IB), a full-time student or

(c) a disregarded person in table 28.4 – for example, students, education leavers, care leavers, people who are severely mentally impaired and refugees from Ukraine.

Notes:

- In England, working age CTR is based on local rules, which are usually different (para 29.17).
- There are no non-dependant deductions at all if you (the claimant) or your partner are disabled as described in para 6.22.

T6.3 CTRE(PR) 9(2)(f), sch 1 para 8(1),(2),(7),(8); CTRW(PR) 9(2)(f), sch 1 para 3(1),(2),(7),(8); sch 6 para 5(1),(2),(7),(8); CTRSW 90(1),(2),(7),(8); CTRSP 3(2)(f), 48(1),(2),(7),(8); SI 2025/39 reg 5; SI 2025/59 reg 15; SSI 2025/24 regs 4, 14

Chapter 7 **Your home**

- Occupying your home: paras 7.1-5.
- Getting benefit on two homes: paras 7.6-10.
- Moving home: paras 7.11-27.

Occupying your home

7.1 The general rule is that you can only get UC, SPC or HB towards accommodation that:

(a) is in the UK and

(b) you normally occupy as your home.

This also applies to support for mortgage interest (SMI) (para 27.8).

Types of accommodation

7.2 Your home can be:

(a) a dwelling – for example a house, flat, caravan, mobile home, or houseboat or

(b) part of a dwelling – for example a room in a hostel or in someone else's home.

A dwelling includes any land or buildings which form part of it. Or it can include somewhere converted, such as when two flats have been knocked together to form a single home (R(H) 5/09; CH/1895/2008). It doesn't include business premises or somewhere used only for a holiday.

Your normal home

7.3 Whether you normally occupy accommodation as your home is decided in your and your benefit unit's particular circumstances (CH/2521/2002). It means more than paying housing costs or having the right to live there: it means being physically present – though exceptions can arise (R(H) 9/05). If you have more than one home (in the UK or abroad), only one can be your normal home. This is decided on the facts, including how much time you and your family spend in each of them.

Short-term accommodation

7.4 Your home can be somewhere short-term, e.g. if you move a lot or are staying in a hostel or refuge. But it must be a 'home' in the ordinary sense, and this doesn't normally include night shelters where you have no right to live during the day (OR v SSWP).

7.1 UC sch 3 para 1(1); LMI sch 3 paras 3(1), 12(1); PC sch 2 para 4(1); HBP 7(1); HBW 7(1)

7.2 UC sch 3 para 1(4); LMI 2(1) – 'dwelling', sch 3 paras 3(1), 12(1); PC 1(2) – 'dwelling occupied as the home', sch 2 para 4(1); HBP 2(1) – 'dwelling occupied as the home', 7(1); HBW 2(1), 7(1)

7.3 UC sch 3 para 1(1)-(3); LMI sch 3 paras 3(1),(2), 12(1),(2); PC sch 2 para 4(1),(2); HBP 7(1),(2); HBW 7(1),(2)

7.4 OR v SSWP and Isle of Anglesey County Council [2013] UKUT 65 (AAC)

Repairs to your normal home

7.5 When you move somewhere temporary because of repairs to your normal home, you can get benefit towards your housing costs on:

(a) your temporary home if you don't pay housing costs on your normal home or the housing costs on your normal home have stopped

(b) your normal home in any other case.

For (a) to apply, the repairs must be essential and of a kind that can't be done while you remain in your normal home (SH v LB Southwark).

Benefit on two homes

7.6 You can get UC, SPC or HB towards housing costs on two homes (but only two) if:

(a) you are a social renter with a large family (UC and HB only) (para 7.7)

(b) you are waiting for adaptations for a disability (para 7.15)

(c) you are unavoidably liable for housing costs on two homes (SPC and HB only) (para 7.24)

(d) you are absent from your normal home due to a fear of violence (para 8.14) or

(e) you are a student couple (SPC and HB only) (para 8.24).

In any other case you can only get UC, SPC or HB on your normal home.

Social renters with a large family

7.7 You can get UC or HB towards your rent on two homes without time limit if:

(a) you were housed in two rented homes by a social landlord (para 11.2) (UC) or by the council (HB)

(b) this was because of the number of children/young persons in your benefit unit and

(c) you normally occupy both homes with those children/young persons.

Calculating benefit for two homes

7.8 When you qualify for benefit towards your housing costs on two homes, a single calculation of benefit covers both homes. For HB this applies even if the two homes are in different council areas (MB v Selby DC).

7.9 In the single calculation:

(a) the two amounts for housing costs are added together

(b) deductions due to income and non-dependants are only made once

(c) the bedroom tax applies to the combined number of bedrooms in the case of large families, or each home separately in other cases.

7.5 UC sch 3 para 3; LMI sch 3 paras 5, 13; PC sch 2 para 4(5); HBW 7(4); HBP 7(4)
SH v LB of Southwark [2023] UKUT 198 (AAC)

7.6 UC sch 3 paras 1(2), 4(1),(2), 5(1),(2), 6(1),(2); LMI sch 3 paras 6, 7, 14(1),(2), 15(1),(2); PC sch 2 para 4(6); HBW 7(6); HBP 7(6)

7.7 UC sch 3 para 4; HBW 7(6)(c); HBP 7(6)(c)

7.8 MB v Selby DC [2011] UKUT 5 (AAC)

7.9(c) UC sch 3 para 4(2); HBW 7(6)

Getting benefit on two homes if you live in STA

7.10 The rules about getting benefit on two homes apply to supported or temporary accommodation (STA) as well as general accommodation. For example, you can get HB on a domestic violence refuge at the same time as getting UC or HB on general accommodation.

Example: Benefit on two homes: fear of violence

Jenny rents a council flat where she is on UC. Her former partner threatens her outside her home. Jenny goes to a refuge and starts action to enable her to return to her flat. The refuge is one that meets the definition of STA (table 13.1(c)).

- Jenny can continue to get UC towards the rent on her council flat, and can get HB towards the rent on the hostel at the same time for up to 12 months (paras 7.6, 8.14).

Moving home

The date of your move

7.11 When you move home, the date of your move is the day you physically transfer from one home to another, along with any members of your benefit unit who are moving with you, though there can be exceptions if your move is delayed at the last moment (R(H) 9/05). It doesn't mean the date on the letting agreement (if different) or the day you start getting your new home ready (R(H) 9/05, CH/1911/2006).

The date your benefit changes

7.12 Your UC, SPC or HB changes to take account of the housing costs on your new home. This happens:

(a) in UC, from the beginning of the assessment period containing the date of your move

(b) in SPC/HB, from the date of your move.

But if you are on HB and move to a different council area, you need to claim HB or UC as described in table 2.3 and paras 25.16-19.

Benefit for a period before you move in or after you move out

7.13 In the situations in the rest of this chapter, you can get:

(a) UC on a new home that you can't move into

(b) SPC or HB on a new home that you can't move into or

(c) SPC or HB on an old home that you have left but still have to pay for.

7.10 UCTP 6A(2),(4); UC sch 3 para 6(1),(2); HBW 7(6); HBP 7(6)

7.12 UC(D&A) sch 1 para 20; SS(D&A) 7(2)(a); HBW 79(2),(2A),(2B); HBP 59(2),(2A),(2B)

7.13 UC sch 3 paras 5, 7, 8; LMI sch 3 paras 7, 14, 16, 17; PC sch 2 para 4(6)(c),(7); HBW 7(6)(e),(8); HBP 7(6)(e),(8)

7.14 The maximum period is:

(a) one month for UC – so you can get UC on a new home from the start of the assessment period before the one containing the date of your move

(b) four weeks for HB/SPC – so you can get HB/SPC on a new home for four weeks before the date of your move, or HB/SPC on an old home for four weeks after the date of your move.

Waiting for adaptations for a disability

7.15 You can get UC, SPC or HB on a home you haven't moved into if:

(a) you are liable for housing costs there

(b) you haven't been able to move in because you were waiting for it to be adapted to meet your disability needs or those of a member of your benefit unit and

(c) your delay in moving was necessary and reasonable.

7.16 In UC (but not SPC or HB), you or the member of your benefit unit must also be getting one of the following disability benefits:

(a) the daily living component of PIP

(b) the standard or enhanced rate of the daily living component of ADP

(c) the middle or highest rate of the care component of DLA, SADLA or CDP

(d) attendance allowance or PADP or an equivalent benefit (para 21.18).

7.17 The adaptations (para 7.15(b)) can include furnishing, carpeting and redecorating as well as changes to your new home's fabric or structure (R (Mahmoudi) v Lewisham LBC).

7.18 In these cases:

(a) if you are liable for housing costs on just your new home (the home you are waiting to move into) you can get UC, SPC or HB there for up to one month/four weeks

(b) if you are also liable for housing costs on your old home, you can get UC and HB (but not SPC) towards your housing costs on both during this period

(c) in either case, you should ask for benefit on your new home as soon as you start being liable for housing costs there, but the payment isn't made until you move in.

7.14 UC sch 3 paras 5(4), 7(3), 8(2); LMI sch 3 paras 7(1), 14(4), 16(2), 17(2); PC sch 2 para 4(6)(c),(7); HBW 7(6)(e),(8); HBP 7(6)(e),(8)

7.15 UC sch 3 paras 5(1),(2), 7; LMI sch 3 paras 7(1),(2), 14; PC sch 2 para 4(7)(c)(i); HBW 7(8)(c)(i); HBP 7(8)(c)(i)

7.16 UC sch 3 paras 5(3), 7(2); LMI sch 3 para 14(3)

7.17 R (Mahmoudi) v Lewisham LBC [2014] EWCA Civ 284

7.18 UC sch 3 paras 5(2), 7(1); LMI sch 3 paras 7(1), 14(2); PC sch 2 para 4(6),(7); HBW 7(6)(e),(8)(c)(i); HBP 7(6)(e),(8)(c)(i)

Example: Benefit on two homes: waiting for adaptations

Wolfgang rents a bedsit and is offered the tenancy of a flat nearer work. He takes on the tenancy and moves in three weeks later after adaptations make it suitable for his wheelchair. He is on the daily living component of PIP.

- If Wolfgang is on HB, he can get HB towards the rent on both the bedsit and the flat for those three weeks; or if he is on UC, he can get UC towards the rent on them both for the whole of the assessment period in which he becomes liable for rent on the flat (para 7.15, 7.18).

Waiting to leave hospital or a care home

7.19 You can get UC, SPC or HB on a home you haven't moved into if:

(a) you are liable for housing costs there

(b) you haven't been able to move in because you were waiting to leave an NHS or independent hospital or a care home

(c) if you have a partner, they were also waiting to leave hospital or a care home (this condition applies to UC but not SPC or HB) and

(d) your delay in moving was reasonable (this condition applies to SPC and HB but not UC).

7.20 In these cases:

(a) you can get UC, SPC or HB towards housing costs on your new home (the home you are waiting to move into) for up to one month/four weeks

(b) you should ask for benefit on your new home as soon as you start being liable for housing costs there (or else ask for your benefit to be backdated), but the payment isn't made until you move in.

Waiting for local welfare assistance

7.21 You can get SPC or HB (but not UC) on a home you haven't moved into if:

(a) you are liable for housing costs there

(b) you haven't been able to move in because you were waiting for local welfare assistance (para 31.24) to help with the move or setting up home and

(c) your delay in moving was reasonable.

7.19 UC sch 3 para 8(1); LMI sch 3 paras 7(1),(4), 17(1); PC sch 2 para 4(7)(c)(iii); HBW 7(8)(c)(iii); HBP 7(8)(c)(iii)

7.20 UC sch 3 para 8(2); LMI sch 3 paras 7(1), 17(2); PC sch 2 para 4(7)(b); HBW 7(8)(b); HBP 7(8)(b)

7.21 LMI sch 3 paras 7(1),(3); PC sch 2 para 4(7)(c)(ii); HBW 7(8)(c)(ii); HBP 7(8)(c)(ii)

7.22 In SPC and HB, you (or your partner if you are in a couple) must also meet one of the following conditions:

(a) you are over pension age or

(b) you have limited capability for work (or for work-related activity) (para 4.15) or

(c) you qualify for a disability premium (paras 18.26-28) or

(d) you have a child under 6 or

(e) you qualify for a disabled child premium for a child or young person in your benefit unit (para 18.14).

7.23 In these cases:

(a) if you are liable for housing costs on just your new home (the home you are waiting to move into) you can get UC, SPC or HB there for up to one month/four weeks

(b) if you are also liable for housing costs on your old home, you can only get benefit towards one home – this means whichever of them counts as your normal home during this period

(c) you should ask for benefit on your new home as soon as you start being liable for housing costs there, but the payment isn't made until you move in.

Unavoidable liability for housing costs

7.24 You can get SPC or HB (but not UC) on a home you have left but still have to pay for if:

(a) you remain liable for housing costs there (for example, you have to pay for a notice period) and

(b) your liability couldn't reasonably have been avoided.

7.25 Whether your liability could reasonably have been avoided depends on the facts and any alternatives that were open to you (CH/4546/2002), such as whether and when you gave notice to your landlord.

7.26 In these cases:

(a) if you are liable for housing costs on just your old home (the home you have left) you can get UC, SPC or HB there for up to one month/four weeks

(b) if you are also liable for housing costs on your new home, you can get benefit towards your housing costs on both during this period

(c) in either case, you usually need to ask for benefit to continue on your old home.

7.22 LMI sch 3 paras 7(3); PC sch 2 para 4(7)(c)(ii); HBW 7(8)(c)(ii); HBP 7(8)(c)(ii)

7.23 LMI sch 3 para 7(1); PC sch 2 para 4(7)(b); HBW 7(8)(b); HBP 7(8)(b)

7.24 PC sch 2 para 4(6)(c); HBW 7(6)(d); HBP 7(6)(d)

7.26 PC sch 2 para 4(6)(c); HBW 7(6)(d),(10); HBP 7(6)(d),(10)

7.27 This rule is sometimes called the 'overlapping benefit rule'. It can apply whether:

(a) you have moved to a house, flat etc or

(b) you have gone into a hospital, care home or prison (HBGM A3.688 example 3) or

(c) you left your old home due to fear of violence (para 8.14) and don't yet have a new address or don't want to say where it is.

Example: Unavoidable liability (overlapping benefit)

Barnaby gets HB on a private rented flat. He is offered a housing association house in the same area and has to take up the tenancy there on the following Monday. He gives notice to his old landlord and is liable for rent on both homes for the overlap period.

- He can get HB on both homes during the overlap for up to four weeks (paras 7.24, 7.26).

Chapter 8 **Temporary absences**

- General conditions and how the time limits work: paras 8.1-10
- Absences in Great Britain: paras 8.11-29
- Absences abroad: paras 8.30-40

General rules

8.1 This chapter explains when you can get UC, SPC and HB during an absence from your normal home.

8.2 We use the following terms:

(a) 'absences in the UK' – this means absences within England, Scotland, Wales or Northern Ireland

(b) 'absences abroad' – this means absences anywhere else in the world.

In the rules about (a), the law refers to Great Britain, but reciprocal arrangements (the last two items in the footnote) then extend it to Northern Ireland.

Summary

8.3 The main rule is that you can only get benefit up to the time limit in this chapter. If you are away for longer than that:

(a) for absences in the UK, you stop getting benefit towards your housing costs

(b) for absences abroad, you stop getting benefit altogether.

If your absence is partly in the UK and partly abroad, see para 8.40.

General conditions

8.4 During an absence (in the UK or abroad), you have to meet the following conditions in order to get UC/SPC/HB on your normal home:

(a) you must intend to return – in other words your absence must be temporary

(b) your expected absence (and your actual absence) mustn't exceed the time limit

(c) you must have been getting UC/SPC/HB immediately before the absence began

(d) in SPC and HB, your home mustn't have been let out (or sub-let) to someone else

(e) in UC, paying UC during the absence must be reasonable.

8.2 WRA 4(1)(c), 11(2)(a),(3)(c); SPCA 1(2)(a); SSCBA 130(1)(a); SI 2020/129 sch para 2; SI 2016/1050

8.3 WRA 4(1)(c), 11(1),(3)(c); SPCA 1(2)(a),(5); SSCBA 130(1)(a), 137(2)(a),(b),(h); UC 10, 11, 25(1)(c),(4), sch 3; PC 3, sch 2 paras 1(1)(a), 4; HBW 7; HBP 7

8.4 UC 11(1), 25(1)(c),(4), sch 3 paras 1(1), 6(1)(c),(4), 9; PC 3(1), sch 2 paras 1(1)(a), 4(9)-(12); HBW 7(13),(13D),(16); HBP 7(13),(13D),(16)

Your intention to return

8.5 During an absence in the UK, you can only get UC, SPC or HB towards your housing costs if you intend to return to your normal home. During an absence abroad, you can only get benefit (towards living or housing costs) if you intend to return to the UK.

8.6 In each case, your intention can depend on the outcome of events (e.g. in the case of absences due to a fear of violence), but your return must be possible within the time limit. Wanting to return is not enough if your return is in fact impossible (CSHB/405/2005).

The time limits

8.7 The time limits for all absences are summarised in tables 8.1 and 8.2. You can only get benefit if:

(a) your absence is unlikely to exceed the time limit or

(b) in exceptional circumstances, it is unlikely to 'substantially' exceed the time limit and

(c) in either case, it hasn't yet reached the time limit.

8.8 Condition (b) above only applies to SPC and HB cases in which the limit is 52 weeks. It can apply if a stay in hospital or other unanticipated events mean you may be absent for up to 15 months (HBGM A3.532). Condition (a) applies in other SPC and HB cases and all UC cases.

Counting the time limits

8.9 The time limits apply to absences that are continuous (R v Penwith DC ex parte Burt). The day you go away counts as a day of absence, but the day you return does not (Slough BC v PK). And so long as you return for at least 24 hours, going away again starts a new absence with a new time limit (HBGM A3.460).

How the time limits affect your benefit

8.10 During an absence from home, the time limits apply as follows:

(a) if your absence is likely to be within the time limit, you get benefit throughout your absence (AM v SSWP) but

(b) if your absence is likely to exceed the time limit, your benefit ends on the first day of the assessment period or benefit week in which your absence begins – in other words, you don't get benefit during any of your absence (para 33.34).

If the circumstances surrounding your absence change, each period is decided separately.

8.5 WRA 4(1)(c); SPCA 1(2)(a); SSCBA 130(1)(a); UC 11(1), sch 3 paras 6(1), 9(1); PC 3(1), sch 2 paras 1(1)(a), 4(10),(11); HBW 7(13)(a),(13D)(a),(16)(a); HBP 7(13)(a),(13D)(a),(16)(a)

8.7 UC 11(1), sch 3 paras 6(4), 9; PC 3(1), sch 2 paras 1(1)(a), 4(9)-(12); HBW 7(13),(13D),(13G),(16)(a),(d); HBP 7(13),(13D),(13G),(16)(a),(d)

8.8 PC 6(7), sch 2 para 4(9),(11)(a),(d),(12); HBW 7(16)(d); HBP 7(16)(d)

8.9 R v Penwith HBRB ex parte Burt (1990) QBD 22 HLR 292
Slough BC v PK (HB) [2019] UKUT 128 (AAC)

8.10 UC 11(1), sch 3 para 9(1); PC 3(1), sch 2 para 4(10),(11)(d); HBW 7(13),(13D),(16)(d); HBP 7(13),(13D),(16)(d)
AM v SSWP (UC) [2024] UKUT 137 (AAC)

Examples: Time limits for absences

These examples relate to tables 8.1 and 8.2.

1. A short absence in the UK

Ernest is on UC and his assessment periods begin on 18th of each month. He goes to visit a friend for two months, leaving his home on 15 November and returning on 15 January.

- His absence is less than six months, so he continues to get UC towards his housing costs and living costs while he is away.

2. A longer absence in the UK

Erica is on UC and her assessment periods begin on 8th of each month. She goes to stay with a friend for eight months, leaving her home on 15 November and returning on 15 July.

- Her absence is longer than six months, so her UC continues but she stops getting UC towards her housing costs.
- The first full day she is absent is 16 November.
- Her UC stops including her housing costs from the beginning of the assessment period containing that date, which is 8 November.

3. A short absence abroad

Ernestina is on UC and her assessment periods begin on 13th of each month. On 6 July she goes abroad to visit relatives. She intends to return to the UK on 1 August.

- Her absence is less than one month, so she continues to get UC towards her housing costs and living costs while she is away.

4. A longer absence abroad

Emilio is on UC and his assessment periods begin on 23rd of each month. On 15 August he goes abroad to visit relatives. He intends to return to the UK on 15 December.

- His absence is longer than one month, so his UC stops altogether (both for his housing costs and living costs).
- The first full day he is absent is 16 August.
- His UC stops from the beginning of the assessment period containing that date, which is 23 July.

Absences in the UK

8.11 This section explains when you can get benefit towards your housing costs during an absence within the UK. If you don't qualify under the rules in this section, you can't get UC, SPC or HB towards your housing costs, but you can get UC or SPC towards your living costs so long as you meet the basic conditions (tables 2.1, 2.2).

The general rule for absences in the UK

8.12 The general rule applies to all absences within the UK unless a longer time limit is given later in this section. For example, it applies to working away from home and holidays in the UK.

8.13 In these cases, the time limit is:

(a) six months in UC

(b) 13 weeks in SPC and HB.

Table 8.1 **Time limits for absences in the UK**

	Reason for absence	UC time limit	SPC/HB time limit
(a)	General rule	Six months	13 weeks
(b)	Fear of violence	12 months	52 weeks
(c)	Receiving medical treatment	Six months	52 weeks
(d)	In a care home to try it out	Six months	13 weeks
(e)	In a care home for respite care	Six months	52 weeks
(f)	Providing care	Six months	52 weeks
(g)	Studying or training	Six months	52 weeks
(h)	In prison pending trial	Six months	52 weeks

Note: For repairs to your home see para 7.5, and for prison, remand and bail see paras 8.25-29.

Example: Going away for work

Robin rents a private flat in Cornwall and is on UC. He gets a live-in job in Berkshire that is expected to last for three months.

- While he is away, Robin can get UC towards the rent on his flat (para 8.13) (but his income from the job is included in assessing the amount of his UC).

8.12 WRA 11(2)(a); SI 2020/129 sch para 2; SI 2020/677 sch para 2; UC 25(1),(4), sch 3 paras 6, 9; PC 3(1), sch 2 paras 1(1)(a), 4(9)-(12); HBW 7(13),(16)(d); HBP 7(13),(16)(d)

8.13 UC sch 3 para 6(1); PC sch 2 para 4(10); HBW 7(16)(d); HBP 7(16)(d)

T8.1 UC sch 3 paras 1(1), 6(4), 9; PC sch 2 paras 1(1)(a), 4(8)-(12); HBW 7(11)-(13),(16); HBP 7(11)-(13),(16)

Absences in the UK due to a fear of violence

8.14 If you are absent from your normal home due to a fear of violence, you can get benefit towards your housing costs on:

(a) your normal home or

(b) the place you are staying or

(c) both, if you are liable for housing costs on both.

8.15 In each case, the time limit is:

(a) 12 months in UC

(b) 52 weeks in SPC and HB.

You must intend to return to your normal home when it becomes safe and reasonable to do so. If you don't intend to return, you can get a further four weeks' SPC or HB to cover your notice period at your (now former) home (para 7.24).

8.16 A 'fear of violence' means a fear of violence towards yourself or a member of your benefit unit either:

(a) in your normal home (whoever it would be from) or

(b) outside your normal home from:

- your former partner (UC, SPC and HB) or
- a close relative (para 9.30) (SPC only).

No violence needs actually to have occurred so long as your fear of it is reasonable (CH/1237/2004).

Example: Fear of violence

Morgana gets UC towards the rent on her council flat. Her partner lives with her and he begins to threaten her with violence. She goes to stay in a refuge, but she intends to return to her flat and has got her parents to tell her ex-partner to leave.

- She can get UC for up to twelve months towards the rent on her flat because she intends to return (para 8.15). She can also get HB towards the rent on the refuge (paras 7.6, 7.10).

Absences in the UK providing care

8.17 Providing care means:

(a) you are providing medically approved care to someone or

(b) you are caring for a child whose parent/guardian is away from their home to receive medical treatment or medically approved care.

8.15 UC sch 3 paras 6(4), 9(3); PC sch 2 para 4(11)(c)(x),(d),(12); HBW 7(6)(a),(16)(d)(i); HBP 7(6)(a),(16)(d)(i)

8.16 UC sch 3 para 6(1)(b); PC sch 2 para 4(6)(a),(11)(c)(x); HBW 7(6)(a),(16)(c)(x); HBP 7(6)(a),(16)(c)(x)

8.17 PC sch 2 para 4(11)(c)(v),(vi); HBW 7(16)(c)(v),(vi); HBP 7(16)(c)(v),(vi)

8.18 If you are absent from your normal home due to providing care, you can get benefit towards your housing costs (on your normal home) during an absence of up to:

(a) six months in UC (under the general rule in para 8.12).

(b) 52 weeks in SPC and HB.

Absences in the UK receiving care or medical treatment

8.19 Receiving care or medical treatment means:

(a) you are in hospital or a similar institution

(b) you are in a care home (paras 8.21-23)

(c) you are receiving medical treatment or medically approved care or convalescence somewhere else

(d) you are accompanying a member of your benefit unit who is receiving medical treatment or medically approved convalescence.

8.20 If you are absent from your normal home due to receiving care or medical treatment, you can get benefit towards your housing costs (on your normal home) during an absence of up to:

(c) six months in UC (under the general rule in para 8.12).

(d) 52 weeks in SPC and HB.

Example: A long stay in hospital

Michaela gets pension age HB on her rented home. She has a serious accident and her doctors expect her to be in hospital for between nine and 15 months.

- She can get HB because her expected absence is unlikely to substantially exceed 52 weeks (para 8.8)

Absences in the UK in a care home

8.21 For the rule in para 8.22, care homes include residential homes, nursing homes, independent (non-NHS) hospitals and Abbeyfield Homes.

8.22 If you are absent from your normal home because you are in a care home, you can get benefit towards your housing costs (on your normal home) during an absence of up to:

(a) six months in UC (under the general rule in para 8.12)

(b) 52 weeks in SPC and HB but

(c) 13 weeks in SPC and HB if you are trying the care home out to see if it will suit you as your future home.

8.18 UC sch 3 para 9(1); PC sch 2 para 4(11)(d),(12); HBW 7(16)(d)(i); HBP 7(16)(d)(i)

8.19 PC sch 2 para 4(11)(c)(ii),(iii),(vii),(ix); HBW 7(16)(c)(ii),(iii),(vii),(ix); HBP 7(16)(c)(ii),(iii),(vii),(ix)

8.20 UC sch 3 para 9(1); PC sch 2 para 4(11)(d),(12); HBW 7(16)(d)(i); HBP 7(16)(d)(i)

8.21 PC 1(2) – 'care home', 'independent hospital'; HBW 7(18) – 'residential accommodation'; HBP 7(18)

8.22 UC sch 3 para 9(1); PC sch 2 para 4(8),(9),(11)(c)(ix); HBW 7(11),(12),(16)(c)(ix); HBP 7(11),(12),(16)(c)(ix)

8.23 You can try out more than one care home and the 13 weeks limit in SPC and HB starts again for each one, but only until you have been absent from your normal home for 52 weeks overall. If and when you decide to stay in a care home, you can get a further four weeks' SPC or HB to cover your notice period at your (now former) home (para 7.24).

Example: A care home

Betella gets UC towards the rent on her flat. She goes into a care home for a three-month trial period. Then she decides to stay and gives a month's notice to the landlord of her flat.

- She can get UC towards the rent on her flat for up to six months, so this includes the trial period in the care home and the notice period to the landlord of her flat.

Absences in the UK studying or training

8.24 If you are away from home studying, or training on a government scheme, you can get benefit as follows:

(a) in UC, for up to six months (under the general rule in para 8.12)

(b) in SPC and HB, for up to 52 weeks towards housing costs on:

- your normal home or
- your term-time home if you don't have housing costs on your normal home or
- both homes if you are in a couple and it is reasonable and unavoidable for you to have two homes.

But if your term-time home becomes your normal home, you can get benefit there in the normal way.

In prison, on remand or on bail

8.25 The following paragraphs explain when you can get benefit on your normal home if you are a sentenced prisoner, remand prisoner or living away from home because you are on bail in approved premises or elsewhere. The rules differ between UC, SPC and HB, but in all the benefits:

(a) the rules for sentenced prisoners also apply to prisoners on temporary release

(b) you can't get benefit if you are detained in hospital.

8.23 PC sch 2 para 4(8),(9); HBW 7(11),(12); HBP 7(11),(12)

8.24 UC sch 3 paras 1(1), 9(1); PC sch 2 para 4(6)(b),(11)(c)(viii),(d); HBW 7(6)(b),(16)(c)(viii),(d); HBP 7(6)(b),(16)(c)(iii),(d)

8.25 WRA 6(1)(a); SPCA 2(3),(6); UC 2 – 'prisoner', 19(1)(b),(c),(4); PC 1(2) – 'prisoner', 6(2),(3), sch 3 para 2; HBW 7(14),(15); HBP 7(14),(15)

UC in prison, on remand or on bail

8.26 You can get UC towards your housing costs during an absence of up to six months if:

(a) you are a sentenced prisoner, a remand prisoner or on bail

(b) you are a single person

(c) you were getting UC immediately beforehand (or had claimed and were entitled to it) and this was for at least one full assessment period (SSWP v AH) and

(d) you haven't yet been sentenced or have been sentenced but aren't expected to serve more than six months.

In these cases, your UC it is recalculated to include just your housing costs element.

SPC in prison, on remand or on bail

8.27 You can't get SPC while you are a sentenced prisoner. But you can get SPC towards your housing costs during an absence of up to 52 weeks if you are a remand prisoner or on bail. In this case, your SPC is recalculated to include just your housing costs element and amounts for children and young persons (para 3.24).

HB in prison, on remand or on bail

8.28 You can get HB towards your housing costs:

(a) during an absence of up to 13 weeks if you are a sentenced prisoner and your overall absence (including time you were absent on remand or bail) is unlikely to exceed 13 weeks or

(b) during an absence of up to 52 weeks if you are a remand prisoner or on bail

8.29 You are likely to meet condition (a) above if your sentence is up to six months (which is 13 weeks after remission) or ten months if you are qualify for home detention curfew (HBGM A3.512-18). If you don't meet that condition, you can get four weeks' HB to cover your notice period at your (now former) home (para 7.24). This four weeks also applies if you are detained in hospital (HBGM A3.430-32).

Examples: Remand and serving a sentence

Gabriel gets UC on a rented flat. He is arrested and sent to prison. He is on remand for three months, and then serving a sentence of two years.

- Gabriel can get UC towards the rent on his flat while he is on remand. After that he can't get UC because he is expected to serve more than six months (para 8.28).
- But if he was in a couple, his partner could claim UC towards the rent during his absence.

8.26 UC 19(1)(b),(2),(3); SSWP v AH [2023] UKUT 274 (AAC)

8.27 SPCA 2(3),(6); PC 1(2) – 'prisoner', 6(2)(a),(3),(6)(d),(7),(9),(10)

8.28 SSCBA 130(1)(a), 137(2)(h); HBW 7(13),(16)(c)(i),(d)(i),(16A); HBP 7(13),(16)(c)(i),(d)(i),(16A)

8.29 HBW 7(7); HBP 7(7)

Absences abroad

8.30 This section explains when you can get benefit (including benefit towards your housing costs) during an absence abroad. If you don't qualify under the rules in this section, you can't get UC, SPC or HB at all (towards your living costs or housing costs).

Table 8.2 **Time limits for absences abroad**

	Reason for absence	UC time limit	SPC/HB time limit
(a)	General rule	One month	Four weeks
(b)	Fear of violence	One month	Four weeks in SPC 26 weeks in HB
(c)	Death in the family	Two months	Eight weeks
(d)	Receiving medical treatment	Six months	26 weeks
(e)	Mariners and continental shelf workers	Six months	26 weeks
(f)	HM forces	No limit	26 weeks
(g)	Crown servants	No limit	Four weeks

The general rule for absences abroad

8.31 The general rule applies to all absences abroad unless a longer time limit is given later in this section. For example, it applies to working, studying, training, providing care and holidays abroad.

8.32 In these cases, the time limit is:

(a) one month in UC

(b) four weeks in SPC and HB.

Absences abroad due to a fear of violence

8.33 If you are absent abroad due to a fear of violence (as described in para 8.16), you can get benefit towards your housing costs on your normal home for up to:

(a) one month in UC/four weeks in SPC (under the general rule in para 8.31)

(b) 26 weeks in HB.

You must intend to return to your normal home when it becomes safe and reasonable to do so. If you don't intend to return, you can get a further four weeks' SPC or HB to cover your notice period at your (now former) home (para 7.24).

8.30 WRA 4(1)(c),(5); SPCA 1(2)(a),(5); SSCBA 130(1)(a), 137(2)(a),(h); SI 2020/129 sch para 2; SI 2020/677 sch para 2; UC 11; PC 3; HBW 7(13D)-(13G),(17C); HBP 7(13D)-(13G),(17C)

T8.2 UC 10(1), 11(1)-(4); PC 3(1)-(3); HBW 7(13C)-(13G),(17C),(17D); HBP 7(13C)-(13G),(17C),(17D)

8.31 UC 11(1); PC 3(1)(a); HBW 7(13C),(13D),(17D); HBP 7(13C),(13D),(17D)

8.32 UC 11(1); PC 3(1)(a); HBW 7(13D),(17D); HBP 7(13D),(17D)

8.33 UC 11(1); PC 3(1)(a); HBW 7(16)(c)(x),(d)(ii),(17C); HBP 7(16)(c)(x),(d)(ii),(17C)

Absences abroad due to a death in the family

8.34 If you are absent abroad due to a death in the family, you can get benefit for up to:

(a) two months in UC

(b) eight weeks in SPC and HB.

But this applies only if it is unreasonable to expect you to return within the first month/four weeks.

8.35 A 'death in the family' means the death of:

(a) a member of your benefit unit (your partner, child or young person) or

(b) a close relative (para 9.30) of you or of a member of your benefit unit.

Absences abroad receiving medical treatment

8.36 If you are absent receiving medical treatment abroad, you can get benefit for up to:

(a) six months in UC

(b) 26 weeks in SPC and HB.

8.37 Receiving medical treatment abroad means:

(a) in UC and SPC:

- you are being treated by or under a qualified practitioner for an illness or physical or mental impairment or
- you are having convalescence or care which results from an illness or physical or mental impairment you had before you left GB or
- you are accompanying a member of your benefit unit whose absence is for one of the above reasons

(b) in HB:

- you are in hospital or a similar institution or
- you are receiving medical treatment or medically approved care or convalescence or
- you are accompanying a member of your benefit unit who is receiving medical treatment or medically approved convalescence.

Mariners and continental shelf workers

8.38 If you are abroad because you are a mariner with a UK contract of employment, or a continental shelf worker in UK, EU or Norwegian waters, you can get:

(a) UC for up to six months

(b) HB for up to 26 weeks.

8.34-35 UC 11(2); PC 3(2); HBW 7(13E); HBP 7(13E)

8.36 UC 11(3); PC 3(3); HBW 7(16)(d),(17C); HBP 7(16)(d),(17C)

8.37 UC 11(3),(5) – 'medically approved', 'qualified practitioner'; PC 3(3),(4); HBW 7(16)(c)(ii),(iii),(18) – 'medically approved'; HBP 7(16)(c)(ii),(iii),(18)

8.38 UC 11(4),(5) – 'continental shelf worker', 'designated area', 'mariner', 'prescribed area'; HBW 7(13F),(13G),(18) – 'continental shelf worker' etc; HBP 7(13F),(13G),(18)

HM Forces and Crown servants

8.39 If you are abroad because you are a member of HM Forces or a Crown servant, or the partner of someone who is, you can get:

(a) UC without time limit so long as you were habitually resident in the UK before you left (para 40.43)

(b) HB for up to 26 weeks (HM Forces) or four weeks under the general rule in para 8.31 (Crown servants).

Absences partly in the UK and partly abroad

8.40 If your absence is partly within the UK and partly abroad:

(a) decide which time limits apply to:

- your absence within the UK (the UK time limit) and
- your absence abroad (the abroad time limit)

(b) the UK time limit continues to run during the parts of your absence that you spend abroad

(c) if the abroad time limit runs out, your UC/SPC/HB stops and

- you can't get UC or SPC again until you make a claim for them
- you can't get HB again until you not only return to the UK but also move back into your home (regardless of whether the UK time limit has run out or not).

In HB these rules are specified in the law, but in UC and SPC they follow from the law about individual absences and about claims.

8.39 UC 10; HBW 7(13F),(13G); HBP 7(13F),(13G)

8.40 HBW 7(13A),(13B),(13C),(17A),(17B),(17D); HBP 7(13A),(13B),(13C),(17A),(17B),(17D)

Chapter 9 **Liability for housing costs**

- Summary of main rules: paras 9.1-5
- What liability is: paras 9.6-14
- Who is treated as liable: paras 9.15-20
- Excluded liabilities: paras 9.21-38

Summary

9.1 You can get UC, SPC or HB towards the housing costs on your home if:

(a) you are liable or treated as liable for them and

(b) your liability isn't excluded.

9.2 For rent and service charges, meeting these conditions is usually shown by your letting agreement or a letter from your landlord and the answers to questions about your tenancy. For mortgage interest it is usually shown by your mortgage agreement or similar document.

9.3 You are liable for housing costs (and can get benefit towards them) if:

(a) you are a single person and you are liable

(b) you are in a couple and both of you are liable

(c) you are in a couple and you are liable but your partner is not or

(d) you are jointly liable for housing costs in a house share (in this case you get benefit towards a share of the housing costs).

9.4 You can be treated as liable for housing costs (and can get benefit towards them) if:

(a) you are in a couple and your partner is liable but you are not

(b) someone else is liable but you make the payments or

(c) your landlord agrees you can work on your home rather than pay rent.

9.5 But you are treated as not being liable for housing costs (and can't get benefit towards them) if your liability is a sham, isn't commercial, is contrived, or is excluded for other reasons.

9.1 WRA 11(3)(b); UC 25(1)(b),(3), sch 2; SSCBA 130(1)(a), 137(2)(i),(j); HBW 8, 9; HBP 8, 9; SPCA 2(3)(b); PC 6(6)(c), sch 2 paras 1(1)(a), 3

9.3 UC 25(3)(a)(i); HBW 8(1)(a); HBP 8(1)(a); PC sch 2 paras 1(1)(a), 3(a),(c)

9.4 UC 25(3)(a)(ii), sch 2 paras 1-3; HB 8(1)(b)-(d); HBP 8(1)(b)-(d); PC sch 2 paras 3, 13(4)

9.5 UC 25(3)(a), sch 2 para 10; HBW 9(1)(a),(l); HBP 9(1)(a),(l)

What liability is

9.6 Liability for housing costs means having a legal obligation to pay them. 'A liability to make payments imposes legally enforceable conditions on the parties to the agreement. If one party breaks the agreement, the other party has the right to go to court to seek redress' (ADM F2081). Further details for renters are in table 9.1.

Table 9.1 **Liability of renters**

(a) *What is liability:* You are liable for rent if your obligation to pay it is legally enforceable – a moral obligation is not enough (R v Rugby HBRB ex parte Harrison).

(b) *Whether an agreement must be in writing:* Most letting agreements are in writing in the form of a contract or of a letter that gives the necessary details. But there is no requirement for this (HBGM A3.50). An agreement by word of mouth is sufficient to create a legally enforceable liability (R v Poole BC ex parte Ross) except in the (rare) case of tenancies with a fixed term of over three years (Law of Property Act 1925, s54).

(c) *Your right to a written statement in Wales:* In Wales you have the right to a written statement of your contract from your landlord with 14 days of moving in. You can recover any money paid if your landlord fails to provide it. But any repayment is compensation (not rent) and this doesn't change the rule in (b) (Renting Homes (Wales) Act 2016, s31, 35, 87).

(d) *Sham liability:* If evidence shows that there is no intention to enforce the terms of your letting agreement, this can indicate the agreement is a sham so you aren't liable and can't get HB or UC towards your rent (R(H) 3/03).

(e) *Your circumstances:* It isn't possible to grant a tenancy to yourself (Rye v Rye). And if you already have the right to occupy your home (e.g. as joint owner) no-one can grant you a letting on it (e.g. another joint owner) so you can't be liable.

(f) *Your landlord's circumstances:* Normally your landlord has a legal interest in the dwelling as an owner or tenant but this is not necessarily the case (CH/2959/2006 Bruton v London and Quadrant HT, Lambeth LBC v Kay).

(g) *If you have an attorney or appointee:* An attorney or appointee (paras 32.7-8) can enter a letting agreement for you thus making you liable for rent – even when your attorney is your landlord (AD v Nottingham CC).

(h) *If you are incapable of understanding your agreement:* If you are legally incapable of understanding your letting agreement (e.g. you are under 18 or have a mental disability), the law can be more complicated. In England and Wales, your letting agreement is likely to be valid so you are liable for rent (Wychavon DC v EM). Or if it isn't valid, you are likely to be liable or treated as liable under section 7 of the Mental Capacity Act 2005 or under the common law principle of paying for necessaries (Wychavon/EM). In Scotland, your liability needs to be decided on a 'transaction by transaction approach' (Glasgow CC v AL), and in some cases your letting agreement may not be valid so you aren't liable for rent and can't get HB or UC towards it.

(i) *Non-payment or arrears of rent:* If your landlord is unlikely to evict you if you don't pay, this can be evidence that you are not liable. Most landlords expect to end an agreement if a tenant doesn't pay, and in some cases, arrears may suggest you aren't liable (CH/1849/2007). However, not paying your rent 'even for an extensive period' or paying less than your agreement says (even if your landlord has agreed to this), doesn't without other evidence mean you aren't liable (FH v Manchester CC).

(j) *If your landlord breaks their own occupation agreement by renting to you:* If by granting your letting your landlord has broken their own occupation agreement on your dwelling (e.g. because it says they mustn't rent it out), your own letting agreement is still valid so you are liable for rent (Governors of Peabody Donation Fund v Higgins) until and unless the landlord's right to occupy is terminated.

(k) *If your landlord breaks the law by renting to you:* A contract (including a tenancy) that is made with knowledge that carrying it out involves a criminal act, is not enforceable (Nayyar v Denton Wilde Sapte). For example, if your home had a prohibition/closing order (Housing Act 2004, s32; Housing (Scotland) Act 1987, s122) on it when your landlord offered you a tenancy. The law is less clear if the order was made after the start of the tenancy and/or in England and Wales the agreement may be varied by a first-tier tribunal (Housing Act 2004, s34). But in some parts of the UK different rules apply if your landlord needs a licence but does not have one – see (l) to (n).

(l) *If your landlord needs a licence for a house in multiple occupation (HMO) in Scotland:* It is an offence to let an HMO in Scotland without a council licence (Housing (Scotland) Act 2006, s154) so the rule in (k) applies. But the council can also make an order to suspend your rent, so your liability is nil (Housing (Scotland) Act 2006, s144(1)).

(m) *If your landlord needs an HMO or other licence in England or Wales or has a banning order:* In England and Wales if your home should be licensed but isn't, the law says your agreement is enforceable (despite the rule in (k)): Housing and Planning Act 2016, s24, Housing Act 2004, s73. But you can apply to a first-tier tribunal for a rent repayment order, or the council can if your rent was paid by HB or UC (Housing and Planning Act 2016, s43-45; Housing Act 2004, s73). In England, this also applies if your landlord has a banning order (Housing and Planning Act 2016, s40).

Table continued ➤

T9.1 R v Rugby BC HBRB ex parte Harrison (1994) 28 HLR 36
R v Poole BC ex parte Ross (1995) 28 HLR 351 (QBD)
Rye v Rye [1962] AC 496
Bruton v London and Quadrant HT [1999] UKHL 26, [2000] 1 AC 406
AD v Nottingham CC [2013] UKUT 128 (AAC)
Lambeth LBC v Kay [2006] UKHL 10, [2006] 2 AC 465
Wychavon DC v EM (HB) [2012] UKUT 12 (AAC) reported as [2012] AACR 41
Glasgow CC v AL (HB) [2011] UKUT 354 (AAC) reported as [2012] AACR 20
The Governors of Peabody Donation Fund v Higgins [1983] 1 WLR 1091, 10 HLR 82 (CA)
Nayyar v Denton Wilde Sapte [2009] EWHC 3218, [2010] PNLR 15
https://www.rentsmart.gov.wales

(n) *If your landlord/agent doesn't have a licence to manage property in Wales:* Anyone who carries out private rented property management in Wales must have a management licence from Rent Smart Wales [www]. If your landlord/agent doesn't have one the council can apply for a rent repayment order, or a rent stop order (so your liability is nil) (Housing (Wales) Act 2014, s30, 32).

Tenancies

9.7 You can get UC or HB towards your rent if you have a tenancy (table 10.1). A tenancy is often described as a stake in the land. It is a contract that:

(a) gives you the right to occupy a dwelling and to exclude others from it ('exclusive possession') (Street v Mountford)

(b) requires you to pay rent and

(c) is for a length of time that can be established (a 'term certain') – in practice this means that it is either 'periodic' (e.g. a weekly tenancy with no end date) or 'fixed term' (e.g. a tenancy for six months).

Security for secure and assured tenants

9.8 A secure or assured tenancy (in Wales secure and standard contracts) gives you additional 'security' so that you can continue to live there even after the contract term has expired (and an ordinary 'notice to quit' has no effect). If you remain, your landlord must give you a 'notice of seeking possession' [www] and get a court order to evict you. But your security and status as a secure or assured tenant is lost if the dwelling stops being your only or principal home.

Licences and permission to occupy

9.9 You can get UC or HB towards your rent if you have a licence or permission to occupy (table 10.1). A licence is an agreement that gives you the right to occupy and requires you to pay rent (a 'fee') but doesn't give you the right to exclude others. Licences are used in hostels and supported accommodation where the landlord (licensor) can place others in the dwelling and/or require you to move rooms (AG Securities v Vaughan). Payments for permission to occupy ('use and occupation payments') are usually accepted by social landlords from people who are not a tenant or licensee, for example a person who remains after a tenancy has ended but hasn't got the right to succeed to the tenancy.

9.7 Street v Mountford [1985] UKHL 4, [1985] AC 809

9.8 Housing Act 1985, s81, 82; Housing Act 1988, s1(1)(b), 5; Renting Homes (Wales) Act 2016, s220(2), 232
Protection from Eviction Act 1977, s.2, 3(1)
In England, Form 6A for an assured shorthold tenancy, or Form 3 for any other assured tenancy
www.gov.uk/guidance/assured-tenancy-forms

9.9 AG Securities v Vaughan [1988] UKHL 8, [1990] 1 AC 417

Secure and standard contracts in Wales

9.10 In Wales, you can get UC or HB towards your rent if you have 'secure contract' or 'standard contract'. These terms are used for tenancies and licences, and 'contract-holder' is used for both tenants and licensees.

Mesne profits

9.11 You can get HB towards your rent if you pay mesne profits, but not UC (table 10.1). Mesne profits are payable after your tenancy or right to occupy has terminated.

9.12 A tenancy can end for various reasons, for example when its fixed term ends. But the landlord can usually only obtain possession by getting a court order (para 9.8). In some cases, accepting rent may mean the landlord creates a new tenancy, so instead the landlord claims compensation for the lost rent – in the law these payments are called 'mesne profits' (or in Scotland 'violent profits'). Landlords sometimes call these use and occupation payments, charges or fees (although in the law these are not the same as mesne profits).

Mesne profits for secure and assured tenants

9.13 Most social and private renters are either secure or assured tenants (in Wales, secure or standard contract-holders). In these cases, mesne profits can arise when your landlord:

(a) says you have stopped occupying the dwelling as your 'only or principal home' and have therefore lost your security which arises from your assured or secure (or contract-holder) status and

(b) issues you with a notice to quit under common law (paras 9.7-8).

Any payments you make up to the date the notice to quit expires are rent (as the tenant), but after that are mesne profits (as a trespasser).

9.14 But mesne profits don't normally arise for secure or assured tenants (or secure or standard contract holders) when the landlord:

(a) has issued you with a 'notice of seeking possession' under one of the Housing Act(s) grounds (e.g. because you have rent arrears) to end your tenancy and

(b) applies to the court for a possession order to evict you.

Any payments you make up to and including your eviction date (including those made after the possession order but before the eviction) are rent, not mesne profits.

9.10 Renting Homes (Wales) Act 2016, s7, 8

9.11 UC 25(2)(a), sch 1 para 2(a)-(e); HBW 12(1)(c); HBP 12(1)(c); HB(CP) Old 12(1)(c) in sch 3 para 5(1)

9.13 Housing Act 1985, s81; Housing Act 1988, s1(1)(b); Renting Homes (Wales) Act 2016, s220(2)

When you are treated as liable

If your partner is liable but you are not

9.15 If your partner is liable for the housing costs on your home but you are not, you are treated as liable (and can get UC, SPC or HB towards them). There are no further conditions, and in UC this rule applies even when you are in a couple but claiming UC as a single person.

If your ex-partner is liable

9.16 You are treated as liable for the housing costs on your home (and can get UC, SPC or HB towards them) if:

(a) your ex-partner is liable for them but isn't paying them and

(b) you are paying them so you can continue living there.

In HB there are no further conditions. But in UC and SPC you have to show that it is reasonable to treat you as liable. And in UC you have to show that it would be unreasonable to expect you to make other arrangements.

Examples: Treated as liable for rent

1. When your ex-partner is liable but you are paying

Megan and Ffion are a couple on UC, but the tenancy of their home is only in Ffion's name. Ffion leaves and stops paying the rent. The landlord agrees that Meghan can stay so long as she pays the rent.

- Assuming the DWP agrees this is reasonable, Megan can get UC towards the rent (para 9.16).

2. When someone else is liable but you are paying

Zubin lives in a rented flat as a sole tenant, with Gill his adult daughter who is on UC. Zubin goes abroad for a long period and stops paying rent. The landlord agrees that Gill can stay so long as she pays the rent.

- Assuming the DWP agrees this is reasonable, Gill can get UC towards the rent (paras 9.18-19).

3. When you carry out work instead of paying rent

Spencer rents a flat for £700 a month and is on pension age HB. The flat is in a poor condition and the landlord says that if Spencer does the redecoration, he can miss the next monthly payment.

- Assuming the council accepts this is reasonable, Spencer can get HB towards that month's rent (para 9.20).

9.15 UC sch 2 para 1(1)(b),(2); HBW 8(1)(b); HBP 8(1)(b); PC sch 2 para 3(a)

9.16 UC sch 2 para 2; HBW 8(1)(c)(i); HBP 8(1)(c)(i); PC sch 2 para 3(b)

If a young person is liable

9.17 You are treated as liable for the housing costs on your home (and can get UC, SPC or HB towards them) if a young person (or child) in your benefit unit is liable for them. In UC there are no further conditions. But in SPC and HB you have to show that you need to pay the housing costs in order to continue living in your home and it is reasonable to treat you as liable.

If someone else is liable

9.18 You are treated as liable for the housing costs on your home (and can get UC, SPC or HB towards them) if:

(a) the person who is liable for the housing costs on your home isn't paying them

(b) you are paying them so you can continue living there and

(c) it is reasonable to treat you as liable.

In HB and SPC there are no further conditions. But in UC you have to show that it would be unreasonable to expect you to make other arrangements.

9.19 The person who is liable (but isn't paying) could be a relative or friend who has gone away permanently or for longer than the temporary absence rules allow (table 8.1), the executor of someone who has died, or a company or other body (R(H) 5/05). In all cases, the reason you are paying the housing costs must be in order to keep your home (Babergh DC v GW; FK v Wandsworth BC).

When you do work on your home rather than pay rent

9.20 You can get UC, SPC or HB towards rent or service charges if your landlord has agreed to let you carry out work on your home rather than pay rent, but only in the case of reasonable repairs and redecorations, and only up to a reasonable amount. In UC this has no time limit, but in SPC and HB there is a time limit of eight weeks.

Excluded liabilities

9.21 You can't get UC, SPC or HB towards your housing costs if your liability is excluded. Table 9.2 summarises all the types of excluded liability.

9.22 Courts and tribunals have decided many appeals about the exclusions for renters whose landlords are related to them and found that they don't breach human rights (R v Secretary of State for Social Security ex parte Tucker, R (Painter) v Carmarthenshire County Council, R(H) 9/04, R(H) 5/06).

9.17 UC sch 2 para 1(1)(a); HBW 8(1)(c)(ii); HBP 8(1)(c)(ii); PC sch 2 para 3(b)

9.18 UC sch 2 para 2; HBW 8(1)(c)(ii); HBP 8(1)(c)(ii); PC sch 2 para 3(b)

9.19 Babergh DC v GW (HB) [2017] UKUT 40 (AAC)
FK v Wandsworth DC (HB) [2016] UKUT 570 (AAC)

9.20 UC sch 2 para 3; HBW 8(1)(d); HBP 8(1)(d); SPC sch 2 para 13(4)

9.21 WRA 11(3)(b); UC 25(3), sch 2 paras 5-10; SSCBA 137(2)(i); HBW 9; HBP 9; PC 6(6)(c), sch 2 paras 3(a), 5

9.22 Tucker v Secretary of State for Social Security [2001] EWCA Civ 1646, [2002] HLR 27
R (Painter) v Carmarthenshire County Council [2001] EWHC Admin 308

Table 9.2 **Excluded liabilities**

Exclusions for renters, owners and shared owners

(a) You aren't in fact liable for housing costs, or your liability is a sham (para 9.23)

(b) Your liability isn't on a commercial basis (para 9.24)

(c) Your liability was contrived in order to obtain benefit (para 9.25)

(d) Your liability was increased to recover arrears you owe on your current or former home – in this case only the increase is excluded (para 9.26)

Further exclusions for renters

(e) Your landlord lives with you and is a family member or close relative (paras 9.27-28)

(f) Your landlord is a company and an owner, director or employee is a family member or close relative (para 9.31)

(g) Your landlord is a trustee of a trust and a beneficiary or trustee is a family member or close relative (para 9.32)

(h) You are a renter who used to be a non-dependant in your home (HB only) (para 9.33)

(i) You are a renter who used to own your home (HB only) (paras 9.34-35)

(j) You are a renter and your home is tied to your job (HB only) (para 9.36)

Further exclusions for owners

(k) You are an owner and your payments are due to a member of your household (para 9.37).

Note: All the exclusions apply to UC and HB except as shown. Only exclusions (a) and (k) apply to SPC.

If you aren't liable or your liability is a sham

9.23 You can't get UC, SPC or HB towards your housing costs if:

(a) you aren't liable for them – in other words, you haven't provided evidence that you have to pay them in order to occupy your home or

(b) you have a sham (pretended) liability – in other words, you have provided evidence but the arrangements between you and your landlord or mortgage lender show there was no intention to create a genuine liability.

In (a), it is up to you to provide evidence of your liability, but in (b) it is up to the DWP or the council to show that your liability is a sham (R(H) 3/03).

T9.2 UC 25(3), sch 2 paras 5-10; HBW 9, 12(2)(f); HBP 9, 12(2)(f); PC sch 2 paras 1(1), 3(a), 5

9.23 UC 25(1); HBW 12(1); HBP 12(1); PC sch 2 para 1(1)

If your liability isn't on a commercial basis

9.24 You can't get UC or HB towards your housing costs if your liability isn't on a commercial basis. The decision about this must take into account your individual circumstances (UC and HB) and whether the terms of the agreement are legally enforceable (HB only). It is up to the DWP or the council to show that your liability isn't commercial, not up to you to show that it is. Table 9.3 gives a summary of the case law and DWP guidance is in ADM F2081-84.

If your liability was contrived to obtain or increase your benefit

9.25 You can't get UC or HB towards your housing costs if your liability was contrived to obtain benefit or to increase the amount. It is up to the DWP or the council to show that your liability was contrived, not up to you to show that it wasn't. Table 9.3 gives a summary of court and tribunal decisions for renters and DWP guidance is in ADM F2140-46.

Table 9.3 **Commerciality, contrivance and renters**

Commerciality

(a) *What makes a letting commercial:* The primary consideration is about what was agreed between you and your landlord rather than what in fact happens. Not only the financial arrangements between you and your landlord but all the terms of your agreement should be taken into account (R v Sutton LBC ex parte Partridge; ADM F2084). Each case must be considered on its individual facts and is a matter of judgment (R(H) 1/03). It is necessary to consider whether your letting agreement contains terms that are not enforceable in law (CH/2899/2005). The arrangements between you should be at 'arm's length' (R v Sheffield HBRB ex parte Smith).

(b) *Claiming UC/HB and rent arrears:* Claiming UC or HB towards your rent can be evidence that your agreement is commercial (Warwick DC v SSWP). If your landlord accepts what you get from UC/HB rather than your contractual rent this doesn't by itself mean your letting is non-commercial (CH/1076/2002), nor does your landlord's failure to chase up arrears or take possession proceedings against you (FH v Manchester CC).

(c) *Personal and moral considerations:* If your letting is in fact commercial, friendliness and kindness between you and your landlord doesn't make it non-commercial (R v Poole BC ex parte Ross, CH/4854/2003, HMRC v CA). Conversely, if your letting is in fact non-commercial, the fact that it was drawn up in a way that meets your moral or religious beliefs doesn't make it commercial (R(H) 8/04).

(d) *Lettings between family members or friends:* A letting between family members may or may not be commercial. The family arrangement is not decisive by itself. If the letting enables a disabled family members to be cared for more easily, this is not

Table continued ➤

9.24 UC 25(3)(a)(i); HBW 9(1)(a),(2); HBP 9(1)(a),(2)

9.25 UC 25(3)(b), sch 2 para 10; HBW 9(1)(l); HBP 9(1)(l)

decisive by itself. Each case depends on its individual circumstances (CH/296/2004, CH/1096/2008, CH/2491/2007). For example, a letting of an annexe to a disabled son was commercial (SG v Epping Forest DC), as was a letting by a son to his terminally ill mother (CE v Maldon DC), and a letting to a friend in their time of trouble (CH/1097/2004). See also (j).

(e) *Low rents:* Having a low rent doesn't by itself make your letting non-commercial (CE/Maldon DC); ADM F2083).

(f) *Statutory tenancies:* A statutory tenancy is one created by law, usually at the end of a contractual tenancy. This does not make it non-commercial (CH/4081/2004).

(g) *If the circumstances of your letting change:* If your letting was commercial when it began, it can become non-commercial if there is an identifiable reason for this (CH/3497/2005).

Contrivance

(h) *What makes a letting contrived:* Your liability for rent must have been contrived as a way of gaining UC or HB towards your housing costs or increasing its amount. The word 'contrived' implies abuse of the UC/HB scheme (in the sense of taking improper advantage, not necessarily bad faith) and there must be evidence that this was a primary or dominant purpose of the agreement (R v Solihull HBRB ex parte Simpson, CH/39/2007, ADM F2142). The circumstances and intentions of both you and your landlord should be taken into account (R v Barking and Dagenham HBRB ex parte Mackay, R v Sutton HBRB ex parte Keegan).

(i) *If there is no advantage:* Your letting can't be contrived if no advantage is gained by you or your landlord (MP v Sutton LBC).

(j) *Lettings between family members or providing support:* If your landlord is a relation of yours (e.g. your parent) this does not by itself mean your letting is contrived (Solihull case), but your letting may be treated as non-commercial. See also (d).

(k) *High rents and lettings to people on low incomes:* Having a high rent doesn't mean your letting is contrived (R v South Gloucestershire HBRB ex parte Dadds). There is no objection to landlords letting to people on low incomes to make a profit unless

T9.3 UC 25(3), sch 2 para 10; NIUC 26(3), sch 2 para 10
R v Sutton HBRB ex parte Partridge (1994) 28 HLR 315 (QBD)
R v Sheffield HBRB ex parte Smith (1994) 28 HLR 36 (QBD)
Warwick DC v SSWP and CH (HB) [2020] UKUT 240 (AAC)
FH v Manchester CC [2010] UKUT 43 (AAC)
R v Poole HBRB ex parte Ross (1995) 28 HLR 351 (QBD)
HMRC v CA [2009] UKUT 13 AAC
SG v Epping Forest DC [2011] UKUT 41 (AAC)
CE v Maldon DC (HB) [2015] UKUT 565 (AAC)
R v Solihull MBC ex parte Simpson (1993) 26 HLR 370 (QBD)
R v Barking and Dagenham HBRB ex parte MacKay [2001] EWHC Admin 234
R v Sutton HBRB ex parte Keegan (1992) 27 HLR 92 (QBD)
MP v Sutton LBC (HB) [2021] UKUT 193 (AAC)
R v South Gloucestershire HBRB ex parte Dadds (1997) 29 HLR 700 (QBD)
R v Manchester CC ex parte Baragrove Properties (1991) 23 HLR 337 (QBD)

their charges and profits show abuse (CH/39/2007, R v Manchester CC ex parte Baragrove Properties). And if you can't afford your rent or know that you will have to claim UC or HB to pay it, this is not evidence that your letting is contrived (Solihull case), though the DWP suggests it could be if you could have avoided this and still been adequately housed (ADM F2145-46).

If your liability is increased to cover your arrears

9.26 You can't get UC or HB towards an increase in your housing costs if the increase:

(a) is designed to recover arrears you owe from past periods (either on your current home or a former home) and

(b) is done on an individual basis (rather than on an across-the-board basis).

If you rent from someone who is related to you (UC rules)

9.27 You can't get UC towards your rent or service charges if your landlord:

(a) is your partner or

(b) is a child or young person in your benefit unit or

(c) lives in the accommodation and is a close relative (paras 9.29-30) of you, your partner or a child or young person in your benefit unit.

Examples: Excluded liabilities

1. When you rent from a close relative you live with

Violetta owns a house which she lives in with her adult daughter Clara, who pays her £150 a week. Clara claims UC and says this is her rent.

- Clara can't get UC towards this as her landlord lives with her and is her close relative (para 9.27).

2. When you rent from a close relative you don't live with

Andy owns flats and rents them out. When one of the flats becomes vacant, Andy's mother Margaret moves there and claims pension age HB. Andy tells the council that this is so that Margaret has somewhere decent to live and so that he still receives the rental income.

- Although Margaret is Andy's close relative, she doesn't live with him so she isn't excluded from HB on that basis. Assuming the council will accept that Margaret is liable for the rent on the flat, that the letting is commercial, and that it is not contrived, she can get HB there (paras 9.22-25, 9.28).

9.26 UC sch 2 para 9; HBW 11(3); HBP 11(2)

9.27 UC sch 2 para 5

If you rent from someone who is related to you (HB rules)

9.28 You can't get HB towards your rent or service charges if your landlord:

(a) is your partner or

(b) is your ex-partner (whether they lived with you in your current or a former home) or

(c) is the parent or adoptive parent of a child under 16 in your benefit unit or

(d) lives in the accommodation and is a close relative (paras 9.29-30) of you or your partner.

Lives with you

9.29 Your landlord lives in the accommodation with you if you share at least some essential living accommodation (CH/542/2006), even if you have exclusive possession of one of the rooms (CH/3656/2004). Sharing just a kitchen may be enough to count as living with you (CPC/1446/2008), as may sharing a house but being unable to make use of the shared areas due to disability (CPC/3379/2008). A 'landlord' includes one of joint landlords (South Lanarkshire Council v DG), for example if you rent from a couple who are joint landlords and one of them is the other parent of your child.

Close relative

9.30 A 'close relative' means:

(a) a parent, parent-in-law or step-parent; or

(b) a daughter/son, daughter/son-in-law or step-daughter/son; or

(c) a sister/brother or half-sister/brother (Bristol CC v JKT); or

(d) the partner of any of these.

It is the legal not the blood relationship that is used (R(SB) 22/87). An adopted child's parents are his or her adoptive parents, and their other children (natural or by adoption) are his or her brothers and sisters.

If your landlord is a company related to you

9.31 You can't get UC or HB towards your housing costs if:

(a) your landlord is a company and

(b) any of the following are an owner or director of the company:

- you or your partner (UC and HB) or
- a person who lives with you and is a close relative (paras 9.29-30) of yours/your partner's (UC and HB) or
- a child or young person in your benefit unit (UC only) or
- a person who lives with you and is a close relative of theirs (UC only).

9.28 HBW 9(1)(b)-(d), 12(2)(f); HBP 9(1)(b)-(d), 12(2)(f)

9.29 South Lanarkshire Council v DG (HB) [2018] UKUT 417 (AAC)

9.30 UC 2 – 'close relative'; HBW 2(1) – 'close relative'; HBP 2(1)
Bristol CC v JKT (HB) [2016] UKUT 517 (AAC)

9.31 UC sch 2 para 6; HBW 9(1)(e),(3); HBP 9(1)(e),(3)

But you can get HB in these cases if you can show that your letting was for a genuine reason rather than being contrived to take advantage of the benefit rules. In UC only, an owner is defined as someone who holds at least 10% of the company's shares (ADM F2110-17), and this may be a useful rule of thumb in HB.

If your landlord is a trust related to you

9.32 You can't get UC or HB towards your housing costs if:

(a) your landlord is a trustee of a trust and

(b) any of the following are a beneficiary or trustee of the trust:

- you or your partner (UC and HB) or
- a person who lives with you and is a close relative (paras 9.29-30) of yours/your partner's (UC and HB) or
- a child or young person in your benefit unit (UC only) or
- a person who lives with you and is a close relative of theirs (UC only).

But (except when a child in your benefit unit is a beneficiary of the trust) you can get HB in these cases if you can show that your letting was for a genuine reason rather than being contrived to take advantage of the benefit rules.

If you are a renter who used to be a non-dependant

9.33 You can't get HB towards your housing costs if you used to be a non-dependant (para 6.1) of someone who lived in your home then and continues to live in your home now. But you can get HB in these cases if you can show that:

(a) you were in fact a tenant beforehand rather than a non-dependant (LB of Hammersmith and Fulham v FJ) or

(b) your rent liability was created for a genuine reason rather than being contrived to take advantage of the HB scheme.

If you are a renter who used to own your home

9.34 You can't get HB towards your housing costs if you or your partner were an owner or long leaseholder of your current home at any time in the past five years – even if you have since moved out and then back in (CH/3698/2008). But you can get HB in these cases if you can show that you had to give up ownership in order to continue living there.

9.32 UC sch 2 para 7; HBW 9(1)(e),(f),(3); HBP 9(1)(e),(f),(3)

9.33 UC sch 2 para 8; HBW 9(1)(g),(3); HBP 9(1)(g),(3)
LB of Hammersmith and Fulham v FJ [2023] UKUT 203 (AAC)

9.34 HBW 9(1)(h),(ha); HBP 9(1)(h),(ha)

9.35 It is usually accepted as reasonable to have given up ownership if:

(a) your home was about to be repossessed or

(b) you sold it to a housing association under a mortgage rescue scheme or

(c) (in the case of a shared owner) you sold back some or all of the percentage you were buying.

These may have been your only option (HBGM A3.282-288), even if stress made you sell your home more quickly than you needed to (R(H) 6/07, LP v v SSWP). In other situations, it might be reasonable to get work or take in a tenant to avoid having to sell (CH/1586/2004), but not to use a credit card to pay your mortgage (KH v Sheffield CC). Selling your home due to a moral compulsion is not likely to be regarded as reasonable (CH/3853/2001). Good general advice can be found in circular A5/2009.

If you are a renter living in tied accommodation

9.36 You can't get HB towards your housing costs if you or your partner are required to live in your home as a condition of your employment (in other words, your home is 'tied' to your job). For example, this could apply to a caretaker of a block of flats who is required to live in one of the flats. But this rule only applies during your employment, not once you are retired (HBGM A3.291).

If you are an owner and pay housing costs to someone in your household

9.37 If you are an owner you can't get benefit towards service charge payments if you pay them to a family member or anyone else who lives in your household (para 5.9).

Decisions and appeals about excluded liabilities

9.38 If the DWP or the council refuses you benefit towards your housing costs, it must send you a decision notice explaining this (para 38.1). The notice should give clear findings of fact (RC v Maldon DC) and state which exclusion applies to you. In some cases more than one exclusion may apply (ADM F2144) and the notice should make this clear without muddling them up (CSHB/718/2002). You can appeal about all the exclusions (chapter 39).

9.35 LP v SSWP (UC) [2018] UKUT 322 (AAC)
KH v Sheffield CC [2008] UKUT 11 (AAC)

9.36 HBW 9(1)(i); HBP 9(1)(i)

9.37 UC sch 2 para 8; PC sch 2 para 3(a)

9.38 UC(D&A) 7, 51; HBW 90(1), sch 9 para 14(b); HBP 71(1), sch 8 para 14(b)
RC (deceased) v Maldon DC [2012] UKUT 333 (AAC)

Chapter 10 **Rent and eligible rent**

- What is rent: paras 10.1-6
- What is eligible rent and which rules apply to you: paras 10.7-14
- When your eligible rent can be restricted and when you are protected against this: paras 10.15-30

Rent

10.1 You can get UC or HB towards your rent if:

(a) you are a renter or shared owner

(b) the payments you make count as rent and

(c) the payments are eligible for UC or HB.

This chapter explains these (along with certain owner-occupier payments that SPC can meet). You must also meet the conditions in chapter 2.

Actual and eligible rent and housing costs

10.2 In this guide:

(a) your 'actual' rent or housing costs means the total rent and service charges you are liable to pay on your home (tables 10.1 and 10.2)

(b) your 'eligible' rent or housing costs means the charges UC, SPC or HB can meet (para 10.7).

Renter

10.3 We use 'renter' to mean any kind of rent-payer:

(a) whether landlord and tenant law regards you as a tenant or licensee (table 10.1)

(b) whether you rent your home or are a shared owner and

(c) whether you are a sole renter or joint renter (para 10.11).

Shared owners

10.4 You are a 'shared owner' if you are part renting and part buying your home. This is also called having an equity sharing agreement.

10.1 WRA 11(1),(3)(a); SSCBA 130(2); UC 25(2), sch 1 paras 2, 7; HBW 2(1) – 'rent', 12(1); HBP 2(1), 12(1)

10.2(a) UC 25(2), sch 1 paras 2, 7; HBW 2(1) – 'rent', 12(1), Old 12(1); HBP 2(1), 12(1), Old 12(1)

10.2(b) UC sch1 para 8, sch 4 paras 22-25, 33-35; HBW 12B(2), B13(1), 13(2)-(4), 13D(1),(5); HBP 12B(2), B13(1), 13(2)-(4), 13D(1),(5)

10.3 WRA 11(1),(3)(a); UC 25(2)(a), 26(2);
SSCBA 130(2); HBW 2(1) – 'rent', 12(1),(2)(a), Old 12(1),(2)(a); HBP 2(1), 12(1),(2)(a), Old 12(1),(2)(a)

10.4 UC 26(6); HBW 2(1) – 'shared ownership lease'; HBP 2(1)

Landlord

10.5 Your 'landlord' means the person you have a legal liability to pay rent to. It doesn't mean your managing agent. And if your landlord has leased the property from a superior landlord, it doesn't mean them.

10.6 For example:

(a) if your legal liability to pay rent is to a housing association, then they are your landlord even if they have leased the property from a private landlord

(b) if your legal liability to pay rent is to a private landlord, they are your landlord even if a housing association manages your tenancy on their behalf

(c) if your liability to pay rent is to the council, they are your landlord even if the council manages their homes through a separate company (typically an 'arms-length management organisation' or 'tenant management organisation': ALMO/TMO)

(d) if you are a lodger your landlord is the person your rent is due to (e.g. if you are a lodger of a council tenant your landlord is the council tenant, not the council).

Table 10.1 **Payments that count as rent**

Payments that count as rent in UC and HB

(a) Rent payable under a tenancy (para 9.7)

(b) Rent payable under a shared ownership tenancy

(c) Payments for a licence or permission to occupy (para 9.9)

(d) Payments made by boarders and lodgers

(e) Service charges you have to pay as a condition of occupying your home

(f) Payments for a croft and croft land

(g) Payments for a charitable housing association almshouse

(h) Rent and site charges if you rent a caravan or mobile home, or just site charges if you own it

(i) Rent, mooring charges and berthing fees if you rent a houseboat or just mooring charges and berthing fees if you own it

---

10.5 WRA 11(1); UC 25(1),(2); SSCBA 130(1)(a); HBW 12(1), Old 12(1); HBP 12(1), Old 12(1)

T10.1 UC 25(2)(a),(c), sch 1 para 2; HBW 2(4),12(1),(2)(a), Old 12(1),(2)(a); HBP 2(4),12(1),(2)(a), Old 12(1),(2)(a);

T10.1(e) UC 25(2)(c), sch 1 paras 7, 8; HBW 12(1)(e), Old 12(1)(e); HBP 12(1)(e), Old 12(1)(e)

T10.1(f) UC sch 3 para 2; HBW 2(4)(d); HBP 12(1)(e), Old 12(1)(e)

T10.1(g) UC sch 1 para 2(e); HBW 12(1)(h); HBP 12(1)(h)

T10.1(h) UC sch 1 para 2(d); HBW 2(4)(b), 12(1)(g); HBP 2(4)(b), Old 12(1)(g)

T10.1(i) UC sch 1 para 2(c); HBW 2(4)(c), 12(1)(f); HBP 2(4)(c), 12(1)(f)

Payments that count as rent in UC and SPC but not HB

(j) Payments on most armed forces accommodation and Crown tenancies (HBGM A3.210-218)

Payments that count as rent in HB but not UC

(k) Rent payable on supported or temporary accommodation (chapter 13)

(l) Mesne profits (in Scotland, violent profits) payable after your tenancy or right to occupy has terminated (para 9.11)

(m) Payments under a rental purchase agreement (HBGM A4.140)

Note: A houseboat includes a narrow boat suitable for permanent residence (R(H) 9/08), and mooring charges include a continuous cruiser licence (this is required if you don't have a permanent mooring) (AB v LB Camden).

Table 10.2 **Payments that don't count as rent**

These payments don't count as rent and you can't get UC or HB towards them.

(a) Mortgage and similar payments if you are an owner or shared owner

(b) Ground rent if you are an owner or shared owner

(c) In mixed residential and business accommodation that part of your rent that relates to business premises

(d) Payments on care homes and independent (non-NHS) hospitals

(e) Payments for bail and probation hostels ('approved premises')

(f) Payments for a tent or similar moveable structures and related site fees

(g) Payments on some night shelters (para 7.4)

(h) Payments on any accommodation if your letting is non-commercial, contrived or otherwise excluded from benefit (table 9.3)

(i) Payments under a co-ownership scheme (HBGM 4.270-74)

Note: You can get help with the housing costs in (a) as part of your SMI (para 27.2) or those in (b), (f) and (i) as part of your SPC (para 17.16).

T10.1(j) UC 25(2)(a), sch 1 para 2; HBW 2(1) – 'Crown tenant', 12(2)(e), Old 12(2)(e); HBP 12(2)(e), Old 12(2)(e); PC sch 2 paras 1(1), 13(1)(e)

T10.1(k) UC sch 1 paras 3(h),(i), 3A, 3B; UCTP 6A(2)

T10.1(l) UC 25(2)(a), sch 1 para 2; HBW 12(1)(c), Old 12(1)(c); HBP 12(1)(c), Old 12(1)(c)

T10.1(m) UC 25(2)(a), sch 1 para 2; HBW 12(1)(i), Old 12(1)(i); HBP 12(1)(i),(4) Old 12(1)(i,(4)

T10.1 (note) AB v LB of Camden (HB) [2020] UKUT 158 (AAC)

T10.2 UC 25(2)(a),(c), sch 1 paras 2, 3; HBW 7(5), 9(1)(k),(4), 11(2), 12(2),(4), Old 12(2),(4); HBP 7(5), 9(1)(k),(4), 12(2),(4) Old 12(2), (4)

T10.2 (note) PC sch 2 paras 1(1), 13(1)(a),(d),(f)

Eligible rent

What is eligible rent

10.7 Your 'eligible rent' means the amount of rent (including service charges) that you can get UC or HB for. It can be equal to or lower than your actual rent. Table 10.3 summarises which rules apply.

How does your eligible rent affect your benefit

10.8 Your eligible rent is used:

(a) in UC, in the calculation of your housing costs element (HCE) (para 16.32)

(b) in HB, in the calculation of your maximum HB (para 18.2).

In each case, the higher your eligible rent is, the more UC/HB you get.

How eligible rent is calculated in UC

10.9 In UC, there are two methods of calculating eligible rent:

(a) the social renter rules for social renters and

(b) the LHA rules for private renters.

How eligible rent is calculated in HB

10.10 In HB, there are four methods:

(a) the social renter rules for social renters and

(b) the LHA rules for private renters unless (c) or (d) apply

(c) the rent referral rules for boarders, hostels, mobile homes, caravans, houseboats and pre-2008 HB claims and

(d) the old scheme rules for exempt accommodation.

There are also rare rules for pre-1996 claims and pre-1989 tenancies (paras 12.44-45).

10.7 WRA 11(4); UC 26(1),(2); SSCBA 130A; HBW 11(1); HBP 11(1)

10.8 WRA 8(2), 11(1); UC 23, 25; SSCBA 130(1), 130A; HB 70; HB66+ 50

10.9 UC sch 4 paras 1(4), 20, 22, 25(2), 30, 33, 34, 35(3)

10.10 HBW 11(1), Old 12(3)-(5), 12B, 12C, B13, 13D(1),(4),(5); HBP 11(1), Old 12(3)-(5), 12B, 12C, 13D(1),(4),(5)

Table 10.3 **Which eligible rent rules apply to you**

	Which UC rules apply	Which HB rules apply
(a) Council tenants		
■ All cases	Social renter rules	Social renter rules
(b) Registered housing association tenants		
■ You have a market rent tenancy	LHA rules	LHA rules
■ Your landlord provides or arranges care, support or supervision so that your home qualifies as exempt accommodation (table 13.1(a))	Can only get HB	Old scheme rules
■ Otherwise	Social renter rules	Social renter rules
(c) Tenants of non-profit landlords (unregistered housing associations, charities, voluntary organisations, county councils in England)		
■ Your landlord provides or arranges care, support or supervision so that your home qualifies as exempt accommodation (table 13.1(a))	Can only get HB	Old scheme rules
■ Otherwise	As (d) below	As (d) below
(d) Private tenants		
■ You live in a hostel, mobile home, caravan or houseboat	LHA rules	Rent referral rules
■ You are a boarder	LHA rules	Rent referral rules
■ Your HB claim began before 7 April 2008	N/A	Rent referral rules
■ Otherwise	LHA rules	LHA rules

Note: Different rules apply to some large or expensive accommodation (paras 10.15-18) and in HB to some pre-1996 and pre-1989 tenancies (paras 12.44-45). For the HB rules about who is a boarder, see para 12.37.

T10.3 UC 26(2),(4),(5), sch1 paras 3, 3A, 3B, sch 4 paras 2 – 'provider of social housing', 20, 22, 23, 25, 30; 31, 33, 34, UCTP 6A(2) SSAA 134(1A),(1B) – 'rent rebate', 'rent allowance'; HBW 12B(1), A13(2), 13(1), 13C(2),(5), 13D(10), 14(1),(2)(b); HBP 12B(1), 13(1), 13C(2),(5), 13D(10), 14(1),(2)(b)

Sole and joint renters

10.11 Several rules in chapters 11-13 depend on whether you are:

(a) a sole renter

(b) a joint renter with just a member of your benefit unit (para 5.2)

(c) a joint renter with someone who shares your household but isn't in your benefit unit (e.g. a friend or relation)

(d) a joint renter with someone who shares your dwelling but isn't in your benefit unit and has a separate household (e.g. a workmate).

Chapter 5 explains who is in your benefit unit and in your household.

Joint renter's share of the rent

10.12 If you are a joint renter with someone who isn't in your benefit unit (e.g. a friend, relation or workmate), your eligible rent is calculated using a share of the actual rent on your home (paras 11.13-14, 12.9, 13.18).

Examples: Joint renters

1. Two joint renters

Flora and Jean are friends who rent a two-bedroom flat. The total rent is £750 per month and they each pay half of this. Flora reaches pension age and claims pension age HB.

- Flora can get HB towards her share of the rent, which is £375 a month (para 10.14).

2. Two joint renters one with children

Dan and Luke are friends who are joint tenants of a three-bedroom house. The total rent is £300 per week. Dan uses two bedrooms and pays two thirds of the rent because his children often come to stay. Luke uses one bedroom and pays one third of the rent. Dan loses his job and claims UC towards his £200 per week.

- Assuming the DWP accepts that this is a reasonable share of the rent, Dan can get UC towards it (para 10.13).

Joint renter's share in UC

10.13 In UC, the DWP decides your share by:

(a) dividing the amount for your dwelling by the total number of joint renters (including yourself)

(b) then multiplying it by the number of joint renters (including yourself) who are in your benefit unit.

If this produces an unreasonable result, the DWP can decide your share by taking into account the factors in para 10.14. This may apply to you if you are a joint renter whose other joint renter(s) have left, so you are now liable for the full rent. This is sometimes referred to as an 'untidy' tenancy. DWP guidance refers to it as an 'absent joint tenant case' and advises that you are 'liable for the total rent' (OG file 095).

10.12 UC sch 4 paras 24, 35

10.13 UC sch 4 paras 24, 35

Joint renter's share in HB

10.14 In HB, your share of the eligible rent is decided by the council by taking into account:

(a) the number of joint renters – including those who aren't eligible for benefit (Nagshabandi v Camden LBC)

(b) how you actually split your rent and service charges – for example you may have a written agreement

(c) any other relevant circumstances – for example the number of rooms each of you occupies, and whether the other renters are living there or not (CH/3376/2002).

If you don't provide this information, the council is likely to decide the share in another way, for example it could use the method in para 10.13.

Restrictions and protections

UC eligible rent restrictions

10.15 The following UC rules can restrict your eligible rent to a lower figure:

(a) the bedroom tax if you are a social renter (para 11.17)

(b) housing payment determinations if you are a social renter (para 11.25)

(c) the LHA rules if you are a private renter (para 12.8).

UC protections against restrictions

10.16 The following protections apply in UC cases:

(a) you are protected against the bedroom tax for up to three months if you have had a death in your home (paras 33.31-32)

(b) in Scotland, you are usually fully protected against the bedroom tax (para 31.11)

(c) you are protected against housing payment determinations if the DWP decides it is not appropriate to use them (para 11.28)

(d) in England and Wales you may be able to get help from discretionary housing payments.

HB eligible rent restrictions

10.17 The following HB rules can restrict your eligible rent to a lower figure:

(a) the bedroom tax if you are a social renter with a working age claim (para 11.17)

(b) the LHA rules, rent referral rules or old scheme rules if you are a private renter (chapters 12-13) or in rare cases rent from a housing association (para 12.26)

(c) the default rule in rare cases (para 11.32).

10.14 HBW 12B(4), 12C(2), B13(2)(c), 13D(4),(12) – 'cap rent'; HBP 12B(4), 12C(2), 13D(4),(12)
Nagshabandi v Camden LBC HBRB [2002] EWCA Civ 1038, [2002] All ER(D) 293, [2003] HLR 280

10.15 UC sch 4 paras 22 (step 1), 25, 32, 34 (step 4), 36

10.16 UC 37, sch 4 paras 32(4)

10.17 HBW 12B(6), B13(2), 13(2),(3),(5),(7), Old 13(3), 13D(4),(5); HBP 12B(6), 13(2),(3),(5), Old 13(3), 13D(4),(5)

HB protections against restrictions

10.18 The following protections apply in HB cases:

(a) you are protected against all the restrictions if:

- you have had a death in your home within the past 12 months (para 10.19) or
- you could afford your home within the past 13 weeks (para 10.22)

(b) you are protected against the old scheme restrictions without a time limit if you live in exempt accommodation and are a protected occupier (para 10.25)

(c) you may be able to get other help as described in chapter 31.

Examples: Protections against eligible rent restrictions

1. Claiming HB following retirement

Hudson makes a claim for pension age HB after he retires. His actual rent is high. He moved to this address when he was in a well-paid job and could easily afford the rent and outgoings. He has not been on HB in the last 52 weeks.

- Because of the protection for people who could formerly afford their home, Hudson's eligible rent must not be restricted in any way for the first 13 weeks of his award of HB. During those weeks, his eligible rent is his actual rent minus amounts for any ineligible services (paras 10.22-24).

2. Claiming HB following a bereavement

Mirah makes a claim for pension age HB after the death of her husband. She has not moved since her husband's death. Her actual rent is high.

- Because of the protection for people who have had a bereavement, Mirah's eligible rent must not be restricted in any way until the first anniversary of her husband's death. Until then, her eligible rent is her actual rent minus amounts for any ineligible services (paras 10.19-21).

3. Bereavement while on HB

Reuben is on HB and his mother Lois lives with him as his non-dependant. His eligible rent takes account of the fact that he qualifies for two bedrooms (chapter 14) and is £175 per week. Following Lois's death he only qualifies for one bedroom

- Because he has been bereaved while on HB, Reuben's eligible rent must not be reduced below £175 per week until the first anniversary of his mother's death (paras 10.19-21).

4. Bereavement while on UC

If Reuben in example 3 had been on UC rather than HB, he would instead qualify for a bereavement run-on for three months (paras 33.31-32).

10.18 Bedroom tax: HBW 12BA(2),(3),(6)
LHA: HBW 12D(2),(3),(5); HBP 12D(2),(3),(5)
Old scheme: HBW/HBP Old 13(5),(7) in HB(CP) sch 3 para 5(2)
Rent referral: HBW 13(8), 13ZA(1); HBP 13(6), 13ZA(1)

The HB protection if you have had a death in your home

10.19 This HB protection applies if you meet the following conditions when you make your claim for HB or while you are on HB:

(a) a linked person in your home (para 10.29) has died within the past 12 months (including occupiers who were temporarily absent, but not including yourself)

(b) it was your home on the date of their death (chapter 7)

(c) you have not moved since then and

(d) the reduction didn't begin before the death occurred.

10.20 This protection lasts for the 12 months following the date of the person's death. If you stop receiving HB and then make a new claim at the same address within the 12 months, the protection resumes until 12 months after the date of the person's death (but it isn't extended). If you move, the protection ends.

10.21 If you weren't on HB on the date of the person's death, your eligible rent always equals:

(a) your actual rent (para 10.2)

(b) minus an amount for ineligible service and other charges (table 15.3).

If you were on HB on the date of the person's death, your eligible rent must not be reduced below whatever it was immediately beforehand (but it is increased or reduced if any other rule requires this).

The HB protection if you could previously afford your home

10.22 This HB protection applies if you meet the following conditions when you make your claim for HB:

(a) you or a linked person in your home (para 10.29) could afford the financial commitments there when your liability for rent was entered into (no matter how long ago that was) and

(b) you haven't received HB for any period during the 52 weeks before your award of HB starts, or in a couple neither of you have.

10.19 Bedroom tax: HBW 12BA(3)
LHA: HBW 12D(3); HBP 12D(3)
Old scheme: HBW/HPW Old 13(5) in HB(CP) sch 3 para 5(2)
Rent referral: HBW 13(8), 13ZA(1); HBP 13(6), 13ZA(1)

10.20 Bedroom tax: HBW 12BA(5)
LHA: HBW 12D(7)(a); HBP 12D(7)(a)
Old scheme: HBW/HBP Old 13(5), Old 13ZA(2) in HB(CP) sch 3 para 5(2),(3)
Rent referral: HBW 13ZA(1); HBP 13ZA(1)

10.21 Bedroom tax: HBW 12BA(3)
LHA: HBW 12D(3); HBP 12D(3)
Old scheme: HBW/HBP Old 13(5) in HB(CP) sch 3 para 5(2)
Rent referral: HBW 2(1) – 'reckonable rent', 13ZA(1); HBP 2(1), 13ZA(1)

10.22 Bedroom tax: HBW 12BA(6),(7)
LHA: HBW 12D(5),(6); HBP 12D(5),(6)
Old scheme: HBW Old 13(7),(8); HBP Old 13(7),(8)
Rent referral: HBW 13ZA(3),(4); HBP 13ZA(3),(4)

10.23 This protection lasts for the first 13 weeks you are on HB. It ends after those 13 weeks, or if sooner, when your HB ends. You can't get the protection again until there has been a break in your HB of at least 52 weeks.

10.24 While this protection applies to you, your eligible rent always equals:

(a) your actual rent (para 10.2)

(b) minus an amount for ineligible service and other charges (table 15.3).

Additional protection for old scheme cases

10.25 This HB protection applies if you meet the following conditions when you make your claim for HB or while you are on HB:

(a) your home is exempt accommodation (table 13.1(a)) and

(b) you or a linked person in your home are a protected occupier (paras 10.28-29).

10.26 This protection doesn't have a time limit. It lasts for as long as you meet the conditions.

10.27 While this protection applies to you, your eligible rent mustn't be reduced unless:

(a) there is cheaper suitable alternative accommodation available – this means accommodation you could move into at the date of the decision (HBGM para A4.1222) and

(b) it is reasonable to expect you to move – taking account of the effect on retaining your employment and on children/young persons who would have to change school.

For case law about these conditions, see table 13.5.

Who is a protected occupier

10.28 You are a protected occupier if:

(a) you have reached pension age or

(b) you have at least one child or young person in your benefit unit or

(c) you have limited capability for work as decided by the DWP (CH/4424/2004) (GSH paras 223-225).

A linked person is also a protected occupier if (a) or (c) applies to them.

10.23 Bedroom tax: HBW 12BA(6),(7)
LHA: HBW 12D(5),(6); HBP 12D(5),(6)
Old scheme: HBW Old 13(7),(8); HBP Old 13(7),(8)
Rent referral: HBW 13ZA(3),(4); HBP 13ZA(3),(4)

10.24 Bedroom tax: HBW 12BA(6)
LHA: HBW 12D(5); HBP 12D(5)
Old scheme: HBW Old 12(3), Old 13(7); HBP Old 12(3), Old 13(7)
Rent referral: HBW 12C(2),13ZA(3); HBP 12C(2), 13ZA(3)

10.25 HBW/HBP Old 13(4) in HB(CP) sch 3 para 5(2)

10.26 HBW/HBP Old 13(4) in HB(CP) sch 3 para 5(2)

10.27 HBW/HBP Old 13(4),(9)(b) in HB(CP) sch 3 para 5(2)

10.28 HBW/HBP Old 13(4)(a),(ca),(cb),(d) in HB(CP) sch 3 para 5(2)

Who is a linked person

10.29 A 'linked person' means:

(a) your partner or a child or young person in your benefit unit or

(b) a relative of you or your partner who has no separate right to occupy the dwelling – for example, a non-dependant, lodger, tenant, or joint tenant of yours.

10.30 For this rule, a 'relative' means:

(a) a parent, daughter, son, sister, or brother

(b) a parent-in-law, son-in-law, daughter-in-law, step-son, step-daughter, including equivalent relations arising through civil partnership

(c) a partner of any of the above or

(d) a grandparent, grandchild, aunt, uncle, niece, or nephew.

10.29 HBW/HBP 2(1) – 'linked person'; HBW/HBP Old 13(10),(11) in HB(CP) sch 3 para 5(2)

10.30 HBW/HBP 2(1) – 'close relative', 'couple', 'relative'

Chapter 11 **Social renters**

- When the social renter rules apply: paras 11.1-11
- How your eligible rent is calculated using the social renter rules: paras 11.12-16
- The bedroom tax for social renters: reductions and exceptions: paras 11.17-24
- Social renters with unreasonably high rents: paras 11.25-33

When the social renter rules apply

11.1 The social renter rules apply to social renters on UC and HB. In some cases, they also apply to private renters living in caravans, mobile homes and houseboats (para 12.30) or private or housing association renters with pre-1989 tenancies (para 12.45).

Who is a social renter

11.2 You are a 'social renter' if you are a renter or shared owner and rent your home from a social landlord. Your landlord is a social landlord if it is a local council or a registered housing association.

Local councils

11.3 The social renter rules apply to you if you rent from a local council. This means:

(a) in England, a unitary district or borough council, a London borough, the City of London, the council of the Isles of Scilly or (in UC) a county council or parish council

(b) in Wales, a county or county borough council or (in UC) a community council

(c) in Scotland, a local council.

11.4 But in HB only, the LHA, rent referral or old scheme rules apply to you (chapters 12-13) if you rent from a county council in England that doesn't administer HB (i.e. a two-tier council area).

11.2 UC 2 –'local authority', sch 4 para 2 –'provider of social housing'
SSAA 134(1A),(1B), 191 – 'housing authority', 'local authority', ; Housing and Regeneration Act 2008, s.68-70;
HBW 13C(5)(a), 14(2)(b), sch 2 para 3(1)(a),(1A); HBP 13C(5)(a), 14(2)(b), sch 2 para 3(1)(a),(1A)

11.3 UC 2 –'local authority', sch 4 paras 1(4)(c), 2 – 'provider of social housing', 30
SSAA 134(1),(1A), 191 – 'housing authority', 'local authority'; HBW 12B(1), 12BA(1),(2), A13(1); HBP 12B(1)

11.4 SSAA 134(1),(1B), 191 – 'housing authority', 'local authority'; HBW 13C(1),(2), 13(1), 14(1); HBP 13C(1),(2), 13(1), 14(1);
HB(CP) sch 3 para 4(10) – 'exempt accommodation'

Housing associations

11.5 The social renter rules apply to you if you rent from a registered housing association. This means:

(a) in England, a landlord (other than a local council) that is registered as a non-profit making provider of social housing with the Regulator of Social Housing or

(b) in Wales and Scotland, a social landlord registered with the Welsh or Scottish government.

11.6 But the HB old scheme rules apply to you if you live in exempt accommodation (chapter 13).

11.7 And the LHA rules apply to you (chapter 12) if your home isn't exempt accommodation and you rent from:

(a) an unregistered housing association or

(b) in England only, a profit-making registered housing association and you have a market rent tenancy.

Stock transfers

11.8 You are a stock transfer tenant if your tenancy started with the council and was transferred to a registered or unregistered housing association.

11.9 If you transfer to a registered housing association:

(a) in UC, the social renter rules apply to you (including the bedroom tax) (regardless of rent increases)

(b) in HB, the social renter rules apply to you (including the bedroom tax) until or unless you have a rent increase that makes your rent unreasonably high, at which point the rent referral rules apply to you (chapter 12).

11.10 If you transfer to an unregistered housing association:

(a) in UC, the LHA rules apply to you (chapter 12) (regardless of rent increases)

(b) in HB, the social renter rules apply to you (without the bedroom tax) if you have an old tenancy (para 12.45) otherwise until or unless you have a rent increase that makes your rent unreasonably high (or your home is unreasonably large, if it was transferred before 7 October 2002), at which point LHA rules apply to you.

11.5 UC sch 4 paras 1(4)(c), 2 – 'provider of social housing', 'registered social landlord', 30
HBW 2(1) – 'registered housing association', 13C(5)(a), sch 2 para 3(1)(a),(1A); HBP 2(1), 13C(5)(a), sch 2 para 3(1)(a),(1A)

11.6 UCTP 2(1) – 'specified accommodation', 6A(2); UC sch 1 paras 1 – 'exempt accommodation', 3(h), 3A(2);
HBW 13C(5)(b); HBP 13C(5)(b); HB(CP) sch 3 para 4(1)(b)

11.7 UC sch 4 paras 1(4), 2 – 'provider of social housing', 20, 30
Housing and Regeneration Act 2008, s.68, 69; HBW 13C(2),(5), 14(1), sch 2 para 3(1)(a),(1A);
HBP 13C(2),(5), 14(2)(b), sch 2 para 3(1)(a),(1A)

11.9 UC sch 4 paras 1(4)(c), 2 –'provider of social housing', 30
HBW 12BA(1),(2), A13(1)(a), 13(1), 13C(5)(a),(c), 14(2)(b), sch 2 paras 3(2), 11; HBP 13(1), 13C(5)(a),(c), 14(2)(b), sch 2 paras 3(2), 11

11.10 UC sch 4 paras 1(4)(c), 2 –'provider of social housing', 30
HBW 12B(1),(2); A13(1),(2)(a), 13C(1),(5)(c), 14(1),(2)(b), sch 2 para 11; HBP 12B(1),(2), 13C(5)(c), 14(1),(2)(b), sch 2 para 11

Charities and voluntary organisations

11.11 Charities and voluntary organisations usually have social aims. But if they aren't a registered housing association, the LHA, rent referral or old scheme rules apply if you rent from them (chapters 12-13).

Eligible rent: the social renter rules

11.12 Your eligible rent is worked out using:

(a) the general rule if you are a sole renter or jointly rent with someone in your benefit unit (your partner, child or young person) or

(b) the joint renter rule if you are a joint renter with someone not in your benefit unit (e.g. a friend, relation or workmate).

The general rule

11.13 The general rule for social renters is that your eligible rent equals:

(a) your actual rent (para 10.2)

(b) minus an amount for ineligible service and other charges (table 15.3)

(c) minus a further amount if you are a renter (not a shared owner), have a working age claim, and have more bedrooms than the bedroom tax allows (para 11.22).

Examples: Eligible rent for social renters

1. A couple with children

Tom and Jacquie are on UC and have three children. They rent a three-bedroom house from a social landlord. Their rent is £600 per month and doesn't include any service charges.

- Their eligible rent is £600 per month (para 11.13).

2. Two joint tenants

Jane and Cora are sisters and are each on HB. They jointly rent a two-bedroom flat from a social landlord. The rent there is £180 per week and doesn't include any service charges.

- Each one's eligible rent is £90 per month (para 11.14).

11.11 UC sch 4 paras 1(4)(b), 2 – 'provider of social housing', 20; HBW 13C(2),(5), 14(1); HBP 13C(2),(5), 14(1); HB(CP) sch 3 para 4(1)(b),(10) – 'exempt accommodation'

11.12 UC sch 4 paras 33, 34, 35; HBW 12B(2),(4); B13(2)(a),(c); HBP 12B(2),(4)

11.13 UC sch 4 paras 3, 33, 34; HBW 12B(2),(4); B13(2); HBP 12B(2),(4)

The joint renter rule for UC

11.14 In UC, if you have a joint renter who isn't in your benefit unit:

(a) first, the eligible rent for your dwelling is worked out – this is:
- your actual rent
- minus an amount for ineligible charges

(b) then it is shared between the joint renters (para 10.13).

In these cases, the bedroom tax doesn't apply.

The joint renter rule for HB

11.15 In HB, if you have a joint renter who isn't in your benefit unit:

(a) first, the eligible rent for your dwelling is worked out – this is:
- your actual rent
- minus an amount for ineligible charges
- minus a further amount if you are a renter (not a shared owner), have a working age claim and have more bedrooms than the bedroom tax allows

(b) then it is shared between the joint renters (para 10.14).

The bedroom tax is decided as though you and your joint renters were one unit (para 14.29).

Eligible rent if you qualify for a rent discount

11.16 Some social landlords have rent discount schemes that reduce your rent when you pay it promptly or online. In such cases, the full amount is usually regarded as your eligible rent. For example, if your rent is £100, this is nonetheless your eligible rent even if you can get a reduction for paying on time. However, this only applies when the DWP has approved the rent discount scheme (ADM F3251-52).

The bedroom tax for social renters

11.17 The bedroom tax reduces your eligible rent if you have more bedrooms than you qualify for. Unless you fall within the exceptions in table 11.1, it applies to:

(a) UC in all cases

(b) HB if you are under pension age, or in a couple and both of you are under pension age.

11.18 This means you get less UC or HB, except in Scotland where you can usually get a discretionary housing payment that cancels out the reduction (para 31.11). In HB law the reduced amount of your eligible rent is called the 'maximum rent social sector'.

11.14 UC sch 4 paras 2 – 'listed persons', 3, 33, 35(3)-(5)

11.15 HBW 12B(4), B13(2); HBP 12B(4)

11.16 UC sch 4 paras 30, 32A; HBW 12(2A),(2B), Old 12(6A),(6B); HBP 12(2A),(2B), Old 12(6A),(6B)

11.17 UC sch 4 para 34, 36(2)-(4); HBW 12BA(2), B13(2),(3)

11.18 HBW 12BA(2), A13(1)

Table 11.1 **Exceptions to the bedroom tax**

Exceptions that apply to UC and HB

(a) You are a shared owner

(b) You live in sanctuary scheme accommodation (para 11.19)

Exceptions that only apply to UC

(c) You have a joint renter who isn't in your benefit unit (para 11.14)

(d) You have had a death in your home within the past three months (para 10.16)

Exceptions that only apply to HB

(e) You are over pension age (over 66), or in a couple and at least one of you is

(f) You live in exempt accommodation (table 13.1(a)) or temporary accommodation (para 11.20)

(g) You pay site charges or mooring fees for a caravan, mobile home or houseboat (para 11.21)

(h) You rent from a registered housing association and the council has referred your rent to the rent officer (para 11.30)

(i) You are a stock transfer tenant of an unregistered housing association (para 11.10)

(j) You have had a death in your home within the past 12 months (para 10.19)

(k) You could afford your home when you took it on and are in your first 13 weeks on HB (para 10.22)

Note: Exception (f) applies whether you are on HB by itself or HB with UC/SPC.

Examples: The bedroom tax for social renters

1. One extra bedroom

Amelia and Owen are social renters on UC and have two children under 10. They rent a three bedroom house and no-one else lives with them. The eligible rent for the house is £1,000 per month.

- They qualify for two bedrooms, one for themselves and one for the children. Because their home has one bedroom more than this, their eligible rent is reduced by 14% (£140) to £860 per month (para 11.22).

2. Two extra bedrooms

Violet is a social renter on UC. She rents a three-bedroom house and no-one else lives with her. The eligible rent for the house is £1,000 per month.

- She qualifies for one bedroom. Because her home has two bedrooms more than this, her eligible rent is reduced by 25% (£250) to £750 per month (para 11.22).

T11.1 UC 37, sch 4 paras 2 – 'listed persons', 35(4), 36(5),(6)
HBW 12BA, A13(1),(2), 14(2)(b), sch 2 paras 3(1)(a),(1A), 11; HB(CP) sch 3 para 4(1)(b)

Sanctuary scheme accommodation

11.19 In UC and HB, the bedroom tax doesn't apply to you if you rent from a social landlord and live in sanctuary scheme accommodation that meets the following conditions:

(a) it is part of a scheme that provides additional security for your home

(b) you – or someone in your home – have been the victim of actual or threatened domestic violence (para 13.9)

(c) this was from your partner or former partner, or your or their son, daughter, stepchild, grandchild, parent, stepparent, grandparent, sister, brother, aunt, uncle, niece, nephew or first cousin

(d) that person no longer lives with you (unless they are a young person) and

(e) a professional person or any public, voluntary or charitable body provides confirmation of (a) and (b).

Temporary accommodation

11.20 In HB, the bedroom tax doesn't apply if you live in temporary accommodation. This means:

(a) your home was made available to you by the council you claim HB from or a registered housing association (para 11.5) under an arrangement with the council, for the purpose of:

- satisfying a homelessness duty owed to you following your application for assistance (e.g. permanent housing wasn't available) or
- preventing you from becoming homeless (as defined in the homeless persons legislation) and

(b) the accommodation is:

- 'board and lodging' (para 42.24(a))
- 'leased' (para 42.24(b)) or
- 'licensed' (para 42.24(c)).

Caravans, mobile homes and houseboats

11.21 In UC and HB, the bedroom tax applies in the normal way to rent on a caravan, mobile home or houseboat. But in HB only, it doesn't apply to site charges or mooring fees if you pay these as a separate amount (FT v Perth and Kinross Council).

11.19 UC sch 4 para 36(6); HBW A13(2)(f),(5) – 'sanctuary scheme'

11.20 HBW A13(2)(e),(3),(4)

11.21 FT v Perth and Kinross Council and SSWP (HB) [2019] UKUT 43 (AAC)

The amount of the reduction

11.22 The bedroom tax is calculated by comparing the number of bedrooms you have in your home (living rooms aren't taken into account) with the number of bedrooms you qualify for. Then your eligible rent is:

(a) reduced by 14% if your home has one bedroom more than you qualify for

(b) reduced by 25% if your home has two or more bedrooms more than you qualify for.

The reduction for joint renters (HB only)

11.23 If you have a joint renter who isn't in your benefit unit (e.g. a friend, relation or workmate), the bedroom tax doesn't apply in UC. But in HB it applies to the eligible rent for your dwelling before it is shared between the joint renters (para 11.15).

How many bedrooms do you qualify for

11.24 You qualify for the number of bedrooms described in chapter 14. This takes into account:

(a) the people in your benefit unit (you, your partner, children and young persons) and

(b) any non-dependants you have.

In HB, it can also include other occupiers of your home (para 14.26).

Unreasonably high rents

UC if you have a high rent

11.25 If you are a social renter on UC and your rent is considered to be unreasonably high, the DWP can refer the details to the rent officer to make a housing payment determination (HPD). This never applies if your home is in the Affordable Rent programme. In other cases, it is rare and is only likely to apply if your rent is at least £50 per week higher than the LHA figure that would apply if you were a private renter (ADM F3253).

The rent officer's housing payment determination

11.26 The rent officer:

(a) compares your rent with what a landlord could reasonably be expected to obtain

(b) takes account only of accommodation that matches yours as far as possible in terms of council area, number of bedrooms, landlord type (council or housing association) and state of repair and

(c) excludes service charges for care, support and supervision.

11.22 UC sch 4 para 36(2)-(4); HBW B13(2)(b),(3)

11.23 HBW B13(2)(c)

11.24 UC sch 4 paras 8-12; HB B13(5)-(7)

11.25 UCROO 5, sch 2 paras 1, 2, 3(c); UC sch 4 paras 3, 32(1),(2)

11.26 UCROO sch 2 para 3(a),(b)

11.27 The rent officer may determine that your rent is reasonable, in which case the DWP mustn't reduce your eligible rent.

11.28 Or the rent officer may tell the DWP what would be a reasonable amount. In this case:

(a) the DWP uses the rent officer's figure to calculate your eligible rent unless this wouldn't be appropriate and

(b) if the rules about joint tenants (para 11.14) or the bedroom tax (para 11.17) also apply to you, they apply after this rule.

The rent officer can correct HPDs in the same way as they can correct LHA figures and areas (para 12.22).

11.29 When the DWP adopts the rent officer's redetermination your UC housing costs reduce on the first day of the next assessment period following the redetermination.

HB if you have a high rent

11.30 In HB, if you rent from a registered housing association and your rent is considered to be unreasonably high, the council can refer the details to the rent officer as in para 12.26.

11.31 If your rent is reduced as a result of a referral to the rent officer, the reduced rent takes effect from the first day of the benefit week following the date on which the council received the rent officer's determination.

The HB default rule

11.32 The default rule is very rare. It only applies in HB, and only to cases that don't count as exempt accommodation (table 13.1(d)). It says that if your eligible rent appears greater than 'it is reasonable to meet by way of HB', the council can reduce it to 'such lesser sum as seems reasonable'.

11.33 The rule could possibly be used when none of the other rules can be applied (AA v Chesterfield DC). It has been used in the past in the case of a council tenant (Burton v Camden LBC). When it is used, the council must consider your personal circumstances (R (Laali) v Westminster CC).

11.27 UCROO sch 2 para 1; UC sch 4 para 32(3)

11.28 UCROO sch 2 para 2; UC sch 4 para 32(4)

11.29 UC(D&A) 30, 35(14)

11.30 HB(D&A) 7(2)(c), 8(6A)(b)

11.31 HBW 14(1),(2)(b), sch 2 para 3(1)(a),(1A),(2)(b); HBP 14(1),(2)(b), sch 2 para 3(1)(a),(1A),(2)(a),(b)

11.32 HBW 12B(6); HBP 12B(6)

11.33 HBW 12B(1); HBP 12B(1)
AA v Chesterfield DC and SSWP [2011] UKUT 156 (AAC)
Burton v Camden LBC [2000] UKHL 8, [2000] 2 AC 399
R (Laali) v Westminster CC HBRB [2002] HLR 179 (QBD)

Chapter 12 **Private renters**

- The private renter rules and when they apply: paras 12.1-5
- How your eligible rent is calculated using the LHA rules: paras 12.6-9
- Which LHA figure applies to you: paras 12.10-16
- How the LHA figures are set: paras 12.17-24
- How your eligible rent is calculated using the rent referral rules: paras 12.25-41
- Eligible rent for old HB claims and tenancies: paras 12.42-45

The private renter rules

12.1 'Private renter rules' is an umbrella term for three methods of calculating eligible rent:

(a) the LHA rules — if you are a private renter on UC or HB (para 12.6)

(b) the rent referral rules — only if you are a private renter on HB (para 12.25) and

(c) the old scheme rules — only if you are a private renter on HB (para 13.16).

See paras 11.4-11 for which one applies to you.

Who is a private renter

12.2 You are a 'private renter' if you rent from any landlord who isn't a local council or registered housing association (paras 11.3-7).

Examples of private renters

12.3 You are a private renter if you rent from:

(a) a private landlord (whether you live in their home or they live elsewhere)

(b) a lettings agency or company

(c) an unregistered housing association

(d) a charity or non-profit-making voluntary organisation (unless it is also a registered housing association)

(e) anyone else (except a local council or registered housing association).

Which rules apply if you are on UC

12.4 Private renters on UC can get:

(a) HB under the old scheme rules if you live in exempt accommodation or

(b) UC under the LHA rules for housing costs in any other case.

12.2 UC sch 4 paras 1(4)(b), 2 – 'provider of social housing', 20; SSAA 134(1A),(1B); HBW 13C(2),(5)(a); HBP 13C(2),(5)(a)

12.4 UC sch 1 paras 1 – 'exempt accommodation', 2, 3(h), 3A(2), sch 4 paras 1(4)(b), 20; UCTP 2 – 'specified accommodation', 6A(2); HBW 13C(5)(b); HBP 13C(5)(b); HB(CP) sch 3 para 4(1)(b)

Which rules apply if you are on HB

12.5 Private renters on HB can get:

(a) HB under the old scheme rules if you live in exempt accommodation

(b) HB under the rent referral rules if you are a boarder, live in a hostel, mobile home, caravan or houseboat, or have a pre-2008 HB claim or

(c) HB under the LHA rules in any other case.

The rules can apply differently for pre-1996 HB claims and pre-1989 tenancies (paras 12.42-45).

Eligible rent: the LHA rules

When do the LHA rules apply

12.6 The LHA rules apply to:

(a) all private renters whose housing costs are included in their UC

(b) all private renters on HB unless you live in exempt accommodation, or are a boarder, live in a hostel, mobile home, caravan or houseboat, or have a pre-2008 HB claim (para 12.25).

Eligible rent

12.7 Your eligible rent is worked out using:

(a) the general rule if you are a sole renter or jointly rent with someone in your benefit unit (your partner, child or young person) or

(b) the joint renter rules if you are a joint renter with someone not in your benefit unit (e.g. a friend, relation or workmate).

The general rule

12.8 The general LHA rule for private renters is that your eligible rent equals the lower of:

(a) your actual rent and

(b) the local housing allowance (LHA) that applies to you (para 12.10).

Your actual rent includes all service and other charges (para 10.2).

12.5 UCTP 2 – 'specified accommodation', 6A(2); HBW 13C(2),(5)(b)-(e), 14(1),(2)(b), sch 2 paras 4-9; HBP 13C(2),(5)(b)-(e), 14(1),(2)(b), sch 2 paras 4-8; HB(CP) sch 3 para 4(1)(b)

12.6 UC sch 1 paras 3(h), 3A(2), sch 4 paras 1(4)(b), 20; UCTP 6A(2); HBW 13C(2),(5)(b)-(e); HBP 13C(2),(5)(b)-(e)

12.7 UC sch 4 paras 23, 24; HBW 12B(4), 13D(4),(5),(12) – 'cap rent'; HBP 12B(4), 13D(4),(5),(12)

12.8 UC sch 4 paras 2 – 'listed persons', 22, 23, 24(3); HBW 13D(4),(5); HBP 13D(4),(5)

Examples: Eligible rent for private renters

1. A single person

Rod is a single person aged 74 and is on HB. He rents a bedsit from a private landlord. His actual rent is £200 a month. Rod qualifies for the LHA for one-bedroom shared accommodation and this is £195 a month.

- His eligible rent is £195 per month (para 12.8 and table 12.2).

2. A couple with a child

Anna and Noah are on UC and have a child aged 14. They rent a house from a private landlord. Their actual monthly rent is £750 a month. They qualify for the LHA for a two-bedroom dwelling and this is £700 per month.

- Their eligible rent is £700 per month (para 12.8).

3. Three joint tenants

Radu, Antonin and Olexandr are friends in their 40s. They jointly rent a three-bedroom house from a private landlord. Their total actual rent is £1,200 a month, and each of them pays £400 a month. Only Radu is on UC. He qualifies for the LHA for a one-bedroom dwelling and this is £350 per month.

- Radu's eligible rent is £350 per month (para 12.9).

The joint renter rule

12.9 If you have a joint renter (other than your partner, child or young person) your eligible rent equals the lower of:

(a) your share of the actual rent on your dwelling, calculated as in paras 10.13-14 and

(b) the LHA that applies to you (excluding your joint renter(s)).

Which LHA figure applies to you

12.10 The LHA figure that applies to you is the one for:

(a) the size of accommodation you qualify for under the bedroom tax (para 12.11) and

(b) the area your home is in.

This means the figure changes if you qualify for a different size of accommodation or move to a new area.

12.9 UC sch 4 paras 22, 24(1),(2),(4); HBW 12B(4), 12D(2)(a), 13D(4),(5),(12); HBP 12D(2)(a), 13D(4),(5),(12)

12.10 UC sch 4 para 25(2); HBW 13D(1) – 'occupiers'; HBP 13D(1)

Sizes of accommodation

12.11 LHAs are set by the rent officer (para 12.17), who provides figures for:

(a) one-bedroom shared accommodation

(b) one-bedroom self-contained accommodation

(c) two-bedroom dwellings

(d) three-bedroom dwellings and

(e) four-bedroom dwellings (this is the maximum number of bedrooms in LHA cases).

How many bedrooms you qualify for

12.12 You qualify for the number of bedrooms described in chapter 14 (up to a maximum of four). This takes into account:

(a) the people in your benefit unit (you, your partner, children and young persons) and

(b) any non-dependants you have.

In HB, it can also include other occupiers of your home (para 14.29).

Examples: Which LHA for private renters on UC

1. A single person aged 24

Unless she is in an excepted group, she qualifies for the LHA for one-bedroom shared accommodation.

2. A single person aged 58

He qualifies for the LHA for one-bedroom self-contained accommodation.

3. A couple

They qualify for the LHA for one-bedroom self-contained accommodation.

4. A couple with a son aged 9 and a daughter aged 7

The couple qualify for the LHA for a two-bedroom dwelling.

5. The son in example 4 reaches the age of 10

Because the children are no longer expected to share a bedroom (table 14.1), the couple qualify for the LHA for a three-bedroom dwelling.

6. Three joint tenants who are not related

They are all under 35 and none of them is in an excepted group (table 12.1). So each one qualifies for the LHA for one-bedroom shared accommodation.

7. Two brothers who are joint tenants

They are in their 40s, and the daughter of one of them lives with him. So that brother qualifies for the LHA for a two-bedroom dwelling. The other brother qualifies for the LHA for one-bedroom self-contained accommodation.

12.11 UC(ROO) 4(1)(a), sch 1 para 1; HB(ROO) 4B(2A), sch 3B para 1

12.12 UC sch 4 paras 8-10, 25(1); HBW 13D(2),(3),(12) – 'occupiers'; HBP 13D(2),(3),(12)

One-bedroom shared or self-contained accommodation

12.13 There are two LHAs for one-bedroom accommodation: one for self-contained and one for shared accommodation. For example, single people who live in shared accommodation usually qualify for the LHA for shared accommodation. The full details differ between UC and HB rules and are in tables 12.1 and 12.2.

12.14 Qualifying for the shared accommodation LHA (rather than the self-contained one) has been found not to amount to unlawful discrimination in the case of people with a disability (CM v Bradford MBC).

When does your home count as self-contained

12.15 In HB, the rules in table 12.2 depend on whether your home is self-contained (table 12.2). It counts as self-contained only if you have exclusive use of:

(a) one room plus a bathroom and toilet (in the bathroom or separately) and a kitchen or cooking facilities; or

(b) at least two rooms (counting only bedrooms and living rooms, and ignoring other facilities whether you share them or not).

'Exclusive use' means the right to exclude others; and this must be a legal right, not just what happens in practice: AA v Chesterfield DC and JS v SSWP. This has applied in the case of a couple who separated but remained in their home as joint tenants with a legal agreement that they each had exclusive use of part of it (DC v LB Bromley).

Hostels for homeless people

12.16 You qualify for self-contained accommodation (rather than shared) if you have lived in one or more hostels for homeless people for at least three months. This means a building that:

(a) provides non-self-contained domestic accommodation, with meals or adequate food-preparation facilities

(b) is either:

- managed or owned by a registered housing association or
- run on a non-commercial basis, and wholly or partly funded by a government department or agency or local council or
- managed by a registered charity or non-profit-making voluntary organisation

(c) has the general purpose of providing accommodation together with care, support or supervision, in order to assist homeless people to be rehabilitated or resettled and

(d) is not a care home or independent (non-NHS) hospital.

12.13 UC sch 4 paras 27, 28; HB 13D(2)(a),(b); HB66+ 13D(2)(a),(b)

12.14 CM v Bradford MBC and SSWP [2020] UKUT 285 (AAC)

12.15 HB 13D(2)(b); HB66+ 13D(2)(b)
AA v Chesterfield DC and SSWP [2011] UKUT 156 (AAC)
JS v SSWP and Cheshire West and Chester BC (HB) [2014] UKUT 36 (AAC)
DC v LB Bromley (HB) [2018] UKUT 416 (AAC)

12.16 UC sch 4 para 29(4),(10) – 'hostel', 'hostel for homeless people';
HBW 2(1) – 'young individual' (para (h) of that definition), 2(1A),(1B), 13D(2)(a)

Table 12.1 **The UC rules for one-bedroom LHAs**

UC category of accommodation

Single people over 35

(including people in a couple but claiming as a single person)

■ All cases	Self-contained
Single people under 35	
■ If you are in excepted groups (a)-(g)	Self-contained
■ Otherwise	Shared
Couples	
■ All cases	Self-contained

UC excepted groups

Disability, care-leavers, ex-offenders

(a) You are receiving:
- the middle or highest rate of the care component of DLA, SADLA or CDP
- the standard or enhanced rate of the daily living component of PIP or ADP or
- attendance allowance or PADP or an equivalent benefit (para 21.18)

(b) You are over 18 but under 25 and were in social services care before the age of 18

(c) You are an ex-offender and are managed under a MAPPA (multi-agency public protection) agreement

Foster parents, homelessness, domestic violence, modern slavery

(d) You are a foster parent or have a child placed with you for adoption

(e) You have (at any time) occupied one or more hostels for homeless people (para 12.16) for one or more periods totalling at least three months

(f) You are a victim of, or have been threatened with, domestic violence that occurred after you reached 16 and was from your partner or former partner, or your or their son, daughter, stepchild, grandchild, parent, stepparent, grandparent, sister, brother, aunt, uncle, niece, nephew or first cousin

(g) You are a victim of modern slavery and this has been confirmed by the Home Office Competent Authority or other competent authority under the Trafficking Convention of 2005 (HB A6/2022).

T12.1 UC 2 'attendance allowance', sch 4 paras 27, 28, 29

T12.1(a)-(c) UC 2 'attendance allowance', sch 4 para 29(2),(5),(6)-(9)

T12.1(d)-(g) UC sch 4 para 29(4),(9A),(9B),(9C),(10)

Table 12.2 **The HB rules for one-bedroom LHAs**

HB category of accommodation	
Single people over 35	
■ If your home is self-contained (para 12.15)	Self-contained
■ Otherwise	Shared
Single people under 35	
■ If you are in excepted groups (a) or (b)	Self-contained
■ If you are in excepted groups (c)-(f) and your home is self-contained	Self-contained
■ Otherwise	Shared
Couples	
■ If your home is self-contained	Self-contained
■ If one or both of you are in excepted groups (a) or (b)	Self-contained
■ Otherwise	Shared

HB excepted groups

Disability, care-leavers, ex-offenders

(a) You meet the conditions for a severe disability premium (para 18.20)

(b) You are under 25 and were in social services care after the age of 16

(c) You are an ex-offender over 25 but under 35 and are managed under a MAPPA agreement

Foster parents, homelessness, domestic violence, modern slavery

- Excepted groups (d)-(g) are the same as in table 12.1.

Note: The rules in this table apply to LHA cases (para 12.13) and also to rent referral cases (table 12.4(f)).

T12.2 HB 2(1) – 'young individual', 13D(2)(a),(b)

How the LHA figures are set

12.17 The LHA figures are set by the rent officer, a government employee who is independent of the DWP. They were published online in late January 2025 [www] and apply as follows:

(a) in UC, from the start of your assessment period that begins on or after 7 April 2025 (the first Monday in the new tax year) or

(b) in HB, from 1 April 2025.

How LHA figures are calculated

12.18 April 2025's LHA figures are the same as April 2024's. These were set at the 30th percentile of rents using data in the year ending on 30 September 2023, or in some cases mainly in London are limited to a national maximum.

12.19 The 30th percentile means the highest rent within the bottom 30% of rents on accommodation which:

(a) is the correct size and in the correct area

(b) is rented on an assured tenancy and is in a reasonable state of repair

(c) includes eligible service charges but not ineligible ones

(d) excludes rents paid by people on UC or HB (to avoid the effect UC/HB could have on rent levels).

The LHA figure for a larger category of dwelling can't be lower than the LHA for a smaller one.

LHA areas

12.20 LHA areas are called 'broad rental market areas' (BRMAs) and are defined by postcodes. They are drawn up by the rent officer so that:

(a) a 'person could reasonably be expected to live there having regard to facilities and services for the purpose of health, education, recreation, personal banking and shopping, taking account of the distance by travel, by public and private transport, to and from those facilities and services'

(b) they contain 'residential premises of a variety of types' held as a 'variety of tenancies' and

(c) they contain 'sufficient privately rented premises' to ensure that the LHA figures 'are representative of the rents that a landlord might reasonably be expected to obtain in that area'.

They can only be changed with the DWP's consent.

12.17 UC sch 4 paras 25(2),(5); UC(ROO) 4; SI 2025/5
HBW 13C(1),(3), 13D(1),(10) – 'relevant date'; HBP 13C(1),(3), 13D(1),(10); HB(ROO) 4B(2A),(2B),(3B); HB(D&A) 7A(2), 8(15)
https://lha-direct.voa.gov.uk/search.aspx

12.18 UC(ROO) 4(2), sch 1 paras 2(2), 7; HB(ROO), 4B(2B),(3B), sch 3B paras 2(2), 3A; SI 2024/11 regs 2-4

12.19 UC(ROO) sch 1 paras 3, 5; HB(ROO) 2 – 'rent', sch 3B para 2(4)-(8)

12.20 UC(ROO) 3(2)-(4); HB(ROO) 4B(1A), sch 3B paras 4, 5

12.21 There are currently 152 BRMAs in England, 22 in Wales, and 18 in Scotland. On average they are about twice the size of council areas, but their boundaries don't follow council or jobcentre areas. The rules in para 12.20 were introduced after large rental market areas were challenged in R (Heffernan) v the Rent Service.

Correcting rent officer figures and areas

12.22 If the rent officer finds a technical error in an LHA figure or in a BRMA they can correct it (para 39.46). But matters of professional judgment can only be challenged by judicial review (para 39.43).

12.23 When the rent officer makes a correction that increases your UC or HB, the increase goes back to when the original figure applied from. So you get your arrears of benefit back to then.

12.24 But when the rent officer makes a correction that reduces your UC or HB:

(a) your UC reduces from the assessment period after the one in which the DWP receives the correction

(b) your HB reduces from the date the rent officer makes the correction.

So in each of these cases you haven't been overpaid benefit.

Eligible rent: the rent referral rules

When do the rent referral rules apply

12.25 The rent referral rules apply if:

(a) you are on HB

(b) you are a private renter and

(c) either:

- you live in a hostel
- you live in a caravan, mobile home or houseboat
- you are a boarder or
- you have a pre-2008 HB claim (para 12.43).

12.26 In rare cases the rent referral rules also apply if your landlord is a registered housing association and:

(a) your rent is considered to be unreasonably high (para 11.30) or

(b) you have a pension age claim and your home is unreasonably large (para 14.4).

They never apply if you get UC towards your rent.

12.21 R (Heffernan) v the Rent Service [2008] UKHL 58, reversed by SI 2008/3156

12.22 UC(ROO) 6(2)(a); HB(ROO) 7A(4)

12.23 UC(D&A) 19(2), 21; HBW 2(1) – 'amended determination', 18A(3); HBP 2(1), 18A(3); HB(D&A) 4(3), 6

12.24 UC(D&A) 30, 35(14); HBW 2(1) – 'amended determination', 18A(2); HBP 2(1), 18A(2); HB(D&A) 7(2)(c), 8(6)

12.25 HBW 13(1), 13C(2),(5)(d),(e), 14(1); HBP 13(1), 13C(2),(5)(d),(e), 14(1)

12.26 UC sch 4 paras 20, 25; HBW A13(1)(a), 13(1), 13C(5)(a), 14(1),(2)(b), sch 2 para 3(2); HBP 13(1), 13C(5)(a), 14(1),(2)(b), sch 2 para 3(2)

Hostels

12.27 If you live in a hostel and have a private landlord, your eligible rent is calculated using:

(a) the LHA rules if your housing costs are met by UC

(b) the old scheme rules in HB if the hostel is exempt accommodation (table 13.1(a))

(c) the rent referral rules in HB in other cases.

If you have a social landlord, it is calculated using the social renter rules.

12.28 A hostel is a building that:

(a) provides accommodation for residents or a class of residents that is neither separate nor self-contained

(b) together with either meals or adequate facilities for preparing food

(c) which is not a care home, independent hospital or Abbeyfield Home and

(d) meets at least one of the operating conditions in para 12.29.

12.29 The operating conditions are that the building is:

(a) managed by a charity or voluntary organisation which provides care, support or supervision to help people be rehabilitated or resettled within the community or

(b) run on a non-commercial basis, and wholly or partly funded by a government department or agency or local authority or

(c) managed or owned by a registered housing association (para 11.5).

In (a), the provision of care, support or supervision may mean your home is exempt accommodation in which case it falls under the old scheme rules (para 13.24).

Caravans, mobile homes and houseboats

12.30 If you live in a caravan, mobile home or houseboat and pay site fees or mooring charges, your eligible rent is worked out as follows:

(a) if your housing costs are met by UC, it is calculated using the social renter rules if you rent from a social landlord, or the LHA rules if your rent from a private landlord

(b) in HB, it is calculated using the social renter rules but without the bedroom tax, if:

- you pay your site fees or mooring charges to a council that administers HB (whether or not you also pay rent for your dwelling and whether or not your rent is paid to the same or a different landlord) or
- you live on a gypsy or traveller site and your landlord is an English county council

(c) in HB in any other case, it is worked out using the rent referral rules.

12.27 UC sch 1 paras 3(h), 3A(2), sch 4 paras 20, 25(1),(2); HBW 13(1), 13C(5)(d)(ii), 14(1); HBP 13(1), 13C(5)(d)(ii), 14(1); HB(CP) sch 3 para 4(1)(b)

12.28-29 HBW 2(1) – 'hostel'; HBP 2(1)

12.30 UC sch 4 paras 1(4), 2 – 'provider of social housing', 20, 25, 30, 33 SSAA 134(1A),(1B); HBW 12B(1), A13(2)(c), 13(1), 13C(5)(d)(i), 14(2)(b), sch 2 para 3(1)(b),(c),(4); HBP 12B(1), 13(1), 13C(5)(d)(i), 14(2)(b), sch 2 para 3(1)(b),(c),(4)

Boarders

12.31 If you are a boarder and have a private landlord, your eligible rent is calculated using:

(a) the LHA rules if your housing costs are met by UC

(b) the rent referral rules in HB.

If you are a boarder and have a social landlord, your eligible rent is calculated using the social renter rules.

Eligible rent and rent determinations

12.32 In rent referral and old scheme cases, the council refers the details of your rent to the rent officer, who makes one or more rental valuations known as 'rent determinations'. The council uses these determinations to calculate your eligible rent (para 12.38). In the law this is called the 'maximum rent'. Table 12.4 gives the names of the determinations and explains the calculation.

12.33 But if you live in exempt accommodation the rent officer's determinations are advisory (HBGM A4.1061, 4.1125) and your eligible rent is calculated as described in chapter 13.

When the council refers your rent to the rent officer

12.34 The council refers details of your rent to the rent officer:

(a) when you claim HB

(b) when you move into a new home

(c) when you have a relevant change in your circumstances (table 12.3)

(d) when 52 weeks have passed since the council's last referral

(e) up to one month before you move into a new home or renew your tenancy agreement, if you and your landlord request this (HBGM A4.2050-70).

12.35 But:

(a) if the rent officer has already provided figures for your home (for example, because someone else claimed HB while they were living there), the council uses these, so long as they don't relate to different circumstances (table 12.3) and less than 52 weeks have passed since they were provided or

(b) if you live in a hostel (para 12.28), the council makes one referral to the rent officer each year for each type of room (single, double, shared, etc).

12.31 UC sch 4 paras 1(4), 2 – 'provider of social housing', 20, 25, 30, 33; HBW 13C(5)(e), 13D(10), 114A(3)-(5); HBP 13C(5)(e), 13D(10), 95A(3)-(5)

12.32 Housing Act 1996, s122; HB(ROO) 3, sch 1; HBW 13(2),(3),(5),(7), 14(1), 114A(1)(a),(6); HBP 13(2),(3),(5), 14(1), 95A(1)(a),(6)

12.33 HB(CP) sch 3 para 5(2), Old 13(3)

12.34 HBW 14(1)(a)-(h),(8) – 'change relating to a rent allowance'; HBP14(1)(a)-(h),(8)

12.35 HBW 14(1)(f),(g),(2),(7), sch 2 para 2; HBP 14(1)(f),(g),(2),(7), sch 2 para 2

The information the council gives the rent officer

12.36 The council gives the rent officer details of:

(a) your tenancy

(b) your rent

(c) which eligible and ineligible charges are included in your rent and

(d) the occupiers of your home.

The rent officer's decision about who is a boarder

12.37 If your rent includes an element for meals, the rent officer makes a board and attendance determination. This decides whether the meals amount to 'substantial board and attendance'. If they do, the rent referral rules apply to you; if they don't, the LHA rules apply. To count as 'board and attendance', there must be an element of preparation, service and clearing away ('attendance') on the premises. And as a rule, anything valued at over 15% of the rent is taken to be 'substantial' and anything under 10% is not (Rent Officer Handbook [www]).

How the rent officer's figures are used to calculate your eligible rent

12.38 Table 12.4 shows the figures the rent officer gives the council and how these are used to calculate your eligible rent (except in exempt accommodation: table 13.1(a)). The rent officer either confirms your rent is reasonable, or makes one or more of the determinations in table 12.4 if it is too high or your home is too large. The rent officer's handbook [www] provides guidance about how the rent officer sets the figures.

When rent officer figures take effect

12.39 The rent officer figures take effect as follows:

(a) when you claim HB, the figures take effect from the day your HB starts

(b) when your circumstances change, the figures take effect when the change itself takes effect (chapter 33)

(c) when 52 weeks have passed, the figures take effect:

- if they go up and your rent is due weekly or in multiples of weeks, on the day after the 52 weeks run out, or if that isn't a Monday, on the preceding Monday
- if they go up and your rent is due monthly, on the day after the 52 weeks run out or
- if they go down, on the day the council receives the rent officer's figures or, if that isn't a Monday on the following Monday.

12.36 HBW 114A(6)-(9); HBP 95A(6)-(9)

12.37 HBW 13C(5)(e), 13D(10), 114A(3)-(5); HBP 13C(5)(e), 13D(10), 95A(3)-(5)
https://tinyurl.com/RO-handbook see section on HB referrals, boarders

12.38 HBW 12C, 13(2),(3),(5)(a),(7); HBP 12C, 13(2),(3),(5)

12.39 HB(D&R) 7A(3), 8(6A); HBW 14(1)(f),(g); HBP 14(1)(f),(g)

Appeals about rent and service charges

12.40 If you live in exempt accommodation (table 13.1(a)) all decisions about rent and services are made by the council and appeals go to a first-tier tribunal (para 39.4).

12.41 In other rent referral cases:

(a) the council values most ineligible service and other charges (table 12.4(a)-(g)), and appeals about these go to a first-tier tribunal (para 39.4)

(b) the rent officer makes all the determinations used in setting your eligible rent and values some less common service charges (table 12.4(h)), and appeals about these (known as redeterminations) go to another rent officer (you can't appeal to a first-tier tribunal about them).

Table 12.3 **Relevant changes in rent referral cases**

Rent determinations are required in all these situations (paras 12.25-26):

Changes that could affect the size of accommodation you qualify for

(a) There is a change in the number of occupiers – but this doesn't apply if you live in a hostel (para 12.28).

(b) A child in your home reaches the age of 10 or 16 – but only if your most recent rent determination included a size-related rent determination (table 12.4(b)).

(c) The household composition of the occupiers changes – but only if your most recent rent determination included a size-related rent determination (table 12.4(b)).

(d) You start or stop qualifying for an additional bedroom for any of the reasons in para 14.32 (foster parents, overnight carers, and disabled people who need their own bedroom).

(e) You start to meet the conditions for a single room rent determination (table 12.4(f)).

Other changes

(f) There is a substantial change in the terms of your letting (other than rent) or the condition of your home.

(g) Your rent increases under a term of your letting (CH/3590/2007) – but only if, in your most recent rent determination, your claim related rent (table 12.4(d)) equalled your actual rent minus all ineligible charges.

Note: Other changes in the amount of your rent don't count as a 'relevant change'.

12.40 CSPSSA sch 7 para 6(1); HB(CP) sch 3 para 5(2), old 13

12.41 CSPSSA sch 7 para 6(1),(2)(c); HBW 15-18; HBP 15-18; HB(ROO) 4, 4A, 4C, 4D, 4E

T12.3 HB 14(1)(c),(8) – 'change relating to a rent allowance', sch 2 para 2; HB66+14(1)(c),(8), sch 2 para 2

Table 12.4 **Eligible rent in rent referral cases**

Rent officer figures

(a)	Significantly high rent determination	This is provided when your rent is high compared with rents in the area you live in.
(b)	Size-related rent determination	This is provided when your home is larger than you need (chapter 14).
(c)	Exceptionally high rent determination	This is provided when your home is at the top end of the market.
(d)	Claim-related rent	The rent officer always provides this. It equals the lowest of (a)-(c). Or if none of these applies to you, it equals your actual rent minus all ineligible charges.
(e)	Local reference rent	This is the mid-point of rents for your kind of accommodation in the area you live in. The rent officer provides this if it is lower than (d).
(f)	Single room rent	This is the mid-point of rents for one-bedroom shared accommodation in the area you live in. It only applies if you are the sole occupier of your home and don't fall within any of the excepted groups (table 12.2) (a 'young individual'). The rent officer provides this if it is lower than (d).

Eligible rent and ineligible charges

Your eligible rent equals the lowest of (d)-(f). But all the figures have to be adjusted by the council or the rent officer to exclude ineligible service charges (table 15.2).

(g)	Ineligible charges valued by the council	■ Water charges (para 15.16) ■ Cleaning of your own accommodation (para 15.13) ■ Fuel for your own accommodation (para 15.13) ■ Meals (using the standard figures) (table 15.5) ■ Support and related services (para 15.23)
(h)	Ineligible charges valued by the rent officer	■ Acquisition of furniture (para 15.7) ■ Day-to-day living expenses not included in (g) (table 15.2) ■ Charges that are not related to the provision of adequate accommodation (para 15.11)

T12.4(a)-(f) HBW 2(1) – 'young individual', 13(1)-(7); HBP 13(1)-(7); ROO sch 1 paras 1-6(1)

T12.4(g)-(h) ROO sch 1 paras 6(2A),(3), 7; HB 13(7), 114A(3)(d)-(f),(4),(6),(8)(a); HB66+ 13(7), 95A(3)(d)-(f),(4),(6),(8)(a)

Exceptions

- If you have one or more joint tenants who are not a member of your family (para 6.11), the figures apart from (f) are apportioned between you.
- If you live in a caravan, mobile home or houseboat, determination (b) doesn't apply.
- If you live in a hostel (paras 12.27-29), determinations (e) and (f) don't apply.
- If your landlord is a registered housing association, determination (f) doesn't apply.

Eligible rent: old HB claims and tenancies

12.42 This section describes the rules that apply if you have an old HB claim or old tenancy. These rules are all rare.

HB claims made in or before 2008

12.43 Your eligible rent is worked out using the rent referral rules rather than the LHA rules if:

(a) you are a private renter (paras 12.2-3) and

(b) you have been getting HB continuously since 6 April 2008 or earlier.

But if you also meet the conditions in para 12.44, the old scheme rules apply rather than the LHA rules or rent referral rules.

HB claims made in or before 1996

12.44 Your eligible rent is worked out using the old scheme rules rather than the LHA rules or rent referral rules if:

(a) you are a private renter (paras 12.2-3)

(b) you have been getting HB continuously since 1 January 1996, ignoring breaks of four weeks or less and

(c) you have not moved home since then, or moved only because your home was made uninhabitable by fire, flood or natural disaster.

Registered rent and similar tenancies

12.45 Your eligible rent is worked out using the social renter rules, but without the bedroom tax, if:

(a) you are a private renter (paras 12.2-3) and

(b) your tenancy (whether its rent has been registered or not) began before:

- 15 January 1989 in England and Wales
- 2 January 1989 in Scotland.

T12.4 exceptions	ROO 6(2), 7; HB 2(1) – 'young individual' (para (a) of that definition), 12C(2); HB66+ 12C(2)
12.43	HBW 13(1), 13C(2)(a)-(c), 14(1); HBP 13(1), 13C(2)(a)-(c), 14(1)
12.44	HB(CP) sch 3 para 4(1)(a),(2),(3),(10) – 'first date', 'second date'
12.45	HBW 12B(1), A13(2)(a), 13C(5)(c), 14(2)(b), sch 2 paras 4-8; HBP 12B(1), 13C(5)(c), 14(2)(b), sch 2 paras 4-8

Example: Eligible rent in a rent referral case

Suzie is aged 52 and has been getting HB on her home since 2007. She lives in a flat and currently pays her private landlord £110 per week which includes some ineligible services. She falls within the rent referral rules (para 12.43) and the council refers her rent to the rent officer because 52 weeks have passed. The rent officer sets only a claim-related rent of £110 per week and a service charge determination of £5 per week.

- Her eligible rent equals her claim related rent (£110.00 per week) minus her service charge determination (£5.00 per week) which is £105.00 per week (table 12.4).

Chapter 13 **Supported accommodation**

- What is supported and temporary accommodation and related definitions: paras 13.1-10
- Benefits you can get: paras 13.11-14
- Eligible rent in STA and rent restrictions in old scheme cases: paras 13.15-25

Supported and temporary accommodation (STA)

13.1 This chapter is about supported and temporary accommodation. It only applies to the kinds of accommodation in tables 13.1 and 13.2.

Table 13.1 **The four kinds of supported accommodation**

(a) Exempt accommodation

- You rent from a non-profit landlord (para 13.6) and either
- Your landlord provides you with care, support or supervision (CSS) or
- Your landlord arranges for it to be provided by someone else.

(b) Managed accommodation

- You rent from a non-profit landlord
- Someone other than your landlord provides you with CSS and
- You were provided with the accommodation because you need CSS.

(c) Domestic violence refuges

- You rent from a non-profit landlord or from a local council (para 13.8)
- The refuge is non-permanent and is for people escaping domestic violence and
- You were provided with the accommodation for that reason.

(d) Local council hostels

- The hostel is owned or managed by a local council
- It provides non-self-contained, domestic accommodation
- It provides meals or facilities for preparing food and
- Your landlord or someone else provides you with CSS.

T13.1 UC sch 1 paras 1 – 'exempt accommodation', 3A; UCTP 2(1) – 'specified accommodation'; HBW 75H; HB(CP) sch 3 para 4(10) – 'exempt accommodation'

Table 13.2 **Temporary accommodation**

- You pay rent to the council or a registered housing association (para 11.5)
- Your home was provided by the council because you were homeless or to prevent you being homeless (as defined in homelessness law) and
- Your home isn't exempt accommodation (table 13.1(a)).

Guidance about supported accommodation

13.2 Guidance about supported accommodation is in:

(a) the DWP's 'Housing benefit guidance for supported housing claims' (GSH) and

(b) the DLUHC's 'Supported housing: national statement of expectations' [www].

In England, the Supported Housing (Regulatory Oversight) Act 2023 allows the government to require landlords or managing agents of supported housing (table 13.1) to apply for a licence from their local council under national or local rules. Licensing schemes (and other new council enforcement powers) are intended to improve quality and value for money (GSH para 11). These new licensing schemes are expected to come into force some time in 2025 or 2026 (table 1.4). See table 9.1 for how licensing affects HB entitlement.

Supported accommodation and related definitions

Supported accommodation

13.3 Many kinds of accommodation can be described as being supported in a general sense. But in this guide, 'supported accommodation' (which is called 'specified accommodation' in the law) means only accommodation in table 13.1. It is divided into exempt accommodation, managed accommodation, domestic violence refuges and local council hostels, and includes accommodation that meets the criteria for more than one of these.

13.4 In November 2023, there were an estimated 634,000 accommodation units in Great Britain that were supported in the general sense, of which 215,770 met the definitions in table 13.1 and so counted as 'supported accommodation'. These had an average eligible rent of £247 a week. They were mainly exempt accommodation (table 13.1(a)) with working age renters.

T13.2 UC sch 1 para 3B; UCTP 2(1) – 'temporary accommodation'

13.2 www.gov.uk/government/publications/housing-benefit-guidance-for-supported-housing-claims
www.gov.uk/government/publications/supported-housing-national-statement-of-expectations

13.3 UCTP 2(1) – 'specified accommodation'; HBW 75H

13.4 MHCLG/DWP, Supported housing review 2023: executive summary, paras 26, 51

13.5 Supported accommodation can be short-term or long-term, and people may live there due to:

(a) physical or sensory disabilities, learning disabilities or poor mental health
(b) problems related to homelessness, domestic abuse, drugs or alcohol
(c) needing support as a care leaver, young parent or older person
(d) needing support as an armed forces veteran, ex-offender, migrant or refugee
(e) rough sleeping or not having a settled way of life.

Non-profit landlord

13.6 Most supported accommodation has a 'non-profit landlord' (table 13.1). This means:

(a) a registered or unregistered housing association (paras 11.5-7)
(b) a registered charity or a charity that is exempt from registration
(a) a voluntary organisation (para 13.7) or
(b) a county council in England – but only in an area that also has district councils.

They must be your immediate landlord (CH/3900/2005; East Hertfordshire DC v KT), and not, for example, the superior landlord or a managing agent.

Voluntary organisation

13.7 A 'voluntary organisation' means a 'body, other than a public authority or council, the activities of which are carried on otherwise than for profit' – for example, a community interest company, community benefit society or co-operative registered with the Financial Conduct Authority. Whether a landlord meets this description can involve looking at all the circumstances (not just the landlord's written constitution), and it is a 'commercial reality' that a voluntary organisation is likely to have contracts with profit-making third parties (Wirral BC v MF).

Local council

13.8 A 'local council' means a district, borough or city council in England or any council in Scotland or Wales.

Domestic violence

13.9 'Domestic violence' includes controlling or coercive behaviour, violence, or psychological, physical, sexual, emotional, financial or other abuse, regardless of the gender or sexuality of the victim. The domestic violence doesn't have to be from a partner or family member; it can be from others, including a neighbour or landlord (GSH para 83).

13.5 MHCLG/DWP, Supported housing review 2023: executive summary, para 21

13.6 UC sch 1 para 3A(6) – 'relevant body'; HB(CP) sch 3 para 4(10) – 'exempt accommodation'
East Hertfordshire DC v KT [2009] UKUT 12 (AAC)

13.7 UC sch 1 para 1 – 'voluntary organisation'; HBW/HBP 2(1) – 'voluntary organisation'
Wirral BC v MF and Salisbury Independent Living [2013] UKUT 291 (AAC) reported as [2014] AACR 12

13.8 UC sch 1 para 3A(6) – 'relevant body'; SSAA 134(1), 191 – 'housing authority', 'local authority'

13.9 UC 98, sch 1 para 3A(6) – 'domestic violence'; HBW 2(1) – 'domestic violence', 75H

Care, support or supervision (CSS)

13.10 'Care, support or supervision' is part of the definition of most kinds of supported accommodation. This phrase has its ordinary English meaning, and has been considered in many appeals (table 13.3). The DWP recognises that 'the needs of tenants living in supported housing... vary greatly' and gives useful advice about how councils should check what services are provided, that there is a need for them, and that the provision is more than minimal (GSH paras 136-137, 142-155).

Table 13.3 **Care, support or supervision**

(a) Meaning of care, support or supervision (CSS)

This part of the table applies to supported accommodation generally (table 13.1).

Meaning of CSS: Supported accommodation means 'accommodation in which a measure of care, support or supervision is provided to assist the occupants with the practicalities of day-to-day living' and the phrase 'care, support or supervision' has its ordinary English meaning (R(H) 2/07 confirmed in R(S) v Social Security Commissioners and Others).

Availability of CSS: The CSS must be available in reality to the tenant, and there must be a real prospect that they will find the service of use (R(H) 4/09 and Bristol CC v AW).

Meaning of 'support': 'Support' might well be characterised as 'the giving of advice and assistance to the claimant in coping with the practicalities of [their] life, and in particular [their] occupation of the property' (Chorley BC v IT). It is more than ordinary housing management (Chorley/IT; MMcF v Sefton BC).

Continuity of support: The support provided must be ongoing (R(H) 4/09). Help with gaining exemption from the council tax because the tenant is severely mentally impaired is more like a setting up cost and is not enough (Chorley/IT).

Need for and provision of 'support': 'What matters is simply whether support is provided to more than a minimal extent, and it is... implicit that support is not "provided" unless there is in fact some need for it (Salford CC v PF).

Dwellings in a group: A dwelling in a group (e.g. sheltered accommodation) doesn't qualify as supported accommodation just because other dwellings in the group do: CSS must be provided to that particular dwelling (CH/1289/2007).

Amount of CSS: CSS must be more than minimal. An average of ten minutes per tenant per week was not enough (in R(H) 7/07), but three hours per tenant per week might be

---

13.10 UC sch 1 para, 3A(2),(5); HBW 75H(3),(5); HB(CP) sch 3 para 4(10) – 'exempt accommodation'

T13.3 R(S) v Social Security Commissioner and Others [2008] EWHC 3097 Admin and [2009] EWHC 2221 Admin
Bristol CC v AW [2009] UKUT 109 (AAC)
Chorley BC v IT (HB) [2009] UKUT 107 (AAC) reported as [2010] AACR 2
MMcF v Sefton BC (HB) [2016] UKUT 403 (AAC)
Salford CC v PF [2009] UKUT 150 (AAC)
DW v Oxford CC [2012] UKUT 52 (AAC)
AG v South Ayrshire Council (HB) [2017] UKUT 110 (AAC) reported as [2018] AACR 18
Allerdale BC v JD and Others (HB) [2019] UKUT 304 (AAC)

enough (in CH/1289/2007). Just helping with HB claims and reviews, and carrying out safety and security inspections, was not more than minimal; but 'proactively considering what physical improvements or alterations to the properties could be usefully made' in the case for adaptations for disability could be enough (Chorley/IT). In the test of what is or is not minimal it is 'unfortunately inherent... that some landlords may just about scrape over the line... while others will not do so' (DW v Oxford CC).

When there is no relevant history: In a new development it is necessary to look at what is contemplated (Bristol CC v AW).

(b) Provision of CSS in exempt accommodation

This part of the table applies only to exempt accommodation (table 13.1(a)).

CSS provided by the landlord: A landlord can provide CSS by making arrangements for it, or by paying for someone to do it (Chorley/IT).

CSS provided on behalf of the landlord: For CSS to be provided 'on behalf of' the landlord, there must be 'a sense of agency between the [CSS provider and the landlord], or... a contract, or something akin to it'. A joint venture is not enough; nor is a contract between the CSS provider and e.g. social services (R(S) v Social Security Commissioner, confirming R(H) 2/07).

CSS provided by landlord as well as care provider: The landlord may provide CSS without being the principal provider of it to that particular tenant (Chorley/IT).

Landlord not registered to provide CSS: In Scotland, if CSS is in fact provided but the landlord isn't registered to provide it under the Public Services Reform (Scotland) Act 2010, this leaves the landlord open to legal action, but doesn't stop the claimant's home being exempt accommodation (AG v South Ayrshire Council).

Availability of CSS from elsewhere: 'The likely nature, extent and frequency of [the CSS], and the extent of support available to the claimant from elsewhere' are to be taken into account in considering whether the CSS provided by a landlord is more than minimal (Chorley/IT).

Who pays for the CSS? It is irrelevant that the landlord is (or is not) paid to provide the CSS by someone else (Chorley/IT).

Support vs housing management: 'Support' means that the landlord does more than an ordinary landlord would do (R(H) 4/09). It is more than ordinary housing management, e.g. repairs and maintenance. But if the tenancy agreement 'imposes unusually onerous repairing and maintenance obligations on the landlord', this can amount to support as can the fact that a claimant's disabilities impose a 'materially greater burden on the landlord' (Chorley/IT). Intensive (enhanced) housing management activities may be support for exempt accommodation purposes but not an ineligible service. 'The two provisions are capable of operating independently' (Allerdale BC v JD).

Live-in carers: While the presence of a live-in carer may or may not amount to CSS (depending on who provides the carer), the case law on carers can affect whether the size of the accommodation is reasonable.

Benefits in STA

The benefits you can get

13.11 If you live in STA, you can get:

(a) HB from the council towards your housing costs (whether you have a working age or pension age claim) and

(b) UC or SPC from the DWP towards your living costs.

So, unless you only qualify for HB, you have to make two separate claims.

What HB can help with

13.12 You can get HB towards your rent and eligible services, but you can't get HB (or UC/SPC) towards ineligible services such as support or related charges (chapter 15). Ineligible charges may be paid by your landlord or someone else (e.g. social services or another non-profit body) or you may have to pay for them or contribute towards them yourself. You and your landlord may have to give lengthy details about your rent and service charges, so the council can check your home counts as STA and decide which service charges are eligible for HB.

Decisions and appeals about STA

13.13 Decisions about whether your home counts as STA are made by the council, and you can appeal to the council about this in the usual way (chapter 39).

13.14 If you are claiming UC, the DWP follows the council's decision (OG, file 167). If the council decides your home doesn't count as STA, you should go back and ask the DWP to include your housing costs in your UC. The DWP says that your UC housing costs 'will be revised back to the date you originally declared you were living in the accommodation' (GSH paras 64-68).

Eligible rent in STA

13.15 Your eligible rent is worked out using:

(a) the 'old scheme' rules if you live in exempt accommodation or

(b) the ordinary private or social renter rules in any other kind of STA (paras 11.12-24 and paras 12.6-9 and 12.32-38).

Table 13.4 summarises which eligible rent rules apply, and how living in STA affects other benefit rules.

13.11 WRA sch 5 para 2(1); UC sch 1 paras 3(h),(i), 3A, 3B; UCTP 6A(2)

13.12 HBW/HBP 12(1)(a),(b),(e),(3), sch 1; HBW/HBP Old 12(1)(a),(b),(e) in HB(CP) sch 2 para 5(1)

13.13 UCTP 6A(2)

13.14 UC(D&A) 9, 21

13.15 HB(CP) sch 3 para 4(1)

The old scheme rules

13.16 The old scheme HB rules apply if you live in exempt accommodation (table 13.1(a)) or in rare cases if you have a pre-1996 claim (para 12.44). They are called 'old scheme' because the pre-1996 rules continue to apply to them.

Eligible rent in the old scheme

13.17 The general rule for old scheme cases is that your eligible rent equals:

(a) your actual rent (para 10.2)

(b) minus an amount for ineligible service and other charges (table 15.2).

But your eligible rent may in some cases be restricted (paras 13.19-25).

Joint renters

13.18 If you have at least one joint renter who isn't in your benefit unit (e.g. a friend, relation or workmate), the result of the calculation in para 13.17 is shared between the joint renters (para 10.14).

Table 13.4 **Treatment of HB and UC in STA**

Type of accommodation	**(A) HB eligible rent**	**(B) Bedroom tax**	**(C) Benefit cap in HB and UC**	**(D) UC work allowance**
(a) Exempt accommodation	Old scheme rules	Exempt	HB not counted	Higher
(b) Managed accommodation	Social or private renter rules	Yes	HB not counted	Higher
(c) Domestic violence refuges	Social or private renter rules	Yes	HB not counted	Higher
(d) Local council hostels	Social renter rules	Yes	HB not counted	Higher
(e) Temporary accommodation (homeless)	Social renter rules	Exempt	HB only counted if you aren't on UC	Lower

Notes:

- Working age claimants in accommodation types (a) to (e) claim HB for help with their rent instead of the UC housing costs element
- Columns (B) to (D) don't apply to pension age claimants

13.16 HB(CP) sch 3 para 4(1)

13.17 HBW/HBP Old 12(1),(3) in HB(CP) sch 3 para 5(1)

13.18 HBW/HBP Old 12(5) in HB(CP) sch 3 para 5(1)

T13.4 (col A) HB 11(1), A13(1), 13(1), 13C(1),(5)(a),(b), 14(2)(b), sch 2 para 3; HB(CP) sch 3 para 4(1)(b

T13.4 (col B) HB A13(1)(c),(2)(e) T13.4 (col C) UC 80(2A); HB 75C(2)(a) T13.4 (col D) UC 22(2); UCTP 5A

Example: Eligible rent in exempt accommodation

Orlando rents a room in a house that has been converted to provide accommodation for six residents and meets the definition of 'exempt accommodation' (table 13.1(a)). His total actual rent is £335.00 per week and his eligible rent is £247.05 per week as shown below (para 13.17 and chapter 15). This leaves Orlando with £87.95 per week to pay himself, unless the landlord funds any of the excluded amounts from other sources (para 15.30).

Weekly figures	**Actual rent**	**Eligible for HB**	**Excluded from HB**
Rent (core rent)	£234.00	£234.00	—
His share of council tax on the house	£3.00	£3.00	—
His share of fuel, water charges and cleaning in communal areas	£9.00	£9.00	—
All meals (£35.95 is the standard amount: table 15.5)	£37.00	£1.05	£35.95
Fuel and water charges for his own accommodation	£25.00	—	£25.00
Counselling and support	£27.00	—	£27.00
Totals	**£335.00**	**£247.05**	**£87.95**

Rent restrictions in old scheme cases

13.19 In old scheme cases, the council can restrict your eligible rent if:

(a) your rent is unreasonably high
(b) your home is unreasonably large
(c) you have a rent increase that is unreasonably high or
(d) you have a rent increase that is less than 12 months after the previous rent increase, and this is unreasonable.

There have been many court cases about rent restrictions in the old scheme, and they are summarised in table 13.5. For guidance see GSH paras 203-241.

13.19 HBW/HBP Old 13(3), Old 13ZA(1) in HB(CP) sch 3 para 5(2),(3)

Table 13.5 **Rent restrictions under the old scheme**

These cases apply to exempt accommodation and pre-1996 HB claims (para 13.16).

Decisions about unreasonably high rents: The authority must decide:

- what would be suitable alternative accommodation (including what services are needed)
- what the rent would be for such accommodation and
- whether your actual rent is unreasonably high by comparison.

Unreasonably high for claimant rather than landlord: The authority must decide whether 'the rent is unreasonably high for the claimant to have to pay', rather than unreasonably high for a particular landlord to charge given the amount of public funding the landlord receives or the costs they incur (SS v Birmingham CC).

'Unreasonably high': This means more than just 'higher' (Malcolm v Tweeddale DC HBRB).

Suitability of alternative accommodation: The authority must have 'sufficient information to ensure that like is being compared with like [...] Unless that can be done, no safe assessment can be made of the reasonableness of the rent in question or the proper level of value' (Malcolm v Tweeddale DC HBRB). Your home should be compared with 'more suitable' rather than 'less suitable' accommodation (BM v Vale Royal BC).

Decisions about past periods: A decision about a past period should be made as if it was being made then. If evidence about that period is unavailable or unclear, findings of fact must be made about what was likely to have been the case (BM v Vale Royal BC).

Decisions about the amount of a reduction: The authority should:

(a) consider whether any circumstances may make a small reduction appropriate;

(b) decide the appropriate level of a reduction; and

(c) be able to say how it arrived at (b).
(Mehanne v Westminster CC HBRB and R v Beverley BC ex parte Hare).

Limits to reductions: Your eligible rent must not be reduced below the cost of suitable alternative accommodation (R v Brent LBC ex parte Connery).

Table continued ➤

T13.5 R v Beverley DC HBRB ex parte Hare (1995) 27 HLR 637 (QBD)
SS v Birmingham CC and SSWP [2016] EWCA Civ 1211, [2017] 1 WLR 2251, reported as [2017] AACR 8
Malcolm v Tweeddale DC HBRB (1991) 1994 SLT 1212 (CS)
BM v Vale Royal BC [2009] UKUT 162 (AAC)
R v Westminster HBRB ex parte Mehanne [2001] UKHL 11, [2001] 2 All ER 690, [200] 1 WLR 539
R v Brent LBC ex parte Connery [1990] 2 All ER 353, (1989) 22 HLR 40 (QBD)
R v East Devon DC HBRB ex parte Gibson (1993) 25 HLR 487 (QBD)
R v Sefton MBC ex parte Cunningham (1991) 23 HLR 534 (QBD)

> *People who are protected renters:* availability of suitable alternative accommodation: Although suitable alternative accommodation must be available if you are a protected renter (para 10.25), this doesn't mean the authority is expected to find a home for you. It is 'quite sufficient if an active market is shown to exist in houses in an appropriate place at the appropriate level' (the level your eligible rent is reduced to). So long as the authority has evidence of this, it is sufficient 'to point to a range of properties, or a bloc of property, which is available without specific identification of particular dwelling houses' (R v East Devon DC HBRB ex parte Gibson). If the authority doesn't have this evidence, it shouldn't reduce your eligible rent (CH/4306/2003).
>
> *People who are protected renters:* reasonableness of being expected to move: If you are a protected renter, the authority should have evidence that it has taken into account the effect a move would have (para 10.27) on employment and schooling (R v Sefton MBC ex parte Cunningham).

Suitable alternative accommodation

13.20 The council decides what is 'unreasonable' by making a comparison with suitable alternative accommodation. When doing so it must (or for rent increases, may) take into account:

(a) your and the comparable accommodation's nature, facilities and security of tenure

(b) the age and state of health of the occupiers of your home (para 13.24).

For example, 'if you are disabled or elderly you might have special needs and require expensive or larger accommodation' (HBGM para A4.1171).

13.21 The council normally only looks at alternative accommodation in its own area. If there is nothing comparable there, it can look outside its area but not at 'other parts of the country where accommodation costs differ widely from those which apply locally' (HBGM para A4.1172).

How much can the council reduce your eligible rent

13.22 When a rent restriction applies, the council reduces your eligible rent to the level of rent for suitable alternative accommodation or it can make a smaller reduction. It mustn't simply adopt the rent officer's figures (para 13.25).

13.20 HBW/HBP Old 13(9) in HB(CP) sch 3 para 5(2)

13.22 HBW/HBP Old 13(3), Old 13ZA(1) in HB(CP) sch 3 para 5(2),(3)

Protection against old scheme rent restrictions

13.23 There are three protections against rent restrictions in old scheme cases. These apply as follows:

(a) for 12 months if you have had a death in your home

(b) for 13 weeks if you could previously afford your home or

(c) without time limit if you or an occupier of your home have reached pension age, or have a child or young person, or have limited capability for work.

Only protection (a) applies in the case of in-year rent increases (para 13.9(d)), but in other cases they all apply. For the details see paras 10.19-30.

Occupiers the council takes into account

13.24 The council takes the following occupiers into account when it is deciding what is suitable alternative accommodation and whether the protections against rent restrictions apply:

(a) you and your benefit unit

(b) relatives of you or your partner who have no separate right to occupy the dwelling and

(c) only when the council is considering whether your home is unreasonably large, any other occupier.

'Relative' means the same as in para 10.30. For example, (b) includes your grown up children or your parents who live with you as non-dependants.

Rent officer figures and subsidy

13.25 The council refers all old scheme cases to the rent officer (para 12.25) unless you rent your home from a registered housing association. The rent officer's figures can mean the council gets less subsidy (chapter 42), but they aren't binding in old scheme cases. This means (R v Brent LBC ex p Connery) that the council:

(a) mustn't take subsidy into account when it decides whether your rent, accommodation size or rent increase is unreasonable, or any matter relating to the protections against the restrictions'

(b) may take subsidy into account when deciding the amount of a reduction, but shouldn't reduce your eligible rent on financial grounds alone (HBGM para A4.1173).

13.23 HBW/HBP Old 13(4),(5),(7), Old 13ZA(2) in HB(CP) sch 3 para 5(2)

13.24 HBW/HBP Old 13(10),(11) in HB(CP) sch 3 para 5(2)

13.25 R v Brent LBC ex parte Connery [1990] 2 All ER 353, (1989) 22 HLR 40 (QBD)

Chapter 14 **The size of your home**

- How many bedrooms you qualify for and how this affects your eligible rent: paras 14.1-10
- What counts as a bedroom: paras 14.11-25
- Which occupiers are included: paras 14.26-31
- Qualifying for additional bedrooms: paras 14.32-43

Size and eligible rent

14.1 This chapter applies to UC and HB for renters, not shared owners or owners. It explains how your eligible rent can be reduced if your home is larger than you need.

14.2 For social renters this is usually called the 'bedroom tax', and in the law it is called the 'under-occupancy deduction' in UC or the 'maximum rent (social sector)' in HB. For private renters it is part of the LHA or rent referral rules, and in the law it is called the 'cap rent' in UC or 'maximum rent' in HB.

If you fall within the social renter rules

14.3 If you have a working age claim and your eligible rent is calculated using the social renter rules (para 11.1):

(a) you qualify for the number of bedrooms in table 14.1 (with no upper limit)

(b) your eligible rent is normally reduced if you have more bedrooms than this in your home (paras 11.13).

These rules only apply to UC and working age HB.

14.4 The bedroom tax doesn't apply to pension age HB. Instead, your eligible rent could be restricted under the rent referral rules for registered housing associations (para 12.26) or the default rule for council tenants (para 11.32). In practice both of these are rare.

14.1 UC sch 4 paras 25(1),(2), 36(1),(5); HBW 12B(1), A13(2)(b), B13(2)(b), 13(2),(3),(5), 13C(5)(a), 14(2)(b), sch 2 paras 3, 11A; HBP 12B(1), 13(2),(3),(5), 13C(5)(a), 14(2)(b), sch 2 paras 3, 12; HB(ROO) sch 1 paras 2-5, 9, sch 2

14.2 UC sch 4 paras 25(1),(2), 36(1); HBW B13(1), 13(1), 13D(1); HBP 13(1), 13D(1)

14.3 UC sch 4 paras 8(2)(b), 9, 10, 36(1); HBW A13(1),(2)(d), B13(2)(b),(5)

14.4 HBW A13(2)(d); HBP 12B(6), 13(1), 13C(5)(a), 14(1),(2)(b), sch 2 para 3(2)(a)

If you fall within the LHA rules

14.5 If your eligible rent is calculated using the LHA rules (para 12.6):

(a) you qualify for the number of bedrooms in table 14.1, but only up to a maximum of four

(b) if you qualify for only one bedroom, there are further rules about which category applies to you (paras 12.13)

(c) your eligible rent is normally limited to the LHA figure for the size (or category) of accommodation you qualify for (para 12.8).

These rules apply to UC and both working age and pension age HB.

If you fall within the rent referral rules

14.6 If your eligible rent is calculated using the rent referral rules (para 12.25):

(a) you qualify for the number of bedrooms (with no upper limit) and living rooms in table 14.1

(b) your eligible rent is normally limited to the rent officer's determination for the size (or category) of accommodation you qualify for (table 12.4)

(c) if you qualify for only one bedroom, there are further rules about which category applies to you (table 12.4(f)).

These rules apply to both working age and pension age HB.

If you fall within the old scheme rules

14.7 If your eligible rent is calculated using the old scheme rules (para 13.16), this chapter doesn't apply. But other rules about the size of your home may affect your HB (para 13.19).

Unlawful discrimination

14.8 The courts have decided that the rules in this chapter don't unlawfully discriminate against:

(a) claimants who have a disabled adult child living with them (JD v UK)

(b) separated parents with shared care of a child (R (Cotton and Others) v SSWP)

(c) gypsy travellers (FT v Perth and Kinross Council).

Other cases resulted in changes to the law so that the rules no longer discriminate against adults and children who are disabled (R (Daly and Others) v SSWP) or against women living in sanctuary schemes (A v UK).

14.5 UC sch 4 paras 8(2)(a), 9, 10, 26; HBW 13D(1)-(3); HBP 13D(1)-(3)

14.6 HBW 13(2),(3); HBP 13(2),(3); HB(ROO) sch 1 paras 4-6, sch 2

14.7 HBW 12B(1), A13(1)(c), 13C(2),(5)(b); HBP 12B(1), 13C(2),(5)(b); HB(CP) sch 3 para 4(1)(b)

14.8 JD and A v UK [2019] ECHR 753
R (Cotton and Others) v SSWP [2014] EWHC Admin 3437
R (Daly and Others) v SSWP [2016] UKSC 58
FT v Perth and Kinross Council and SSWP (HB) [2019] UKUT 43 (AAC)

Table 14.1 **The size rules**

(a) Bedrooms (all cases)

You qualify for one bedroom for each of the following occupiers:

- each couple (including you and your partner if you are a couple)
- each single person aged 16 or over (including yourself if you are single)
- two children under 16 of the same sex
- two children under 10 of the same or opposite sex
- any other child aged under 16.

Children are expected to share bedrooms in whatever way results in the smallest number of bedrooms. But young persons aren't expected to share a bedroom, and in most cases nor are non-dependants (para 14.28).

(b) Additional bedrooms (all cases)

One or more additional bedrooms can be allowed for each the following (paras 14.32-43):

- a foster parent or pre-adoptive parent
- a couple who can't share a bedroom due to disability
- a child who can't share a bedroom due to disability or
- an adult who requires overnight care.

(c) Living rooms (rent referral cases only)

When the social renter or LHA rules apply, living rooms are ignored. But when the rent referral rules apply, you qualify for living rooms as follows:

- one if there are one to three occupiers of your home (regardless of age)
- two if there are four to six occupiers
- three if there are seven or more occupiers.

(d) Further rules (private renters only)

- When the LHA rules apply, the maximum number of bedrooms you can qualify for (including additional bedrooms) is four
- When the LHA or rent referral rules apply, there are further rules about one bedroom accommodation (para 12.13 and table 12.4(f)).

T14.1(a) UC sch 4 para 10(1),(2); HBW B13(5); HB(ROO) sch 2 para 1

T14.1(b) UC sch 4 para 12(A1),(1),(2),(8),(9); HBW B13(6),(7); HB(ROO) sch 2 paras 1A, 1B

T14.1(c) HB(ROO) sch 2 para 2

T14.1(d) UC sch 4 para 26; HBW 13D(2)(c); HBP 13D(2)(c)

Examples: How many bedrooms you qualify for

The rules in these cases are the same for UC and HB (table 14.1) except as in example 7.

1. A single person who is the only occupier

She qualifies for one bedroom. If she is a private renter, see tables 12.1-2 for whether she qualifies for shared or self-contained accommodation.

2. A couple who are the only occupiers

They qualify for one bedroom.

3. A single person with three children

He has sons aged 15 and 8 and a daughter aged 13. The sons are expected to share a bedroom. So the household qualifies for three bedrooms.

4. The older son in example 3 reaches 16

Now none of the children are expected to share a bedroom. So the household qualifies for four bedrooms.

5. A couple with four children

They have daughters aged 13 and 4 and sons aged 14 and 8. The children are expected to share bedrooms in the way that results in the smallest number of bedrooms (the daughters sharing, and also the sons). The household qualifies for three bedrooms.

6. The couple in example 5 have a baby

The couple now qualify for four bedrooms. No way of sharing bedrooms can result in a lower number.

7. A single person with two non-dependants

In UC, the household qualifies for three bedrooms whether the non-dependants are a couple or two single people, but in HB, the household qualifies for two bedrooms if the non-dependants are a couple or three bedrooms if they are two single people (para 14.28).

Examples including additional bedrooms are later in this chapter.

How bedrooms affect the size rules

14.9 The size rules compare:

(a) how many bedrooms you have and

(b) how many you qualify for (table 14.1).

These depend on what counts as a bedroom (para 14.11) and who occupies your home (para 14.26).

14.10 The rules are designed to prevent under-occupation (SSWP v Nelson), but also to ensure you have an extra bedroom if you need it (para 14.32).

14.10 SSWP v Nelson and Fife Council [2014] UKUT 525 (AAC), reported as [2015] AACR 21

What is a bedroom

14.11 This section explains what counts as a bedroom for the purposes of the UC and HB size rules.

14.12 The regulations don't define 'bedroom': the meaning described in the following paras is derived from decisions made by the Upper Tribunal and the higher courts. The three leading cases are SSWP v Nelson and Fife Council, SSWP v Glasgow CC and IB, and SSWP v Hockley – we refer to these as 'Nelson', 'Glasgow/IB' and 'Hockley'.

14.13 If a room is a bedroom, it counts for the purposes of the bedroom tax. For example:

(a) if you have a bedroom for yourself and a second bedroom for visitors, the bedroom tax may reduce your benefit (paras 14.3-4)

(b) but if the second bedroom is for an overnight carer, you may qualify for an 'extra' bedroom for them (para 14.39) and avoid the bedroom tax.

14.14 If a room isn't a bedroom, it doesn't count for the purposes of the bedroom tax. For example, if you qualify for two bedrooms and have two bedrooms plus a living room, the living room isn't an 'extra bedroom' so it doesn't reduce your benefit (para 14.15).

The main considerations

14.15 Whether a room is a bedroom is decided using the ordinary use of the word 'bedroom' (Nelson). The DWP or council should consider all the factors summarised in this section (SSWP v GM). The main ones are:

(a) whether the room can be used for sleeping in (paras 14.18-21) and

(b) how the room is described in your letting agreement (paras 14.22-24).

The room's vacant state

14.16 Whether a room is a bedroom is decided objectively by reference to the property's vacant state, and ignores how the room is actually used from time to time (Nelson; Glasgow/IB; Hockley). For example, using a bedroom as an office doesn't stop it being a bedroom, and letting someone sleep on a sofa in your living room doesn't make it into a bedroom.

Using a room as a bedroom

14.17 For a room to be a bedroom, there must be enough room for the following (Nelson; SSWP v RR):

(a) a bed

(b) clothes storage

(c) a flat surface of some sort to place necessary items and avoid obvious safety risks

(d) enough free space for dressing and undressing.

14.12 SSWP v Nelson and Fife Council [2014] UKUT 525 (AAC) reported as [2015] AACR 21
SSWP v Glasgow CC and IB [2017] CSIH 35, reported as [2017] AACR 38
SSWP v Hockley and Nuneaton and Bedworth BC [2019] EWCA Civ 1080, reported as [2019] AACR 27

14.15 SSWP v GM and Liverpool CC [2018] UKUT 425 (AAC)

14.17 SSWP v RR (HB) [2018] UKUT 180 (AAC)

Size, shape, access and configuration

14.18 The above requirements can be met in a range of different ways. It all depends on the size and configuration of the room in question and whether a room is suitable to accommodate a bed with sufficient space, height, light, ventilation and privacy (Glasgow/IB). But in all these cases, It should be possible to get into bed from within the room, and there should be somewhere to put clothes and a glass of water, for example a bedside cabinet with drawers (Stevenage BC v ML; M v SSWP)

14.19 A room with space only for a single bed and chest of drawers is likely to be sufficient (Stevenage v ML/M v SSWP). So a room may be a bedroom even if the door would bang into the bed when opened (SSWP v GM), or the door doesn't open all the way (SSWP v JM). A room can be a bedroom even it is an unusual shape, or even if the occupant would have to swing their legs over the bed, or move the bed, to get to one part of the room (SSWP v WT).

14.20 The following factors can also be taken into account:

(a) the number of rooms in the property, their size, layout and function as living/dining space, kitchen, washing/toilet facilities and what other space is available in the property as a whole (Nelson, Glasgow/IB, SSWP v RR)

(b) evidence of how similar rooms/spaces are used in other properties in the area (Nelson).

Who could use the room

14.21 A room is a bedroom if it can be used by any of the people mentioned in the size rules (para 14.26 and table 14(1)(a)-(b)) (Nelson). For example, a child's bedroom is a bedroom even if there are no children in your home. And a room is a bedroom even if it is only suitable for part time use (for example for a visitor or overnight carer) rather than full-time use (Nelson).

The description in the letting agreement

14.22 The DWP or council can take account of the description of the room by the original or current landlord (for example in the letting agreement or marketing materials) or in the plans or designs for the building. This is a starting point that can be of use in borderline cases, rather than being conclusive (Bolton MBC v BF; Nelson; Glasgow/IB; SSWP v RR). For example, a landlord might advertise a property as having three bedrooms, when in reality it has two bedrooms and a small storage space.

Change of use

14.23 Converting a room so that it is objectively different (for example, knocking two bedrooms into one) is part of the assessment of what is a bedroom, but merely using it for a different purpose is not (Glasgow/IB, Hockley). Historic uses of a room are not normally relevant. For example, when a council divided several one-bedroom flats to make them two-bedroom flats, that didn't mean that they still only had one bedroom (CB v Manchester CC).

14.18 Stevenage v ML (HB) [2016] UKUT 164 (AAC)
M v SSWP (UC) [2017] UKUT 443 (AAC)

14.19 SSWP v JM and Liverpool CC (HB) [2020] UKUT 337 (AAC)
SSWP v WT and Redcar and Cleveland BC [2019] UKUT 372 (AAC)

14.22 Bolton MBC v BF (HB) [2014] UKUT 48 (AAC)

14.23 CB v Manchester CC and SSWP [2015] UKUT 556 (AAC)

Overcrowding

14.24 The law on overcrowding sets a limit for the dwelling based on the number of living rooms, the floor area and ceiling height of each of those rooms, the age and sex of the occupiers and whether they are a couple. The occupiers are free to set their own sleeping arrangements and are only bound by the overall limit, not the permitted number for each room. Although, these rules are separate from the benefit rules, they can sound 'warning bells' that a room with very small dimensions may not be a bedroom (Nelson; Stevenage v ML; M v SSWP).

Illegal occupation

14.25 A room contaminated with asbestos can't be counted as a bedroom (E v Bristol CC), and it seems likely that any accommodation which it would be illegal to occupy (for example, because it has a prohibition order/closing order) wouldn't count as a bedroom.

Which occupiers are included

14.26 In UC and HB, the following occupiers of your home are taken into account in deciding how many bedrooms you qualify for:

(a) you and your partner

(b) children and young persons in your benefit unit (chapter 5)

(c) any non-dependants you have (chapter 6) and

(d) in HB only, other occupiers of your home (para 14.29).

Children and young persons

14.27 A child or young person is included as an occupier even if the 'two child limit' means they are not included in your maximum UC or your applicable amount in HB (paras 19.3-4 and 19.15). But the following are not included:

(a) a foster child

(b) or child or young person placed with you for adoption

(c) a child or young person who normally lives somewhere else (for example with their other parent).

In cases (a) and (b) see instead para 14.33

Non-dependants

14.28 In UC you qualify for one bedroom for each non-dependant in your home. In the case of a non-dependant couple, this means two bedrooms (one each). In HB you qualify for one bedroom for each single non-dependant and one bedroom for each non-dependant couple.

14.24 Housing Act 1985, s.323-326; Housing (Scotland) Act 1987, s135-137

14.25 E v Bristol CC (HB) [2018] UKUT 287 (AAC)

14.26 UC sch 4 paras 9(1), 10(1); HBW B13(5); 13D(3),(12) – 'occupiers'; HBP 13D(3),(12); HB(ROO) sch 2 para 1

14.27 UC 4(2), sch 4 para 9(1)(c),(2)(c),(g),(3); HBW 2(1) – 'child', 20(1), 21(3),(4); HBP 2(1), 20(1), 21(3),(4)

14.28 UC sch 4 paras 8, 9(1)(c), 10(1)(c); HBW 13(5)(a),(b), 13D(3)(a),(b); HBW 13D(3)(a),(b); HB(ROO) sch 2 para 1(a),(b)

Other occupiers

14.29 Other occupiers of your home are included as an occupier in HB but not UC. For example, this applies to lodgers and joint renters in your household.

People who are temporarily absent

14.30 You and your benefit unit can be included during a temporary absence, and in practice the DWP or council is likely to do this when you or they meet the conditions in chapter 8. The same normally applies to non-dependants (though in their case there is also a special rule for armed forces absences).

Non-dependants in the armed forces

14.31 If you have a non-dependant son, daughter or step-son/daughter who is in the armed forces, they are included as an occupier during periods they are away on operations. There is no time limit (except in rent referral cases), so long as they were a non-dependant in your home before they went away and intend to return to your home afterwards.

Additional bedrooms

14.32 You qualify for an additional bedroom for:

(a) a foster parent or pre-adoptive parent
(b) a couple who can't share a bedroom due to a disability
(c) a child who can't share a bedroom due to a disability or
(d) an adult who requires overnight care.

You can qualify for one additional bedroom for each of (a) to (d) and in some cases more than one. The details are in this section.

Fostering and pre-adoption

14.33 You qualify for an additional bedroom if you or your partner:

(a) are a foster parent and
- have a child or young person placed with you or
- are waiting for a placement or between placements – but only up to 12 months/ 52 weeks in each period or

(b) are a pre-adoptive parent and have a child placed with you for adoption.

14.29 UC sch 4 para 9(1); HBW B13(5), 13D(3),(12) – 'occupiers', 114A(9); HBP 13D(3),(12), 95A(9); HB(ROO) 2(1) – 'occupier', sch 2 para 1

14.30 UC sch 4 paras 10(3)(a), 11; HBW 3(1), 7(1),(2), 21(1), B13(5), 13D(12) – 'occupiers', 114A(9); HBP 3(1), 7(1),(2), 21(1), 13D(12); HB(ROO) 2(1) – 'occupier', sch 2 para 1

14.31 UC sch 4 paras 9(1)(c), 10(1)(c), 11(1),(4),(5)(d); HBW B13(8), 13D(12) – 'occupiers'; HBP 13D(12)
Rent referral: HBW/HBP 7(13F),(13G),(18) – 'member of Her Majesty's forces posted overseas'; HB(ROO) 2(1) – 'occupier', sch 2 para 1(b)

14.32 UC sch 4 para 12; HBW B13(5)(za),(zb),(6), 13D(3)(za),(ba),(3A); HBP 13D(3)(za),(ba),(3A); HB(ROO) sch 2 paras 1(za),(ba), 1A

14.33 UC sch 4 para 12(1)(b),(4),(5); HBW 2(1) – 'qualifying parent or carer', B13(6)(b), 13D(3A)(b); HBP 2(1), 13D(3A)(b); HB(ROO) sch 2 paras 1A(b), 3

Example: A foster parent

Jasper and Isla are foster parents. They have two sons aged 13 and 11, and two foster daughters aged 12 and 9.

- They qualify for one bedroom for themselves, and one for their two sons. Although they do not qualify for a bedroom for the foster daughters under the general rules (table 14.1), they qualify for one additional bedroom as foster parents (para 14.32). So they qualify for three bedrooms in all.

14.34 In HB for social renters only, you also qualify for an additional bedroom for each other occupier of your home who meets the conditions in para 14.33(a) or (b).

Couples who can't share a bedroom

14.35 You qualify for an additional bedroom if:

(a) you are in a couple

(b) due to your or your partner's disability, you aren't reasonably able to share a bedroom with them and

(c) you or your partner are receiving:

- the daily living component of PIP or ADP at the standard or enhanced rate
- the middle or highest rate of the care component of DLA, SADLA or CDP or
- attendance allowance or PADP.

But in HB, you only qualify if you have an actual bedroom that is additional to those in table 14.1(a).

14.36 In HB (for social and private renters) only, you also qualify for an additional bedroom for each other couple in your home who meet the above conditions.

14.34 HBW B13(7)(b), 13D(3A)(b); HBP 13D(3A)(b); HB(ROO) sch 2 para 1A(b)

14.35 UC sch 4 para 12(1)(d),(6A); HBW 2(1) – 'member of a couple who cannot share a bedroom', B13(5)(za), 13D(3)(za); HBP 2(1), 13D(3)(za); HB(ROO) sch 2 paras 1(za), 3

14.36 HBW B13(6)(ab), 13D(3A)(a)(iii); HBP 13D(3A)(a)(iii); HB(ROO) sch 2 para 1A(a),(iii)

Disabled children who can't share a bedroom

14.37 You qualify for an additional bedroom if:

(a) you have a child (under 16) in your benefit unit or you have a non-dependant who has a child

(b) due to the child's disability, they can't reasonably share a bedroom with another child and

(c) the child is receiving the middle or highest rate of the care component of DLA or CDP.

But in HB, you only qualify if you have an actual bedroom that is additional to those in table 14.1(a).

14.38 Whether a child can 'reasonably share a bedroom with another child' is considered in the circumstances of the particular case. For example, it applies if there would be a danger to a child they shared with, or significantly disturb their sleep (ADM para F3135).

Examples: Disabled people who can't share a bedroom

1. A couple

Under the general rules (table 14.1) they qualify for one bedroom. But the couple can't share a bedroom due to the partner's disability.

- An additional bedroom is allowed, so they qualify for two bedrooms (para 14.35).

2. A single person with two children under 10

Under the general rules they qualify for two bedrooms. But one of the children can't share a bedroom because of his disability.

- An additional bedroom is allowed, so they qualify for three bedrooms (para 14.37).

3. A couple with two children under 10

Under the general rules they qualify for two bedrooms. But one partner in the couple is disabled and can't share bedroom and one child is disabled and can't share a bedroom.

- Two additional bedrooms are allowed, so they qualify for four bedrooms.

14.37 UC sch 4 para 9(1)(c), 12(1)(c),(6); HBW 2(1) – 'child who cannot share a bedroom', B13(5)(ba), 13D(3)(ba); HBP 2(1), 13D(3)(ba); HB(ROO) sch 2 paras 1(ba), 3

14.38 UC sch 4 para 12(6)(b); HBW 2(1) – 'child who cannot share a bedroom'; 2(1)

People who require overnight care

14.39 You qualify for an additional bedroom if:

(a) a person in your home (para 14.41) requires overnight care on a regular basis

(b) one or more carers stay overnight in your home to provide it and

(c) the person is receiving:

- the daily living component of PIP or ADP at the standard or enhanced rate
- the middle or highest rate of the care component of DLA, SADLA or CDP or
- PADP, armed forces independence payment or constant attendance allowance paid as part of an industrial injury or war disablement pension.

But in HB, you only qualify if there is an actual bedroom provided for the carer(s) – this means a room which has a bed in it or is used for sleeping in (Bolton MBC v BF).

14.40 In HB, you don't need to be receiving a benefit in (c) above if you have other evidence to show that you need overnight care – for example you receive other relevant benefits (SD v Eastleigh BC).

14.41 The person who requires overnight care can be:

(a) you or your partner

(b) a child or young person in your benefit unit

(c) a non-dependant in your home

(d) a foster child or child placed with you for adoption

(e) in HB only, any other occupier of your home.

Example: Someone who requires overnight care

Milo and Grace are a couple and no-one else lives with them. Milo receives the daily living component of personal independence payment, and a rota of carers stay every night of the week to care for him. At the weekend Grace provides overnight care for him.

- They qualify for one bedroom under the general rules (table 14.1), and one additional bedroom because the carers provide regular overnight care (para 14.39). So they qualify for two bedrooms in all.

14.39 UC sch 4 paras 9(1), 12(A1),(3); HBW 2(1) – 'person who requires overnight care', B13(6)(a),(ab), 13D(3A)(a); HBP 2(1), 13D(3A)(a); HB(ROO) sch 2 para 1A(a)
Bolton MBC v BF (HB) [2014] UKUT 48 (AAC)

14.40 HBW 2(1) – 'person who requires overnight care'; HBP 2(1)
SD v Eastleigh BC (HB) [2014] UKUT 325 (AAC)

14.41 UC sch 4 paras 9(1), 12(A1); HBW B13(6)(a),(ab),(9); 13D(3A)(a); HBP 13D(3A)(a); HB(ROO) sch 2 para 1A(a)

14.42 The care does not have to be every night or on the majority of nights; but must be provided regularly –which means 'habitually, customarily or commonly', not just 'on occasion' or 'when needed': SD v Eastleigh BC.

14.43 You can qualify for one or more additional bedrooms under this rule as follows:

(a) in UC you qualify for one for each person who meets the conditions

(b) in HB for social renters you qualify for two (if a person in para 14.41(a)-(d) meets the conditions and so does a joint tenant) or one (in other cases)

(c) in HB for private renters you qualify for one.

14.42 UC sch 4 para 12(A1),(2),(9)(a); HBW B13(6)(a),(ab),(7)(a); 13D(3A)(a); HBP 13D(3A)(a); HB(ROO) sch 2 para 1A(a)

Chapter 15 **Service charges**

- Eligible and excluded charges: paras 15.4-22
- Support and similar service charges: paras 15.23-30
- Classifying charges and calculating costs: paras 15.31-36
- Unreasonable service charges: paras 15.37-42

15.1 Your rent or other payments may include charges for services or other items. The charges could be towards fuel, water, council tax, communal areas, support, and so on.

15.2 This chapter describes which charges you can get UC or HB towards (for SPC see chapter 17). It applies to renters, shared owners and owners. But it doesn't apply to renters who fall within the LHA scheme because their benefit is worked out in a different way (para 12.8).

15.3 The DWP gives helpful advice in:

(a) *Universal credit service charges guidance for social landlords* (GSL)

(b) *Housing benefit guidance for supported housing claims* (GSH) paras 166-193 and

(c) *Housing benefit guidance manual* (HBGM) paras A4.700-950.

Eligible and excluded charges

15.4 A service charge is an amount you are charged for the provision of 'services or facilities for the use or benefit of' the occupiers of your home (para 15.17). It is either:

(a) 'eligible' – it can be met by benefit if it meets all the conditions in para 15.5 or

(b) 'excluded' (ineligible) – it can never be met by benefit.

The conditions for getting benefit

15.5 You can get benefit towards a service charge if it meets all the following conditions:

(a) the charge must be for an eligible kind of service, not an excluded kind (tables 15.1-3)

(b) paying the charge must be a condition of occupying your home (para 15.6)

(c) the charge must not be for an item that will become yours (para 15.7)

(d) the charge must not be for an item that could be paid for by public funds (UC only) and

(e) the service and charge must be reasonable (paras 15.38-41).

But different rules apply if the charge counts as rent (para 15.17).

15.5 UC 25(2)(c), sch 1 paras 7(1) 8(2)-(6); HBW 12(1)(e), 12(2)(d), sch 1; HBP 12(1),(e), 12(2)(d), sch 1; HBW/HBP Old 12(1)(e), Old 12(2)(d)

15.6 UC sch 1 para 8(3); HBW Old 12(1)(e), 12(1)(e); HBP Old 12(1),(e), 12(1)(e)

A condition of occupying your home

15.6 You can only get benefit towards service charges that are a condition of occupying your home (table 10.1). If you are given a choice about whether to pay for any services you receive, you can't get benefit towards those particular ones.

If an item will become yours

15.7 When a landlord provides furniture, domestic items or household equipment, they sometimes only charge for them for a fixed time, after which the items belong to you. These charges are excluded from benefit.

Which charges are eligible for UC and HB

15.8 Tables 15.1-3 explain which charges are eligible for UC and HB and which are excluded from them. The law is drawn up in different ways for the two benefits, but in practice the effect is the same.

Table 15.1 **Eligible service charges in UC**

Eligible service charges

The law lists these categories as eligible for UC. Charges that count as part of your rent are also eligible (para 15.17).

Maintaining the general standard of accommodation (Category A)

- External window cleaning on upper floors
- For owner occupiers and shared owners only, separately identifiable payments for maintenance and repairs (internal and external)

General upkeep of communal areas (Category B)

- Ongoing maintenance and cleaning of communal areas
- Supply of water, fuel and other commodities to communal areas

Basic communal services (Category C)

- Provision of basic communal services
- Ongoing maintenance, cleaning and repair in connection with basic communal services

Accommodation-specific charges (Category D)

- Use of essential items in your own home, such as furniture and domestic appliances

Excluded service charges

Charges not in the above categories are excluded

15.7 UC sch 1 para 8(6)(b); HBW Old 12(2)(d), 12(2)(d); HBP Old 12(2)(d), 12(2)(d)

15.8 UC 25(2)(a),(c), sch 1 para 7(1), 8(4); HBW Old 12(3), 12B(2) sch 1; HBP Old 12(3), 12B(2) sch 1

T15.1 UC 25(2)(a),(c), sch 1 para 8(4), categories A to D, sch 4 para 3

Table 15.2 **Eligible and excluded service charges in HB**

Charges that count as part of your rent are also eligible (para 15.17).

Eligible service charges

- Fuel for communal areas
- Cleaning and window cleaning of communal areas
- Furniture and household equipment
- Most other communal services
- Any charge relating to the provision of adequate accommodation

Excluded service charges

- Fuel for your own accommodation
- Meals
- Cleaning and window cleaning of your own accommodation
- Counselling and support
- Any day-to-day living expense

Table 15.3 **Examples of eligible and excluded service charges**

These lists combine UC and HB law with examples from DWP advice (ADM paras F2072-74 and F2077, GSH para 177, GSL paras 19-20, HBGM A4.730). Charges that count as part of your rent are also eligible (para 15.17).

(a) Examples of eligible service charges

- Furniture and household equipment (e.g. cookers, washing machines, crockery, cutlery)
- Heating, lighting and water charges for communal areas
- Cleaning and maintenance of communal areas including communal lifts and phones
- Secure building access (e.g. keypads, CCTV and concierges) (ET v Rossendale BC)
- Ground maintenance (e.g. lawn mowing, tree and hedge management, litter removal and lighting for access areas)
- Tenant parking (for cars or bikes) excluding security costs
- Laundry facilities, children's play areas, garages and mobility scooter sheds

Table continued ➤

T15.2 HBW sch 1 paras 1, 2, 5, 6; HBP sch 1 paras 1, 2, 5, 6

- Health and safety charges
- Refuse collection and TV/wireless aerials for receiving a free service
- Most other communal charges
- In HB, services relating to the needs of residents the accommodation is for (CIS/1460/1995; Liverpool CC v NM) – for example, residents with disabilities or vulnerable young people
- A proportion of staff management and administration costs relating to eligible services.

(b) Examples of excluded service charges

- Food of any kind
- Medical and personal services of any kind, including personal care
- Nursing care and personal alarm systems
- Equipment and adaptations relating to disability or infirmity
- Counselling and support
- Heating, lighting and water charges for your own accommodation
- Cleaning your own accommodation and having your laundry done
- Gardening in your own garden (CP v Aylesbury Vale DC, CH/755/2008)
- Recreational facilities and subscription/fee-based TV
- TV licences, transport, leisure/sports facilities and other day-to-day living expenses
- A proportion of staff management and administration relating to excluded services.

Communal charges

15.9 'Basic communal charges', and charges for communal areas, are eligible for UC (table 15.1). Charges relating to 'the provision of adequate accommodation', including charges for communal areas, are eligible for HB (table 15.2). In practice charges meeting either description are eligible for both UC and HB.

Basic communal services

15.10 In UC, basic communal services are those that are available to everyone in the accommodation.

T15.3 ET v Rossendale BC [2010] UKUT 222 (AAC)
Liverpool CC v NM (HB) [2015] UKUT 532 (AAC) reported as [2016] AACR 19
CP v Aylesbury Vale DC (HB) [2011] UKUT 22 (AAC)

15.9 UC sch 1 para 8(4) category C; HBW sch 1 paras 1(g), 5; HBP sch 1 paras 1(g), 5

15.10 UC sch 1 para 8(4), category C

Provision of adequate accommodation

15.11 In HB, the courts have said (R v Swansea HBRB ex p Littler/R v St Edmundsbury HBRB ex p Sandys) that:

(a) what is meant by the 'provision of adequate accommodation' is fairly narrow and is restricted to only those services that are necessary for the enjoyment of your home (for example, a lift in a block of flats and costs associated with maintaining it)

(b) in deciding what is necessary for the enjoyment of the dwelling, no account can be taken of your personal needs. It is only the adequacy of the accommodation that counts, not your ability to take advantage of it.

Communal areas

15.12 'Communal areas' include both internal and external communal areas. If you live in STA (table 13.1(a)-(d)) or sheltered or extra care housing, they also include common rooms such as sitting rooms, offices and meeting rooms (Oxford CC v Basey, Liverpool CC v NM).

Fuel, cleaning and window cleaning

15.13 The following charges are eligible for UC and HB if they are for communal areas (para 15.12), but excluded from benefit if they are for your own accommodation:

(a) fuel including payments for gas, electricity, etc, standing charges and other supply costs

(b) cleaning

(c) internal window cleaning and

(d) external window cleaning on upper floors.

15.14 Charges that combine amounts for communal areas with amounts for your accommodation therefore have to be separated out (Liverpool CC v NM). The DWP or council uses your or your landlord's actual or estimated figures for this. But for fuel in HB cases only, the amount in table 15.4 is used if no other evidence is available.

Meals

15.15 Charges for meals or food (including preparation costs) are excluded from benefit. In UC, the actual cost is excluded. In HB, the amounts in table 15.5 are always excluded instead.

15.11 UC sch 1 para 8(4) category C; HBW sch 1 para 1(g); HBP sch 1 para 1(g)
R v Swansea HBRB ex p Littler [1998] EWCA Civ 1214, 48 BMLR 24
R v St Edmundsbury HBRB ex p Sandys [1997] EWHC Admin 711, 30 HLR 800

15.12 UC sch 1 para 8(4) category B; HBW sch 1 para 8 – 'communal areas'; HBP sch 1 para 8
Oxford CC v Basey [2012] EWCA Civ 115 reported as [2012] AACR 38
Liverpool CC v NM (HB) [2015] UKUT 532 (AAC) reported as [2016] AACR 19

15.13 UC sch 1 para 8(4) category B, sch 4 para 31; HBW sch 1 paras 1(a)(iv),(g), 5; HBP sch 1 paras 1(a)(iv),(g), 5

15.14 HBW sch 1 paras 5, 6; HBP sch 1 paras 5, 6

15.15 UC sch 1 para 8(6)(c); HBW sch 1 paras 1(a)(i), 2; HBP sch 1 para 1(a)(i),(2)

Table 15.4 **HB standard weekly fuel deductions 2025-26**

If the claimant and any family occupy more than one room	
Fuel for heating	£35.25
Fuel for hot water	£4.10
Fuel for lighting	£2.85
Fuel for cooking	£4.10
Fuel for any other purpose	NIL
Fuel for all the above	£46.30
If the claimant and any family occupy one room only	
Fuel for heating and any hot water and/or lighting	£21.10
Fuel for cooking	£4.10
Fuel for any other purpose	NIL
Fuel for all the above	£25.20

Note: Standard weekly deductions for fuel in 2025-26 remain unchanged from the previous year.

Table 15.5 **HB standard weekly meals deductions 2025-26**

A separate amount is assessed and deducted for each person whose meals are provided.

If at least three meals are provided every day	
For the claimant, and each other person from the first Monday in September following his or her 16th birthday	£35.95
For each child	£18.25
If breakfast only is provided	
For the claimant, and each other person of any age	£4.35
All other cases	
For the claimant, and each other person from the first Monday in September following his or her 16th birthday	£24.00
For each child	£12.00

T15.4 HBW sch 1 para 6(2),(3); HBP sch 1 para 6(2),(3); SI 2025/295 regs 23, 24

T15.5 HBW sch 1 para 2(2)-(5); HBP sch 1 para 2(2)-(5); SI 2025/295 regs 23, 24

Water charges

15.16 If you pay water charges to your landlord, they are usually regarded as part of your rent rather than service charges (para 15.17). They are eligible for UC and HB if they are for communal areas (para 15.12), but excluded from benefit if they are for your own accommodation. The DWP or council decides how much to deduct using the figure billed by the water company, or a proportion of it if your home is only part of a dwelling.

Charges that are part of your rent rather than service charges

15.17 The law sometimes makes the following distinction:

(a) a charge counts as a service charge if:

- it relates to services or facilities for the use or benefit of the occupier(s) of your home and
- it benefits you rather than your landlord or leaseholder

(b) but a charge counts as part of your rent if:

- it relates to the property and isn't attributable to a service and
- it benefits the landlord or leaseholder rather than you.

15.18 All charges that count as rent are eligible for benefit, except for water charges as described in para 15.16. But in some cases your overall eligible rent could be restricted (paras 10.15-18).

Landlord overheads

15.19 The following landlord costs or overheads count as part of your rent (paras 15.17) rather than a service charge (ET v Rossendale BC) and are eligible for benefit:

(a) mortgage repayments (or rent if the landlord leases the property from someone else)

(b) landlord insurance and similar payments (DWP correspondence)

(c) licence fees and council tax when the landlord has to pay these (e.g. in an HMO)

(d) property maintenance including repairs, replacements and redecoration

(e) testing fire, smoke, gas and electricity alarms

(f) installing, repairing and maintaining adaptations to your home such as a stair lift (Pembrokeshire County Council v EL)

15.16 UC sch 1 para 8(7), sch 4 para 31; HBW Old 12(3)(a),(6), 12B(2)(a),(5), sch 1 para 1(a)(iv),(g); HBP Old 12(3)(a),(6), 12B(2)(a),(5), sch 1 para 1(a)(iv),(g)

15.17 UC sch 1 para 7(2); HBW Old 12(7), 12(8); HBP Old 12(7), 12(8)

15.18 UC 26(2), sch 1 paras 2(a), 3(g), 7(2), 8(7), sch 4 para 3; HBW 12(1)(a), 12B(2),(5), sch 1 para 3(3); HBP 12(1)(a), 12B(2),(5), sch 1 para 3(3)

15.19 ET v Rossendale BC [2010] UKUT 222 (AAC) correspondence from DWP ministers office 2024, ref TO2024/59794
Pembrokeshire County Council v EL [2011] UKUT 513 (AAC)
Wigan MBC v VF [2009] UKUT 28 (AAC)
Birmingham CC v IB [2009] UKUT 116 (AAC)

(g) space for a live-in carer if you are charged for their room (Wigan MBC v VF, Birmingham CC v IB)

(h) other items that are properly considered in setting the rent, such as a sinking fund for property maintenance, bad debt provision, and the cost of vacant lettings (voids) (CH/3528/2006; ET v Rossendale BC).

Owners on UC – exclusions and waiting period

15.20 If you are an owner (including a leaseholder, but not a shared owner) and are on UC:

(a) you can't get UC towards your service charges if you have any kind of earned income and

(b) in any other case, you have to complete a waiting period before you can get UC for your service charges.

These don't apply if you are on HB or SPC.

15.21 The service charge waiting period is nine months during which:

(a) you must have been liable for service charges on your home and

(b) you must have qualified for UC throughout, or any combination of UC and new-style JSA or ESA.

This waiting period is different from the SMI waiting period for mortgage interest (paras 27.10-13).

Owners and shared owners – maintenance charges

15.22 Charges for internal and external maintenance are eligible for UC if you are a leaseholder (whether you are an owner or shared owner), or for HB if you are a shared owner, but not for SPC (para 17.20). This includes repairs and improvements unless you have taken out a loan to cover the costs (in which case you may be able to get SMI: table 27.1(b)). The example shows how service charges for a leaseholder are calculated.

Example: Service charges for a leaseholder

Harry is a leaseholder on UC and his assessment periods begin on the first day of each month. He pays the freeholder for eligible maintenance charges. The freeholder sends Harry bills each February for estimated charges for the following financial year and each May for the finalised balance for the preceding financial year.

1. The DWP averages each new amount over a year as follows (DMG volume 13 para 78487):

- In February the DWP awards Harry one twelfth of the annual amount of the estimated bill, for each assessment period beginning with the one in which the DWP receives the bill (or if later the one containing 1 April) and
- In May the DWP awards Harry one twelfth of the annual amount of the balance bill, for each assessment period beginning with the one in which the DWP receives the bill.

15.20 UC 26(3)-(5), sch 5 paras 4, 5

15.21 UC 26(3), sch 5 paras 5, 6

15.22 UC sch 1 para 8(4) – category C; PC sch 2 para 13(2)(c),(7); HBW sch 1 para 1(g); HBP sch 1 para 1(g)

2. For example:

- In February 2025 Harry sends the DWP the estimated bill for 2025-26, so the DWP awards him one twelfth of this for each month beginning on 1 April 2025 and
- In May 2025 Harry sends the DWP the finalised balance for 2024-25 so the DWP awards him one twelfth of this for each month beginning on 1 May 2025.

Support and similar service charges

15.23 This section is about support and similar service charges. The rules apply to anyone on UC or HB, but mainly arise in relation to HB for supported and temporary accommodation (STA) (table 13.1).

The exclusion from benefit

15.24 Charges for all the following are excluded from benefit:

(a) support and counselling

(b) medical services

(c) personal care and other personal services

(d) emergency alarm systems (used to call for assistance in the event of a fall, etc).

These charges have to be identified and when necessary the costs have to be separated out (paras 15.31-36).

Meaning of 'support'

15.25 'Support' and similar terms have their ordinary English meanings (R(H) 2/07). For example, support can include a wide range of activities for people who are vulnerable and typically includes:

(a) setting up your home and staying safe and secure in it

(b) dealing with tenancy or related problems

(c) applying for benefits and using local services

(d) budgeting

(e) keeping healthy and well and

(f) activities relating to the reason you are vulnerable.

15.26 A charge is likely to be a support charge (and therefore excluded from benefit) if it:

(a) helps you manage your tenancy (e.g. helps you claim benefit) or make use of the facilities (Chorley BC v IT (HB)) or

(b) varies in intensity according to your personal needs.

15.24 UC sch 1 paras 3A(2)-(4), 8(4); HBW sch 1 para 1(c)-(f); HBP sch 1 para 1(c)-(f); HB(CP) sch 3 paras 4(1)(b),(10)

15.26 Chorley BC v IT (HB) [2009] UKUT 102 (AAC), reported as [2010] AACR 2

How providing support affects HB

15.27 HB has two linked rules for landlords who provide support, and it is usually the case that the advantage of (a) outweighs the disadvantage of (b):

(a) providing care, support or supervision usually means your home is exempt accommodation (table 13.1(a)) and your eligible rent is less likely to be restricted than in ordinary accommodation but

(b) a charge for providing support or counselling isn't eligible for HB and usually has to be paid for in some other way (para 13.12).

What constitutes 'support' needs to be considered in the context of each rule (Allerdale BC v JD), but in practice it typically means the same for both (a) and (b).

15.28 It is sensible for landlords to provide services that are eligible for HB rather than excluded [MHCLG/DWP's *Supported housing review 2023: executive summary,* paras 42, 48, 49 [www]], such as:

(a) increased housing management (usually eligible) instead of support services (excluded) or

(b) a warden, security guard or concierge (usually eligible) instead of a support worker (excluded).

Renaming an excluded service charge doesn't make it eligible: the service that is provided has to change (CH/3528/2006).

Example: Charges in exempt accommodation

Pavel rents a room in a hostel that meets the definition of 'exempt accommodation' (table 13.1(a)). His rent is made up of the following weekly payments:

- £190 for rent – this is eligible for HB
- £10 for annual safety tests and testing alarms – this is eligible for HB
- £4 for council tax – this is eligible for HB
- £2 for communal water charges – this is eligible for HB
- £7 for fuel for communal areas – this is eligible for HB
- £3 for water charges for his own accommodation – this is excluded
- £20 for fuel for his own room – this is excluded
- £40 for counselling and support – this is excluded

His actual rent is the total of all the items, which is £276 pw. His eligible rent is the total of the four eligible items, which is £213 pw.

15.27 UC sch 1 para 3A(2)-(4); HBW sch 1 para 1(f); HBP sch 1 para 1(f); HB(CP) sch 3 paras 4(1)(b),(10)
Allerdale BC v JD and Others (HB) [2019] UKUT 304 (AAC)

Staff management and administration costs

15.29 In supported accommodation, staff management and administration costs often include a mixture of services. The general rule (ET v Rossendale BC) is that they:

(a) are eligible for HB when they relate to eligible rent and service charges such as maintaining the property and cleaning communal areas but

(b) are excluded when they relate to excluded services such as support and counselling and

(c) are excluded if and to the extent that they are excessive (paras 15.38-41).

Services provided free of charge

15.30 If your landlord doesn't charge you for a service, you aren't liable for the cost so you can't get benefit towards it (HBGM A4.1950). This mainly applies in supported accommodation when support, counselling and other services are funded by public or other bodies, donations, other activities of the landlord or provided by volunteers (GSH paras 161-162).

Classifying charges and calculating costs

15.31 Your landlord normally tells you which service and other charges they provide and how much they cost. If you are a social renter or live in STA, your landlord should always do this (GSL paras 3, 6, 24-25).

Working out the cost of charges

15.32 The DWP or council normally accepts your landlord's figures for services but:

(a) if your landlord doesn't give a value, the DWP or council must decide how much is fairly attributable to them and

(b) if your landlord doesn't apportion a charge between eligible and excluded parts, the DWP or council should do this (or in some cases in HB the council can use standard figures: paras 15.14-15).

Dividing costs between units of housing

15.33 In shared or multi-occupied accommodation (including much STA):

(a) some costs (e.g. water charges) can reasonably be averaged across a number of similar units but

(b) other costs (e.g. support) should be apportioned separately for each unit of accommodation to fairly reflect the differences in what is actually provided to each resident (R(PC) 1/07).

15.29 UC sch 1 para 8(4),(5); HBW sch 1 paras 1(f),(g), 4; HBP sch 1 paras 1(f),(g), 4
ET v Rossendale BC [2010] UKUT 222 (AAC)

15.32 UC sch 1 para 7(2)(b); HBW sch 1 para 3(1); HBP sch 1 para 3(1)

15.33 UC sch 1 para 7(2); HBW/HBP Old 12(6), 12B(5)

Dividing charges in supported accommodation

15.34 In supported accommodation, your landlord and the council need to divide your rent and service charges into eligible and excluded elements and decide how much these are (Allerdale BC v JD and GSH para 189).

15.35 Charges that combine eligible and excluded amounts therefore have to be separated out, often by calculating or estimating a fair percentage that applies to each (ADM paras F2073-74). An average is not sufficient; each case (or type of case) needs to be calculated separately (R(PC) 1/07). For example, if a manager is responsible for both maintenance staff (an eligible cost) and support staff (an excluded cost), a fair proportion of the manager's time, salary and other costs needs to be allocated to each of these, and calculated separately for each renter if appropriate.

Misclassified costs

15.36 If the amounts you pay are misclassified, the DWP or council must correct them whether that increases or reduces your eligible rent (Wigan MBC v VF, CH/3528/2006). The label matters less than what is actually provided, so a payment for a service is a service charge even if your letting agreement calls it rent (Wigan MBC v VF, CH/3528/2006, Allerdale BC v JD and others).

Unreasonable service charges

15.37 This section only applies to service charges, not charges that count as rent (para 15.17). The rules apply to renters and shared owners, but not to renters who fall within the LHA or rent referral schemes (paras 12.6, 12.25), nor to owners (ADM para F2066).

Charges for unreasonable services

15.38 You can't get UC or HB towards service charge payments if:

(a) in UC, they don't 'relate to services or facilities of such description as it is reasonable to provide' or

(b) in HB, they aren't 'connected with the provision of adequate accommodation' (para 15.11).

For example, a charge for a gym, swimming pool, bar, shop or café is not eligible (GSL para 20).

Unreasonably high service charges

15.39 Your UC may be reduced if you or your landlord have provided an unreasonably high figure for an eligible service. A figure is considered to be unreasonably high if the costs and charges are not of 'a reasonable amount'. In this case the DWP usually asks you for your comments (GSL paras 32-36). They may then ask the rent officer for a housing payment determination and can use their figure instead of the one you or your landlord provided (para 11.25).

15.34 Allerdale BC v JD and Others (HB) [2019] UKUT 304 (AAC)

15.36 Wigan MBC v VF [2009] UKUT 28 (AAC)
Allerdale BC v JD and Others (HB) [2019] UKUT 304 (AAC)

15.38 UC sch 1 para 8(5), sch 4 para 32; HBW sch 1 para 4; HBP sch 1 para 4

15.39-41 UC sch 1 para 8(5), sch 4 para 32; UC(ROO) 5, sch 2 para 2; HBW sch 1 para 4; HBP sch 1 para 4

15.40 Your HB may be reduced if you or your landlord have provided an unreasonable high figure for an eligible service. A figure is considered to be excessive if:

(a) it is 'excessive in relation to the service provided... having regard to the cost of comparable services' or

(b) there is other evidence that it is excessive – for example, that the landlord could provide the service with fewer staff (ET v Rossendale BC).

In this case, the council decides what it considers to be reasonable and uses that figure instead of the one you or your landlord provided.

15.41 The DWP advises the council's benefit department to work with other departments and councils to establish what is reasonable (GSH para 165), and to take account of the landlord's explanation of how the charge was arrived at (GSH para 181).

Unreasonably low service charges

15.42 Your benefit may be reduced if you or your landlord have provided an unreasonably low figure for an excluded service. A figure is considered to be unreasonably low if:

(a) in UC, the costs and charges are not of 'a reasonable amount' or

(b) in HB, the charges are low taking account of comparable services.

The DWP or council decides what it considers to be reasonable and uses that figure instead of the one you or your landlord provided.

15.42 UC sch 1 paras 7(2); HBW sch 1 para 3(2); HBP sch 1 para 3(2)

Chapter 16 **Calculating UC**

The UC calculation

16.1 This chapter explains how UC is calculated. UC has monthly assessment periods, so all the figures are monthly. For more on monthly figures, see paras 1.17-25.

Maximum UC

16.2 'Maximum UC' means the maximum amount of UC that you could qualify for. It is the total of:

(a) a standard allowance for you (and your partner if you are making a joint claim)

(b) child elements for children and young persons in your benefit unit

(c) additions for each child or young person who is disabled

(d) additions (called 'elements') if you have limited capability for work, are a carer, or have childcare costs

(e) a housing costs element towards your rent and/or service charges and

(f) a transitional element if you have migrated from legacy benefits to UC (para 26.1).

This chapter explains who qualifies for each of these and table 16.1 gives the amounts.

Your UC

16.3 The monthly amount of your UC is:

(a) your maximum UC

(b) minus:

- 55% of your earned income and
- 100% of your unearned income.

Only certain kinds of unearned income are taken into account (table 21.1), and if you qualify for a work allowance this is disregarded from your earned income (para 22.27).

16.2 WRA 8(2); UC 23

16.3 WRA 8(3); UC 22(1)

Reductions in your UC

16.4 Your UC can be reduced if:

(a) the two-child limit applies to you (chapter 19)

(b) the benefit cap applies to you (chapter 20)

(c) a sanction applies to you (para 4.24)

(d) an advance of UC is recovered (paras 34.19 and 34.22)

(e) part of your UC is paid to a third party (para 35.21 and table 35.3)

(f) an overpayment is recovered (para 37.4 and table 37.1).

Table 16.1 **UC allowances and additional elements: 2025-26**

	Monthly amount
Standard allowance	
■ single under 25	£316.98
■ single aged 25 or over	£400.14
■ couple both under 25	£497.55
■ couple at least one aged 25 or over	£628.10
Child element	
■ higher rate	£339.00
■ lower rate	£292.81
Disabled child addition	
■ higher rate	£495.87
■ lower rate	£158.76
Work capability elements	
■ LCW element	£158.76
■ LCWRA element	£423.27
Carer element	£201.68
Childcare costs element	
■ maximum for one child	£1031.88
■ maximum for two or more children	£1768.94

Note: You are awarded each of the allowances and additional amounts that you qualify for, plus a housing costs element and a transitional element if you qualify for them (paras 16.32, 26.1).

16.4 WRA 10(1A), 26(1), 27(1), 96(2); SSAA 5(1)(r), 71ZB(1), 71ZC(1); OPR 10, 11; POA 10; UC(C&P) 60

T16.1 UC 36; SI 2025/295 sch 13

Examples: Amount of UC

All figures are monthly and none of the claimants have capital.

1. Single renter aged 23, no income

Sean's eligible rent is £400.

Maximum UC

- standard allowance £316.98
- housing costs element (eligible rent) £400.00
- total £716.98

Amount of Sean's UC £716.98

2. Couple over 25, renters, two children aged 8 and 10, unearned income only

Polly and Patrick's eligible rent is £1250. Polly receives £500 maintenance for the children (this is disregarded) plus £300 for herself (this is counted).

Maximum UC

- standard allowance £628.10
- two child elements (£339.00 + £292.81) £631.81
- housing costs element (eligible rent) £1250.00
- total £2509.91

Income deduction

- unearned income £300 x 100% – £300.00

Amount of Polly and Patrick's UC £2209.91

- Note that the benefit cap may apply (table 20.1).

Other UC calculation rules

16.5 There is no lower limit to the amount of UC, so if you qualify for 1p per month you are awarded it. Amounts used in UC are rounded to the nearest whole penny, halfpennies being rounded upwards.

Standard allowances and child additions

Standard allowance

16.6 Everyone qualifies for a standard allowance. You get:

(a) the single rate if you are a single person, or in a couple but claiming UC as a single person (para 2.9) or

(b) the couple rate if you are a joint claim couple (para 2.8).

If you are in a polygamous marriage see para 2.34.

16.5 WRA 5; UC 6(1), 17

16.6 WRA 9; UC 36

Child element

16.7 You qualify for a child element for each child or young person in your benefit unit. The amount is decided as follows:

(a) if at least one child/young person was born before 6 April 2017 you get
   - the higher rate for one child/young person and
   - the lower rate for each of the others

(b) otherwise, you get the lower rate for each child/young person.

But if you have more than two children born on or after 6 April 2017, you may be affected by the two child limit (chapter 19).

Disabled child addition

16.8 The disabled child addition has two rates:

(a) you get the higher rate for each child or young person who is:
   - entitled to the highest rate of the care component of DLA, SADLA or CDP or
   - entitled to the enhanced rate of the daily living component of PIP or ADP or
   - certified as blind or severely sight-impaired by a consultant ophthalmologist;

(b) you get the lower rate for each child or young person who is entitled to DLA, SADLA, PIP, CDP or ADP, but does not meet the conditions in (a).

You get a disabled child addition for every child/young person who meets these conditions, even if the number of your child elements is affected by the two-child limit.

Work capability elements

16.9 There are two work capability elements:

(a) the LCWRA element is for people who have limited capability for work and work-related activity (LCWRA)

(b) the LCW element was abolished on 3 April 2017, but it can continue to be awarded for people who have limited capability for work (LCW) and don't meet the conditions for an LCWRA element.

If you meet the conditions for a carer element as well as either of these, see table 16.2.

16.7 WRA 10(1),(1A); UC 24(1), 36; UCTP 43

16.8 WRA 10(2); UC 24(2)

16.9 WRA 12(1)(b); WRWA 16; UC 27(1); SI 2017/204 reg 7(2), sch 2 paras 8-15

LCWRA element

16.10 You qualify for an LCWRA element if:

(a) you have limited capability for work and work-related activity (LCWRA) (para 4.15)

(b) you meet the earnings condition (para 16.12) and

(c) you meet one of the following conditions (or in a joint claim couple at least one of you does):

- you have completed a waiting period (para 16.14)
- you are swapping from an LCW element to an LCWRA element
- you are terminally ill (para 16.18) or
- you claimed UC while you were on ESA, SDA, IB or IS, or getting national insurance credits in their place at that time (JW v SSWP).

LCW element

16.11 You only qualify for an LCW element if:

(a) you have had limited capability for work (LCW) since before 3 April 2017

(b) you meet the earnings condition (para 16.12) and

(c) either:

- you have been on UC since before 3 April 2017 or
- you claimed UC while you were on ESA, SDA, IB or IS, or getting national insurance credits in their place, and you claimed that benefit or those credits before 3 April 2017.

If you are in a joint claim couple, only one of you has to meet these conditions.

The earnings condition

16.12 If you have earnings at or above the 16-hour threshold, you can't get an LCW or LCWRA element unless:

(a) you are on PIP, DLA, SADLA, attendance allowance, ADP, CDP, PADP or an equivalent benefit (para 21.18); or

(b) you have one of the medical conditions in table 4.3.

The 16-hour threshold

16.13 The 16-hour threshold for a single person is what you would earn for working 16 hours per week at the national living wage (table 4.2). From 6 April 2025, the amount is £846.56 per month.

16.10 UC 27, 28(1),(5),(6), 40(5), 41(2), sch 9 para 1
JW v SSWP (UC) [2022] UKUT 117 (AAC)
PR v SSWP (UC) [2023] UKUT 290 (AAC)

16.11 SI 2017/204 reg. 7(2), sch 2 paras 8-15

16.12 UC 41(2)

16.13 UC 6(1), 41(3)

The LCWRA waiting period

16.14 The LCWRA waiting period is three months beginning with:

(a) the day you first provide medical evidence – this can include a doctor's note or self-certificate (KS v SSWP) or

(b) the day you request an LCWRA element in the situations in para 16.12(a) or (b).

Your LCWRA element is then awarded from the beginning of the assessment period following the one in which the three months end.

UC during the waiting period

16.15 During the waiting period you don't get an LCWRA element. But if the amount of your income means you would qualify for UC with the LCWRA element and wouldn't qualify without it, you are awarded UC of one penny a month. This is so that you can count as being on UC.

Examples: The LCWRA waiting period

1. A new UC claim

John is awarded UC from 26 July, so his assessment periods begin on the 26th of each month. On 19 August, he provides medical evidence and the DWP agrees he qualifies for an LCWRA element.

- His waiting period runs from 19 August to 18 November (three months)
- He is awarded the LCWRA element from 26 November (the first day of his assessment period).

2. A break in UC

Helen is on UC, and her assessment periods begin on the fifth of each month. On 21 September she provides medical evidence and the DWP agrees she qualifies for an LCWRA element. Then her UC stops from the 5 October to 4 February.

- Her waiting period runs from 21 September to 20 December (three months)
- She is awarded the LCWRA element from 5 February.

Breaks in UC during or after the waiting period

16.16 If you have a break in your UC of no more than six months:

(a) you don't have to complete a new waiting period when you reclaim; but

(b) if your waiting period was incomplete, it continues to run during the break, and after it if necessary.

You only have to start a new waiting period after a break in your UC of more than six months.

16.14 UC 28(2),(6)
KS v SSWP [2025] UKUT 15 (AAC)

16.15 UC 28(7)

16.16 UC 28(3),(4)

Starting and stopping qualifying for an element

16.17 When you start qualifying for the LCWRA element, you can get arrears if you are terminally ill or in some other situations (para 33.27). If you stop qualifying for either element, you shouldn't normally be told you have been overpaid benefit (para 33.28).

People who are terminally ill

16.18 Being terminally ill means suffering from a progressive disease which is likely to lead to death within 12 months. No matter how long it takes you to inform the DWP about this, you are awarded the LCWRA element back to when you became terminally ill (para 33.26).

Claiming UC while you are on ESA

16.19 ESA assesses capability for work in the same way as UC:

(a) the ESA 'work-related activity component' is equivalent to UC's LCW element

(b) the ESA 'support component' is equivalent to UC's LCWRA element

(c) if you claim UC while you are getting an ESA component, you qualify for the equivalent element in your UC

(d) if you claim UC while you are in ESA's 13-week assessment period, it continues to run as part of UC's waiting period (which in this case is 13 weeks, not three months).

Carer element

16.20 You qualify for the carer element if:

(a) you are the carer of a severely disabled person (they could be someone in your household, including your partner, or someone outside it)

(b) you provide regular and substantial care for them for at least 35 hours per week

(c) you don't receive any earned income for this and

(d) you get carer's allowance, or meet the conditions for it, or would meet the conditions except that your earnings are too high.

If you meet the conditions for an LCW or LCWRA element as well as this, see table 16.2.

Shared care for one person

16.21 Only one person can count as the carer for a particular disabled person, so only one person can get the carer element for them. If two or more people meet the conditions, you choose who is to count as the carer, or if you don't the DWP chooses.

16.17 UC(D&A) 35(9), sch 1 paras 25, 28

16.18 UC(D&A) 2 – 'terminally ill', sch 1 para 28

16.19 UC 2 – 'ESA regulations', 40(1)(a)(ii)

16.20 WRA 12(2)(c); UC 29(1), 30

16.21 UC 29(3)

Couples caring for two people

16.22 If you are claiming UC as a joint claim couple and you each meet the conditions in relation to a different severely disabled person, you get two carer elements (one each).

Table 16.2 **Carer element and LCW/LCWRA elements**

This table explains which element(s) you get if you meet the conditions for both an LCW/LCWRA element and a carer element.

Single people who meet the LCWRA condition

(a) You get the LCWRA element (but not the carer element)

Single people who meet the LCW condition

(b) You get the carer element (but not the LCW element).

Couples who meet the LCWRA condition

(c) You get the LCWRA element.

(d) You also get one carer element (never two), but only if:

- both of you meet the LCWRA condition and one or both of you meet the carer condition, or
- one of you meets the LCWRA condition and the other one meets the carer condition.

Couples who meet the LCW condition

(e) You get two carer elements (but no LCW element) if both of you meet the carer condition.

(f) You get one carer element if one of you meets the carer condition. You also get the LCW element, but only if the other one meets the LCW condition.

Childcare costs element

16.23 You qualify for a childcare costs element if you meet the work condition and the childcare costs condition described below. The amount is:

(a) 85% of the monthly childcare charges you pay (paras 16.28-31) or

(b) If lower, the maximum amount in table 16.1.

16.22 UC 29(2)

T16.2 UC 29(4)

16.23 WRA 12(1); UC 34(1)

The work condition for single people

16.24 If you are a single person you must meet at least one of the following conditions:

(a) you are in employment, self-employment or other paid work (para 22.2)

(b) you have an offer to start paid work in your current or next assessment period

(c) you ceased paid work in your current or previous assessment period or

(d) you are receiving statutory sick, maternity, paternity, shared parental, parental bereavement or adoption pay or maternity allowance.

The work condition for couples

16.25 If you are in a couple (even if you are claiming UC as a single person):

(a) both of you must meet the work condition in para 16.24 or

(b) one of you must meet the work condition and the other one must be unable to provide childcare because they:

- have limited capability for work or for work and work-related activity (paras 4.15-20) or
- get the carer element (para 16.20) or carer's allowance, or meet the conditions for it, or would meet the conditions except that their earnings are too high or
- are temporarily absent from your household (chapter 8).

Example: Childcare element and amount of UC

Kate is 29 and has a child of 10. She works and pays a registered childminder £500 a month. Her eligible rent is £800 a month and she has no non-dependants. She has no capital, and her earnings (after deducting the work allowance) are £1500 a month.

Maximum UC

■ Standard allowance	£400.14
■ Child element (higher rate)	£339.00
■ Childcare element (85% of £500)	£425.00
■ Housing costs element (eligible rent)	£800.00
■ Total	£1964.14

Amount of UC

■ Maximum UC	£1964.14
■ Earned income deduction (55% of £1500)	– £825.00
■ Monthly amount of UC	£1139.14

16.24 UC 32(1)(a),(2)

16.25 UC 34(1)(b)

The childcare costs condition

16.26 You meet the childcare costs condition if you (or your partner if you are in a joint claim couple) have paid childcare charges for a child in your benefit unit. This applies even if the number of your child elements is affected by the two child limit.

16.27 You stop meeting the condition on:

(a) the child's 16th birthday or

(b) if later, the first Monday in September following their 16th birthday.

Which childcare charges are included

16.28 Childcare charges only count for these purposes if they enable you to:

(a) continue in employment, self-employment or other paid work; or

(b) take up paid work in your current or next assessment period or

(c) maintain arrangements you had if you:

- ceased paid work in your current or previous assessment period or
- are receiving statutory sick, maternity, paternity or adoption pay or maternity allowance.

16.29 The childcare charges must be paid to:

(a) a registered childminder, childcare agency or equivalent (including an approved childcare provider outside Great Britain) or

(b) an out-of-school-hours (or pre-school age) scheme provided by a school as part of its school activities.

16.30 The following are excluded:

(a) childcare provided by the child's 'close relative' (para 9.30) or foster parent in the child's home

(b) childcare paid for by anyone else, for example an employer, or the government in connection with any work-related activity or training you are undertaking

(c) childcare the DWP considers excessive for the extent of your or your partner's paid work.

16.26 UC 33(1)(a)

16.27 UC 2 – 'child', 33(1)(a)

16.28 UC 32(2), 33(1)(b)

16.29 UC 35(1)-(5)

16.30 UC 34(2),(3), 35(7),(8)

Which month's childcare charges

16.31 In each assessment period, you can get a childcare element towards charges that:

(a) you report to the DWP during that assessment period or the next one (or later in special circumstances: para 33.16) and

(b) you paid:

- in the current assessment period for childcare provided in that assessment period or a previous one or
- in the two previous assessment periods for childcare in the current assessment period.

This is sometimes called the 'proof of payment' rate. It only applies to charges you have actually paid (R (Salvato) v SSWP).

Other elements

Housing costs element (HCE)

16.32 You qualify for a housing costs element (HCE) towards your eligible housing costs. These are made up of:

(a) your rent and service charge payments if you are a renter or shared owner or

(b) your service charge payments if you are an owner.

Chapters 10-15 explain how much of these UC can meet.

Amount of HCE

16.33 The amount of your HCE equals:

(a) your eligible rent and service charge payments if you are a renter or shared owner or

(b) your service charge payments if you are an owner.

If you are a renter or shared owner and have one or more non-dependants living with you, your HCE is reduced by the amount they are expected to contribute (chapter 6).

Transitional element

16.34 You only qualify for a transitional element if you have migrated from legacy benefits to UC. Chapter 26 explains who qualifies and how much for.

16.31 UC 33(1)(za), 34A(1)
R (Salvato) v SSWP [2021] EWCA Civ 1482

16.32 UC 25, 26, sch 4, sch 5

16.33 UC 26(2),(3), sch 4, sch 5

16.34 UCTP 52, sch 2 para 4

Chapter 17 **Calculating SPC**

- The calculation of SPC guarantee credit (the main calculation): paras 17.3-7
- Allowances and additions: paras 17.8-14
- Housing costs addition: paras 17.15-21
- The calculation of SPC savings credit: paras 17.22-26

SPC guarantee credit and SPC savings credit

17.1 There are two kinds of state pension credit (SPC):

(a) SPC guarantee credit – this ensures you have a minimum income (for example it can top up your pension) and

(b) SPC savings credit – this provides a top up to people with a modest income from pensions and savings but is being phased out.

You can receive either kind or both. In this guide, 'SPC' means SPC guarantee credit unless we state otherwise.

17.2 SPC (of both kinds) has weekly benefit periods, so all the figures are weekly. For more on weekly figures, see paras 1.17-25.

The SPC calculation

17.3 This section explains how SPC guarantee credit is calculated. The starting point for this is your 'maximum SPC'.

Maximum SPC

17.4 Maximum SPC (in the law, your 'appropriate minimum guarantee') means the maximum amount of SPC you could qualify for. It is the total of:

(a) a standard allowance for you (and your partner if you have one)

(b) amounts for children and young persons in your benefit unit

(c) additions for each child or young person who is disabled

(d) additions if you are a carer, or are severely disabled

(e) an amount towards your allowable housing costs and

(f) a transitional element if you have migrated from tax credits to SPC (para 26.25-26).

This chapter explains who qualifies for each of these and table 17.1 gives the amounts.

17.1 SPCA 1(3), 2, 3; PC 6, 7

17.2 PC 1(2) – 'benefit week', 6(1),(5),(8), 17(1), sch 2 para 13(1), sch 2A paras 9(1), 10

17.4 SPCA 2(3),(5),(7),(8); PC 6(1),(4),(5),(6)

Your SPC

17.5 The weekly amount of your SPC guarantee credit is:

(a) your maximum SPC

(b) minus 100% of your earned and unearned income.

Only certain kinds of unearned income are taken into account (table 21.1(a)-(i)), and part of your unearned and earned income is disregarded (table 21.1(j)-(y) and table 22.4).

Reductions in your SPC

17.6 Your SPC guarantee credit can be reduced if:

(a) part of your SPC is paid to a third party (paras 35.26 and 35.40)

(b) an overpayment is recovered (paras 36.9 and 37.4-7)

(c) you have been convicted of benefit fraud or agreed to pay a penalty (para 37.20).

Other SPC calculations rules

17.7 If your SPC is between 1p and 9p per week:

(a) it is paid to you if you get state pension or another benefit it can be paid with

(b) otherwise, it isn't paid but you count as having 'underlying entitlement' (table 18.1).

Amounts in SPC are rounded, with fractions of a penny being rounded in whichever way benefits you.

Allowances and additions

Allowances for you and your partner

17.8 Everyone qualifies for a standard allowance (in the law, your 'standard minimum guarantee'). You get:

(a) the single rate if you are a single person

(b) the couple rate if you are in a couple or

(c) the couple rate if you are in a polygamous marriage, plus the polygamous spouse rate for each husband or wife beyond two (but see paras 2.34-36).

17.5 SPCA 2(1),(2), 15; PC 15

17.6 SSAA 5(1)(p); 71(1),(11)(ab); SSFA 6A(1)(b), 6B, 7; SS(C&P) 35, sch 9; SS(LB) 3A; SS(PAOR) 3,4, 11, 15; SS(LB) 1A, 2, 3A

17.7 PC 13, 24A

17.8 SPCA 2(3); PC 6(1), sch 3 para 1(5)

Table 17.1 **SPC allowances and additional amounts 2025-26**

Standard allowance	
■ single person	£227.10
■ couple	£346.60
■ polygamous spouse	£119.50
Child allowance	
■ higher rate	£78.10
■ lower rate	£67.42
Disabled child addition	
■ higher rate	£114.12
■ lower rate	£36.54
Carer addition	
■ claimant/partner/each	£46.40
Severe disability addition	
■ single rate	£82.90
■ double rate	£165.80

Note: You are awarded each of the allowances and additional amounts that you qualify for, plus a housing costs addition if you qualify for it (para 17.15).

Allowances for children and young persons

17.9 You qualify for an allowance for each child or young person in your benefit unit.

17.10 The amount is decided as follows:

(a) if at least one child/young person was born before 6 April 2017 you get

- the higher rate for one child/young person and
- the lower rate for each of the others

(b) otherwise you get the lower rate for each child/young person.

Unlike UC, there is no two-child limit.

T17.1 PC 6(1),(5),(8), sch 2A paras 9(1), 10; SI 2025/295 reg 29

17.9 PC 6(6)(d),(11)

17.10 PC sch 2A paras 9(1), 10

Disabled child addition

17.11 The disabled child addition has two rates:

(a) you get the higher rate for each child or young person who is:

- entitled to the highest rate of the care component of DLA, SADLA or CDP or
- entitled to the enhanced rate of the daily living component of PIP or ADP
- certified as blind or severely sight-impaired by a consultant ophthalmologist

(b) you get the lower rate for each child or young person who is entitled to DLA, PIP or (in Scotland) a disability payment, but does not meet the conditions in (a).

Carer addition

17.12 You qualify for a carer addition if:

(a) you receive carer's allowance or carer support payment or

(b) you are entitled to either payment but don't receive it (para 18.19) or

(c) you stopped receiving or being entitled to either payment (for any reason) within the past eight weeks.

If you are in a couple, you get one carer addition for each of you who meets these conditions.

Severe disability addition

17.13 You qualify for a severe disability addition if you meet the following conditions:

(a) you are severely disabled

(b) you don't have any non-dependants living with you and

(c) your carer doesn't receive carer's allowance, carer support payment or the UC carer element.

The details of these conditions are in paras 18.22-24.

17.14 Single people qualify for the single rate of severe disability premium if you meet all three conditions. Couples qualify for:

(a) the double rate if you both meet all three conditions

(b) the single rate if one of you meets all three conditions and the other one meets only the first two conditions

(c) the single rate if you (the claimant) meet all three conditions, and your partner has been certified by a consultant ophthalmologist as severely sight impaired or blind.

17.11 PC 6(6)(d),(11), sch 2 para 9(2),(3)

17.12 PC 6(6)(a),(8), sch 1 para 4

17.13 PC 6(4), sch 1 para 1

17.14 PC 6(5)

Examples: Calculating SPC

1. A single person aged 73

James lives in a leasehold flat. He pays service charges of £30 pw that are eligible for SPC. He has no income or capital.

Maximum SPC (appropriate minimum guarantee):

■ allowance for single person	£227.10
■ eligible housing costs	£30.00
James has no income to deduct so his weekly SPC is	£257.10

2. A non-dependant moves in

James's adult daughter Sora moves in and a non-dependant deduction of £126.65 applies for her (table 6.2). This reduces James's eligible housing costs from £30 to nil (para 17.17).

Maximum SPC

■ allowance for single person	£227.10
■ eligible housing costs	£0.00
James's weekly SPC is now	£227.10

3. A couple aged 87 and 94

Robert and Patricia live in a leasehold flat. They pay service charges of £27.40 pw that are eligible for SPC. They have state and private pensions totalling £333.90 per week and capital under £10,000.

Maximum SPC

■ allowance for couple	£346.60
■ eligible housing costs	£27.40
■ total	£374.00
Minus their weekly income	£333.90
Robert and Patricia's weekly SPC is	£40.10

Housing costs addition

Housing costs

17.15 HB and SMI cover most housing costs (table 10.1 and table 27.1), and in most cases you have to claim these as well as SPC.

17.16 But you can get a housing costs addition in your SPC towards housing costs that:

(a) aren't included in HB or SMI (table 10.1 and table 27.1) and

(b) are listed in table 17.2.

In each case you must meet the housing costs conditions in chapter 2.

17.15 SSCBA 130; WRWA 18; HBP 12(1), 26; LMI 3(2)(a), sch 1 paras 1-3

17.16 PC 6(6)(c), sch 2 paras 1(1), 5, 13

Table 17.2 **Housing costs you can get SPC for**

(a) Rent or ground rent on a long tenancy

A long tenancy is one where the lease is made by deed, registered with the land registry, and granted for a specified number of years exceeding 21, or for a fixed term with a promise in the agreement for perpetual renewal (unless it is sub-let, and the original lease was for less than 21 years). It includes a lease granted for life because the law treats these as a 90-year agreement.

(b) Service charges if you are an owner or long leaseholder

Chapter 15 and paras 17.18-20 explain which of these SPC can meet.

(c) Payments in a co-ownership scheme

You are a co-owner if you rent from a housing association (para 11.5) and under the terms of the agreement you will be entitled to a payment based on the value of your home when you cease to be a member of the scheme. A co-owner is different from a shared owner, because a shared owner is buying a percentage of their home (para 10.4).

(d) Payments in a Crown tenancy or licence

You are a Crown tenant/licensee if your landlord is the Crown or a government department. But this doesn't apply if your home is managed by the Crown Estates Commission or the landlord is the Duchy of Cornwall or Lancaster, and in this case you can get HB (table 10.1).

(e) Rentcharges

A rentcharge (or chief rent) is an annual fee paid by a freehold homeowner to a third party who has no other interest in the property. No new rentcharges can be created after 21 July 1977.

(f) Tents and site fees

If your home is a tent, housing costs are allowed for the hire of the tent and the pitch it stands on.

Amount of housing costs addition

17.17 The amount of your housing costs addition equals:

(a) your eligible housing costs (table 17.2)

(b) minus any non-dependant housing cost contributions that apply to you (chapter 6).

But if you get (or could get) HB towards your housing costs, you can't get SPC towards them.

T17.2 PC sch 2 para 13(1)(a)-(f),(6) – 'co-ownership scheme', 'Crown tenant', 'housing association', 'long tenancy'

17.17 PC sch 2 paras 1(1), 13, 14

Service charges for owners and long leaseholders

17.18 If you are an owner or long leaseholder (table 17.2), only certain service charges are eligible for SPC as described in chapter 15. Your freeholder, landlord or managing agent usually sends an estimated bill for the year to come and sends a final adjustment after the end of the year.

17.19 The eligible part of each bill you receive (whether an estimate or an adjustment):

(a) is taken into account when the bill is issued, or when you tell the DWP about it if this is later, and

(b) is averaged over the 52 weeks following that date.

See also para 15.22 and the example there.

Repairs and improvements

17.20 A charge for minor repairs and maintenance is eligible for SPC. But work to make your home habitable is excluded – for example, the following are excluded:

(a) provision of washing or sanitary facilities (bath, shower, lavatory) and drainage facilities

(b) repairs to the heating system

(c) provision of damp proof measures or insulation

(d) provision of ventilation or natural lighting

(e) provision of lighting or power sockets

(f) repairs of unsafe structural defects

(g) adapting the dwelling for the needs of a disabled person, or to provide additional bedrooms so that children or young persons of the opposite sex can sleep separately.

Business premises

17.21 If your home forms part of a building that is liable for both business rates and council tax, your housing costs are in proportion to the residential part of the building only. That fraction is the current market value of the residential part of the building divided by the combined market values of the business and residential parts. If the building was built or converted before 1 April 1990 the rateable values (as of 31 March 1990) are used instead.

17.18 PC sch 2 para 13(2)

17.19 PC sch 2 para 13(3)

17.20 PC sch 2 para 13(2)(c),(7)

17.21 PC sch 2 para 6

SPC savings credit

17.22 This section explains how SPC savings credit is calculated.

17.23 Savings credit is being phased out. You can now only get it if:

(a) you are single and reached pension age before 6 April 2016 or

(b) you are a couple and

- both of you reached pension age before 6 April 2016, or
- at least one of you qualified for savings credit before that date and has been continuously entitled to it since then.

Amount of SPC savings credit

17.24 You can only get SPC savings credit if your qualifying income is above the savings credit threshold (para 17.25). In this case, your weekly SPC savings credit equals:

(a) 60% of the amount by which your 'qualifying income' exceeds your savings credit threshold, up to the savings credit limit (para 17.26) or

(b) the savings credit limit minus 40% of the amount by which your 'total income' exceeds your maximum SPC.

Terminology

17.25 In the above calculation:

(a) 'qualifying income' means your total income calculated in the same way as for SPC guarantee credit (para 17.3), but excluding new-style JSA, new-style ESA, SDA, maternity allowance and maintenance payments for you or your partner from a former spouse

(b) the 'savings credit threshold' is £198.27 per week if you are a single person or £314.34 per week if you are in a couple

(c) 'total income' is calculated in the same way as for SPC guarantee credit (para 17.5) but without the exclusions in (a)

(d) 'maximum SPC' means the same as it does for SPC guarantee credit (para 17.4).

The savings credit limit

17.26 Your SPC savings credit is limited to £17.30 per week if you are a single person or £19.36 per week if you are in a couple. (In the law it is called your maximum savings credit.)

17.23 SPCA 3(1), 3ZA; PC 7A

17.24 SPCA 3(2)-(7); PC 7(1)(b),(c)

17.25 SPCA 3(4); PC 7(2), 9; SI 2025/295 reg 29(3)

17.26 SPCA 3(7); PC 7(1)(a)

Chapter 18 **Calculating HB**

- The calculation: paras 18.1-7
- Personal allowances: paras 18.8-12
- Amounts for children: paras 18.13-17
- Carer premium and severe disability premium: paras 18.18-24
- Additional amounts that only apply if you are working age: paras 18.25-32
- People in hospital: paras 18.33

The HB calculation

18.1 This chapter explains how HB is calculated. HB has weekly benefit periods, so all the figures are weekly. For more on weekly figures, see paras 1.17-25.

Maximum HB

18.2 'Maximum' HB means the maximum amount of HB you could qualify for. It is:

(a) your weekly eligible rent (chapters 11-13)

(b) minus any non-dependant deductions that apply to you (chapter 6).

Your HB

18.3 If you are on a passport benefit (table 18.1) you qualify for maximum HB. In any other case you qualify for:

(a) maximum HB

(b) minus 65% of your excess income.

Excess income

18.4 Excess income represents the income you have after meeting your basic living needs. It equals:

(a) 100% of your earned and unearned income

(b) minus your applicable amount (para 18.5).

Only certain kinds of unearned income are taken into account (table 21.1), and part of your earned income is disregarded (para 22.30).

18.2 SSCBA 130(1)(b), 130A; HBW 70; HBP 50

18.3 SSCBA 130(1)(b),(c)(3); HBW 71, sch 4 para 12, sch 5 paras 4, 5, sch 6 paras 5, 6; HBP 26, 51

18.4 SSCBA 130(1)(c)

Applicable amount

18.5 Your 'applicable amount' represents your basic living needs. It is the total of:

(a) a personal allowance for you (and your partner if you have one)

(b) additions for children and young persons in your benefit unit and

(c) additional amounts (called 'premiums' or 'components' in the law) if you or someone in your benefit unit are a carer, or are disabled or long-term sick.

This chapter explains who qualifies for each of these and table 18.2 gives the amounts.

Reductions in your HB

18.6 Your HB can be reduced if:

(a) the two-child limit applies to you (para chapter 19)

(b) the benefit cap applies to you (chapter 20)

(c) an overpayment is recovered (paras 36.10-14 and 37.4-7)

(d) you have been convicted of benefit fraud or agreed to pay a penalty (para 37.19).

Other HB calculations rules

18.7 If your HB is under 50p per week it isn't awarded. Amounts used in HB are rounded to the nearest whole penny, halfpennies being rounded upwards.

Table 18.1 **Passport benefits**

You are on a passport benefit if you are:

(a) on SPC guarantee credit or have 'underlying entitlement' to it (para 17.7)

(b) on UC in supported or temporary accommodation (table 13.1)

(c) on UC during the two-week run-on period (para 25.8)

(d) on ESA(IR) or not receiving it due to a sanction.

Notes:

- In cases (a)-(d), you qualify for maximum HB (paras 18.3-4).
- You aren't 'on' UC if you have a nil award during a reclaim period (paras 22.8-12) (Ipswich BC v TD).
- JSA(IB) and IS were also passport benefits before they were replaced by UC.

18.5 SSCBA 135(1); HBW 22(1); HBP 22(1)

18.6 SSAA 75; SSFA 6B, 7; WRA 96; HBW 75D, 93(2),(3), 102(1); HBP 74(2),(3), 83(1); SS(LB) 1A, 2, 17, 18

18.7 SSCBA 134(4); HBW 75; HBP 56

T18.1 UCTP 8A(a); HBW 2(3),(3A), sch 4 para 12, sch 5 paras 4, 5, sch 6 paras 5, 6; HBP 2(5), 26, 51
CTRE(PR) 2(6), sch 1 para 13; CTR(DS) 2(3),(4),(6), 28, 35, 37, sch 7 para 14, sch 8 paras 8, 9, sch 10 paras 8, 9
Ipswich BC v TD and SSWP (HB) [2024] UKUT 117 (AAC)

Examples: Calculating HB

Claimant on a passport benefit

Olivia is on a passport benefit (table 18.1). She has no non-dependants. Her eligible rent is £105.00 per week.

Claimants on a passport benefit get maximum benefit – which equals their eligible rent.

Olivia's weekly HB equals	£105.00

Claimant not on a passport benefit

Noah and Sophia are not on any of the passport benefits. They have no non-dependants. Their joint weekly income exceeds their applicable amount by £20.00. Their eligible rent is £130.00 per week.

Claimants with excess income get maximum benefit minus a percentage of their excess income.

Eligible rent	£130.00
minus 65% of excess income (65% x £20.00)	£13.00
Noah and Sophia's weekly HB equals	£117.00

Claimant on ESA(IR) with working non-dependant

Nathan is on ESA(IR). His eligible rent is £150.00 per week. His 26-year-old son Leo lives with him. Leo earns £600 per week gross for a 35-hour week.

Claimants on ESA(IR) get maximum benefit, which in this case involves a non-dependant deduction. Leo works at least 16 hours per week and the level of his gross income means the highest deduction applies in HB (table 6.2).

Eligible rent	£150.00
minus non-dependant deduction	£126.65
Nathan's weekly HB equals	£23.35

Claimant on ESA(IR) with non-dependant on new-style JSA

Leo in the previous example loses his job and starts receiving new-style JSA.

The calculation is as above, except that now the lowest deduction applies in HB (table 6.2).

Eligible rent	£150.00
minus non-dependant deduction	£19.65
Nathan's weekly HB equals	£130.35

Personal allowances

Allowances for you and your partner

18.8 Everyone qualifies for a personal allowance. You get:

(a) the single rate if you are a single person

(b) the couple rate if you are in a couple or

(c) the couple rate if you are in a polygamous marriage, plus the polygamous spouse rate for each husband or wife beyond two.

Pension age rates

18.9 For single people:

(a) the old pension age rates apply if you reached 66 before 1 April 2021

(b) the new pension age rates apply if you reached 66 on or after that date.

18.10 For couples and polygamous marriages:

(a) the old pension age rates apply if you both (or all) reached 66 before 1 April 2021

(b) the new pension age rates apply if at least one of you reached 66 on or after that date.

Working age rate

18.11 The working age rate applies if you are:

(a) a single person under 66 or

(b) in a couple or polygamous marriage and both (or all) of you are under 66.

Lower rate

18.12 The lower age rate only applies if you are:

(a) a single person under 25 or a lone parent under 18, and aren't on the main phase of ESA or

(b) in a couple or polygamous marriage both (or all) under 18, and you (the claimant) aren't on the main phase of ESA.

The main phase of ESA starts at week 14 of your ESA award and follows the assessment phase.

18.8 HBW 2(1) – 'couple', 22(1)(a); 23(1)(a),(b), sch 3 paras 1, 1A; HBP 2(1), 22(1)(a),(5), sch 3 para 1
CTRE(PR) 4, 5, sch 1 para 6(1)(a),(2), sch 2 para 1; CTRE(DS) 4, 5, 25(1)(a),(2), 26(1)(a), 27, sch 2 para 1, sch 3 paras 1, 2

18.9 HBP sch 3 para 1(1),(2); CTRE(PR) sch 2 para 1(1),(2); CTRE(DS) sch 2 para 1(1),(2)

18.10 HBP sch 3 para 1(4),(5); CTRE(PR) sch 2 para 1(3),(4); CTRE(DS) sch 2 para 1(3),(4)

18.11 HBW sch 3 para 1(1)(a),(b),(2)(a),(b),(3)(a),(b); CTRE(DS) sch 3 para 1(1)(a),(b),(2),(3)

18.12 HBW sch 3 paras 1(1)(c),(2)(c),(3)(c); CTRE(DS) sch 3 para 1(1)(c)

Table 18.2 **HB allowances and additional amounts 2025-26**

Personal allowances

Single person	new pension age rate	£227.10
	old pension age rate	£244.40
	working age rate	£92.05
	lower rate	£72.90
Couple	new pension age rate	£346.60
	old pension age rate	£366.00
	working age rate	£144.65
	lower rate	£110.15
Polygamous spouse	new pension age rate	£119.50
	old pension age rate	£121.60
	working age/lower rate	£52.60
Child or young person	usually up to two amounts	£84.66

Additional amounts: any age

Disabled child premium	each child/young person	£81.37
Enhanced disability premium (child)	each child/young person	£32.75
Family premium	old HB cases	£19.48
Carer premium	claimant/partner/each	£46.40
Severe disability premium	single rate	£82.90
	double rate	£165.80

Additional amounts: working age only

Disability premium	single person	£43.20
	couple	£61.65
Enhanced disability premium (adult)	single person	£21.20
	couple	£30.25
Support component	single person/couple	£48.50
WRA component	single person/couple	£36.55

Note: You are awarded each of the personal allowances and additional amounts you qualify for.

T18.2 HBW sch 3 paras 1-3, 20, 25, 26; HBP sch 3 paras 1-3, 12; SI 2025/295 sch 4-7

Amounts for children

Allowances for children and young persons

18.13 You qualify for a personal allowance for each child or young person in your benefit unit. But if you are on working age HB and have more than two children born on or after 6 April 2017, you may be affected by the two-child limit (chapter 19). The two-child limit stopped applying to pension age HB on 8 June 2024.

Disabled child premium

18.14 You qualify for a disabled child premium for each child or young person in your benefit unit who:

(a) receives PIP (either component at any rate) or (in Scotland) ADP
(b) receives DLA (either component at any rate) or (in Scotland) SADLA or CDP
(c) receives armed forces independence payment (young persons only)
(d) has been certified by a consultant ophthalmologist as severely sight impaired or blind or
(e) has regained sight within the past 28 weeks.

Enhanced disability premium for a child

18.15 You qualify for an enhanced disability premium (as well as a disabled child premium) for each child or young person who receives:

(a) the enhanced rate of the daily living component of PIP or (in Scotland) ADP
(b) the highest rate of the care component of DLA or (in Scotland) SADLA or CDP or
(c) armed forces independence payment (young persons only).

If a child or young person dies

18.16 If a child or young person dies who met the conditions for the disabled child premium or the enhanced disability premium for a child, these continue for eight weeks after their death.

Family premium

18.17 The family premium has been abolished, but you still qualify for it if:

(a) you were entitled to HB on 30 April 2016
(b) you have had at least one child or young person in your benefit unit since then (not necessarily the same one throughout) and
(c) you haven't made a new claim for HB since then (e.g. following a break in your entitlement or a move to a new local authority area).

18.13 HBW 22(1)(b),(2); HBP 22(1)(b),(5A); CTRE(PR) sch 1 para 6; CTRE(DS) 25, 26; (CTRE) SI 2017/1305 reg 7

18.14 HBW sch 3 para 16; HBP sch 3 para 8; CTRE(PR) sch 2 para 8; CTRE(DS) sch 2 para 8, sch 3 para 13

18.15 HBW sch 3 para 15; HBP sch 3 para 7; CTRE(PR) sch 2 para 7; CTRE(DS) sch 2 para 7, sch 3 para 12

18.16 HBW sch 3 para 15(1A), 16(c); HBP sch 3 para 7(2), 8(c); CTRE(PR) sch 2 paras 7(2), 8(c); CTRE(DS) sch 2 paras 7(2), 8(c), sch 3 paras 12(2), 13(c)

18.17 (HB) SI 2015/1857 reg 4; (CTRE) SI 2015/2041 reg 3

Examples: Applicable amounts

1. Pension age couple, no children

A couple in their 70s claim HB. They do not have any disabilities.

Personal allowance	
■ Couple, old pension age rate	£366.00
Total weekly applicable amount	£366.00

2. Working age single person, one child

A single person aged 30 claims HB on supported accommodation. She has one child aged three. Neither of them has any disabilities. The claimant gets carer's allowance for caring for her mother.

Personal allowances	
■ Single person, working age rate	£92.05
■ One child	£84.66
Additional amount	
■ Carer premium	£46.40
Total weekly applicable amount	£223.11

3. Pension age single person, one disabled child

A single person who has just reached 66 claims HB. Her grandson aged eight lives with her, and he gets the mobility component of DLA.

Personal allowances	
■ Single person, new pension age rate	£227.10
■ One child	£84.66
Additional amount	
■ Disabled child premium	£81.37
Total weekly applicable amount	£393.13

4. Working age couple, two children, one disabled

A couple in their 40s are on HB (para 2.17). They have two children aged 11 and 13. One child gets the enhanced rate of the daily living component of PIP.

Personal allowances	
■ Couple, working age rate	£144.65
■ Two children	£169.32
Additional amounts	
■ Disabled child premium	£81.37
■ Enhanced disability premium (child)	£32.75
Total weekly applicable amount	£428.09

Carer premium

18.18 You qualify for a carer premium if:

(a) you receive carer's allowance or carer's support payment

(b) you are entitled to either payment but don't receive it (para 18.19) or

(c) you stopped receiving or being entitled to carer's allowance (for any reason) within the past eight weeks.

If you are in a couple, you get one carer premium for each of you who meets these conditions.

18.19 You can be entitled to carer's allowance (but not receive it) when:

(a) you are getting another social security benefit (e.g. state pension) that stops carer's allowance being paid (an 'overlapping' benefit)

(b) you are on a government training scheme

(c) you meet the conditions for carer's allowance and have made a claim for it (Insurance Officer v McCaffrey, SSWP v Nelligan, CIS/367/2003).

The main condition for getting carer's allowance is that you provide care to a severely disabled person with a qualifying benefit for 35 hours per week.

Severe disability premium

18.20 You qualify for a severe disability addition if you meet the following conditions:

(a) you are severely disabled

(b) you don't have any non-dependants living with you and

(c) your carer doesn't receive carer's allowance, carer's support payment or the UC carer element.

The details of these conditions are in paras 18.22-24.

18.21 Single people qualify for the single rate of severe disability premium if you meet all three conditions. Couples qualify for:

(a) the double rate if you both meet all three conditions in paras 18.22-24

(b) the single rate if one of you meets all three conditions and the other one meets only the first two conditions

---

18.18 HBW sch 3 para 17; HBP sch 3 para 9; CTRE(PR) sch 2 para 9; CTRE(DS) sch 2 para 9, sch 3 para 14

18.19 SSAA 1(1); HBW sch 3 paras 17(1), 19; HBP sch 3 paras 9(4), 11
CTRE(PR) sch 2 paras 9(4), 11; CTRE(DS) sch 2 paras 9(4), 11
Insurance Officer v McCaffrey [1985] 1 All ER 5 (HL); SSWP v Nelligan [2003] EWCA Civ 555

18.20 HBW sch 3 para 14(1),(2); HBP sch 3 para 6(1),(2)
CTRE(PR) sch 2 para 6(1),(2); CTRE(DS) sch 2 para 6(1),(2), sch 3 para 11(1),(2)

18.21 HBW sch 3 paras 14(3), 20(6); HBP sch 3 paras 6(3)-(5), 12(1)
CTRE(PR) sch 2 paras 6(3)-(5), 12(1); CTRE(DS) sch 2 paras 6(3)-(5), 12(1), sch 3 paras 11(3), 17(2)

(c) the single rate if you (the claimant) meet all three conditions, and your partner:
- has been certified by a consultant ophthalmologist as severely sight impaired or blind (or has regained sight within the past 28 weeks) or
- gets one of the benefits in para 18.22.

The first condition: severely disabled

18.22 The first condition is that you must receive one of the following benefits (or would do so except that you are in hospital):

(a) the daily living component of PIP or ADP

(b) the middle or highest rate of the care component of DLA, SADLA or CDP

(c) attendance allowance or PADP

(d) constant attendance allowance paid with an industrial injury or war disablement pension or

(e) armed forces independence payment.

The second condition: no non-dependants

18.23 The second condition is that you must have no non-dependants living with you (para 6.1) apart from non-dependants who:

(a) receive a benefit in para 18.22 or

(b) have been certified by a consultant ophthalmologist as severely sight impaired or blind or

(c) have regained sight within the past 28 weeks.

The third condition: no carer benefits

18.24 The third condition is that no-one must be receiving carer's allowance or the carer element of UC for caring for you. For this rule, your carer:

(a) counts as getting carer's allowance, carer support payment or carer element if they stop because you are in hospital but

(b) doesn't count as getting any of these during a period in which they are backdated (this means that your carer's arrears don't cause your HB to be overpaid) and

(c) doesn't count as getting carer's allowance if another social security benefit stops it being paid (para 18.19(a)).

18.22 HBW 2(1) – 'attendance allowance', sch 3 para 14(2)(a)(i),(b)(i); HBP 2(1), sch 3 para 6(2)(a)(i),(b)(i)
CTRE(PR) 2(1), sch 2 para 6(2)(a),(b); CTRE(DS) 2(1), sch 2 para 6(2)(a),(b), sch 3 para 11(2)(a),(b)

18.23 HBW sch 3 para 14(4),(5); HBP sch 3 para 6(4)-(7)
CTRE(PR) sch 2 para 6(4)-(7); CTRE(DS) sch 2 para 6(4)-(7), sch 3 para 11(4),(5)

18.24 HBW sch 3 paras 14(6),(7) 19; HBP sch 3 paras 6(8), 11
CTRE(PR) sch 2 paras 6(8), 11; CTRE(DS) sch 2 paras 6(8), 11, sch 3 paras 11(6),(7), 16

Additional amounts: working age only

18.25 The additional amounts in the rest of this chapter only apply if:

(a) you are single and under pension age (under 66) or

(b) you are in a couple and you (the claimant) are under pension age (regardless of the age of your partner).

Disability premium for an adult

18.26 Single people qualify for the single rate of the disability premium if:

(a) you are under pension age

(b) you aren't on ESA or ESA credits and

(c) you meet the disability condition in para 18.28.

18.27 Couples qualify for the couple rate if:

(a) you (the claimant) are under pension age

(b) you (the claimant) aren't on ESA or ESA credits and

(c) you meet the disability condition in para 18.28, or your partner is also under pension age and they meet that condition.

The disability condition

18.28 You meet the disability condition if:

(a) you receive:

- PIP or ADP (either component at any rate)
- DLA, SADLA or CDP (either component at any rate)
- attendance allowance or PADP
- constant attendance allowance paid with an industrial injury pension or war disablement pension
- armed forces independence payment or
- war pensioner's mobility supplement

(b) you have been certified by a consultant ophthalmologist as severely sight impaired or blind

(c) you have regained sight within the past 28 weeks or

(d) you get DWP payments for car running costs or have an invalid vehicle supplied by the NHS.

The same applies to your partner if they are under pension age.

18.25 HBW 5, 22(d)-(f); CTRE(PR) 3; CTRE(DS) 3, 26(1)(d)-(f)

18.26 HBW sch 3 paras 12, 13(9); CTRE(DS) sch 3 paras 9, 10(8)

18.27 HBW sch 3 para 20(5); CTRE(DS) sch 3 para 17(1)

18.28 HBW sch 3 para 13(1)(a),(2); CTRE(DS) sch 3 para 10(1)(a),(2)

Enhanced disability premium for an adult

18.29 Single people qualify for the single rate of the enhanced disability premium if:

(a) you are under pension age and

(b) you receive:

- the enhanced rate of the daily living component of PIP or (in Scotland) ADP
- the highest rate of the care component of DLA or (in Scotland) SADLA or CDP
- armed forces independence payment or
- the support component of ESA or equivalent ESA credits.

18.30 Couples qualify for the couple rate if:

(a) you (the claimant) are under pension age and

(b) you receive one of the benefits in para 18.29(b), or your partner is also under pension age and they receive one of the first three of those benefits.

It is not enough if your partner gets the support component of ESA or equivalent ESA credits.

Support component

18.31 Single people qualify for a support component in your HB if:

(a) you are under pension age and

(b) you are entitled to the support component of ESA or equivalent ESA credits.

18.32 Couples qualify for a support component in your HB if:

(a) you (the claimant) are under pension age and

(b) at least one of you is entitled to the support component or ESA or equivalent ESA credits.

People in hospital

18.33 If you or someone in your benefit unit goes into hospital, you usually continue to be entitled to HB unless your absence is likely to be longer than 52 weeks (paras 8.19-20). Table 18.3 shows how going into hospital can affect your premiums.

18.29 HBW sch 3 para 15(1); CTRE(DS) sch 3 para 12(1)

18.30 HBW sch 3 para 20(9); CTRE(DS) sch 3 para 17(5)

18.31-32 HBW sch 3 paras 21, 21A, 24; CTRE(DS) sch 3 paras 18, 19, 22

Table 18.3 **Premiums for people in hospital**

How PIP and DLA affect HB

(a) If you or your partner go into hospital, PIP/DLA/ADP or CDP stop after four weeks. If this is the only reason they stop:

- disability premium continues
- enhanced disability premium (adult) continues
- severe disability premium ends if you are a single person, but continues at the single rate if you are a couple (or polygamous marriage) and were previously getting the couple rate.

(b) If a young person aged 18 or over goes into hospital, PIP/DLA/ADP or CDP stop after four weeks.

If this is the only reason they stop:

- disabled child premium continues
- enhanced disability premium (child) continues.

They also continue if a child or young person under 18 goes into hospital, because in their case PIP/ADP/DLA/CDP don't stop.

How carer's allowance affects HB

(c) If you or your partner go into hospital, carer's allowance stops after 12 weeks. If this is the only reason it stops:

- carer premium continues for a further eight weeks (making 20 weeks in total).

(d) If the person you or your partner care for goes into hospital, PIP/DLA/ADP or CDP stop after four weeks. If this is the only reason they stop:

- carer premium continues for a further eight weeks (making 12 weeks in total).

Note:

The four weeks in (a) and (d) don't have to be continuous but can be made up of two or more periods which are less than 29 days apart.

T18.3(a) HBW sch 3 paras 13(1)(a), 14(5), 15(1)(b),(c),(ca),(2), 20(6)(b); HBP sch 3 paras 6(7), 7(1)(a),(b),(ba) CTRE(PR) sch 2 paras 6(7), 7(1); CTRE(DS) sch 2 paras 6(7), 7(1), sch 3 paras 10(1), 11(5), 12(1),(3), 17(2)

T18.3(b) HBW sch 3 paras 15(1)(b),(ba),16(a),(d),(da); HBP sch 3 paras 7(1)(a),(b),(ba), 8(a),(d),(da) CTRE(PR) sch 2 paras 7(1)(a),(ab),(b), 8(a),(d); CTRE(DS) sch 2 paras 7(1), 8(a), sch 3 paras 12(1),13

T18.3(c) HBW sch 3 para 17(2)(b),(4)(b); HBP sch 3 para 9(2)(b) CTRE(PR) sch 2 para 9(2)(b); CTRE(DS) sch 2 para 9(2)(b), sch 3 para 14(2)(b),(4)(b)

T18.3(d) HBW sch 3 para 17(2)(b),(4)(b); HBP sch 3 para 9(2)(b) CTRE(PR) sch 2 para 9(2)(b); CTRE(DS) sch 2 para 9(2)(b), sch 3 para 14(2)(b),(4)(b)

Chapter 19 **The two-child limit**

- The two-child limit in UC: paras 19.3-13
- The two-child limit in HB: paras 19.14-18

Who is affected by the two-child limit

19.1 The 'two-child limit' applies to UC and working age HB. It only affects you if:

(a) you have more than two children or young persons in your benefit unit and

(b) at least one of them was born on or after 6 April 2017 (when the two-child limit was first introduced).

The two-child limit doesn't amount to unlawful discrimination (SC, CB and Others v SSWP).

19.2 The two-child limit affects:

(a) how many child elements you can get in UC (para 16.7) and

(b) how many personal allowances you can get in working age HB (para 18.13).

It never affects the number of bedrooms you qualify for (chapter 14) or any other aspect of UC or HB. And it never applies to SPC or (since 8 June 2024) pension age HB.

The two-child limit in UC

How the two-child limit works in UC

19.3 If you have one child/young person you get one child element in your UC. Or if you have two you get two child elements.

19.4 But if you have three or more, you get a child element in your UC for:

(a) each child/young person who has full protection (para 19.5) and

(b) the oldest two other children/young persons (decided by their date of birth, or time of birth for twins, etc) and

(c) any other child/young person who:

- has third child protection (para 19.6) or
- was born before 6 April 2017 (para 19.7).

These rules are applied in the order (a), (b), (c) – this is illustrated in the examples.

19.1 WRA 10(1A); UC 24A; UCTP 43; HBW 22(1)(b)
SC, CB and Others v SSWP [2021] UKSC 26

19.2 WRA 10(1A),(4); UC 24A; PC sch 2A para 9; HBW 22(1)(b)(2); HBP 22(1)(b); SI 2024/611 regs 2, 6

19.3 WRA 10(1A); UC 24(1), 36

19.4 UC 24A, 24B

Full protection

19.5 In UC, 'full protection' can apply to any child/young person (whether your first, second, third, etc). The qualifying conditions relate to:

(a) adoption (para 19.8) or

(b) non-parental care (para 19.9).

Third child protection

19.6 In UC, 'third child protection' can only apply to your third or subsequent child/young person (counting only those that don't have full protection) (AT v SSWP). The qualifying conditions relate to:

(a) multiple births (twins etc) (para 19.10) or

(b) non-consensual conception (para 19.11).

Born before 6 April 2017

19.7 In UC, you get a child element for every child/young person who was born before 6 April 2017, and this continues for as long as they continue to be children/young persons (paras 5.18-19).

Adoption

19.8 In UC, a child/young person has full protection (para 19.5) if he or she:

(a) is adopted by you or your partner or

(b) is placed for adoption with you or your partner.

But this doesn't apply if you or your partner are their parent or step-parent (except as in para 19.13). And it doesn't apply to adoptions arranged directly from outside the British Isles.

Non-parental care

19.9 In UC, a child/young person has full protection (para 19.5) if he or she:

(a) is looked after by you or your partner under formal arrangements made (now or before they reached 16) by social services or a court, or confirmed by you or your partner being entitled to guardian's allowance for them or

(b) is looked after by you or your partner under informal arrangements (made by you or your partner) if they would otherwise be likely to enter local authority care (in practice a social worker will be asked to confirm this) or

(c) is a child whose parent is also a child (under 16) and in your benefit unit (paras 5.20-27) – for example, if you have a 15-year-old daughter with a baby, this means the baby.

But (a) and (b) don't apply if you or your partner are their parent or step-parent.

19.5 UC 24A(1)(za)(i), 24B(2A), sch 12 paras 3, 4

19.6 UC 24A(1)(b)(ii), 24B(2A), sch 12 paras 2, 5
AT v SSWP (UC) [2023] UKUP 148 (AAC)

19.7 UC 24A(1)(b)(i),(3)

19.8 UC sch 12 para 3

19.9 UC sch 12 para 4

Multiple births (twins, etc)

19.10 In UC, a child/young person has third-child protection (para 19.6) if he or she was born to you or your partner and:

(a) is the second-born of twins, both of whom are in your benefit unit (paras 5.17-27) or

(b) is the second-born or later-born of triplets or a larger multiple birth, counting only those in your benefit unit.

Non-consensual conception

19.11 In UC, a child/young person has third-child protection (para 19.6) if he or she was born to you or your partner as a result of non-consensual intercourse with a person who doesn't (or doesn't now) live with you, for example due to rape or controlling or coercive behaviour.

19.12 In UC, because this is an extremely sensitive issue, the DWP accepts evidence (ADM para F1024):

(a) from a third party it has approved for this purpose, normally a health professional, registered social worker or specialist charity or

(b) that the person has been convicted of a relevant offence or

(c) that the Criminal Injuries Compensation Authority has made a relevant award to you.

Step parents

19.13 In UC, the protections in paras 19.8 and 19.10-12 continue if:

(a) you are a step-parent of a child/young person and

(b) you were previously getting UC as a couple with their parent or adoptive parent and

(c) you have remained on UC since then with no break longer than six months.

The same applies if you were getting CTC, JSA(IB) or IS within the six months before your UC began.

Examples: The two-child limit

The examples use 'child' to include both children and young persons. Except when stated, none of them qualify for full protection or third child protection (paras 19.5-6).

1. Three children all born before 6 April 2017

A single person has three children, all born before 6 April 2017. She gets three child elements as follows.

■ First child	Yes (oldest two)
■ Second child	Yes (oldest two)
■ Third child	Yes (born before 6.4.17)

19.10 UC 24B(1),(2), sch 12 para 2

19.11 UC sch 12 para 5

19.13 UC 2 – 'step-parent', 24A(1)(za)(ii),(b)(ii), sch 12 para 6

2. Three children, two born before 6 April 2017

A couple have three children, two born before 6 April 2017. They get two child elements as follows.

- First child — Yes (oldest two)
- Second child — Yes (oldest two)
- Third child — No (not born before 6.4.17)

3. Three children, all born on or after 6 April 2017

A single person has three children, all born on or after 6 April 2017. He gets two child elements as follows.

- First child — Yes (oldest two)
- Second child — Yes (oldest two)
- Third child — No (not born before 6.4.17)

4. Three children, younger two are twins

A couple have three children, all born on or after 6 April 2017. The younger two are twins. They get three child elements as follows.

- First child — Yes (oldest two)
- Second child (older twin) — Yes (oldest two)
- Third child (younger twin) — Yes (third-child protection)

5. Three children, older two are twins

A couple have three children, all born on or after 6 April 2017. The older two are twins. They get two child elements as follows.

- First child (older twin) — Yes (oldest two)
- Second child (younger twin) — Yes (oldest two)
- Third child — No (no third-child protection)

6. Five children, two adopted

A single person has two adopted children, and three other children born after 6 April 2017. He gets four child elements as follows.

- Adopted child — Yes (full protection)
- Adopted child — Yes (full protection)
- First other child — Yes (oldest other two)
- Second other child — Yes (oldest other two)
- Third other child — No (no third-child protection)

7. Adopted child and twins

A couple have one adopted child, and three other children born after 6 April 2017. The youngest two are twins. They get four child elements as follows.

- Adopted child — Yes (full protection)
- First other child — Yes (oldest other two)
- Second other child (older twin) — Yes (oldest other two)
- Third other child (younger twin) — Yes (third-child protection)

The two-child limit in working age HB

How the two-child limit works in HB

19.14 The two-child limit only applies to working age HB. If you have one child/young person in your family, you get a personal allowance for him or her in your HB. Or if you have two, you get personal allowances for each of them.

19.15 But if you have three or more, you only get two personal allowances for them in your HB unless you have been on HB since before 6 April 2017.

If you have been on HB since before 6 April 2017

19.16 This exception to the two-child limit applies if:

(a) you have been entitled to HB continuously since before 6 April 2017

(b) you have had no breaks in your entitlement and

(c) you haven't had to reclaim because of moving to a new local authority area.

19.17 In this case, you qualify for an HB personal allowance for each child/young person who:

(a) was included in your benefit unit then and

(b) is included in your benefit unit now (even if they were absent in between).

19.18 If only one child/young person in your benefit unit meets the conditions in paras 19.16-17, you can get an HB personal allowance for one more. But if two meet the conditions, you can't get an HB personal allowance for any more.

19.14 HBW 22(1)(b)

19.15 HBW 22(1)(b); SI 2017/376 reg 9(1),(2)

19.16 SI 2017/376 reg 9(1),(2)

19.17 SI 2017/376 reg 9(1)-(3)

19.18 SI 2017/376 reg 9(4)-(9)

Chapter 20 **The benefit cap**

- Summary and main rules: paras 20.1-9
- Benefit cap exceptions: paras 20.10-16

Summary and main rules

Who is affected by the benefit cap

20.1 The benefit cap can only affect your benefit if you have a working age claim. It applies to UC if you are on UC, or HB if you are on working age HB. It never applies to SPC or pension age HB.

20.2 The amount of the benefit cap is in table 20.1. Your UC or HB is reduced if the total of your welfare benefits (table 20.2) exceeds this. But there are exceptions relating to work, disabilities, carers, people with war pensions (table 20.3), supported and temporary accommodation (table 20.4), and pension age claimants who have transferred from tax credits to UC (paras 25.33-34).

Table 20.1 **The amount of the benefit cap**

Your household	Annual benefit cap in Greater London	Annual benefit cap elsewhere
(a) Single person with no children/young persons	£16,967	£14,753
(b) Single person with one or more children/young persons	£25,323	£22,020
(c) Couple with or without children/young persons	£25,323	£22,020

Notes:

- Greater London means the London boroughs and the City of London.
- Only children/young persons in your benefit unit are taken into account.
- In UC, if you are in a couple but claiming as a single person, (a) or (b) applies to you, but your partner's benefits are included in the benefit cap calculation.
- To convert the benefit cap to a monthly or weekly figure see para 1.25.

20.2 WRA 96; UC 78, 79; HBW 75A

T20.1 WRA 96(5A); UC 80A(2); HBW 75CA(2)

20.3 The Supreme Court has held that the benefit cap doesn't discriminate unlawfully (R (SG and others) v SSWP; R (DA and others) v SSWP; R (DS and others) v SSWP).

How the benefit cap reduces your UC or HB

20.4 When your total welfare benefits exceed the benefit cap, the excess is deducted from your UC or HB. Your HB mustn't be reduced below 50p in any week – this is so you can apply for a discretionary housing payment (paras 18.7, 20.5).

Table 20.2 **Your total welfare benefits**

Benefits that are taken into account

The following benefits are added together to give the total of your welfare benefits:

(a) universal credit (in UC only)
(b) housing benefit (in HB only)
(c) JSA(IB), ESA(IR) and IS (in HB only)
(d) child tax credit (in HB only)
(e) new-style JSA and ESA
(f) child benefit
(g) maternity allowance
(h) severe disablement allowance
(i) widowed parent's allowance
(j) bereavement allowance (but not bereavement support payments)

Notes:

- In a couple, your partner's benefits are included (even if you are claiming UC as a single person).
- If you become a couple while you are on UC, and your new partner is on HB but not UC, their benefits aren't included during the assessment period in which you become a couple.
- If you are on UC, the childcare element isn't taken into account (para 20.6).
- Benefits (and the benefit cap itself) are converted to a monthly amount in UC or a weekly amount in HB (para 1.25).
- Benefits are counted before any reductions are made for recovering overpayments, administrative penalties, third party deductions or sanctions.
- For the HB benefit cap, the DWP usually provides the council with the figures (HB A15/2013).

20.3 R (SG and others) v SSWP [2015] UKSC 16; R (DA and others) v SSWP [2019] UKSC 21; R (DS and Others) v SSWP [2019] UKSC 21

20.4 UC 79(1), 81(1),(3); HBW 75A, 75D

T20.2 WRA 96(10) – 'welfare benefit'; UC 79(1), 80; HBW 75A, 75C

Discretionary housing payments

20.5 You may be able to get a discretionary housing payment from your local council (para 31.4) if:

(a) your UC calculation included a housing costs element (para 16.32) and your UC is reduced because of the benefit cap or

(b) your HB is reduced because of the benefit cap.

Example: The UC benefit cap

Amelia and her children are renting their home in London (it isn't supported accommodation). She is on UC and her total welfare benefits exceed the benefit cap, so her UC is calculated as follows:

■ Amelia's UC without the benefit cap	£1,820.00 per month
■ Her other benefits in table 20.2	£860.20 per month
■ Her total welfare benefits	£2,680.20 per month
■ Benefit cap (£25,323 annually)	£2,110.25 per month
■ Reduction in UC due to the benefit cap	£569.95 per month
■ Amelia's UC is reduced to	£1,250.05 per month

Deduction for childcare costs

20.6 In UC only, if you qualify for the childcare costs element, it is excluded from the total of your welfare benefits (table 20.2). This ensures you get the full amount of the childcare element even if the benefit cap reduces the rest of your UC to nil.

Decisions about the benefit cap

20.7 If you are on UC, the DWP makes all the decisions about whether the benefit cap applies to you and how much it is. If you are on HB, the DWP usually tells the council when to apply the benefit cap (HB A15/2013).

When the benefit cap starts

20.8 If your total welfare benefits exceed the benefit cap when you claim UC or HB, the benefit cap starts then.

20.5 DFA 1(2) – 'relevant award of universal credit', 2(1)

20.6 UC 81(2)

20.7 HB 75B

20.8 UC 79(1),(2); HBW 75A, 75G – 'reference period'

20.9 If your total welfare benefits start to exceed the benefit cap during your award of UC or HB:

(a) the UC benefit cap starts on the first day of the assessment period in which that happens – or later if you qualify for a grace period (paras 20.12-14)

(b) the HB benefit cap starts when the council makes the decision about it.

The rule in (b) is intended to ensure you aren't overpaid HB as a result of the benefit cap being imposed for a period in the past.

Benefit cap exceptions

General exceptions

20.10 The benefit cap doesn't apply to you if you fall within any of the exceptions in table 20.3. If you are in a couple, it doesn't apply if either of you fall within the exceptions (and in UC this is the case even when you are claiming as a single person).

Exceptions during a grace period

20.11 The benefit cap doesn't apply during the 'grace period' you get in UC or HB after your earnings reduce or end (table 20.3(c),(d)) .

Calculating the grace period in UC

20.12 If your earned income (or in the case of a couple, your combined earned income) reduces below the 16-hour threshold (para 16.13) or ends while you are on UC:

(a) your grace period starts on the first day of the assessment period in which that happens

(b) it lasts for nine months (in other words, nine assessment periods) – but the benefit cap doesn't apply to you until the assessment period following the one in which the grace period ends.

20.13 If you ceased paid work before your entitlement to UC began (or in a couple either of you did):

(a) your grace period starts on the day after you or your partner ceased paid work

(b) it lasts nine months – but the benefit cap does not apply to you until the assessment period following the one in which the grace period ends.

Calculating the grace period in HB

20.14 If you or your partner stop work, your grace period starts on the following Monday.

20.9 UC(D&A) 23(1), 34, sch 1 para 20; HB(D&A) 7(2)(r), 8(14F)

20.10 WRA 96(4)(c); UC 82, 83; HBW 75E, 75F

20.11 UC 82(1); HBW 75E(1)

20.12 UC 82(1),(2)(a)

20.13 UC 82(1),(2)(b)

20.14 HBW 75E(3),(5)

Grace periods for couples

20.15 If you are in a couple and you each separately meet the conditions for a (UC or HB) grace period, a grace period applies to each of you, and you can use whichever one is current.

Examples: The UC benefit cap and the grace period

1. A reduction in earned income

Aarna has been on UC for over 12 months. She has had earned income at or above the 16-hour threshold throughout that time, so no benefit cap has applied to her (table 20.3(a)). Her assessment periods start on the 23rd of each month. She loses her job on 31 March.

Aarna's grace period (table 20.3(c)) begins on 23 March and lasts nine months until 22 December. The benefit cap applies to her from 23 December.

2. Losing paid work then claiming UC

Ishir has been working for many years with earned income at or above the 16-hour threshold. He loses paid work on 15 January. When he claims UC a few weeks later, he is awarded it from 26 February. So his assessment periods begin on the 26th of each month.

Ishir's grace period (table 20.3(c)) begins on 16 January and lasts nine months until 15 October. The benefit cap applies to him from the first day of his next assessment period, which is 26 October.

Exceptions for supported or temporary accommodation

20.16 If you live in supported or temporary accommodation (table 13.1) you may not be affected by the UC or HB benefit cap, but if you are you can only be affected by one of these. The details about this are in table 20.4.

Table 20.3 **Benefit cap exceptions**

Current work: exception to UC benefit cap

(a) You are receiving (or in a couple you are jointly receiving) earned income equal to or above the 16-hour threshold – this means what you would earn for working 16 hours per week at the national living wage (para 16.13)

Starting work: exception to HB benefit cap

(b) You are receiving a four-week extended payment of HB after starting work

Table continued ➤

20.15 UC 82(1)(a),(2)(a); HBW 75E(4)

20.16 UC sch 1 paras 3A, 3B; HB 75C(2)(a), 75F(1)(g)

T20.3 UC 6(1A)(za), 82(1), 83(1); HBW 72E, 73E, 75E(1),(2), 75F(1)

Grace period following recent work: exception to UC benefit cap

(c) You are in a grace period of nine months (paras 20.12-13) and:

- you had earned income at or above the 16-hour threshold in each of the 12 months before you left work and
- your earned income ends or drops below the 16-hour threshold while you are on UC, or ended before you claimed UC

Grace period following recent work: exception to HB benefit cap

(d) You are in a grace period of 39 weeks after leaving work (para 20.14) and:

- you were working during at least 50 of the 52 weeks before you left and
- you weren't claiming JSA(IB), ESA(IR) or IS during those weeks

Disabilities, carers and war pensions: exceptions to the UC and HB benefit caps

(e) Your UC includes an LCWRA element or carer element (paras 16.10, 16.20) (only applies in UC)

(f) You are getting:

- PIP, DLA, ADP, CDP, or armed forces independence payment
- attendance allowance, PADP or an equivalent benefit (para 21.18)
- carer's allowance or carer support payment
- guardian's allowance
- industrial injuries benefit
- ESA that includes a support component
- a war pension (para 21.24)

(g) A child or young person in your benefit unit is getting:

- PIP, DLA, SADLA or CDP
- carer's allowance or carer support payment

Notes:

- For couples, 'you' includes your partner, except when you are claiming UC as a single person.
- You count as being on a benefit even when it has stopped due to you being in hospital.
- If you live in supported or temporary accommodation, see table 20.4.
- For the HB benefit cap, the DWP usually tells the council when these exceptions apply, apart from those relating to war pensions (HB A15/2013).

Table 20.4 **Calculating the benefit cap and accommodation types**

Your main benefit for living costs and your accommodation type	UC benefit cap		HB benefit cap	
	UC housing costs/HB	**Other benefits**	**HB**	**Other benefits**
(a) UC, general accommodation	Count in full	Count in full	N/A	N/A
(b) UC, supported accommodation	HB not counted	Count in full	HB not counted	UC not counted
(c) UC, temporary accommodation	HB not counted	Count in full	HB not counted	UC not counted
(d) Legacy benefits, general accommodation	N/A	N/A	Count in full	Count in full
(e) Legacy benefits, supported accommodation	N/A	N/A	HB not counted	Count in full
(f) Legacy benefits, temporary accommodation	N/A	N/A	Count in full	Count in full

Notes:

- For UC, 'other benefits' include all other UC elements except childcare costs (para 20.6), plus benefits (e) to (j) in table 20.2.
- For HB, 'other benefits' include (c) to (j) in table 20.2.

T20.4 WRA 96(10) – 'welfare benefits'; UC 80(2A); HBW 75C(2)(a), 75F(1)(g)

Chapter 21 **Income**

- General rules about income and capital: paras 21.1-9
- Unearned income: paras 21.10-11
- Benefits and pensions: paras 21.12-25
- Income from maintenance, fostering/adoption and rent: paras 21.26-30
- Student and miscellaneous income: paras 21.31-45

General rules

21.1 This and the following chapters explain how your income and capital are assessed for benefit purposes. They describe which kinds of income and capital are counted and which are 'disregarded' (which means ignored).

21.2 Your income and capital are assessed for two main reasons:

(a) if you have capital over £16,000 you can't get UC or HB, but you can get SPC (para 24.2) and

(b) your income, including assumed income from capital, affects how much UC, SPC and HB you get (paras 16.3, 17.5, 18.3-4).

Whose income and capital is included

21.3 The assessment of your benefit takes into account:

(a) your income and capital if you are a single person

(b) your and your partner's income and capital if you are in a couple.

In this guide, 'your' income and capital includes the income and capital of both you and your partner. Income or capital of a child or non-dependant is never taken into account.

21.4 Your partner's income and capital is always included with yours – even if you are in a couple but claiming UC or SPC as a single person (para 2.9, 2.15). And if you are claiming SPC or HB as a polygamous marriage, the income and capital of all the members of the marriage are included (for UC and mixed age couples in SPC/HB see paras 2.34-36).

21.2 WRA 5; SPCA 2(1),(2); SSCBA 130(3), 134(1); UC 22(1); HBW 43, 71; HBP 43, 51
CTRE(PR) 11(2), sch 1 paras 1, 3(f); CTRE(DS) 14(f), 17(f), 23(1)

21.3 SPCA 5; SSCBA 136(1); PC 14; HBW 25(1),(3), sch 5 para 21; HBP 23(1),(3)
CTRE(PR) 11(1),(2), CTRE(DS) 33(1),(2), sch para 25

21.4 WRA 5(2); SPCA 12(2)(d); SSCBA 136(1); UC 18(2), 22(3); PC 14, sch 3 para 1(4); HBW 25(1),(2); HBP 23(1),(2)
CTRE(PR) sch 1 para 11; CTRE(DS) 33

Distinguishing capital from income

21.5 The distinction between capital and income is usually straightforward. For example:

(a) capital includes savings, investments and property, but some capital is disregarded

(b) income includes earnings, maintenance and benefits, but some income is disregarded.

21.6 A particular payment you receive might be capital (for example an inheritance) or income (for example earnings). This depends on 'the true characteristics of the payment in the hands of the recipient', not what the payment is called by the person paying it (Minter v Hull City Council).

21.7 However, a payment of income can turn into capital. For example, if you receive wages, benefits etc monthly, what you haven't spent by the end of the month becomes part of your capital (CH/1561/2005).

Examples: Assessing income

1. A couple claiming UC

Geoff and Julia are claiming UC and have two children at school. Geoff works and has net earnings (after the work allowance has been deducted) of £491 pcm. Julia receives child maintenance from the children's father and child benefit. They have £3,962 in a savings account.

Their monthly income is assessed as follows:

- The child benefit and child maintenance are disregarded (para 21.26 and table 21.2)
- The earnings are counted (chapter 16) £491 pcm
- They do not have assumed income from their capital (para 24.3)
- Total monthly income £491 pcm

2. A single person claiming pension age HB

Jacqui is claiming pension age HB. She receives a state pension and a private pension totalling £274 pw. She has £12,620 in a savings account.

Her weekly income is assessed as follows:

- The pensions both count as her income (para 21.20) £274 pw
- She has assumed income from her capital (para 24.3) £6 pw
- Total weekly income £280 pw

21.6 Minter v Kingston upon Hull City Council [2011] EWCA Civ 1155 reported as [2012] AACR 21

Monthly income for UC

21.8 UC is a monthly benefit and uses monthly income. Unearned income is converted to a monthly figure as described in para 1.19. But employed and self-employed earnings are usually taken into account in full in the month you receive them (paras 22.8-15).

Weekly income for SPC and HB

21.9 SPC and HB are weekly benefits and use weekly income. Earned and unearned income are converted to a weekly figure as described in para 1.21.

Unearned income

21.10 Tables 21.1 and 21.2 summarise which kinds of unearned income are counted and which are disregarded. But if you are on any of the passport benefits (table 18.1), the whole of your income and capital is disregarded in the assessment of HB.

21.11 All kinds of unearned income are calculated net of any tax paid on them.

Table 21.1 **Unearned income**

Payments that mainly count as your unearned income

(a) Some social security benefits (table 21.2)

(b) Retirement pensions (paras 21.20-23)

(c) Maintenance for you, your partner or a non-dependant (para 21.27)

(d) Rent you receive from a lodger in your home (HB only) (para 21.29)

(e) Student income if you are working age (paras 21.33-34)

(f) In some cases, certain insurance payments (para 21.36)

(g) Some income from trusts, annuities and equity release (paras 21.38-40)

(h) Royalties, copyright and patent payments (para 21.44)

(i) Assumed income from capital (para 24.3)

Payments that are mainly disregarded

(j) Most war pensions (paras 21.24-25)

(k) Maintenance for a child or young person (para 21.26)

Table continued ➤

21.8 UC 54(1), 61(2), 73(1)

21.9 PC 1(2) – 'benefit week', 17(1); HBW 27(1), 29(1), 30(1), 31(1); HBP 30(1) CTRE(PR) sch 1 para 24(1); CTRE(DS) 47(1), 48(1), 49(1), 57(1)

21.10 SPCA 15(1)(a)-(j), 16(1)(za)-(n); UC 66(1)(a)-(m); PC 15(1),(5), 16; HBW 40(1),(2); HBP 29(1)(b)-(x) CTRE(PR) sch 1 para 16(1)(b)-(x); CTR(DS) 39(1)(b)-(x), 54(1),(2)

21.11 PC 17(10); HBW sch 5 para 1; HBP 33(12); CTRE(PR) sch 1 para 17(13); CTR(DS) 40(13), sch 8 para 4

T21.1(a)-(s) See the paragraphs referred to

(l) Most rent you receive on property other than your home (para 21.30)
(m) Student income if you are pension age (para 21.32)
(n) Fostering and adoption payments (para 21.28)
(o) Discretionary housing payments and other council payments (para 21.42)
(p) Training allowances and sports funding awards (para 21.31)
(q) Personal injury payments (para 21.37)
(r) Charitable and voluntary payments (para 21.41)
(s) Payments for certain disasters etc (para 21.43)
(t) Victoria Cross and George Cross payments
(u) Government fuel and cost of living payments
(v) Expenses paid if you are part of a service user group or work for a charity
(w) Juror's allowances
(x) Payments for health service supplies and prison visits
(y) Payments in kind (in other words, in goods rather than money or vouchers).

Note: This table gives the main rules. For exceptions, see the paragraphs referred to.

Social security benefits

21.12 Table 21.2 lists which DWP social security benefits are counted as part of your income and which are disregarded.

21.13 All Scottish social security benefits are disregarded except for carer support payment up to the same amount as carer's allowance, and the whole of any employment injury assistance.

Counted and disregarded benefits

21.14 The counted benefits are included as your income in the period they relate to. So arrears of them are included as income in the past, and this may mean you have been overpaid benefit (para 36.23). If deductions are made from them, the gross amount (before the deductions) is used.

T21.1(t) UC sch 10 para 19; PC 15(1); HBW sch 5 para 10; HBP 29(1); CTRE(DS) sch 8 para 15

T21.1(u) Social Security (Additional Payments) Act 2023, s.8

T21.1(v) UC 55(3)(b); PC 17A(3)(f); HBW 35(2)(d), sch 5 paras 2, 2A; HBP 35(2)(f)
CTRE(PR) sch 1 paras 18(2)(f), 23(3); CTRE(DS) 41(2)(f), 46(3), 51(2)(d), sch 8 paras 5, 6

T21.1(w) UC 66(1); PC 15(1); HBW sch 5 para 39; HBP 29(1); CTRE(DS) sch 8 para 44

T21.1(x) UC 66(1); PC 29(1); HBW sch 5 paras 44-46; HBP 29(1); CTRE(DS) sch 8 paras 46-48

T21.1(y) UC 55(2); PC 17A(3)(a); HBW 35(1)(k),(3), sch 5 para 23; HBP 35(1)(g),(3)
CTRE(PR) sch 1 para 18(1)(g),(3); CTR(DS) 41(1)(g),(3), 51(1)(l),(3), sch 8 para 28

21.13 UC 66(1); PC 15(1)(ra)-(rh); HBW sch 5 paras 68-74; HBP 29(1)(j)(xviib)-(xviih),(4)(g), sch 5 para 25
CTRE(PR) sch 1 para 16(1)(j)(xx)-(xxvi); CTRE(DS) 39(1)

21.14 UC 66(1)(b), 73(1); PC 15(3); HBW 31(2), 40(5),(5A); HBP 29(3), 33(6);
CTRE(PR) sch 1 paras 16(2), 17(7); CTRE(DS) 39(2), 40(7), 49(2), 54(3),(4)

Table 21.2 **Social security benefits**

Benefits that count as your unearned income

(a) The savings credit of SPC (in HB only) (para 21.19)
(b) New style JSA and ESA (the new style contributory benefits: para 1.12)
(c) Maternity allowance
(d) Carer's allowance
(e) Severe disablement allowance
(f) Industrial injuries benefit apart from increases for attendance
(g) Bereavement allowance
(h) Widow's pension
(i) Widowed mother's/parent's allowance (except for the first £10 in SPC or £15 in HB)
(j) Payments from a foreign government that are similar to any of the above

Benefits that are disregarded

(k) PIP, DLA, attendance allowance and equivalent benefits (para 21.18)
(l) Child benefit and guardian's allowance
(m) UC, HB and the guarantee credit of SPC
(n) ESA(IR) and (before they were replaced by UC) JSA(IB) and IS
(o) Most Scottish social security benefits (para 21.13)
(p) Bereavement support payments
(q) Other benefits not in this table (except in working age HB).

Note: See para 21.20 for state pension. Statutory sick, maternity, paternity and adoption pay count as earnings (table 22.1).

T21.2(a) HBP 27(4)(a); CTRE(PR) sch 1 para 14(2)(a); CTRE(DS) 36(2)(a)

T21.2(b)-(h) UC 66(1)(b)(i)-(ix); PC 15(1); HBW 40(1),(6); HBP 29(1)(j); CTRE(PR) sch 1 para 16(1)(j); CTRE(DS) 39(1)(j), 54(1)

T21.2(i) PC sch 4 paras 7, 7A; HBW sch 5 para 16; HBP sch 5 paras 7, 8; CTRE(PR) sch 5 paras 7, 8; CTRE(DS) sch 6 paras 7, 8, sch 8 para 21

T21.2(j) SPCA 15(1)(f); UC 66(1)(c),(da); PC 15(2); HBW 40(1); HBP 29(1)(k); CTRE(PR) sch 1 para 16(1)(k); CTRE(DS) 39(1)(k), 54(1)

T21.2(k) UC 66(1)(b); PC 15(1)(a)-(c); HBW sch 5 paras 6, 9; HBP 29(1)(j)(i)-(v); CTRE(PR) sch 1 para 16(1)(j); CTRE(DS) 39(1)(j), sch 8 paras 11, 14

T21.2(l) UC 66(1)(b); PC 15(1)(g),(j); HBW sch 5 paras 50, 65; HBP 29(1)(j)(vi),(vii); CTRE(PR) sch 1 para 16(1)(j)(vi),(vii); CTRE(DS) 39(1)(j)(vi),(vii), sch 8 paras 52, 66

T21.2(m) UC 66(1)(b); PC 15(1)(l); HBW sch 5 para 4; HBP 26, 29(1)(j)(zi),(xi); CTRE(PR) sch 1 paras 13, 16(1)(j)(zi),(xi); CTRE(DS) 28, 35, 37, 39(1)(j)(zi),(xi), sch 8 para 42

T21.2(n) HBW sch 5 paras 4, 5; CTRE(DS) sch 8 paras 8, 9

T21.2(o) UC 66(1)(b); PC 15(1)(ra)-(rh); HBW sch 5 paras 68-74; HBP 29(1)(j)(xviib)-(xviih); CTRE(PR) sch 1 para 16(1)(j)(xx)-(xxvii); CTRE(DS) 39(1)(j)(xx)-(xxvii), sch 8 paras 69-75

T21.2(p) UC 66(1)(b); PC 15(1)(n); HBW sch 5 para 67; HBP 29(1)(j)(xiii); CTRE(PR) sch 1 para 16(1)(j); CTRE(DS) 39(1)(j), sch 8 para 68

T21.2(q) UC 66(1)(b); PC 15(1)(za)-(s); HBW 40(1); HBP 29(1)(j); CTRE(PR) sch 1 para 16(1)(j); CTRE(DS) 39(1)(j), 54(1)

21.15 Before 6 April 2025, CTC counted as income in working age HB, but not in UC, SPC and pension age HB. And WTC counted as income in SPC and pension and working age HB, but not in UC.

21.16 In most cases, when benefits are disregarded as income, arrears of them are disregarded as capital for 12 months (table 24.2(o)).

Overlapping benefits

21.17 'Overlapping benefits' (ones you can't be paid because you get other benefits) are disregarded. For example, carer's allowance can't be paid (so isn't counted) if you get maternity allowance or retirement pension.

Benefits equivalent to attendance allowance

21.18 The following benefits are equivalent to attendance allowance:

(a) increases in industrial injuries benefit for constant attendance or exceptionally severe disablement

(b) increases in a war disablement pension for attendance, constant attendance or exceptionally severe disablement

(c) armed forces independence payments (these are covered separately in the law but are treated the same way as attendance allowance)

(d) payments for attendance under the Personal Injuries (Civilians) scheme and

(e) adult disability payment (ADP), child disability payment (CDP) and PADP in Scotland.

The savings credit of SPC

21.19 The savings credit of SPC counts as income in HB only, and only if you aren't also on the guarantee credit. The council doesn't assess your income in the normal way. Instead it:

(a) uses the DWP's figure for your income (this is called the SPC 'assessed income figure')

(b) adds the amount of your savings credit and

(c) adjusts the result to take account of additional disregards that apply in HB compared with SPC, in relation to local schemes for war pensions, maintenance for an adult, and earnings (paras 21.25, 21.27, table 22.4(b)).

The council also uses the DWP's figure for your capital unless and until your capital goes above £16,000.

21.17 UC 66(1)(a),(b); PC 15(4); HBW 40(1); HBP 29(3),(4); CTRE(PR) sch 1 paras 16(2),(3); CTRE(DS) 39(2),(3), 54(1)

21.18 UC 66(1)(b)(ix); PC 15(1)(c)-(e),(rh); HBW 2(1) – 'attendance allowance', sch 5 paras 9, 73; HBP 2(1), 29(1)(j)(iaa),(ib),(ic),(iii)-(v), sch 5 para 2 CTRE(PR) 2(1), sch 1 para 16(1)(j)(iii)-(v), sch 5 para 2; CTRE(DS) 2(1), 39(1)(j)(iii)-(v), sch 6 para 2, sch 8 para 14

21.19 HBP 27(1),(4); CTRE(PR) sch 1 para 14(1),(2); CTRE(DS) 36(1),(2)

State and other retirement pensions

21.20 All the following count in full as your income:

(a) state pension (old and new)

(b) occupational retirement pensions

(c) personal retirement pensions

(d) payments from retirement annuities

(e) payments from the Payment Protection Fund and

(f) foreign state retirement pensions.

21.21 If you get an amount for your partner this is included. But if a court has ordered that part of your pension must be paid to someone else (e.g. your former partner), that part is disregarded (CH/1672/2007).

Deferring state pensions

21.22 State pension starts when you reach pension age (66). If you defer it until a later date, it isn't included as your income until it starts. If you then get an increased amount, the increased amount is included as your income. And if you receive a lump sum (because of deferring it), the lump sum is disregarded as capital until the pension starts.

Deferring other pensions

21.23 If you defer an occupational or personal pension or choose not to receive it, it is nonetheless included as your unearned income (para 21.45). But this only applies if you are aged 66 or over. It never applies if you are under 66 or transferred from tax credits to UC or SPC (paras 25.33-34).

War pensions

21.24 We use 'war pensions' to mean:

(a) pensions under the Armed Forces Pensions and Compensation schemes for war disablement and war widows, widowers and bereaved civil partners

(b) equivalent payments from the UK government and from non-UK governments, including those paid to the victims of Nazi persecution.

21.20 SPCA 16(1); UC 66(1)(a),(da), 67; PC 15(2),(3), 16; HBW 35(2)(c), 40(1); HBP 29(1)(c),(d),(t),(x), 35(2)(c) CTRE(PR) sch 1 paras 16(1)(c),(d),(t),(x), 18(2)(c); CTRE(DS) 39(1)(c),(d),(t),(x), 41(2)(c), 51(2)(c), 54(1)

21.22 UC 74(3),(4); PC sch 5 paras 23A, 23AA; HBP 41(2),(3),(8BA)-(8BD), sch 6 paras 26A, 26AA CTRE(PR) sch 1 para 22(2),(3),(11A)-(11D), sch 6 paras 28, 28A; CTRE(DS) 45(2),(3),(11A)-(11D), sch 9 paras 28, 28A

21.23 UC 74(3),(4); PC 18; HBW 42(2)(c); HBP 41; CTRE(PR) sch 1 para 22; CTRE(DS) 45, 56(2)(c)

21.24 UC 2 'war disablement pension'; SPCA 17 – 'war disablement pension', 'war widow's or widower's pension'; PC 17(5)(a)-(b); HBW 2(1) – 'war disablement pension', 'war pension', 'war widow's pension', 'war widower's pension'; HBP 2(1); CTRE(PR) 2(1); CTRE(DS) 2(1)

21.25 In UC all these payments are disregarded in full. But in SPC and HB:

(a) mobility supplement, payments equivalent to attendance allowance, and pre-1973 special payments are disregarded in full

(b) the first £10 per week of any other war pension is disregarded

(c) most councils have a local HB scheme that disregards the rest.

The government pays councils up to 75% of the cost of local HB schemes (para 42.27) but decisions about them are not appealable to a tribunal (table 39.1).

Maintenance for a child or young person

21.26 Maintenance for a child or young person is disregarded in full.

Maintenance for you, your partner or a non-dependant

21.27 Maintenance for you, your partner or a non-dependant is counted as income in full. But in HB only, the first £15 is disregarded if:

(a) you have at least one child or young person in your benefit unit and

(b) the maintenance is paid by your or your partner's former partner.

Fostering, adoption and social care

21.28 The following payments made by local councils are disregarded:

(a) fostering, adoption and special guardianship payments

(b) boarding out, community care and direct care payments and

(c) payments to care leavers or to avoid children going into care.

Rent from a lodger in your home

21.29 In UC, income you receive from a lodger in your home is disregarded in full (ADM para H5112). In SPC and HB it depends on whether you provide the lodger with meals:

(a) if you do provide meals, £20 of the rent you receive is disregarded and only half of the remainder counts as your income

(b) if you don't provide meals, £20 of the rent you receive is disregarded and all of the remainder counts as your income.

Rule (a) applies if you provide 'at least some meals' that are cooked or prepared by you (or anyone other than the lodger or a member of their family) in your home or associated premises.

21.25 SPCA 15(1)(g),(h); SSAA 134(8); UC 66(1); PC 15(5)(a),(aa)-(ac),(b), sch 4 paras 1-6; SI 2007/1619 sch
HBW 2(1) – 'attendance allowance', sch 5 paras 8, 9, 15, 53-55; HBP 2(1), 27(4)(g), 29(1)(e)-(h),(l),(m), sch 5 paras 1-6
LGFA sch 1A para 2(2); CTRE(PR) sch 1 para 16(1), sch 5 paras 1-6; CTRE(DS) 2(1), 39(1), sch 6 paras 1-6, sch 8 paras 13, 14, 20, 54-56

21.26 UC 66(1)(d); PC 15(5)(d); HBW sch 5 para 47A; HBP 29(1)(o); CTRE(PR) sch 1 para 16(1)(o); CTRE(DS) 39(1)(o), sch 8 para 50

21.27 UC 66(1)(d); PC 15(5)(d); HBW sch 5 para 47; HBP 29(1)(o), sch 5 para 20;
CTRE(PR) sch 1 para 16(1)(o), sch 5 para 20; CTRE(DS) 39(1)(o), sch 6 para 20, sch 8 para 49

21.28 SPCA 15(1); UC 66(1); HBW sch 5 paras 25-28A, 57; HBP 29(1); CTRE(PR) sch 1 para 16(1); CTRE(DS) sch 8 paras 30-34, 59

21.29 UC 66(1); PC 15(5)(e),(i), sch 4 paras 8, 9; HBW sch 5 para 42; HBP 29(1)(p),(v), sch 5 paras 9, 10;
CTRE(PR) sch 1 para 16(1)(p),(v), sch 5 paras 9, 10; CTRE(DS) 39(1)(p),(v), sch 6 paras 9, 10, sch 8 paras 26, 27

Examples: Letting out a room

1. UC if you have a lodger

Allegra and Bob are on UC. They rent out a spare room to a lodger for £100 pw.

- Their income from the lodger (para 21.29) is disregarded and has no effect on the amount of their UC

2. HB if you have a lodger whose rent doesn't include meals

Henry and Lucy are on HB. They rent out a spare room to a lodger for £80 pw inclusive of fuel and water, but not meals.

- Their income from the lodger (para 21.29) is £80 minus £20, which is £60 pw.

3. HB if you have a lodger whose rent includes meals

Flora and Benny are on HB. They rent out a spare room to a lodger for £90 pw inclusive of fuel, water and meals.

- Their income from the lodger (para 21.29) is £90 minus £20, which is £70, the result being divided by two, which is £35 pw.

Rent from other property

21.30 There are two rules about rent you receive on property that isn't your home:

(a) the general rule is that the rent is disregarded as your income, and included as your capital after you have met the costs of the letting

(b) but in UC and working age HB only, if the property's capital value is itself disregarded (table 24.2), the rent counts as your unearned income after you have met the costs of the letting.

Government training allowances and sports funding awards

21.31 Allowances for taking part in a government training scheme and awards for sports funding are assessed as follows:

(a) amounts for your housing costs and living expenses count as your income

(b) amounts paid in place of UC count as your income

(c) all other amounts are disregarded in full for 52 weeks (training scheme) or 26 weeks (sports awards).

21.30 UC 66(1)(m), 72(3); PC 17(8), sch 4 para 18; HBW sch 5 para 17; HBP 29(1)(i), 33(11), sch 5 para 22; CTRE(PR) sch 1 paras 16(1)(i), 17(12); CTRE(DS) 39(1)(i), 40(12), sch 8 para 22

21.31 UC 66(1)(f),(g); HBW sch 5 paras 13, 59, sch 6 paras 35, 50; CTRE(DS) sch 8 paras 18, 61, sch 10 paras 39, 54

Table 21.3 **Student income: UC and working age HB**

(a) Student income if you get, or could get, a student loan

The following count as income:

- 30% of your student loan if you are on a postgraduate master's degree course
- All of your student loan if you are on an any other full-time advanced course
- Grants towards the maintenance of your partner or child
- Grants towards your rent payments

All other grants and learner support or hardship funds are disregarded.

(b) Student income if you can't get a student loan

The whole of any grant you get counts as income except for:

- Special support loans for students on means tested benefits
- Student fee loans
- Grants towards books, equipment, travel expenses, disability, childcare costs and tuition/examination fees
- Grants towards a home other than your term-time address
- Grants towards term-time residential study away from your educational establishment
- Grants towards anyone not in your benefit unit
- Bursary fund payments and educational maintenance allowances for 16-19 year olds in non-advanced education
- All learner support or hardship funds

Note: Reduced loans and grants

If your student loan or grant is reduced because your parent (or anyone else) is expected to contribute, the contribution is included whether or not they pay it. If it is increased for extra weeks, the increase is included. If you have chosen not to take a student loan (or to take a reduced amount), the full amount you could receive is included.

T21.3(a) UC 68(2),(3), 69(1),(1A), HBW 53(1) – 'grant income', 59(1),(6), 64(1),(4A); CTRE(DS) 73(1), 76(1),(6), 81(1),(6)

T21.3(b) UC 68(4), 70; HBW 59(2),(3), 64A, 64B, 65, sch 5 para 11, sch 6 para 51; CTRE(DS) 76(2),(3), 81(6), 82, sch 8 para 16, sch 10 para 55

T21.3 Note: UC 68(5), 69(2),70; HBW 53(1) – 'grant income', 59(7), 64(3),(4); CTRE(DS) 73(1), 76(7), 81(3),(4)

Student income

21.32 'Student income' means income from loans and grants. In SPC and pension age HB it is disregarded in full.

21.33 In UC, your annual student income is calculated as shown in table 21.3. Then:

(a) the resulting figure is averaged over however many of your UC assessment periods end within your current academic year (excluding the summer vacation or longest vacation unless it is for less than one month) and

(b) £110 is disregarded in each of those assessment periods.

21.34 In working age HB, your annual student income is calculated as shown in table 21.3. Then:

(a) £693 is disregarded from this annual amount

(b) the result is averaged over the weeks in your current academic year (excluding the summer vacation or longest vacation unless it is for less than one month) and

(c) If the income includes a loan, a further £10 is disregarded in each of those weeks.

Using other income towards your student expenses

21.35 In working age HB only, if your student expenditure exceeds what your loan or grant provides, the balance can be deducted from other income that is intended for this purpose. For example, this could apply if you take a job to cover your expenditure, but not to a job you would have regardless of being a student, nor to social security benefits (CIS/3107/2003).

Insurance payments

21.36 Insurance payments count as your income if they are paid under a policy you took out to insure yourself against losing income due to illness, accident or redundancy. But this only applies to UC and working age HB, and in working age HB it is limited to policies covering mortgage and loan repayments.

Personal injury payments

21.37 Payments of income that you receive for a personal injury are disregarded in full. This is restricted to payments for physical or mental injury, not injury to feelings (DR v SSWP).

21.32 UC 66(1)(e), 68(1); PC 15(1); HBW 53(1) – 'grant', 'grant income', 'standard maintenance grant', 'student loan'; HBP 29(1) CTRE(PR) sch 1 para 16(1); CTRE(DS) 39(1), 73(1)

21.33 UC 68(1),(7), 71

21.34 HBW 59(3), 64(2),(5); CTRE(DS) 76(3), 81(2),(5)

21.35 HBW 63; CTRE(DS) 80

21.36 SPCA 15(1); UC 66(1)(h); HBW sch 5 para 29; HBP 29(1); CTRE(PR) sch 1 para 16(1); CTRE(DS) 39(1), sch 8 para 35

21.37 UC 75; PC sch 4 paras 13, 14; HBW 41(5), sch 5 para 14(1); HBP sch 5 paras 14, 15; CTRE(PR) sch 5 paras 14, 15; CTRE(DS) 55(5), sch 6 paras 14, 15, sch 8 para 19(1) DR v SSWP (UC) [2024] UKUT 196 (AAC)

Income from trusts

21.38 Payments of income from a trust are assessed as follows:

(a) in UC and working age HB, they count as your income, unless the trust is made up of personal injury compensation in which case they are disregarded

(b) in SPC and pension age HB, they are disregarded in full, unless they are towards housing costs or living expenses, in which case only the first £20 is disregarded and the rest counts as your income.

Income from annuities

21.39 Payments of income from annuities count in full as your income, unless the annuity is made up of personal injury compensation in which case the payments are disregarded.

Income from equity release

21.40 In SPC and pension age HB, payments of income from equity release schemes count in full as your income. In UC they are disregarded as income but included in your capital. In working age HB, the law is not quite clear, but it appears that they count as income because there is no clear obligation to repay (R(IS) 6/03, R(H) 8/08).

Charitable and voluntary payments

21.41 Charitable and voluntary payments are disregarded in full. For example, these could be from a charity, family, or friends.

Local council discretionary welfare payments

21.42 The following discretionary welfare payments made by local councils are disregarded:

(a) discretionary housing payments (para 31.2)

(b) local welfare assistance payments (para 31.24) and

(c) payment for support services that aren't eligible for benefit (para 15.30).

Payments for disasters, emergencies, medical negligence and miscarriages of justice

21.43 Government-funded payments for disasters, emergencies, medical negligence, and miscarriages of injustice are disregarded in full. For example, these include payments resulting from the Post Office Horizon scandal, payments to Victims of Overseas Terrorism, Windrush payments, payments for historical child abuse and vaccine damage payments.

21.38 UC 66(1)(j); PC sch 4 para 11; HBW sch 5 para 14(1)(c); HBP sch 5 para 12; CTRE(PR) sch 5 para 12; CTRE(DS) sch 6 para 12, sch 8 para 19(1)(c)

21.39 SPCA 15(1)(d), 16(1)(h)-(j); UC 46(3), 66(1)(i); HBW 41(2), sch 5 para 14(1)(d); HBP 29(1)(d), 33(11), sch 5 paras 14, 15, sch 6 para 29 CTRE(PR) sch 1 paras 16(1)(d), 17(12), sch 5 paras 14, 15, sch 6 para 32;
CTRE(DS) 39(1)(d), 40(12), 55(2), sch 6 paras 14, 15, sch 8 para 19(1)(d), sch 9 para 32

21.40 UC 46(3); PC 1(2) – 'equity release scheme', 15(1)(j); HBP 29(1)(w),(8); CTRE(PR) sch 1 para 16(1)(w),(5)(a); CTRE(DS) 39(1)(w),(5)

21.41 SPCA 15(1); UC 66(1); HBW sch 5 para 14(1)(a),(b); HBP 29(1); CTRE(PR) sch 1 para 16(1); CTRE(DS) 39(1), sch 8 para 19(1)(a),(b)

21.42 SPCA 15(1); UC 66(1); HBW sch 5 paras 31A, 62, 63; HBP 29(1); CTRE(PR) sch 1 para 16(1); CTRE(DS) sch 8 paras 37, 64, 65

21.43 SPCA 15(1); UC 66(1), 76; PC sch 5 paras 13, 15; HBW sch 5 para 35, sch 6 para 24, 34, 55, 63; HBP 29(1), sch 6 paras 14, 16, 26I
CTRE(PR) sch 1 para 16(1), sch 6 paras 14, 16, 16A; CTRE(DS) sch 8 para 41, sch 9 paras 14, 16, 16A, sch 10 paras 29, 38, 59, 67

Royalties, copyright and patent payments

21.44 Royalties, copyright, patent and similar payments are included as part of your income. They count as:

(a) earned income if you are the first owner of the right to receive them (e.g. you are the writer of a book) or

(b) unearned income if you are anyone else (e.g. you have inherited the right to receive them).

In working age HB, (a) is usually counted as part of your self-employed income (table 23.1). In SPC and pension age HB, the law spells out the distinction between (a) and (b), and the payments are normally assumed to be annual and averaged over a year. For UC, the distinction between (a) and (b) is less clear; and when the payments are earnings it appears they are taken into account in full in the month in which you receive them, but when they are unearned income it appears they are assumed to be annual and averaged over a year.

Income available on application

21.45 You are counted as having unearned income equal to any amount that would be available to you if you applied for it. In UC and working age HB this applies to any income that is counted for benefit purposes, but not normally social security benefits (HBGM BW2.680, 682) and in the case of working age HB not occupational or private pensions (para 21.23). In SPC and pension age HB it only applies to retirement pension income. Income included because of this rule is sometimes called 'notional income'.

21.44 UC 66(1)(m), 73(2),(3); PC 15(5)(f), 17(4),(5)(9)(b),(9A); HBW 37(3),(4); HBP 29(1)(q),(r), 33(4),(5),(8),(8A) CTRE(PR) sch 1 paras 16(1)(q),(r), 17(5),(6),(9),(10); CTRE(DS) 39(1)(q),(r), 40(5),(6),(9),(10), 53(3),(4)

21.45 UC 74; PC 18; HBW 42(2); HBP 41; CTRE(PR) sch 1 para 22; CTRE(DS) 45, 56(2)

Chapter 22 **Employed earnings**

- General rules about employed earnings: paras 22.1-7
- Assessment rules in UC: paras 22.8-17
- Assessment rules in SPC and HB: paras 22.18-23
- Reclaim periods and surplus earnings in UC: paras 22.24-26
- The work allowance and earnings disregards: paras 22.27-30

General rules

Earned income

22.1 Earned income means:

(a) employed earnings as described in this chapter

(b) self-employed earnings as described in chapter 23 and

(c) any other paid work (for example if you are paid for a one-off job).

What are employed earnings

22.2 Employed earnings mean:

(a) earnings you receive under an employment contract (wages, salary, etc)

(b) earnings you receive because you hold an office, e.g. as a company director, councillor or member of clergy and

(c) earnings from any other paid work (work for which payment is made or expected).

22.3 The assessment of your benefit takes into account your own earnings if you are single, or your and your partner's earnings if you are in a couple (paras 21.3-4). But if you are on any of the passport benefits (table 18.1), the whole of your income and capital (including earnings) is disregarded in the assessment of HB.

Calculating employed earnings

22.4 Employed earnings are assessed after deducting tax, national insurance etc, and a work allowance or earnings disregards if you qualify. Table 22.1 and tables 22.3-6 give the details.

22.1 SPCA 17(1) – 'earnings'; UC 2 – 'earned income', 55(1), 57(1); PC 17A(1), 17B(1); HBW 2(1) – 'earnings', 35(1), 37(1); HBP 2(1), 35(1), 38(1) CTRE(PR) 2(1), sch 1 paras 18(1), 21(1); CTRE(DS) 2(1), 41(1), 44(1), 51(1), 53(1)

22.2 SSCBA 2(1)(a); UC 52; PC 17A(5); HBW 2(1) – 'employed earner'; HBP 2(1); CTRE(PR) 2(1); CTRE(DS) 2(1)

22.3 WRA 5(2); SPCA 5; SSCBA 136(1); UC 22(1); PC 14; HBW 25(1); HBP 23(1); CTRE(PR) sch 1 para 11(1),(2); CTRE(DS) 33(1),(2)

22.4 UC 22(1), 55(5); PC 17(9)(a),(10), 17A(4A); HBW 36(1)-(3); HBP 36(1),(2); CTRE(PR) sch 1 para 19(1),(2); CTRE(DS) 42(1),(2), 52(1)-(3)

Table 22.1 **Employed earnings**

(a) Amounts that are included

These count as employed earnings:

- Your wages or salary
- Statutory sick, maternity, paternity, adoption and parental bereavement pay
- Taxable expenses, e.g. for travel between home and work
- Tax and national insurance refunds made through PAYE (in UC only) (SK v SSWP)
- Councillor's allowances (ADM H3038-3049)
- Holiday pay, retainers, bonuses, commission and tips
- Payments in lieu of notice
- Surplus earnings (para 22.24)

(b) Amounts that are deducted

These are deducted from the total of (a):

- Your income tax and national insurance contributions
- Your tax-deductible pension contributions (in UC)
- Half of your tax-deductible pension contributions (in SPC and HB)
- Tax-deductible donations you make under a payroll giving scheme (in UC only)
- A work allowance in UC or earnings disregards in SPC and HB if you qualify for them (tables 22.3-6)

(c) Amounts that aren't included

These don't count as employed earnings:

- Non-taxable expenses, e.g. for travel between workplaces
- Employee benefits, e.g. free use of your employer's facilities
- Tax and national insurance refunds (in SPC and HB)
- Redundancy payments (in most cases these count as part of your capital)
- Charitable or voluntary payments
- Expenses you are paid to take part in a service user group
- Bounty payments for part-time fire-fighters and lifeboat workers, auxiliary coastguards and members of the territorial army or similar reserve forces

T22.1(a) UC 55(2)-(4),(4A); PC 17A(2)(a)-(k); HBW 35(1)(a)-(k); HBP 35(1)(a)-(k); CTRE(PR) sch 1 para 18(1)(a)-(m); CTRE(DS) 41(1)(a)-(k), 51(1)(a)-(l)

T22.1(b) UC 55(5); PC 17(10), 17A(4A); HBW 36(2),(3); HBP 36(1),(2); CTRE(PR) sch 1 para 19(1),(2); CTRE(DS) 42(1),(2), 52(2),(3)

T22.1(c) UC 55(2),(3); PC 17(9)(a), 17A(3),(5); HBW 35(1)(b),(2), 36(2), 46(1), sch 4 paras 1, 2; HBP 35(1)(b),(2) CTRE(PR) sch 1 para 18(1)(b),(2); CTRE(DS) 41(1)(b),(2), 51(1)(b),(2), 52(2), 64(2), sch 7 paras 1, 2, 9

If you are paid less than the going rate

22.5 If you work for less than the going rate for local comparable services or for nothing, you can be counted as having employed or self-employed earnings equal to the going rate. But this doesn't apply to work that is:

(a) for a charitable or voluntary organisation if it is reasonable to provide the services cheaper or free

(b) for someone who doesn't have the means to pay or to pay more or

(c) part of a government training programme.

Depriving yourself of earnings

22.6 If you arrange to receive lower employed earnings in order to get UC or more UC (or your employer arranges this), the DWP can treat you as having the earnings that you have deprived yourself of.

Trade disputes

22.7 If you are in a trade dispute:

(a) in UC, you are treated as receiving whatever employed earnings you would have apart from the dispute

(b) in working age HB, (a) doesn't apply (LB Ealing v Saville) but any strike pay you receive is included as unearned income

(c) in SPC and pension age HB, (a) and (b) don't apply.

Assessment rules in UC

22.8 Each assessment period is one month (para 32.23). In each assessment period, the UC calculation uses your current actual earnings and deductions for that month – whereas other benefits use an average based on a past period.

22.9 This means that the earnings you receive in a particular assessment period:

(a) are used to calculate your UC in that assessment period and

(b) affect the amount of UC you are paid seven days after that assessment period ends.

You need to report changes in earnings promptly to make sure you don't get less UC than you should.

22.5 UC 60(3),(4); HBW 42(9),(10); CTRE(DS) 56(6),(7)

22.6 UC 60(1),(2)

22.7 UC 56; PC 15(5) 18(1); HBW 35(1), 40(1); HBP 29(1), 41(1) CTRE(PR) sch 1 para 11(1); CTRE(DS) 39(1), 41(1), 45(1), 51(1), 54(1)
R v LB Ealing HBRB ex p Saville (1986) 18 HLR 349 (QBD)

22.8 UC 54(1), 61(2)

22.9 UC 54(1)

Monthly earnings and shifted pay days

22.10 If you are paid monthly, your UC assessment periods nearly always contain exactly one pay day. But if your payment date is shifted (e.g. to avoid a weekend or bank holiday) you may receive two payments in the same UC assessment period. In this case, the DWP should reallocate the shifted payment to ensure only one payment is taken into account in each of your assessment periods (ADM memo 27/20). The DWP doesn't apply the rule automatically, so you normally need to ask it to do so each time this situation arises.

Weekly, fortnightly and four-weekly earnings

22.11 Your UC assessment periods contain:

(a) four pay days if you are paid weekly, or five in some months

(b) two pay days if you are paid fortnightly, or three in some months

(c) one pay day if you are paid four-weekly, or two in some months.

The courts have decided this is not irrational (R (Pantellerisco and others) v SSWP; SSWP v LM).

22.12 Your UC is lower or nil in months with an extra pay day. If it is nil, you get a six-month UC reclaim period, during which you can get UC as soon as you qualify again (typically the following month), and in some cases you may have surplus earnings (paras 22.24-26).

Examples: Employed earnings and UC

1. Making a claim for UC while working

Alishea realises she can get UC while she is working. She makes a UC claim on 10 September, so her first assessment period is the month from 10 September to 9 October.

- Alishea's UC for the month from 10 September to 9 October is calculated using the earnings she receives in that month, and is paid on 17 October.

2. Changes in earnings while on UC

Rhys is working and on UC. His UC assessment periods start on the 14th of each month and his earnings vary every month.

- Rhys's UC for the month from 14 March to 13 April is calculated using the earnings he receives in that month, and is paid on 21 April.
- His UC for the month from 14 April to 13 May is calculated using the earnings he receives in that month, and is paid on 21 May.
- And so on.

22.10 UC 61(6)

22.11 UC 61(2)
R (Pantellerisco and others) v SSWP [2021] EWCA Civ 1454, [2021] PTSR 1922, [2021] WLR(D) 513
SSWP v LM [2023] UKUT 72 (AAC)

22.12 UC 54A(1); UC(C&P) 32A

Starting a new job while you are on UC

22.13 If you start a job while you are on UC:

(a) your first earnings are used to calculate your UC in the assessment period containing the day you receive them

(b) they affect the amount of UC you are paid seven days after that assessment period ends.

If the level of your wages or salary means you stop qualifying for UC, you don't get UC in the assessment period containing the day you receive your first earnings.

Leaving a job while you are on UC

22.14 If you leave a job while you are on UC:

(a) your final wages or salary are used to calculate your UC in the assessment period containing the day you receive them

(b) they affect the amount of UC you are paid seven days after that assessment period ends.

Examples: Starting and leaving a job while on UC

1. Starting a job while on UC – monthly earnings

Tobias is on UC and his UC assessment periods start on the 8th of each month. He starts work on 1 June and is paid monthly. His first earnings are paid on 25 June.

- The earnings Tobias receives on 25 June are used in the calculation of UC for the assessment period running from 10 June to 9 July.
- So his UC goes down (to a lower amount or nil) on 15 July.

2. Starting a job while on UC – weekly earnings

Molly is on UC and her UC assessment periods start on the 12th of each month. She starts work on 24 June and is paid once a week.

- The earnings Molly receives during the assessment period running from 12 June to 11 July are used in the calculation of UC for that assessment period.
- So her UC goes down (to a lower amount or nil) on 19 July.

3. Leaving a job while on UC

Evanna is working and on UC. Her UC assessment periods start on the 5th of each month. She leaves work on 20 June and receives her last earnings on that day.

- The earnings Evanna receives during the assessment period that runs from 5 June to 4 July affect the amount of UC she is paid on 12 July.
- She receives no earnings during the assessment period running from 5 July to 4 August, so her UC goes up on 12 August.

22.13-14 UC 54(1)

Arrears of earnings

22.15 If you receive a payment of employed earnings for a past period (e.g. arrears following a pay rise) it is taken into account in the UC assessment period in which you receive it (NM v SSWP; LP v SSWP).

Information about your earnings

22.16 The DWP gets details of your earnings from HMRC through the Real Time Information System (RTI), and uses these to calculate your UC. If you disagree with HMRC's figures, you can ask the DWP to look at this. The DWP calls this an 'RTI dispute'. If the DWP tells you it can't use the HMRC arrangements, you need to report your earnings to the DWP each month.

Estimating earnings

22.17 The DWP can estimate your employed earnings if your employer (or you) provide unreliable information or no information, or are late providing information (SSWP v RW).

Assessment rules in SPC and HB

The period earnings relate to

22.18 Your employed earnings are taken into account in the period they relate to, based on an average over a reference period that gives a fair and accurate weekly amount.

22.19 When you first claim SPC or pension age HB, the DWP or council uses your current pay if you work regular hours and your pay is stable. Otherwise, they average your payments over:

(a) one complete cycle if your work follows a cycle (for example you work two weeks on, one week off) or

(b) the most recent two months (if you are paid monthly) or four weeks (if you are paid weekly).

22.20 When you first claim working age HB, the council averages your payments over the most recent two months (if you are paid monthly) or five weeks (if you are paid weekly), or in either case it can choose a more representative period. If you haven't been employed for two months or five weeks and haven't yet been paid, the council can ask you to get an estimate from your employer.

22.15 UC 54(1)
NM v SSWP (UC) [2021] UKUT 46 (AAC)
LP v SSWP (UC) [2018] UKUT 332 (AAC)

22.16 UC 61(2)

22.17 UC 61(3),(4),(5)
SSWP v RW (rule 17) (UC) [2017] UKUT 347 (AAC)

22.18 PC 17(1); HBW 29A; HBP 33(2A),(3A); CTRE(PR) sch 1 para 17(3A),(4A)

22.19 PC 17(1),(2); HBP 33(1),(2); CTRE(PR) sch 1 para 17(1)-(3); CTRE(DS) 40(1)-(3)

22.20 HBW 29(1),(2); CTRE(DS) 47(1),(2)

22.21 Your earnings are reassessed at regular intervals (often annually) or when there is a change in your earnings, for example when you change jobs.

Information about your earnings

22.22 If you are claiming SPC or HB, you need to report your employed earnings to the DWP or council. You should do this when you first claim, when your earnings change, and at other times if you are asked to.

Arrears of earnings

22.23 If you receive a payment of employed earnings for a past period, it is taken into account in the (past) weeks the payment relates to. This usually means that you have been overpaid SPC or HB (paras 36.9-10).

Reclaim periods and surplus earnings in UC

When does the surplus earnings rule apply

22.24 The surplus earnings rule only applies during the six-month reclaim period you get when you stop qualifying for UC because your earnings are too high. During a re-claim period, your UC is kept open for six months in case you become entitled to UC (para 33.35).

Information about earnings during the reclaim period

22.25 If you have employed earnings, HMRC continues to provide the DWP with details about them during the reclaim period. If you are self-employed, you should continue to provide the DWP with details of your earnings. This means that if you become entitled to UC, you can reclaim UC using your journal rather than having to make a full claim.

How surplus earnings are calculated and carried forward

22.26 Your surplus earnings are calculated and carried forward as described in table 22.2. But surplus earnings are never carried forward if you are a recent victim of domestic violence (table 4.1(l)).

22.21 SS(D&A) 6(2)(a); HB(D&A) 7(2)(a); CTRE(PR) sch 1 para 46(8),(9); CTRE(DS) 107(8),(9)

22.22 SS(C&P) 7(1); SS(D&A) 16(1),(3), 17(4); HBW 86(1), 88(1); HBP 67(1), 69(1); HB(D&A) 11; CTRE(PR) sch 8 paras 7(4), 9(1),(2); CTRE(DS) 113(4), 115(1),(2)

22.23 SPCA 17 – 'earnings'; SI 1996/2745 reg 7; HBW 29A; HBP 33(2A),(3A); CTRE(PR) sch 1 para 17(3A),(4A)

22.24 UC 54A(1); UC(C&P) 32A(1)

22.25 UC 54A(2), 61(2); UC(C&P) 32A(2)

22.26 UC 54A(5)

Example: Surplus earnings in UC

Roger is on UC. His only income is from employed earnings. He earns the same amount each month and also gets an annual bonus. In a month with no bonus, he qualifies for UC of £123.45. This year, his annual bonus is £3,200 (after deductions for tax and national insurance).

- The income from the bonus is taken into account in his assessment period containing the date it is paid. In that assessment period he doesn't qualify for UC, but does qualify for a reclaim period during which his surplus earnings are carried forward as follows (table 22.2).
- In the first month, £224.45 of the bonus is needed to reduce his UC to nil (because 55% of £224.45 is £123.45), so £2,975.55 of his bonus is unused. Deducting the allowance of £2,500 leaves £475.55 to carry forward as surplus earnings.
- In the second month, £224.45 of the carried forward surplus earnings is needed to reduce his UC to nil, so £251.10 of his bonus is unused. Deducting the allowance of £2,500 leaves nil to carry forward as surplus earnings.
- In the third month, he has no surplus earnings, so he gets UC of £123.45.

The work allowance and earnings disregards

22.27 The work allowance or earnings disregards are deducted from your earned income (whether from employment or self-employment or both). If you are in a couple, they are deducted from your combined earnings (even if you are claiming as a single person (para 2.9).

22.28 The deductions can be described as the amounts you are allowed to 'keep' before your earned income affects the amount of your benefit.

The UC work allowance

22.29 If you are claiming UC you may qualify for a work allowance (table 22.3).

The SPC and HB earnings disregards

22.30 If you are claiming HB you may qualify for:

(a) a standard disregard (table 22.4)

(b) an additional disregard (table 22.6)

(c) a childcare disregard (table 22.5).

If you are claiming SPC, you only qualify for (a).

22.27 UC 22(1)(b); PC 17(9)(a); HBW 36(2), 38(2); HBP 33(8)(a); CTRE(PR) sch 1 para 17(9); CTRE(DS) 40(9), 52(2), 61(2)

22.29 UC 22(1)(b)

22.30 PC 17(9)(a), sch 6; HBW 27(1)(c), 36(2), 38(2), sch 4; HBP 30(1)(c), 33(8)(a), sch 4
CTRE(PR) sch 1 paras 17(9), 24(1),(c), sch 4; CTRE(DS) 40(9), 52(2), 57(1)(c), 61(2), sch 5, sch 7

Example: Earnings and the UC work allowance

Penny is single and claiming UC. She is over 25 and has one child. Her monthly eligible rent is £600. Her employed earnings (after deductions for tax and national insurance) are £1,035 pcm. She qualifies for a work allowance of £411 (table 22.3) and this leaves £624 pcm. Penny's monthly UC is calculated as follows.

■ Standard allowance	£400.14
■ Plus child element (higher rate)	£339.00
■ Plus housing costs element (eligible rent)	£600.00
■ Equals maximum UC	£1339.14
■ Deduction for earned income £624 × 55%	– £343.20
■ Amount of Penny's monthly UC	£995.94

Example: Earnings and the HB earnings disregards

Rosa is single and on HB. Her only income is from employed earnings of £366.30 pw, from which her employer deducts £34.88 for tax and national insurance and £12.32 as a pension contribution. Rosa qualifies for a standard earnings disregard (table 22.4) and her weekly earnings are calculated as follows.

■ Gross earnings	£366.30
■ Minus tax and national insurance	– £34.88
■ Minus half the pension contribution	– £6.16
■ Minus standard earnings disregard	– £5.00
■ Amount of Rosa's weekly net earnings	£320.26

Table 22.2 **Surplus earnings**

This table explains how to assess surplus earnings during the six-month re-claim period that follows a break in your UC because your earnings were too high.

(a) Calculate 'surplus earnings' in the first month you don't qualify for UC

- Start with your monthly earned income.
- Deduct the work allowance if you qualify for one (table 22.3).
- Deduct your 'nil UC threshold' (see below).
- Deduct an allowance of £2,500.
- Any remaining earnings count as surplus earnings.

(b) Carry forward surplus earnings to next month

- Add your surplus earnings to your earned income (if any) in the next month.
- Deduct the work allowance if you qualify for one.
- Calculate UC using the resultant amount (paras 16.2-5) to see whether you now qualify.
- If you do qualify, you are awarded UC (and you no longer have surplus earnings).
- If you don't, repeat steps (a) and (b) until the end of the six-month review period.

(c) The nil UC threshold

- Start with your maximum UC (para 16.2).
- Deduct unearned income (if any).
- Work out how much earned income is needed, so that 55% of it exactly reduces your UC to nil.
- This amount of earned income is your nil UC threshold.

T22.2 UC 54A(3),(4),(6); SI 2015/345 reg 5; House of Commons Deposited Paper DEP2025-0134

Table 22.3 **The UC work allowance 2025-26**

Conditions

This allowance only applies to UC. You qualify if you are working (employed or self-employed) and:

(a) you have at least one child or young person in your benefit unit or

(b) you have limited capability for work (LCW or LCWRA) (para 4.15) or are in a couple and at least one of you does.

Amount

Lower rate: £411 per month

- Renters in general accommodation
- Renters in temporary accommodation (table 13.2)
- Shared owners
- Owners who qualify for a housing costs element (para 16.32)

Higher rate: £684 per month

- Renters in supported accommodation (table 13.1(a)-(d))
- Owners who don't qualify for a housing costs element (para 16.32)
- People with no housing costs

T22.3 UC 22(1)(b),(2); UCTP 5A; SI 2025/295 reg 32

Table 22.4 **The SPC/HB standard earnings disregard**

Conditions and amounts

Everyone who has earned income qualifies for this disregard in SPC or HB. You qualify for the first amount you meet the conditions for, or if you are in a couple, at least one of you meets the conditions for.

(a) 'Permitted work': £195.50 per week (HB only)

You qualify if you or your partner:

- get new style ESA, ESA credits, or severe disablement allowance and
- are doing work the DWP has approved (e.g. you are trying out your ability to work).

(b) Lone parents: £25 per week in HB, £20 per week in SPC

You qualify if you are a lone parent.

(c) Sickness or disability: £20 per week

The main conditions are that you qualify if you or your partner:

- get a disability premium (para 18.26)
- would get a disability premium except that you are over pension age
- get a severe disability premium (para 18.20) or
- get main phase ESA or ESA credits (in HB only).

(d) Carers: £20 per week

You qualify if you or your partner get carer's allowance or a carer premium in your SPC or HB (para 18.18).

(e) Special occupations: £20 per week

You qualify if you or your partner are a part-time fire-fighter or lifeboat worker, auxiliary coastguard or member of the territorial army or similar reserve forces.

(f) Others: couples £10 per week, single people £5 per week

You qualify if none of (a)-(e) apply.

T22.4 PC 17(9)(a); HBW 36(2), 38(2); HBP 33(8)(a), sch 4 para 1(a)

T22.4(a) HBW sch 4 para 10A; HBP sch 4 para 5A; CTRE(PR) sch 4 para 6; CTRE(DS) sch 5 para 6, sch 7 para 12

T22.4(b) PC sch 6 para 1; HBW sch 4 para 4; HBP sch 4 para 2; CTRE(PR) sch 4 para 2; CTRE(DS) sch 5 para 2, sch 7 para 5

T22.4(c) PC sch 6 paras 4, 4A; HBW sch 4 para 3; HBP sch 4 para 5; CTRE(PR) sch 4 para 5; CTRE(DS) sch 5 para 5, sch 7 para 4

T22.4(d) PC sch 6 para 3; HBW sch 4 paras 5, 6; HBP sch 4 para 4; CTRE(PR) sch 4 para 4; CTRE(DS) sch 5 para 4, sch 7 paras 6, 7

T22.4(e) PC sch 6 paras 2, 2A, 2B; HBW sch 4 paras 8, 9; CTRE(DS) sch 7 paras 9, 10

T22.4(f) PC sch 6 para 5; HBW sch 4 paras 9, 10; HBP sch 4 para 7; CTRE(PR) sch 4 para 7; CTRE(DS) sch 5 para 8, sch 7 paras 10, 11

Table 22.5 **The HB childcare earnings disregard**

Conditions

This disregard only applies to HB, not SPC. You qualify if you meet the following conditions or are in a couple and at least one of you does.

(a) You or your partner pay childcare charges to:

- a registered childminder, out-of-school-hours scheme or other recognised provider or
- someone who provides the childcare in your home, but not if they are your partner or the child's relative (para 10.30).

(b) The charges are for at least one child in your benefit unit who hasn't yet reached:

- the first Monday in September following their 15th birthday or
- if they meet the conditions for a disabled child premium (para 18.14), the first Monday in September following their 16th birthday.

(c) If you are single, you work at least 16 hours per week (every week or on average).

(d) If you are in a couple, one of you works at least 16 hours per week and the other:

- also works at least 16 hours per week or
- has a limited capability for work (para 4.15) or
- gets a disability premium (para 18.26) or
- would get a disability premium except for being over pension age.

Amount

(e) The disregard equals the weekly amount of childcare charges you pay, up to a maximum of:

- £175 per week if the charges are for one child
- £300 per week if the charges are for two or more children.

Note: This disregard applies even when the care is not being provided due to the illness of the carer or the child, so long as the care is expected to resume (Carmarthenshire County Council v LT).

T22.5(a) HBW 28(8); HBP 31(8); CTRE(PR) sch 1 para 25(8); CTRE(DS) 58(8)

T22.5(b) HBW 28(6); HBP 31(6); CTRE(PR) sch 1 para 25(6); CTRE(DS) 58(6)

T22.5(c) HBW 28(1)(a); HBP 31(1)(a); CTRE(PR) sch 1 para 25(1)(a); CTRE(DS) 58(1)(a)

T22.5(d) HBW 28(1),(b),(c),(11); HBP 31(1)(b),(c),(11); CTRE(PR) sch 1 para 25(1)(b),(c),(10); CTRE(DS) 58(1)(b),(c),(11)

T22.5(e) HBW 27(1)(c),(3), HBP 30(1)(c),(3); CTRE(PR) sch 1 para 24(1)(c),(3); CTRE(DS) 57(1)(c),(3)

T22.5 (note) Carmarthenshire County Council v LT [2022] UKUT 224 (AAC)

Table 22.6 **The HB additional earnings disregard**

Conditions and amount

This disregard only applies to HB, not SPC. You qualify if you meet at least one of the following conditions or are in a couple and at least one of you does. The amount is £17.10 per week in all cases.

(a) You or your partner are aged 25 or more and work at least 30 hours per week

(b) You or your partner work at least 16 hours per week and have at least one child or young person in your benefit unit

(c) You or your partner work at least 16 hours per week and:

- get a support component (para 18.31) or
- have a limited capability for work (para 4.15) or
- get a disability premium (para 18.26) or
- would get a disability premium except for being over pension age.

T22.6 HBW sch 4 para 17; HBP sch 4 para 9; CTRE(PR) sch 4 para 10; CTRE(DS) sch 5 para 10, sch 7 para 18

Chapter 23 **Self-employed earnings**

- General rules about self-employed earnings: paras 23.1-5
- Business expenses: paras 23.6-12
- Assessment rules in UC: paras 23.13-17
- Assessment rules in SPC and HB: paras 23.18-19
- The UC minimum income floor: paras 23.20-25

General rules

What are self-employed earnings

23.1 Self-employed earnings mean earnings from any kind of trade, profession or vocation in which you are aren't employed by someone else. You can be self-employed as a sole trader or in a partnership.

23.2 The assessment of your benefit takes into account your own earnings if you are single, or your and your partner's earnings if you are in a couple (paras 21.3-4), and in some cases can include illegal earnings (SSWP v MA). But if you are on any of the passport benefits (table 18.1), the whole of your income and capital (including earnings) is disregarded in HB.

Calculating self-employed earnings

23.3 Self-employed earnings are assessed after deducting business expenses, tax, national insurance etc, and a work allowance or earnings disregards if you qualify. See table 23.1.

Table 23.1 **Self-employed earnings**

Your self-employed earnings equal the total of the amounts in (a) minus the total of the amounts in (b).

(a) Amounts that counted as your income

- Your business receipts
- Payments in kind to your business (this means in goods, not money)
- Royalties, copyright, patent and similar payments when they are paid as part of your business

Table continued ➤

23.1 SSCBA 2(1)(b); UC 53(1) – 'self-employed earnings', 57(1); PC 17(1) – 'earnings'; HBW 2(1) 'self-employed earner', 37(1); HBP 2(1), 38(1) CTRE(PR) 2(1), sch 1 para 21(1); CTRE(DS) 2(1), 44(1), 53(1)

23.2 WRA 5(2); SPCA 5; SSCBA 136(1); UC 22(1)(b); PC 14; HBW 25(1); HBP 23(1); CTRE(PR) sch 1 para 11(1),(2); CTRE(DS) 33(1),(2) SSWP v MA [2024] UKUT 131 (AAC)

23.3 UC 57(2), 58, 59; PC 17(10),(11), 17B(1),(5),(6); HBW 38, 39; HBP 39, 40; CTRE(PR) sch 1 para 29, 30; CTRE(DS) 61, 62

- the value of assets you sell or stop using for your business (if you earlier claimed them as an expense)
- Surplus earnings (para 22.24)

(b) Amounts that are deducted from your income

- Your allowable business expenses
- Your income tax and national insurance contributions (para 23.4)
- Your tax-deductible pension contributions (in UC)
- Half of your tax-deductible pension contributions (in SPC and HB)
- A work allowance (in UC) if you qualify for it (table 22.3)
- Earnings disregards (in SPC and HB) if you qualify for them (tables 22.4-6)

Notes:

- Only your actual earnings and expenses are used, not 'drawings' (money you choose to take from your business) (ADM H4168-70)
- Only earnings you have received are included in (a), not earnings you are owed (until it is paid) (ADM H4158)
- Loans and capital payments aren't included in (a) – they count as capital instead
- If you are liable for VAT, you can choose whether to include VAT in both (a) and (b), or to exclude VAT from both (ADM H4125-26)
- The rules about surplus earnings, the UC work allowance and the SPC/HB earnings disregards are the same for self-employed people as they are for employed people (chapter 22).

Income tax and national insurance contributions

23.4 In SPC and HB, the DWP/council calculates your liability for income tax and NICs as follows (this is called a 'notional' amount because it can differ from what HMRC charges you):

(a) start with your total annual self-employed earnings (table 23.1(a))
(b) deduct your allowable annual business expenses para 23.6)
(c) deduct £12,570 (the income tax personal allowance) to give your 'taxable income'
(d) your liability for tax is 20% of your taxable income
(e) your class 4 NICs are 6% of your taxable income (class 2 NICs were abolished from 6 April 2024).

In UC, the DWP uses the actual amount of tax and NICs you pay (para 23.16).

T23.1(a) UC 57(2),(4),(5); PC 17(9A), 17B(1),(3),(4); HBW 30(2), 37(1),(3); HBP 33(8A), 38(1) CTRE(PR) sch 1 paras 17(10), 21(1); CTRE(DS) 40(10), 44(1), 48(2), 53(1),(3),(4)

T23.1(b) UC 22(1)(b),(2), 57(2); PC 17B(1),(5)(a),(6); HBW 38(1)-(3); HBP 33(8),(8A), 39(1),(2) CTRE(PR) sch 1 paras 17(9),(10) 29(1),(2); CTRE(DS) 40(9),(10), 61(1)-(3)

T23.1(note) UC 57(2),(4),(5), 58(2); PC 17B(1),(5)(b); HBW 37(1), 38(6),(8)(b); HBP 38(1), 39(5),(7)(b) CTRE(PR) sch 1 paras 21(1), 29(5),(7)(b); CTRE(DS) 44(1), 53(1), 61(6),(8)(b)

23.4 UC 55(5); PC 17(10), 17B(5),(6); HBW 39; HBP 40; CTRE(PR) sch 1 para 30; CTRE(DS) 62

Example: Assessing self-employed earnings

Lesley is a self-employed plumber on UC. She provides the following information for a particular month. She used her van wholly for business purposes and all her expenses are allowable. So her self-employed earnings are calculated as follows (tables 23.1, 23.2):

■ Income received	£2,492
■ Minus the following expenses	
■ Use of van	– £314
■ Buying in stock for use in trade	– £170
■ Payment to sub-contractor	– £80
■ Telephone, postage, stationery	– £76
■ Advertising, subscriptions	– £42
■ Business use of home (para 23.10)	– £18
■ Tax/NI paid to HMRC	– £68
■ Amount of Lesley's monthly self-employed earnings	£1,724

If you are paid less than the going rate

23.5 In UC and working age HB if you work for less than the going rate for local comparable services or for nothing, you can be counted as having self-employed earnings equal to the going rate. But this doesn't apply to work that is:

(a) for a charitable or voluntary organisation if it is reasonable to provide the services cheaper or free

(b) for someone who doesn't have the means to pay or to pay more

(c) part of a government training programme.

Business expenses

23.6 Business expenses are allowable if:

(a) they are wholly and exclusively incurred for your business

(b) they aren't unreasonable (e.g. they aren't excessive) and

(c) they aren't excluded.

Table 23.2 summarises which business expenses are allowable and which are not.

23.5 UC 52(b), 60; HBW 27(4), 42(9)-(11); CTRE(PR) sch 1 para 30; CTRE(DS) 62

23.6 UC 58(1),(3); PC 17B(5)(b); HBW 38(3)(a),(8)(a); HBP 39(2)(a),(7)(a); CTRE(DS) 56(6)-(9)

Table 23.2 **Self-employed business expenses**

(a) Amounts that are allowable

- Advertising and subscriptions to trade and professional bodies
- Computer, telephone, postage, stationery and delivery costs
- Transport and vehicle costs and hire and leasing charges
- Materials, supplies, stock and protective clothing
- Bank charges, insurance costs, and accountancy and legal fees
- Staff costs and payments to subcontractors
- Premises costs, e.g. rent, rates and fuel
- An amount for working from home
- Setting up and expansion costs (in UC only)
- Capital repayments on loans for repairs and replacements (in SPC and HB)
- Interest you pay on any business loans, but in UC only this is limited to £41 per month
- Unused losses (in UC only) (para 23.7)

(b) Amounts that are excluded

- Setting up and expansion costs (in SPC and HB)
- Capital repayments on any loan (except as in (a))
- Expenditure on non-depreciating assets
- Depreciation
- Business entertainment

Unused losses

23.7 'Unused losses' are allowable business expenses that:

(a) you haven't yet claimed in your UC and

(b) you incurred during your current UC award, during a break in your UC no longer than six months, or during a UC award prior to such a gap.

Expenses for mixed purposes

23.8 If you have expenses which are partly for business and partly for private purposes, you can only claim for your business use. Paras 23.9-12 give special rules that can apply. In all other cases, you need to make a calculation or estimate.

T23.2(a) UC 58(1),(2),(3A); PC 17B(5)(b); HBW 38(4),(6),(8)(b); HBP 39(3),(5),(7)(b); CTRE(PR) sch 1 para 29(3),(5),(7)(b); CTRE(DS) 61(4),(6),(8)(b)

T23.2(b) UC 58(3); PC 17B(5)(b); HBW 38(5); HBP 39(4); CTRE(PR) sch 1 para 29(4); CTRE(DS) 61(5)

23.7 UC 57A; CTRSW 52

23.8 UC 58(1); CTRSW 53

UC allowance for use of motor vehicle

23.9 This monthly UC allowance is:

(a) for use of a car or van: 45p per mile for the first 833 miles, plus 25p per mile after that

(b) for use of a motorcycle: 24p per mile.

In the case of a car, you can claim this allowance but you can't make your own calculation or estimate. In the case of a van or motorbike, you can either claim the allowance or make your own calculation or estimate.

UC allowance for business use of your home

23.10 This monthly UC allowance depends on the number of hours you spend at home on income-generating activities in that month. It is:

(a) for at least 25 hours: £10

(b) for more than 50 hours: £18 or

(c) for more than 100 hours: £26

You can either claim this allowance or make your own calculation or estimate.

UC disallowance for personal use of business premises

23.11 This monthly UC disallowance applies to premises you mainly use for business purposes but also occupy for personal use (e.g. your business is running a care home and you live there or stay there):

(a) if only you occupy the premises: £350

(b) if you and one other person do so: £500

(c) if you and two or more other people do so: £650

This amount is deducted from your total allowable expenses on the premises in the month.

SPC/HB allowance for childminders

23.12 In SPC, and HB, if you are a self-employed childminder you don't need to calculate your expenses. This is because expenses are always assumed to equal two-thirds of your income.

23.9 UC 59(2); CTRSW 54(2)

23.10 UC 59(3); CTRSW 54(3)

23.11 UC 59(4); CTRSW 54(4)

23.12 PC 17B(5)(b); HBW 39(3)(b); HBP 40(3)(b); CTRE(PR) sch 1 para 30(4)(b); CTRE(DS) 62(4)(b)

Assessment rules in UC

23.13 Each assessment period is one month (para 32.23). In each assessment period, the UC calculation uses your current actual earnings and deductions for that month – whereas other benefits use an average based on a past period.

22.14 This means that the self-employed earnings you receive in a particular assessment period:

(a) are used to calculate your UC in that assessment period and

(b) affect the amount of UC you are paid seven days after that assessment period ends.

Arrears of earnings

23.15 If you receive a payment of self-employed earnings for a past period (e.g. because a customer is late paying a bill), it is taken into account in the UC assessment period in which you receive it.

Example: Self-employed earnings and UC

Ernestina is self-employed and on UC. Her UC assessment periods start on 14th of each month.

- Ernestina's UC for the month from 14 March to 13 April is calculated using her self-employed earnings in that month, and is paid on 21 April.
- Her UC for the month from 14 April to 13 May is calculated using her self-employed earnings in that month, and is paid on 21 May.

Information about your earnings

23.16 You need to report your self-employed earnings, expenses and deductions to the DWP every month. You should aim to do this by the end of each of your assessment periods, but the DWP can allow you longer in an assessment period in which they reduce.

Estimating earnings

23.17 The DWP can estimate your self-employed earnings if you provide unreliable information or no information or are late providing information (SSWP v RW).

23.13 UC 54(1); CTRSW 44, 47(1)

23.14 UC 54(1); CTRSW 47(1),(2), 51(2)

23.15 UC 57(2), step 1; CTRSW 47(1), 51(2) step 1

23.16 UC 61(1)

23.17 UC 54(2); CTRSW 47(2)
SSWP v RW (rule 17) (UC) [2017] UKUT 347 (AAC)

Assessment rules in SPC and HB

The period earnings relate to

23.18 When you claim SPC or HB, your self-employed earnings are assessed as follows:

(a) they are averaged over your most recent business year and converted to a weekly figure (para 1.21) or

(b) the DWP/council can choose a more representative period (CH/329/2003; CC v Braintree DC) or ask you for an estimate if you are just starting up.

Your earnings are reassessed at regular intervals (often annually) or when there is a change in your business circumstances, for example when your income drops due to a change in the market.

Information about your earnings

23.19 If you are claiming SPC or HB, you need to give details of your self-employed earnings to the DWP or council. You should do this when you first claim, when your earnings change, and at other times if you are asked to.

The UC minimum income floor

23.20 The DWP can treat you as having earnings equal to the 'minimum income floor' if your self-employed earnings are lower than this and you are not in a start-up period. The remainder of this chapter gives the details.

Who does the minimum income floor apply to

23.21 The minimum income floor applies if:

(a) you are in 'gainful self-employment' – this means your business is your main employment and is 'organised, developed, regular and carried on in the expectation of profit'

(b) you are required to carry out all the work-related activities in para 4.6 and

(c) you aren't in a UC start up period (para 23.24).

23.18 PC 17B(3); SS(D&A) 6(2)(a); HBW 30(1); HBP 37(1); HB(D&A) 7(2)(a); CTRE(PR) sch 1 para 20(1); CTRE(DS) 43(1), 48(1)
CC v Braintree DC [2013] UKUT 104 (AAC)

23.19 SS(C&P) 32(1),(1B); SS(D&A) 17(1); HB(D&A) 13(1),(2); HBW 86(1), 88(1); HBP 67(1), 69(1); CTRE(PR) sch 8 para 7(4); CTRE(DS) 113(4)

23.20 UC 62(2),(3); CTRSW 56(1),(2)

23.21 UC 62(1),(5), 63(1)(a); CTRSW 56(1),(2)

How the minimum income floor works

23.22 The minimum income floor works as follows:

(a) if you are a self-employed single person and your monthly earnings are below your minimum income floor, you are counted as having earnings equal to your minimum income floor or

(b) if you are in a couple, one or both of you are self-employed, and your combined monthly earnings are below your combined minimum income floors, you are counted as having earnings equal to your combined minimum income floors.

In each case, 'monthly earnings' mean earnings from all kinds of employment or self-employment (after deductions for tax, national insurance etc).

Amount of the minimum income floor

23.23 Each single person and each partner in a couple has their own minimum income floor. It equals what you would earn for working 35 hours per week at your rate of the national minimum wage (table 4.2). But the DWP can agree to use a lower number of hours per week (and therefore a lower minimum income floor) if you have a disability, ill health or caring responsibilities for a child or adult.

The UC start-up period

23.24 You qualify for a UC start-up period (during which the minimum income floor doesn't apply to you) if:

(a) you are taking active steps to increase your earnings up to your minimum income floor

(b) you haven't begun a UC start-up period for your type of business at any time before and

(c) you haven't begun a UC start-up period for any other type of business within the past five years.

If you migrate to UC from legacy benefits your start up period begins from the date you transfer.

23.25 Your start-up period lasts for 12 months beginning with the assessment period in which the DWP agrees you are in 'gainful self-employment' (para 23.21(a)). It is brought to an early end if you stop being in gainful self-employment or stop taking steps to increase your earnings.

23.22 UC 62(2),(3),(4)(b); CTRSW 56(1),(2)

23.23 UC 88(1),(2), 90(2),(3); CTRSW 56(1),(2)

23.24 UC 63(1),(2); CTRSW 56(4)

23.25 UC 63(1),(3), 64; CTRSW 56(4)

Chapter 24 **Capital**

- General rules about capital and how it affects your benefit: paras 24.1-3
- Assessing capital and disregarded capital: paras 24.4-14
- Notional capital: paras 24.15-21

General rules

24.1 This chapter explains how capital is assessed. It describes which kinds of capital are counted and which are disregarded. But if you are on any of the passport benefits (table 18.1), the whole of your capital and income are disregarded in the assessment of HB.

The capital limit

24.2 You can't get UC or HB if your capital (after allowing for disregards) is over the capital limit of £16,000. But you can get SPC because it doesn't have a capital limit.

Assumed income from capital

24.3 Your capital is assumed to provide you with income as follows:

(a) the first £6,000 or £10,000 of your capital is ignored

(b) your assumed income is calculated on the remainder of your capital as described in table 24.1.

Table 24.1 **How capital affects your benefit**

	(a) Capital limit	(b) Assumed income from capital
UC	£16,000	£4.35 per month for each £250 (or part £250) of capital between £6,000 and £16,000
Working age HB	£16,000	£1 per week for each £250 (or part £250) of capital between £6,000 and £16,000
Pension age HB	£16,000	£1 per week for each £500 (or part £500) of capital between £10,000 and £16,000
SPC	None	£1 per week for each £500 (or part £500) of capital above £10,000

24.2 WRA 5(1)(a),(2)(a); SSCBA 134(1); UC 18; HBW 43; HBP 43; CTRE(PR) 11(2); CTRE(DS) 20, 23

24.3 UC 72(1); PC 15(6)(a); HBW 52(1); HBP 29(2)(a); CTRE(PR) sch 1 para 37; CTRE(DS) 71, 72

T24.1 UC 18, 72(1); PC 15(6); HBW 43, 52(1),(6); HBP 29(2), 43; CTRE(PR) 11(2), sch 1 para 37; CTRE(DS) 20, 23, 71, 72

Assessing capital

What is capital

24.4 Capital means any kind of holding that has a clear monetary value (HBGM para BW1.70). It includes:

(a) money in a bank or other account

(b) shares and investments

(c) lump sums you receive (e.g. an inheritance)

(d) property that isn't your home

(e) any other category of holding that has a clear monetary value (HBGM para BW 1.70)

(f) in some cases income you haven't spent (para 21.7)

(g) in some cases 'notional capital' (para 24.15).

Examples: Capital and assumed income

1. Capital and assumed income in UC

Leroy is claiming UC. He in his 40s and has £14,085 in his bank account. Of this, £2,000 is an insurance payment he received three weeks ago to replace his motorbike after an accident. He has no other capital.

Assessment:

- Disregard the insurance payment of £2,000 (table 24.2(m))
- So his capital is £12,085.00
- Calculate assumed income from capital:
- Deduct £6,000 from his capital £6,085.00
- Rounded up, this contains 25 lots of £250
- So his assumed income is 25 x £4.35 (table 24.1) £108.75

2. Capital and assumed income in pension age HB

Nadia and Idris are claiming pension age HB. They are in their 80s and have £15,085 in their bank account. Of this, £3,000 is arrears of attendance allowance they received three months ago after winning an appeal. They have no other capital.

Assessment:

- Disregard the arrears of £3,000 (table 24.2(o))
- So their capital is £12,085.00

  Calculate assumed income from capital:
- Deduct £10,000 from their capital £2,085.00
- Rounded up, this contains five lots of £500
- So their assumed income is 5 x £1 (table 24.1) £5.00

Whose capital counts

24.5 The assessment of your benefit takes into account your own capital if you are single, or your and your partner's capital if you are in a couple (paras 21.3-4). It never includes capital belonging to a child or young person in your benefit unit.

Calculating capital

24.6 Each item of your capital is calculated as follows:

(a) start with its current market or surrender value

(b) then disregard 10% if selling it would involve costs

(c) then disregard any debt or charge secured on it.

But see para 24.13 for capital held outside the UK.

Jointly held capital

24.7 If you own a capital item jointly with one or more other people, you are assumed to own it in equal shares unless you provide evidence that it should be divided in some other way.

The capital value of property

24.8 Property you own that isn't disregarded (table 24.2) counts as capital and is valued as described in paras 24.6-7. If you have rented it out, this is taken into account in valuing it. For example the presence of a sitting tenant can reduce the value of a dwelling (CH/1953/2003). If ownership of a property is in dispute, it may have no value until the dispute is settled.

Capital held for you in a trust

24.9 Money held for you in a trust is disregarded if the trust holds a personal injury payment for you. Any other money held in a trust for you is:

(a) disregarded in all cases for the purposes of the capital limit

(b) counted in SPC and pension age HB for the purposes of assumed income from capital (para 24.3)

(c) disregarded in UC and working age HB for those purposes.

Capital you hold for someone else

24.10 If you are looking after someone else's capital for them, it counts as their capital, not yours. For example, you might be looking after money belonging to your child or to someone you have power of attorney for. It's up to you to provide evidence that the money isn't yours, but you don't need to be a formally documented trustee for them (JK v SSWP).

24.5 WRA 5(2); SPCA 5; SSCBA 136(1); PC 14; HBW 25, 44, 45; HBP 23, 25, 28, 44; CTRE(PR) sch 1 paras 11, 15, 31; CTRE(DS) 33, 37, 38, 63

24.6 UC 49(1); PC 19; HBW 47; HBP 45; CTRE(PR) sch 1 para 32; CTRE(DS) 65

24.7 UC 47; PC 23; HBW 51; HBP 49 CTRE(PR) sch 1 para 36; CTRE(DS) 70

24.8 HBW 44(1) sch 6 paras 7, 33; HBP 33(11), 44(1), sch 6 paras 5, 28
CTRE(PR) sch 1 paras 17(12), 31(1), sch 6 paras 5, 31; CTRE(DS) 40(12), 63(1), 64(5), sch 9 paras 5, 31, sch 10 paras 10, 37

24.9 HBW sch 6 para 14, 14A; HBP 33(11), sch 6 paras 17, 30
CTRE(PR) sch 1 para 17(12), sch 6 paras 17, 33; CTRE(DS) 40(12), sch 9 paras 17, 33, sch 10 paras 17, 18

24.10 JK v SSWP (JSA) [2010] UKUT 437 (AAC)

Instalments of capital

24.11 Instalments of capital count as capital, except when an outstanding instalment would take your capital over £16,000, in which case it counts as unearned income.

Interest and other income from capital

24.12 Interest and other income from capital count as your capital from the day they are due, except when the capital is disregarded, in which case they count as your unearned income. For example this applies to interest on a savings account, or rent you receive on a property that isn't your home (para 21.30).

Capital outside the UK and commission

24.13 Capital in a country outside the UK is included as your capital. Its value is the market value in that country, unless the country has a prohibition against bringing the money to the UK, in which case it is what a willing buyer in the UK would pay for it. Commission for converting capital into sterling is disregarded.

Disregarded capital

24.14 Table 24.2 lists the kinds of capital that are disregarded when your benefit is assessed.

Table 24.2 **Disregarded capital**

The time limits of six months/26 weeks (where shown in this table) can be extended when reasonable.

(a) Your home

The value of your home is disregarded along with any land or buildings which form part of it.

(b) The home of a pension age or disabled relative

In UC, they must be a close relative (para 9.30) who is over 66 or has limited capability for work (LCW or LCWRA) (para 4.15). In SPC and HB, they can be a close relative or a grandparent, grandchild, aunt, uncle, niece or nephew, who is over 66 or 'incapacitated' in the ordinary English sense of the word.

24.11 UC 46(4); HBW 41(1), sch 6 para 18; CTRE(DS) 55(1), sch 10 para 22

24.12 UC 72(3); PC 15(6), 17(8), sch 4 para 18, sch 5 para 25; HBW 46(4); HBP 29(2), 33(11), sch 5 paras 22, 24
CTRE(PR) sch 1 paras 17(12), 37, sch 5 paras 22, 23; CTRE(DS) 55(1), 40(12), 64(5), 71, 72, sch 6 paras 22, 23

24.13 UC 49(2),(3); PC 20, sch 5 para 21; HBW 48, sch 6 para 23; HBP 46, sch 6 para 23
CTRE(PR) sch 1 para 33, sch 6 para 23; CTRE(DS) 55(1), 66, sch 9 para 23, sch 10 para 28

24.14 UC 48(1),(2), 75-77, sch 10; PC 17(8), sch 5; HBW 44(2), sch 6; HBP 44(2), sch 6;
CTRE(PR) sch 1 para 31(2), sch 6; CTRE(DS) 55(1), 63(2), sch 9, sch 10

T24.2(a) UC sch 10 para 1; PC sch 5 para 1A; HBW sch 6 para 1; HBP sch 6 para 26
CTRE(PR) sch 6 para 26; CTRE(DS) sch 9 para 26, sch 10 para 4

T24.2(b) UC sch 10 para 2; PC sch 5 para 4(a); HBW sch 6 para 4(a); HBP sch 6 para 4(a)
CTRE(PR) sch 6 para 4(a); CTRE(DS) sch 9 para 4(a), sch 10 para 7(a)

(c) Your partner's home

This applies when your relationship hasn't ended but you live apart (para 5.10).

(d) Your former home

You must have moved out because your relationship with your partner ended and at least one of the following must apply:

- they are a lone parent and live in it as their home or
- you ceased to occupy it within the past six months/26 weeks.

(e) Your home and other property you are waiting to sell

This applies to a home or any other property you are taking reasonable steps to dispose of, and began doing so within the past six months/26 weeks.

(f) Your future home

It must be a home you intend to occupy and at least one of the following must apply:

- you acquired it within the past six months/26 weeks or
- you are taking steps to obtain possession of it, and first sought legal advice about this or began proceedings within the past six months/26 weeks or
- you are carrying out essential repairs or alterations to make it fit for occupation, and began doing so within the past six months/26 weeks.

(g) Money for buying a home

Money you intend to use to buy a home is disregarded, so long as you are actively pursuing this intention (EAM v SSWP). In UC and working age HB, you must have received the money within the past six months/26 weeks from:

- the proceeds of the sale of your former home or
- a grant from a local council towards buying a home
- the return of a housing association deposit.

In SPC and pension age HB, you must have been given the money within the past year with the sole purpose of buying a home.

Table continued ➤

T24.2(c) UC sch 10 para 3; PC sch 5 para 4(b); HBW sch 6 para 4(b); HBP sch 6 para 4(b)
CTRE(PR) sch 6 para 4(b); CTRE(DS) sch 9 para 4(b), sch 10 para 7(b)

T24.2(d) UC sch 10 para 5; PC sch 5 para 6; HBW sch 6 para 25; HBP sch 6 para 6
CTRE(PR) sch 6 para 6; CTRE(DS) sch 9 para 6, sch 10 para 30

T24.2(e) UC sch 10 para 6; PC sch 5 para 7; HBW sch 6 para 26; HBP sch 6 para 7
CTRE(PR) sch 6 para 7; CTRE(DS) sch 9 para 7, sch 10 para 31

T24.2(f) UC sch 10 para 4; PC sch 5 paras 1-3; HBW sch 6 paras 2, 27, 28; HBP sch 6 paras 1-3
CTRE(PR) sch 6 paras 1-3; CTRE(DS) sch 9 paras 1-3, sch 10 paras 5, 32, 33

T24.2(g) UC sch 10 para 13; PC sch 5 paras 17, 19(a); HBW sch 6 paras 3, 11(b), 38(a); HBP sch 6 paras 18, 20(a)
CTRE(PR) sch 6 paras 18, 20(a); CTRE(DS) sch 9 paras 18, 20(a), sch 10 paras 6, 14(b), 41(a)
EAM v SSWP(UC) [2020] UKUT 247 (AAC)

(h) Housing association deposits

This applies when you pay a deposit to a housing association in advance of taking on a shared ownership tenancy.

(i) Local council grants for repairs or alterations

In UC and working age HB you must have received the grant within the past six months/26 weeks, in SPC and pension age HB within the past year.

(j) Business assets

These are disregarded while you are self-employed. And if you ceased business because of incapacity, they are disregarded for six months/26 weeks so long as you are taking reasonable steps to dispose of them.

(k) Personal possessions

This applies to any physical assets other than land, property or business assets (R(H) 7/08), except in working age HB if you bought them in order to reduce your capital and thereby obtain benefit or increase it.

(l) Money in a life insurance policy, annuity, pension scheme or funeral plan contract

The disregard of money in a funeral plan contract doesn't apply to working age HB.

(m) Insurance pay-outs

Payments for loss or damage to your home or personal possessions are disregarded for six months/26 weeks (UC and working age HB) or one year (SPC and pension age HB).

(n) Personal injury payments

These are disregarded for 12 months, and then without time limit if they are held in a trust or administered by a court or under a court's direction.

(o) Arrears of social security benefits

Arrears of the following are disregarded as capital for 12 months/52 weeks. Then, in SPC and HB (and UC if you have migrated from a legacy benefit), if the arrears are £5,000 or more and were paid to correct an official error, they are disregarded for as long as you remain on benefit:

T24.2(h) UC sch 10 para 12; PC sch 5 paras 17, 19(a); HBW sch 6 para 11(a); HBP sch 6 paras 18, 20(a) CTRE(PR) sch 6 paras 18, 20(a); CTRE(DS) sch 9 paras 18, 20(a), sch 10 para 14(a)

T24.2(i) UC sch 10 para 15; PC sch 5 paras 17, 19(b); HBW sch 6 para 10(b); HBP sch 6 paras 17, 20(b) CTRE(PR) sch 6 paras 17, 20(b); CTRE(DS) sch 9 paras 17, 20(b), sch 10 para 13(b)

T24.2(j) UC sch 10 paras 7, 8; PC sch 5 paras 9, 9A; HBW sch 6 para 8; HBP sch 6 paras 9, 10 CTRE(PR) sch 6 paras 9, 10; CTRE(DS) sch 9 paras 9, 10, sch 10 para 11

T24.2(k) UC 46(2), 50(2); PC sch 5 para 8; HBW sch 6 para 12; HBP sch 6 para 8 CTRE(PR) sch 6 para 8; CTRE(DS) sch 9 para 8, sch 10 para 15

T24.2(l) UC 46(3), sch 10 paras 9-11; PC sch 5 paras 10, 11, 22, 23, 26; HBW sch 6 paras 13, 17, 31, 32; HBP 33(11), sch 6 paras 11, 12, 24, 29 CTRE(PR) sch 1 para 17(12), sch 6 paras 11, 12, 24, 32; CTRE(DS) 40(12), sch 9 paras 11, 12, 24, 32, sch 10 paras 16, 21, 35, 36

T24.2(m) UC sch 10 para 14; PC sch 5 paras 17, 18; HBW sch 6 para 10(a); HBP sch 6 paras 18, 19 CTRE(PR) sch 6 paras 18, 19; CTRE(DS) sch 9 paras 18, 19, sch 10 para 13(a)

T24.2(n) UC 75; PC sch 5 para 16; HBW 41(5), sch 6 paras 14, 14A, 45, 46; HBP sch 6 para 17 CTRE(PR) sch 6 para 17; CTRE(DS) 55(5), sch 9 para 17, sch 10 paras 17, 18, 50, 51

- PIP, DLA, attendance allowance, and in Scotland ADP, CDP and PADP
- an increase for constant attendance or exceptionally severe disablement paid with an industrial injury or war pension
- armed forces independence payment (AFIP)
- UC, SPC (guarantee credit or savings credit), ESA(IR), JSA(IB) and IS
- bereavement support payment
- maternity allowance
- most other Scottish social security benefits

(p) Other council, government and special payments

The following are disregarded for 12 months/52 weeks:

- fostering and adoption payments
- discretionary housing payments and other council payments (para 21.42)
- the £2,500 or £3,500 addition paid in the first month of bereavement support
- payments for disasters, emergencies, miscarriages of justice and medical or official negligence (para 21.43)
- Victoria Cross and George Cross payments
- payments in kind (in other words, in goods rather than money or vouchers)

Notional capital

24.15 Notional capital means capital you are treated as having but don't actually possess. In UC, SPC and HB, this can happen if:

(a) you spend money to gain benefit or

(b) you are effectively an owner or partner of a company.

In SPC and HB it can happen for other reasons too, but these are all rare.

If you spend money to gain benefit (deprivation of capital)

24.16 You are counted as having capital equal to any amount you have spent or given away in order to obtain benefit or increase it. This is called 'depriving' yourself of capital.

T24.2(o) UC sch 10 paras 18, 18A; UCTP 10A; PC sch 5 paras 17, 20, 20A; HBW sch 6 paras 9, 9A; HBP sch 6 paras 18, 21, 22
CTRE(PR) sch 6 paras 18, 21, 22; CTRE(DS) sch 9 paras 18, 21, 22, sch 10 para 12

T24.2(p) UC sch 10 paras 17, 18A, 19, 20; PC sch 5 para 23C, 23D, 23E
HBW sch 6 paras 9(1), 12, 19, 19A, 20A, 47, 57-62; HBP sch 6 paras 21(1)(e),(f),(2)(k), 26D, 26F, 26G, 26H
CTRE(PR) sch 6 paras 8, 21, 29, 29B, 29C; CTRE(DS) sch 9 paras 8, 21, 29; sch 10 paras 12, 15, 23-25, 52, 61-64

24.15 UC 50(1), 77(1),(2); PC 21(1),(3),(5); HBW 49(1),(5),(7); HBP 47(1),(3),(5); CTRE(PR) sch 1 para 34(1),(3),(5); CTRE(DS) 67(1),(7),(9)

24.16 UC 50(1); PC 21(1); HBW 49(1); HBP 47(1); CTRE(PR) sch 1 para 34(1); CTRE(DS) 67(1)

24.17 This rule can only apply if:

(a) you have actually spent the capital or given it away (JM v SSWP)

(b) you knew what you were doing (R(H) 1/06) and

(c) your purpose was to obtain the benefit in question (SH v Tower Hamlets LBC).

24.18 This rule doesn't apply when you spend capital to:

(a) pay off or reduce any debt you owe or

(b) buy goods or services that are reasonable in your circumstances.

This exclusion is stated in the law for UC, SPC and pension age HB, but for working age HB it follows from the case law (para 24.17).

24.19 Your notional capital reduces each month (UC) or week (SPC and HB) by the amount it has caused you to lose (as illustrated in the example). In HB only, if you make a claim that is unsuccessful (due to your notional capital being included), the council calculates the rate of reduction once and continues to use that as a fixed deduction. You can then make a further HB claim at any time and:

(a) if your claim is successful, you are awarded HB again

(b) if your claim is unsuccessful and there has been a gap of least 26 weeks, the rate of reduction is recalculated

(c) if your claim is unsuccessful and there has been a gap of less than 26 weeks, the rate of deduction isn't recalculated.

Example: How notional capital reduces

Juan is on UC. He has actual capital of £15,000 and with this he would qualify for UC of £350 per month. But he is found to have notional capital of £2,000 as well, which means his total capital is £17,000.

Initial calculation of reduction in notional capital:

- In the first three UC months (assessment periods) his capital is over £16,000, so he doesn't qualify for UC.
- In those three months, his total loss (due to the notional capital) is £1,050.
- This reduces his notional capital to £950 and his total capital to £15,950.

Next calculation of reduction in notional capital:

- He no longer has capital over £16,000.
- When his UC is calculated in the fourth month he qualifies for £200.
- In that month, his loss (due to the notional capital) is £150.
- This reduces his notional capital to £800 and his total capital to £15,800

The calculation continues on a monthly basis until his notional capital reduces to nil.

24.17 JM v SSWP [2009] UKUT 145 (AAC); SH v Tower Hamlets LBC [2011] UKUT 500 (AAC)

24.18 UC 50(2); PC 21(2); HBP 47(2); CTRE(PR) sch 1 para 34(2); CTRE(DS) 67(2)

24.19 UC 50(3); PC 22; HBW 50; HBP 48; CTRE(PR) sch 1 para 35; CTRE(DS) 68, 69

If you are effectively an owner or partner of a company

24.20 You are counted as having notional earnings from a company if:

(a) the company is a property business or carries on a trade

(b) it isn't an intermediary or a managed service company that pays your earnings and

(c) your relationship to it is equivalent to that of a sole trader or partner.

24.21 In this case:

(a) the company's income or your share of it is counted as your notional earnings and

(b) the company's value (the value of its assets) or your share of it is counted as your notional capital but

(c) while you are working for the company, that notional capital is disregarded.

24.20 UC 77(1),(2),(3)(b); PC 21(3),(4); HBW 49(5),(6); HBP 47(3),(4); CTRE(PR) sch 1 para 34(3),(4); CTRE(DS) 67(7),(8)

Chapter 25 **Migration to UC**

Migration

25.1 This chapter describes what happens when you transfer from legacy benefits to UC (or in some cases SPC: para 25.32). This is called 'migration'. Chapter 26 gives the rules about transitional protection, and table 25.1 summarises the main points from both chapters. If you disagree with a decision about migration or transitional protection, you can ask the DWP to reconsider it or appeal to a tribunal.

Kinds of migration

25.2 There are three kinds of migration:

(a) 'voluntary migration' is when you transfer to UC because you choose to claim it (para 25.11)

(b) 'natural migration' is when you transfer because a legacy benefit you were on has ended or you become a couple with someone already on UC (para 25.21)

(c) 'managed migration' is when you transfer because the DWP has sent you a migration notice (para 25.22).

Migration timetable

25.3 Most claimants who were on legacy benefits have now transferred to UC (or SPC). During 2025-26, there remain some claimants on ESA(IR) (with or without HB). The DWP expects to transfer all remaining cases (and close all remaining legacy benefits) by March 2026 (table 1.4).

25.2 WRA 36, sch 6 paras 1, 4; UCTP 7, 8, 44, 46

Table 25.1 **UC migration dates and transitional element**

Type of migration	(A) Start of UC	(B) End of HB and ESA(IR)	(C) Transitional element
(a) Voluntary migration: you choose to claim UC	Date of UC claim	Two weeks after (B)	Only if severely disabled
(b) Natural migration: one of your legacy benefits ends	Date of UC claim	Two weeks after (B)	Only if severely disabled
(c) Natural migration: you become a couple with someone on UC	Start of assessment period in which you become a couple	Day before (A)	No
(d) Managed migration: you claim UC by the deadline day	Date of UC claim	Two weeks after (B)	Yes
(e) Managed migration: you claim UC after the deadline day but by the final deadline	Deadline day	Two weeks after (B)	Yes
(f) Managed migration: you claim UC after the final deadline	Date of UC claim	Two weeks after (B)	No
(g) Managed migration: you don't claim UC	Not entitled to UC until you claim it	Two weeks after (B)	No

Notes:

- HB continues in supported or temporary accommodation (table 13.1)
- UC can be backdated (table 32.2) in all cases except (e) and (g)
- UC can be postdated in case (d) to fit in with your legacy benefit payments
- If there is a gap between your legacy benefits and UC, you can get a UC advance (para 34.19)

The legacy benefits and when they end

25.4 The remaining legacy benefits are working age HB (except in supported or temporary accommodation) and ESA(IR) (table 1.4). When you make a claim for UC:

(a) your legacy benefits stop and

(b) you can't get legacy benefits in the future but

(c) you may qualify for transitional protection if you are worse off on UC than on legacy benefits (chapter 26).

These apply even if you claim UC by mistake or withdraw your claim.

Two-week HB run-on

25.5 You get a two-week run-on of HB overlapping with the beginning of your UC if:

(a) you are on HB when you make your UC claim and

(b) you don't live in supported or temporary accommodation (table 13.1).

This is called a 'transitional housing payment' in the law.

Amount of two-week HB run-on

25.6 If your transfer to UC is part of voluntary or natural migration, you get 'maximum HB' during the two-week run-on, regardless of the level of your income. This means your eligible rent minus any non-dependant contributions that apply, calculated by the HB rules in chapter 17 (so if you have a rent-free week this appears to mean nil for that week).

25.7 If your transfer to UC is part of managed migration, your HB during the two-week run-on continues at the same amount it is on the first day of the run-on (so no changes of circumstance are taken into account after that first day).

Two-week ESA(IR) run-on

25.8 If you are on ESA(IR) when you make your UC claim, you get a two-week run-on of that benefit overlapping with the beginning of your UC. This is in addition to the HB run-on if you qualify for it (para 25.5).

Transitional protection

25.9 If you transfer to UC as part of voluntary or natural migration, you can get:

(a) the two-week run-ons

(b) the transitional SDP element only if you are severely disabled (para 26.8)

(c) protection for some self-employed people (para 23.24).

25.4 UCTP 5(1), 6A, 7, 8; SI 2013/983

25.5 UCTP 8(2A), 8A, 46(1)(a)

25.6 UCTP 8A(a)

25.7 UCTP 2(1) – 'notified person', 8A(c)

25.8 UCTP 8B

25.9 UCTP 8A, 8B, 63, sch 2 paras 1-4, sch 3; UC 63(1)(a)

25.10 If you transfer to UC as part of managed migration, you can get:

(a) the two-week run-ons (paras 25.5-8)

(b) the main transitional element (para 26.3)

(c) the transitional capital disregard (para 26.21)

(d) protection for some students (table 3.1)

(e) protection for some self-employed people (para 23.24)

(f) protection against the notional income rule if you delay claiming your retirement pension (para 21.23)

(g) the age condition waived if you transferred from WTC (para 25.33).

Voluntary migration

Choosing to claim UC

25.11 'Voluntary migration' is the term used when you transfer to UC because you choose to claim it. You can do this at any time, usually because you are sure you will be better off on UC. However, if you aren't sure, claiming UC is risky because you can't go back (para 25.4).

25.12 In voluntary migration cases:

(a) your UC starts on the day you claim UC or the day it is backdated to (table 32.2)

(b) your HB (except in supported or temporary accommodation) and ESA(IR) end two weeks later

(c) you are only eligible for a UC transitional element if you are severely disabled (para 26.8).

Choosing to remain on legacy benefits

25.13 If you don't transfer to UC as part of voluntary migration, you can remain on any legacy benefits you are already on until natural or managed migration applies to you. But you can't make any further claims for legacy benefits except as in paras 25.14-15

25.14 You can claim HB in supported or temporary accommodation (table 13.1) at any time. (HB paid for STA doesn't count as a legacy benefit.)

25.10 UCTP 2(1) – 'notified person', 44(6), 48, 50(1), 51(1), 60

25.11 SI 2013/983, art 4; UCTP 6A, 8(1),(2),(2A)

25.12 UCTP 8(2),(2A), 8A, 8B, sch 2 para 3

25.13 SI 2013/983, art 4; UCTP 8(2),(2A)

25.14 UCTP 6A(2)

25.15 You can only claim HB in general accommodation (accommodation that isn't STA) if:

(a) you (and your partner in a couple) have reached pension age or

(b) you are in the UC assessment period in which you (or the younger partner in a couple) reach pension age or

(c) you are in a couple or polygamous marriage, with one under pension age and one over, and you (the HB claimant):

- reached pension age before 15 May 2019 and
- have been on SPC or HB (as a mixed age couple or polygamous marriage) since before that date or

(d) you are in a couple or polygamous marriage, with one under pension age and one over, and your partner(s) can't get UC because of being an excluded migrant, absent from the UK, a prisoner, hospital detainee, member of a religious order, or under 18 years old.

In the situation in (d), you can only get HB as if you were a single person.

Natural migration

25.16 'Natural migration' is the term used when you transfer to UC because:

(a) one of your legacy benefits has ended (para 25.17) or

(b) you become a couple with someone already on UC (para 25.20).

Claiming UC when a legacy benefit ends

25.17 If your entitlement to a legacy benefit ends (under the rules for that benefit), you can no longer claim other legacy benefits to replace it. So you have to claim UC (or be worse off), and this causes any other legacy benefits you are on to end (para 25.4).

25.18 For example this happens when:

(a) you lose ESA(IR) because of starting work or increasing your hours or earnings

(b) you lose ESA(IR) because of becoming fit for work

(c) you lose HB because of moving areas or

(d) you lose ESA(IR) or HB for other reasons.

25.19 In this case:

(a) your UC starts on the day you claim UC or the day it is backdated to (table 32.2)

(b) your HB (except in supported or temporary accommodation) and ESA(IR) end two weeks later

(c) you are only eligible for a UC transitional element if you are severely disabled (para 26.8).

25.15 UCTP 6A(3)-(5); SI 2019/37

25.17 SI 2013/983 art 4; UCTP 6A(1), 8(2),(2A)

25.19 UCTP 8(2),(2A), 8A, 8B, sch 2 para 3

Becoming a couple with someone on UC

25.20 If you become a couple with someone who is already on UC, you become part of their UC claim and this causes all your legacy benefits to end.

25.21 In this case:

(a) your new joint UC claim begins from the first day of your partner's assessment period in which you became a couple

(b) your HB (except in supported or temporary accommodation) and ESA(IR) end on the day before your joint UC claim begins

(c) you aren't eligible for a UC transitional element.

Examples: Natural migration to UC

1. Becoming fit for work

Ava is on ESA(IR), CTC and HB. She becomes fit for work and this means her ESA(IR) ends.

- In the past she could have claimed JSA(IB) but she can no longer do so.
- She claims UC so her CTC and HB also end.
- She can't in the future claim any of the legacy benefits.
- She can't in the future claim any of the legacy benefits.

2. Moving home to a new area

Evie is on ESA(IR) and HB. She moves to a new area and this means her HB ends.

- In the past she could have claimed HB in the new area but she can no longer do so.
- She claims UC so her ESA(IR) also ends.
- She can't in the future claim any legacy benefits.

25.20 UCTP 7(1),(2),(6)

25.21 UC 21(3B); UCTP 5(2)(b)(iii), 7(2),(7), 12A, sch 2 para 2

Managed migration

25.22 'Managed migration' is the term used when you transfer to UC because the DWP:

(a) sends you a migration notice giving you a deadline to claim UC (para 25.23) and

(b) ends your legacy benefits whether or not you claim UC (paras 25.28-30).

Your migration notice

25.23 The DWP sends you a migration notice saying:

(a) that your legacy benefits will end and you will need to claim UC instead

(b) what you need to do and what will happen if you don't do it

(c) when your 'deadline day' and 'final deadline' are (para 25.25).

If you are in a couple (or polygamous marriage), the DWP normally sends this to each of you.

What you need to do

25.24 You should claim UC by your deadline day, or at the latest by your final deadline. This ensures that:

(a) there is no gap between your legacy benefits and UC and

(b) you get a transitional element if you need it (para 26.3).

Your deadline day and final deadline

25.25 In the rules about migration to UC:

(a) your 'deadline day' means the day after your legacy benefits run out. It is usually at least three months after your migration notice

(b) your 'final deadline' is one month after your deadline day.

If you claim UC on or before your final deadline, the day before your UC starts is called your 'migration day'.

Extending the deadline day and final deadline

25.26 You (or someone on your behalf) can ask the DWP to extend your deadline day, or the DWP can do this without a request. When your deadline day is extended, so is your final deadline, so it is still one month later.

25.22 UCTP 44, 46

25.23 UCTP 44(1),(2)

25.24 UCTP 46, 48

25.25 UCTP 44(3), 46(3),(4), 48, 49

25.26 UCTP 45

25.27 There must be a 'good reason' for an extension and the DWP decides this on the merits of each individual case. For example, the DWP is likely to agree to an extension [www] if:

(a) you are in hospital or have to go to hospital
(b) you have a mental health condition
(c) you have a disability
(d) you have learning difficulties
(e) you are homeless
(f) you have caring responsibilities or
(g) you have a domestic emergency.

If you claim UC by the deadline day

25.28 If you claim UC on or before your deadline day:

(a) your UC starts on the day you make your UC claim
(b) your UC can be backdated for up to one month if you meet the conditions (table 32.2)
(c) your UC can be postdated for up to one month, usually to fit in with your legacy benefit payments
(d) your HB (except in supported or temporary accommodation) and ESA(IR) end two weeks later
(e) you are eligible for the transitional element and capital disregard (paras 26.3, 26.21).

These rules mean there is no gap between your legacy benefits and your UC.

If you claim UC after the deadline day but by the final deadline

25.29 If you claim UC after your deadline day but on or before your final deadline:

(a) your UC starts on your deadline day (it is automatically backdated to that day, and can't be backdated further)
(b your HB (except in supported or temporary accommodation) and ESA(IR) end two weeks later
(c) you are eligible for the transitional element and capital disregard (paras 26.3, 26.21).

These rules mean there is no gap between your legacy benefits and your UC.

25.27 UCTP 45; Explanatory Memo to the SSAC on the draft Managed Migration Regulations 2018, para 36 https://tinyurl.com/MM-SSAC-Memo-2018

25.28 UCTP 44(1), 46(1), 48, 49, 50(1), 58; UC(C&P) 10, 26

25.29 UCTP 46(1),(3), 48, 49, 50(1)

If you claim UC after the final deadline

25.30 If you claim UC after your final deadline:

(a) your UC starts on the day you make your UC claim

(b) your UC can be backdated for up to one month if you meet the conditions (table 32.2)

(c) your HB (except in supported or temporary accommodation) and ESA(IR) end two weeks later

(d) you aren't eligible for the transitional element or capital disregard.

These rules mean there is a gap between your legacy benefits and your UC.

If you become a couple or a single person during migration

25.31 If you become a single person or a couple between getting legacy benefits and claiming UC:

(a) your legacy benefits end the day before each of you claim UC (whether you both claim UC on the same day or not) but

(b) you aren't eligible for the transitional element or capital disregard.

Examples: Managed migration to UC

1. UC claim made by the deadline day

James is a single person on ESA(IR) and HB. The DWP issues him a migration notice in February, giving him a deadline day of 14 May. He claims UC (as a single person) on 11 May.

- His UC starts on 11 May (para 25.28).
- The last day of his HB and ESA(IR) is 24 May.
- He is eligible for a UC transitional element if he would otherwise be worse off.

2. UC claim made after the deadline day but by the final deadline

Josie and Andrew are a couple on ESA(IR) and HB. The DWP issues a migration notice in March, giving them a deadline day of 12 June. They claim UC (as a couple) on 24 June.

- Their UC starts on 12 June (para 25.29).
- The last day of their HB and ESA(IR) is 25 June.
- They are eligible for a UC transitional element if they would otherwise be worse off.

25.30 UCTP 46(1), 48, 49, 50(1)

25.31 UCTP 44(1),(4), 48, 50(2)

Migration for pension age claimants

25.32 Pension age claimants on tax credits are being transferred to UC or SPC as part of managed migration. These transfers began on 8 June 2024 and are expected to be completed by December 2025. For transitional protection in these cases, see paras 26.25-26.

Pension age transfers from WTC (with or without CTC) to UC

25.33 If you are a pension age claimant and were getting WTC (with or without CTC) but aren't entitled to SPC for any reason, you can transfer to UC and the normal UC age limits are waived without time limit. If you later become entitled to SPC, you can choose to claim it at any time. In all these cases, your UC stops as soon as:

(a) you claim SPC or

(b) your transitional element or capital disregard ends (or would end if you qualified for one) or

(c) one year (12 assessment periods) after your UC begins.

In other respects, all the rules in paras 25.21-31 apply to you.

Pension age transfers from CTC (but not WTC) to SPC

25.34 If you are a pension age claimant getting CTC (but not WTC), you transfer to SPC. Your migration notice is issued by HMRC (not the DWP) and is called a 'tax credit closure notice'. In other respects, all the rules in paras 25.21-31 apply to you, except that they are governed by separate law.

25.32 SI 2024/611 regs 2-4; SI 2025/3 regs 6, 7

25.33 UCTP 60A

25.34 SI 2019/167 arts 3A, 3B

Chapter 26 **Transitional protection**

The transitional elements

26.1 The transitional elements help avoid you being worse off when you transfer from legacy benefits to UC (or in some cases to SPC: paras 26.25-26). There are two kinds:

(a) the 'main transitional element' is for people who transfer to UC as part of managed migration (para 26.3)

(b) the 'transitional SDP element' is for disabled people who transfer to UC as part of voluntary migration, or natural migration caused by the end of a legacy benefit (para 26.8).

This chapter explains how the amount is calculated. The DWP does this calculation automatically; it isn't checked until or unless you request a revision or appeal.

26.2 The rule in (b) avoids discrimination for people whose ESA(IR), JSA(IB) or IS included a severe disability premium (R (TP, AR & SXC) v SSWP, R (TP & AR No 3) v SSWP, AB & F v SSWP).

The main transitional element

Who qualifies for the main transitional element

26.3 You qualify for a main transitional element if:

(a) you transferred to UC as part of managed migration (para 25.22)

(b) you made your UC claim on or before your final deadline (paras 25.28-29)

(c) your indicative UC is less than your total legacy benefits (para 26.4) and

(d) your claims for legacy benefits and for UC were as a single person in both cases, or as a couple with the same partner in both cases (including, in the case of UC, a couple claiming as a single person: para 2.9).

26.2 R(TP, AR and SXC) v SSWP [2020] EWCA Civ 37;
R(TP and AR No 3) v SSWP, AB and F v SSWP [2022] EWHC 123 (Admin)

26.3 UCTP 46(4), 48, 50(1)(b), 52(1)

Your total legacy benefits and your indicative UC

26.4 In the rules about the main transitional element:

(a) your 'total legacy benefits' means your legacy benefits as calculated in table 26.1

(b) your 'indicative UC' means your UC as calculated in table 26.2.

Both of these are calculated as at the day before your UC starts (in the law called your 'migration day'). They can be slightly different from the actual amounts you receive.

Table 26.1 **Your total legacy benefits**

Your 'total legacy benefits' are used to work out your transitional element when you transfer to UC due to managed migration (paras 25.22-31). In all cases:

- use the following figures as at the day before your UC starts
- convert them to a monthly amount (as shown in brackets)
- add them together to give your total legacy benefits.

(a) HB

- Use the council's HB figure (x 52÷12), ignoring any adjustments for rent-free periods.
- But exclude HB entirely if you live in supported or temporary accommodation (table 13.1).

(b) JSA(IB), ESA(IR) or IS

- Use the DWP's figure (x 52÷12), and include any amount of JSA(IB)/ESA(IR) that is classified as being JSA(C)/ESA(C).

(c) CTC and/or WTC

- Use HMRC's daily figure (x 365÷12).

(d) Benefit cap and sanctions

- The benefit cap and its exceptions all apply (chapter 20), but ensuring that it is not deducted twice (i.e. not from the HB figure in (a) and from the total).
- Don't make deductions for sanctions etc (para 16.4(c)-(f)).

26.4 UCTP 49, 52(1), 53, 54

T26.1 UCTP 49, 53

Table 26.2 **Your indicative UC**

Your 'indicative UC' is used to work out your transitional element when you transfer to UC due to managed migration (paras 26.5-6). In all cases:

- use the following figures as at the day before your UC starts
- convert them to a monthly amount (as shown in brackets)
- use the ordinary rules (para 16.3) to calculate your indicative UC.

(a) Standard allowance and elements

- Use the figures in table 16.1 for these (except as in (c) below).

(b) Children and young persons in your benefit unit

- If you were on CTC, include the same children/young persons as in your CTC.
- Otherwise, use the UC rules to decide who to include.

(c) Childcare costs element

- If you were on WTC, use the WTC figure (x 52÷12) for this.
- Otherwise, use the UC rules to decide this.

(d) Housing costs element

- Use the UC rules to decide this.

(e) Earned income

- If you were on CTC/WTC, use HMRC's annual figure (x 1÷12), then the DWP decides how much to deduct for tax and national insurance.
- If you were on JSA(IB)/ESA(IR)/IS (but not CTC/WTC), use the DWP's figure (x 52÷12).
- If you were only on HB, use the council's figure (x 52÷12).

(f) Unearned income and capital

- The DWP decides these using information about your legacy benefits from you.
- But if you were on CTC/WTC, any capital over £16,000 is disregarded (para 26.21).

(g) Benefit cap and sanctions

- The benefit cap and its exceptions all apply (chapter 20).
- Don't make deductions for sanctions etc (para 16.4(c)-(f)).

T26.2 UCTP 49, 54

How much main transitional element – first month

26.5 In your first UC assessment period, your main transitional element equals:

(a) the total of your legacy benefits (table 26.1)

(b) minus your indicative UC (table 26.2).

This usually means that your first month's UC (when calculated with the transitional element) equals your total legacy benefits. The same applies to para 26.6.

26.6 If your indicative UC is nil, your transitional element equals the total of your legacy benefits plus your excess income. 'Excess income' means:

(a) 55% of your earned income and 100% of your unearned income (calculated as in chapters 21-23, and after deducting any disregards and work allowance you qualify for)

(b) minus your maximum UC (para 16.2).

This rule ensures you still get a transitional element when your excess income is greater than your indicative UC but less than your total legacy benefits. (It covers situations where your supposed indicative UC is negative (table 26.2)).

How much main transitional element – subsequent months

26.7 In your second and subsequent UC assessment periods, your main transitional element stays the same as in paras 26.5-6 unless and until it reduces or ends (para 26.14).

The transitional SDP element

26.8 The transitional SDP element is for people who lost a severe disability premium (SDP) as a result of transferring from legacy benefits to UC. It helps with the loss of that premium and the other disability amounts described in this section.

Who qualifies for the transitional SDP element

26.9 You qualify for a transitional SDP element if:

(a) you transferred to UC as part of voluntary migration (paras 25.11), or natural migration caused by the end of a legacy benefit (para 25.17), but not when you transfer to UC because you become a couple with someone already on UC (para 25.20)

(b) you or your partner met the conditions for a severe disability premium in your JSA(IB), ESA(IR) or IS (para 26.10) no more than one month before your UC began

(c) you or your partner also met those conditions on the day your UC started and

(d) your claims for legacy benefits and for UC were as a single person in both cases, or as a couple with the same partner in both cases (including, in the case of UC, a couple claiming as a single person: para 2.9).

26.5 UCTP 55(1),(2)(a)

26.6 UCTP 55(1)(b)

26.7 UCTP 55(2)(b),(c)

26.9 UCTP 63, sch 2 paras 3, 7

26.10 You must have been getting (or entitled to) a severe disability premium in your JSA(IB), ESA(IR) or IS (para 26.9(b)). Getting the premium in just your HB is not enough, but in this case you may be able to get a discretionary housing payment (para 31.9).

Conditions for a severe disability premium

26.11 You meet the conditions for a severe disability premium if:

(a) you receive one or more of the following disability benefits:
- the daily living component of PIP or ADP or
- the middle or highest care rate of the care component of DLA or CDP or
- attendance allowance or
- constant attendance allowance paid with an industrial injury or war disablement pension or
- an armed forces independence payment and

(b) you have no non-dependants living with you (chapter 6) apart from non-dependants who receive any of the disability benefits in (a), or are (or were within the last 28 weeks) certified as severely sight impaired or blind and

(c) no-one receives carer's allowance or the carer element of UC for caring for you.

26.12 The severe disability premium has two rates:

(a) single people get the single rate if you meet all the conditions in para 26.11

(b) couples get the double rate if you both meet all the conditions

(c) couples get the single rate if:
- one of you meets all the conditions and
- the other meets the first two conditions (para 26.11(a) and (b)) or is certified as severely sight impaired or blind.

How much transitional SDP element

26.13 Your transitional SDP element is calculated as follows:

(a) in your first UC assessment period, it equals the total of the amounts in table 26.3 that apply to you

(b) in your second and subsequent UC assessment periods, it stays the same as in (a) unless and until it reduces or ends (para 26.14)

26.10 UCTP 2(1) – 'severe disability premium'

26.11-12 UCTP sch 2 paras 5, 6

26.13 UCTP 55(2), 63

Table 26.3 **Transitional SDP element 2025-26**

	Single person	Couple
(a) Standard amount		
You qualify for a standard amount as follows if you got a severe disability premium (SDP) in your JSA(IB)/ESA(IR)/IS.		
■ If you got the single rate of SDP in JSA(IB)/ESA(IR)/IS, and qualify for an LCWRA element in UC	£143.37	£143.37
■ If you got the single rate of SDP in JSA(IB)/ESA(IR)/IS, and don't qualify for an LCWRA element in UC	£340.50	£340.50
■ If you got double rate of SDP in JSA(IB)/ESA(IR)/IS (regardless of whether you qualify for an LCWRA element in UC)	n/a	£483.88
(b) Additional amounts		
If you qualify under (a), you also qualify for all the following that apply.		
■ If you got an enhanced disability premium in JSA(IB)/ESA(IR)/IS	£91.15	£130.22
■ If you got a disability premium in JSA(IB)/ESA(IR)/IS	£186.64	£266.94
■ Each child for whom you got a disabled child premium in JSA(IB)/ESA(IR)/IS or a disabled child element in WTC/CTC	£192.07	£192.07

Note: The single person amount applies to single people and to couples claiming as a single person. The couple amount applies to joint claim couples.

T26.3 UCTP 63, sch 2 para 5, sch 3 paras 4, 5; SI 2025/295 reg 33

Example: The transitional SDP element

James is a single person aged 53. He lives in a rented flat and gets HB and ESA(IR) which includes a disability premium and a severe disability premium.

James moves to a new area. He claims UC and qualifies for a UC LCWRA element. His transfer to UC is part of natural migration (para 25.17) and he qualifies for a transitional SDP element (para 26.8).

In his first UC assessment period, his transitional SDP element is (table 26.3):

- £143.37 towards the loss of his severe disability premium and
- £186.64 towards the loss of his disability premium
- totalling £330.01 pcm.

In subsequent UC assessment periods, he will continue to get £330.01 pcm unless or until his transitional SDP element reduces or ends (para 26.14).

How transitional elements change and end

26.14 The following rules apply to both the main transitional element and the transitional SDP element. They explain how your transitional element reduces. If it reduces to nil, it is never reinstated (except as described in para 26.20).

Changes that reduce your transitional element

26.15 The general rule is that if you are awarded an allowance, element or addition in your UC, or their amount increases for any reason (e.g. when they are up-rated), your transitional element reduces by the same amount. But there are exceptions to this, and the full details are in table 26.4.

26.16 Your transitional element doesn't reduce (or change at all) when:

(a) you stop qualifying for an allowance, element or addition in your UC, or their amount reduces for any reason or

(b) your income or capital change.

26.14 UCTP 55(3)
26.15-16 UCTP 55(2),(4)

Table 26.4 **How transitional elements reduce**

Situation	Effect on your transitional element
(a) You are awarded a UC housing costs element when you move from STA to general accommodation	Your transitional element doesn't change
(b) You are awarded a housing costs element, or an increase in its amount, for any other reason	Your transitional element reduces by the same amount as the award or increase
(c) You are awarded an LCWRA element and your carer element ceases as a result (table 16.2)	Your transitional element reduces by the difference between the LCWRA element and the carer element
(d) You are awarded a childcare costs element, or an increase in its amount	Your transitional element doesn't change
(e) You are awarded any other UC allowance, element or addition, or an increase in their amount	Your transitional element reduces by the same amount as the award or increase

Notes:

- This table applies to the main transitional element and the transitional SDP element.
- The rule in (a) is included in UC regulations from 1 June 2025, but has applied since 19 February 2024 when the upper tribunal decided (SSWP v JA).
- The rule in (c) isn't yet included in UC regulations, but has applied since 29 January 2025 when the upper tribunal decided (SSWP v MJ).

T26.4 UCTP 55(2)-(6) and SI 2025/3 reg 6(8) inserting UCTP 55(5A) from 1 June 2025
SSWP v JA (UC) [2024] UKUT 52 (AAC)
SSWP v MJ [2025] UKUT 35 (AAC)

Examples: How changes affect your transitional element

1. Moving home

Ryan is getting UC which includes a housing costs element of £600.00 pcm and a transitional element of £230 pcm. In June 2025, he moves home and at his new home his housing costs element is £700 pcm.

- His housing costs element increases by £100 pcm
- So his transitional element reduces by £100 pcm to £130 pcm (table 26.4(b)).

2. Moving from STA to general accommodation

Sarah lives in STA (table 13.1) and is getting HB towards her rent there. She also gets UC which includes a transitional element of £150 pcm. In June 2025, she moves into general accommodation where her housing costs element is £650 pcm.

- She is awarded a housing costs element of £650 pcm for the first time.
- Her transitional element doesn't reduce but stays at £150 pcm (table 26.4(a)).

End of transitional element

26.17 Your transitional element ends if and when:

(a) the amount reduces to nil (under the rules in para 26.15) or

(b) you were getting UC as a single person and start claiming as a couple or

(c) you were getting UC as a couple and start claiming as a single person or as a couple with a different partner or

(d) your earned income has reduced or ended as in paras 26.18-19 or

(e) you stop being entitled to UC (para 26.20).

It isn't reinstated except as described in para 26.20.

Reduction of earned income: main rule

26.18 Except as explained in para 26.19, your transitional element ends if your earned income:

(a) was at or above the administrative earnings threshold (para 4.11) in your first UC assessment period but

(b) is lower than that (or nil) in any three consecutive assessment periods.

26.17 UCTP 55(3), 56(2)-(4), 57(1)

Exception for pension age transfers from tax credits

26.19 If you transfer from WTC to UC (para 25.33):

(a) during your first 12 UC assessment periods, matters relating to earned income (whether it starts, increases, reduces or ends) never end your transitional element and

(b) after that, your transitional element only ends if your earned income (or in the case or a couple, your combined earned income) is less than someone would earn for working 16 hours per week at the national living wage (table 4.2), which is £846.56 per month.

Gaps in your entitlement to UC

26.20 Your transitional element:

(a) ends as soon as you stop qualifying for UC

(b) is reinstated after a gap in your UC that is due to an increase in your earned income and is less than three assessment periods

(c) isn't reinstated after any other gap in your UC.

When the transitional element is reinstated as in (b), its amount is the same as if you had been on UC throughout. This rule can apply any number of times and is particularly important for people who receive non-monthly earnings (paras 22.10-11).

The transitional capital disregard

Who qualifies for a transitional capital disregard

26.21 You qualify for a transitional capital disregard if:

(a) you transferred to UC as part of managed migration (para 25.22)

(b) you made your UC claim on or before your final deadline (paras 25.28-29)

(c) on the day before your UC started, you were on CTC or WTC or both and you had capital over £16,000

(d) your claims for legacy benefits and for UC were as a single person in both cases, or as a couple with the same partner in both cases (including, in the case of UC, a couple claiming as a single person: para 2.9).

26.20 UCTP 56(2), 57(2)

26.21 UCTP 48, 49, 51

How the disregard works

26.22 The disregard applies to all your capital over £16,000. This means that:

(a) your capital doesn't stop you qualifying for UC (para 24.2) and

(b) only the first £16,000 of your capital counts as providing you with an assumed income (para 24.3).

End of transitional capital disregard

26.23 Your transitional capital disregard ends if and when:

(a) your capital reduces below £16,000 or

(b) you were getting UC as a single person and start claiming as a couple or

(c) you were getting UC as a couple and start claiming as a single person or as a couple with a different partner or

(d) your earned income has reduced or ended as in paras 26.18-19 or

(e) you have received UC for 12 successive assessment periods, or (if you have breaks in your UC that are due to an increase in your earned income), for 12 assessment periods not counting the gaps or

(f) you stop being entitled to UC (para 26.24).

It isn't reinstated except as described in para 26.24.

Gaps in your entitlement to UC

26.24 Your transitional capital disregard:

(a) ends as soon as you stop qualifying for UC

(b) is reinstated after a gap in your UC that is due to an increase in your income and is less than three assessment periods

(c) isn't reinstated after any other gap in your UC.

When the transitional capital disregard is reinstated as in (b), its amount is the same as if you had been on UC throughout. This rule can apply any number of times and is particularly important for people who receive non-monthly earnings (paras 22.10-11).

26.22 UCTP 51(2)

26.23 UCTP 50(2), 51(3),(4), 56(2)-(4), 57(2)

26.24 UCTP 56(2), 57(2)

Transitional protection for pension age claimants

Transitional protection if you transfer to UC

26.25 If you transfer from WTC (with or without CTC) to UC, you qualify for one or both of the transitional elements and/or the transitional capital disregard in the normal way. All the rules in para 26.4-24 apply to you.

Transitional protection if you transfer to SPC

26.26 If you transfer from CTC (without WTC) to SPC, and your SPC is lower than your CTC was, you qualify for a 'transitional amount'. This equals the difference between your weekly amount of CTC and your weekly amount of SPC. The detailed rules including how it reduces, and ends are mostly similar to those in paras 26.4-24.

26.25 PC 6(6)(e), sch 2B as inserted by SI 2024/611 reg 4(3),(5)

26.26 PC 6(6)(e) sch 2B as inserted by SI 2024/611 reg 4(3),(5)

Chapter 27 **Support for mortgage interest**

- Who can get SMI: paras 27.1-9
- The SMI waiting period if you are on UC: paras 27.10-13
- The amount of your SMI: paras 27.14-19
- How to get SMI: paras 27.20-28

Who can get SMI

27.1 If you are an owner or shared owner, you can get support for mortgage interest (SMI) towards your mortgage interest or related payments (table 27.1). The SMI payments you receive are a loan secured on your home (and in the law are called 'loans for mortgage interest').

The conditions for getting SMI

27.2 You can get SMI if you meet the following conditions (or in a couple, at least one of you does):

(a) you are an owner or shared owner (paras 27.5-6)

(b) you are liable for mortgage interest or alternative finance payments (table 27.1)

(c) the payments are due on your home (chapter 7)

(d) you are on UC, SPC or a legacy benefit (paras 27.3-4) and

(e) in the case of UC (but not SPC), you complete a three-month SMI waiting period (para 27.10).

In this chapter we use 'mortgage interest payments' to include alternative finance payments unless otherwise stated.

People on UC or SPC

27.3 You can only get SMI if:

(a) you qualify for UC

(b) you qualify for SPC or would qualify for it if your mortgage interest payments were included as part of your maximum SPC.

People on a legacy benefit

27.4 You can also get SMI if you qualify for ESA(IR) or (before they were replaced by UC) JSA(IB) or IS. In this case there is a 39-week SMI waiting period but otherwise the rules are mostly the same as for SPC.

27.1 WRWA 18(1); LMI 3(1),(2)(a), sch 1 paras 2(1), 5(1)

27.2 WRWA 18(1)-(5),(8); LMI 3(1),(2), 8(1)(b),(c)

27.3 LMI 2(1) – 'single claimant', 'SPC claimant', 'UC claimant', 2(2)(aa), 3(1),(2)

27.4 LMI 2(1) – 'legacy benefit', 'legacy benefit claimant', 'qualifying period' 3(2), 8(1)(b)

Owners

27.5 You count as an owner if:

(a) you and/or your partner are liable for mortgage interest on your home as a freeholder or leaseholder or

(b) you are paying the mortgage interest because the person who is liable isn't doing so (the details are the same as in para 9.18) or

(c) you have a reasonable arrangement to share the mortgage interest with the person who is liable (this only applies if you are on SPC).

You can get SMI towards your mortgage interest payments (table 27.1) and also UC or SPC towards your service charges (chapter 15).

Shared owners

27.6 You are a shared owner if you have an equity sharing agreement. This means:

(a) in England and Wales, you are buying a percentage of the value of your home (typically 25%, 50% or 75%) on a shared ownership lease

(b) in Scotland, you are jointly buying your home with your landlord and have the right to purchase their share.

You can get SMI towards your mortgage interest payments (table 27.1) and also UC or HB towards your rent and service charges (chapters 10,15).

Joint owners and shared owners

27.7 If you are a joint owner or joint shared owner with someone who is not in your benefit unit, your SMI is awarded towards your share of the mortgage interest payments. The DWP decides the share based on your circumstances. It is usually the same as your share of your rent and service charges (para 10.13).

SMI if you have two lots of housing costs

27.8 The following rules apply to owners and shared owners:

(a) if you rent somewhere temporary due to a fear of violence (para 8.14), you can get UC, SPC or HB there as well as SMI on your normal home (for UC this is limited to 12 months)

(b) If you move out due to essential repairs you can get help with your mortgage or rent on your temporary home or normal home, but not both (para 7.5)

(c) if you are unavoidably liable for housing costs on two homes (e.g. when you move home) (para 7.24), you can get SMI on one and SPC or HB on the other, or SMI on both

(d) if you are a student couple and have to live apart in order to attend your courses (para 8.24), you can get SMI on one and SPC or HB on the other.

27.5 LMI 2(1) – 'relevant accommodation', 3(2)(a), sch 1 paras 2(1),(2), 5(1),(2); UC 25(1),(2), 26(3) sch 5 paras 1, 3; PC 6(6)(c), sch 2 paras 1(1), 13(1)(b)

27.6 UC 26(6)

27.7 LMI 3(3)

27.8 LMI 3(2)(c), sch 3 paras 4-6, 13, 15

Rules (a) and (b) apply whether you are on UC or SPC, but rules (c) and (d) only apply if you are on SPC.

SMI if you are temporarily absent from your home

27.9 If you are temporarily absent from your normal home, you can continue to get SMI there so long as you intend to return. The time limits are the same as in table 8.1 (depending on whether you claimed SMI with UC or SPC).

Examples: Support for mortgage interest

1. SMI paid with UC

Marcia is a homeowner who qualifies for UC. At the time of her claim, she owes £100,000 to her mortgage lender. She completes the three-month SMI waiting period and then qualifies for SMI:

- Total outstanding capital £100,000
- Multiply by standard rate of interest 3.66% to give annual SMI £3,660
- Divide by 12 to give Marcia's monthly SMI £305.00

2. SMI paid with SPC

Curtis is a homeowner who has unearned income and qualifies for SPC. At the time of his claim, he owes £100,000 to his mortgage lender. There is no SMI waiting period, so he qualifies for SMI:

- Total outstanding capital £100,000
- Multiply by standard rate of interest 3.66% to give annual SMI £3,660
- Divide by 52 to give Curtis's weekly SMI (usually paid four-weekly) £70.38

3. SMI paid with no SPC

Curtis's unearned income increases so that it is £20.38 above his maximum SPC (para 17.4). He stops qualifying for SPC but continues to qualify for SMI:

- His weekly SMI when he was on SPC £70.38
- Subtract amount by which his income exceeds his maximum SPC – £20.38
- Curtis's weekly SMI is now £50.00

27.9 LMI 3(2)(c), sch 3 paras 9, 10, 18

Table 27.1 **The payments SMI can meet**

(a) Mortgage/loan interest for people on UC

People on UC can get SMI towards any mortgage or loan that is secured on your home (whether to purchase your home or not).

(b) Mortgage/loan interest for people on SPC

People on SPC can only get SMI towards a mortgage or loan that is secured on your home and is:

- to purchase your home or increase your equity in it
- to provide any of the following:
  - a bath, shower, sink or toilet
  - ventilation, natural or electric lighting, insulation, damp-proofing, drainage or fuel storage
  - food cooking, preparation and storage facilities
  - repairs to heating systems and unsafe structural defects
  - adaptations for a disabled person
  - separate bedrooms for two people of opposite sexes aged 10 or over but under 20 or
- to pay off another mortgage or loan that met the above conditions.

(c) Special cases for people on SPC

If you took out the mortgage or loan while you were on SPC (or in a break in entitlement to SPC of up to 26 weeks), it must be:

- to purchase a new home better suiting the needs of a disabled person
- to purchase a new home providing separate bedrooms for two people of opposite sexes aged 10 or over but under 20
- to replace an earlier mortgage/loan – but in this case your SMI is limited to the SMI you got on the earlier mortgage/loan or
- taken out while you were on HB – but in this case your SMI is limited to the amount of your HB plus any housing costs you were getting in your SPC or a legacy benefit.

(d) Alternative finance arrangements for people on UC or SPC

People on UC or SPC can get SMI towards an alternative finance arrangement that is recognised by UK law and is to purchase your home or increase your equity in it. These avoid the payment of interest and are sometimes called 'Islamic mortgages'. For example, the following are included:

T27.1(a) LMI sch 1 para 5(1),(2)

T27.1(b) LMI sch 1 para 2(1)(a),(2),(4)-(6)

T27.1(c) LMI sch 1 para 3

T27.1(d) LMI sch 1 paras 2(2)(b), 5(3),(4)

- purchase and resale (murabaha)
- diminishing shared ownership (musharaka)
- profit share agency (mudaraba/wakala)
- investment bonds (sukuk).

Note: Mortgages and loans qualify under (b) or (c) whether you have already carried out the purpose mentioned there or plan to carry it out within the next six months (FMcC v DfC).

The SMI waiting period

27.10 If you are an owner or a shared owner and are on UC, you have to complete a waiting period before you can get SMI towards your mortgage interest payments or any of the payments in table 27.1 (the waiting period never applies if you are on SPC).

27.11 The SMI waiting period is three months (three consecutive assessment periods), during which:

(a) you are liable for mortgage interest payments on your home (or the other payments in table 27.1) and either:

(b) you qualify for UC throughout the waiting period or

(c) you began the waiting period while you were on JSA, ESA or IS and transferred from that benefit to UC with no gap between them longer than one month.

27.12 Note that if you are an owner (not a shared owner) there is a separate waiting period (which sometimes has different rules) before you can get help with service charges in UC (paras 15.20-21).

Other SMI waiting period rules

27.13 The following rules also apply:

(a) if you stop meeting the conditions in para 27.11, you have to complete a new SMI waiting period

(b) if you become a couple or single person during the SMI waiting period, it continues to run

(c) if you become a couple with someone who was previously getting SMI payments on SPC your SMI starts immediately (there is no waiting period)

(d) once you are getting SMI, if there is a break in your UC of six months or less, your SMI restarts when your UC restarts without you having to complete a new SMI waiting period.

T27.1 (note) FMcC v DfC [2016] NICom 70 reported as [2017] AACR 22

27.10 LMI 8(1)(b),(c)

27.11 LMI 2(1) – 'qualifying period', 21

27.12 UC sch 5 paras 1(4), 5-7

27.13 LMI 2(1) – 'qualifying period', 8(1)(ba),(bb), 9(8)

The amount of your SMI

SMI calculations

27.14 SMI is calculated as a monthly amount if you are on UC, or a weekly amount if you are on SPC. Table 27.2 gives the calculation.

Table 27.2 **The amount of your SMI**

(a) The amount you owe

Start with:

- The capital you owe on your mortgage, loan or alternative finance arrangement (table 27.1) or
- Your share of it if you are a joint owner or joint shared owner or
- If lower, the capital limit (para 27.17)

(b) The calculation

- Multiply by the standard rate of interest (para 27.16) to give the annual amount
- Convert this to a monthly or weekly figure (para 1.19)
- If you are on UC and have a mortgage or loan protection policy, subtract the monthly or weekly amount you receive.

(c) Deductions for non-dependants

- If you are on SPC, deduct any amounts for non-dependants that apply to you (table 6.2 and para 6.23). (There are no deductions for non-dependants if you are on UC.)

Annual SMI recalculations

27.15 Your SMI is recalculated on each anniversary date of the day you became entitled to SMI. The recalculation takes into account the capital you currently owe and the current standard rate of interest.

The standard rate of interest

27.16 The standard rate of interest used to calculate SMI is the average mortgage rate published by the Bank of England. On 30 March 2025 it was 3.66%. Changes in the standard rate are published online along with the date they take effect [www].

27.14 LMI 11(1) step 4, 12(1) step 3

T27.2(a) LMI 10, 11(1) steps 1-3, 12(1) steps 1-2, (3)

T27.2(b) LMI 10, 11(1) step 4, 12(1) step 3, 14A

T27.2(c) LMI 14

27.15 LMI 11(4),(5), 12(4),(5)

27.16 LMI 13 www.gov.uk/support-for-mortgage-interest/what-youll-get

The capital limit

27.17 The capital limit is:

(a) £200,000 for UC

(b) £100,000 for SPC.

This capital limit applies to the combined amount of your mortgage interest payments (table 27.1), except when you qualify for SMI on two homes (para 27.8) in which case it applies to each home separately.

Increasing the capital limit for disability adaptations

27.18 This rule only applies to SMI towards a mortgage or loan, not alternative finance payments. The capital limit is increased if:

(a) you, your partner, or a child or young person in your benefit unit:
- gets the daily living component of PIP, or (in Scotland) ADP
- gets the middle or highest rate of the care component of DLA
- gets attendance allowance or equivalent benefit (para 21.18) or
- is 75 or over and meets the disability condition in para 18.28 and

(b) you have a mortgage, loan or alternative finance arrangement that was for adaptations meeting that person's disablement needs.

27.19 In this case, the £200,000/£100,000 capital limit applies to capital you owe for anything other than the adaptations, and the capital you owe for the adaptations is added to this.

How to get SMI

The DWP's offer of SMI

27.20 When you claim UC or SPC you should tell the DWP that you are liable for mortgage interest payments. The DWP then sends you a written offer of SMI, saying that SMI is a loan secured on your home and registered with the Land Registry, what the main terms and conditions are, and where to get independent advice.

27.21 You can choose whether to accept or refuse the DWP's offer. If you refuse (or don't reply) you can't get SMI, but you can still get benefit towards your service charges (owners and shared owners) and rent (shared owners). And you can ask for SMI again at any time.

27.17 LMI 11(2), 12(2)

27.18 LMI 2(1) – 'disabled person', 11(3), sch 3 para 14(3); PC sch 2 para 1(2)(a) (as it was on 05/04/2018)

27.19 LMI 11(3)

27.20 LMI 3(1)

27.21 LMI 4, 5

How the DWP pays your SMI

27.22 The DWP pays your SMI to your lender (this is free of any charge to them) and has approved most lenders for this purpose. The payments are made monthly in arrears. If your lender isn't approved or chooses not to receive payments, the DWP pays you.

27.23 Your lender must use the payments in the following order:

(a) towards your current interest

(b) towards your arrears of interest

(c) towards the capital amount you owe

(d) towards any other debts you owe the lender.

Interest you owe on your SMI

27.24 The DWP charges monthly compound interest on the SMI you have received. This equals the weighted average interest rate on conventional gilts [www]. The rate can change each January and July, and on 1 January 2025 the rate was 4.1%.

Obligatory repayments

27.25 You have to repay the SMI and interest you owe when:

(a) your home is sold, transferred or disposed of, other than to your partner or as in para 27.27 or

(b) you die, or in the case of a couple, the last of you who owns your home dies.

But you (or your estate) aren't normally required to repay more than the amount your home sold for, unless this was below the market value.

Voluntary repayments

27.26 You can choose to make repayments of the SMI and interest you owe at any time, so long as each repayment (other than the final one) is at least £100. You can ask for a completion statement in which the DWP tells you the balance you owe, and this remains valid for 30 days.

27.22 WRWA 19(7),(8); LMI 17, sch 4 para 7

27.23 LMI 17, sch 4 paras 4, 5

27.24 LMI 15 www.gov.uk/support-for-mortgage-interest/repaying-your-loan

27.25 LMI 16(1)-(7)

27.26 LMI 16(8),(9)

Transferring what you owe to a new home

27.27 When you move home, you can transfer the SMI and interest you owe to your new home so long as:

(a) you inform the DWP in advance of your plans

(b) your solicitors write to the DWP agreeing to transfer the charge on your old home to your new home and

(c) the purchase of your new home is completed within 12 weeks of the sale of your old home.

The DWP can agree to pay your solicitor's costs in transferring the charge and add this to the SMI you owe.

Appeals

27.28 You can appeal about your entitlement or amount of SMI. The appeal is dealt with in the same way as UC or SPC (chapter 39).

27.27 LMI 16A

27.28 SSA 8(3)(bc), 9(1), 10(1), 12(1), 28(3)(k), 39(1A); FTPR 22(1)

Chapter 28 **Council tax**

- What is council tax and who is liable to pay it: paras 28.1-21
- Reducing your council tax bill: paras 28.22-30
- Claims, awards and appeals: paras 28.31-36

What is council tax

28.1 Council tax is a tax on dwellings that helps to pay for local services. It applies in England, Scotland and Wales.

28.2 Local councils send out the bills for council tax. In most cases:

(a) one or more residents of a dwelling are liable for council tax there, but in some cases the owner/landlord is liable instead;

(b) the amount of your bill depends on which valuation band your dwelling is in and whether you qualify for any reduction.

This chapter gives the details and the exceptions.

Council tax bands

28.3 The amount of council tax depends on what valuation band a dwelling is in:

(a) in England and Scotland there are eight bands, from A to H;

(b) in Wales there are nine, from A to I.

You can find out which band your home is in online [www]. The amounts for each band are always in proportion to band D (table 28.1).

Dwellings

28.4 There is one council tax bill per dwelling. A 'dwelling' is a single domestic property, for example a house, a flat, a mooring with a houseboat or a pitch with a mobile home. (The last two are 'hereditaments', but we use 'dwellings' for all of them in this guide.) Shops, offices, warehouses, factories and other non-domestic property are subject to business rates (not council tax). Non-domestic property includes holiday lets. In England they must have been available for at least 140 days and actually let for at least 70 days in the previous year.

Your home

28.5 Your 'home' is the dwelling where you live or mostly live. The law calls this your 'sole or main residence'.

28.2 LGFA 1

28.3 LGFA 5(1),(2) www.gov.uk/council-tax-bands www.saa.gov.uk

28.4 LGFA 3, 4, 7; Local Government Finance Act 1988, s66(2B); SI 2022/217

28.5-6 LGFA 6(2),(5)

Table 28.1 **Council tax bands**

Band	Proportion: England and Wales	Proportion: Scotland
A	6/9 of band D	240/360 of band D
B	7/9 of band D	280/360 of band D
C	8/9 of band D	320/360 of band D
D	–	–
E	11/9 of band D	473/360 of band D
F	13/9 of band D	585/360 of band D
G	15/9 of band D	705/360 of band D
H	18/9 of band D	882/360 of band D
I (Wales only)	21/9 of band D	

Residents and occupiers

28.6 The people living in a dwelling are either:

(a) 'residents' – over 18-year-olds who live there as their sole or main residence, including householders, lodgers and non-dependants (paras 28.7-9); or

(b) other occupiers – under 18-year-olds and people with no sole or main residence or whose sole or main residence is elsewhere.

Only residents can be liable for council tax (para 28.10) but both residents and other occupiers can affect whether you qualify for a reduction (para 28.22).

Householders

28.7 We use 'householders' (not a legal term) for residents of a dwelling who own or rent it. You can be a sole householder, householder couple, or joint householder (paras 28.13-16).

Lodgers

28.8 A lodger is someone over 18 who pays a commercial rent to you (or your partner) to live in part of your home.

Non-dependants

28.9 A non-dependant is someone over 18 who:

(a) lives in your home – for example a son, daughter, other relative or friend or a sponsored Ukrainian (table 28.3); but

(b) isn't your partner, young person (para 5.19), joint householder, or a lodger (para 6.14).

T28.1 LGFA 5(1),(2), 36(1)

28.6 LGFA 6(5)

Who is liable for council tax

28.10 This section explains when the residents of a dwelling are liable for council tax (paras 28.11-16) and when the owner/landlord is liable instead (paras 28.17-21).

When the residents are liable

28.11 The general rule is that liability for council tax falls on the resident(s) of a dwelling. If there is more than one, it falls on the resident(s) with the highest legal interest which is the first of the following:

(a) the freehold owner;

(b) the leasehold owner;

(c) the tenant;

(d) the licensee;

(e) any other resident(s).

If you are a couple who reside together and you are liable as in (a)-(e), your partner is also liable, even when they have a lesser interest.

'FTS/SMI' and care leavers

28.12 The rules in paras 28.13-16 refer to people who are full-time students (FTS) or severely mentally impaired (SMI) as described in table 28.4(a),(b). In Wales only, these rules also apply to care leavers aged under 25 (table 28.4(d)) in the same way as to people who are FTS/SMI, except that if the only resident is a care leaver (or all the residents are) you aren't exempt.

Sole householders

28.13 If you are a single person (para 5.4) and own or rent your home just in your name:

(a) you are liable for council tax on your home; but

(b) when you are FTS/SMI, your home is exempt from council tax unless other adults live with you who aren't FTS/SMI or in table 28.3(a) or you live in an HMO (para 28.17).

Householder couples who are joint owners/tenants

28.14 If you are a couple (para 5.5) and own or rent your home in both your names:

(a) you are both jointly liable for council tax on your home; but

(b) when one of you is FTS/SMI, only the other is liable; or

(c) when both of you are FTS/SMI, your home is exempt from council tax unless other adults live with you who aren't FTS/SMI or in table 28.3(a) or you live in an HMO (para 28.17).

28.11 LGFA 6(1)(2)(a)-(e), 9(1),(2)

28.12 LGFA 6(4),(4A),(4B), sch 1 paras 2, 4

28.13 LGFA 6(1),(2)(a)-(e)

28.14 LGFA 6(1)

Householder couples: only one an owner/tenant

28.15 If you are a couple and one partner owns or rents your home but the other partner doesn't:

(a) you are both jointly liable for council tax on your home; or

(b) when only the owner/renter partner is FTS/SMI, you are both jointly liable; but

(c) when only the non-owner/renter partner is FTS/SMI, only the owner/renter partner is liable; or

(d) when both of you are FTS/SMI, your home is exempt from council tax unless other adults live with you who aren't FTS/SMI or in table 28.3(a).

These rules were confirmed in E v Sandwell MBC, which is not binding case law but is widely accepted as correct (CTGM 8.3.8(b)).

Joint householders

28.16 If you are single or a couple and own or rent your home with one or more others (e.g. relatives or friends in a house-share):

(a) you are all jointly liable for council tax on your home; but

(b) when one or more of you is FTS/SMI, only the other(s) are liable; or

(c) when all of you are FTS/SMI, your home is exempt unless other adults live with you who aren't FTS/SMI or in table 28.3(a) or you live in an HMO (para 28.17).

When the owner is liable not the residents

28.17 Non-resident owners are liable if there are no residents in the dwelling (para 28.21). Additionally, in the classes of dwelling in table 28.2, the owner/landlord is liable for the council tax, not the resident(s). This is the case even if all the occupiers are FTS/SMI or under 18, because the council tax exemptions in table 28.3 don't apply.

Houses in multiple occupation

28.18 A house in multiple occupation (HMO) is a building that:

(a) has been constructed or adapted for occupation by more than one household; or

(b) is inhabited by one or more people each of whom:

- is a tenant of or has a licence to occupy only part of the dwelling, or
- has a licence to occupy but is not solely or jointly liable to pay rent for the whole dwelling.

The adaptation in (a) can be adding locks to rooms, converting the use of a room, etc, depending on the details of the individual case (CTGM 8.3.5).

28.15 LGFA 6(3),(4), 9(1),(2)

28.16 LGFA 6(3),(4)

28.17 LGFA 8, CT(LO) 2

28.18 Table 15.2 Class C as amended by SI 1993/151 and SI 1995/620

Table 28.2 **Owner liable not residents**

(a) A house in multiple occupation (para 28.18).
(b) A bail/probation hostel or hostel providing personal care (para 28.20(a),(b)).
(c) A care home or independent hospital.
(d) A dwelling occupied by a minister of religion.
(e) A dwelling occupied by a religious community (table 28.4(l)).
(f) A second home occupied only by live-in staff and their families.
(g) A dwelling provided to asylum seekers by the Home Office.
(h) An empty dwelling (para 28.21).

Note:

- If you live in an HMO or hostel, your rent usually includes an amount towards the landlord's council tax.

28.19 The most familiar example of an HMO is a house where the landlord lets out rooms separately and there is a shared bathroom/WC, kitchen and/or living room. But any dwelling that meets the conditions in para 28.18 is an HMO for council tax purposes, even if it doesn't count as an HMO for Housing Act licensing or other purposes.

Hostels

28.20 A hostel is:

(a) a bail or probation hostel ('approved premises');

(b) a building or part of a building used solely or mainly for residential accommodation that is provided in non-self-contained units, together with personal care for people who are elderly, disabled, have a past or present alcohol or drug dependence or a past or present mental disorder; or

(c) a dwelling (including a night shelter) that provides non self-contained accommodation:
- for people with no fixed abode or settled way of life; and
- where the individual lettings are licences rather than tenancies.

T28.2(a)-(g) LGFA 8(1)-(3); CT(LO) 2, Classes A to F
T28.2(a) CT(LO) 2, Class C substituted by SI 1993/151, amended by SI 1995/620 reg 2
T28.2(b),(c) CT(LO) 2, Class A as substituted by SI 2003/3125, amended by SI 2015/643
T28.2(d) CT(LO) 2, Class E amended by SI 1995/620 reg 3
T28.2(e) CT(LO) 2, Class B
T28.2(f) CT(LO) 2, Class D
T28.2(g) CT(LO) 2, Class F added by SI 2000/537
T28.2(h) LGFA 6(1),(2)(f)
28.20 LGFA sch 1 paras 7, 10; in DDO 6 definition: 'hostel' as substituted by SI 2003/3121 art 4

Empty dwellings

28.21 There are many council tax rules about dwellings that have no occupiers, or only have occupiers at certain times of the year. National law sets classes of dwellings and local councils decide how much to alter the council tax on them. So, the landlord/owner:

- may be liable for an empty homes premium or second home premium (meaning they have to pay more than if the home was occupied) or
- may qualify for a discount (though most councils don't allow the 50% discount that used to apply to empty dwellings).

You should be able to obtain details from your local council for the area your empty dwelling is in.

Reducing your council tax bill

28.22 You can get help with council tax if you qualify for:

(a) an exemption (para 28.23);

(b) a disability reduction (para 28.24);

(c) a discount (para 28.26); and/or

(d) a council tax rebate (chapter 29).

Your council may also offer discounts for prompt payment or for payment by one of its preferred methods.

Council tax exemptions

28.23 When a dwelling is exempt, no one has to pay council tax on it. Your council tax bill should show you have nothing to pay. Table 28.3 lists all the classes of exempt dwelling.

Council tax disability reductions

28.24 When you qualify for a disability reduction:

(a) your council tax is reduced to the amount for the next band down – for example, for homes in band D the bill is reduced to the amount for band C;

(b) if your home is in band A (the lowest band) your bill is reduced by one sixth.

28.21 LGFA 11, 11A, 11B, 11C; SI 2003/3011 as amended by SIs 2004/926, 2005/416, 2005/2886, 2012/2964, 2019/1458, 2024/1007, 2025/8

28.22 LGFA 4, 11, 13, 13A

28.23 LGFA 4(1)-(4)

28.24 LGFA 13(1),(4),(6),(7); CT(RD) 4 as amended by SI 1999/1004

Table 28.3 **Council tax exempt dwellings**

(a) A dwelling whose only occupiers are any combination of:
- full time students (table 28.4(a))
- people who are severely mentally impaired (table 28.4(b))
- in Scotland and Wales, young care leavers (table 28.4(d))
- people from Ukraine who have leave under the Homes for Ukraine scheme, and in Scotland, people from Ukraine whose leave gives access to public funds (table 40.3) or
- under 18-year-olds.

(b) An unoccupied dwelling left empty by a student or someone who became a student within six weeks after leaving.

(c) A hall of residence predominantly for students.

(d) An unoccupied dwelling whose owner/renter (the last person liable for council tax):
- resides elsewhere to receive personal care
- resides elsewhere to provide personal care
- is in hospital or long-term care
- has died within the last six months or
- is detained in prison or hospital.

(e) An unoccupied dwelling that is owned by a charity and was in use by the charity within the last six months.

(f) In Wales, an unoccupied dwelling that has been vacant:
- for less than six months or
- for less than 12 months and which requires major repairs or structural changes to make it habitable.

(g) An unoccupied dwelling awaiting occupation by a minister of religion.

Table continued ➤

T28.3(a) CT(ED) Class N substituted by SI 1993/150, amended by SI 1995/619, SI 2005/2865; Class S added by SI 1995/619; Class U substituted by SI 1999/536; Classes N, S and U amended by SI 2022/439

T28.3(b) CT(ED) Class K substituted by SI 1993/150

T28.3(c) CT(ED) Class M amended by SI 1993/150 and SI 1994/539

T28.3(d) CT(ED) Class I substituted by SI 2003/3121; Classes D, E, F and J amended/substituted by SI 1994/539, Class E amended by SI 2005/2865

T28.3(e) CT(ED) Class B, amended by SI 1994/539

T28.3(f) CT(ED) Classes A and C abolished in England by SI 2012/2965

T28.3(g) CT(ED) Class H

(h) An unoccupied dwelling whose owner/renter (the person who would now be liable for council tax) is bankrupt.

(i) An unoccupied dwelling that has been repossessed by a mortgage lender.

(j) An unoccupied dwelling whose occupation is prohibited by law or by a planning restriction.

(k) UK armed forces accommodation owned by the Secretary of State for Defence.

(l) Visiting forces accommodation.

(m) A dwelling where the liable resident has diplomatic immunity.

(n) An empty houseboat mooring or mobile home pitch.

(o) An unoccupied annex or dwelling, that can't be let separately due to a planning restriction.

(p) An annex or self-contained part of a property occupied by a dependant relative who is over 65, or severely mentally impaired (table 28.4(b)), or substantially and permanently disabled.

Notes:

- A Ukrainian who has leave under the Homes for Ukraine scheme is disregarded when deciding if the dwelling is unoccupied in items (b), (d), (e), (g)-(i) and (o).
- None of the exemptions apply to HMOs, hostels or any dwelling where the owner is liable, not the residents (table 28.2).
- All exemptions apply in England and Wales. In Scotland (a)-(l) apply with some differences, and there are further exemptions including sheltered housing owned by a housing association and a dwelling which is the main residence of people seeking asylum who have been resettled under a UK government programme.

T28.3(h) CT(ED) Class Q added by SI 1993/150, amended by SI 1994/539

T28.3(i) CT(ED) Class L

T28.3(j) CT(ED) Class G substituted by SI 2006/2318

T28.3(k) CT(ED) Class O amended by SI 1992/2941

T28.3(l) CT(ED) Class P added by SI 1992/2941

T28.3(m) CT(ED) Class V added by SI 1997/656, definition – 'dependent relative' in class amended by SI 1998/291

T28.3(n) CT(ED) Class R added by SI 1994/539

T28.3(o) CT(ED) Class T added SI 1995/619

T28.3(p) CT(ED) Class W added by SI1997/656, definition – dependent relative in class amended by SI 1998/291

T28.3 notes CT(ED) 2(1),(3A) – 'relevant Ukrainian person', amended by SI 2022/439

Who gets a disability reduction

28.25 You qualify for a disability reduction if:

(a) you are disabled, or at least one disabled adult or child has their home with you; and

(b) your home provides:

- an additional kitchen or bathroom for the disabled person's use; or
- an additional room (not a kitchen, bathroom or toilet) used predominantly to meet their special needs; or
- sufficient floor space to use a wheelchair if they need one; and

(c) this is of major importance to the disabled person's well-being, taking account of the nature and extent of their disability; and

(d) you make a written application for it (see also para 28.34).

Your home doesn't need to have been specifically adapted. For example, it could be that the disabled person has to have a separate bedroom or a bedroom downstairs.

Council tax discounts

28.26 When you qualify for a discount, your council tax is reduced by 25%. This is called a 'single occupancy' discount).

Who gets a discount

28.27 Discounts depend on how many adults there are in your home (this means people over 18) and how many of them are 'disregarded persons' (table 28.4).

28.28 When you are the only adult in your home, you qualify for:

(a) a 25% discount; or

(b) a 50% discount if you are a disregarded person (table 28.4).

28.29 When there are two adults in your home (including you), you qualify for:

(a) a 25% discount if one of you is a disregarded person; or

(b) a 50% discount if you both are.

28.30 When there are three or more adults in your home, you qualify for:

(a) a 25% discount if all but one of you are disregarded persons; or

(b) a 50% discount if you all are.

28.25 CT(RD) 3(1),(3)

28.26 LGFA 11(1)-(3), 11A(1)-(4)

28.27-30 LGFA 11(1)-(3)

Examples: Council tax discounts

1. Single person with discount

June owns her home and is the only person who lives there.

- She qualifies for a 25% discount – because she is the only adult there.

2. Couple with no discount

Jane and John are a couple. They rent their home and are the only people who live there.

- They don't qualify for a discount – because there are two adults and neither are disregarded persons.

3. Couple with discount

Geoff and Gina are a couple. They rent their home and Geoff is severely mentally impaired.

- They qualify for a 25% discount – because there are two adults and one is a disregarded person (table 28.4(b)).

4. Single person plus non-householder

Geri rents her home. Her father lives with her and is on the guarantee credit of SPC.

- Geri can't get a discount – because there are two adults, and neither are disregarded.
- But she can get second adult rebate – because her father is a non-dependant with a low income (para 30.29).

Claims, awards and appeals

Claims and awards

28.31 The council uses information you provide, or that it already holds, to decide:

(a) who is liable for council tax; and

(b) who qualifies for exemptions, disability reductions or discounts.

When your liability increases, you have 21 days to inform the council, otherwise you can incur a penalty. When it reduces there is no time limit (para 28.34) but the longer you leave it, the more difficult it may be to provide any evidence the council needs.

28.31 CT(A&E) 11, 16; CT(RD) 5

Table 28.4 **Council tax disregarded persons**

The following 'disregarded persons' affect discounts (paras 28.27-30), non-dependant deductions in main CTR (table 6.3) and second adult rebate (paras 30.28-33). Definitions (a) and (b) also apply for exemptions (table 28.3). Details for Scotland and Wales may differ in some cases.

(a) Full-time students

Anyone who:

- is on a one-year or longer UK or EU course at level 3 or above (A levels, degrees etc) and is expected to study at least 21 hours per week, for at least 24 weeks per year
- is under 20 and is on a three-month or longer UK or EU course and is expected to study for at least 12 hours per week during term times
- is studying to be included for the first time in the nursing register
- is a foreign language assistant registered with the British Council or
- is under 20 and left one of these courses during May to October – this applies until 31 October in the year they leave.

(b) People who are severely mentally impaired

Anyone who has a medical certificate confirming they have a severe impairment of intelligence and social functioning, and receives (or would receive but for being over 66):

- the daily living component of PIP or (in Scotland) the standard or enhanced rate of the daily living component of ADP
- the middle or highest rate of the care component of DLA or (in Scotland) SADLA or CDP
- attendance allowance, PADP or an equivalent benefit (para 21.18)
- the LCW or LCWRA element of UC
- SDA or
- in Scotland, ESA.

(c) Under 20-year olds for whom child benefit is payable

Anyone aged under 20 for whom child benefit could be paid (para 5.19).

Table continued ➤

T28.4(a)-(m) LGFA 11(5), sch 1

T28.4(a) LGFA sch 1 paras 4, 5; DDO 4, sch 1 paras 2-7; DDR 3 Class C; SI 1993/149; SI 1994/543; SI 2006/3396 art 2(2)(b)

T28.4(b) LGFA sch 1 para 2; DDO 3; SI 1994/543; SI 2013/388 sch para 12; SI 2013/591 sch para 5; SI 2013/630 reg 55

T28.4(c) LGFA sch 1 para 3

(d) Care leavers under 25/26 (Wales and Scotland only)

Anyone who:

- is under 25 (Wales) or 26 (Scotland)
- was in local authority care at any time after age 16, but has since left care and
- in Wales only, was in care between the ages of 14 and 16 for one or more periods totalling at least three months (but ignoring any short-term placements intended to last less than four weeks).

Many English councils offer a similar reduction using CTR (paras 29.14, 29.19).

(e) Youth trainees under 25

Anyone under 25 who is undertaking government funded youth training.

(f) Apprentices

Anyone who is studying for an accredited qualification as part of their employment and is paid no more than £195 per week.

(g) Carers

Any carer who provides care for at least 35 hours per week to someone in your home, if the person they care for gets or could get:

- the daily living component of PIP or ADP
- the middle or highest rate of the care component of DLA or SADLA or
- attendance allowance, PADP, or an equivalent benefit (para 21.18).

But in Scotland in each case, the award must be at the enhanced/highest/higher rate. The carer can be a relative or friend of the person they care for; but not their partner, nor (in the case of a child/young person under 18) their parent.

(h) Live-in care workers

Any carer who:

- provides care to someone in your home
- was introduced by a local council, government department or charity and
- is paid no more than £44 per week.

(i) Night shelter and homeless hostel residents

Anyone who, on any day has his/her sole or main residence under a licence agreement in a resettlement/homeless hostel or night shelter (para 28.20(c)) that mainly provides non-self-contained accommodation.

T28.4(d) See Appendix 4

T28.4(e) LGFA sch 1 para 4(1); DDO 4, sch 1 para 8; SI 2006/3396 art 2(2)(c)

T28.4(f) LGFA sch 1 para 4(1); DDO 4, sch 1 para 1; SI 2006/3396 art 2(2)(a)

T28.4(g) LGFA sch 1 para 9(1)(b),(g); DDR 2; sch paras 3, 4; SI 1994/540; SI 1996/637; SI 2013/388 sch para 3; SI 2013/591 sch para 6; SI 2013/725

T28.4(h) LGFA sch 1 para 9(1),(2)(a)-(g); DDR 2; sch paras 1, 2; SI 2006/3395 reg 4

T28.4(i) LGFA sch 1 para 10

(j) Care home and hospital residents

Anyone whose sole or main residence is an NHS hospital, independent hospital or care home, or hostel that provides personal care for people who require it due to old age, disability, mental disorder or past or present alcohol or drug dependence (para 28.20(b)).

(k) Prisoners, bail hostel residents and hospital detainees

For details about who is a prisoner or hospital detainee see para 3.23.

(l) Members of religious communities

Any member who is maintained by the community and has no money of their own (apart from an occupational pension).

(m) Non-British partners of students

Any spouse or civil partner who is not permitted to work or claim benefits.

(n) Diplomats etc

Anyone who has diplomatic immunity or is a member of visiting forces, and in some cases their spouse, civil partner or dependants.

(o) Persons evacuated from Ukraine and other resettled asylum seekers

A person who has leave under the Homes for Ukraine sponsorship scheme, and in Scotland a person seeking asylum who entered the UK under a relocation or resettlement scheme.

Changes to your council tax bill

28.32 When your circumstances change, your council tax starts, changes or ends on the exact day. For example, when you move:

(a) your council tax on the new home starts on the day of your move;

(b) your council tax on the old home ends on the day before (or later in some cases if you leave it empty).

Council tax reconsiderations

28.33 You can ask the council to reconsider decisions it makes about council tax liability, exemptions, disability reductions and discounts. (For reconsiderations about council tax rebates, see paras 29.52-54.)

T28.4(j) LGFA sch 1 paras 6, 7; DDO 6(b) definition: 'hostel' as substituted by SI 2003/3121 art 4

T28.4(k) LGFA sch 1 paras 1, 7; DDO 2, 6(a) definition: 'hostel' as substituted by SI 2003/3121 art 4

T28.4(l) LGFA sch 1 para 11; DDR 3 Class B

T28.4(m) LGFA sch 1 para 11; DDR 3 Class A, Class E; SI 1995/620 reg 4

T28.4(n) LGFA sch 1 para 11; DDR 3 Class A, Class D, Class F; SI 1992/2942 reg 2; SI 1995/620 reg 4; SI 1997/657

T28.4(o) LGFA sch 1 para 11; DDR3 Class G added by SI 2022/439 reg 2

28.32 LGFA 2

28.33 LGFA 15, 16

Mistakes about liability

28.34 When there has been a mistake about whether or when you are liable for council tax, or qualify for an exemption or discount, there is no time limit on how far back the council can go. If you make an appeal the Limitation Act 1980 sets a six-year time limit from the date on which 'the cause of action accrued' but the Valuation Tribunal has interpreted this phrase fairly widely (CTGM 10.3.7(b)-(c)). For example, your council must take reasonable steps to find out if you qualify for a discount or an exemption and the tribunal may decide the time limit starts from the date they do this. But if your appeal relates to a disability reduction the time limit runs back from the date you first apply for it (Arca v Carlisle CC).

28.35 A dispute about liability, a discount etc (para 28.34) is not a defence against the council getting a liability order in the magistrates court for unpaid council tax. This is because only a tribunal can decide these disputes (Lone v LB Hounslow).

Council tax appeals

28.36 You can appeal to a valuation tribunal in England and Wales or a first-tier tribunal in Scotland:

(a) within two months of the council's decision letter if they don't give you everything you asked for or

(b) between two and four months after your reconsideration request if the council doesn't respond.

Your appeal is limited to matters raised in your reconsideration request.

28.34 CT(A&E) 8, 14; Arca v Carlisle [2013] RA 248

28.35 Lone v LB Hounslow [2019] EWCA Civ 2206, [2020] 1 WLR 952

Chapter 29 **Council tax rebates**

- Who can get CTR: paras 29.1-12
- Local CTR/CTR classes: paras 29.13-19
- Discretionary CTR: paras 29.20-23
- Exclusions from CTR: paras 29.24-34
- CTR claims, changes and reconsiderations: paras 29.35-54

Who can get CTR

29.1 Council tax rebates (CTR) apply in England, Scotland and Wales. This chapter and chapter 30 describe the different kinds of council tax rebate you can get and these are summarised in table 29.1. The law calls them 'council tax reductions' and some councils in England call them council tax support.

Table 29.1 **Kinds of CTR**

(a) National CTR

CTR has national rules that apply in England for pension age claims, and in Wales and Scotland for all claims. It is for when you have a low income, and if you have a non-dependant they may be expected to contribute towards your council tax (para 30.7).

(b) Second adult rebate

SAR has national rules that apply in England for pension age claims and in Scotland for all claims. It is for when you have a non-dependant who stops you getting a discount (para 28.26) but has a low income (paras 30.28-35).

(c) Local CTR/CTR classes

Councils in England must have a local CTR scheme for working age claims, and this is made up of CTR classes (para 29.11). Councils can also have CTR classes for pension age claims in England and all claims in Wales (paras 29.7-9). Local CTR classes have local rules (para 29.13).

(d) Discretionary CTR

Discretionary CTR applies in England and Wales. Councils can award it whether or not you qualify for any of the above (para 29.20).

T29.1 LGFA 13A(1)(c),(2) sch 1A para 2(1)-(4),(9); CTRE(PR) sch 1 paras 1-4; CTRE(DS) 13-18

Residents

29.2 To get any of the kinds of CTR you must be a resident who is liable for council tax (paras 28.6, 28.11). If you are jointly liable with one or more others (apart from just your partner in a couple) the figures used in the main CTR and SAR calculations are shared between you (paras 30.12, 30.35).

Your benefit unit and non-dependants

29.3 Your CTR takes account of you and your benefit unit (paras 5.2-3). Non-dependants (para 6.1) can't get CTR themselves but may affect your CTR (para 30.7).

Working age and pension age

29.4 Working age means under 66 and pension age means 66 or over. Table 29.2 shows whether you can get working age or pension age CTR. Note that the rules for mixed age couples are sometimes different from the other benefits (para 2.3).

Table 29.2 **Pension age or working age CTR**

Single person	
(a) Over 66	Pension age CTR
(b) Under 66	Working age CTR
Couple	
(c) Both over 66	Pension age CTR
(d) Both under 66	Working age CTR
(e) Mixed ages (one over, one under 66):	
■ Claimant is over 66	Pension age CTR
■ Claimant is under 66	Working age CTR

National variations

29.5 Paras 29.6-12 summarise the CTR variations between Scotland, Wales and England. The most notable is that:

(a) CTR for all ages in Scotland and Wales and for pension age claims in England have mainly national rules but

(b) CTR for working age claims in England has mainly local rules.

29.2 LGFA sch 1A para 2(2)(a),(b); CTRE(PR) sch 1 paras 1(1), 2(a), 3(a), 4(1)(a); CTRE(DS) 13(a), 14(a), 15(1)(a), 16(a), 17(a), 18(1)(a)

29.3 LGFA sch 1A para 2(2)(c); CTRE(PR) 9; CTRE(DS) 9

29.4 Pensions Act 1995, sch 4 para 1(6); CTRE(PR) 2(1) definitions: 'pensioner', pensionable age, 'qualifying age for state pension credit'; CTRE(DS) 2(1)

T29.2 CTRE(PR) 3, sch 1 para 2(f), 3(f), 4(e), sch 8 paras 3, 4(1); CTRE(DS) 3, 13(f), 14(g), 15(1)(e), 16(f), 17(g), 18(1)(e), 109(1)

29.5 LGFA sch 1A para 2(1),(3),(8),(9); CTRE(PR) 11(1), 14(1), sch 1 paras 1-4

CTR in Scotland

29.6 Every council in Scotland operates the national CTR rules. The council:

(a) must have CTR and SAR for both pension age and working age claims (chapter 30)

(b) must include the alternative CTR calculation for dwellings in bands E to H (paras 30.8, 30.11) and

(c) must fully disregard war pensions (paras 21.24-25).

Discretionary CTR doesn't apply.

CTR in Wales

29.7 Every council in Wales must have a CTR scheme. This scheme:

(a) must include CTR for both pension age and working age claims (chapter 30)

(b) may lengthen the backdating period (para 29.45) and/or the period of extended CTR (para 30.27)

(c) may increase the disregard for war pensions (para 21.25) and

(d) may have local CTR classes that supplement national CTR.

The council must also provide for discretionary CTR.

29.8 Local CTR classes must follow the rules in paras 29.13-16. They are in practice uncommon. Those that exist are like SAR or council tax discounts, where a flat rate is awarded to people who meet the conditions set by the council.

Pension age CTR in England

29.9 Every council in England must have a CTR scheme for pension age claims, made up of CTR classes. This scheme:

(a) must include main CTR (para 30.3) – this counts as two classes (class A for claimants without excess income and class B for those with excess income)

(b) must include SAR (para 30.3) – this counts as one class (class C)

(c) may increase the disregard for war pensions (para 21.25) and

(d) may have additional CTR classes that supplement CTR and/or SAR (para 29.10).

The council must also provide for discretionary CTR.

29.10 Local CTR classes must follow the rules in paras 29.13-16. They are in practice rare.

29.6 LGFA 80(1),(2); CTS 3, 13(1), 14(1), 57(1); CTRSP 12, 14(1), 14A(1), sch 3 paras 1-2

29.7 LGFA 13(1)(b),(c),(4),(5), sch 1B paras 2(1), 3, 4; CTRW(PR) 14, 21-24, 32, 33, 34(4),(5)

29.8 LGFA 13A(1)(b),(4),(5), sch 1B paras 3-5; CTRW(PR) 3-10, 12, 14-18, 27-29

29.9 LGFA sch 1A para 2(1)-(4),(8),(9); CTRE(PR) 11(1), 14(1), sch 1 paras 1-4

29.10 LGFA 13A(2), sch 1A paras 2, 3, 5; SI 2017/1305, reg 2

Working age CTR in England

29.11 Every council in England must have a CTR scheme for working age claimants made up of CTR classes. This scheme:

(a) must include one or more CTR classes giving the council's primary rules for working age CTR – this is sometimes called 'local CTR' (para 29.12)

(b) may increase the disregard for war pensions (para 21.25) and

(c) may have additional CTR classes that supplement local CTR (para 29.12).

The council must also provide for discretionary CTR.

29.12 All local CTR classes must follow the rules in paras 29.13-16. For examples of local CTR, see paras 29.17-19.

Example: Working age CTR in England

Joyce is a care leaver aged 23. She has lost her job and claims UC and CTR. The DWP awards her UC. Her local council has two CTR classes that apply to her:

- a reduced form of national CTR based on 80% of the council tax (para 29.17) – the council calls this class D
- a flat rate 25% reduction for care leavers under 25 (para 29.19) – the council calls this class G

and people who qualify for both get whichever is the most.

Joyce's CTR claim covers both classes, and she is awarded the council's class D.

Local CTR/CTR classes

29.13 When councils set CTR classes, there are requirements (in paras 29.14-16) about:

(a) basing classes on financial need

(b) following national rules and

(c) setting and changing classes.

Those requirements apply to the CTR classes that make up working age CTR in England (local CTR) and all other CTR classes in England and Wales.

Financial need

29.14 CTR classes must be based on financial need, not on other factors such as length of residence (R (Winder) v Sandwell MBC). This means your or your family's:

(a) own financial circumstances or

(b) membership of a group that is generally at higher risk of being in financial need than the wider population, such as people with disabilities, carers, young care leavers and others.

29.11 LGFA 13A((1)(a),(c),(2),(3), sch 1A para 2(1)-(4)

29.12 LGFA 13A(2), sch 1A paras 2, 3, 5; SI 2017/1305, reg 2

29.13 LGFA sch 1A paras 2(1),(3),(5)-(7),(9), 3(1)-(3), 5; SI 2017/1305, reg 2; CTRE(PR) 11-15, sch 1 paras 1-5

29.14 LGFA 13A(2), sch 1B para 3(4)-(7)
R (Winder) v Sandwell MBC [2014] EWHC 2617 Admin, [2015] PTSR 34

Following national rules

29.15 And all local CTR classes must follow the national CTR rules about:

(a) what is a 'working age' claim
(b) who is included in your household
(c) which migrants and recent arrivals are excluded
(d) certain minimum standards relating to claims, decision notices and appeals.

Setting and changing CTR classes

29.16 All CTR classes apply and can be changed from 1 April each year. Councils must:

(a) consult with local residents about classes and changes to them – this must be done in a 'meaningful way' (R (Moseley) v Haringey LBC)
(b) include transitional rules when changes to schemes end or reduce your entitlement and
(c) publish details of their classes and how you can apply (which most councils do on their website).

Any changes in CTR classes must be confirmed by 11 March (in Wales, 31 January) in time for the new financial year starting on 1 April.

Local CTR: classes based on national CTR

29.17 Some councils have CTR classes for working age claims that adopt the national CTR rules in full (the 'default scheme'). Many more have variations on national CTR that do one or more of the following:

(a) reduce the amount of council tax that can be met by CTR (this is often the only variation)
(b) set a minimum award
(c) reduce the upper capital limit
(d) increase or restructure the non-dependant contributions and the income bands
(e) vary the assessment of different kinds of income
(f) increase the excess income taper above 20%
(g) limit or remove entitlement to backdated CTR
(h) limit or remove entitlement to SAR or
(i) set their own rates for some or all of the allowances, premiums and components in the calculation of the applicable amount.

These schemes have the advantages of sensitivity to changes in income and being similar to other benefits, but the disadvantages of requiring frequent changes in the award.

29.15 LGFA sch 1A para 2(9); CTRE(PR) 3-15, sch 7, sch 8
R (Moseley) v Haringey LBC [2014] UKSC 56, [2014] 1 WLR 3947, [2014] PTSR 1317

29.16 LGFA sch 1A paras 3(1),(3),(5), 5(1)-(6); SI 2017/1305 reg 2

29.17 LGFA 13A(2), sch 1A para 2(2),(4)

Local CTR: classes based on income bands

29.18 Some councils have working age CTR classes that are based on income bands. Usually your CTR equals a high percentage of your council tax if you are in the lowest income band, which reduces for higher income bands. These classes have the advantage of simplicity and less frequent changes in your CTR, but the disadvantage of sudden jumps from one amount of CTR to another (or to nil) when your income crosses between bands.

Local CTR: other kinds of classes

29.19 Some councils have CTR classes that are like SAR or council tax discounts, where a flat rate discount is awarded for a group-based financial need, for example, for young care leavers (para 29.14).

Discretionary CTR

29.20 Discretionary CTR applies in England and Wales, not Scotland. Councils can award it based on your individual or group-based financial need (para 29.14).

29.21 You can get discretionary CTR:

(a) to top up your national CTR, SAR or local CTR or

(b) you don't qualify for these (e.g. your income is too high or you are excluded: para 29.24).

This could reduce the amount of council tax you have to pay to a lower figure or to nil.

29.22 The council can treat any claim for CTR as a request for discretionary CTR. But in practice you need to make it clear in writing that you are asking for discretionary CTR, and if the council requires you to request it in a particular way (e.g. on a form) it must tell you.

29.23 You can appeal almost any decision about discretionary CTR to a tribunal (para 39.5).

Exclusions from CTR

29.24 You may be excluded from:

(a) main CTR and SAR if you are absent from home (paras 29.25-32)

(b) main CTR and SAR if you are a migrant (para 29.33)

(c) main CTR (not SAR) if you are a full-time student (para 29.34)

(d) main CTR (not SAR) if you have capital over £16,000 (para 24.2).

In the case of local CTR/CTR classes, councils must apply exclusion (b) to working age and pension age claims and (d) to pension age claims. They can choose whether to apply any of the other exclusions. None of the exclusions apply to discretionary CTR.

29.18 LGFA 13A(2), sch 1A para 2(2),(4)

29.19 LGFA 13A(2),(3), sch 1A para 2(1)-(4)

29.20 LGFA 13A(1)(c),(6),(7)

29.21 LGFA 13A(1)(c),(6), sch 1A para 2(2),(4)

29.22 LGFA 13A(1)(c),(6),(7); CTRE(PR) sch 7 para 9(2)

29.24 LGFA sch 1A para 2(9); CTRE(PR) 11-13; sch 1 paras 2(b),(d), 3(b),(d), 4(1)(b),(d), 5; CTRE(DS) 13-24, 75(1),(2)

Absences from home

29.25 You are excluded from national CTR (including SAR) for each full day you (the claimant) are absent from your home unless you meet one of the conditions in paras 29.26-32. The national rules vary between England, Wales, and Scotland and in each case depend on whether the absence is within or outside Great Britain.

England: temporary absence

29.26 In England, national CTR follows the HB rules for absences within and outside Great Britain (chapter 8).

Wales: temporary absence

29.27 In Wales, national CTR follows the HB rules for absences within Great Britain (chapter 8).

29.28 For absences outside Great Britain, you can get CTR:

(a) for up to 52 weeks if are absent because:
- you or your family member are receiving medically approved treatment or convalescence other than in a care home (para 8.19)
- you are receiving or providing medically approved care other than in a care home (para 8.17) or
- you are on a government training course (para 8.24) or

(b) in any other case, for up to 13 weeks following the HB general rule (para 8.12).

Scotland: your home and temporary absence

29.29 In Scotland, you can sometimes get CTR on two homes, on a home before you move in or after you have moved out, or if you move out while repairs are done. The rules are the same as for HB (chapter 7). But the rules about temporary absence also apply.

29.30 For absences within Great Britain, CTR follows the HB rules in chapter 8 (13 or 52 weeks).

29.31 For absences outside Great Britain, you can get CTR:

(a) without time limit if it is due to your employment as a member of HM armed forces, a mariner, a continental shelf worker, an aircraft worker or a Crown servant

(b) for up to 52 weeks in the same circumstances as in Wales (para 29.28(a)) and

(c) during a period in which your absence is disregarded (meaning CTR can continue), provided you were entitled to CTR immediately before that period started.

29.25 CTRE(PR) sch 1 paras 2(b), 3(b), 4(1)(b), 5(1); CTRE(DS) 13(b), 14(b), 15(1)(b), 16(b), 17(b), 18(1)(b), 19(1); CTRW(PR) 22(b), 23(b), 24(b), 25(b), 26(1); CTRW(DS) 13(b), 14(b), 15(b), 16(b), 17(1); CTRSW 13(1),(3)(b), 14(1),(3)(b), 15(1),(2); CTRSP 14(1),(3)(b), 14A(1),(3)(b), 15(1),(2)

29.26 CTRE(PR) sch 1 para 5; CTRE(DS) 19

29.27 CTRW(PR) 26(2)-(4); CTRW(DS) 17(2)-(4)

29.28 CTRW(PR) 26(2)(b),(c),(3)(c),(d),(e),(g); CTRW(DS) 17(2)(c),(d),(3)(c),(d),(e),(g)

29.29 CTRSW 9; CTRSP 5

29.30 CTRSW 15(2)-(4); CTRSP 15(2)-(4)

29.31 CTRSW 15(4)(c),(d),(e),(g), 17, 18; CTRSP 15(4)(c),(d),(e),(g), 17, 18

29.32 A period of absence outside Great Britain is disregarded:

(a) for up to six months if your absence is due to:

- your medical treatment for an illness or disability by an appropriately qualified practitioner
- you accompanying a member of your benefit unit or a close relative for medical treatment or
- you undergoing medically approved convalescence as result of treatment of an illness or disability, provided you had that illness or disability before leaving Great Britain

(b) for up to two months if your absence is due to the death of a member of your benefit unit or a close relative and it is unreasonable to expect you to return within one month or

(c) for up to one month for any other absence.

Migrants

29.33 You are excluded from national CTR, SAR and local CTR/CTR classes if you (the claimant) are a migrant or have recently arrived in the UK, unless you are on UC, SPC, JSA(IB), ESA(IR) or IS, or in one of the eligible groups in table 40.1.

Full-time students

29.34 You are excluded from main CTR (but not SAR) if you (the claimant) are a working age full-time student in Scotland or Wales, unless you are on SPC, or ESA(IR) (or in Scotland, UC), or are in one of the eligible groups. These are normally the same as in HB (table 3.2). But note that the rules can differ for local CTR classes, and also that students can be exempt or a disregarded person for council tax purposes (tables 28.3, 28.4) whether or not eligible for benefits.

CTR claims and changes

29.35 The rules in this section apply to national CTR and SAR. In England and Wales councils can have their own rules for local CTR/CTR classes and discretionary CTR.

Claims

29.36 To get CTR you have to make a claim to the council that sends your council tax bill:

(a) in England and Wales, you have to make a separate CTR claim to the council even if you are claiming UC or SPC at the same time

---

29.32 CTRSW 18; CTRSP 18

29.33 CTRE(PR) 12, 13; CTRE(DS) 21, 22; CTRW(PR) 28, 29; CTRW(DS) 19, 20; CTRSW 16, 19; CTRSP 16, 19

29.34 CTRE(DS) 20, 24, 75(1),(2); CTRW(PR) 31, sch 11 para 3(1),(2); CTRW(DS) 18, 22, 72(1),(2); CTRSW 20(1)-(3)

29.36 CTRE(PR) sch 1 paras 2(f), 3(g), 4(1)(e), sch 7 paras 2, 3, 9; CTRE(DS) 13(f), 14(g), 15(1)(e), 16(f), 17(g), 18(1)(e), sch 1 paras 2, 3, 11 CTRW(PR) 22(f), 23(g), 24(f), 25(g), sch 12 paras 2, 3, 11; CTRW(DS) 13(f), 14(g), 15(f), 16(g), sch 1 paras 2, 3, 11; CTRSW 13(3)(c), 23-25; CTRSP 14(3)(c), 63, 64

(b) in Scotland, when you claim UC, the DWP tells the council and the council treats this as if you had made a CTR claim; but when you claim SPC and in all other situations, you have to make a separate CTR claim to the council.

(In CTR law, claims are called 'applications' and claimants are called 'applicants'.)

Advance claims

29.37 You can make an advance claim for CTR:

(a) up to 17 weeks (in Wales, 13 weeks) before your 66th birthday or

(b) up to 17 weeks (in Wales, 13 weeks) before you expect to qualify for pension age CTR

(c) up to 13 weeks before you expect to qualify for working age CTR or

(d) in England and Scotland, up to eight weeks before you expect to become liable for council tax.

In (a)-(c) for example, this could be because you know your income will go down.

How to claim

29.38 You can claim CTR on your council's claim form or in most areas by telephone or online [www]. If you are in a couple, one of you ('the claimant') makes the claim for you both.

Help with claiming

29.39 You can ask the council or an advice organisation to help with your claim, or you can ask a family member or friend. If you can't manage your financial affairs, an attorney can claim for you, or the council can appoint someone to do this.

Information and evidence

29.40 You should provide the information and evidence the council reasonably needs, including personal, family and household details and your (and your partner's) capital, income and (except in Scotland) national insurance number. The council can request this when you claim or at any time during your CTR award, and should allow you at least one month to provide it.

Decisions about your CTR

29.41 Chapter 39 gives the rules about decision notices. For reconsiderations and appeals see paras 29.52-54 and chapter 38.

29.37 CTRE(PR) sch 8 para 5(6),(7); CTRE(DS) 110(6),(7); CTRW(PR) sch 13 para 2(7); CTRW(DS) 108(7); CTRSW 20(5),(6); CTRSP 65(2),(3)

29.38 CTRE(PR) sch 7 paras 2, 3, sch 8 para 4(1); CTRE(DS) 109(1), sch 1 paras 2, 3; CTRW(PR) sch 12 paras 2, 3, sch 13 para 1; CTRW(DS) 107(1), sch 1 paras 2, 3 www.gov.uk/apply-council-tax-reduction

29.39 CTRE(PR) sch 8 para 4; CTRE(DS) 109; CTRW(PR) sch 13 para 1; CTRW(DS) 107

29.40 CTRE(PR) sch 8 para 7; CTRE(DS) 113; CTRW(PR) sch 13 para 5; CTRW(DS) 111; CTRSW 27; CTRSP 66

The date your CTR starts

29.42 Your CTR starts:

(a) in England and Scotland, on the Monday following your date of claim or backdated date of claim (paras 29.44-46) or

(b) in Wales, on your exact date of claim or backdated date of claim.

29.43 But your CTR starts on the day your council tax starts if that is in the same benefit week (para 29.2) as your date of claim or backdated date of claim.

Date of claim

29.44 In England and Wales your date of claim is the earliest of the following dates:

(a) the day the council received your CTR claim

(b) the day you told the council you wanted to claim CTR, so long as the council received your CTR claim within one month

(c) the day your partner died or you separated from them (if they were previously the CTR claimant), so long as the council received your CTR claim within one month

(d) the day your UC or guarantee credit of SPC began, as long as the council received your CTR claim within one month of the DWP receiving your UC/SPC claim

(e) the day your council tax started if you are on UC or guarantee credit of SPC, so long as the council received your CTR claim within one month of that.

In Scotland some of these rules are varied and are closer to HB rules.

Backdating

29.45 For pension age CTR claims, your date of claim (para 29.44) is backdated for three months in all cases. For working age CTR claims, it is backdated for up to six months in Scotland or three months in Wales (or longer: para 29.7), but only if you have 'good cause'. In England, some councils include similar working age rules in their local CTR scheme.

29.46 'Good cause' is decided in the same way as in HB (table 32.3). You may qualify if you were too ill to claim, were wrongly advised, or had some other good reason for not claiming CTR earlier.

29.42 CTRE(PR) sch 1 para 45(1); CTRE(DS) 106(1); CTRW(PR) sch 1 para 39(1), sch 6 para 45(1); CTRW(DS) 104(1); CTRSW 33(1); CTRSP 58(1)

29.43 CTRE(PR) sch 1 para 45(2); CTRE(DS) 106(2); CTRW(PR) sch 1 para 39(2), sch 6 para 45(2); CTRW(DS) 104(2); CTRSW 33(2); CTRSP 58(2)

29.44 CTRE(PR) sch 7 paras 2-7, sch 8 para 5; CTRE(DS) 110, sch 1 paras 2-7
CTRW(PR) sch 12 paras 2-7, sch 13 para 2; CTRW(DS) 108, sch 1 paras 2-7; CTRSW 26, 30; CTRSP 65, 71

29.45 CTRE(PR) sch 8 para 6; CTRE(DS) 111, 112; CTRW(PR) sch 13 paras 3, 4; CTRW(DS) 109, 110; CTRSW 26(7),(8); CTRSP 62

The date your CTR changes or ends

29.47 You should tell the council about any change that could affect your CTR. Your CTR changes when there is a change in your income, capital, family, household, or other circumstances. It only ends when:

(a) your liability for council tax ends
(b) you move out of the council's area
(c) you stop meeting the conditions for CTR (e.g. you are excluded: para 29.24) or
(d) the CTR calculations give a figure of nil or a negative figure.

29.48 In most cases, your CTR changes or ends:

(a) in England and Scotland, on the Monday following the change
(b) in Wales, on the exact day of the change.

But changes in your council tax take effect the exact day, and some changes relating to non-dependant deductions or finding a job are delayed (paras 6.24, 30.27).

Payments of CTR

29.49 Your CTR is awarded (or 'paid') by crediting it to your council tax account – so you have less council tax to pay. If you are jointly liable for council tax the council can pay you instead if it considers it would be 'inappropriate' to credit it to your account. If you have already paid your council tax bill in full, a payment is made to you.

Shortfalls and excess CTR

29.50 If your CTR was calculated incorrectly in the past (for example because the wrong facts were used) it must be recalculated. There are two possibilities:

(a) if you were awarded too little CTR, the shortfall (or 'underpayment') is awarded as in para 29.49
(b) if you were awarded too much CTR, the excess (or 'overpayment') is recovered by increasing your council tax bill or by sending you an invoice.

Official error overpayments in Scotland

29.51 In Scotland, if you were overpaid CTR due to an official error and you could not have reasonably been expected to realise that you were being overpaid at the time it arose, or when you were notified of your award, the overpayment is not recoverable (table 36.2). An 'official error' means a mistake by the council, or someone acting for the council or providing services to the council. It is not an official error however if you, or someone acting for you, caused or materially contributed to the mistake (table 36.1).

29.47 CTRE(PR) sch 1 para 46(1); CTRE(DS) 107(1); CTRW(PR) sch 1 para 40(1), sch 6 para 46(1); CTRW(DS) 105(1); CTRSW 34(1); CTRSP 59(1)

29.48 CTRE(PR) sch 1 para 46(1)-(4); CTRE(DS) 107(1)-(4); CTRW(PR) sch 1 para 40(1)-(4), sch 6 para 46(1)-(4); CTRW(DS) 105(1)-(4); CTRSW 34(1)-(4); CTRSP 59(1)-(3)

29.49-50 CTRE(PR) sch 8 para 14; CTRE(DS) 118; CTRW(PR) sch 13 para 10; CTRW(DS) 116; CTRSW 21 sch 5; CTRSP 19A, sch 7 LGFA 13A(1)(a),(b); CT(A&E) 1(2) – 'discount', 20, 24; SI 2013/3086; SI 2013/62

29.51 CTRSW 21; CTRSP 19A

CTR reconsiderations and appeals

29.52 You can ask the council to reconsider any CTR decision. Your request should

(a) be sent to the council in writing

(b) say what matter you are asking the council to reconsider

(c) give your grounds and

(d) be within the time limit if there is one.

You can't appeal to a tribunal unless you have asked for a reconsideration first and any matter you want to be considered at appeal must be raised at the reconsideration stage.

29.53 The time limit is:

(a) in England, each council can set its own time limit (or decide not to have one)

(b) in Wales, one month

(c) in Scotland, two months.

29.54 The council should write to you with its decision and should normally do this within two months of your request. If the council doesn't respond or if you don't get everything you have asked for you can appeal to a tribunal within the time limit (paras 39.5, 39.23).

29.52 LGFA 16(1),(4),(6), 81(1),(4),(6); CTRE(PR) sch 7 para 8(1),(2); CTRW(PR) sch 12 para 8(1); CTRSW 93(2),(3); CTRSP 70A(2),(3)

29.53 LGFA sch 1A para 2(6); CTRW(PR) sch 12 para 8(2); CTRSW 93(3); CTRSP 70A(3)

29.54 LGFA 16(7),(8), 81(7),(8); CTRE(PR) sch 7 para 8(3); CTRW(PR) sch 12 paras 9, 10; CTRSW 93(4), 94(1),(2); CTRSP 70A(4), 70B(1),(2)

Chapter 30 **National CTR and SAR**

- National CTR: paras 30.1-4
- Calculating main CTR: paras 30.5-13
- Applicable amount for main CTR: paras 30.14-19
- Income and capital for main CTR: paras 30.20-27
- Second adult rebate: paras 30.28-35

30.1 This chapter explains who can get national CTR and SAR and how they are calculated. It gives the national rules (table 29.1).

30.2 National CTR applies:

(a) in Scotland and Wales whether you are working age or pension age

(b) in England if you are pension age.

Working age claims in England have local CTR rules (paras 29.11-12) but the rules in this chapter describe the 'default scheme' which most councils follow or modify (para 29.17).

30.3 The two kinds of national CTR:

(a) 'main' CTR which is based on your income or

(b) in England and Scotland, 'second adult rebate' which is based on the income of other adults who live with you.

If you qualify for both kinds you get whichever is the higher.

Benefit weeks

30.4 National CTR is awarded for benefit weeks which always start on a Monday, or on a daily basis if you only qualify for part of a benefit week.

30.2 CTRE(PR) 11(1), 14, sch 1 paras 1-4; CTRE(DS) 12-18; CTRW(PR) 21-25; CTRW(DS) 12-16; CTRSW 13(1), 14(1); CTRSP 14(1), 14A(1)

30.3 CTRE(PR) sch 1 paras 2-4; CTRE(DS) 13-18; CTRW(PR) 22-25; CTRW(DS) 12-22; CTRSW 13(1), 14(1); CTRSP 14(1), 14A(1)

30.4 CTRE(PR) 2(1) – 'reduction week' 2(1); CTRE(DS) 2(1); CTRW(PR) 2(1); CTRW(DS) 2(1); CTRSW 4(1); CTRSP 2(1)

Main CTR

Who can get main CTR

30.5 You can get main CTR if:

(a) you are a resident who is liable for council tax (para 28.11)

(b) you aren't excluded due to an absence (para 29.25)

(c) you aren't an excluded migrant or student (paras 29.33-34)

(d) you don't have capital over £16,000 (para 30.21) and

(e) your income is low enough (para 30.10).

Calculating main CTR

30.6 To calculate your main CTR first calculate your weekly eligible council tax, then work through paras 30.7-13. This is:

(a) your annual council tax after any disability reduction or discount that applies

(b) divided by 365 (or 366 in a leap year) then multiplied by seven.

If your liability starts after 1 April, divide your bill by the number of days in the financial year it covers.

Maximum CTR

30.7 'Maximum CTR' means the maximum amount of CTR you could qualify for. It is:

(a) your weekly eligible council tax

(b) minus any non-dependant deductions that apply to you (chapter 6).

Maximum CTR for bands E to H in Scotland

30.8 If your home is in Scotland and in council tax band E to H, your maximum CTR is either the amount in para 30.7 or the following amount, whichever would give you more main CTR:

(a) a fixed percentage of your weekly council tax which is:

- 7½% of your weekly council tax (para 30.6) if your home is in band E
- 12½% if it is in band F
- 17½% if it is in band G or
- 22½% if it is in band H

(b) minus any non-dependant deductions.

30.5 CTRE(PR) 11-13, sch 1 paras 1-3, 5; CTRE(DS) 12-14, 16, 17, 19-24; CTRW(PR) 21-31; CTRW(DS) 12-22; CTRSW 13-20, 66; CTRSP 14, 14A, 15-19, 40

30.6-7 CTRE(PR) sch 1 para 7(1); CTRE(DS) 29(1); CTRW(PR) sch 1 para 2(1), sch 6 para 4(1); CTRW(DS) 27(1); CTRSW 79(1); CTRSP 47(1)

30.8 CTRSW 79(2),(3); CTRSP 47(1A),(1B)

Your CTR

30.9 If you are on a passport benefit (table 18.1) you qualify for maximum CTR.

30.10 In any other case you qualify for:

(a) maximum CTR

(b) minus 20% of your excess income.

Excess income

30.11 Excess income represents the income you have after meeting your basic living needs. It equals:

(a) your weekly income (para 30.20) minus your applicable amount or

(b) in Scotland, if your home is in council tax bands E to H your weekly income minus:

- £321 (single people with no children or young persons) or
- £479 (others).

In Scotland, in cases where both (a) and (b) apply you get whichever results in the higher award.

Examples: National CTR

1. A single person on SPC with a non-dependant

Darra lives in England and is on the guarantee credit of SPC. His council tax is £30 per week. He has one non-dependant, his daughter. She works full-time and has gross income of £600 pw, so her non-dependant contribution is £15.35 pw (table 6.3).

Weekly council tax	£30.00
Minus non-dependant deduction	– £15.35
Equals weekly national CTR	£14.65

2. A band H home in Scotland

Dolores and Diane live in a band H home in Scotland. Their council tax is £45 per week. They have net income of £500 pw. For the ordinary main CTR calculation, this is too high for them to qualify (para 30.10). But for the alternative calculation, it is £21 above the threshold of £479 (para 30.11).

22½% of weekly council tax	£10.13
Minus 20% of £21	– £4.20
Equals weekly national CTR	£5.93

30.9 CTRE(PR) 2(6), sch 1 para 13; CTRE(DS) 2(3),(4),(6), 35, sch 7 para 14, sch 8 paras 8, 9, sch 10 paras 8, 9
CTRW(PR) 2(3),(4),(6), sch 1 para 7, sch 8 para 14, sch 9 paras 8, 9, sch 10 paras 8, 9;
CTRW(DS) 2(3),(4),(6), 32, sch 6 para 14, sch 7 paras 8, 9, sch 9 paras 8, 9;
CTRSW 4(1) – 'qualifying income-related benefit claimant', 13(11); CTRSP 23

30.10 CTRE(PR) sch 1 paras 3(f)(ii), 10(2),(3); CTRE(DS) 14(f)(ii), 17(f)(ii), 32(2),(3)
CTRW(PR) 23(f)(ii), 25(f)(ii), sch 1 para 4(2),(3), sch 6 para 6(2),(3); CTRW(DS) 14(f)(ii), 16(f)(ii), 29(2),(3)
CTRSW 13(6),(9)(a),(b), 14(5),(7)(a),(b); CTRSP 14(5),(8)(a),(b), 14A(5),(7)(a),(b)

30.11 CTRE(PR) sch 1 para 3(f)(ii); CTRE(DS) 14(f)(ii), 17(f)(ii); CTRW(PR) 23(f)(ii), 25(f)(ii); CTRW(DS) 14(f)(ii), 16(f)(ii)
CTRSW 13(4),(6)(b)(ii), 14(1),(5)(b)(ii); CTRSP 14(3A),(5)(b)(ii), 14A(1),(5)(b)(ii)

National CTR if you are jointly liable

30.12 If you are jointly liable for council tax with someone other than your partner (para 28.16), your maximum CTR (para 30.7) is calculated:

(a) on your share of the weekly council tax based on equal shares between all the jointly liable occupiers ignoring any excluded students (para 29.34) – e.g. if three are jointly liable it is a third, or if one of the three is an excluded student, it is a half and

(b) each non-dependant deduction is shared equally between whichever of you the non-dependant lives with – if they live only with you, it applies wholly to you.

Other CTR calculations rules

30.13 The minimum payment is one penny so many councils calculate the weekly council tax to six decimal places, otherwise the figures used (income, tapered excess) are rounded to the nearest penny.

Applicable amount

30.14 Your 'applicable amount' represents your basic living needs. It is calculated by your council (paras 30.15-19).

Applicable amounts if you are on UC in England and Wales

30.15 In England and Wales for national CTR if you have a UC award your applicable amount is:

(a) the DWP's maximum UC figure

(b) multiplied by 12 and the result divided by 52.

In a polygamous marriage the UC received by a spouse of the second or subsequent marriage is ignored.

Applicable amounts for other people

30.16 Except for claimants on UC in England and Wales, everyone qualifies for a personal allowance. These are awarded using the same rules as for HB (paras 18.8-12) using the figures in table 30.1 except that:

(a) the working age lower rate only applies to single people (para 18.12(a)): couples both aged under 25 receive the ordinary working age rate

(b) in Scotland, for working age claims, if you are in a polygamous marriage, each spouse beyond the first couple in the marriage is ignored (and so is any of their income).

In England and Wales, the allowance for each additional spouse in a polygamous marriage is calculated by deducting the appropriate rate for a single person from the rate for a couple.

30.12 CTRE(PR) sch 1 paras 7(1),(3)-(5); CTRE(DS) 29(1),(3)-(5) (Scotland and Wales see appendix 3)

30.13 CTRE(PR) 2(2), sch 1 paras 7(1), 10(1)-(3); CTRE(DS) 2(2), 29(1), 32(1)-(3) (Scotland and Wales see appendix 3)

30.15 CTRE(DS) 28; CTRW(PR) sch 6 para 3; CTRW(DS) 26

30.16 CTRE(PR) sch 1 para 6(1)(b), sch 2 para 1; CTRE(DS) 25(1)(b), 26(1)(b), sch 2 para 2, sch 3 para 3; CTRW(PR) sch 1 para (1)(b), sch 2 para 2, sch 6 para 1(1)(b), sch 7 para 3; CTRW(DS) 23(1)(b), 24(1)(b), sch 2 para 2, sch 3 para 3; CTRSW 35(b), sch 1 para 2; CTRSP 20(b), sch 1 para 3

Table 30.1 **Weekly CTR applicable amounts 2025-26**

Personal allowances		
Single person	new pension age rate	£227.10
	old pension age rate	£244.40
	working age rate	£92.05
	working age rate (Wales)	£98.10
	lower rate	£72.90
	lower rate (Wales)	£77.65
Couple	new pension age rate	£346.60
	old pension age rate	£366.00
	working age rate	£144.65
	working age rate (Wales)	£154.00
Child or young person	each	£84.66
	each (Scotland)	£105.85
Additional amounts: any age		
Disabled child premium	each child/young person	£81.37
Enhanced disability premium (child)	each child/young person	£32.75
Family premium	transitional (old cases)	£19.48
Severe disability premium	single rate	£82.90
	double rate	£165.80
Carer premium	claimant/partner/each	£46.40
Additional amounts: working age only		
Disability premium	single person	£43.20
	couple	£61.65
Enhanced disability premium (adult)	single person	£21.20
	couple	£30.25
Support component	single person/couple	£48.50
WRA component	single person/couple	£36.55

Note: In England, working age rates aren't set by law but councils usually adopt the HB figures in this table as part of their local CTR scheme (paras 29.11, 29.17).

T30.1 CTRE(PR) sch 2 paras 1, 12; CTRE(DS) sch 2 paras 1-3, 12; sch 3 paras 1-4, 17; SI 2025/39; CTRW(PR) sch 2 paras 1-3, 12; sch 7 paras 1-4, 17; CTRSW sch 1 paras 1-4, 17; SI 2025/59; CTRSP sch 1 paras 1-4, 13; SSI 2025/24

30.17 You qualify for a personal allowance for a child or young person:

(a) in England, from 1 April 2025, for each child or young person in your benefit unit in pension age claims, but for working age local CTR you may be affected by the two-child limit (chapter 19)

(b) in Scotland and Wales, for each child or young person in your benefit unit.

30.18 In Scotland, the allowance for each child/young person is 25% higher than the HB figure (table 30.1).

30.19 Additional amounts (premiums and components) follow the HB rules (paras 17.14-33). For CTR law in England see the footnotes to those paras and in Scotland and Wales, appendix 3. The CTR figures are in table 30.1.

Income and capital for main CTR

How income is calculated for main CTR

30.20 Your income for main CTR is calculated:

(a) if you have an award of UC, using the rules in paras 30.22-24

(b) if you have an award of SPC, savings credit only (para 17.1), in the same way as for HB (para 21.19) except in Scotland war pensions are disregarded in full

(c) if (a) and (b) don't apply, using the HB rules in chapters 21 to 23.

You don't need to calculate your income if you get a passport benefit (para 30.9).

How capital is calculated for main CTR

30.21 Your capital (including the capital limit and tariff income) for main CTR is calculated:

(a) for all claims in England and Wales and for pension age claims in Scotland, using the HB rules for working age or pension age claims as appropriate

(b) for all working age claims in Scotland, using the UC rules (converted to a weekly figure by multiplying by 12 and dividing by 52).

The UC and HB rules for capital are in chapter 24.

30.17 CTRE(PR) sch 1 para 6(1)(b), sch 2 para 2; CTRE(DS) 25(1)(b), 26(1)(b), sch 2 para 2, sch 3 para 3; CTRW(PR) sch 1 para (1)(b), sch 2 para 2, sch 6 para 1(1)(b), sch 7 para 3; CTRW(DS) 23(1)(b), 24(1)(b), sch 2 para 2, sch 3 para 3; CTRSW 35(b), sch 1 para 2; CTRSP 20(b), sch 1 para 3

30.18 See policy note to SSI 2016/253

30.19 CTRE(PR) sch 1 para 6(1)(c),(d), sch 2; CTRE(DS) 25(1)(c),(d), 26(1)(c)-(f), sch 2, sch 3; CTRW(PR) sch 1 para 1(1)(c),(d), sch 2, sch 6 para 1(1)(c)-(f), sch 7; CTRW(DS) 23(1)(c),(d), 24(1)(c)-(g), sch 2, sch 3; CTRSW 35(c)-(h), sch 1; CTRSP 20(c)-(d), sch 1

30.20 CTRE(PR) sch 1 paras 13, 14; CTRE(DS) 36-38, 47-56; CTRW(PR) sch 1 paras 8, 9, sch 6 paras 10-19; CTRW(DS) 33-25, 44-53; CTRSW 38-44; CTRSP 25, 26

30.21 CTRE(PR) 11(2), sch 1 paras 15, 31-37, sch 6; CTRE(DS) 20, 23, 38, 63-72, sch 9, sch 10; CTRW(PR) 30, sch 1 paras 9, 25-31, sch 5, sch 6 paras 26-33, sch 10; CTRW(DS) 18, 21, 35, 60-69, sch 8, sch 9; CTRSW 66-76, sch 4; CTRSP 26, 27(2), 40-46, sch 4

Calculation of income in England and Wales: if you get UC:

30.22 In national CTR if you have an award of UC, the council uses DWP's figure of your income:

(a) adds your UC award and

(b) converts the total into a weekly figure by multiplying by 12 and dividing by 52.

No other adjustments are made to DWP's income figure except in accordance with your local CTR rules. For example, no earnings disregard is applied (table 22.4) unless your local CTR rules say so.

Calculation of income in Scotland: if you have a UC award

30.23 These rules apply in Scotland if you have a UC award, including a 'nil award' (paras 22.24, 33.36).

30.24 The council calculates your income based on the same monthly assessment periods as your UC. Your income is the total of:

(a) your earned income using the UC earned income rules (including the rules about surplus earnings and the minimum income floor unless it is unreasonable to do so), but:

- deducting the HB standard earned income disregards (table 22.4) (not the work allowance), then
- if appropriate, an amount equivalent to 85% of the weekly UC childcare costs element (para 16.23)

(b) your unearned income that would be counted under the UC rules

(c) if received, the lower of:

- your UC transitional element and elements for children (e.g. for a disabled child or for childcare costs), or the capped amount if it is capped
- the amount of your UC award.

The council calculates each of these, but it may use figures the DWP supplies if it chooses. In each case the weekly figure is found by multiplying the monthly figure by 12 and dividing by 52.

All other cases

30.25 In all other cases (i.e. if you don't get UC, SPC or a passport benefit), the council calculates your income and capital in the same way as for HB except:

(a) in England and Scotland, any payments you receive in connection with the Homes for Ukraine scheme are disregarded in working age and pension age claims

(b) in Scotland, for all working age claims (UC and non-UC) your unearned income is calculated in the same way as for UC (para 21.10).

30.22 CTRE(DS) 37; CTRW(PR) sch 6 para 9; CTRW(DS) 34

30.23 CTRSW 4(1) – 'award of universal credit'

30.24 CTRSW 42(1),(2), 43, 44(1), 57(1),(2)(d), 78

30.25 CTRE(PR) 17 (as inserted by SI 2023/16 reg 5), sch 1 para 15; CTRE(DS) 38, 47-56; CTRW(PR) sch 1 para 9, sch 6 paras 10-19; CTRW(DS) 35, 44-53; CTRSW 57(1), sch 4 para 43; CTRSW 27(1), sch 4 para 30J

Changes in income and capital

30.26 Changes in your income and capital are usually taken into account:

(a) in England and Scotland, from the Monday following the change

(b) in Wales, from the exact day of the change.

Starting work and extended CTR

30.27 You get four weeks extended CTR if:

(a) you have been on JSA(IB), ESA or IS (not UC or SPC) for at least 26 weeks and

(b) this ends because you start work or increase your hours or earnings.

During those four weeks, your national CTR continues at the level it was beforehand, but in England local CTR may apply instead.

Second adult rebate

30.28 SAR applies:

(a) in Scotland whether you are working age or pension age

(b) in England if you are pension age.

It doesn't apply in Wales (table 29.1) and working age SAR in England usually has different rules (paras 29.9-12).

Who can get SAR

30.29 You can get SAR if:

(a) you meet the liability condition (para 30.30)

(b) you have at least one second adult with a low enough income (paras 30.31-33)

(c) you don't have any lodgers who pay a commercial rent to live in part of your home

(d) you aren't excluded due to an absence (para 29.25)

(e) you aren't an excluded migrant (para 29.33).

For SAR, your own income is completely ignored and so is your capital, even if it is over £16,000. If you qualify for both national CTR and SAR, you get whichever of them is worth more.

30.26 CTRE(PR) sch 1 para 46(1); CTRE(DS) 107(1); CTRW(PR) sch 1 para 40(1), sch 6 para 46(1); CTRW(DS) 105(1); CTRSW 34(1); CTRSP 59(1)

30.27 CTRE(DS) 95-98; CTRW(PR) sch 6 paras 34-37; CTRW(DS) 93-96; CTRSW 80-88

30.28 CTRE(PR) 14(2), sch 1 para 4; CTRE(DS) 15, 18; CTRSW 13(1)(b),(3),(7); CTRSP 14(1)(b),(3),(6)

30.29 CTRE(PR) sch 1 paras 4(1),(2), 9(1), sch 6 para 27; CTRE(DS) 15(1),(2), 18(1),(2), 31(1), sch 9 para 27, sch 10 para 49; CTRSW 13(1)(b),(3),(7),(9)(c); CTRSP 14(1)(b),(3),(6),(8)(c)

SAR liability condition

30.30 You meet the SAR liability condition if:

(a) you are a sole householder (para 28.13) or

(b) you are a householder couple or two joint householders (paras 28.14-16) and:

- one of you is a disregarded person (table 28.4) or
- both of you are or

(c) you are three or more joint householders (para 28.16) and:

- all but one of you are disregarded persons or
- all of you are.

Second adults

30.31 A second adult is an adult (over 18) in your home who:

(a) is a non-dependant (para 6.1) but

(b) isn't a disregarded person (table 28.4).

Amount of SAR

30.32 If your second adult is on SPC, JSA(IB), ESA(IR), IS or in Scotland, UC with no earned income, your SAR is:

(a) 25% of your weekly council tax (para 30.34) or

(b) 100% of your weekly council tax if you (the claimant) are an excluded student (para 29.34).

When you have more than one second adult, they must all be on the benefits mentioned.

30.33 Otherwise, your SAR is:

(a) 7½% of your weekly council tax if your second adult's gross weekly income is below £358 pw in England or £365 pw in Scotland or

(b) 15% of your weekly council tax if it is below £276 pw in England or £269 pw in Scotland.

A second adult's gross weekly income is worked out in the same way as in para 6.25. When your second adult is in a couple, both their incomes are combined. And when you have more than one second adult, all their gross weekly incomes are combined.

30.30 CTRE(PR) sch 1 paras 4(2),(3), 9(2),(3); CTRE(DS) 15(2),(3), 18(2),(3), 31(2),(3); CTRSW 13(1)(b),(3),(7),(8), 91(2),(3); CTRSP 14(1)(b),(3),(6),(7), 56(2),(3)

30.31 CTRE(PR) sch 1 para 4(2),(3), sch 3 para 1(1); CTRE(DS) 15(2),(3), 18(2),(3), sch 4 para 1(1); CTRSW 13(1)(b),(3),(7),(8), 91(2),(3), sch 2 para 1(1); CTRSP 14(1)(b),(3),(6),(7), 56(2),(3), sch 5 para 1(1)

30.32 CTRE(PR) sch 1 paras 9(1), 10(4), sch 3 paras 1, 3; CTRE(DS) 31(1), 32(4), sch 4 paras 1, 3; CTRSW 13(9)(c), 91(2),(3), sch 2 paras 1, 3; CTRSP 14(8)(c), 56(2),(3), sch 5 paras 1, 3

30.33 CTRE(PR) sch 3 paras 1, 3; CTRE(DS) sch 4 paras 1, 3; CTRSW sch 2 para 1; CTRSP sch 5 para 1; SI 2025/39 reg 7; SSI 2025/24 regs 6, 17

Weekly council tax for SAR

30.34 For SAR, your weekly council tax means the amount due on your home in the current benefit week (para 30.4) after any disability reduction but before any discount. (This ensures that discounts and SAR calculations are based on the same amount.)

SAR if you are jointly liable

30.35 If you are jointly liable for council tax with someone other than your partner, the result of the SAR calculation (paras 30.32-33) is shared equally between all of you. So, if there are three jointly liable people and two are a couple, the couple's share is two thirds.

Examples: Second adult rebate

1. A single person with one second adult

Dorinder has too much capital to qualify for national CTR. Her council tax is £36 per week. She has one second adult, her son, who works full-time and has gross income of £301 pw.

- Weekly SAR of 7½% of council tax £2.70

2. Discount plus SAR

Dan is a carer (table 28.4(g)). He cares for his mother who is a second adult and is on SPC. His council tax is £30 per week.

- Weekly discount of 25% of council tax £7.50
- Plus weekly SAR of 25% of council tax £7.50

30.34 CTRE(PR) sch 3 para 1(2); CTRE(DS) sch 4 para 1(2); CTRSW sch 2 para 1(2); CTRSP sch 5 para 1(2)

30.35 CTRE(PR) sch 1 para 9(2),(3) ; CTRE(DS) 31(2),(3); CTRSW 91(2),(3); CTRSP 56(2),(3)

Chapter 31 **Discretionary housing payments**

- Discretionary housing payments and who can get them: paras 31.2-6
- What DHPs are used for: paras 31.7-11
- DHP limits, amounts, claims and appeals: paras 31.12-19
- Government grants towards DHPs: paras 31.20-23
- Other local and national welfare schemes: paras 31.24-35

31.1 This chapter describes the other kinds of financial assistance you may be able to get from your local council. There are two kinds:

(a) discretionary housing payments (DHPs) throughout the UK and

(b) local welfare assistance in England and similar payments in Scotland and Wales.

DHPs and who can get them

31.2 Your council can award you a discretionary housing payment (DHP) if you need further help towards your rent or related housing costs. To get a DHP you must meet the conditions in para 31.4. But DHPs are discretionary, so (except in para 31.11) you may not get a DHP even if you meet the conditions.

31.3 The DHP scheme is administered by the council that administers HB (the housing authority). Councils are expected to take government guidance into account, which is:

(a) in England and Wales, the DWP's Discretionary housing payments guidance manual, May 2022 ('GDHP') and

(b) in Scotland, the Scottish discretionary housing payment guidance manual, March 2024 ('SGDHP').

Councils should publicise the DHP scheme and any rules and conditions they apply.

Basic conditions for DHPs

31.4 You can get a DHP in any kind of rented accommodation. The basic conditions are:

(a) you must be entitled to HB or

(b) you must be entitled to a UC housing costs element and

(c) in either case, you must appear to require some further financial assistance in order to meet housing costs,

In condition (b), the guidance adds that you must have completed your first UC assessment period (GDHP para 11, SGDHP para 4.1).

31.2 CSPSSA 69(2)(b); DFA 2(2); SSA(Scot) 88(1)

31.3 CSPSSA 69(1),(7); SSA(Scot) 88(1), 90, 91(1)

31.4 CSPSSA 69(1); DFA 2(1); Scotland Act 1998, sch 5, part 2, section F1, exception 6; SSA(Scot) 88(2),(3)

Requiring financial assistance

31.5 DHP law doesn't define what requiring 'some further financial assistance' means. It is up to councils to choose how to interpret the phrase. Usually, you will need to show that you are unable to meet all or part of your housing costs from your available income. And in Scotland, Ministers have provided councils with a list of priority groups (SGDHP section 10).

31.6 If you or your partner get a DLA mobility component, the council must ignore this. They should also consider ignoring any DLA care component or PIP daily living component (Hardy v Sandwell MBC).

What DHPs are used for

Housing costs that DHPs can help with

31.7 You can get DHPs towards:

(a) your rent

(b) any eligible service charges you pay (para 15.8)

(c) rent in advance and rent deposits

(d) other lump sum costs associated with a housing need such as removal costs (GDHP paras 5, 8-9, 18, SGDHP paras 3.1, 10.1).

Housing costs that DHPs can't help with

31.8 You can't get a DHP to help with:

(a) any ineligible service charges you pay (para 15.8)

(b) council tax or water charges

(c) increases in your HB to recover ineligible rent arrears (para 9.26)

(d) reductions in your benefit to recover overpaid HB/UC

(e) reductions in your benefit due to sanctions relating to job-seeking, child support or benefit offences.

But in Scotland you may be able to get a DHP towards (d) or (e) if your situation is exceptional (SGDHP para 7.4).

31.6 R (Hardy) v Sandwell MBC [2015] EWHC 890 (Admin), [2015] PTSR 1292

31.7 CSPSSA 69(2)(b); DFA 2(1)(b),(2); SSA(Scot) 88(1)

31.8 CSPSSA 69(2)(a); DFA 3; SSA(Scot) 89(2),(3), 91(1),(2)

What DHPs can be used for

31.9 DHPs can be awarded if your HB or UC housing element is lower than your eligible rent. For example, when:

(a) your eligible rent is restricted by the LHA or other rules (chapters 11-13)

(b) you are affected by the bedroom tax or the benefit cap (paras 31.10-11)

(c) your HB or UC is reduced by the 65%/55% calculation taper (paras 16.3, 18.3)

(d) your HB or UC is reduced because you have a non-dependant (para 6.17)

(e) you are threatened with homelessness and a DHP can help avoid this

(f) you need help with a rent deposit or rent in advance to help you move into a new home

(g) you are fleeing violence and qualify for HB or UC on two homes (para 7.6) (GDHP paras 28-29, SGDHP paras 16.1-4)

(h) you are moving to supported or temporary accommodation and there is a gap between the end of UC on your old home and the start of HB on your new one (para 33.20).

Bedroom tax and benefit cap

31.10 DHPs can help (throughout GB) if your HB/UC is reduced as a result of the bedroom tax (para 11.17) or the benefit cap (chapter 20).

31.11 And in Scotland only, the Scottish Government has told councils that it expects them to award a DHP to meet the full amount of the reductions under:

(a) the bedroom tax for all social renters (SGDHP para 5.2) unless your HB is reduced to nil (para 31.4) and

(b) the benefit cap in all cases (SGDHP para 6.5).

DHP limits, amounts, claims and appeals

DHPs awarded for a fixed or open-ended period

31.12 DHPs can be awarded:

(a) for a short fixed period – in this case you may need to reapply several times

(b) for a longer fixed period – the guidance says this may be appropriate 'if a claimant has ongoing needs, such as a disabled person living in specially adapted accommodation' (GDHP para 17)

(c) for an open-ended period – in this case the council can end the period at any time.

In these cases, the total of your HB/UC including the DHP must not be greater than your eligible rent if you are on HB or your housing costs element if you are on UC.

31.9 DFA 3, 4; SSA(Scot) 88(1), 90(c)

31.11 SSA(Scot) 88(2), 91(1),(2)

31.12 CSPSSA 69(2)(b),(d),(g); DFA 2(2)(b), 4, 5; SSA(Scot) 90(c)

DHPs awarded as a lump sum

31.13 DHPs can also be awarded as a lump sum, for example:

(a) towards a deposit or rent in advance or

(b) 'for past housing costs (arrears of rent) on the ground that [you are] currently receiving full housing benefit' (Gargett v Lambeth LBC).

In these cases, there are no limits to the amount.

Backdating DHPs

31.14 DHPs can be awarded for a past period, but only for a period for which you were entitled to HB or a UC housing element. They can't be awarded for a period before your HB/UC started, and in Scotland they can't be backdated more than 12 months (SGDHP para 11.1).

Making a claim for DHPs

31.15 You can usually make a claim for DHPs in writing, online or by telephone, or someone can claim on your behalf if this is reasonable (GDHP para 27, SGDHP para 15.1). Some councils have a special DHP form you can use. In Scotland you can use the Government's website to find your council's claim form [www], or councils can award a DHP without you making a claim (SGDHP para 13.1).

31.16 You should provide information and evidence you are asked for when you claim (GDHP para 25, SGDHP para. 14). And if your circumstance change in a way that could affect your DHPs, you (and the person they are paid to if this is different) should tell the council about this.

Payments of DHPs

31.17 The council can pay your DHP:

(a) to you

(b) to someone else if appropriate (e.g. someone acting on your behalf or your landlord) or

(c) to your rent account if you are a council tenant.

If you are overpaid, the overpayment can be recovered.

Decisions and notifications

31.18 When you claim a DHP the council should give you written notice of its decision, including reasons, as soon as reasonably practicable. The notice should say when your DHP

31.13 R (Gargett) v Lambeth LBC [2008] EWCA Civ 1450, [2009] PTSR 1434

31.14 CSPSSA 69(1); DFA 2(1), 5(2); SSA(Scot) 88(2), 91(2)(a)

31.15 CSPSSA 69(2)(e); DFA 6(1); SSA(Scot) 90(a), 91(2)(b)
www.mygov.scot/discretionary-housing-payment

31.16 CSPSSA 69(2)(f); DFA 6(1); SSA(Scot) 91(2)(b)

31.17 DFA 6(2); SSA(Scot) 88(4)

31.18 DFA 6(3); SSA(Scot) 91(2)(c)

starts and (if it is for a fixed period) when it will end. The DWP says that councils should 'avoid unnecessary delay, considering that an application for DHPs is often to deal with an immediate need' (GDHP para 31).

Reviews and appeals

31.19 You can ask the council to review any decision about DHPs. The council decides how to carry out reviews and who deals with them (GDHP para 33, SGDHP para 18.2). You can't appeal to a tribunal about DHPs, but in limited circumstances you may be able to apply for judicial review (para 39.43).

Government grants towards DHPs

Government grants: England and Wales

31.20 In England and Wales the DWP makes grants to councils towards their expenditure on DHPs. In 2025-26 the amounts for each council are in circular S9/2024 and the total is £100 million. The council must submit a claim for an estimated amount by 31 October, and submit its final claim by 30 April.

31.21 English and Welsh councils that have spent their grant can continue to award DHPs from their own funds, but only up to 2½ times the total grant. Any underspend is returned to the DWP.

Government grants: Scotland

31.22 The Scottish Government makes grants to Scottish councils towards their expenditure on DHPs. These include:

(a) the full cost of DHPs awarded for the bedroom tax and the benefit cap (para 31.11) and

(b) a fixed amount towards the cost of other DHPs.

In 2025-26 the total amount for both is £99.2 million (Scottish Budget 2025-26 [www]).

31.23 Scottish councils that have spent their grant can continue to pay DHPs from their own funds (with no limit) or may refuse to consider any further applications for DHPs. Any underspend is returned to the Scottish government.

31.19 SSA(Scot) 90(d), 91(2)(b),(c)

31.20 CSPSSA 70(2)(b); The Discretionary Housing Payments (Grants) Order 2001, No. 2340, reg 3(2)

31.21 CSPSSA 70(3); The Discretionary Housing Payments (Grants) Order 2001, No. 2340, reg 7(1)

31.22 SSA(Scot) 91(1), 92(1),(2)
www.gov.scot/policies/social-security/support-with-housing-costs/
www.gov.scot/publications/scottish-budget-2025-2026 (page 40)

31.23 SSA(Scot) 92(3),(5)

Welfare assistance in England

31.24 In England, you may be able to get help from your council's:

(a) local welfare assistance scheme (LWA) (also called discretionary welfare assistance) or

(b) household support fund (HSF).

31.25 These are not part of the UC, HB or DHP schemes. They may be run by your district or county council, or sometimes by two or more councils working together. Payments are discretionary, so you shouldn't rely on getting help.

Who can get an LWA payment

31.26 LWA payments can be a grant or a loan, but many councils provide help only or mainly on a non-cash basis. There are no national rules or guidance for LWA schemes and no government funding, so some councils don't make any LWA payments.

31.27 Councils that make LWA payments usually do so if you are 'in need' and without the money to meet it. Most LWA schemes are to help you:

(a) avoid becoming homeless

(b) avoid entering institutional care (e.g. residential care, hospital, or prison)

(c) set up home after leaving institutional care or

(d) meet a crisis and avoid harm.

Most councils exclude payments you could get a DHP for, and many exclude payments towards rent and mortgages.

Who can get an HSF payment

31.28 During 2025-26, the government provides funding to county and unitary councils for HSF payments. Councils have to follow government guidance about what HSF payments can meet [www]. This includes:

(a) energy and water bills

(b) food

(c) essentials linked to energy or food, such as home insulation or energy efficient fridges, slow cookers and other appliances that help reduce energy bills

(d) wider essentials, such as phone bills, repairs to a car or fuel to prevent a crisis

(e) advice and preventative support – for example, the council could fund a local debt advice service or a community group to provide a warm space and

(f) housing costs other than mortgage payments not covered by UC/HB or a DHP – in an emergency or exceptional circumstances, it could include 'historic rent arrears'.

31.24 Localism Act 2011, s1

31.26 Localism Act 2011, s1

31.28 Local Government Act 2003, s31; Localism Act 2011, s1
www.gov.uk/government/publications/household-support-fund-guidance-for-local-councils

Welfare assistance in Wales

31.29 In Wales, you may be able to get help from the discretionary assistance fund (DAF). You can get a grant for:

(a) an 'emergency assistance payment' (EAP) or

(b) an 'individual assistance payment' (IAP).

This is administered by the Welsh government, and you can apply online [www].

31.30 To get an emergency assistance payment you must:

(a) be in extreme financial hardship

(b) be in a crisis and in need of immediate financial support and

(c) have no other money and considered all other responsible lenders (e.g. a credit union).

31.31 To get an individual assistance payment you must be getting UC, guarantee credit, ESA(IR), IS or JSA(IB). You can only get a payment if:

(a) you are leaving care (a care home, hospital or prison) to live independently

(b) you need it to prevent you from going into care

(c) you are setting up home after an unsettled way of life

(d) you need to move quickly due to relationship breakdown or domestic violence or

(e) you are going to care for a prisoner or young offender released on temporary licence.

Welfare assistance in Scotland

31.32 In Scotland, you may be able to get help from the Scottish Welfare Fund (SWF). You can get:

(a) a crisis grant – to help with an emergency such as a fire, flood or losing work or

(b) a community care grant (CCG) – to help you or someone you care for live independently such as if you are leaving care, prison, you are escaping domestic abuse or starting a settled way of life after being homeless.

This is administered by local councils on behalf of the Scottish government, and you can apply online [www].

31.33 To get a crisis grant or CCG you must be on a 'low income'. You don't have to be on UC/SPC/ESA(IR) but your application is more likely to succeed if you are. You are unlikely to get CCG if you have more than £700 savings, or £1,200 if you have a pension.

31.34 You can only get three crisis grants within a 12 month period unless exceptional circumstances apply.

31.35 You can't get a grant for rent or mortgage payments, rent in advance, repair costs or any housing costs that could be covered by a DHP.

31.29 Government of Wales Act 2006, s70
www.gov.wales/discretionary-assistance-fund-daf

31.30 www.gov.wales/discretionary-assistance-fund-daf/eligibility

31.32 The Welfare Funds (Scotland) Act 2015; SSI 2016/107
www.mygov.scot/scottish-welfare-fund/

Chapter 32 **Making a claim**

- How to claim: paras 32.1-13
- Information and evidence: paras 32.14-22
- UC assessment periods: paras 32.23-26
- Start dates: paras 32.27-35
- Backdating: paras 32.36-45

How to claim

32.1 This chapter is about claims for UC, SPC and HB. You can only get these benefits if you make a claim or someone claims them on your behalf. Claims for UC and SPC go to the DWP, and claims for HB go to your local council. When you claim affects when your benefit starts, and if you claim a benefit by more than one method, the earliest one is used to decide when your benefit starts.

Claims for UC

32.2 You normally claim UC on an online form [www] and this takes up to 40 minutes. You may be able to claim by phone instead, but only if you have a good reason for not claiming online, for example, you don't have regular access to the internet, or have a physical or mental health condition that stops you from claiming online.

Claims for SPC

32.3 You can claim SPC on an online form if you have already claimed your state pension [www], or by phone using the SPC claim line (0800 99 1234). Or you can ask the claim line to send you a form you can post or visit the DWP office and claim in person.

Claims for HB

32.4 Most councils ask you to claim HB online. It is usually also possible to get a printed claim form and send it in, or to start a claim by telephone.

32.1 SSAA 1(1)(4)(za),(ab),(b), UC(C&P) 8; SS(C&P) 4ZC(1)(k), 4D(1),(3),(6A), HBW 83(1),(4A), 83A; HBP 64(1),(5A), 64A

32.2 UC(C&P) 8(1)-(3), sch 2 paras 2, 4
www.universal-credit.service.gov.uk/start

32.3 SS(C&P) 4ZC(1),(2)(k), 4D(2),(3),(6A), sch 9ZC
https://apply-for-pension-credit.service.gov.uk/start

32.4 HBW 83(1),(4)(b),(4A), 83A, sch 11 paras 2, 4; HBP 64(2),(5)(b),(5A), sch 10 paras 2, 4

Claiming HB at the same time as SPC/UC

32.5 If you claim SPC, you can tick a box indicating that you pay rent. This counts as an HB claim even if the council isn't made aware of it until later (CP/3477/2003), though the council will still need details of your rent. If you claim UC and live in supported or temporary accommodation, there is no equivalent rule, so you need to make separate claims for HB and UC.

Help with claiming

32.6 You can phone Citizens' Advice for help with UC claims, budgeting and payments using their DWP-sponsored 'Help to Claim' service [www] and if you do the DWP is allowed to share information with them if it is used to assist you. Citizens' Advice also provides advice on SPC and HB. You may also be able to get help with claiming from your local council or a jobcentre.

Attorneys and appointees acting for you

32.7 If you have an attorney who acts for you, or someone appointed by a court to act for you, they can claim benefit on your behalf. In any other case, a friend or relation aged 18 or over can apply to act as your 'appointee', or a firm or organisation can do this (e.g. a solicitor or charity). They should apply in writing to the DWP (UC and SPC) or the council (HB). If you already have an appointee for one benefit, the DWP/council should accept the appointee for other benefits.

32.8 An attorney or appointee has all the rights you have in connection with your claim or award or benefit, including making a claim (but not after your death: R(IS) 3/04), reporting changes in your circumstances, receiving payments, and requesting a reconsideration or appeal. An appointee can stop acting on your behalf if they write to the DWP or council giving notice of one month/four weeks.

The decision about your claim

32.9 The DWP or council only has to decide your claim once the following conditions are met:

(a) you have completed the claim according to the instructions (on the form or by telephone or online)

(b) you have provided any information and evidence required

(c) in the case of an SPC phone claim, you have signed a written statement confirming the details of your claim

(d) in the case of a UC online claim, the computer has accepted your claim and you have logged out (GDC v SSWP).

32.5 HBP 64(5)(a),(6)(a),(7)

32.6 SI 2012/1483, Regs 2 – 'universal support initiative', 5(1)(h), 10(1)(e), 16(d), 17(3)(c)
www.citizensadvice.org.uk/about-us/contact-us/contact-us/help-to-claim/

32.7 UC(C&P) 57(1)-(3),(6); SS(C&P) 33(1),(1A)-(1C); HBW 82(2),(3),(5); HBP 63(2),(3),(5)

32.8 UC(C&P) 57(4),(5),(7),(8); SS(C&P) 33(2),(3); HBW 82(4),(6); HBP 63(4),(6)

32.9 UC(C&P) 8(1)-(4), 37(2), sch 2 paras 2, 4, 5; SS(C&P) 4ZC(2)(k), 4D(6B),(6C), 7(1), sch 9ZC paras 2, 4, 6; HBW 83(4B),(4C), 83A, 86(1), sch 11 paras 2, 4, 6; HBP 64(5C),(5D), 64A, 67(1), sch 10 paras 2, 4, 6
GDC v SSWP (UC) [2020] UKUT 108 (AAC)

Incomplete claims

32.10 Your claim is incomplete if you don't meet the above conditions. If you don't meet conditions (a) to (c), the DWP/council should write to you saying what you need to do and giving you a month to do it. Otherwise, your claim is void and you can only get benefit if you start again.

Your decision letter

32.11 The DWP or council must send you a decision letter:

(a) saying whether you qualify and

(b) if you do qualify, giving the amount or

(c) if you don't qualify, saying why not – this must be included in HB decision letters, and in practice is usually included in UC/SPC decision letters.

Chapter 36 gives more information about this.

Amending and withdrawing a claim

32.12 You can amend or withdraw your claim at any time before a decision is made on it. If you withdraw it, the DWP or council takes no further action on it.

The UC online journal

32.13 If you claimed UC online, you get access to an online journal through your UC online account [www]. The DWP uses this to tell you the outcome of your claim, and to send you other messages include items for your 'to-do list'. You use it to reply and send the DWP other messages and requests.

Information and evidence

32.14 You have to provide information and evidence the DWP/council needs when:

(a) you make a claim

(b) your circumstances change

(c) the DWP or council is checking your entitlement and

(d) you are overpaid.

32.10 UC(C&P) 8(5),(6), 37(2),(3); UC(D&A) sch 3 para 1(c); SS(C&P) 4D(6D),(6E),(10),(11), 7(1); SS(D&A) sch 2 para 5(f); HB(D&A) sch para 1; HBW 83(4D),(4E),(7),(8),(8A); HBP 64(5E),(5F),(8),(9),(9A)

32.11 UC(D&A) 7(1),(3)(b); SS(D&A) 3ZA(1),(3)(b); HBW 90(1), sch 9 paras 9, 10, 14; HBP 71(1), sch 8 paras 9, 10, 14

32.12 UC(C&P) 30, 31; SS(C&P) 5; HBW 87; HBP 68

32.13 UC(C&P) 3, sch 2 paras 1, 2
www.gov.uk/sign-in-universal-credit

32.14 SSAA 5(1A),(2)(za),(ab),(e); UC(C&P) 37(2), 38(2); UC(D&A) 45;
SS(C&P) 7(1), 32(1); SS(D&A) 17(1),(2)(b); HBW 83(1), 86(1); HB(D&A) 13(1),(2)(b)

What the DWP or council needs to know

32.15 The DWP or council needs to know about:

(a) you and the people who live with you

(b) your housing costs

(c) your income and capital, including details of your bank or similar account

(d) your national insurance number (para 32.20) and

(e) any other matter that could affect your entitlement to benefit or its amount.

But for UC and SPC where the information or evidence about your housing costs is incomplete the DWP can decide your claim based on what it has.

Who must provide the information and evidence

32.16 In UC, SPC and HB, you are responsible for providing the information and evidence. If you are a couple claiming SPC or HB, this responsibility belongs only to you (the claimant), but if you are a couple claiming UC, the responsibility belongs to both of you (whether you are claiming as a single person or jointly).

Time limit when you make a claim

32.17 When you are making a claim you should provide the information and evidence within one month. If you do, it counts as having been provided when you made your claim (para 32.10). The DWP or council can allow longer than a month for this if it is reasonable to do so.

Using information from a third party

32.18 The DWP or council can require a third party to provide information or evidence relevant to your claim, and they should normally do this within one month. In UC, HB and SPC this includes your pension fund holder. In UC and HB, it also includes your employer, landlord, a rent officer (para 11.25) or your childcare provider.

Using information from the DWP to assess HB

32.19 When the council assesses HB, it can use information provided by the DWP. For example, if you are on a passport benefit, you automatically qualify for maximum HB (para 18.2). But:

(a) if the DWP has refused you a passport benefit, the council can't refuse you HB without making its own assessment of your circumstances (Rossendale BC v RM) and

(b) if you have no income, the council can't refuse you HB because you 'ought' to claim UC or SPC.

32.15 UC(C&P) 37(3),(6),(7), 38(3),(7),(9); UC(D&A) 39(4); SS(C&P) 7, 32; SS(D&A) 13(1); HBW 88; HBP 69

32.16 UC(C&P) 37(2),(4),(5); SS(C&P) 7(1); HBW 86(1); HBP 67(1)

32.17 UC(C&P) 37(3); SS(C&P) 7(1); HBW 86(1); HBP 67(1)

32.18 UC(C&P) 37(6),(7), 41; SS(C&P) 7(4)-(6); HBW 28(10), 29(2)(b), 86(5)-(7), 117-121; HBP 31(10), 67(5)-(7), 98-102

32.19 SSAA 7A, 7B; SI 2007/2911 reg 5; HBW 108, 112; HBP 89, 93
Rossendale BC v RM (HB) [2017] UKUT 362 (AAC)

National insurance numbers

32.20 When you claim UC, SPC or HB, you have to give your own national insurance number (NINo), along with your partner's if you are claiming as a couple. But:

(a) you never have to give a NINo for a child, young person or non-dependant

(b) in HB, you don't have to give your (or your partner's) NINo if you live in a hostel (para 12.30) and

(c) in SPC and HB, you don't have to give your partner's NiNo if they require leave to be in the UK but don't have it (para 40.19).

If you don't have a NINo, your UC can be paid if it is likely that one will be issued (Bui v SSWP (CA)), but you can't get a UC advance (para 34.23). SPC, HB and other benefits can't be paid until a Nino is actually issued (Bui v SSWP (UKUT)), but then you get arrears of benefit back to the start of your claim.

If you don't have particular evidence

32.21 When the DWP or council request evidence (or 'verification'):

(a) you should try and provide what they asked for

(b) if you don't have the evidence they asked for, you should provide alternative evidence if you can

(c) if you don't have any evidence of a particular matter, 'the absence of verification does not necessarily mean something isn't true' (RA v SSWP).

For example, if you don't have the evidence of identity the DWP or council requested, they must consider whether you are who you say you are based on any evidence you do have (PHC v SSWP). Or if you only have incomplete evidence of your housing costs, the DWP should decide your claim based on what you do have.

Providing incorrect information

32.22 If you provide incorrect information you could be liable for prosecution resulting in a fine and/or a prison sentence of up to three months (six months if you were dishonest). A landlord (including a company) could also be liable for prosecution if they assist you to provide incorrect information.

32.20 SSAA 1(1A)-(1C); UC(C&P) 5; PC 1A; HBW 4; HBP 4
R(Bui) v SSWP [2023] EWCA Civ 566, [2024] PTSR 162
R(Bui) v SSWP [2022] UKUT 189 (AAC) reported as [2023] AACR 9

32.21 RA v SSWP (UC) [2024] UKUT 207 (AAC)
PHC (formerly HCU) v SSWP (UC) [2024] UKUT 340 (AAC)

32.22 SSAA 111A, 112, 115; UC(C&P) 38; SS(C&P) 32(1B),(1C), 32ZA; HBW 88, 88A; HBP 69, 69A

UC assessment periods

32.23 UC uses monthly assessment periods, whereas SPC and HB use benefit weeks (para 1.9). UC's 'whole month' approach simplifies the administration of benefit and avoids numerous changes if your circumstances change a lot (paras 33.12, 33.35, 33.37).

Your assessment periods

32.24 Your assessment periods are decided as follows:

(a) your first assessment period begins on the day your UC starts (para 32.30)

(b) after that, they begin on the same day of each following month, with adjustments for the ends of months as described in table 32.1.

Table 32.1 **UC assessment periods**

If your first assessment period starts on the day of the month in column 1, your following assessment periods start on the day of the month in column 2 (a), (b) or (c).

1 – Start of first assessment period	**2 – Start of following assessment periods**		
	(a) Except February	(b) February not in a leap year	(c) February in a leap year
1st to 28th	Same as 1	Same as 1	Same as 1
29th	29th	27th	28th
30th	30th	27th	28th
31st	Last day (30th or 31st)	28th	29th

Assessment periods if your start date changes

32.25 Your UC start date can change due to backdating or because the DWP used the wrong date. When this happens, the DWP can change the start date of:

(a) all your assessment periods (so they are still one month) or

(b) just the first assessment period (so that it is longer or shorter than one month).

In the second case, your UC is calculated on a daily basis.

32.23 WRA 7; UC 21(1)

32.24 UC 21(1),(2)

T32.1 UC 21(2)

32.25 UC 21(2A), 21A

Assessment periods when your circumstances change

32.26 When your circumstances change, your assessment periods don't change (chapter 33). In most cases:

(a) your new amount of UC is awarded from the first day of the assessment period in which the change takes place or

(b) if you stop qualifying for UC, your UC ends on the last day of the previous assessment period.

If you become a couple and each of you previously had different assessment periods, the DWP uses the assessment periods of whichever of you means your UC changes or ends earlier.

The date your benefit starts

Date of claim and start date

32.27 This section explains the two steps used to decide when your benefit starts:

(a) first work out your date of claim

(b) then use that to work out your start date.

Date of claim for UC and SPC

32.28 Your date of claim for UC or SPC is whichever is the earliest of the following:

(a) the date the DWP received your properly completed online or paper claim form

(b) the date you phoned the DWP to claim or

(c) the date you first notified the DWP that you needed online assistance to claim.

If you are asked to provide information or evidence, the above dates only apply if you do so within one month of when it was requested.

Date of claim for HB

32.29 Your date of claim for HB is whichever is the earliest of the following:

(a) the date the council received your properly completed online or paper claim form

(b) the date you phoned the council to claim

(c) the date you first notified the council that you wanted to claim

(d) the date your partner (who was on HB) died or you separated – so long as you make your claim within one month of the death or separation

(e) if you are on UC or SPC, the date that benefit began – so long as the council received your HB form within one month of the DWP receiving your UC or SPC form or

(f) if you are on UC or SPC, the date your liability for rent began – so long as the council received your HB form within one month of the liability beginning.

32.26 WRA 7(1), UC(D&A) sch 1 para 20

32.28 UC(C&P) 8(5),(6), 10, 37(3); SS(C&P) 4(2),(6A),(6E),(11)

32.29 HBW 83(1),(4A),(4E),(5)(aa)-(e),(8), 83A, sch 11 para 4; HBP 64(1),(5A),(5F),(6)(a)-(e),(9), 64A, sch 10 para 4

If you are asked to complete a form or to provide information or evidence, the above dates only apply if you do so within one month of when it was requested.

Start date for UC

32.30 Your UC starts on your date of claim. But there are exceptions for advance claims and backdated claims (paras 32.25, 32.35-36), for reclaims (para 33.35, and also for claims by people migrating from legacy benefits (chapter 25).

Start date for SPC

32.31 Your SPC starts on the first day of the benefit week following your date of claim. And your benefit week starts on your state pension payment day (para 34.10).

Start date for HB

32.32 Your HB starts on the Monday following your date of claim. But there are exceptions for new homes, daily rents, advance claims and backdated claims (paras 32.33-36).

Example: Date of claim and start date in UC

Mason (aged 40) makes an online claim for UC on 5 May.

- His date of claim is 5 May
- His UC starts on 5 May (para 32.30)
- His UC assessment periods start on the 5th of the month.

HB start date when you move to a new home

32.33 This rule applies when you become liable for rent for the first time such as moving into a new home, whether you are claiming working age HB in supported or temporary accommodation, or pension age HB in any accommodation. In these cases, if your date of claim for HB is in the same benefit week (Monday to Sunday) as your rent liability starts, your HB starts on:

(a) the day your rent liability starts or

(b) the day you move in, if this is later (SL v Renfrewshire Council).

HB start date if your rent is due daily

32.34 This rule applies if your rent is due on a daily basis, but only if you live in a hostel (para 12.27) or temporary accommodation (para 11.20). In these cases, your HB always starts on the day your rent liability began, so long as that it is no more than a year ago.

32.30 UC(C&P) 26(1)

32.31 SS(C&P) 16A(1),(4)

32.32 HBW 2(1) – 'benefit week', 76(1); HBP 2(1), 57(1)

32.33 HBW 76(2); HBP 57(2)(a)
SL v Renfrewshire Council [2014] UKUT 411 (AAC)

32.34 SSAA 1(2); HBW 76(3)-(5), 79(8); HBP 57(2)(b),(3),(4), 59(8)

Advance claims

32.35 You can make a claim for benefit to start on a future date (an 'advance claim') as follows:

(a) you can claim UC up to one month in advance

(b) you can claim SPC up to four months in advance

(c) you can claim pension age HB up to 17 weeks in advance

(d) you can claim working age HB for supported or temporary accommodation up to 13 weeks in advance.

These rules can be used if you are moving home, your job is coming to an end, you are approaching pension age, you are planning to retire, or for other reasons. They don't apply if you aren't habitually resident in the UK or Ireland (para 40.36).

Backdating

32.36 'Backdating' means you get benefit for a period before you claimed it. This section gives the rules that apply to SPC, UC and HB. In the law, backdating is also called 'extending the time limit for claiming'.

Backdating SPC

32.37 SPC is automatically backdated for three months. You don't have to request this or give any reasons: it applies in all cases.

Backdating SPC if the DWP awards you another state benefit

32.38 This rule applies if:

(a) you claim SPC but you are unsuccessful

(b) you or a member of your benefit unit then claim some other state benefit within 10 days of your SPC claim (this applies to any state benefit except PIP, UC, HB and CTR)

(c) that other benefit means you are entitled to SPC after all and

(d) you make another claim for SPC within three months of being notified of the award of the other benefit.

In these cases, your SPC is backdated to the date of your original SPC claim (the claim that was unsuccessful), no matter how much time has passed since then.

32.35 UC(C&P) 10(1), 32; SS(C&P) 4E, 13D; HBW 83(10),(11); HBP 64(11),(12)

32.37 SS(C&P) 19(2),(3)(i)

32.38 SS(C&P) 6(16)-(18),(22),(26)

Backdating UC

32.39 UC can only be backdated for one month, and only if:

(a) one or more of the circumstances in table 32.2 applies to you (or if you are in a joint claim couple, to each of you)

(b) as a result, you couldn't reasonably have been expected to make your UC claim earlier (para 32.41) and

(c) you request backdated UC:

- when you make your claim or
- within one month of getting the decision letter about your claim.

All three conditions must be satisfied for you to qualify (CK v SSWP). The time limit in (c) can in some cases be extended (para 38.27), (SSWP v Miah, confirming AM v SSWP).

Table 32.2 **Backdated UC: conditions**

To qualify for backdating one or more of the following must have meant you couldn't reasonably have claimed UC earlier.

(a) You have a disability.

(b) You had an illness that prevented you from making a claim and you have given the DWP medical evidence that confirms this.

(c) You were unable to make a claim online because the official computer system was inoperative – but even an overwhelming amount of traffic may not mean the system counts as inoperative (NK v SSWP).

(d) You were in a couple and the DWP decided not to award you UC (or ended your UC) because your partner didn't accept the claimant commitment, and you are now making a claim as a single person.

(e) You were previously on HB, JSA, ESA, IS, CTC or WTC, and you weren't told it would end until after it had ended -- for example, this applies to HB when you move to a new council area but weren't told it would end until your new local council tells you (CP v SSWP).

Note: These circumstances can't be extended to match the wider range of possibilities in table 32.3 (CU v SSWP). But note that the 'good cause' test doesn't apply (CU v SSWP).

32.39 UC(C&P) 26(2),(3)
CK v SSWP [2024] UKUT 331 (AAC)
SSWP v Miah [2024] EWCA Civ 186, [2024] 1 WLR 3012
AM v SSWP (UC) [2022] UKUT 242 (AAC)

T32.2 UC 26(3)
NK v SSWP (UC)[2023] UKUT 65 (AAC)
CP v SSWP (UC) [2020] UKUT 309 (AAC)
CU v SSWP [2024] UKUT 32 (AAC)

32.40 The online UC claim form doesn't have a question about backdating, though the DWP is understood to be considering whether to include one. Your circumstances may make it clear to the DWP that you qualify (WB v SSWP), but it is always advisable to request backdating using your online journal as soon as you can.

Couldn't reasonably have claimed UC earlier

32.41 For the condition in para 32.39(b), 'the test is whether in the whole circumstances you can show that you did what any reasonable person would have done to ascertain their rights' (CSJSA/811/06). If you have a disability, the DWP should consider 'what a hypothetical person with your disability could reasonably have been expected to do, given your knowledge of the benefit system and the possibilities for acquiring information about benefit entitlements and procedures available to you' (CU v SSWP). If you were notified late that your legacy benefits would end (table 32.2(e)), the DWP should consider whether any further delay by you was a reasonable result of the late notification (PR v SSWP and Allerdale BC).

Backdating pension age HB

32.42 Pension age HB is automatically backdated for three months.

Table 32.3 **Backdated working age HB: case law**

To qualify for backdated working age HB, you must have 'good cause' for not claiming earlier (para 32.44).

- *Case law about other benefits:* Pre-1997 case law about other benefits that used good cause remains binding on HB (CH/5221/2001).
- *Reasonableness:* Good cause includes 'any fact that would probably have caused a reasonable person to act as the claimant did' (CH/4501/2004 approving C.S. 371/49). What is 'reasonable' is objective rather than subjective (UH v Islington LBC).
- *Ignorance of rights and attempts to ascertain them:* Claimants are expected to take reasonable steps to ascertain what their rights may be, but 'cannot always be assumed to have an understanding of public administration' (C.S. 371/49). Though ignorance of itself is not good cause, it may be a factor to take into account since the law does not 'require a person to be acquainted with the "rules and regulations"' (UH/Islington).

Table continued ➤

32.40 WB v SSWP (UC) [2022] UKUT 332 (AAC)

32.41 CU v SSWP [2024] UKUT 32 (AAC)
PR v SSWP and Allerdale BC (HB) [2023] UKUT 34 (AAC)

32.42 HBP 64(1)

T32.3 HBW 83(12)
UH v Islington LBC [2010] UKUT 65 (AAC)
SSWP v PG (JSA) [2015] UKUT 616 (AAC)

- *A mistaken belief reasonably held:* Good cause can include a firmly held misunderstanding which amounts to a mistaken belief reasonably held, particularly when the claimant has not been careless or attempted to obtain benefit they are not entitled to (CH/4501/2004 approving earlier cases). This could include believing that you don't have to pay housing costs (and so don't have to claim HB) if you are on a passport benefit (CH/4501/2004), or that you can't get HB if you haven't paid national insurance contributions (CH/2198/2008).
- *Illness:* Good cause is related not to the severity or seriousness of an illness but to the resulting incapability of the claimant to claim (CH/5135/2001).
- *Mental incapacity:* In deciding good cause, a mentally disabled person is treated as having their mental age, not their chronological age (CH/393/2003).
- *Inability to speak English:* By itself, an inability to speak English is not normally good cause (CH/3579/2003).
- *Not receiving a document from the council:* Good cause can include non-receipt of a document from the council (e.g. requesting information and evidence) if this meant your HB stopped and you have reapplied (CH/3402/2005).
- *Misleading or incorrect advice:* Misleading or incorrect advice from a competent source such as a solicitor, law centre or Citizen's Advice is usually good cause (CS 50/50, R(U) 9/74, CI/37/95). So is relying on official literature or online material such as gov.uk or the council's website (SSWP v PG). In some situations, a competent source could include the council's housing department or a housing officer.
- *Who has to have good cause:* Only you (the claimant) have to show good cause not, for example, your partner (CH/3817/2004).
- *Good cause and qualifying for HB:* If you have good cause your claim is backdated even if you only qualify for HB for part of the backdated period (CH/1237/2004). But the council doesn't have to consider whether you have good cause if you don't qualify for any of the backdated period (CH/996/2004).

Example: Backdating SPC and HB

Johnny claims SPC on 12 July. He sees that he also needs to claim HB towards his rent, and does this on 31 July.

- His SPC is automatically backdated three months to 12 April {para 32.37).
- His HB is also backdated to 12 April (para 32.45).

Backdating working age HB

32.43 Working age HB can only be backdated for one month, and only if:

(a) you live in STA (table 13.1) (since no-one else can now claim working age HB: table 2.3).

(b) you have 'good cause' for not claiming earlier (table 32.3) and

(c) you request backdated HB:

- when you make your HB claim or
- within one month of getting the decision letter about your claim or in some cases later (para 38.34).

32.44 If you claim UC and HB, and then the council decides your home isn't STA, the DWP should backdate your UC for housing costs 'to the date you originally declared you were living in the accommodation' (Housing benefit guidance for supported housing claims, paras 64-68).

If you claim HB when you claim SPC or UC

32.45 If you claim pension age HB within a month of claiming SPC guarantee credit, or working age HB within a month of claiming UC, your HB is backdated to the same date as your guarantee credit or UC.

32.43 HBW 83(12),(12A)

32.44 UC(C&P) 2 – 'official error', 9

32.45 HBW 83(5)(aa),(b); HBP 64(1A),(6)(a)

Chapter 33 **Changes of circumstance**

- Reporting changes: paras 33.1-8
- When changes take effect: paras 33.9-34
- UC reclaim periods: paras 33.35-40
- Suspending, restoring and terminating benefit: paras 33.41-46

Reporting changes

Changes you should report

33.1 You should tell the DWP (UC and SPC) or the council (HB) about 'relevant changes' in your circumstances. This means changes which you might reasonably be expected to know could affect:

(a) your continuing entitlement to benefit

(b) the amount of benefit awarded or

(c) the payment of benefit.

33.2 These include moving home, changes in rent (except council tenants on HB), income or capital, and any other change that relates to you, your benefit unit, non-dependants, or someone you are caring for.

33.3 Additionally, if you are on HB:

(a) you must tell the council if you stop qualifying for UC, JSA(IB), ESA(IR) or IS but

(b) the DWP tells the council if you stop qualifying for SPC.

Exception for some older SPC awards

33.4 If were over 75 on 5 April 2016 and you have been on SPC since then, you may have an assessed income period during which you don't need to report changes in your private pensions or capital (DMG chapter 83). But this concession ends when your SPC ends, you become a couple or a single person, or your partner reaches age 65.

33.1-2 UC(C&P) 38(1),(4); SS(C&P) 32(1),(1B); HBW 88(1); HBP 69(1)

33.3 HBW 88(3)(d),(6); HBP 69(6),(8)

33.4 SPCA 7(6), 9(1),(4); PC 12

How to report changes

33.5 For UC you can use your online journal to report changes (para 32.13) or you may be given a contact point. For SPC and HB you can usually report changes by phone or online.

33.6 The DWP or council may require information and evidence about the change and you should provide this within 14 days (one month for HB) or longer if reasonable. The DWP or council then decides how the change affects your UC or HB and sends you a decision letter about this (chapter 38).

Changes others should report (as well as you)

33.7 The responsibility to report relevant changes also applies to:

(a) your partner as well as you if you are claiming UC as a couple

(b) someone acting for you and

(c) your landlord or another third party when part of your UC, SPC or HB is paid to them.

Failing to report a change

33.8 If you fail to report a change of circumstances promptly you could be liable for prosecution resulting in a fine and/or a prison sentence of up to three months (six months if you knew you weren't telling the truth). A landlord (including a company) who is paid UC/SPC/HB could also be liable for prosecution if they fail to report that you have moved out or that your liability for rent/housing costs has ended.

When changes take effect

33.9 This section explains when changes of circumstances take effect. It applies to changes that you (or someone else) report.

33.10 The same rules apply to changes the DWP/council becomes aware of without you (or anyone else) reporting them, but as if the day the DWP/council takes action is the day you reported the change.

Advantageous and disadvantageous

33.11 The rules distinguish between:

(a) 'advantageous' changes – which increase your benefit or reinstate it and

(b) 'disadvantageous' changes – which reduce or end your benefit.

33.5 UC(C&P) sch 2 paras 2, 4; UC(D&A) 3(1), 4; SS(C&P) 32ZA(1),(2)(h), sch 9ZC paras 2, 4; SS(D&A) 2(a); HBW 88(1), 88A(1), sch 11 paras 2, 4; HBP 69(1), 69A(1), sch 10 paras 2, 4

33.6 UC(D&A) 33(2)-(4); SS(C&P) 32(1),(1B); HB(D&A) 7(5)

33.7 UC(C&P) 38(1),(4); SS(C&P) 32(1),(1B); HBW 88(1); HBP 69(1)

33.8 SSAA 111A, 112, 115; UC(C&P) 38; SS(C&P) 32(1B),(1C), 32ZA; HBW 88, 88A; HBP 69, 69A

33.9 UC(D&A) 35(1), sch 1 paras 20, 21; SS(D&A) 7(2)(a),(b),(c)(v), sch 3B; HB(D&A) 8(4)(b)

33.10 UC(D&A) 35(1), sch 1 para 29; SS(D&A) 7(2)(bb); HB(D&A) 8(4)(a)

33.11 UC(D&A) sch 1 paras 20, 21, 29; SS(D&A) 7(1),(2)(a),(b), sch 3B paras 1(b), 2(a); HB(D&A) 8(2)-(4); HBW 79(1); HBP 59(1)

Advantageous changes reported on time

33.12 If you report an advantageous change within the time limits in paras 33.15-16, your benefit increases from:

(a) for UC, the beginning of the assessment period in which the change occurs

(b) for HB, the Monday following the day the change occurs, but a different rule applies to rent increases (para 33.17)

(c) for SPC:

- if your income changes or you or your partner become entitled to AA/PIP, the first day of the benefit week after the one in which the change occurs (or first day of the benefit week in which the change occurs if it is that very day)
- in any other case, the first day of the benefit week in which the change occurs (or following week if it is impracticable).

Advantageous changes reported late

33.13 But if you report an advantageous change outside the time limits (paras 33.15-16), your benefit increases from:

(a) for UC, the beginning of the assessment period in which you report the change

(b) for HB, the Monday following the day you report it or

(c) for SPC, the beginning of the benefit week in which you report it.

The effect is that you get less benefit than you would have if you had reported the change promptly.

Disadvantageous changes whenever reported

33.14 Whenever you report a disadvantageous change, your benefit reduces from:

(a) for UC, the beginning of the assessment period in which the change occurs

(b) for HB, the Monday following the day it occurs or

(c) for SPC:

- if your income changes, the first day of the benefit week after the one in which the change occurs (or first day of the benefit week in which the change occurs if it is that very day)
- in any other case, the first day of the benefit week in which the change occurs (or the following week if it is impracticable).

33.12 UC(D&A) 35(1), sch 1 para 20; SS(D&A) 7(1)(a),(2)(a), sch 3B paras 1(b), 2; HB(D&A) 8(2); HBW 79(1); HBP 59(1)

33.13 UC(D&A) 35(1), sch 1 para 21; SS(D&A) 7(2)(b); HB(D&A) 8(3)

33.14 UC(D&A) 35(1), sch 1 para 20; SS(D&A) 7(1),(2)(c)(v), sch 3B paras 1(b), 2; HB(D&A) 8(2); HBW 79(1); HBP 59(1)

What counts as notifying an advantageous change on time

33.15 Notifying an advantageous change 'on time' means:

(a) you report it by the end of the assessment period in which it occurs (UC) or

(b) you report it within one month of the day the change occurs (SPC and HB) or

(c) the DWP/council agrees you can report it up to 12 months later than (a) or (b).

33.16 The DWP/council can agree to you reporting an advantageous change up to 12 months later if:

(a) there are special circumstances why you couldn't report the change earlier (para 38.36) and

(b) it is reasonable to allow you extra time.

The later you report the change, the more compelling your reasons have to be.

Examples: Changes of circumstances

1. An increase in UC

Abigail is working and getting UC, and her assessment periods begin on the 26th of each month. She starts paying a childminder to look after her son on 6 June and qualifies for more UC because she is entitled to a childcare costs element.

- If she reports this to the DWP by 25 June, her UC increases from 26 May (the start of her assessment period)

2. A reduction in UC

Desmond is getting UC and his assessment periods begin on the 21st of each month. His daughter moves out on 1 October, and he qualifies for less UC because he is no longer entitled to a bedroom for her.

- Whenever he reports this to the DWP, his UC reduces from 21 September (the start of his assessment period).

3. An increase in HB

Barney is retired and is getting HB. On Saturday 26 July 2025, he replaces his car and qualifies for more HB because his capital has gone down.

- If he reports this to the council by 26 August, his HB increases from Monday 28 July (the start of his next benefit week).

4. A rent increase in UC

Clodagh is getting UC and her assessment periods begin on the 5th of each month. Her rent is due monthly and goes up on 1 July.

- If she reports this to the DWP by 4 July, her UC increases from 5 June (the start of her assessment period).

33.15 UC(D&A) 35(1), 36(3),(9), sch 1 paras 20, 21; SS(D&A) 7(2)(a), 8(3)(b); HB(D&A) 8(3)(b), 9(2)(b)

33.16 UC(D&A) 36(3)-(7); SS(D&A) 8(4),(5); HB(D&A) 9(3),(4)

5. A rent increase in HB

Elvira is getting HB in supported accommodation. Her rent is due weekly and goes up on Wednesday 1 October 2025.

- If she reports this to the council by 1 November, her HB increases from Tuesday 1 October.

Rent increases and becoming liable for rent

33.17 If your rent or service charges change:

(a) for UC/SPC, the general rules apply (paras 33.11-16) including if you take on responsibility for them because the liable person isn't paying (paras 9.16-19)

(c) your HB changes on the day your rent increases or reduces, except that if you report an increase late your HB changes on the day you report the increase.

You should report such changes promptly (except in the case of council tenants on HB). If you delay reporting an increase in your rent or other housing costs you could lose benefit.

33.18 You should tell the DWP or council as soon as possible about changes to your housing costs. Your landlord may be asked to confirm these. You should normally report changes whether or not part or all of your benefit is paid to your landlord – though if it is, the landlord has a responsibility in law to report them too.

New LHA and rent officer figures

33.19 Changes to LHA figures in April take effect as described in para 12.17, and changes to rent officer figures take effect as described in para 12.39.

Moving home

33.20 When you move home, you should report your new housing costs to the DWP or council. The general rules (paras 33.11-16) apply to changes in your UC or SPC. But changes in HB take effect as follows:

(a) if you continue to qualify for HB, it changes on the exact day of your move

(b) if you start or stop qualifying for HB on two homes, it changes on that exact day

(c) if you stop qualifying for HB, it ends at the end of the benefit week containing the day of your move (or on the exact day if you have a daily liability for rent).

33.17 UC(D&A) sch1 paras 20, 21; SS(D&A) 7(1),(2)(a),(b), sch 3B para 1(b); HB(D&A) 7(2)(a),(c), 8(2),(3); HBW 79(2); HBP 59(2)

33.18 UC(C&P) 38(1),(4); UC(D&A) 39(4), sch 1 para 21; SS(C&P) 32(1),(1B); SS(D&A) 7(2)(b), 13(1); HB(D&A) 8(3); HBW 88(1); HBP 69(1)

33.20 UC(D&A) 39(1),(4), sch 1 paras 20, 21; SS(D&A) 7(1)(a),(2)(a),(b),(c), sch 3B para 1(b); HB(D&A) 8(2),(3); HBW 79(2A),(8); HBP 59(2A),(8)

When changes take effect: special cases

When you start or leave work

33.21 If you (or your partner) start or leave work (employment or self-employment):

(a) your UC changes as explained in paras 22.13-14

(b) your HB changes on the Monday following your first day of employment/self-employment or the first day you aren't employed/self-employed.

When your social security benefits change

33.22 This rule applies when there is a change in your entitlement to social security benefits (in practice this means all DWP and equivalent Scottish benefits), or in the entitlement of a member of your benefit unit. It applies when another benefit starts, changes or ends.

33.23 In these cases, the change takes effect from:

(a) in UC, the start of the assessment period in which the social security benefit changes

(b) in HB, the day the social security benefit changes

(c) in SPC the first day of the benefit week in which the change occurs (or following week if it is impracticable).

This rule applies no matter how late you tell the DWP about the change (since the DWP should already know what benefits it is paying you).

Benefits uprating

33.24 Your UC/SPC/HB changes due to the annual uprating as follows:

(a) UC, from the first assessment period that starts on or after 6 April

(b) SPC (and other DWP benefits), from the first day of your benefit week that contains the first Monday that falls on or after 6 April or

(c) HB, from the first Monday in April if your rent is paid weekly (or exact multiples) or 1 April in any other case – and whichever applies your other DWP benefits are treated as being uprated on the same day.

Changes in capability for work

33.25 The general rules (paras 33.11-16) apply when you start or stop qualifying for a work capability element (para 16.9), but there are three special cases (paras 33.26-28).

33.26 If you start to qualify for an LCWRA element because you are terminally ill (para 16.18), your UC increases (to include that element) from the beginning of the assessment period containing the date you became terminally ill, no matter how long ago that was. This rule means you don't lose UC as a result of any kind of delay.

33.21 HBW 79(1); HBP 59(1)

33.22 SSA 8(3); UC(D&A) 2 – 'relevant benefit'

33.23 UC(D&A) sch 1 para 31(1),(2)(a); SS(D&A) 6(2)(e),(ee), 7(2)(c)(v),(7), sch 3B paras 7, 8; HB(D&A) 7(2)((i), 8(2),(14); HBW 79(1); HBP 59(1)

33.24 SSAA 150(10)(a),(10ZB), 150A(7); UC(D&A) sch 1 paras 32, 33; SS(D&A) 6(2)(a); sch 3B para 1(b); HBW 42(8), 79(3); HBP 41(9),(10), 59(3)

33.26 UC(D&A) 23(2), sch 1 para 28

33.27 If you start to qualify for an LCWRA element because there is new medical evidence (or the DWP changes its mind about the medical evidence), your UC increases (to include that element) from the beginning of the assessment period containing the date you started qualifying for it, no matter how long ago that was.

33.28 If you stop qualifying for an LCWRA or LCW element but couldn't reasonably have been expected to know you no longer qualify (or that you should report this to the DWP), your UC reduces (to remove that element) from the first day of your assessment period in which the DWP makes its decision about this. This rule means you haven't been overpaid UC.

Reaching pension age

33.29 You can claim SPC and pension age HB up to four months/17 weeks in advance (para 32.35). If you do:

(a) your date of claim for SPC and pension age HB (paras 32.28-29) is the exact day you (or your partner) reach pension age and

(b) your UC continues until the end of the assessment period containing that day.

33.30 This results in you getting both SPC and UC for a short period during which your state pension is included as income in both those benefits (but not your SPC or UC).

The UC bereavement run-on

33.31 In UC only, you qualify for a bereavement run-on if one of the following has died:

(a) your partner if you were claiming UC as a couple

(b) a child or young person who was in your benefit unit

(c) a non-dependant or

(d) a person you were caring for, if you qualified for the UC carer element for caring for them.

33.32 The bereavement run-on lasts for three months – the assessment period containing the date of the death and the next two assessment periods. During this time, your maximum UC (para 16.2) is calculated as though the person hadn't died, but changes in your financial and other circumstances are taken into account in the normal way.

33.27 UC(D&A) sch 1 paras 23-24

33.28 UC(D&A) sch 1 para 25

33.29 SPCA 15(1)(c), 16(1); UC(D&A) sch 1 para 26; UCTP 6A(3)-(5); SS(C&P) 4E, 13D; UC 66(1)(a),(b); PC 15(1)(za); HBP 29(1)(j)(zi), 64(11),(12)

33.31 UC 37

33.32 UC 37

Changes ending UC, SPC or HB

33.33 Your UC, SPC or HB ends when a change in your circumstances means you no longer meet the conditions of entitlement (chapter 2).

33.34 In these cases, your benefit ends on:

(a) the last day of the assessment period before the one in which the change occurs (UC)

(b) the last day of the benefit week in which the change occurs (SPC) or

(c) the Sunday at the end of the benefit week containing the day the change occurs (HB) or where you leave accommodation where the rent is charged daily (para 32.34), the day the change occurs.

Your benefit can also stop if you fail to provide information and evidence (para 33.44).

UC reclaim periods

33.35 If you don't qualify for UC or your UC stops, your claim is kept open for a six-month reclaim period. During this period, you can provide information about your circumstances, and if you qualify again you can make a rapid reclaim via your journal. Reclaim periods only apply to UC and are intended as a simple route back to UC particularly if you have tried work and it didn't work out (OG April 2024 file 138).

Who gets a reclaim period

33.36 You get a six month reclaim period when:

(a) you make a claim for UC but don't qualify because your earnings are too high or

(b) you are on UC and it stops because your earnings are too high or

(c) you are on UC and it stops for any other reason.

In each case, the reclaim period runs for six assessment periods (six months) starting with the first assessment period in which you don't qualify for UC. But this only applies while you meet the basic conditions in table 2.1. Your online journal tells you when you are in a reclaim period.

During the reclaim period

33.37 During your reclaim period:

(a) you can continue to log on to your online journal to report your income and changes in your circumstances

(b) if the DWP was getting details of your employed earnings from HMRC (para 22.16), this continues

(c) the DWP carries forward your 'surplus earnings' in some cases (para 22.26)

(d) your assessment periods continue with the same start dates and

(e) if you become (re-)entitled to UC, you can re-claim using your journal (OG file 138).

33.34 UC(D&A) 35(1), sch 1 para 20; SS(D&A) 7(1),(2)(c)(v), sch 3B paras 1(b), 2(a); HB(D&A) 8(2); HBW 79(8); HBP 59(8)

33.35 UC 21(3C); UC(C&P) 32A; Parliament Deposited Papers DEP 2024-0442

33.36 UC 21(3C); UC(C&P) 32A

33.37 UC 21(3C)(b), 54A(1),(2), 61(2); UC(C&P) 32A(2)

Reclaim periods for earnings

33.38 If your reclaim period relates to your earnings (para 33.36(a),(b)):

(a) you get UC from the first day of the assessment period in which you become entitled to UC (or if later, from the first assessment period after that for which you submit your earnings)

(b) in that assessment period, you get a full month's UC.

You get a new reclaim period every time you stop qualifying for UC due to the level of your earnings. But if you don't qualify for all of the six months, you can't get UC until you make a full UC claim (para 32.2).

Reclaim periods when you stop earning

33.39 If your reclaim period relates to your earnings, but you then stop earning:

(a) you can only make a rapid reclaim via your journal if you do so within seven days of ceasing work (or longer if the DWP agrees)

(b) you get UC from the first day of the assessment period in which you become entitled to UC

(c) in that assessment period, your earnings are only taken into account on a daily basis during the period in which you were earning.

Other reclaim periods

33.40 If your reclaim period relates to anything other than earnings (para 33.36(c)):

(a) you get UC from the first day of the assessment period in which you become entitled to UC

(b) in that assessment period, you get a full month's UC.

33.38 UC 21(3C)(a); UC(C&P) 26(5), 32A(2)

33.39 UC 22A(1),(3)

33.40 UC 22A(2)

Suspending, restoring, and terminating benefit

Suspending benefit

33.41 Suspending benefit means that the DWP or council stops all or part of your payments for the time being. It can do this when:

(a) it has a doubt about:
- whether you qualify for benefit
- how much you qualify for or
- whether you have been overpaid or

(b) it is considering an appeal or an appeal is pending:
- against a tribunal or court decision in your own case or
- against a tribunal or court decision in another person's case and it could affect your case.

33.42 If the DWP or council needs information or evidence, it:

(a) must request this

(b) must allow you at least 14 days (UC and SPC) or one month (HB) to provide it or to show that it doesn't exist or is impossible to obtain and

(c) can only suspend your benefit if you don't.

Restoring benefit

33.43 Restoring benefit means that the DWP or council pays you benefit again. It must do this as soon as it is satisfied that:

(a) you qualify for benefit

(b) you have provided any information or evidence required or shown that it doesn't exist or is impossible to obtain and/or

(c) there is no longer an appeal pending (or there is no longer time for an appeal to be made).

In HB the law adds that this must be within 14 days. But in all the benefits it is in practice usually quicker.

33.41 SSA 21; CSPSSA sch 7 para 13; UC(D&A) 44(1),(2); SS(D&A) 16(1),(3); HB(D&A) 11(1),(2)

33.42 SSA 22; CSPSSA sch 7 para 14; UC(D&A) 45(1),(2),(4); SS(D&A) 17(1),(2),(4); HB(D&A) 13(1),(2),(4)

33.43 UC(D&A) 46; SS(D&A) 20(1)(a),(2),(3); HB(D&A) 12

Terminating benefit

33.44 Terminating benefit means you don't get any more payments and your entitlement ends. The DWP or council can only do this if:

(a) it suspended your payments in full

(b) it required you to provide information or evidence

(c) more than one month has passed and

(d) you haven't provided the information or evidence or shown that it doesn't exist or is impossible to obtain.

33.45 The DWP or council can only terminate benefit from the same date it was suspended from (CH v LB Lewisham). If your benefit should have stopped from an earlier date the rules in paras 33.11-34 apply.

Reconsiderations and appeals

33.46 You can ask for a reconsideration about suspending, restoring or terminating your benefit. And you can appeal to a tribunal about a decision to terminate your benefit or to alter it when it is restored, but you can't appeal about a decision to suspend your benefit or to restore it without altering it (table 39.1).

33.44 SSA 23; CSPSSA sch 7 para 15; UC(D&A) 47; SS(D&A) 18; HB(D&A) 14

33.45 CH v LB Lewisham (HB) [2020] UKUT 71 (AAC)

33.46 UC(D&A) 10, sch 3 para 7; SS(D&A) 3(8), sch 2 para 24; HB(D&A) 4(6), sch para 5

Chapter 34 **Payments**

34.1 This chapter explains how and when your UC, SPC or HB are paid to you. Chapter 35 explains when they can be paid to your landlord or a third party.

How and when UC and SPC are paid

How UC and SPC are paid

34.2 UC and SPC are paid into your bank, building society or other account. For couples claiming UC, this can be an account in one name or joint names, and if you can't agree whose account it should be paid into, the DWP decides. Or if it is in your interests and the circumstances are exceptional, the DWP can split the payments between you.

If you can't use a bank account

34.3 If you are refused a bank account because you don't have the right documents, the DWP will usually refer you to the 'Help to Claim' service first (para 32.6). If you can't use a bank or similar account, the DWP will consider payment using:

(a) the payment exception service

(b) a hospital account

(c) someone else's bank account on your behalf.

The DWP will consider these for your first payment or a limited period only (OG file 106).

34.4 The payment exception service allows you to collect your UC or SPC using a payment card or voucher code at any Post Office or PayPoint outlet [www] (ADM B1006). The voucher code is sent by text/email or can be collected from the jobcentre. Each voucher is limited to £100 and expires after 90 days (OG file 106).

34.2 SSAA 5(1)(i),(2)(za),(ab); UC(C&P) 46(1), 47(5); SS(C&P) 21(1)

34.3 www.gov.uk/payment-exception-service

34.5 If you are a long-term in-patient your UC or SPC can be paid into the hospital's account. Unless the hospital is acting as your appointee, the DWP requires your and the hospital's consent to do this (OG file 106).

Payments to someone on your behalf

34.6 If you have an attorney or appointee (para 32.7) your UC or SPC can be paid into their account, or a joint account if you have one with them. If you don't have an attorney or appointee, the DWP can pay all or part of your UC to someone on your behalf (for example a relative, friend or carer) if you get their consent and it is necessary to protect your interests. This method is only used if the other options have been considered and ruled out (OG file 106).

How you spend your benefit

34.7 There is no obligation on you to spend your benefit in any particular way. It makes sense to pay your rent with your HB or your UC/SPC housing costs element, but you aren't obliged to (DPP v Huskinson). However, if you don't use it to pay these, your benefit could be paid to your landlord instead of you (chapter 35).

'Your interests'

34.8 'Your interests' means:

(a) your own interests

(b) your partner's interests if you are a couple (even if you are claiming UC as a single person)

(c) the interests of a child or young person in your benefit unit or

(d) in UC only, the interests of a person you get a UC carer element for.

When UC is paid

34.9 UC is usually paid monthly within seven days after the last day of the assessment period, or if this isn't possible as soon as reasonably possible afterwards. In certain circumstances it can be paid more frequently if you ask for this (para 34.37).

34.6 SSAA 5(1)(i),(2)(za),(ab); UC(C&P) 46(1), 57, 58(1); SS(C&P) 21(1); 33(1), 34(1)

34.7 DPP v Huskinson [1988] Crim LR 620

34.8 UC(C&P) 47(6), 58(1); SS(C&P) 34(1)

34.9 UC(C&P) 47(1),(2)

When SPC is paid

34.10 Unless your SPC started before 6 April 2010, it is usually paid fortnightly or four weekly on the same day as your state pension, according to the last two digits of your national insurance number as follows:

(a) 00 to 19 – Monday

(b) 20 to 39 – Tuesday

(c) 40 to 59 – Wednesday

(d) 60 to 79 – Thursday

(e) 80 to 99 – Friday

It can be paid at longer intervals (up to 13 weeks) if you qualify for less than £1 per week.

Payment of arrears

34.11 The DWP can pay arrears of UC or SPC in a single sum. Or it can pay them in instalments if you agree to this (or both agree in a joint claim couple) or the DWP considers it is necessary for protecting your interests.

Paying benefit if you die

34.12 If you die, the DWP or council can pay or distribute your UC, SPC or HB to your personal representatives (executor) or next of kin (or in UC and SPC, your legatees or creditors). A written application for these payments has to be made within 12 months after your death, or later if the DWP or council agrees.

Benefit due more than a year ago

34.13 You lose the right to any payment you haven't received within 12 months after it became due. This applies to UC, SPC and HB when you die, and also to UC and SPC (but not HB) in other circumstances. The rule has been confirmed (CDLA/2807/2003), but the period can be extended if you have continuous good cause from a date within the 12 months to when you write requesting the payment (R(S) 2/63).

34.10 SS(C&P) 22C, 22CA, 26B, 26BA

34.11 UC(C&P) 47(2); SS(C&P) 21ZA

34.12 SSAA 5(1)(q),(2)(za),(ab),(e); UC(C&P) 56; SS(C&P) 30(1),(2), HBW 97(1),(3); HBP 78(1),(3)

34.13 SSAA 5(1)(m),(2)(za),(ab),(e); UC(C&P) 55, 56(6); SS(C&P) 30(3),(4)(4B), 38; HBW 97(3); HBP 78(3)

When the amount you get paid is reduced

34.14 The amount you get paid may be less than your full award if deductions are made to repay an advance or to repay other debts as described in this chapter and chapter 35. Deductions may also be made from your award to pay a penalty (para 37.19) or a sanction (para 4.26).

Priority between benefit deductions

34.15 If you have more than one of these they are usually applied in turn until the full amount has been repaid, before starting on the next according to the following order of precedence (OG file 055):

(a) a fraud penalty

(b) a sanction

(c) a new claim or change of circumstances advance

(d) a benefit transfer advance

(e) a budgeting advance

(f) third party deductions for rent arrears etc according to the priority for these (table 35.3).

In the case of (f) more than one can be applied but only up to the maximum amount.

34.16 Only one fraud penalty or sanction can be paid at a time, but in the case of a sanction it can apply to both members of a joint claim couple. If a sanction is in place and a penalty needs to be applied, it will replace the sanction until it is repaid. If a penalty or sanction is being deducted repayment of an advance is postponed until it is repaid (OG file 055).

34.17 From April 2025, with the exception of a sanction the maximum amount that can be deducted from your award at any time is 15% of your standard allowance (table 35.2).

UC advance payments

34.18 This section explains who can get a UC advance payment. These payments are repayable from your future payments of UC/SPC. DWP guidance is available online [www].

Kinds of UC advance

34.19 If you have claimed UC or SPC you may be able to get:

(a) a new claim advance if you are waiting for your first payment following your claim

(b) a change of circumstances advance, if you are waiting for your UC or SPC to increase following a change of circumstances

(c) a benefit transfer advance if you are migrating from legacy benefits to UC

(d) a budgeting advance if you need help with one-off expenses while you are on UC (para 34.27)

In the law these are also called 'payments on account'.

How to get an advance

34.20 If you need a UC advance, you can apply using your online journal (para 32.13), call the UC helpline or speak to your work coach.

Amount and payment

34.21 The DWP decides the amount of your UC advance. The maximum amounts are given in table 34.1, along with the minimum amount for budgeting advances. Advances are paid within three working days into your bank account or on the same day if you are in immediate need (OG file 008).

Repaying an advance

34.22 When you apply for an advance, the DWP should inform you it is repayable. Most advances are recovered by making deductions from your ongoing UC payments. The maximum repayment period is:

(a) 24 months for a new claim advance

(b) 24 months for a budgeting advance or

(c) six months for change of circumstances advance.

But in exceptional circumstances your repayments can be delayed for up to three months (new claims), six months (budgeting) or one month (change of circumstances) (OG files 005, 006, 007, 008).

34.18 SSAA 5(1)(r),(2)(za)
www.gov.uk/guidance/universal-credit-advances
https://depositedpapers.parliament.uk/depositedpaper/2286620/files

34.19 SS(PAB) 3(1)(a),(e), 5(1)(a)-(d),(2), 6, 11, 12(1); UCTP 17

Table 34.1 **Maximum amounts of UC advances**

New claim and benefit transfer advances

Your maximum advance is worked out (OG, files 005, 008) as follows:

(a) work out your expected UC award

(b) if (a) is more than 3.6 times your standard allowance, your maximum advance is 3.6 times your standard allowance

(c) in any other case, your maximum advance is your expected award.

Rule (b) ensures that your maximum repayment is never more than 15% of your standard allowance (para 34.22).

Changes of circumstances advance

DWP guidance (OG, file 007) says the maximum is 50% of the estimated increase in your UC or 90% of your standard allowance whichever is less.

Budgeting advance

Your maximum budgeting advance is worked out as follows (OG file 006):

(a) work out 3.6 times your standard allowance

(b) if you have existing deductions that are a higher priority (para 34.15) multiply these by 24 and deduct them from the total in (a)

(c) compare with the overall maximum depending on your benefit unit:

- single person with no children/young persons £348
- couple with no children/young persons £464
- single person or couple with at least one child/young person £812

Your maximum budgeting advance is the lower of (a) or (c). This is reduced pound for pound by any capital you have above £1,000 (excluding disregarded capital). If the result is less than £100 (or if you request less than £100), you can't get a budgeting advance.

Who can get a new claim, transfer or change of circumstances advance

34.23 To get a new claim, benefit transfer or change of circumstances advance (para 34.19(a)-(c)):

(a) you must explain why you are applying

(b) you must show that you are 'in need' and

(c) in the case of a new claim advance of UC, you must have been allocated a national insurance number.

But you don't have to show you are in need if you are asking for an advance because there is a gap between the end of your legacy benefits and the start of your UC.

T34.1 SS(PAB) 15

34.23 SS(PAB) 5, 6, UCTP 17

Who is 'in need'

34.24 You are in need if there is a serious risk of damage to your health and safety or that of a member of your benefit unit. The DWP also treats you as being in need if you are unable to manage until your next scheduled payment (OG file 008).

Who can get a budgeting advance

34.25 To get a budgeting advance (para 34.19(d)) you must meet the following conditions (OG file 006):

(a) you are on UC

(b) during the past six months, you haven't earned more than £2,600 (single person) or £3,600 (couple)

(c) you have repaid any previous budgeting advances and are likely to repay this one and

(d) either:

- you have been getting UC, SPC, HB, JSA(IB), ESA(IR) or IS for at least six months continuously or
- the advance is to help you start or stay in work and you can't get help from the Flexible Support Fund.

If the advance is to help you stay in work and you have been on UC for less than six months the earnings limit is worked out pro-rata (e.g. a couple on UC for four months, £2400).

34.26 Only one budgeting advance can be paid at a time and you cannot apply for another until your current one has been repaid (OG file 006).

What expenses can budgeting advances help with

34.27 Budgeting advances can help with:

(a) you or your partner getting employment or self-employment or

(b) intermittent expenses, such as furniture, household equipment, clothing and footwear.

The DWP says it also considers rent and removal expenses when you move home; home improvements, maintenance and security; and funeral expenses (OG file 006).

The Flexible Support Fund

34.28 The FSF provides discretionary non-repayable grants to help people claiming UC with work-related expenses (OG file 068). You can ask your work coach for this, and the guidance says the DWP should always consider a grant before making a budgeting advance (OG file 006).

34.24 SS(PAB) 7(1)

34.25 SS(PAB) 12(1),(2), 13, 14

34.27 SS(PAB) 12(1),(2)

34.28 Employment and Training Act 1973, s2

Help managing your money

34.29 This section describes the help the DWP can provide with budgeting once your UC or SPC is in payment. If you struggle to manage finances because your UC or HB doesn't cover your rent you can request a discretionary housing payment (chapter 31).

Money management advice

34.30 You can ask for general advice about managing your money from the DWP, an advice agency (e.g. Citizens Advice) or you can use the free 'Money Helper' website [www]. The website has an online Budget Planner to help manage your spending and a debt advice locator to find free face-to-face debt advice in your area.

Other help managing your payments

34.31 If you find it difficult to manage your money you can also ask the DWP:

(a) to make a UC alternative payment arrangement and/or

(b) to make payments to your landlord to reduce your arrears or to other creditors for certain priority debts (paras 34.44-45) and

(c) if you live in Scotland your housing element can be paid to your landlord and/or you can be paid more frequently under the 'Scottish Choices' scheme.

You can request any of these or, except for Scottish Choices, your landlord can (paras 35.12-16).

UC alternative payment arrangements

34.32 If you are on UC and have difficulty managing your money the DWP can make an 'alternative payment arrangement' (APA) to the normal way UC is paid (paras 34.2, 34.9) (OG file 108). These are considered in the following order of priority:

(a) a 'managed payment to landlord' (MPTL) of your UC housing element (paras 35.17-20)

(b) more frequent payments (paras 34.37-39)

(c) split payment of your award between you and your partner (paras 34.40-43)

The DWP considers requests for these according to its guidance [www]. If you request any of these the DWP always gives priority to a MPTL and only applies (b) or (c) to what remains (OG file 108).

34.33 Alternative payment arrangements are usually for people with the support needs in table 34.2. The DWP should tell you when it is considering starting, changing or stopping these so that you can give your views. If you ask the DWP to reconsider a MPTL because the benefit cap has been applied, the guidance says the MPTL must be removed regardless of your support needs (OG file 108).

34.30 www.moneyhelper.org.uk/en/benefits/universal-credit

34.32 SSAA 5(1)(i),(p),(r),(2)(za),(ab),(3B),(6); SS(PAB) 4-6; UC(C&P) 47(1),(6)
www.gov.uk/government/publications/universal-credit-alternative-payment-arrangements/

Table 34.2 **People with support needs**

These factors are from the DWP's *Guidance: Alternative payment arrangements* [www]. The DWP takes them into account when considering alternative payment arrangements (para 34.32), including whether to pay your UC to your landlord (para 35.17).

Tier 1 factors

These indicate you have a 'highly likely/probable' need for alternative payment arrangements.

(a) You have drug, alcohol or other addiction problems, e.g. gambling

(b) You have learning difficulties, e.g. with literacy and/or numeracy

(c) You have severe or multiple debt problems

(d) You are in supported or temporary accommodation

(e) You are homeless

(f) You are a victim of domestic violence or abuse

(g) You have a mental health condition

(h) You are currently in rent arrears, e.g. under threat of eviction or repossession

(i) You are aged 16 or 17 or a care leaver

(j) You have multiple and complex needs

Tier 2 factors

These indicate you have a 'less likely/possible' need for alternative payment arrangements.

(k) Payments are being made from your UC to a third party, e.g. for fines, utility arrears

(l) You are a refugee or asylum seeker

(m) You have a history of rent arrears

(n) You were previously homeless or in supported accommodation

(o) You have a physical or mental disability

(p) You have just left prison or hospital

(q) You are recently bereaved

(r) You have problems using English

(s) You are ex-services

(t) You are not in education, employment or training

T34.2 Alternative payment arrangements, part 5, Annex A

Managed payments and Scottish Choices

34.34 In Scotland, if you don't meet the criteria for a managed payment (MPTL) you can ask the DWP to pay your UC housing element to your landlord with or without more frequent payments (para 34.39). Your right to request these is called 'Scottish Choices'.

34.35 You can request Scottish Choices at any time after your first payment. If have recently claimed UC, you will be offered Scottish Choices after your first payment. You can cancel your Scottish Choices payment at any time.

34.36 Your landlord cannot request Scottish Choices but can ask for APA. If the DWP decides to apply an APA (requested by you or your landlord) it supersedes your Scottish Choices payment. Scottish Choices payments to your landlord are paid on your normal payment day or on another cycle agreed between the DWP and your landlord.

More frequent payments

34.37 If you are finding it difficult to budget monthly and meet the criteria for an APA you can ask to have your UC divided up and paid more frequently. These can only be made after the end of your first assessment period and in most cases half your UC is paid on the normal payment date and the remaining half 14 or 15 days later (OG file 108). If you pay rent a MPTL is applied first and more frequent payments made on what remains.

34.38 The guidance says that in very exceptional circumstances payments can be paid four times a month. In this case a quarter of your UC is paid on your normal payment day and the rest at seven- or eight-day intervals after (OG file 108).

34.39 In Scotland, if you don't meet the criteria for an APA, you can request your UC is paid twice monthly, with or without payments to your landlord (para 34.34).

Split payments

34.40 Your UC payment can be divided between you and your partner – this is called a split payment. The guidance says this can be done in very exceptional circumstances and should only be considered to prevent hardship to you or your family in specific situations such as domestic abuse (OG file 108).

34.41 The guidance (OG file 108) says the DWP must consider a split payment if:

(a) you tell them financial mismanagement and/or financial abuse is taking place

(b) you tell them there is domestic abuse

(c) you tell them that your partner cannot or will not budget for you or your families basic day-to-day needs.

34.34 UC(C&P)(Scot) 2(1), 4(1),(2)

34.35 UC(C&P)(Scot) 2(2),(3), 3, 4(3),(4), 5

34.36 UC(C&P)(Scot) 2(4), 4(6)

34.37 SSAA 5(1)(i); UC(C&P) 47(1)

34.39 UC(C&P)(Scot) 2

34.40 SSAA 5(1)(i),(3B); UC(C&P) 47(6)

34.42 When a split payment is made the larger percentage is allocated to the person with the primary responsibility for childcare. If you pay rent a managed payment is made to your landlord and what remains is split (OG file 108).

34.43 The UC payment system does not allow a second verification of bank details. To ensure the right person is paid you must verify your bank details by attending in person at the jobcentre. After the first payment any subsequent payments are made automatically (OG file 108).

Other help to manage your money (third-party payments)

34.44 In addition to an APA you can also ask the DWP to pay part of your UC to your landlord towards your rent arrears, or to someone else for certain priority debts such as fuel, water, council tax (chapter 35). These are sometimes called 'direct' or 'third-party' payments.

34.45 Third-party payments can also be made from your SPC (but the rules differ slightly to UC) and your council can pay your HB to your landlord if you have difficulty paying your rent. The DWP can also sometimes make third party payments to your landlord for charges that aren't covered by your HB or SPC housing costs (chapter 35).

How and when HB is paid: council tenants

Rent rebates

34.46 HB for council tenants is called a 'rent rebate'. You don't get a payment yourself. Instead your HB is paid straight into your rent account, so you have less rent to pay. This only applies if you rent from the council that administers HB. It doesn't include tenants of a different council or an English county council.

When rent rebates are paid

34.47 You should get your first rebate within 14 days of your claim or as soon as practicable. The council usually makes subsequent payments on the days your rent is due.

Exceptions

34.48 Your HB is paid as a rent allowance (para 34.49) rather than a rent rebate if:

(a) you live in a houseboat, mobile home or caravan and pay mooring or site charges to the council but pay rent to a non-profit, private or other landlord or

(b) you live in a property that is subject to a management order or empty dwelling management order and the council is collecting your rent rather than your landlord.

34.44 SSAA 5(1)(p); UC(C&P) 60, sch 6

34.45 SSAA 5(1)(p); SS(C&P) 35, sch 9

34.46 SSAA 134(1A),(2),(5),191 – 'rent rebate and rent allowance'

34.47 HBW 91(3); HBP 72(3)

34.48 HBW 91A; HBP 72A

How and when HB is paid: other tenants

Rent allowances

34.49 HB for housing association, non-profit and private landlords (and anyone who isn't a council tenant) is called a 'rent allowance'. Your HB is paid to you by crediting it into your bank, building society or other account. Or part or all of your HB can be paid to your landlord or a third party (chapter 35).

34.50 The council may agree to pay you by cheque if you don't have a bank account (R (Spiropoulos) v Brighton and Hove CC) (HBGM para A6.120) or can't withdraw money because you have an overdraft. Or it may advise you how to open a basic bank account.

Payments to someone on your behalf

34.51 In rent allowance cases, if you have an attorney or appointee your HB can be paid to them. If you don't have an attorney or appointee, the council can pay all or part of your HB to a 'nominee'. This means someone who meets the same conditions as an appointee (para 32.7) but deals only with your payments.

When rent allowances are paid

34.52 You should get your first payment within 14 days of your claim or as soon as practicable. If you don't you qualify for a payment on account.

34.53 The council usually makes subsequent payments every two or four weeks or monthly, and you can insist on two-weekly payments if your HB is more than £2 per week. Or the council can pay you (but not your landlord) weekly if this in your interests or paying over longer periods could lead to an overpayment.

34.49 SSAA 134(1B),(2), 191 – 'rent rebate and rent allowance'

34.50 HBW 91(1), 94(1); HBP 72(1), 75(1)
R (Spiropoulos) v Brighton and Hove CC [2007] EWHC 342 (Admin)

34.51 HBW 94(2),(3); HBP 75(2),(3)

34.52 HBW 91(3); HBP 72(3)

34.53 HBW 92(1),(5),(6); HBP 73(1),(5),(6)

HB payments on account

34.54 This section explains who can get HB payments on account. These are repayable from your future payments of HB.

Who can get payments on account

34.55 Payments on account are only available in rent allowance cases (whether you are a housing association, non-profit, private or other tenant). In these cases:

(a) you qualify for payments on account if:
- 14 days have passed since the council received your claim and
- the council hasn't yet decided whether you qualify for HB or how much you qualify for

(b) but you don't qualify for payments on account if this is because you have failed (with no good reason) to provide information and evidence the council requested.

Condition (b) only applies to you yourself; if your landlord or someone else has failed to provide information or evidence, this doesn't stop you getting payments on account.

How to get payments on account

34.56 If you meet the conditions in para 34.55, the law says you are automatically entitled to payments on account (R v Haringey LBC ex parte Ayub) (HBGM para A6.158). In practice you may well need to ask the council, or your landlord can do this if your HB is likely to be paid to them.

Amount and payment

34.57 The council decides the amount of your HB payments on account. It should:

(a) make a first payment on account within 14 days of getting your claim and

(b) continue making payments on account until it decides whether you qualify for HB and if so, how much you qualify for.

Payments on account are paid in the same way as rent allowances (paras 34.49-50). Overpayments are always recoverable (chapter 36).

34.54 HBW 93(2),(3); HBP 74(2),(3)

34.55 SSAA 5(1)(r),(2)(e); HBW 93(1); HBP 74(1)

34.56 HBW 93(1); HBP 74(1)
R v Haringey LBC ex parte Ayub (1993) 25 HLR 566 (QBD)

34.57 HBW 93(1); HBP 74(1)

Chapter 35 **Payments to landlords and others**

- General rules about payments to landlords: paras 35.1-11
- Landlords and UC: paras 35.12-16
- UC payments to landlords towards rent: paras 35.17-25
- SPC payments to landlords towards rent: paras 35.26-33
- UC/SPC for other payments: paras 35.34-40
- Limits on UC/SPC paid to landlords etc: paras 35.41-42
- HB payments to landlords towards rent: paras 35.43-49

General rules

35.1 The DWP or council can pay all or part of your benefit to your landlord towards your:

(a) current rent or other housing costs (UC, SPC and HB) and/or

(b) arrears of rent or other housing costs (UC and SPC only).

These payments are sometimes called 'direct payments'. In UC and SPC, they are also called 'managed payments' for (a) and 'third party payments' for (b).

35.2 This chapter covers UC, SPC and HB and table 35.1 gives a summary.

35.3 DWP guidance relating to UC only is in:

(a) *UC and rented housing: guide for landlords* ('UC guide for landlords')

(b) *UC Guidance: Alternative Payment Arrangements* and

(c) *UC Third Party Payments Creditor/Supplier Handbook.*

Payments to landlords and deductions from your benefit

35.4 The part of your UC/SPC/HB that is paid to your landlord, can also be described as a 'deduction' from the UC/SPC/HB paid to you. If your SPC is insufficient, the balance can be deducted from your state pension or certain other benefits (this doesn't apply in the case of UC or HB).

35.5 In UC and SPC, if you have several debts (e.g. utility bills as well as rent) the payments and therefore also the deductions are made in the order, and subject to the limits, in para 35.41.

35.1 SSAA 5(1)(p),(2)(za),(ab),(e); UC(C&P) 58, 60; SS(C&P) 34(1), 35(1); HBW 95, 96; HBP 76, 77

35.3 www.gov.uk/government/publications/universal-credit-and-rented-housing--2
www.gov.uk/government/publications/universal-credit-alternative-payment-arrangements
www.gov.uk/government/publications/how-the-deductions-from-benefit-scheme-works-a-handbook-for-creditors

35.4 UC(C&P) 60; SS(C&P) 35(1), sch 9 para 1 – 'specified benefit'

35.5 UC(C&P) sch 6 paras 3(1), 4(1), 5(1); SS(C&P) sch 9 paras 8(1),(2), 9(1A)

Rent and rent arrears

35.6 In this chapter, 'rent' includes service charges (eligible or ineligible) you are liable for as a renter or owner, and 'rent arrears' includes arrears of service charges. The arrears must relate to your current home, but can have built up while you were on UC/SPC/HB or before you claimed them.

Landlords and agents

35.7 The DWP can make payments of UC or SPC to:

(a) your landlord or

(b) an agent if the landlord uses an agent to collect the rent.

Your landlord can be a council, housing association, non-profit organisation, private or other landlord.

35.8 The council can make payments of HB to:

(a) your landlord if your landlord collects your rent but

(b) your landlord's agent if the agent collects your rent.

The rules don't apply if your landlord is the council, but do apply for all other landlords.

35.9 In this chapter 'landlord' means either a landlord or an agent as described above.

Requests for payments to landlords

35.10 You (or your landlord) can ask the DWP or council to pay part of your benefit to your landlord (paras 35.13-16). In UC you can use your online journal, call the UC helpline, or speak to your work coach. In SPC/HB you can phone the DWP/council. You usually need to explain why it is in your interests to do this and give any supporting evidence such as your rent arrears.

Decision letters

35.11 When the DWP or council decides to make payments to your landlord (or changes the amount), it sends both you and your landlord a decision letter, saying:

(a) that payments will be made to the landlord and

(b) how much will be paid to the landlord.

This is a legal requirement in HB for all decisions, and the importance of this was emphasised in R(H) 1/08 and R(H) 2/08. The DWP usually also does this for UC and SPC decisions and must do so after any mandatory reconsideration.

35.6 SSCBA 130(1)(a); UC(C&P) sch 6 para 7(2)-(4),(8); SS(C&P) sch 9 paras 1 – 'housing costs', 'rent', 2(1)(a)-(c); HBW 2(1) – 'rent', 12(1); HBP 2(1), 12(1)

35.7 UC(C&P) 58(1), sch 6 para 7(5); SS(C&P) 35(1), sch 9 paras 2(1), 3(1), 4(1), 4A(2), 5(3)

35.8 HBW 95(1), 96(4); HBP 76(1), 77(4)

35.10 UC(C&P) 58(1), sch 6 para 7(1)-(5); SS(C&P) 35(1), sch 9 paras 3(1), 5(1); HBW 95(1), 96(1),(3A); HBP 76(1), 77(1),(3A)

35.11 UC(D&A) 51; SS(D&A) 28; HB(D&A) 3(1)(a),(e); HBW 2(1) – 'person affected', 90(1), sch 9 para 11; HBP 71(1), sch 8 para 11

Table 35.1 **Rent payments to landlords**

Benefit	Conditions	Normal amount paid to landlord
(a) Payments to landlord towards your rent		
UC in England and Wales	Payment to your landlord is in your interests (paras 35.18-20)	The whole of your UC housing costs element (para 16.34)
UC in Scotland	You request payment to your landlord, or payment to your landlord is in your interests	The whole of your UC housing costs element
SPC	The DWP is paying towards your arrears of rent or was doing so but the arrears are now cleared	The whole of your HB
HB	You have eight weeks' rent arrears or meet one of the other conditions in table 35.4	The whole of your HB
(b) Payments to landlord towards your rent arrears		
UC	You have rent arrears (of any amount)	10% or 15% of your UC standard allowance (table 35.2)
SPC	You have four weeks' rent arrears or £100 if you live in a hostel, and meet the other conditions in paras 35.27-29	£4.65 per week of your SPC
HB	You are on SPC or ESA	The DWP pays £4.65 per week of your SPC or ESA

Notes:

- 'Rent' includes eligible and ineligible service charges and 'landlord' includes an agent (paras 35.7-9). If you live in a hostel and have ineligible service charges, see also para 35.31.
- If the DWP pays the normal amount towards your rent arrears it can also pay any ongoing fuel, water and other hostel charges included in your rent and continue to pay these when the arrears are cleared.

T35.1 UC(C&P) 58(1), sch 6 para 7(3); UC(C&P)(Scot) 4; SS(C&P) sch 9 para 5(1),(1A),(6),(7); HBW 95(1); HBP 76(1)

Landlords and UC

Social landlords

35.12 The DWP can provide a social landlord (para 11.2) with this information on request:

(a) whether you (the tenant) have claimed UC
(b) the amount of your housing costs element
(c) when your next UC payment is due and
(d) whether this is your first payment.

Trusted partners and the landlord portal

35.13 Most social landlords are also DWP trusted partners and have access to the DWP landlord portal [www] which means they can also:

(a) verify rent details you have given (but not give the rent details for you) and
(b) tell the DWP you meet the criteria for your UC to be paid to them (described later in this chapter) and the DWP can accept this after asking for your comments (para 35.16).

Other landlords

35.14 Any other landlord or agent can:

(a) apply for your UC to be paid to them and
(b) call the UC helpline to track their application if they can answer some basic security questions about you (*UC guide for landlords*).

Data protection law prohibits the DWP from providing other information about tenants unless they are present or consent to this.

Landlord requests for payment of UC

35.15 Your landlord can request payments of UC towards your rent or rent arrears. They can use the online 'Application for a direct rent payment or rent arrears deduction' [www] and will need to explain why they are requesting this and give evidence of any arrears you have.

Giving your views before the DWP pays UC to your landlord

35.16 Since 16 January 2025, the DWP must ask for your comments before paying any part of your UC to a landlord (including a trusted partner) or anyone else mentioned in this chapter (R (Roberts) v SSWP). This gives you the chance to dispute the existence or amount of rent arrears or other debts (R (Timson) v SSWP) (ADM2026-28). You can also dispute whether it is in your interests to have deductions made or whether you can afford them.

35.12 WRA 131(1),(11),(12); SS(Info WS) 5(1)(g),(h),(3A), 10(1)(a),(e)

35.13 WRA 131(1),(11)(g),(12); SS(Info WS) 10(1)(a)
www.gov.uk/government/publications/universal-credit-landlord-portal-and-trusted-partner-scheme-for-social-landlords

35.14 WRA 131(1),(11)(g); SSAA 123(1),(9)(e); UC(C&P) sch 6 paras 6, 7; UC(D&A) 10, sch 3 para 1(n)

35.15 https://directpayment.universal-credit.service.gov.uk/

35.16 R (Roberts) v SSWP and Guinness Partnership Trust [2025] EWHC 51 Admin, [2025] WLR(D) 53
R (Timson) v SSWP [2023] EWCA Civ 656, [2023] WLR(D) 277, [2023] PTSR 1616

UC payments to landlords for rent

35.17 The DWP can make payments from your UC to your landlord. These can be towards rent (including service charges) in any kind of accommodation where you can get UC. The payments can be towards your current rent or rent arrears or both.

Current rent

35.18 The DWP can pay part or all of your UC to your landlord towards your current rent if:

(a) it is in your interests to pay your landlord (this applies throughout GB) (paras 35.19-20) or

(b) in Scotland only, you choose to have it paid to your landlord.

'Your' interests include those of another member of your benefit unit or a person you get a UC carer element for.

35.19 The DWP says (*UC guide for landlords*) that you normally qualify if:

(a) you have at least two months' rent arrears

(b) you have repeatedly underpaid your rent and have at least one month's rent arrears

(c) you were previously on HB and your HB was paid to your landlord

(d) you have support needs as described in table 34.2 or

(e) there are other reasons why it is in your interests to do so.

35.20 The DWP also says (ADM D2021-23) that:

(a) payments are a 'first priority' if:

- you have a history of persistent misspending and
- you are threatened with eviction or repossession of your home and
- you have no other suitable means of dealing with the debt

(b) but payments are not usually made if:

- you agree to clear the debt or
- there is evidence that you're determined to do so or
- paying your landlord isn't in your interests.

Rent arrears

35.21 The DWP can pay part of your UC to your landlord towards your rent arrears if:

(a) the arrears relate to your current home (not a former home) and

(b) your earnings (if any) aren't above the work allowance (para 35.23).

35.17 UC(C&P) 58(1), 60

35.18 UC(C&P) 58(1); UC(C&P)(Scot) 4(1)

35.19 www.gov.uk/government/publications/universal-credit-and-rented-housing--2/

35.21 UC(C&P) sch 6 para 7(4),(6),(7)

35.22 You must also be:

(a) on UC and it includes a housing costs element (HCE) or

(b) on both UC and HB in supported or temporary accommodation.

In the law, (b) only refers to exempt accommodation (table 13.1(a)), but in practice the DWP applies it to any supported or temporary accommodation (tables 13.1 and 13.2).

Earnings not above the work allowance

35.23 This rule has two parts:

(a) your earnings must be below (or equal to) the work allowance (table 22.3) in the month before the payments start and

(b) once the payments have started, they continue unless and until your earnings have been above the work allowance for three consecutive UC assessment periods.

If you are in a couple, this rule applies to your combined earnings.

Amount and frequency of UC payments to landlords

35.24 For payments of UC towards your current rent:

(a) the DWP usually pays your landlord the full amount of your housing costs element (HCE), but it can pay less (or nil) if you have difficulty budgeting or support needs (table 34.2)

(b) the payments are made to your landlord monthly, to match your payments of UC.

35.25 For payments of UC towards rent arrears:

(a) the DWP pays your landlord between 10% and 15% of your UC standard allowance (table 16.1) – these amounts are in table 35.2

(b) the payments are calculated monthly, but paid to your landlord in 12 of the 13 four-week cycles that occur over the year.

Table 35.2 **UC monthly amounts for rent arrears 2025-26**

Your circumstances	Minimum amount: 10% of standard allowance	Maximum amount: 15% of standard allowance
Single under 25	£31.70	£47.55
Single 25 or over	£40.01	£60.02
Couple both under 25	£49.76	£74.63
Couple one or both over 25	£62.81	£94.22

35.22 UC(C&P) sch 6 para 7(2)

35.23 UC(C&P) sch 6 para 7(6),(7)

35.24 UC(C&P) 58(1)

35.25 UC(C&P) sch 6 paras 2(2), 7(5)

T35.2 UC(C&P) sch 6 para 7(5)

Example: UC payments to a landlord

Luke is a single tenant aged 42. He rents from a housing association and has rent arrears. He is on UC and qualifies for a standard allowance of £400.14 and a housing costs element of £800.00, totalling £1200.14.

The DWP decides to pay the following monthly amounts to Luke's landlord:

- a payment for current rent equal to Luke's HCE (para 35.24) £800.00
- a payment for rent arrears at the maximum amount (table 35.2) £60.02
- total £860.02

Luke gets the balance of his UC, which is £340.12, and this is paid each calendar month. His landlord gets £800.00 towards Luke's current rent on a calendar monthly cycle (para 35.24) but gets £60.02 towards Luke's rent arrears on 12 out of 13 four-weekly cycles (para 35.25).

SPC payments to landlords for rent

35.26 The DWP can make payments from your SPC to your landlord for rent. These can be towards:

(a) arrears of rent and service charges that are covered by HB and

(b) other payments included in your rent that aren't covered by HB (e.g. fuel, water).

These payments can be towards ongoing costs or arrears or both. If the DWP makes either kind the council must pay your HB to your landlord (table 35.4).

Payments towards rent arrears

35.27 The DWP can, If you consent, pay part of your SPC to your landlord towards your rent arrears if:

(a) you are getting HB towards all or part of your rent

(b) the arrears relate to your current home (not a former home)

(c) they are at a certain level (para 35.29) and

(d) you are on SPC (guarantee credit or savings credit).

Minimum rent arrears for payments to be made

35.28 If you live in a hostel (para 12.27) the DWP can, If you consent, pay part of your SPC to your landlord if your service charge arrears (para 35.31) exceed £100.

35.26 SS(C&P) sch 9 paras 2(1), 4A, 5; HBP 76(1)(a)

35.27 SS(C&P) sch 9 paras 5(1),(1A)

35.28 SS(C&P) sch 9 paras 5(1A)

35.29 In any other case your rent arrears:

(a) must be at least four times your weekly rent and

(b) either:

- the arrears have built up or continued over at least eight weeks or
- they have built up or continued over less than eight weeks and the DWP considers it is in your interests or those of your benefit unit to make payments to your landlord.

Current service charges for fuel and water in general accommodation

35.30 If your rent includes charges towards fuel and/or water the DWP can pay part or all of your SPC to your landlord towards your current charges if:

(a) the amount deducted doesn't exceed the maximum (para 35.41) and

(b) either:

- it is paying the landlord towards your rent arrears (para 35.29) or
- it was paying towards arrears, but the arrears have now cleared, and it is satisfied it is in the interests of your family to continue making them.

Current service charges for fuel etc in a hostel

35.31 if you live in a hostel and are on HB as well as SPC, the DWP can, if you consent, pay part of your SPC towards your current charges for ineligible fuel, water, cleaning, meals and laundry (paras 15.13-16, table 15.3). The DWP uses the council's figure for these charges or makes an estimate if that figure isn't available. These payments can be made whether you have arrears or not. The maximum amounts (para 35.41) don't apply.

Amount and frequency of SPC payments to landlords

35.32 For payments of SPC towards:

(a) your fuel, water and other ineligible hostel charges paid as part of your rent, the DWP usually pays the full amount

(b) arrears, the DWP pays your landlord £4.65 per week.

In both cases, the payments are made to your landlord four-weekly [www].

35.33 But the DWP may pay your landlord a lower amount if these payments exceed the maximum amount or if other deductions are being made towards other debts (para 35.42).

35.29 SS(C&P) sch 9 paras 5(1)(c)

35.30 SS(C&P) sch 9 para 5(3),(5),(7)

35.31 SS(C&P) sch 9 para 4A(1),(2)

35.32 SS(C&P) sch 9 paras 2(3), 4A(3),(4); 5(3),(6),(7)
www.gov.uk/government/publications/how-the-deductions-from-benefit-scheme-works-a-handbook-for-creditors/

35.33 SS(C&P) sch 9 paras 2(2), 8, 9

UC/SPC for other payments

35.34 The DWP can pay part of your UC/SPC towards:

(a) your service charges if you are a leasehold owner (paras 35.35-38)

(b) certain other housing costs such as rent if you are a Crown tenant and payments to a care home (paras 35.39-40).

UC/SPC payments for owner's service charges

35.35 If you are a leasehold owner, the DWP can pay part of your UC/SPC to your freeholder or managing agent towards:

(a) current payments of your service charges

(b) arrears of your service charges.

Current service charges

35.36 The DWP can pay part of your UC/SPC towards your current service charges if:

(a) for UC, you are in debt with your service charge payments by any amount

(b) for SPC, the DWP:

- is already making payments to the landlord towards your service charge arrears or
- was making payments to your landlord but the arrears have been cleared (or the freeholder/managing agent is prevented from taking legal action under the 'Breathing Space' scheme) and it is your interests (para 34.8) to continue making payments.

The amount of the payment equals the amount of the service charge.

Service charge arrears

35.37 The DWP can pay part of your UC/SPC towards your service charge arrears if:

(a) for UC, the DWP is already making payments towards your current service charges

(b) for SPC, you owe service charges equal to at least half the annual amount, or making the payments is in the overriding interests of your family.

35.38 The amount of the payment equals:

(a) for UC, 5% of your standard allowance (i.e. half the amount in table 35.2)

(b) for SPC, £4.65 per week for each service charge debt up to a maximum of three times that amount.

These amounts also apply to payments for fuel and water arrears (para 35.32).

35.35 UC(C&P) sch 6 para 6(2),(3); SS(C&P) sch 9 para 3(1),(2)

35.36 UC(C&P) sch 6 para 6(2); SS(C&P) sch 9 para 3(1),(2)(b),(4)

35.37 UC sch 6 para 6(3); SS(C&P) sch 9 para 3(1),(4)

35.38 UC sch 6 paras 6(3), 8(4)(a), 9(6)(a); SS(C&P) sch 9 paras 3(2)(a), 6(2)(a), 7(3)(a)

SPC payments for other housing costs

35.39 The DWP can pay part of your SPC towards the following, and in these cases the rules are the same as in paras 35.36-38:

(a) rent on a Crown tenancy where you owe at least half the annual amount, or making payments is in the overriding interests of your family and

(b) any of the other housing costs in table 17.2 except for

- payments for a tent and its site and
- payments for ground rent or rent charges unless you also get a housing costs addition for your owner service charges.

35.40 The DWP can pay part of your SPC to a care home, independent hospital or Abbeyfield home if you failed to budget for your payments there, it is in your interests to make the payments, and making the payments will leave you an income of at least £32.30 per week for your personal expenses.

Limits on UC/SPC paid to landlords etc

35.41 You may have several debts – rent arrears, mortgage arrears and/or debts in table 35.3. In that case, the following are the limits to the amount the DWP can pay towards these from your UC/SPC:

(a) the maximum is usually:

- in UC, 15% of your UC standard allowance, but this limit doesn't apply to current fuel or water charge debts
- in SPC, 25% of your maximum SPC excluding your housing costs (para 17.4)

(b) if the total deductions would cause the maximum to be exceeded, the DWP makes deductions:

- first for sanctions and benefit advances (para 34.15)
- then for other debts following the priority in table 35.3

(c) at any one time the DWP makes deductions:

- in UC, for no more than three debts (including rent arrears)
- in SPC, for no more than three times the standard deductions for housing costs, fuel and water (para 35.38)

(d) the payments mustn't reduce:

- your UC below 1p per month or
- your SPC below 10p per week.

These are often called the 'maximum deductions' that can be taken from your UC/SPC (para 35.4).

35.39 SS(C&P) sch 9 paras 1 – 'housing costs', 3(1)

35.40 SS(C&P) sch 9 para 2(1)(b), 4

35.41 UC(C&P) 60, sch 6 paras 3(1), 4(1),(2), 5; SS(C&P) sch 9 paras 2(2), 8(1),(2),(4), 9(1A),(1B)
In UC law the limit is 40% but guidance limits this to 15%
www.gov.uk/guidance/universal-credit-debt-and-deductions-that-can-be-taken-from-payments

Table 35.3 **Deductions: order of priority**

Deductions from UC

(a) Arrears of service charges if you are an owner

(b) Arrears of rent and service charges at the minimum rate (table 35.2)

(c) Arrears of fuel charges (and current fuel charges if you consent)

(d) Arrears of council tax

(e) Court fines and compensation orders

(f) Arrears of water charges (and current charges if you consent)

(g) Child support maintenance

(h) Recovery of hardship payments (paras 4.30-31)

(i) Overpayment recoveries (including penalties) (table 37.1)

(j) Arrears of credit union and similar loans

(k) Arrears of refugee integration loans

(l) Arrears of rent and service charges at the maximum rate (table 35.2)

Deductions from SPC

(a) Arrears of service charges or other housing costs you get SPC for (para 35.39)

(b) Hostel charges or rent in general accommodation

(c) Arrears of fuel charges (and current fuel charges if you consent)

(d) Arrears of water charges (and current charges if you consent)

(e) Arrears of council tax

(f) Court fines and compensation orders

(g) Arrears of refugee integration loans

(h) Arrears of credit union and similar loans

(i) Tax credits and income tax self-assessment debts

Note: In UC no more than three of the items (a)-(f), (j) and (k) can be made at once (para 35.41(c)).

35.42 Deductions for fuel and water cannot be made without your agreement:

(a) in UC, if their total would exceed 15% of your standard allowance plus any child element

(b) in SPC, if:

- the amount for either would exceed the maximum or
- their total plus the standard amount for rent or service charge arrears would exceed the maximum.

35.42 UC(C&P) sch 6 para 3(3); SS(C&P) sch 9 paras 5(5), 6(6), 7(8), 8(2),(4)

HB payments to landlords

35.43 The council can make payments from your HB to your landlord. These can be towards rent (including service charges). The rules about this:

(a) don't apply if you rent from the council (because in these cases your HB is paid straight into your rent account)

(b) do apply to renters and shared owners in any other kind of accommodation where you can get HB.

Obligatory and discretionary grounds for paying the landlord

35.44 The rules in table 35.4(a) are obligatory – the council must pay the landlord. Those in (b) and (c) are discretionary – the council may pay the landlord. The DWP has given councils guidance on the discretionary grounds (DWP, LHA Guidance 4.001-6.102), but the council must make its own decision (CH/2986/2005).

Table 35.4 **Paying HB to your landlord**

(a) When the council must pay your landlord (LHA and other cases)

- You have eight weeks or more rent arrears, unless it is in your overriding interests not to pay your landlord (para 35.45)
- Part of your SPC or ESA(IR) is being paid to your landlord towards rent arrears or service charges (paras 35.27-31)
- You have died, HB was being paid to your landlord before your death, rent remains due and your landlord makes a request for the balance within 12 months

(b) When the council may pay your landlord (LHA cases)

- Your HB has previously been paid to your landlord under the rules in (a)
- Paying your landlord would help you secure or retain your tenancy
- You are likely to have difficulty managing your finances (para 35.46)
- It is improbable that you will pay your rent (para 35.47)
- The council is considering whether your HB should be paid to the landlord
- You haven't paid your rent, but this only applies to your first payment of HB following your claim or following a change of circumstances
- You've left your home and rent remains due to your landlord after deducting the amount of any deposit held by them (E v Dacorum BC)

35.43 SSAA 134(1A),(1B),(2), 191 – 'rent rebate and rent allowance'

35.44 SSAA 5(1)(p),(q); HBW 95, 96, 97; HBP 76, 77, 78

T35.4(a) HBW 95(1)(a),(b), 97(1),(3),(5); HBP 76(1)(a),(b), 78(1),(3),(5)

T35.4(b) HBW 96(1)(c),(3A),(3B); HBP 77(1)(c),(3A),(3B)
E v Dacorum BC and M (HB) [2017] UKUT 93 (AAC)

(c) When the council may pay your landlord (other cases)

- You have requested payment to your landlord or consented to it
- It is in your interests or those of your benefit unit
- You haven't paid your rent, but this only applies to your first payment of HB following your claim or following a change of circumstances
- You've left your home and rent remains due to your landlord

Notes:

- The council mustn't pay your landlord if they aren't a 'fit and proper person', unless paying them is nonetheless in your interests or those of your benefit unit (para 35.48)
- References to a landlord include an agent (paras 35.7-9)

Eight weeks rent arrears

35.45 The council must pay your HB to your landlord if you have eight weeks or more rent arrears (including eligible and ineligible service charges) unless it is in your overriding interests not to pay your landlord. For this purpose rent arrears includes any amount whose contractual date for payment has passed, 'whether the rent is due in advance or in arrears' (ST v Sunderland CC), so if your rent is due two months in advance, you have at least eight weeks of rent arrears at the outset. The council doesn't have to check every HB claim for rent arrears but must consider any information you or your landlord provide (R v Haringey LBC ex parte Ayub).

Difficulty managing your finances

35.46 The council may pay your HB to your landlord if you are likely to have difficulty managing your finances. For example, this could be because you have difficulty budgeting or are being supported to manage your money.

Improbable that you will pay rent

35.47 The council may pay your HB to your landlord if it is improbable that you will pay your rent. The DWP says the test that should be used is whether the evidence about this is compelling (DWP, LHA Guidance 6.063-064). If the council helped you get your tenancy for this reason, that may amount to sufficient evidence (HB/CTB A26/2009).

T35.4(c) HBW 96(1)(a),(b),(c); HBP 77(1)(a),(b),(c)

35.45 HBW 95(1)(b); HBP 76(1)(b)
ST v Sunderland CC [2019] UKUT 33 (AAC) reported as [2019] AACR 20
R v Haringey LBC ex parte Ayub (1993) 25 HLR 566 (QBD)

35.46 HBW 96(3A)(b)(i); HBP 77(3A)(b)(i)

35.47 HBW 96(3A)(b)(ii); HBP 77(3A)(b)(ii)

If your landlord is not a fit and proper person

35.48 The council mustn't pay your HB to your landlord if they aren't a 'fit and proper person' unless paying them is nonetheless in your 'best interests' and those of your benefit unit. The DWP says (HBGM A6.197-199) that whether your landlord is a fit and proper person relates to their honesty in connection with HB (e.g. they regularly fail to report changes or repay overpayments), not their honesty in connection with anything else, nor that they have been found to be not a fit and proper person to let property under the Housing Acts.

If the council pays the wrong person

35.49 If the council should have paid your landlord but accidentally paid you, there are two rules:

(a) in the obligatory cases in table 35.4(a), the council must nonetheless pay the landlord, and recover what it paid you as an overpayment (Islington LBC v SJ)

(b) in the discretionary cases in table 35.4(b)-(c), the council can't pay the landlord, but the landlord can seek compensation from the council (R(H) 2/08, Wirral MBC v AL), and ask the Ombudsman to intervene.

The reverse is likely to be true if the council should have paid you but accidentally paid your landlord.

35.48 HBW 95(3), 96(3); HBP 76(3), 77(3)

35.49 Islington LBC v SJ [2008] UKUT 31 (AAC)
Wirral MBC v AL [2010] UKUT 254 (AAC)

Chapter 36 **Overpayments**

- What is an overpayment: paras 36.1-7
- Which overpayments can be recovered: paras 36.8-17
- The amount of an overpayment: paras 36.18-26
- Who overpayments can be recovered from (including overpayments of housing costs): paras 36.27-30

What is an overpayment

36.1 If you are paid more benefit than you are entitled to, this is called an overpayment. It is also an overpayment if more benefit than you are entitled to is paid into your rent account, to your landlord or agent or to someone on your behalf. Guidance about UC and SPC is in the *Benefits overpayment recovery guide* (BORG) [www] and for HB is in the *HB overpayments guide* updated to 2023 (HBOG).

36.2 An overpayment only exists and can only be recovered if the DWP/council have carried out the necessary steps, including the revisions and supersessions (para 38.5) that demonstrate there has been an overpayment (CH/3439/2004).

Types of overpayment

36.3 An overpayment is usually due to:

(a) claimant error – you or your partner gave the DWP/council the wrong information, failed to give information or were late providing information

(b) landlord or third party error – your landlord, employer or someone else gave the DWP/council the wrong information or failed to give information or

(c) official error – the DWP/council made a mistake, including an accidental error, or was late acting on information.

(d) external error – there was a fault with banking systems etc (BORG paras 1.19, 1.22).

36.1 SSAA 71ZB(1), 75(1); HBW 99; HBP 80
www.gov.uk/government/publications/benefit-overpayment-recovery-staff-guide
www.gov.uk/government/publications/housing-benefit-overpayments-guide

Decision letters

36.4 The DWP/council must send you a decision letter (or two decision letters) about

(a) your entitlement to benefit (or that you don't qualify) and

(b) the overpayment.

Every overpayment requires an overpayment decision letter as well as a decision about your entitlement (BORG para 1.4). If the DWP/council doesn't send both of these, or doesn't include the details in para 36.5, the overpayment decision has no force or effect (R (IS) 2/96)) so the overpayment can't be recovered (CH/3439/2004, NSP v Stoke CC, LL v SSWP, Godwin v Rossendale BC).

Information in decision letters

36.5 The DWP/council's decision letter(s) should give the following information:

(a) your correct entitlement to benefit

(b) the fact that there has been an overpayment

(c) the overpayment period

(d) the cause of the overpayment and whether it is recoverable

(e) the amount that is recoverable and how it was calculated

(f) who the overpayment is recoverable from

(g) the reasons for the above.

The decision letter(s) should explain these, all of which are listed either in benefit law or in DWP guidance (BORG 3.8). In (c), the individual cause must be explained, not hidden in the sentence 'it was due to a change of circumstances' (R v Thanet ex p Warren Court Hotels).

Overpayments involving more than one cause or person

36.6 When overpayments have different causes or are calculated differently in different periods, decision letters should give details for each period separately (LB Waltham Forest v CA; ADM D1032-35). And when an overpayment is recoverable from more than one person (paras 36.28-29), decision letters should name and be sent to both (CH/3622/2005, R(H) 6/06). In this case, either party can appeal, even if recovery is being made from the other party who doesn't challenge it (R(H) 3/04).

Revisions and supersessions

36.7 Decision letters should usually include the legal terminology, for example making it clear whether an entitlement decision is a 'revision' (a decision that usually goes right back) or a 'supersession' (a decision that usually takes effect from now) (para 38.5).

36.4 SSA 12(6); CSPSSA sch 7 para 6(7); UC(D&A) 7; SS(D&A) 3ZA; HBW 90(1); HBP 70(1)
NSP v Stoke-on-Trent CC and GP (HB) [2022] UKUT 86 (AAC)
LL v SSWP (IS) [2013] UKUT 208 (AAC)
Godwin v Rossendale BC [2002] EWCA Civ 726

36.5 HBW sch 9 para 15; HBP sch 8 para 15
R v Thanet ex p Warren Court Hotels (2000) 33 HLR 32 (QBD)

36.6 SSA 12(4); CSPSSA sch 7 para 6(6)
LB Waltham Forest v CA [2024] UKUT 39 (AAC)

Which overpayments can be recovered

UC overpayments

36.8 All overpayments of UC are recoverable. This is the case even if they were due to official error (S v SSWP). However, if the DWP assured you that you weren't being overpaid and then changed its mind, it may not be able to recover the overpayment; R (on the application of K) v SSWP.

SPC overpayments

36.9 An overpayment of SPC is recoverable if it resulted from:

(a) the late payment of income (e.g. arrears of state or private pension)

(b) your failure to disclose information to the DWP. But in this case, it is only recoverable for the period up to the date when the DWP received the information to correct it (whether provided by you or not) or

(c) a direct credit transfer payment error (e.g. paid twice for the same period).

Other overpayments of SPC aren't recoverable.

HB overpayments

36.10 Not all overpayments of HB are recoverable. The main rules are:

(a) official error overpayments are only recoverable if you could or should have known you were being overpaid but

(b) other overpayments are always recoverable.

HB official error overpayments

36.11 An 'official error' means an error by the DWP, HMRC or council – or someone acting on their behalf (e.g. a contractor or partner organisation). But it doesn't include an error that you (the claimant) or the payee or someone acting on your or the payee's behalf 'materially contributed to'. Case law about this is in table 36.1.

36.12 An official error overpayment of HB is only recoverable if:

(a) you or

(b) someone on your behalf (e.g. an attorney or appointee) or

(c) the person the money was paid to (e.g. your landlord or agent)

could reasonably have been expected to realise it was an overpayment at the time of receiving the payment or a decision letter about it. Case law about this is in table 36.2.

36.8 SSAA 71ZB(1)(a)
S v SSWP (DLA) [2018] UKUT 323 (AAC)
R (on the application of K) v SSWP [2023] EWHC 233 (Admin), [2023] WLR(D) 74, [2023] PTSR 729

36.9 SSAA 71(1),(3),(4),(5A),(11)(ab), 74(1),(3),(4); SS(PAOR) 7, 8, 11

35.10 SSAA 75(1); HBW 100(1),(2); HBP 81(1),(2)

36.11 HBW 100(3); HBP 81(3)

36.12 HBW 100(1),(2),(4); HBP 81(1),(2),(4)

Table 36.1 **HB overpayments: what is official error**

(a) How the council should make the decision

- The council should decide what is the substantial cause of the overpayment viewed in a commonsense way (SN v LB Hounslow), or who really caused the overpayment (KW v Lancaster CC). For this purpose:
- when an overpayment has more than one cause, they must be separated out. If the claimant delayed reporting a change and then the council delayed acting on it, only the second part is official error (AG v Calderdale Council)
- when the facts are in dispute they are decided on the balance of probability. If the claimant says they reported a change but the council has no record of this, it can't be assumed that the council's procedures are infallible (LB Islington v JM)
- for the overpayment not to count as official error, it is only necessary that the claimant or a person acting for them (DG v Bromley LBC) contributed to the error, not necessarily the overpayment (CH/215/2008)
- terms like 'error' and 'mistake' are interchangeable (CH/943/2003).

(b) Overpayment was official error

The following were found to be council error:

- not asking the claimant fundamental questions about eligibility (CH/4228/2006)
- delays in applying to the rent officer (CH/361/2006)
- issuing an out-of-date application form (MB v Christchurch BC)
- a mistake by another department that affected HB (CH/3586/2007)
- a failure by another department to pass information on to benefits staff or advise the claimant to do so (CH/2567/2007).

The following were found to be DWP error:

- telling the claimant it would pass on information to the council and not doing so (CH/3761/2005)
- a DWP decision that an appeal tribunal found to be an error of law (GH v Scarborough BC).

T36.1 HBW 100(2); HBP 81(2)
SN v LB Hounslow [2010] UKUT 57 (AAC)
AG v Calderdale Council (HB) [2016] UKUT 396 (AAC)
DG v Bromley LBC [2024] UKUT 49 (AAC)
GH v Scarborough BC (HB) [2015] UKUT 197 (AAC)
D v Flintshire County Council (unreported) CH/1987/2017
MW v SSWP (ESA) [2023] UKUT 50 (AAC)
KW v Lancaster CC & SSWP [2011] UKUT 266 (AAC)
LB Islington v JM (HB) [2014] UKUT 23 (AAC)
MB v Christchurch BC (HB) [2014] UKUT 201 (AAC)
EE v City of Cardiff (HB) [2018] UKUT 418 (AAC)
R (Sier) v Cambridge CC HBRB [2001] EWCA Civ 1523

(c) Overpayment wasn't official error

The following were found not to be council error:

- not cross-checking an HB claim form against information the claimant had given in a previous claim (R(H) 1/04)
- not asking follow-up questions that would have been prompted if the claimant had given accurate information (EE v City of Cardiff)
- assessing benefit income wrongly, because the claimant hadn't understood which DWP figure to provide (CH/56/2008)
- not anticipating changes in the claimant's benefit income (CH/687/2006, R(H) 2/04) or earnings (CH/3/2008)
- a short delay (of 24 days) in acting on a change the claimant reported (CH/858/2006);
- having poor performance statistics which in any case weren't the cause of the overpayment (D v Flintshire County Council)

The following were found not to be DWP error:

- not notifying the council that a working age passport benefit had ceased – since this is the claimant's duty (table 18.1) not the DWP's (R (Sier) v Cambridge CC)
- not exchanging information between branches of the DWP dealing with different benefits (MW v SSWP).

Other HB overpayments

36.13 Other HB overpayments are always recoverable, whether they are due to claimant, landlord or third-party error.

Special HB cases

36.14 The following kinds of HB overpayment are always recoverable, regardless of whose fault they were:

(a) overpayments of payments on account – when a payment on account (para 34.22) turns out to be too great

(b) future overpayments to council tenants – when the council credited a payment to your rent account for a future period and it turns out to be too great

(c) migration overpayments – when you transferred from HB to UC and the council continued to pay you HB after it should have stopped (table 25.1).

36.13 SSAA 75(1); HBW 100(1); HBP 81(1)

36.14 SSAA 75(2); HBW 93(3), 100(4); HBP 74(3), 81(4); UCTP 10; OPR 11(2)

Table 36.2 **HB overpayments: when should you realise**

(a) How the council should make the decision

The council should decide whether the claimant or payee could have realised there 'was' an overpayment, not 'might be' (CH/858/2006). This includes considering:

- the claimant's knowledge, experience and capacity, generally and in relation to the HB scheme (R v Liverpool CC ex parte Griffiths)
- what the claimant could have realised from the decision notice they received at the time – not the overpayment notice (CH/1176/2003)
- what the claimant could have realised from the payment they received – or in rent rebate cases from the credit to their rent account (CH/1675/2005)
- when payment was to a landlord and the overpayment was due to the claimant moving out, whether the landlord knew they had left (Hastings BC v Hanlon)
- when payment was to a landlord organisation, what the organisation as a whole could have realised (CH/4918/2003)
- when the decision depends on the burden of proof, this falls on the claimant or payee to show they couldn't have realised – not on the council to show they could (CH/4918/2003, CH/3439/2004).

(b) Claimant could have realised

In these cases it was found that the claimant could reasonably have been expected to realise they were overpaid (so the official error overpayment was recoverable):

- the decision notice gave the basis of the HB calculation and this showed reasonably clearly that there was a mistake (CH/2409/2005)
- although the notice omitted the claimant's earnings, it listed their other income (CH/2554/2002)
- although the notice was wrong, the figures it gave were obviously different from the claimant's actual earnings (CH/2943/2007), or rent (ZB v Sheffield CC)
- although the notice was wrong, the claimant didn't attempt to reconcile it with their knowledge of their own situation (CH/2943/2007).

T36.2 HBW 100(2); HBP 81(2)
R v Liverpool CC ex parte Griffiths (1990) 22 HLR 312 (QBD)
Hastings BC v PA & DA Hanlon (HB) [2013] UKUT 232 (AAC) reported as [2014] AACR 4
ZB v Sheffield CC [2008] UKUT 6 (AAC)
DP v East Dorset DC (HB) [2020] UKUT 270 (AAC)
AG v Calderdale Council (HB) [2016] UKUT 396 (AAC)
LB v LB Lambeth and SSWP (HB) [2015] UKUT 237 (AAC)36.15 SSAA 71B(1), 75(1); HBW 102(1) HBP 83(1)

(c) Claimant couldn't have realised

In these cases it was found that the claimant couldn't reasonably have been expected to realise they were overpaid (so the official error overpayment wasn't recoverable):

- the decision notice contained 'bundles of figures' and was so unclear that the claimant wouldn't have realised it was wrong (DB v East Dorset DC)
- the notice was wrong, but was issued so late that the claimant wouldn't have realised it was wrong (AG v Calderdale Council)
- the notice didn't explain that (or how) the claimant's earnings had been averaged (LB v LB Lambeth)
- although the notice didn't include the claimant's retirement income, the claimant might easily have assumed this was because everyone of his age received it (CH/2554/2002)
- the claimant thought the notice might be wrong so queried it more than once, but the council kept making payments, so the claimant assumed the council knew what it was doing (CH/3240/2007)
- the notice gave the wrong figure for income, but the council requested (and the claimant had given) details for the wrong period, so the claimant assumed it was right (CH/1780/2005)
- the notice gave the wrong figure for income, but the social security system in the claimant's home country had different assessment rules, so the claimant thought it was right (CH/858/2006)
- the claimant was not offered help understanding the notice, even though the council knew he had needed help with the claim form (CH/2935/2005).

Waiving recovery

36.15 When an overpayment is recoverable, the DWP or council usually recovers the overpayment when they can (BORG 2.2). But you can ask them to waive recovery, and if you do, you need to give your reasons in full.

36.16 The DWP has said it considers waiving an overpayment when recovery would be detrimental to your or your family's health or welfare, or not in the public interest (BORG para 8.6) but it should also consider doing so in other situations (K v SSWP). DWP guidance to councils says they should take into account your circumstances and whether recovery would cause you or your family hardship (HBOG 2.145-147).

Suspending recovery temporarily

36.17 If you request a reconsideration of the overpayment or appeal about it, the DWP doesn't normally suspend recovery (BORG 4.6, 4.13). But if you are unable to repay an overpayment or have debt problems, you can ask the DWP to suspend recovery temporarily under its 'Breathing Space' debt relief scheme (BORG paras 5.4, 6.32-33).

36.16 R (on the application of K) v SSWP [2023] EWHC 233 (Admin), [2023] WLR(D) 74, [2023] PTSR 729

36.17 SI 2020/1311 regs 5(4), 23-27

The amount of an overpayment

36.18 The amount of an overpayment for a particular period is:

(a) the amount that was actually paid for that period

(b) minus the amount you were properly entitled to for that period.

36.19 But this can be reduced:

(a) in UC, SPC and HB, when the overpayment relates to capital (para 36.20)

(b) in UC and HB, when you move home and are paid benefit on the old home for too long (para 36.22)

(c) in UC, when you are awarded another DWP benefit (para 36.23)

(d) in SPC and HB, when you have 'underlying entitlement' (para 36.24).

Diminishing capital

36.20 An overpayment of UC, SPC or HB is recalculated if:

(a) it occurred because of an error about your capital (no matter who caused the error) and

(b) the overpayment period is over three months in UC or 13 weeks in SPC or HB.

36.21 In these cases:

(a) at the end of the first three months/13 weeks of the overpayment period, the DWP/council treats your capital as reduced by the amount that was overpaid during those three months/13 weeks

(b) this gives an imaginary capital figure which is used to calculate your UC/HB/SPC overpayment after that

(c) steps (a) and (b) are repeated at the end of each complete three months/13 weeks until the end of the overpayment period

(d) but when the council calculates your benefit after the end of the overpayment period, it uses your actual capital (not the imaginary amount).

This rule reflects the fact that if you had received less UC/HB (due to the capital being taken into account) you might have used some of it to meet your living and housing costs (BORG 3.33).

Example: Diminishing capital

Richie is getting UC of £1,000 per month based on having no income or capital. The DWP later finds he had undeclared capital of £18,000 throughout his time on UC.

His overpayment is calculated as follows:

- For the first three months he doesn't qualify for UC (para 24.2). So, his overpayment is £1,000 per month. For three months this is £3,000.

36.19 SSAA 71(6)(a), 71ZB(4); OPR 6, 7, 9; SS(PAOR) 13, 14; HBW 103, 104, 104A; HBP 84, 85, 85A

36.20-21 OPR 7; SS(PAOR) 14; HBW 103; HBP 84

- His capital is then treated as reduced by £3,000 to £15,000. This gives him an assumed income of £156.60 (table 24.1) which reduces his UC entitlement to £843.40 per month.
- For the second three months his overpayment is (£1,000 – £843.40) = £156.60 per month. For three months this is £469.80.
- His capital is then treated as reduced by £469.80 to £14,530.20, and his UC entitlement is recalculated. This procedure is repeated at the end of each complete three months of his overpayment period.

Overpayments of housing costs when you move home

36.22 When you move home, the DWP/council can treat an overpayment of UC or HB for your old home as having been correctly paid on your new one, but only if:

(a) your UC/HB for your old home carried on beyond the date on which it should have stopped

(b) you qualify for UC/HB on your new home and for it to be paid to the same person (you on both homes, or the same landlord/agent on both homes) and

(c) in HB, the two homes are in the same council area.

This rule doesn't apply to council tenants on HB. It also doesn't apply to SPC, though for SPC the underlying entitlement rule usually has the same effect.

UC when another DWP benefit is awarded

36.23 Your UC can be adjusted if:

(a) you are awarded another DWP benefit for a past period and

(b) this reduces your entitlement to UC for that period (because the other benefit counts as income for UC purposes).

In this case, the DWP can treat part of the UC you were paid as having been for the other benefit. This rule doesn't apply to SPC or HB.

Example: The award of another DWP benefit

Lyra is getting UC of £600 per month. Later she is awarded industrial injuries disablement benefit (IIDB) of £45.06 per week for the entire period she has been on UC, and this is taken into account as income of £195.26 per month (para 21.12 and table 21.2).

The DWP decides to treat £195.26 per month of the UC she has been paid as though it was IIDB. So, she does not get her IIDB arrears, but she has not been overpaid.

36.22 OPR 9; HBW 104A; HBP 85A

36.23 SSAA 71ZF; OPR 6

SPC, HB and underlying entitlement

36.24 In SPC the DWP must reduce your overpayment by your underlying entitlement to SPC, UC, JSA(IB), ESA(IR) and IS. In HB the council must reduce your overpayment by your underlying entitlement to HB (except when the rule in para 36.22 applies instead). The underlying entitlement rule doesn't apply in UC.

36.25 'Underlying entitlement' means benefit that would have been awarded if you had kept the DWP/council fully and promptly informed of your true circumstances throughout the overpayment period, including all changes of circumstances no matter how frequent (NS v SSWP).

36.26 This rule undoes failures to report advantageous changes (KS v SSWP) and undoes the effect of reporting them late (para 33.13). But this is only for the purpose of calculating the overpayment so:

(a) all the underlying entitlement that falls within the overpayment period is used to reduce your overpayment, but not underlying entitlement falling outside it

(b) the overpayment can be reduced as far as nil in some cases, but the balance (if there is one) can't be paid to you.

Example: Underlying entitlement

Blythe is on HB. Her non-dependant Gwenyth moved out six months ago, but Blythe did not tell the council until three months ago (and had no special circumstances for the late reporting of this change) so the council removed the non-dependant deduction from three months ago. Today the council discovered that Blythe has undeclared earnings from work over the previous nine months.

The underlying entitlement rule mean the council must reduce the amount of the overpayment (due to Blythe's undeclared earnings from work) by the amount it could not award in relation to Gwenyth moving out. This results in a lower recoverable overpayment; it may even reduce the overpayment to nil, but in no circumstances can it result in Blythe getting more HB.

36.24-25 SS(PAOR) 13; HBW 104(1); HBP 85(1)
NS v SSWP (IS) [2015] UKUT 423 (AAC)

36.26 KS v SSWP (ESA) [2019] UKUT 188 (AAC)

Table 36.3 **Recovery of UC overpaid housing costs**

Reason for overpayment	Who the overpayment is recoverable from
Overpayments of rent and service charges	
(a) Overpayment caused by you (the claimant)	From you (not from the landlord/ agent even if it was paid to them)
(b) Overpayment caused by your landlord or agent	From the landlord/agent (not from you even if it was paid to you)
(c) Other overpayments that were paid to you	From you
(d) Other overpayments that were paid to your landlord or agent	From the landlord/agent
(e) But if your landlord or agent was paid more than your housing costs	The excess is recoverable only from the landlord/agent
Overpayments of rent arrears payments to landlords etc	
(f) Overpayments of payments for arrears of rent (table 35.1) or service charge payments (para 35.36)	From you
(g) But if more was paid than should have been	From the landlord/agent, mortgage lender etc

Notes

- A person has 'caused' an overpayment if it occurred because they misrepresented or failed to disclose a material fact (whether fraudulently or not). The DWP gives extensive advice on this (ADM D1133 onwards) and says that a landlord should only be regarded as having caused an overpayment if they had a legal duty to disclose a fact in question (ADM D1170).
- References to a landlord/agent mean whichever was paid the overpayment, and this applies to an agent even if they have already paid the money to the landlord (R(H) 10/07).

T36.3 SSAA 71ZB(2); OPR 4(4)-(8)

Table 36.4 **Recovery of overpaid HB**

Reason for overpayment	Who the overpayment is recoverable from
Overpayments of rent and service charges	
(a) Overpayment caused by you the claimant)	From you (not from the landlord/agent even if it was paid to them)
(b) Overpayment caused by your landlord or agent	From the landlord/agent (not from you even if it was paid to you)
(c) Overpayment caused by official error if you could or should have realised (para 36.12)	From you
(d) Overpayment caused by official error if your landlord or agent could or should have realised	From the landlord/agent
(e) Other overpayments that were paid to you	From you
(f) Other overpayments that were paid to your landlord or agent	From the landlord/agent

Notes

- 'Causing' an overpayment, and references to a landlord/agent, mean the same as in table 36.3.
- If a landlord or agent warned the council in writing that there may be an overpayment (before the council knew about it) and didn't contribute or collude in the overpayment, the council mustn't recover the overpayment from them unless it was caused by the claimant moving to another address.

T36.4 SSAA 75(3); HBW 101(1),(2); HBP 82(1),(2)

Who can overpayments be recovered from

36.27 The general rule for UC, SPC and HB is that an overpayment can be recovered:

(a) from the payee in all cases, whether this is you the claimant, your attorney/appointee or your landlord/agent

(b) from you, the claimant, even if it wasn't paid to you

(c) from the person who caused the overpayment, even if this is different from (a) and (b)

(d) in UC, from your partner if you are a joint claim couple

(e) in SPC/HB, from your partner if the two of you were a couple at the time of the overpayment and at the time or recovery (but in this case only if it is being recovered from your ongoing SPC/HB as in para 37.4).

Further rules apply to payments of UC housing costs and HB. These are in tables 36.3 and 36.4.

Overpayments recoverable from more than one person

36.28 When:

(a) an overpayment is recoverable from more than one person (e.g. you and your landlord/agent) and

(b) each of them is separately notified about it (Tendring DC v SSWP),

then each of those people have a joint and several liability to repay it (R(H) 6/06). The DWP/council can choose which of them to recover from and change the choice (BORG 2.23), but shouldn't take steps to recover from both at the same time (CH/2583/2007).

36.29 In UC, when an overpayment is recoverable from a couple and the couple then separate, the DWP splits the outstanding overpayment equally between you (BORG para 2.23).

Overpayments recoverable from both you and your landlord

36.30 If an overpayment is recoverable from both you and your landlord/agent, both parties have the right to be notified about the overpayment and to ask for a reconsideration or appeal (paras 39.2, 39.6). These rights are clearly set out in NSP v Stoke on Trent CC.

36.27 SSAA 71(3), 71ZB(2), 74(1),(3),(4), 75(3); OPR 4; SS(POAR) 17; HBW 101(2), 102(1ZA); HBP 82(2), 83(1ZA)

36.28 Tendring DC v SSWP and CD [2024] EWCA Civ 1509

36.30 SSA 12(4); UC(D&A) 49(d); HB(D&A) 3(1)(d); HBW 90(1), sch 9 para 15; HBP 71(1), sch 8 para 15
NSP v Stoke-on-Trent CC and AT (HB) [2020] UKUT 311 (AAC)

Chapter 37 **Recovery of overpayments**

- Summary: paras 37.1-3
- Methods of recovery: paras 37.4-16
- Time limits, bankruptcy, penalties and fraud: paras 37.17-20

Summary

37.1 This chapter explains how the DWP or council can recover an overpayment. It only applies to overpayments that are recoverable as described in chapter 36.

37.2 The DWP/council can recover overpayments of UC, SPC and HB by:

(a) deductions from your UC, SPC or HB

(b) deductions from your other DWP benefits

(c) deductions from your earnings

(d) deductions from blameless tenants' UC or HB that is payable to your landlord

(e) deductions from your landlord's own benefits (or earnings in the case of HB overpayments)

(f) agreement or using court procedures to register the debt.

37.3 These methods apply to the recovery of:

(a) overpaid UC, SPC or HB

(b) UC hardship payments (para 4.30) and advance payments (para 34.22)

(c) overpayments of HB payments on account (para 34.57) if you are no longer on benefit

(d) penalties and court costs relating to overpayments and

(e) overpayments of most other social security benefits.

37.2 SSAA 71ZB(7), 71ZC, 75(4),(7),(8); OPR 10, 20(2); HBW 105, 106, 106A; HBP 86, 87, 87A

37.3 SSAA 71(8),(9),(9A),(10), 71ZB(7), 71ZE(3), 75(4)-(8), 115A(4)(a), 115C(4),(5), 115D(4),(5); OPR 3; HBW 93(2); HBP 74(2)

Methods of recovery

Deductions from your UC, SPC or HB

37.4 The DWP/council can make deductions from your ongoing UC/SPC/HB. When the overpayment is recoverable from you, these deductions:

(a) in the case of UC and HB, mustn't be greater than the maximums in table 37.1

(b) in all cases mustn't reduce your UC below 1p a month, your SPC below 10p a week or your HB below 50p a week.

The DWP/council must consider your personal circumstances rather than automatically deducting the maximums (R (Blundell) v SSWP).

37.5 But there are no limits to the amount that can be deducted from:

(a) your ongoing benefit when the overpayment is recoverable from your landlord/agent or

(b) arrears of UC/SPC/HB when you are awarded these as a lump sum.

In case (a), deductions from the HB paid to your landlord count as recovery from you, not from your landlord, so you (not your landlord) have the right of appeal (R(H) 7/04).

37.6 When deductions are made from your benefit to recover an overpayment, and your benefit (as deducted) is paid to your landlord, this puts you in rent arrears (unless you pay the shortfall yourself).

37.7 But different rules apply if your landlord caused the overpayment and has been convicted of an offence or agreed to pay a penalty as a result. In these cases, your landlord:

(a) is barred from recovering the shortfall (via your rent account or in the courts) as either a rent debt or a non-rent debt and

(b) instead, must credit your rent account with the shortfall until the overpayment is recovered.

The DWP/council must send both you and your landlord a decision letter to tell you this.

Deductions from your other DWP benefits

37.8 When a UC or SPC overpayment is recoverable from you, the DWP can make deductions from other DWP benefits you are getting. For UC overpayments these are UC, SPC, JSA, ESA, state pension, PIP, AA, DLA, carer's allowance, industrial injuries benefit and some others. For SPC overpayments the list omits DLA but is otherwise the same.

37.4 SSAA 71(6)(c), 71ZC(2)(b), 75(5)(b); OPR 10, 11(7), 14(5); SS(POAR) 15(1),(2)(d), 16(7); HBW 102(1),(5); HBP 83(1),(5)
R (Blundell and Others) v SSWP [2021] EWHC 608 (Admin), [2021] WLR(D) 172, [2021] PTSR 1342

37.5 SSAA 71(6)(b), 71ZF; OPR 11(8),(9); SS(POAR) 15, 16(3); HBW 102(1); HBP 83(1)

37.7 SSAA 71ZC(2)(b),(3), 75(5)(b),(6); OPR 15; HBW 107; HBP 88

37.8 SSAA 71(8), 71ZC(1); OPR 10; SS(PAOR) 15

37.9 When an HB overpayment is recoverable from you, the council can ask the DWP to take deductions from most benefits (as above), but only if deductions can't be made from your HB, and only in the case of:

(a) overpayments caused by you or your landlord/agent – these can be recovered from most benefits and

(b) migration overpayments (para 36.14(c)) – these are always recovered from your UC.

Deductions from your earnings

37.10 When a UC/SPC/HB overpayment is recoverable from you, the DWP/council can require your employer to make deductions from your earnings. This is called making a 'direct earnings attachment' (DEA), and is usually only used when no other method is available and you don't come to a voluntary agreement to make payments. Amounts and further details for employers are in the DWP's *Direct Earnings Attachment: an employers' guide* (May 2024) [www].

Deductions from payments to a landlords for blameless tenants

37.11 When an overpayment is recoverable from a landlord, the DWP/council can recover it by making deductions from payments to them of their other tenants' UC or HB. This is called 'recovery from blameless tenants' because the tenants had nothing to do with the overpayment. In these cases:

(a) the DWP/council must tell the landlord which tenant's UC or HB they are recovering in this way, so that the landlord can debit their rent account accordingly

(b) the landlord mustn't put the blameless tenants into rent arrears because of this deduction.

But if the council deducts the money before it has issued the decision notice(s) (para 36.4) the landlord can make a county court claim for repayment (Waveney DC v Jones).

Recovery from a landlord: effect on your rent balance

37.12 Whenever recovery is made from your landlord, your landlord can charge you for the amount they have repaid or deducted from blameless tenants. The law treats your resulting debt as follows.

37.9 SSAA 75(4),(5)(a); HBW 102(1), 104, 105; HBP 83(1), 86, 87

37.10 SSAA 71(8),(9A)-(9C), 71ZD, 75(8)-(10); OPR 17-30; SS(PAOR) 29A, HBW 106A; HBP 87A
www.gov.uk/government/publications/direct-earnings-attachments-an-employers-guide

37.11 SSAA 71ZC(2)(c),(4), 75(5)(c),(6); OPR 11(9); HBW 106(3), sch 9 para 15(2); HBP 87(3), sch 8 para 15(2)
Waveney DC v Jones (1999) 33 HLR 3 (CA)

37.13 In all UC cases (private and council renters), and in HB rent rebate cases (council renters):

(a) the debt doesn't count as rent arrears (R v Haringey LBC ex parte Ayub) unless your letting agreement states that overpayments recovered from the landlord can be charged as additional rent

(b) but the debt can be recorded in your rent account.

This means that when you make payments into your rent account, you should say whether they are for rent or to pay off the debt. If you don't say, the law says the payment is credited against the earliest debt first (which may not be the payment you want the money to go towards).

37.14 But in HB rent allowance cases (private renters), the debt counts as rent arrears and can be recovered in the same ways as any other rent arrears. (This is because HB law was amended after the Haringey and Ayub case.)

Deductions from your landlord's own benefits

37.15 When an overpayment is recoverable from your landlord, the DWP/council can recover it from the landlord's personal entitlement to UC/HB or to most other benefits. The DWP/council can also recover it from the landlord's earnings. These cases are in practice rare.

Recovery by agreement or through the courts

37.16 The DWP/council can recover overpaid benefits by any other lawful method. For example, it could reach an agreement with you about how much you will pay. As a last resort, the DWP can recover overpayments through the county court in England and Wales and through the sheriff court in Scotland. The DWP/council tries to recover court costs when there is a court judgment in its favour. It can add these to the recoverable overpayment and recover them along with it.

37.13 R v Haringey LBC ex parte Ayub (1992) 25 HLR 566

37.14 SSAA 5(1)(p); HBW 95(2); HBP 76(2)

37.15 SSAA 71ZC(2)(a), 75(5)(a); OPR 2 – 'liable person', 10; HBW 106(2), 106A; HBP 87(2), 87A

37.16 SSAA 71ZB(1)(a),(5),(7), 71ZE, 74(1),(2),(4), 75(7)

Table 37.1 **Maximum deductions for overpayments 2025-26**

(a) Maximum monthly deductions from UC

The maximum amounts are 15% of your UC standard allowance. The higher amount for fraud cases no longer applies.

■ Single under 25	£47.55
■ Single 25 or over	£60.02
■ Couple both under 25	£74.63
■ Couple one or both over 25	£94.22

(b) Maximum weekly deduction from SPC

There are no maximum amounts if you were overpaid SPC. The following apply if you were overpaid UC and this is now being recovered from your SPC.

■ Fraud cases	£23.25
■ Other cases	£13.95

(c) Maximum weekly deductions from HB

The maximum weekly deduction is:

■ Fraud cases	£23.25
■ Other cases	£13.95

Plus, in all cases, not more than half of:

- any £5, £10, £20 or £25 earnings disregard (table 22.4)
- any disregard of regular charitable or voluntary payments (para 21.41)
- the £10 disregard of war pensions for bereavement or disablement (para 21.25).

Note: The SPC and HB amounts for fraud cases apply if you have been convicted of an offence or agreed to pay a penalty (para 37.19).

T37.1 OPR 11(2)-(4), 14(2)-(5); HBW 102(2)-(4); HBP 83(2)-(4)

Other rules

Time limits

37.17 In England, Wales and Northern Ireland the DWP/council can't use the courts to enforce recovery (para 37.16) more than six years from the date you were first notified of the decision (paras 36.4-5) but this does not stop it from recovering the overpayment by other means (such as deductions from your future benefit payments). In Scotland the time limit for recovery through the courts is five years from the date you were notified or 20 years for recovery by other methods.

Bankruptcy

37.18 With exceptions in the case of fraud, the DWP can't recover an overpayment it has already identified once you become bankrupt or the overpayment is included in a debt relief order (DRO) in England and Wales or sequestration order in Scotland. This applies to all methods of recovery (SSWP v Payne and Cooper, Re Nortel Companies).

Penalties

37.19 If the DWP considers that an act or omission of yours has resulted in an overpayment, it can offer you a choice between facing prosecution and paying an administrative penalty. The DWP does this for UC, SPC, HB and other benefits (in the case of HB, this is in conjunction with the council). The penalty equals 50% of the recoverable overpayment, subject to a minimum of £350 and a maximum of £5,000. If you choose to pay the penalty, it is payable in addition to repaying the overpayment and recoverable by the same methods. You can also be charged a civil penalty of £50 in relation to overpayments over £65 if you aren't prosecuted.

Fraud

37.20 You (the claimant) can be prosecuted if you make a false statement, supply a false document, or fail to report a change of circumstances that you know will affect your benefit. A landlord or agent can be prosecuted if they make a false statement, supply a false document, or fail to report a change of circumstances that will affect the benefit of a claimant whose benefit is paid to them. This applies to individual landlords/agents, landlord/agent companies, and the officers and staff of these companies as individuals. The penalty in each of these cases can include a fine or a prison sentence.

37.17 Limitation Act 1980, 9(1), 38(11)(a); Prescription and Limitation (Scotland) Act 1973, 6, 7(1), sch 1 para 1(b)

37.18 SSWP v Payne and Cooper [2011] UKSC 60, [2012] 2 AC 1
Re Nortel Companies [2013] UKSC 52, [2014] AC 209

37.19 SSAA 115A; 115C, 115D; OPR 3; SI 2112/1990

37.20 SSAA 111A, 112, 115

Chapter 38 **Decisions and reconsiderations**

General rules

Decision rights

38.1 You can get a written decision about any matter relating to your claim for benefit. In HB the council must issue one, and in UC and SPC the DWP usually does. After that you have the right to:

(a) ask the DWP or council to reconsider it (para 38.20) and

(b) appeal to an independent tribunal (chapter 39).

Who has these rights

38.2 These rights belong to:

(a) you (the claimant) or either of you if you are claiming UC as a couple

(b) your attorney or appointee (para 32.7) or someone managing your UC after your death

(c) a landlord/agent about whether HB should be paid to them (chapter 35)

(d) a landlord/agent about whether an overpayment of UC or HB is recoverable from them (chapter 36)

(e) someone acting for you or for a landlord/agent.

Counting time limits

38.3 Many of the rights in this chapter have a time limit of one month from the date a decision is issued. The date of issue is usually taken to mean the day the decision letter becomes available to view on your online account, or the day it is posted or handed to you. 'One month' means a calendar month counted as follows:

(a) if the date of issue is 17 January, the month runs up to and includes 17 February

(b) if the date of the issue is 31 January, the month runs up to and includes 28/29 February.

The time limit can be extended in special circumstances (para 38.36), and the DWP/council usually accepts requests on the next day (ADM A3049).

38.1 SSA 9(1), 12(1); CSPSSA sch 7 paras 3(1), 6(1); UC(D&A) 5(1), 7(1), 50, 51; SS(D&A) 3(1), 3ZA(1), 26-28; HB(D&A) 4(1), 10; HBW 90(1),(2); HBP 71(1),(2)

38.2 SSA 12(2), 39(1) – 'claimant'; CSPSSA sch 7 para 6(3) – 'person affected'; UC(D&A) 49; SS(D&A) 25; HB(D&A) 3 – 'person affected'

Decisions and determinations

38.4 Benefit law often distinguishes between these terms. The Upper Tribunal has described them as follows (R(IB) 6/03; HMRC v SSWP):

(a) 'a decision upon the actual question whether a claimant is entitled to a particular benefit or not' – this is often called an 'outcome decision'

(b) 'a determination of any matter along the way to a decision'.

For example, a UC determination could be that you have a particular amount of income or capital; and a UC decision would then be that you are entitled to a particular amount of UC or not entitled to UC.

Revisions and supersessions

38.5 Benefit law also distinguishes between these:

(a) a revision is a decision which alters your benefit from the same date as the decision it is altering – it is mainly used when a wrong decision is changed

(b) a supersession is a decision which alters your benefit from a date later than the decision it is altering – it is mainly used for changes of circumstances

(c) a 'closed period supersession' is used when a change of circumstances took place in the past and it has already come to an end – it means your benefit is altered, but only for that past fixed period (CH/2595/2003).

Decisions and decision letters

Decisions

38.6 The DWP/council makes a decision:

(a) when you claim

(b) when your circumstances change

(c) when you are overpaid and

(d) when you ask for a reconsideration.

Time limits for decisions

38.7 In HB the council should normally make a decision within 14 days of getting the information and evidence it needs. In UC, SPC and SMI, no time limit is specified in the law but in straightforward cases the DWP usually makes a decision fairly quickly.

38.4 HMRC v SSWP and GS (TC) [2023] UKUT 9 (AAC)

38.5 SSA 9(1), 10(1); CSPSSA sch 7 paras 3(1), 4(1)

38.6 CSPSSA sch 7 paras 3(1), 4(1); HBW 86(1),(1A), 89(2); HBP 70(2); HB(D&A) 4(1),(2), 7(1),(2)

38.7 HBW 89(2); HBP 70(2)

Decision letters

38.8 In HB the council sends you a decision letter (online or by post) about each decision it makes, and in UC and SPC the DWP does. The decision letter tells you:

(a) what the decision is

(b) the reasons for it (in most cases)

(c) your rights to a written statement, to request a mandatory reconsideration and to appeal.

38.9 There is an exception for UC. When your earned income changes from one assessment period to another, the DWP gets the information from HMRC and changes your UC to your new entitlement but doesn't usually send you a formal decision letter. You still have the decision rights in para 38.1.

Who the decision letter is sent to

38.10 The DWP/council sends decision letters to:

(a) you (the claimant) or both of you if you are claiming UC as a couple – this is usually online

(b) your landlord if it decides to pay UC/HB to them – this is usually by post and gives the amount that will be paid but not your personal or financial details.

Decisions awarding benefit

38.11 If the DWP/council decides you qualify for benefit, its decision letter must tell you that you qualify, how much you qualify for, and other details such as when you will be paid. They must also tell you about your responsibility to report changes in your circumstances.

Decisions refusing benefit

38.12 If the DWP/council decides you don't qualify for benefit, its decision letter must tell you that you don't qualify and give the reason why not. For example, the DWP/council can refuse you benefit if:

(a) you don't meet the conditions of entitlement (chapter 2)

(b) you haven't provided the information or evidence showing that you meet those conditions

(c) your capital, income other circumstances mean you don't qualify or

(d) it is reasonable to assume you don't qualify – this is called making an 'adverse inference'.

In the case of reasons (b) and (d) (which are illustrated in the examples), the DWP/council may say they are 'closing your claim', though this concept is legally questionable (PP v SSWP).

38.8 HBW 90(1),(2), sch 9 paras 2-5; HBP 71(1),(2), sch 8 paras 2-5

38.9 SSAA 159D(2); UC(D&A) 41

38.10 HBW 90(1), sch 9 paras 11, 12; HBP 71(1), sch 8 paras 11, 12; HB(D&A) 3

38.11 HBW sch 9 para 10; HBP sch 8 paras 9, 10

38.12 HBW sch 9 para 14; HBP sch 8 para 14
PP v SSWP (UC) [2020] UKUT 109 (AAC)

Examples: Reasons for refusing a claim

1. Not meeting the conditions of entitlement

Johnny claims UC. He is a single student and tells the DWP that he considers his course is part time. The DWP asks Johnny for evidence of how his university regard the course, but he doesn't provide this.

- Johnny doesn't meet the conditions of entitlement for UC because he hasn't provided the evidence requested (para 38.12(b)).

2. An adverse inference

Glenda claims HB. Her bank account shows that she recently had £20,000, but withdrew £7,000 so that she now has £13,000. The council asks her for evidence of what she used the money for, but she says it was to repay family debts and there is no evidence she can send.

- The council concludes that Glenda must still have the money somewhere, so she doesn't qualify for HB (para 38.12(d)).

How decisions are made

38.13 When the DWP or council makes a decision about your benefit, it should:

(a) identify the facts and

(b) apply the law to those facts.

Deciding the facts

38.14 The DWP/council should only take account of facts that are relevant to your benefit. For example, who lives with you is normally relevant, but their personal characteristics are not.

Balance of probability

38.15 When there is a disagreement about the facts or the facts are uncertain, the DWP/council should decide what they are based on the weight of evidence each way. For this purpose:

(a) evidence shouldn't be taken at face value just because it is given by a government department; the claimant should always be given the opportunity to challenge it if they dispute it (KA v SSWP)

(b) in relation to identity and similar matters, 'the absence of verification does not necessarily mean that something isn't true' (RA v SSWP).

38.15 KA v SSWP [2024] UKUT 248 (AAC)
RA v SSWP (UC) [2024] UKUT 207 (AAC)

Burden of proof

38.16 When there is no evidence about the facts or where the evidence is balanced equally each way, the DWP/council should decide who has to demonstrate what. For example:

(a) when you make a claim, it is up to you to demonstrate who you are and that you are entitled to benefit

(b) when you are told an overpayment is recoverable from you, it is up to the DWP/council to demonstrate this.

Applying the law

38.17 The DWP or council must apply the law fairly, objectively and impartially. The words in statute law (para 1.13) have their ordinary English meaning. But:

(a) some words or phrases are defined in the law – for example 'child' and 'young person' (paras 5.18-19)

(b) some law has been interpreted by Upper Tribunals and courts in case law (para 1.13) – for example deciding whether two people are a couple (paras 5.8-16)

(c) the Supreme Court has decided that the DWP/council or a tribunal may disapply a regulation, order, etc (but not an Act of Parliament) if it breaches the Human Rights Act 1998 (RR v SSWP).

The footnotes in this guide give the details of (a) and (b).

Judgment

38.18 The law uses terms like 'reasonable', 'appropriate', 'suitable', 'good cause' or 'special circumstances' to show that the DWP/council has to make a judgment. Examples include:

(a) whether it is 'reasonable' to award benefit for a home you haven't yet moved into (paras 7.15, 7.19, 7.21)

(b) if you are a social renter, whether it is 'appropriate' to use the rent officer's housing payment determination as your eligible rent (paras 11.27, 11.29)

(c) what is a 'suitable' comparison for the level of rent in exempt accommodation (para 13.20)

(d) whether you have 'good cause' for not claiming earlier (para 32.43)

(e) whether you have 'special circumstances' for a delay in notifying an advantageous change (para 33.16).

You can ask the DWP/council to reconsider any matter of judgment and appeal it to a tribunal (chapter 39).

38.17 RR v SSWP [2019] UKSC 52, [2019] 1 WLR 6430, [2020] 2 All ER 477

Discretion

38.19 A discretion differs from a judgment in the sense that the DWP/council may choose what to do. The law usually says that it 'may' do something to show this. Examples include:

(a) whether to award discretionary housing payments (para 31.2)

(b) who to recover an overpayment from when it is recoverable from more than one person (R(H) 3/04) (paras 36.6, 36.28)

(c) the method selected to recover a recoverable overpayment (para 37.2).

You can ask the DWP to reconsider any matter of discretion but can't appeal it to a tribunal (R(H) 3/04).

Mandatory reconsiderations

38.20 You (or another person in para 38.2) can ask the DWP/council to reconsider any decision it has made. This is usually called a 'mandatory reconsideration' or just a 'reconsideration'. In UC and SPC you have to do this before you can appeal to an independent tribunal (chapter 39). In HB you can request an appeal even if you haven't asked for a reconsideration, but it is often best to ask for a reconsideration first.

What reconsiderations can be about

38.21 Reconsiderations can be about:

(a) whether you qualify for UC

(b) the amount of your UC and how it is calculated

(c) when your UC begins, changes or ends

(d) whether you have been overpaid or

(e) any other matter (unlike appeals to a tribunal there are no exceptions).

For decisions about figures determined by the rent officer see paras 39.44-52.

When you can request a reconsideration

38.22 You can request a reconsideration at any time:

(a) you get a full payment of any arrears that are due to you if you request the reconsideration on time – this usually means within one month (para 38.34) but

(b) you could get a substantially lower payment of arrears if you request the reconsideration late (para 38.32).

38.20 SSA 9(1), 12(3A),(3B); CSPSSA sch 7 para 3(1); UC(D&A) 5(1), 7(2); SS(D&A) 3(1), 3ZA(2); HB(D&A) 4(1)

38.21 UC(D&A) 5(1), 7(5), 10; SS(D&A) 3(1), 3ZA(5); HB(D&A) 4(1),(6)

38.22 SSA 10(1),(5); UC(D&A) 5(1), 21, 24, 35(2),(4); SS(D&A) 3(1), 5(1), 6(2)(b), 7(2)(b); HB(D&A) 4(1), 6, 7(2)(b), 8(4)(b)

How to request a reconsideration

38.23 Your decision letter should tell you how to request a reconsideration. For UC and SPC you can use an online form [www] or print out the DWP's form CRMR1 [www]. Most councils also have online forms for HB. For UC you can alternatively send a letter to Freepost DWP (Universal Credit Full Service). The DWP also accepts reconsideration requests made by telephone or in person [www].

Information and evidence

38.24 When you request a reconsideration, you should provide any new information or evidence you have. If the DWP/council needs further information or evidence, it should request this, and must take it into account if you provide it within one month.

How long should the DWP/council take

38.25 The DWP/council usually deals with reconsiderations reasonably quickly unless they are complex, but no time limit is specified in the law.

Decisions and decision letters about reconsiderations

38.26 The DWP/council can alter any decision that was wrong (SSWP v SV), and sends you a decision letter telling you:

(a) whether it has altered your benefit

(b) if it has, what it has altered and when this takes effect and

(c) your right to appeal to an independent tribunal (chapter 39).

Getting a written statement of reasons

38.27 If the reasons for a decision aren't in your decision letter, you can ask the DWP/council for a written statement of reasons within one month of the decision letter's date of issue. The DWP/council should normally provide this within 14 days of your request or as soon as practicable after that.

When new decisions take effect

38.28 This section explains what happens when:

(a) you ask the DWP/council to reconsider a decision you disagree with (the original decision) and

(b) the DWP/council changes it (makes a new decision).

38.23 UC(D&A) 4; SS(D&A) 2; SS(C&P) 32ZA; HB(D&A) 2, 4(8); HBW sch 11 paras 2, 4; HBP sch 10 paras 2, 4
www.gov.uk/government/publications/challenge-a-decision-made-by-the-department-for-work-and-pensions-dwp

38.24 UC(D&A) 20(2),(3); SS(D&A) 3(2); HB(D&A) 3(5)

38.26 UC(D&A) 51(1),(2)(a); SS(D&A) 28(1)(a),(c); HBW 90(1),(2); HBP 71(1),(2)
SSWP v SV [2023] UKUT 279 (AAC)

38.27 UC(D&A) 51(2)(b),(3); SS(D&A) 28(1)(b),(2); HBW 90(2),(4); HBP 71(2),(4); HB (D&A) 10

38.29 It explains when the new decision takes effect, whether the new decision:

(a) awards you more benefit than the original decision (including when the original decision refused you benefit and the new decision awards benefit) or

(b) awards you less benefit (including when the new decision awards you no benefit).

If you are awarded more benefit

38.30 If you requested a reconsideration within the time limits in paras 38.34-35 and the new decision awards you more benefit (or some benefit instead of none), your benefit increases from the date the original decision took effect (or should have).

More benefit but you were late requesting the reconsideration

38.31 There is an exception if:

(a) you requested a reconsideration outside the time limits in paras 38.34-35 and

(b) the new decision awards you more benefit (or some benefit instead of none).

38.32 In this case, your benefit increases from:

(a) the beginning of the assessment period in which you requested the reconsideration (UC)

(b) the beginning of the benefit week following the one in which you requested it (SPC) or

(c) the beginning of the benefit week in which you requested it (HB).

The effect is that you get less benefit than you would have if you had requested the reconsideration promptly. But note that this rule doesn't apply to official errors (para 38.37).

If you are awarded less benefit

38.33 If you requested a reconsideration and the new decision awards you less benefit (or no benefit), your benefit reduces from the date the original decision took effect (or should have). This rule applies regardless of any time limits.

What counts as requesting a reconsideration on time

38.34 Requesting a reconsideration 'on time' means:

(a) you requested the reconsideration within one month of getting the decision letter or

(b) in UC, you asked for a written statement of reasons within that month, and requested the reconsideration within 14 days of:

- the end of that month, or
- the DWP providing the written statement (if later) or

38.29 UC(D&A) 9(b), 24; SS(D&A) 3(5)(b), 6(2)(b); HB(D&A) 4(2)(b), 7(2)(b)

38.30 UC(D&A) 5(1), 6(1), 21; SS(D&A) 3(1), 4(1), 5(1); HB(D&A) 4(1), 5(1), 6

38.31 UC(D&A) 24; SS(D&A) 6(2)(b); HB(D&A) 7(2)(b)

38.32 UC(D&A) 35(2),(4); SS(D&A) 7(2)(b),(bb); HB(D&A) 8(4)(a),(b)

38.33 UC(D&A) 9(b), 21; SS(D&A) 3(5)(b), 5(1); HB(D&A) 4(2)(b), 6

38.34 UC(D&A) 5(1), 6(3)(c); SS(D&A) 3(1), 4(3); HB(D&A) 4(1),(4), 5(3)

(c) you made your reconsideration request up to 12 months later than (a) or (b) and the DWP/council agrees to extend the time limit (para 38.35).

In SPC and HB, rule (b) is simply that time taken to provide the written statement (or to correct an accidental error) is ignored.

Examples: When reconsiderations take effect

1. A new decision increasing benefit

Eva has been on UC since 9 January and her assessment periods begin on the 9th of each month. She realises that she forgot to tell the DWP that some of her capital comes from an insurance payment in December for flood damage to her home. She asks the DWP to reconsider her UC and the DWP makes a new decision increasing her UC.

- If she requests the change on (or before) 8 February, she is within the time limit and her UC increases from 9 January.
- If she requests the change on 15 February and doesn't have special circumstances for her delay, her UC increases from 9 February.

2. A new decision reducing benefit

Frank has been on UC since 9 January and his assessment periods begin on the 9th of each month. The DWP discovers he has been working since before he claimed UC, and makes a new decision reducing his UC.

- Whenever the DWP makes the change, his UC decreases from 9 January.

Extending the time limit

38.35 The DWP/council can agree to your request for a reconsideration up to 12 months later if there are special circumstances why you couldn't request it earlier and it is reasonable to allow you extra time. The longer you take the more compelling your reasons need to be.

38.36 The law doesn't define 'special circumstances' but the DWP advises the following are included (ADM A3055):

(a) a death or serious illness

(b) not being in the UK

(c) normal postal services being adversely affected

(d) learning or language difficulties

(e) difficulty getting evidence or information to support the application and

(f) ignorance or misunderstanding of the law or time limits.

Correcting official errors

38.37 A decision that was wrong due to official error can be reconsidered and/or corrected without time limit. Your benefit is increased or reduced from the date the original decision took effect or should have done, no matter how long ago.

38.35 UC(D&A) 6(2)-(6); SS(D&A) 4(2)-(6); HB(D&A) 5(2)-(6)

38.36 HB(D&A) 5(5)(a)

38.38 This rule applies to any mistake or accidental error made by the DWP, the council or HMRC, so long as neither you nor anyone else (e.g. your landlord) materially contributed to it.

38.39 It also applies when the DWP/council uses the wrong figure for any of the following (even if you did contribute to it):

(a) a sanction (para 4.24)

(b) a housing payment determination (para 11.25)

(c) the local housing allowance (para 12.10)

(d) the benefit cap (table 20.1) or

(e) a penalty (para 37.19).

Example: Official error

Gertrude claimed UC on 9 January. She had a part-time job when she claimed but it ended on 12 March. She reported this on 13 March, but the DWP didn't act on it. Later, she asks the DWP to change its decision. The DWP accepts this was official error (para 38.37) and makes a new decision increasing her UC.

- Whenever she requests the change, she is awarded the increase in her UC from 9 March – because that is when her UC should have increased (paras 33.12, 38.37).

New law

38.40 New statute law (e.g. an amendment to benefit regulations), takes effect when the law itself says. And new case law takes effect from the date of the judgment. For UC in each case, this means your UC changes on the first day of your next assessment period (or of your current assessment period if the law changes that very day).

'Staying' a decision

38.41 But the DWP/council can 'stay' a decision about your benefit if it depends on the outcome of another case being appealed to the Upper Tribunal or a court (this is sometimes called a lead case or test case). This means that:

(a) for the time being, the DWP/council makes its decision in your case based on the least favourable outcome of the test case (even if that means you don't get any benefit), and tells you that the decision has been stayed

(b) when the judgment is given in the test case, the DWP/council alters its decision in your case in line with the test case, and this takes effect on the date the original decision in your case took effect (or should have).

38.37 UC(D&A) 9(a), 21; SS(D&A) 3(5)(a), 5(1); HB(D&A) 4(2)(a), 6

38.38 UC(D&A) 2 – 'official error'; SS(D&A) 1(3) – 'official error'; HB(D&A) 1(2) – 'official error'

38.39 UC(D&A) 14, 19; HB(D&A) 4(3),(7A),(7H)

38.40 SSA 27; CSPSSA sch 7 para 18; UC(D&A) 35(5), sch 1 para 32(a); SS(D&A) 7(6),(30); HB(D&A) 8(8),(10)

38.41 SSA 25; CSPSSA sch 7 para 16; UC(D&A) 53; SS(D&A) 21; HB(D&A) 15

Chapter 39 **Appeals**

- Making an appeal: paras 39.1-17
- Appeals time limits and procedures: paras 39.18-27
- Tribunal hearings and decisions: paras 39.28-43
- Appeals about rent officer determinations: paras 39.44-52

Making an appeal

Who can appeal

39.1 This chapter explains your right to make an appeal to an independent tribunal. It gives the rules about:

(a) UC, SPC and HB appeals – these go to a First-tier Tribunal and

(b) CTR and council tax appeals – these go a First-tier Tribunal in Scotland, but to a Valuation Tribunal in England and Wales.

The chapter includes the differences between UC, SPC and HB. But it only covers the main variations for CTR and council tax appeals, since these often differ between England, Wales and Scotland.

39.2 The right of appeal belongs to the following:

(a) you the claimant in all cases

(b) for UC appeals, either of you if you are claiming as a couple

(c) for council tax appeals, either of you if you are jointly liable for council tax

(d) your attorney or appointee (para 32.7) or someone managing your claim after your death

(e) a landlord/agent about whether UC or HB should be paid to them (chapter 35)

(f) a landlord/agent about whether an overpayment of UC or HB is recoverable from them (chapter 36)

(g) someone acting for you or for a landlord/agent.

A landlord doesn't have the right of appeal about other matters, such as how much benefit you get or how much your eligible rent is.

39.1 TCEA 3, 7(1),(9); CSPSSA sch 7 para 6(3); SI 2008/2684 reg 3(c)
Local Government Finance Act 1988, sch 11 paras A1, A2(2), 1(1), 2(d); LGFA 16(1), 81(1);
CTRE(PR) sch 7 para 8(3); CTRW(PR) sch 12 para 10; CTRSW 94(1); CTRSP 70B(1)

39.2 SSA 12(2) 39(1) – 'claimant'; CSPSSA sch 7 para 6(3); LGFA 16(1), 81(1); UC(D&A) 49; SS(D&A) 25; HB(D&A) 3;
CTRE(PR) sch 7 para 8(3); CTRW(PR) sch 12 para 10; CTRSW 94(1); CTRSP 70B(1)

Mandatory reconsideration then appeal

39.3 The rules differ between benefits:

(a) in UC and SPC, you must request a mandatory reconsideration (para 38.21) and can only appeal after you get the DWP's response

(b) in HB, you don't have to request a mandatory consideration: you can appeal straight away

(c) in CTR and council tax, you must request a mandatory reconsideration and can appeal whether or not the council responds.

Which decisions are appealable

39.4 All UC, SPC and HB decisions are appealable to a tribunal except as summarised in table 39.1. If a decision is non-appealable, you can nonetheless ask the DWP/council to reconsider it (para 38.20) and in some cases you may be able to apply for judicial review (para 39.43).

39.5 You can appeal any decision to refuse you CTR, or about the amount of your CTR, to a tribunal provided you raised it at the reconsideration stage (para 29.52). This includes any decision about your entitlement that involves the council using its judgment or discretion. For example, a decision not to award discretionary CTR including to reduce an overpayment (DG v Liverpool City Council, SC v East Riding of Yorkshire Council). You can also appeal council tax decisions about liability, exemptions, disability reductions and discounts.

Table 39.1 **Decisions you can't appeal to a tribunal**

(a) General matters

- Whether and when you should be included in managed migration from legacy benefits to UC
- Matters of discretion in UC, SPC and HB (but you can appeal about matters of judgment) (paras 38.13-19)
- Amounts set by the law (e.g. benefit rates, capital limit, benefit cap)
- LHA figures and other rent officer determinations (paras 39.44-52)
- In UC, who gets a carer element when care is shared
- In SPC, HB and CTR, which partner in a couple is to be the claimant

---

39.3 SSA 12(3A),(3B); CSPSSA sch 7 paras 1(2), 6(1),(3); UC(D&A) 7; SS(D&A) 3ZA; CTRE(PR) sch 7 para 8(3); CTRW(PR) sch 12 para 10; CTRSW 94(1); CTRSP 70B(1)

39.4 SSA 12(2)(a); CSPSSA sch 7 para 6(4),(5); UC(D&A) 50(2), sch 3; SS(D&A) 27, sch 2; HB(D&A) 16(1), sch

39.5 LGFA 16, 81, sch 1A para 2(6), sch 1B para 5(1)(b); CTRE(PR) sch 7 para 8; CTRW sch 12 paras 8-10; CTRSW 94(1); CTRSP 70B(1)
DG v Liverpool City Council Appeal No. 4310M140277/CTR
SC v East Riding of Yorkshire Council [2014] EW Misc B46 (VT)

T39.1 SSA 12(2)(a); CSPSSA sch 7 para 6(4),(5); LGFA 16, 81; UC(D&A) 50(2), sch 3; SS(D&A) 27, sch 2; HB(D&A) 16(1), sch
PH and SM v SSWP (DLA) (ESA) [2008] UKUT 404 (AAC)

- In HB and CTR, whether the council should run a local scheme to disregard war pensions
- In CTR in England and Wales, whether the council should change its local CTR schemes

(b) Claims etc

- Who may claim on behalf of someone who is unable to act
- What information and evidence the DWP can require
- Suspending and restoring benefit (but you can appeal about terminating benefit)
- Staying decisions pending a test case
- Challenges to out-of-time reconsiderations unless they involve official error (PH and SM v SSWP)

(c) Payments and overpayments

- How and when benefit is paid
- Getting a UC/SPC advance payment or an HB payment on account – but you can appeal about the amount deducted from future benefit
- Whether your UC/SPC/HB is paid to your landlord towards your rent – but you can appeal about UC/SPC payments to landlords towards rent arrears
- Certain matters (but not all) relating to overpayments (paras 39.6-8)

Appeals about overpayments of UC

39.6 In UC, you can appeal about:

(a) whether there has been an overpayment

(b) the amount of the overpayment and/or

(c) who the overpayment can be recovered from.

You can't appeal about what caused the overpayment, whether it is recoverable or how the overpayment is to be recovered, but you can ask the DWP to reconsider these (para 38.20).

Appeals about overpayments of SPC and HB

39.7 In SPC and HB, you can appeal about:

(a) whether there has been an overpayment

(b) what caused the overpayment and whether it is recoverable

(c) the amount of the overpayment and/or

(d) who the overpayment can be recovered from.

You can't appeal about how the overpayment is to be recovered, but you can ask the DWP/council to reconsider this (para 38.20).

39.6 SSA 12(2)(a), sch 3 para 6B; UC(D&A) 50(2), sch 3 para 15

39.7 SSA sch 3 paras 5, 6; CSPSSA sch 7 para 6(4),(6); SS(D&A) 3(8), sch 2 para 20; HB(D&A) 4(6), sch paras 1(e)-(h), 1A(e)-(g), 3

Appeals about overpayments of CTR

39.8 You can appeal about whether there has been an overpayment and how it has been calculated (but in England and Wales your local scheme may have rules about this). In England and Wales, you can't appeal about adding the overpayment to your liability for the year and sending you a new bill with the revised amount. In Scotland, certain official error overpayments aren't recoverable – the rules are the same as for HB (paras 36.11-12).

How to appeal

39.9 The main ways of appealing are:

(a) in UC or SPC, by using the DWP's form SSCS1, available online [www]

(b) in HB by using the council's own form or

(c) in CTR/council tax using the tribunal's form.

Alternatively, you can send a letter or email to the DWP/council making it clear that you are making an appeal rather than asking for a reconsideration.

Appeals conditions and information you must give

39.10 Your appeal should:

(a) be within the appeal time limit (or explain why your late appeal should be allowed: para 39.20)

(b) be in writing and signed by you or your representative

(c) explain what decision you are appealing about and why (para 39.25)

(d) give your name and address

(e) if you have a representative, give their name and address and say whether you want correspondence about the appeal to go to them or you

(f) give the name and address of any other respondent (para 39.13) and

(g) enclose copies of any other relevant documents.

In the case of UC and SPC appeals, you must enclose a copy of your mandatory request, and also your statement of reasons if you were given one. In the case of CTR and council tax appeals that the council hasn't replied to (para 39.23), you also have to give the date you requested the reconsideration.

39.11 When you appeal, you can ask for your appeal to be decided at a hearing or on the papers. You should also say whether you have particular needs, for example a signer, interpreter or wheelchair access if there is a hearing.

39.8 LGFA 16(1), 81(1); CT(A&E)E 1(2) – 'discount', 'exempt dwelling', 20(2),(3), 30; SI 2012/3086; SI 2013/62; CTRSW 21, CTRSP 19A

39.9 FTPR 22(3), 23(2); SS(D&A) 33(2); HB(D&A) 20(1); VTRE 20A(1); VTRW 30(1); FTSLT sch paras 35(1), 41(1)
www.gov.uk/appeal-benefit-decision/submit-appeal

39.10 FTPR 22(3)-(4), 23(6); VTRE 20A(2); VTRW 30(2); FTSLT sch paras 35(2), 41(3)

39.11 FTPR 2(2)(c), 27(1); VTRE 3(c), 29(1); VTRW 33(1), 37(9)(a); FTSLT sch paras 2(2)(c), 9(3), 46(1)

Where to send your appeal

39.12 It is usually best to appeal online (para 39.9 gives the contact details):

(a) UC and SPC appeals go to Her Majesty's Courts and Tribunals Service (HMCTS), which forwards a copy to the DWP

(b) HB appeals go to the council, which forwards a copy to HMCTS unless your appeal lapses (para 39.26)

(c) CTR appeals go to the First-tier Tribunal for Scotland or in England and Wales to the Valuation Tribunal.

Appellants and respondents

39.13 When you appeal you are called the 'appellant'. The DWP/council (whichever made the decision) is usually called the 'respondent' or 'decision maker'. Anyone else with a right of appeal in the case is also called a respondent (for example, if your landlord made the appeal, both the DWP/council and you are respondents). And you are all 'parties' to the appeal.

Representatives

39.14 You can ask a representative to appeal for you. They could be an advice worker, solicitor, friend or family member. Once you have informed the DWP and tribunal in writing about this, your representative can do anything you could do in relation to your appeal (except for signing a witness statement).

HB appeals that don't meet the information requirements

39.15 If your appeal doesn't meet the requirements in para 39.10, the council may write to you asking you to provide what is missing. For example, it might ask you to clarify which decision you are appealing or why you think the decision is wrong. The council should allow you 14 days to do this and can allow longer. If you provide the information, it is treated as being part of your appeal. If you don't provide the information requested, the council must send your appeal to the tribunal to decide whether it meets the requirements.

39.16 For all HB appeals, the council must do one of the following:

(a) if it agrees with your appeal (either wholly or partly), the council must alter its decision, send you a decision notice about its new decision, and award any arrears of benefit. Your appeal 'lapses'. It isn't sent to the tribunal, but you have one month in which you can make further representations about the council's altered decision and about your appeal

(b) if it disagrees with your appeal, the council must send your appeal to the tribunal.

39.12 FTPR 22(2), 23(2); VTRE 20A(1); VTRW 30(1); FTSLT sch paras 35(1), 41(1)

39.13 FTPR 1(3) – 'appellant', 'decision maker', 'respondent'; FTSLT sch para 1 – 'appellant', 'respondent'

39.14 FTPR 11; VTRE 13; VTRW 36; FTSLT sch para 13

39.15 FTPR 24(1A); HB(D&A) 20(5)-(8)

39.16 FTPR 23(7); HB(D&A) 17(1),(3)-(5)

Failure to forward HB appeals to the tribunal

39.17 The ombudsman has frequently found against councils for placing obstacles in the path of appellants, including failing to forward appeals to the tribunal when required (LGO Focus Report, 2020 [www]).

Appeals time limits and procedures

Time limit for UC and SPC appeals

39.18 You are within the appeals time limit for UC and SPC if your appeal reaches the tribunal:

(a) within one month of the date of your reconsideration decision (paras 38.26) or

(b) up to 12 months later than (a) if the tribunal agrees to extend the time limit (para 39.21).

This means 5pm on the last day or, if that isn't a working day, 5pm on the next working day.

Time limit for HB appeals

39.19 You are within the appeals time limit for HB if your appeal reaches the council:

(a) within one month of the date of your decision letter (para 38.8) or reconsideration decision (paras 38.27) or

(b) if you asked for a written statement of reasons within that month, within 14 days of:

- the end of that month, or
- the council providing the written statement (if later) or

(c) up to 12 months later than (a) if the council decides to extend the time limit (para 39.20), or failing that the tribunal does (para 39.21).

When the council can extend the time limit for HB appeals

39.20 The council can only extend the time limit if:

(a) you or a member of your family has died or suffered illness

(b) you were not resident in the UK

(c) normal postal services were adversely affected or

(d) there are some other special circumstances that are exceptional. For examples see HBGM para C7.91.

But if the council decides not to accept your late appeal, it must forward your appeal to the tribunal to make a decision about that (para 39.16). The tribunal has wider powers than the council to accept late appeals and the council's refusal at this stage doesn't stop it supporting your request.

39.17 FTPR 23(7), 24(1A); HB(D&A) 19(5), 20(7),(8)
https://www.lgo.org.uk/assets/attach/5751/Housing-Benefit-Final.pdf

39.18 FTPR 12, 22(2)(d),(8)

39.19 FTPR 23(2),(5); HB(D&A) 10

39.20 HB(D&A) 19(5A)-(8), 20(7)

When the tribunal can extend the time limit for UC, SPC and HB appeals

39.21 The tribunal can accept an appeal up to 12 months later if:

(a) neither the DWP nor any other party to the appeal objects or

(b) they do object but the tribunal considers the appeal should go ahead. In this case, the tribunal first asks for your comments on the objection.

The tribunal can accept an appeal even after the 12 months has run out if the circumstances are truly exceptional and you have done all you can to obtain a hearing (MZ v SSWP, GJ v SSWP).

39.22 The DWP/council is unlikely to object to your appeal going ahead (ADM A5081, HBGM C7.80-93) if:

(a) you were unable to deal with your reconsideration letter or make an appeal because of illness, mental or physical disability or learning difficulty

(b) you had difficulty obtaining an appeal form or getting a representative

(c) you didn't receive your reconsideration letter

(d) you made your appeal earlier, but it didn't reach the tribunal

(e) you were given wrong advice by the DWP or an advice worker or a solicitor or

(f) (in some cases) you have a very strong case or there is a lot of money involved.

Time limit for CTR and council tax appeals

39.23 You are within the appeals time limit for CTR and council tax if your appeal reaches the tribunal:

(a) for all appeals about council tax liability, exemptions, disability reductions and discounts and CTR appeals in England and Wales, within two months of the date the council responds to your reconsideration letter or within four months of the date of your original request if they don't or

(b) for CTR appeals in Scotland only, within six weeks of the date the council responds to your reconsideration letter, or two months plus six weeks of the date of your original request if they don't (para 29.54).

39.24 For council tax and CTR appeals in England and Wales the time limit isn't usually extended. You can request an extension for 'reasons beyond your control' which is considered by the tribunal president. In Scotland, if your appeal is out of time the tribunal must consider your request to extend the time limit if (and only if) you give your reasons why it is late. In England, Scotland and Wales there is no upper time limit to request an extension.

39.21 FTPR 22(8), 23(4),(5)
MZ v SSWP (UC) [2022] UKUT 292 (AAC)
GJ v SSWP (PIP) [22022] UKUT 340 (AAC)

39.23 LGFA 16, 81; CTRE(PR) sch 7 para 8(3); CTRW(PR) sch 12 para 10; FTSLT sch paras 35(3)(a), 41(4)

39.24 VTRE 21(2),(3),(6); VTRW 29(1),(2),(2A),(5); FTSLT sch paras 35(4), 41(5)

Submissions and documents

39.25 The tribunal ensures that each party to the appeal has the other parties' submissions and relevant documents. You should send your submission with your appeal, saying what decision you disagree with, why you consider it is wrong, and what you think it should be. You shouldn't lose out by not using precise legal terms and references, so long as what you say is clear (ADM A5428). The DWP/council and any other respondent (para 39.13) also makes a submission, and in most cases you are given one month to add a further submission if you wish.

Lapsing appeals the DWP/council agrees with

39.26 The DWP/council can alter its decision and send you a new decision letter if:

(a) in UC, SPC and CTR, it wholly agrees with your appeal or

(b) in HB, it wholly or partly agrees with your appeal.

So long as the result is advantageous to you (e.g. you qualify for more benefit), your appeal 'lapses' (no further action is taken on it). In all other cases the appeal is decided by the tribunal.

'Stayed' appeals

39.27 The DWP/council can 'stay' an appeal if it depends on the outcome of another case being appealed to the Upper Tribunal or a court (this is sometimes called a lead case or test case). This means that:

(a) for the time being, your appeal doesn't go ahead

(b) when the judgment is given in the test case, the DWP/council alters its decision in your case in line with the test case, and this takes effect on the date the original decision in your case took effect (or should have).

For guidance on this for council tax and CTR appeals, see Consolidated Practice Statement Part 2, PS4 paras 12-14 [www].

39.25 FTPR 22(3),(7), 23(6),(7), 24(2)-(7); VTRE 28(2),(3); VTRW 30(5); FTSLT sch paras 36, 42

39.26 SSA 9(6); CSPSSA sch 7 para 3(6); LGFA 16(7), 81(7); UC(D&A) 52; SS(D&A) 30; HB(D&A) 17; CTRE(PR) sch 7 para 8(3); CTRW(PR) sch 12 para 10; CTRSW 94(1); CTRSP 70B(1)

39.27 SSA 25; CSPSSA sch 7 para 16; UC(D&A) 53; SS(D&A) 21; HB(D&A) 15
https://valuationtribunal.gov.uk/app/uploads/2023/04/Consolidated-Practice-Statement-2020-1.pdf

Tribunal hearings and decisions

39.28 In UC, SPC and HB, the tribunal that deals with your appeal normally consists of just one judge, or a judge plus a medically or financially qualified person in appropriate cases. In council tax and CTR appeals, there may be two or three panel members. The tribunal's role is inquisitorial, not adversarial, so it can look afresh at your whole case, not just the part you have appealed.

Tribunal case management and directions

39.29 The tribunal can manage an appeal and issue directions to the parties about it at any time. You or any party can ask the tribunal for directions, or the tribunal can make them without a request. And if you fail to comply with a direction, the tribunal could strike out your appeal (so that it doesn't go ahead).

39.30 For example, a tribunal can do the following (ADM A5428):

(a) set, extend or shorten any time limit

(b) allow or require the parties to provide or amend documents, information, evidence or submissions, or require a third party to release evidence (FN v SSWP)

(c) hold a hearing (or not) and decide how it is run

(d) deal with preliminary matters in advance of a hearing

(e) adjourn or postpone a hearing

(f) join appeals so that they are dealt with together

(g) treat one appeal as a lead case and 'stay' other similar cases until the lead case is decided

(h) transfer proceedings to another court or tribunal in certain circumstances.

How appeals are dealt with

39.31 Every appeal is considered at a hearing unless you, the DWP/council, any other party and the tribunal itself all agree that it can be decided on the papers. Research shows that you have a better chance of success if you attend (along with your representative if you have one).

39.28 TCEA 3(3), 4(3), 22(4), sch 2 para 2(2); FTPR 2; SI 2008/2835, rule 2
https://tinyurl.com/Practice-Statement-FT-members
England : LGFA 1988, sch 11 paras A17, A18; VCCTR 25 as modified by SI 2009/2271 reg 3, sch
Consolidated Practice Statement 2023, Part 1, para 7
Wales: VTRW 37(1),(2),(9)
Scotland: FTSLT sch para 2; SSI 2023/47 reg 3(2)

39.29 FTPR 5(2), 6, 8, 15; VTRE 8, 9, 10; VTRW 37(5),(6),(9); FTSLT sch paras 44, 45

39.30 FTPR 5, 6, 18; VTRE 6, 7, 8; VTRW 37; FTSLT sch paras 4, 5, 44
FN v SSWP (UC) [2022] UKUT 77 (AAC)

39.31 FTPR 27(1); VTRE 29; VTRW 33; FTSLT sch paras 9, 46

Hearings

39.32 Hearings are usually held in person or by video conference [www]. For UC, SPC and HB, you should get at least 14 days' notice of the date, time and venue of your hearing.

At the hearing

39.33 You have the right to:

(a) attend the hearing in person or by video conference

(b) have a representative

(c) have a friend or relative with you for support

(d) put your case

(e) question the DWP/council and any other party about their case.

At the hearing or beforehand, you can ask for the hearing to be adjourned (e.g. if you need to obtain further evidence) or to withdraw your appeal (if the tribunal gives you permission to do so).

Tribunal decisions

39.34 The tribunal reaches a decision once it has considered all the evidence. In reaching its decision the tribunal should:

(a) consider the relevant law including any applicable case law

(b) identify the relevant facts based on the available evidence

(c) where the facts are in doubt or dispute, establish them (if necessary, on the balance of probability) and

(d) apply the law to the relevant facts to arrive at a reasoned decision.

Tribunal decision letters

39.35 The tribunal sends you a decision letter saying:

(a) what its decision is (whether your benefit should change and, if so, how and when)

(b) how to get a statement of reasons and

(c) how and when to make a further appeal.

You may also be told the decision on the day. In council tax and CTR appeals you should get a statement of reasons automatically.

39.32 FTPR 2(1) – 'hearing', 29(1),(2), 30; VTRE 2(1) – 'hearing', 30, 31; VTRW 34, 37(3); FTSLT sch paras 1 – 'hearing', 11, 12
http://sscs.venues.tribunals.gov.uk/Venues/venues.htm
https://valuationtribunal.gov.uk/how-remote-hearings-work/

39.33 FTPR 2(1),(2), 5(1), 11(1),(7), 17, 28, VTRE 13(1),(6), 17; VCCTR 20, 24, 25(6); VTRW 32, 36, 37(6),(7); FTSLT sch paras 4(3), 12(6), 13(1), 15(1), 37, 43

39.35 FTPR 33(1),(2), 34; VTRE 36, 37; VTRW 40(2),(3); FTSLT sch para 17(2),(4),(5)

When tribunal decisions take effect

39.36 If the tribunal changes your benefit, its decision letter either gives the new amounts and dates they take effect or clearly instructs the DWP/council how to work these out (ADM A5501, R(IS) 6/07). The DWP/council should action this as soon as practicable unless it knows that a further appeal is pending.

Statement of reasons

39.37 If the tribunal's decision letter doesn't give its reasons, you can get a statement of reasons by applying to the tribunal up to one month after receiving its decision letter (this can be extended if the tribunal agrees). The statement gives the tribunal's findings of fact as well as its reasons for its decision. It is necessary to have this if you want to make a further appeal.

Record of proceedings

39.38 You can get a copy of the record of proceedings by applying to the tribunal up to 18 months (or longer for council tax) after receiving its decision letter [www]. This means 18 months after the last activity in relation to the decision such as a correction, or from the date the statement of reasons was issued (DT v SSWP). The record gives a summary of the evidence and submissions received by the tribunal. It isn't necessary to have this if you want to make a further appeal but can be useful.

Correcting accidental errors in tribunal decisions

39.39 Accidental errors are errors that fail to record what the tribunal intended. The tribunal can correct these as a result of a request (which could be from you, the DWP/council or another party, or without a request).

Setting aside tribunal decisions

39.40 'Setting aside' a tribunal decision means it is cancelled and the appeal starts again (with a new hearing or a new consideration of the papers). The tribunal can set a decision aside if it is in the interests of justice to do so and

(a) a document wasn't sent to, or wasn't received at any appropriate time by the tribunal or any party (or it was received but there was not sufficient time to properly consider it taking into account the volume of evidence: ST v HMRC); or

(b) any party or representative was not present at a hearing; or

(c) there has been some other procedural irregularity.

The time limit for doing this is one month (but is shorter in council tax and CTR appeals).

39.36 FTPR 33, VTRE 36, 38(9); VTRW 40(2),(3); FTSLT sch paras 17(4),(5), 48, 49; CTRSW 94(4); CTRSP 70B(4)

39.37 FTPR 34(3)-(5), 38(2),(3),(7); VTRE 37; VTRW 40(3); FTSLT sch paras 17(4)

39.38 Practice Statement from the Senior President of Tribunals: social security and child support cases, 1 April 2022
VTRE 41(1),(3); VTRW 43(1),(4)
DT v SSWP [2015] UKUT 509 (AAC)

39.39 TCEA 9(1),(4)(a); TSA 44(1); FTPR 36; VTRE 39; 43(7); VTRW 42(1)(a),(5)(a); FTSLT sch para 21

39.40 TCEA 9(1),(4),(5); TSA 44(1), 43(1),(2); FTPR 37; VTRE 40; VCCTR 31; VTRW 42(1)(a),(5); FTSLT sch para 19
ST v HMRC [2025] UKUT 11 (AAC)

Further appeals and reviews

39.41 For UC/SPC/HB and CTR in Scotland you (or any party to an appeal) may be able to apply for a further appeal as follows:

(a) you can apply to the tribunal which made the decision, for permission to make a further appeal to the Upper Tribunal – this must be on the grounds there was an error of law (not that you just disagree about the facts)

(b) if that is refused, you can apply to the Upper Tribunal for permission.

The time limit for doing this is one month (30 days for CTR), and you are likely to need help from a lawyer or professional advice worker.

39.42 For CTR/council tax in England and Wales you (or any party to an appeal) may be able to apply to the tribunal for permission to make a further appeal to the High Court on the grounds there has been an error of law. The time limit is four weeks.

39.43 For decisions that can't be appealed you may be able to apply to the High Court (Court of Session in Scotland) for them to review it. This is called 'judicial review. You will need professional advice and representation. The time limit is three months [www].

Appeals about rent officer figures

39.44 Correcting errors and appeals about the following matters are dealt with by a rent officer (not a tribunal) and are called 're-determinations' and 'substitute determinations':

(a) local housing allowance (LHA) figures and areas in UC and HB private renter cases (paras 12.22-24)

(b) housing payment determinations in UC (para 11.25)

(c) rent determinations in HB rent referral cases (para 12.32) and

(d) board and attendance determinations in HB private renter cases (including in supported or temporary accommodation) (para 12.37).

39.45 The rent officer (acting on their own) can correct certain errors about any of these. The rent officer must respond to the DWP's request to correct a housing payment determination, but you only have the right to appeal to the rent officer about (c) and (d).

Correcting errors

39.46 The rent officer can only correct technical errors or slips of the pen, for example transposing figures. The rent officer can't correct errors of professional judgment and, except for the information that is incorrect or incomplete, must use the same information used to make the original determination.

39.41 FTPR 38, UTPR 21; FTSLT sch paras 39, 46; SSI 2016/231

39.42 VTRE 43; VCCTR 32; VTRW 44

39.43 www.justice.gov.uk/courts/procedure-rules/civil/rules/part54#54.5

39.44 UC(ROO) 6, sch 3; HBW 15-18; HBP 15-18; HB(ROO) 4, 4A, 4D, 4E, 7A

39.45 CSPSSA sch 7 para 6(2)(c); UC(D&A) sch 3 para 6; UC(ROO) 6(1),(2); HBW 15-18; HBP 15-18; HB(ROO) 4, 4A, 4D, 7A

39.46 UC(ROO) 6(1)-(3); HB(ROO) 7A(1),(2),(4)

Re-determinations in HB

39.47 In HB rent referral cases (including board and attendance determinations), the council can apply to the rent officer for a re-determination. And if you write and ask the council to do this within one month of an HB decision letter, the council must make an application within seven days and include a copy of your request and any information and evidence you provide.

39.48 You or the council can only ask for one redetermination each but if you apply first and the council seeks a second, you can ask for another one.

39.49 The council can also apply to the rent officer for a substitute determination (including a board and attendance determination) at any time if it discovers it made an error in the original referral relating to:

(a) the size of the dwelling
(b) the number of occupiers
(c) the composition of the household or
(d) the terms of the tenancy.

Any substitute determination can also be redetermined in the same way as above.

39.50 A re-determination is made by a different rent officer [www] (known as a re-determination officer) with advice from one or two other rent officers. The outcome is normally sent to the council and you within 20 days.

When the rent officer's new figures take effect

39.51 When the rent officer's new figure increases your UC or HB, the increase goes back to when the original figure applied from. So, you get your arrears of benefit back to then.

39.52 But when the rent officer's new figure reduces your UC or HB:

(a) your UC reduces from the assessment period after the one in which the DWP receives the correction
(b) your HB reduces from the Monday after the rent officer makes the correction.

So, in each of these cases you haven't been overpaid benefit.

39.47 HBW 15(1), 16(1),(2); HBP 15(1), 16(1),(2); HB(ROO) 4(1), 4D(1)

39.48 HBW 15(2), 16(3),(4); HBP 15(2), 16(3),(4)

39.49 HBW 17(1)(a), 18; HBP 17(1)(a), 18; HB(ROO) 4A(1), 4E(1)

39.50 HB(ROO) 2(1) – 'relevant period', 4(1),(3), 4D(2),(3), 4E(1), sch 3 para 2
www.gov.uk/guidance/rent-officer-handbook-housing-benefit-referral/housing-benefit-referral-redetermination

39.51 UC(D&A) 19(2), 21; HB(D&A) 4(3), 6; HBW 18A(3); HBP 18A(3)

39.52 UC(D&A) 30, 35(14); HB(D&A) 7(2)(c), 8(6); HBW 18A(2); HBP 18A(2)

Chapter 40 **Migrants and recent arrivals**

- The rules that apply to migrants: paras 40.2-7
- How the decision is made: paras 40.8-19
- The immigration control test, asylum seekers and refugees: paras 40.20-35
- Habitual residence and the right to reside: paras 40.36-50

40.1 This chapter is about when you can get benefit (UC/SPC/HB/CTR) if you have recently arrived in the UK. It covers everyone, whatever your nationality, and whether you are arriving in the UK for the first time or returning after a time abroad.

Which rules apply

40.2 You are excluded from benefit if:

(a) you are subject to immigration control or

(b) you don't have the right to reside in the British Isles (para 40.37) or Ireland or

(c) you aren't habitually resident in the British Isles or Ireland.

In practice, unless you have EU pre-settled status, if you satisfy (a) you also have a right to reside. In the law the right to reside test is a preliminary step to deciding if you are habitually resident and this is reflected in the way the DWP/council makes and tells you its decision (para 40.40).

40.3 If you are a couple, it is the claimant who must meet these conditions. For UC this can be one or both of you (paras 2.8-9). But making a claim as a couple if your partner is subject to immigration control could affect your right to remain in the UK (paras 40.11-16).

Eligibility of nationals of different parts of the world

40.4 This section identifies which rules apply to you depending on your nationality, followed by a straightforward example of each. Table 40.1 summarises how the three tests apply to all new claims from 1 January 2021.

Nationals of the British Isles and Ireland

40.5 You are entitled to benefit if you:

(a) are a British citizen, Irish citizen, or Commonwealth citizen with the right of abode (table 40.2) and

(b) you are habitually resident in the British Isles or Ireland (paras 40.36-50).

This is because (for benefit purposes) you aren't subject to immigration control and have a right to reside here.

40.2 IAA 115(1),(3); WRA 4(1)(c); SPCA 1(2)(a); SSCBA 130(1)(a), 137(2)(a); UC 9(1),(2); PC 2(1),(2); HBW 10(1)-(3); HBP 10(1)-(3)

40.3 Immigration Act 1971, s2, 3(1)(c); UC 3(3)(b); Immigration Rules, rule 6.2

40.5 IAA 115(3),(9); Immigration Act 1971, s1(1), 2(1), 3ZA; Immigration Rules, rule 5E

Nationals of the European Economic Area and their family members

40.6 If you have EU pre-settled status (or your application to the EU settlement scheme has been accepted but not decided) the rules in chapter 41 apply instead. In any other case, unless you have EU settled status, you are treated as a national from the rest of the world.

Nationals of the rest of the world

40.7 If you are a national from the rest of the world you must satisfy the immigration control test and the habitual residence test to be entitled to benefit.

Table 40.1 **Migrants: who can get benefit**

Nationality/date of entry	Test
British and Irish citizens	
Any date	Habitual residence
EEA and EEA family members	
Entered UK after 31 December 2020	Immigration control and habitual residence
Entered UK before 1 January 2021and granted EU settled status	Habitual residence
Entered UK before 1 January 2021 and granted EU pre-settled status	Right to reside and habitual residence
Entered UK before 1 January 2021, applied to the EU settlement scheme, and awaiting a decision	Right to reside and habitual residence
Rest of the world	
On entry to the UK	Immigration control and habitual residence

Notes

- In law the claimant must pass all three tests but, as the table shows, it is in practice either one or two.
- For EEA member states see table 41.1. For EEA family members the entry date applies to the EEA national they accompany.
- Transitional rules apply to nationals of certain European states (para 40.27).
- Different rules apply to claimants who have claimed asylum.

40.6 Immigration and Social Security Co-ordination (EU Withdrawal) Act 2020, s.1, sch 1 paras 1, 2(2); European Union (Withdrawal Agreement) Act 2020, sch 4 paras 1, 12; SI 2020/1209 regs 3, 4, 11, 12(1)(i); SI 2020/1309, sch 4 paras 1-3

40.7 IAA 115(1),(3); WRA 4(1)(c); SPCA 1(2)(a); SSCBA 130(1)(a), 137(2)(a); UC 9(1),(2); PC 2(1),(2); HBW 10(1)-(3); HBP 10(1)-(3)

T40.1 IAA 115(1),(3); WRA 4(1)(c); SPCA 1(2)(a); SSCBA 130(1)(a), 137(2)(a); UC 9(1),(2); PC 2(1),(2); HBW 10(1)-(3); HBP 10(1)-(3)

Decision-making

40.8 This section covers general matters relevant to this chapter and chapter 41, including decision-making and claims, and how the law and terminology work.

Making a claim

40.9 Your online UC claim or SPC claim form asks you:

(a) if you are British, Irish or a citizen of a different country; and

(b) if you have been out of the UK or Ireland in the past two years.

Most HB/CTR claim forms ask similar questions. Both questions are intended to act as a trigger for further investigation. If you are British/Irish and have not been out of the UK/Ireland in the past two years, the DWP/council normally assumes you pass all three tests.

DWP and council decisions

40.10 If you claim HB the council decides if you are entitled (not the DWP). But the law says you pass the habitual residence and right to reside test if you get ESA(IR)/IS/JSA(IB) or SPC (either kind). In practice if you get one of these the council will accept you pass the immigration control test (HBGM C4.33). These benefits also help you qualify for CTR.

Examples: Eligibility for UC

1. A British citizen

A British citizen has been living abroad for 12 years. During that time, she gave up all her connections in the UK. She has now just come 'home' and has rented a flat here.

The only test that applies to a UK national is the habitual residence test. It is unlikely that she satisfies that test to begin with but she probably will after (say) three months or possibly a shorter period (para 40.45). So, for the time being she can't get UC.

2. National of the EEA who entered the UK before 1 January 2021

An Italian national has been working in the UK for several years. He applied to the EU settlement scheme before 1 July 2021 and has EU pre-settled status. He has recently taken a more poorly paid job. He passes the right to reside test because he is working. So he can get UC.

3. National of the rest of the world

An Indian national arrived in the UK six months ago to be with her family. She was given leave to enter by the Home Office without a 'no public funds' condition, so she is able to claim benefits. She now claims UC.

The two tests that apply to a national of the rest of the world are the immigration control test and the habitual residence test. She passes both tests. So she can get UC.

40.10 SSA 34; SSAA 134(1); HBW 10(3B)(k); HBP 10(4A)(k)

Claiming for others in your benefit unit

40.11 If a member of your benefit unit (partner, child, young person) has leave without access to public funds, you must consider if your claim breaches their leave and you should consult an IAA registered adviser [www] before claiming (paras 40.15-16).

40.12 It is safe to claim if everyone in your benefit unit has settled status, EU pre-settled status or the right of abode (table 40.2). But you should get advice if a person without access to public funds is included in your claim if it results in you getting a higher award.

40.13 In a couple only the claimant must meet the conditions of entitlement to get benefit (chapter 2). For SPC/HB/CTR this is whoever makes the claim, but for UC it usually means both of you (para 2.8).

40.14 If you are in a couple and want to claim UC or SPC but your partner doesn't have access to public funds, you can claim it as a single person (paras 2.9, 2.15) but you only get the single person's allowance.

40.15 If you claim HB or CTR for your partner or a child who can't claim public funds, including them in your claim usually only results in a higher award if you have excess income (para 18.4) or if it cancels a non-dependant charge (para 6.22).

40.16 Claiming UC/SPC as a single person, or HB/CTR as a couple or for a child if it doesn't increase your award, means your partner doesn't breach their leave, but it doesn't guarantee their leave will be renewed when they reapply (para 40.11).

40.17 If both of you aren't subject to immigration control (para 40.21) but only one satisfies the habitual residence test, the eligible partner can get SPC, HB or CTR as a couple, but can only get UC as a single person (para 2.9).

National insurance numbers

40.18 When you claim UC or SPC you must provide your national insurance number (NINo) or have applied for one) (para 32.20). If you are a couple this applies to both of you, unless you are claiming as a single person (paras 40.13-14). If you or your partner have applied for a NINo, the DWP should consider whether you are likely to be allocated one before refusing your claim (R (Bui) v SSWP).

40.19 The same requirement applies when you claim HB or CTR in England and Wales (para 29.40). If your partner needs leave but doesn't have it (e.g. if they applied but it hasn't been decided) you can claim HB without one, but you should get immigration advice before doing so (para 40.11). The council could inform the Home Office but is not obliged to (HBGM C4.219).

40.11-12 Immigration Act 1971, s. 1(1), 2, 3(1),(2), 33(2A); Immigration Rules, rule 6.2 – 'public funds'
www.gov.uk/find-an-immigration-adviser

40.13 WRA 4(1)(c); SPCA 1(2),(3), 2(5); SSCBA 130(1)(a), 137(2)(a); UC 3(3), 9(2); PC 1A, 5(1)(h); HBW 10(1); HBP 10(1)

40.14 UC 3(3)(b), 9(2); PC 1A, 5(1)(h)

40.16 Immigration rules, rule 6.2 – 'public funds'

40.17 WRA 4(1)(c); SPCA 1(2),(3), 2(5); CBA 130(1)(a), 137(2)(a); UC 3(3)(b); PC 5(1)(h); HBW 10(1); HBP 10(1)

40.18 SSAA(1),(1A)-(1C),(4)(za),(ab)
R (Bui) v SSWP [2023] EWCA Civ 566, [2024] PTSR 162

40.19 SSAA(1),(1A)-(1C),(4)(b), 191 – 'income-related benefit'; HBW 4(c); HBP 4(c); CTRE(PR) sch 8 para 7(1)-(3); CTRW(PR) sch 13 para 5(1)-(3)

The immigration control test

40.20 If you are from a country other than the UK or Ireland you must pass the immigration control test to get benefit. (You must also pass the habitual residence test: paras 40.36-50.) A basic understanding of immigration law terminology is useful to understanding benefit decisions. Table 40.2 explains the key terms.

Table 40.2 **Simplified immigration law terminology**

EU settled and pre-settled status

EU settled status is a form of settled status granted through the EU settlement scheme to a person with five years' residence. A person with less than five years gets pre-settled status (a form of limited leave) until then. Both EU settled and pre-settled status are granted with access to public funds. See paras 41.10-11 for more details.

Immigration rules

The legal rules approved by parliament which UKVI officers use to decide whether a person should be given permission ('leave') to enter or remain in the UK.

UK Visas and Immigration (UKVI)

The Home Office division responsible for immigration control and deciding asylum claims (including asylum support).

Leave and settled status

Leave is legal permission to be in the UK for anyone who is subject to immigration control. It can be granted for a fixed period (limited leave) or open ended (indefinite leave) and with or without access to public funds or other conditions. Most limited leave has a 'no public funds' condition. The holder can apply to have their leave extended or conditions varied, provided they apply before the current leave expires (para 40.25). Indefinite leave to enter or remain without conditions is also known as 'settled status'. Partners of British/ settled persons usually get leave in two blocks of 30 months each, after which they can apply for settled status.

Temporary permission to stay

Temporary permission to stay (TPS) is a form of limited leave. It is granted to survivors of trafficking or slavery who do not qualify for any other form of leave where it is necessary to help that person recover from physical or psychological harm, to seek compensation, or help the police investigate the traffickers. TPS is granted for 12 or 30 months, and in either case with access to public funds.

Public funds

UC/SPC/HB/CTR, legacy benefits and most non-contributory benefits count as public funds. It also includes getting housed as homeless by your council or joining their housing waiting list.

Table continued ➤

40.20 IAA99 115(1),(3),(9); CTRE(PR) 13; CTRW(PR) 27, 19; CTRSW 19; CTRSP 19

Sponsorship and maintenance undertaking

A sponsored migrant is someone (typically a partner or elderly relative) who is granted leave to join a family member (a 'sponsor') on the understanding that their sponsor will provide their maintenance and accommodation. If the sponsor signs a written agreement (a 'maintenance undertaking') to this effect the person being sponsored is usually excluded from public funds for five years.

Illegal entrant and overstayer

These refer to a person who needs leave to enter or remain in the UK but does not have it or immigration bail. An illegal entrant is someone who entered the UK without leave. An overstayer is someone who entered with leave, but which has since expired.

Leave outside the rules (LOTR)

This is a form of leave granted by the Home Office using their discretion. It is used for humanitarian cases that don't fit the immigration rules. Discretionary leave and the domestic abuse concession (para 40.34) are both forms of LOTR.

Right of abode and right to reside

'Right of abode' is a term that describes someone who is entirely free of immigration control. It applies to all British citizens and some long-term citizens of Commonwealth countries (e.g. 'Windrush' residents). It doesn't apply to other forms of British nationality (e.g. British national (overseas)). Non-British citizens can apply for a certificate in their passport to confirm their status [www].

'Right to reside' is a wider term that describes any legal authority to live or settle in the UK which includes the right of abode and leave. It is now mainly used to determine rights to benefit and other public services for people with EU pre-settled status based on the pre-Brexit EU free movement rules. It does not include immigration bail (previously 'temporary admission' (Yesiloz v LB Camden).

40.21 The immigration control test stops you getting benefit if:

(a) you require 'leave' but do not have it

(b) your leave has a 'no public funds' condition

(c) you are a 'sponsored' immigrant (table 40.2) or

(d) you have been granted immigration bail (table 40.2) while you wait for a decision from the Home Office) (e.g. if you have claimed asylum).

There are some limited exceptions to (b) and (c) (paras 40.26-27).

40.22 The definition in para 40.21 is only used to decide entitlement to benefits. It isn't used to determine your right to enter or remain in the UK for which anyone without the right of abode or Irish citizenship must apply for leave.

T40.2 Immigration Act 1971, s1(1),(2), 2, 3ZA; Immigration Rules, rule 6(2) – 'public funds'
Yesiloz v LB Camden [2009] EWCA Civ 415 reported as R(H) 7/09
www.gov.uk/right-of-abode/apply-for-a-certificate-of-entitlement

40.21 IAA99 115(9)

40.22 IAA 115(9); Immigration Act 1971, s1(1),(2), 2, 3ZA

People who pass the immigration control test

40.23 You pass the immigration control test if:

(a) you are an Irish citizen

(b) you hold a Commonwealth passport with a certificate confirming your 'right of abode'

(c) you have 'indefinite leave to enter or remain' (settled status), including EU settled status

(d) you have EU pre-settled status

(e) you claimed asylum and you have been granted refugee status, humanitarian protection or discretionary leave (paras 40.31-32).

These are usually confirmed by your passport or other Home Office documents. Except for (e) you must also pass the habitual residence test to get benefit.

People with limited leave

40.24 Most forms of limited leave are granted without access to public funds – for example, this applies to most students and work permit holders. But in certain uncommon situations, limited leave can be granted without conditions either under the immigration rules or outside them. Table 40.3 gives examples when limited leave can be granted with access to public funds.

Table 40.3 **Limited leave with access to public funds**

This table lists some of the situations when a person might be granted limited leave with access to public funds:

(a) a long-term resident based on their 'right to family life' with another British citizen (e.g. their child)

(b) a stateless person who has been granted five years leave for that reason (para 40.33)

(c) a British National (Overseas) from Hong Kong following an application to vary their leave

(d) a person refused settled status due to minor criminal offences or failing the 'life in the UK' test

(e) a person granted leave for any of the reasons (b) to (e) in para 40.39

(f) a person granted temporary permission to stay as a survivor of trafficking or slavery

(g) the partner of a British citizen or a settled person who has experienced domestic violence (para 40.34)

Notes:

- Leave with access to public funds may be granted for other reasons.
- Leave granted under (f) and (g) is outside the immigration rules.
- Leave under (e) to (g) also exempts you from the habitual residence test (para 40.39).

40.23 UC(C&P) 37; SS(C&P) 7; HBW 86; HBP 67; CTRE(PR) sch 8 para 7(4); CTRW(PR) sch 13 para 5(4); CTRSW 27(1); CTRSP 66(1)

40.24 IAA 115(9)(b); Immigration Act 1971, s3(1)(c)

T40.3 Immigration Rules, various

Entitlement when leave starts and ends

40.25 Your entitlement to benefit doesn't always coincide with the decision to grant you leave:

(a) your benefit starts from the date you receive your Home Office confirmation letter or your passport is endorsed, not the date the Immigration Appeal Tribunal allowed your appeal, even though that means confirmation will inevitably follow (MUN v SSWP)

(b) you can apply for your leave to be extended provided you apply before it expires and in the correct form. If you do this, you are treated as having leave until 28 days after your application is decided so you continue to pass the immigration control test until then but

(c) if your application is refused or your existing leave excluded you from public funds you aren't entitled to benefit while you appeal, even if you appealed in time (EE v City of Cardiff).

Exceptions to the immigration control test

40.26 The law allows for exceptions to the immigration control test which are set out in regulations. You are not excluded by the immigration control test if:

(a) you are a 'sponsored immigrant' (table 40.2) who has been resident for at least five years beginning with the date of your entry or the date your sponsor signed the maintenance and accommodation undertaking whichever is the later

(b) you are a 'sponsored immigrant' who has been resident for less than five years but your sponsor (or all them if there is more than one) has died or

(c) in transitional cases, you are a national of a European Convention on Social and Medical Assistance (ECSMA)/ European Social Charter (ESC) treaty member state (para 40.27).

ECSMA/ESC nationals: transitional rules

40.27 If you have leave (including leave without access to public funds) and you are a national of an ECSMA/ESC member state you are entitled to:

(a) CTR in Scotland

(b) SPC and HB if you claimed it before 3 May 2022

(c) UC if you claimed it before 1 January 2021.

You must also satisfy stage two of the habitual residence test (para 40.42). ECSMA/ESC member states are: North Macedonia, Turkey and the EEA member states (table 41.1) other than Bulgaria, Liechtenstein, Lithuania, Romania, Slovenia and Switzerland.

40.25 Immigration Act 1971 s3C
MUN v SSWP [2011] UKUT 373 (AAC)
EE v City of Cardiff (HB) [2018] UKUT 418 (AAC)

40.26 IAA 115(3),(4); SI 2000/636 reg 2(1),(1A), sch part 1 paras 2, 3; CTRE(PR) 13(2); CTRW(PR) 29(3); CTRSW 19(2); CTRSP 19(2)

40.27 SI 2020/1505 regs 1(3), 2(2)(a); SI 2022/449 regs 1-3; SI 2023/47 reg 5; CTRSW 19(2); CTRSP 19(2)

Asylum seekers

40.28 You are an asylum seeker if you have made a claim to be recognised as a refugee under the United Nations Convention because of fear of persecution in your country of origin (typically on political or ethnic grounds).

40.29 While your asylum claim is being processed you fail the immigration control test unless one of the exceptions in para 40.30 applies. If you are destitute, you may be able to get help with your maintenance and/or accommodation from the Home Office [www].

40.30 You can claim benefit while your asylum claim is processed if:

(a) you previously had leave with access to public funds and you claimed asylum before it expired (OG file 142)

(b) you are a couple, and your partner is eligible (paras 40.11-16) (and in this case if you are claiming HB/CTR any payment you get from the Home Office for support counts as income: HBGM para C4.128) or

(c) you claimed asylum as an unaccompanied child (para 40.31), but you may be excluded from UC for other reasons (para 3.6).

Refugees and others granted leave on humanitarian grounds

40.31 Following your claim for asylum the Home Office may:

(a) recognise you as a refugee (i.e. accept your claim for asylum) and grant leave

(b) refuse asylum but grant humanitarian protection (which is a form of leave) or discretionary leave or

(c) refuse asylum but grant temporary permission to stay or discretionary leave (LOTR) or

(d) refuse asylum and not grant leave.

Discretionary leave is usually only granted to unaccompanied children

40.32 If leave is granted it is normally for an initial period of 30 months, and then one further period of 30 months, after which you can usually apply for settled status (table 40.2). Refugee status, humanitarian protection and discretionary leave are usually granted with access to public funds. You are also exempt from the habitual residence test so can claim benefit from the date your status is confirmed.

40.28 Immigration Rules, rule 327

40.29 IAA 115(1),(3),(9)(a); www.gov.uk/asylum-support

40.30 IAA 115(1),(3),(9); WRA 4(1)(c); SPCA 1(2),(3), 2(5); CBA 130(1)(a), 137(2)(a); UC 3(3)(b), 9(2); PC 1A, 5(1)(h); HBW 4(c), 10(1)-(3); HBP 4(c), 10(1)-(3)

40.31 Immigration Rules, rules 327EA-EC, 334, 339C

Stateless persons

40.33 You are a stateless person if you are not recognised as a citizen by the law of any country. A stateless person can be granted leave in the same way as any other non-UK national (e.g. as a student, worker permit holder, etc) but can also apply for leave for that reason. The Home Office says it only grants stateless leave if the applicant does not meet the criteria for asylum or qualify for leave under any other category – although the law does not strictly require this. Stateless leave is for five years with access to public funds [www] so you are entitled to benefit provided you are habitually resident (paras 40.36-50).

Migrant victims of domestic abuse concession

40.34 If you are the partner of a British citizen or a person with settled status (table 40.2) who is experiencing domestic abuse you can apply for the migrant victims of domestic abuse concession [www]. This concession is three months leave with access to public funds but is discretionary (ADM C1674-76; HB circular U2/2012 [www]). It allows you time to make an application to UKVI to settle in the UK. You are entitled to benefit until your application to settle is decided (table 40.3(g), 40.39).

40.35 You should always get specialist immigration advice from an IAA registered adviser [www] before you apply for the concession. Getting the concession does not mean that your application to settle will succeed and if it fails you could lose your right to remain in the UK.

The habitual residence test

40.36 You are not entitled to benefit unless:

(a) you have a 'right to reside' in the British Isles or Ireland and

(b) you are 'habitually resident' in the British Isles or Ireland.

Both (a) and (b) together are the 'habitual residence test'. In practice the DWP/council apply (a) first because the law says if you fail (a) you can't satisfy (b).

40.37 In this guide we use 'British Isles' to mean the UK, the Channel Islands, and the Isle of Man. The British Isles and Ireland together are sometimes called the Common Travel Area.

40.38 The habitual residence test applies to everyone, including British citizens. It stops you getting benefit immediately on your arrival in the UK. But if you meet any of the conditions in para 40.39 you are exempt.

40.33 Immigration Rules, rules Appendix Statelessness
www.gov.uk/government/publications/stateless-guidance/

40.34 UC 9(4)(e); PC 2(4)(h); HBW 10(3B)(h); HBP 10(4A)(h)
www.gov.uk/government/publications/application-for-benefits-for-visa-holder-domestic-violence
https://tinyurl.com/U2-2012

40.35 www.gov.uk/find-an-immigration-adviser

40.36 WRA 4(1)(c),(5); SPCA 1(2)(a),(5); SSCBA 130(1)(a), 137(2)(a); UC 9(1),(2); PC 2(1),(2); HBW 10(1)-(3); HBP 10(1)-(3)

40.37 UC 9(1),(2); PC 2(1),(2); HBW 10(1)-(3); HBP 10(1)-(3); CTRE(PR) 12(1)-(3); CTRW(PR) 27, 28(1)-(3); CTRSW 16(1)-(3); CTRSP 16(1)-(3)

Who is exempt from habitual residence test

40.39 You are exempt from the habitual residence test if:

(a) you applied for asylum and have refugee status, humanitarian protection, or discretionary leave

(b) you have leave granted under the Afghan Citizens Resettlement Scheme (ACRS), the Afghan Relocations and Assistance Policy (ARAP) or you left Afghanistan due to the collapse of the Afghan Government on 15 August 2021

(c) you are a person who has access to public funds who was residing in Ukraine before 1 January 2022 and left due to the Russian invasion on 24 February 2022

(d) you are person who has access to public funds who was residing in Sudan before 15 April 2023 and left due to the escalating violence

(e) you are a person who has access to public funds who was residing in Israel, Palestine, the occupied territories, or Lebanon before 7 October 2023 and left due to the Hamas terrorist attack or subsequent violence

(f) you have leave outside the immigration rules (LOTR) (table 40.2)

(g) you have EU pre-settled status and are self-employed, a worker or a family member of a person who is

(h) you have EU pre-settled status and have permanent residence as a retired person or family member

(i) you are a British citizen, a person with the right of abode (table 40.2) or a person with settled status and you have been deported to the UK from another country or

(j) for HB and working age CTR only, you get one of the DWP benefits in para 40.10.

For these purposes a person with access to public funds includes a British or Irish citizen or Commonwealth citizen with the right of abode (table 40.2).

How habitual residence decisions are made and notified

40.40 DWP decision letters only usually tell you if you failed the test overall (not which part). If you have EU pre-settled status you should consider asking for a statement of reasons. The law about EU rights to reside is complex and decision makers often get it wrong or fail to identify all the possibilities. If the DWP/council decides you have a right to reside it will then go on to consider if you are habitually resident based on your individual circumstances.

40.39 UC 9(1),(4); PC 2(4); HBW 10(1),(3B); HBP 10(1),(4A); CTRE(PR) 12(2),(5); CTRW(PR) 28(2),(5); CTRSW 16(1),(6); CTRSP 16(1),(5)

Who has a right to reside

40.41 You have a right to reside if:

(a) you are a British or Irish citizen

(b) you are a Commonwealth citizen with a right of abode

(c) you have settled status (including EU settled status)

(d) you have limited leave provided you are complying with any conditions or

(e) you have EU pre-settled status, and you have one of the qualifying rights to reside described in para 41.15 (Abdirahman v SSWP).

But immigration bail doesn't count as a right to reside (table 40.2).

Habitual residence stage two: based on your facts

40.42 What counts as habitual residence is a 'question of fact'. It is decided by looking at all the facts in your case; no list of considerations can be drawn up to govern all cases. The DWP gives general guidance on this (ADM C1946-70; HBGM paras C4.87-106).

What is habitual residence

40.43 There are two elements to 'habitual residence':

(a) 'residence': you must actually be resident; your intent or mere physical presence are not sufficient.

(b) 'habitual': there must also be a degree of permanence to your residence (HBGM para C4.80) which implies a more settled state in which you are making your home here. This doesn't mean it must be your only home or that it is permanent, provided it is your genuine home for the time being.

Losing and gaining habitual residence

40.44 You can lose your habitual residence in a single day: for example, if you leave intending to take up long-term residence in another country. But you don't become habitually resident immediately on arrival even if you have the intention to settle. You must be resident for an appreciable period of time and have the intention to settle (R(IS) 6/96).

'Appreciable period of time' and 'intention to settle'

40.45 There is no fixed period that amounts to an appreciable period (R(IS) 2/00). It varies according to your circumstances taking account of the 'length, continuity and nature' of your residence (R(IS) 6/96). But the period is usually between one and three months and there must be powerful reasons to justify a significantly longer period (CIS 4474/2003).

40.41 Abdirahman and Ullusow v SSWP [2007] EWCA Civ 657, [2008] 1 WLR 254, reported as R(IS) 8/07

40.42 UC 9(1); PC 2(1); HBW 10(1),(2); HBP 10(1),(2); CTRE(PR) 12(1),(2); CTRW(PR) 28(1),(2); CTRSW 16(1),(2); CTRSP 16(1),(2)

40.46 Factors used to decide what amounts to an appreciable period include (ADM C1965-69, HBGM C4.85-86):

(a) the length and continuity of your residence
(b) your reasons for coming to the UK
(c) your future intentions
(d) your employment prospects and
(e) your 'centre of interest'.

The relative weighting given to each will depend on the facts in your case but no one factor is ever decisive.

40.47 Your education and qualifications are likely to be significant to your employment prospects (CIS 5136/2007). An offer of work is also good evidence of an intention to settle. If you have stable employment, it is presumed that you reside here, even if your family lives abroad (ADM C1969).

Centre of interest

40.48 Your centre of interest is concerned with the strength of your ties to this country and your intention to settle. It can be shown by (ADM C1966; HBGM C4.105):

(a) the presence of close relatives
(b) the location of your family's personal possessions (e.g. clothing, furniture, transport)
(c) substantial purchases, such as furnishings, which indicate a long-term commitment and
(d) the membership of any clubs or organisations in connection with your hobbies or recreations.

Temporary absence and returning residents

40.49 Once your habitual residence has been established, it resumes immediately on your return from a single short absence (such as a holiday or visiting relatives).

40.50 In considering whether you regain your habitual residence following a longer absence, or repeated absences, the following points need to be considered:

(a) the circumstances in which your habitual residence was lost
(b) your intentions – if your absence was always intended to be temporary (even in the case of longer absences) you are less likely to lose your habitual residence than someone who originally never had an intention to return
(c) your continuing links with the UK while abroad
(d) the circumstances of your return. If you slot straight back into the life you had before you left, you are likely to resume habitual residence more quickly.

Chapter 41 **EEA nationals**

- The EU settlement scheme, time limits and who can apply: paras 41.3-12
- EEA nationals and who can get benefit: paras 41.13-17
- EEA self-employed and worker status: paras 41.18-31
- The right of permanent residence: paras 41.32-38
- EEA family member rights: paras 41.39-44
- Derivative rights, students, and self-sufficient persons: paras 41.45-59

41.1 This chapter is about when you can get benefit (UC/SPC/HB/CTR) if you have applied to the EU settlement scheme but don't have EU settled status. If you have EU settled status your rights to benefit are described in chapter 40.

When this chapter applies

41.2 This chapter only applies to you if:

(a) you had the right to apply to the EU settlement scheme (para 41.6)

(b) you applied within the time limit, or your late application was accepted (para 41.8) and

(c) either:

- you have been granted EU pre-settled status (para 41.11) or
- your application has been accepted (whether in time or late) but has not yet been decided (para 41.12).

The EU Settlement Scheme (EUSS)

41.3 This section describes the main features of the EU settlement scheme. It explains:

(a) what the EU settlement scheme does and how it relates to UK immigration control

(b) who can apply and

(c) the time limits for making an application.

41.4 The EUSS is part of the UK's withdrawal agreement with the EU. It provides a simple route for EEA nationals to settle and get access to public services following the UK's departure from the EU. The are no fees and the scheme is part of immigration rules ('Appendix EU'). The scheme also applies to EEA family members and to certain family members of British citizens. A separate application is required by each person and must be made within the time limit.

41.2 European Union (Withdrawal Agreement) Act 2020, s7; SI 2020/1209 regs 4, 6, 11; SI 2020/1309 reg 83, sch 4 paras 1-3; UC 9(3)(c)(i); PC 2(3A)(a); HBW 10(3AA)(a); HBP 10(4ZA)(a); CTRE(PR) 12(4A)(b)

41.4 European Union (Withdrawal Agreement) Act 2020, s7

41.5 The scheme is only open to EEA nationals who first entered the UK before 11pm on 31 December 2020. For EEA family members, the entry cut-off date applies to the EEA national they accompanied and certain other conditions apply such as the date the relationship started.

Who could apply to the EU settlement scheme

41.6 You had the right to apply to the EU settlement scheme if any of the following apply:

(a) you are a national of an EEA member state (table 41.1) who entered the UK before 1 January 2021 using one of the rights described in this chapter

(b) you accompanied a person in (a) as their family member (table 41.2) and arrived to join them before 1 July 2021

(c) you are the family member of a person who was born in Northern Ireland to a parent who was at that time a British or Irish citizen or had settled status. In this case 'family member' includes a grandchild or great grandchild

(d) you are a non-EEA parent of a British child ('Zambrano' carer) (para 41.51) or

(e) you are the family member of a British citizen who exercised their EU free-movement rights in another EU member state before 1 February 2020 and returned to the UK before 1 January 2021. These are sometimes called 'Surinder Singh' rights after the case that established them.

In each case you must have made an application on time or otherwise had your late application accepted.

Table 41.1 **The European Economic Area (EEA)**

This table shows the EEA member states apart from Ireland. Switzerland isn't an EEA member state but the law treats it as one for these purposes.

Austria	Belgium	Bulgaria
Croatia	Cyprus	Czechia
Denmark	Estonia	Finland
France	Germany	Greece
Hungary	Iceland	Italy
Latvia	Liechtenstein	Lithuania
Luxembourg	Malta	Netherlands
Norway	Poland	Portugal
Romania	Slovakia	Slovenia
Spain	Sweden	Switzerland

41.5 European Union (Withdrawal Agreement) Act 2020, s1A(1)-(3),(6) – 'implementation period', 'IP completion day'

41.6 Immigration rules, Appendix EU, EU 11A, EU12, EU 14, EU 14A, Annex 1 – 'EEA citizen', 'family member of a qualifying British citizen', 'family member of a relevant EEA citizen', 'relevant person of Northern Ireland', 'specified date'

T41.1 EEA 2(1) – 'EEA national', 'EEA State'

EU family members arriving after 31 December 2020

41.7 If you are a family member of an EUSS applicant who arrived in the UK after 31 December 2020 you could enter the UK:

(a) on or before 30 June 2021 using an EEA family permit. You could get this permit if you had a derivative right to reside or the right to reside as an EEA family member (paras 41.39-51) provided that relationship existed before 1 January 2021 or

(b) before or after 30 June 2021 using an EUSS family permit granted on the basis that you are a family member (table 41.2).

The distinction is important because an EUSS family permit does not usually count as qualifying right to reside (paras 41.16-17). The situations described above should be taken only as a broad summary.

Time limit for applications

41.8 The scheme opened on 30 March 2019. Your application is on time if it was made:

(a) on or before 29 March 2022 using your 'Surinder Singh' rights and either:

- you are the dependent child, parent or grandparent of the British citizen you accompany (or their spouse/civil partner) or
- your relationship with the British citizen began before 1 February 2020 or

(b) on or before 30 June 2021 in any other case.

Late applications

41.9 If you didn't apply before the time limit you may be in the UK unlawfully and you should get advice immediately from an IAA registered adviser [www] about making a late application. You must have 'reasonable grounds' for missing the deadline and can't apply after 8 August 2023 if you are a 'Zambrano' carer (para 41.51).

EU settled status and pre-settled status

41.10 If your application is successful you get:

(a) indefinite leave to enter/remain ('settled status') or

(b) limited leave to enter/remain ('pre-settled status').

EU settled and pre-settled are kinds of leave with access to public funds. You can use the online service to view, prove and share your settled or pre-settled status with others [www].

41.11 You get EU settled status once you have completed five years continuous lawful residence and certain other conditions are met (in this case the rules in chapter 40 apply). You get pre-settled status if you have not yet completed the five-year qualification period (and in this case the rules in this chapter apply).

41.8-9 Immigration Rules, Appendix EU (Family Permit)
www.gov.uk/find-an-immigration-adviser

41.10-11 Immigration Rules Appendix EU, EU2, EU3, EU11, EU12, EU14

Rights to benefit while you wait for an EUSS decision

41.12 If you made a late application which has been accepted, your rights to benefit are the same as a person who has pre-settled status (para 41.14). You can claim benefit once you have confirmation your late application has been accepted (ADM memo 30/20, HB circular A10/2021).

Who can get benefit

41.13 This section explains when you are entitled to benefit if:

(a) you have EU pre-settled status (para 41.10) or

(b) your EUSS application has been accepted but not yet decided (para 41.12).

If you have EU settled status your rights to benefit are described in chapter 40.

EU pre-settled status and entitlement to benefit

41.14 If you have EU pre-settled status you are entitled to benefit if:

(a) you have a qualifying right to reside (paras 41.16-17), or possibly in certain other cases and

(b) either you are habitually resident or are exempt from the habitual residence test.

If you are a couple, see paras 41.11-17 for how all these rules apply to you.

Who is exempt from the habitual residence test

41.15 You are exempt from the habitual residence test if your EEA right to reside:

(a) is as a worker, frontier worker or self-employed person (paras 41.18-22)

(b) is a right of permanent residence acquired through retirement (para 41.36)

(c) is as a 'family member' of a worker or self-employed person as defined in table 41.2(a)-(c)

(d) is a right of permanent residence as a family member which you acquired because the EEA national you accompanied:

- has retired or ceased working due to incapacity (paras 41.36-37) or
- has died (para 41.44) or

(e) is as a family member of a person from Northern Ireland (paras 41.6(c)).

You can also be exempt from the test for other reasons (para 40.39).

41.12 SI 2020/1209 regs 4, 6, 11

41.13 SI 2020/1309 sch 4 paras 1-4; UC 9(1),(2); PC 2(1),(2); HBW 10(1)-(3),(3B); HBP 10(1)-(3),(4A); CTRE(PR) 12(2),(3),(5)

41.14 UC 9(4)(a)-(c),(ca)-(cc); PC 2(4)(za)-(zf); HBW 10(3B)(za)-(zf); HBP 10(4A)(za)-(zf); CTRE(PR) 12(5)(a)-(c),(ca)-(cc)

EEA qualifying rights to reside

41.16 All the EEA rights to reside described in the rest of this chapter help you qualify for benefit except:

(a) the right to reside as a jobseeker or as a family member of a jobseeker (para 41.30)

(b) the right to reside as a 'Zambrano carer' (para 41.51)

(c) the right to reside as an EUSS family permit holder (para 41.7) or

(d) EU pre-settled status on its own or with (a), (b) or (c).

Except as described in para 41.17, these exclusions are lawful and don't usually constitute unlawful discrimination (SSWP v AT).

Who can get benefit with a non-qualifying right to reside

41.17 If you have a non-qualifying right to reside you may still be able to get benefit if:

(a) you have pre-settled status without a qualifying right to reside and it is the only way you can 'live in dignified conditions' (SSWP v AT, ADM Memo 06/24) or

(b) you arrived on an EUSS family permit as a partner but have separated due to domestic abuse in circumstances where you otherwise qualify for the domestic abuse concession (para 40.34) (GA v SSWP).

EEA self-employed and worker status

41.18 This section describes who has the right to reside as a self-employed person or a worker and how that status can be retained during sickness, unemployment, etc.

Self-employed people

41.19 You have the right to reside if you are an EEA national and are engaged in self-employed business in the UK. Your self-employment must be 'genuine and effective', and have actually begun, but the ten-hour threshold (para 41.25) doesn't apply. Your self-employed status continues even if you have no current work, provided you continue to look for it (SSWP v AL).

41.20 Marginal or low-income activities such as selling the Big Issue may constitute genuine and effective self-employment (Bristol CC v FV). But low earnings coupled with substantial benefits and lack of business development may not be sufficient (DV v HMRC). The fact that you haven't registered your business with HMRC doesn't mean you aren't self-employed even though you have a legal obligation to do so (CH/3213/2007).

41.16 SSWP v AT (UC) [2023] EWCA Civ 1307

41.17 GA v SSWP (UC) [2024] UKUT 380 (AAC)

41.19 EEA 4(1)(b), 6(1) – 'qualified person', 14(1); SSWP v AL [2010] UKUT 451 (AAC)

41.20 Bristol CC v FV (HB) [2011] UKUT 494 (AAC); DV v HMRC (CHB) [2017] UKUT 155 (AAC)

Workers

41.21 You have the right to reside as a 'worker' if you are an EEA national in paid employment in the UK provided your work meets the minimum requirements (paras 41.23-25).

Frontier workers

41.22 You are a frontier worker if you are a worker or self-employed in the UK, but you are not 'predominantly resident' here. You can retain your frontier worker status in a similar way to a worker while you are temporarily out of work.

Deciding worker status

41.23 To decide whether you are a worker the DWP applies a two-tier test:

(a) the DWP considers you a worker/self-employed (ADM C1487) if your average earnings were at least £1,048 per month/£242 per week (the national insurance primary threshold) for three consecutive months immediately before you claimed UC or

(b) if (a) doesn't apply, it decides according to your individual circumstances by considering:

- whether you are exercising your EU free movement rights (ADM C1495-96), and
- if you are, whether you are engaged in 'remunerative' work which is 'effective and genuine' and not 'on such a small scale to be purely marginal and ancillary'.

Test (a) has no basis in law, so (b) must be properly considered before deciding you aren't a worker (RF v LB Lambeth).

41.24 'Remunerative' has its ordinary meaning: payment for services you provide. The following factors are relevant to determining whether your work is 'effective and genuine' (ADM para C1499):

(a) the period of employment

(b) the number of hours worked

(c) the level of earnings and

(d) whether the work is regular or erratic.

41.25 The number of hours worked is not conclusive, but it is relevant: CH/3733/2007. Ten hours per week can be enough (Rinner-Kuhn) but may be insufficient when the other factors are considered – and not doing ten hours does not automatically exclude you. The factors must always be considered together. Part-time or low paid work is not necessarily marginal or ancillary even if it means you need to claim UC. For example, working three hours a day, five days a week for four months (ADM C1501 and example 4). If you work full time (other than a fixed-term contract) you can acquire worker status in as little as two weeks (Tarola v MSP).

41.21 EEA 4(1)(a), 6(1) – 'qualified person', 14(1)

41.22 European Union (Withdrawal Agreement) Act 2020, s.8; SI 2020/1213, regs 3, 4, 5, 6
UC 9(4)(cb),(cc); HBW 10(3B)(ze),(zf); HBP 10(4A)(ze),(zf); CTRE(PR) 12(5)(cb),(cc)

41.23-24 EEA 4(1)(a); RF v LB Lambeth (HB) [2019] UKUT 52 (AAC)

41.25 EEA 4(1)(a); Rinner-Kuhn Case 171/88, [1989] EOR 2734; Tarola v Minister for Social Protection Case C-483/17

Retained worker/self-employed status: temporary incapacity for work

41.26 You retain your EEA worker/self-employed status if you are temporarily unable to work due to sickness or injury. What counts as being temporary isn't defined and there is no set maximum period. Provided your incapacity isn't permanent and there is a realistic prospect you can return to work in the foreseeable future your worker status is retained (LM v HMRC, De Brito v SSHD). You do not have to show you have 'limited capability for work' (para 4.15) – the test is whether you would be able to do the work you were doing (CIS/4304/2007, (HK v SSWP). If your incapacity is permanent see para 41.37.

Retained worker/self-employed status: pregnancy and childbirth

41.27 If you are a worker and stop working because of pregnancy or recent childbirth you retain your worker/self-employed status as follows:

(a) as a worker, while you are still under contract, even if your leave is unpaid (CIS/4237/2007)

(b) as a worker, if you gave up work or seeking work due to the physical constraints of the late stages of pregnancy or the aftermath of childbirth, provided you start work/seeking work again within a 'reasonable period' after the birth – this usually means up to 52 weeks, starting with 11 weeks before your due date (Saint Prix v SSWP, SSWP v SFF)

(c) as self-employed, if you stop work for maternity leave provided you intend to resume your business (CIS/1042/2008).

Retained worker status: vocational training

41.28 You retain your worker/self-employed status while undertaking vocational training related to your previous employment (or any work if there is no work available that is reasonably equivalent to your last job).

Retained worker status: registered unemployed

41.29 You retain your worker/self-employed status during a period of registered unemployment:

(a) for up to six months if you were employed (in the UK) for less than a year (which could have been for as little as two weeks: para 41.25) or

(b) without time limit if you were employed for at least a year.

The one year's employment need not be continuous (SSWP v MM). Small gaps (up to three months) between leaving work and registering can be ignored (SSWP v MK). You can register as unemployed by making a claim for UC, new-style JSA or national insurance credits (although it is not strictly necessary you qualify for these (CIS 184/2008)).

41.26 EEA 6(2)(a),(4)(a); De Brito v SSHD [2012] EWCA Civ 709
LM v HMRC (CHB) [2016] UKUT 389 (AAC); HK v SSWP [ESA] [2017] UKUT 421 (AAC)

41.27 Saint Prix v SSWP [2012] UKSC 49, [2013] 1 All ER 752, [2014] AACR 18
SSWP v SFF [2015] UKUT 502 (AAC) reported as [2016] AACR 16

41.28 EEA 6(2)(d),(e),(4)(d),(e)

41.29 EEA 6(2)(b),(c),(3),(4)(b),(c),(4A); SI 2020/1309, sch 4 para 4(e)
SSWP v MM [2015] UKUT 128 (AAC); SSWP v MK [2013] UKUT 163 (AAC)

EEA jobseekers

41.30 You are an 'EEA jobseeker' if you have a period of registered unemployment that started immediately after:

(a) you entered the UK (without work) or

(b) six months as a registered jobseeker if you hadn't worked in the UK for at least a year when you stopped working.

Your jobseeker status continues for a maximum period of 91 days if you can show you have 'genuine prospects of work' (ADM C1403-50). But if you have EU pre-settled status (para 41.10) you can continue to live in the UK lawfully after your right to reside as a jobseeker has expired.

The genuine prospects of work test

41.31 The 'genuine prospects of work test' only applies to EEA jobseekers. It doesn't apply if you had worked in the UK for at least a year before becoming unemployed – in this case you retain your worker status for long as you are registered unemployed (KH v Bury MBC, ADM memo 31/20). This rule is confirmed in the modified EEA regulations.

The right of permanent residence

41.32 This section describes who has an EEA right of permanent residence. A different set of rules applies to EEA family members (para 41.41).

41.33 Even though the right is 'permanent' you lose it if:

(a) you failed to apply to the EU settlement scheme by the deadline (para 41.8)

(b) you are absent from the UK for more than two years.

Right of permanent residence: the five-year rule

41.34 You have a permanent right to reside if you are an EEA national with five years continuous residence using one or more of the following rights:

(a) a worker or a retained worker

(b) a self-employed person

(c) a jobseeker

(d) a self-sufficient person or

(e) a student.

You can also count your first three months residence in the UK.

41.30-31 EEA 6(1) – 'jobseeker', 6(5)-(10); SI 2020/1309, sch 4 para 4(e)
KH v Bury MBC and SSWP (HB) [2020] UKUT 50 (AAC)

41.33 Immigration and Social Security Co-ordination (EU Withdrawal) Act 2020, sch 1 para 2(2); SI 2020/1309, reg 83, sch 4 paras 1, 2; EEA 15(3)

41.34 EEA 6(1) – definition: 'qualified person', 13, 14(1), 15(1)(a)

41.35 A period of residence counts as 'continuous' despite a period of absence from the UK if:

(a) in any one year, the total length of your absence(s) is no more than six months (or longer for compulsory military service) or

(b) a single absence of not more than 12 months – so long as the reason is pregnancy, childbirth, serious illness, study, vocational training, a posting in another country, or some other important reason.

Retirement due to old age

41.36 You have a permanent right of residence (ADM C1799-1802) if:

(a) you have retired as a worker before or after reaching pension age, or as a self-employed person after reaching pension age: and

- you worked in the UK for at least 12 months before you retired; and
- you had continuous residence in the UK for more than three years before you retired; or

(b) you retired after reaching pension age (whether you have worked or not) and your spouse/civil partner is a British citizen.

Retirement due to permanent incapacity

41.37 You have a right of permanent residence due to incapacity (ADM C1799-1802) if:

(a) you stopped working due to permanent incapacity and

(b) either:

- your incapacity is the result of an accident at work or an occupational disease which entitles you to ESA, SDA or industrial injuries benefit or private pension
- you had continuous residence in the UK for more than two years immediately before you stopped working or
- your spouse/civil partner is a British citizen.

Retired workers: qualifying periods of work and UK residence

41.38 A period of inactivity in which you are unable to work due to illness, accident, or some other reason 'not of [your] own making' or period in which you retained your worker/self-employed status is counted as employment/self-employment. The residence conditions are counted in the same way as para 41.35.

41.35 EEA 3(2)

41.36 EEA 5(2),(6), 15(1)(c)

41.37 EEA 5(3),(6), 15(1)(c)

41.38 EEA 3(2), 5(7)

EEA family member rights

41.39 This section describes who has the right to reside as an EEA family member and how you can retain your family member rights when the relationship ends.

41.40 You are an EEA family member if you satisfy the conditions in table 41.2. You do not need to be an EEA national yourself (although you can be). Your right to reside lasts for as long as you remain a family member. If you aren't married or in a civil partnership your family member rights usually end when you separate unless you have acquired permanent residence or meet the conditions to retain them (paras 41.42-44).

Right of permanent residence: family members

41.41 You get a right of permanent residence as a family member if:

(a) you are a non-EEA national who has resided in the UK for a continuous period of five years as an EEA family member

(b) you have resided in the UK for a continuous period of five years as a qualified person or as an EEA family member and at the end of that period you were a family member who had a retained right of residence (para 41.42)

(c) the EEA national you accompany has the right of permanent residence through retirement or incapacity (paras 41.36-37) and:

- you were their family member at the point they stopped working and
- at that point you enjoyed the right to reside on the basis that you were their family member or

(d) the family member you accompany is a worker or self-employed person who has died and:

- you were living with them immediately before their death and
- they had continuous residence in the UK for at least the two years immediately before their death or they died because of an accident at work or occupational disease.

Table 41.2 **Who is an EEA family member**

You are an EEA family member if you accompany an EEA national who is self-employed, a worker, a student or a self-sufficient person and you:

(a) are their spouse/civil partner (until divorce/dissolution, not separation or estrangement)

(b) are a direct descendant of that person (e.g. a child or grandchild) or of their spouse or civil partner, and you are

41.40 EEA 7, 8, 14(2)

41.41 EEA 15(1)(b),(d)-(f)

T41.2 EEA 7(1)-(3), 8(2)-(7)

- aged under 21 or
- dependent on them or their spouse or civil partner (for example, because you are studying or disabled)

(c) are a dependent direct relative in ascending line (e.g. a parent or grandparent) or of their spouse or civil partner or

(d) are some other family member (an 'extended family member') who has been admitted to the UK on the basis that you are:

- their partner (in the benefit sense)
- a dependent household member of that person in their country of origin or
- a relative who is so ill that you strictly require personal care from that person.

Note: If the EEA national you accompany is a student without any other right to reside you are only treated as their family member if you are their spouse/civil partner or dependent child (i.e. under 18 or dependent in other ways).

Retained family status: termination of marriage or civil partnership

41.42 You retain your family member status if:

(a) your marriage/civil partnership to the EEA national is terminated

(b) your former spouse/civil partner had the right to reside at least until the termination proceedings began and

(c) either:

- before the termination started (which must occur when your spouse/civil partner is in the UK), the marriage/civil partnership must have lasted for at least three years with both of you living in the UK for at least one of those
- you have custody of the EEA national's child or
- your continued right of residence is warranted by particularly difficult circumstances (e.g. if you experienced domestic abuse during the marriage) and

(d) either:

- you are not an EEA national yourself, but you would be a worker, a self-employed person or a self-sufficient person if you were or
- you are the family member of such a person (in the bullet above).

If you arrived on an EUSS family permit (para 41.7) and have separated due to domestic abuse, see para 41.17.

41.42 EEA 10(1),(5),(6); SI 2020/1309, sch 4 para 4(j)

Retained family status: a child in education and their parent

41.43 You retain your family member status if:

(a) you are the EEA national's child or grandchild (or the child or grandchild of their spouse or civil partner)

(b) the EEA national you accompanied was using one of the rights (a)-(e) in para 41.34

(c) you were attending a course of education in the UK when they left the UK or died and

(d) you are still attending that course.

You retain your family member status if you are the parent with custody of that child.

Retained family status: bereavement

41.44 You retain your family member status if:

(a) the EEA national you accompanied was a worker, self-employed, self-sufficient, a student or had a right of permanent residence

(b) you were resident in the UK for at least a year immediately before their death and

(c) either:

- you are not an EEA national yourself but if you were you would be a worker, a self-employed person or a self-sufficient person or
- you are the family member of such a person (in the sub-bullet above).

Other EEA rights to reside

41.45 This section describes other EEA rights to reside you may have other than acquired through working, looking for work or as an EEA family member. These are:

(a) as a 'primary carer' (para 41.52) of a child/young person ('derivative' rights to reside)

(b) as a student or

(c) as a self-sufficient person.

Derivative rights: primary carer of a child

41.46 You may have the right to reside as the primary carer of a child if:

(a) you are the primary carer of an EEA worker's child who is in education

(b) you are the primary carer of an EEA national child or

(c) you are the non-EEA parent who is the primary carer of a British child.

These rights only apply if none of the others in this chapter do unless your only right to reside is as a jobseeker (para 41.30) (Sandwell MBC v KK). See also para 41.43.

41.43 EEA 10(1),(3),(4)

41.44 EEA 10(1),(2),(6)

41.46 EEA 16(1)-(6),(7)(c)
Sandwell MBC v KK and SSWP (HB) [2022] 123 (AAC)

41.47 These rights are in the EEA regulations but sometimes referred to by the legal cases that established them (e.g. 'Ibrahim'). If (a) or (b) apply you are entitled to benefit if you are habitually resident. If (c) applies you aren't entitled to benefit until such time as you acquire EU settled status, but you may qualify for other financial support from social services (Sanneh v SSWP, Yekini v LB Southwark).

Primary carer of an EEA worker's child in education ('Ibrahim/Teixeira' right)

41.48 You have a right to reside if:

(a) you are the 'primary carer' (para 41.52) of a child/young person

(b) the child (now or at any time in the past) has resided with either one of their parents when that parent was a worker or self-employed person

(c) the child is in 'education' in the UK (para 41.54) and

(d) the child could not continue their education here if you left the UK.

The parent must have been in paid employment or engaged in business as self-employed – retained worker/self-employed status isn't enough and it must have been at a time when their country was a member of the EU. For guidance see ADM C1827-39.

41.49 Your right to reside continues until the child completes their education or reaches 18 but it can continue beyond 18 if they continue to need your 'presence and care' to complete it (ADM para C1835).

Primary carer of an EEA national child ('Chen' right)

41.50 You have the right to reside if:

(a) you are the primary carer of an EEA national child aged under 18

(b) the EEA national child resides in the UK as a self-sufficient person (para 41.55) and

(c) the EEA national child would be unable to continue to live in the UK if you (the primary carer) were to leave for an indefinite period.

To be self-sufficient the child must have comprehensive health insurance – but this includes registration for NHS treatment (para 41.59). After five years you may get the right of permanent residence until your settled status is confirmed (para 41.41).

41.47 UC 9(2),(3)(c)(ii); PC 2(2),(3)(bb),(3A)(b); HBW 10(3),(3A)(bb),(3AA)(b); HBP 10(3),(4)(bb),(4ZA)(b); CTRE(PR) 12(3),(4)(b),(4A)(c)
Sanneh v SSWP [2015] EWCA Civ 49, [2016] QB 455; Yekini v LB Southwark [2014] EWHC 2096 (Admin)

41.48 EEA 16(1),(3),(4),(7)(b),(d); SI 2020/1309, sch 4 para 4(j)
Teixeira v Lambeth LBC and SSHD Case C-480/08
Harrow LBC v Ibrahim and SSHD Case C-310/08

41.49 EEA 16(7)(a)

41.50 EEA 16(1),(2)
Chen and others v Home Secretary [2004] EUECJ C-200/02

Non-EEA parent of British child ('Zambrano carer' right)

41.51 You have a right to reside if:

(a) you are a non-EEA national who is the primary carer (para 41.52) of a British child

(b) that child was resident in the UK before 31 December 2020 and

(c) that child would have been unable to continue living in the UK or EEA if you left the UK for an indefinite period (or if you both did if you share care).

If you share the care equally with someone else who acquired this right before you, the rule in (c) applies as if they are the sole carer.

Primary carer

41.52 For each of the 'derivative rights' above you are the child's 'primary carer' if:

(a) you are their 'direct relative' or legal guardian and

(b) either you have primary responsibility for their care, or you share responsibility equally with one other person. In this case the rule in para 41.48(d) is read as if the child couldn't continue their education if you both left the UK. But if that person's only right to reside in UK is as a primary carer and they acquired it before you became a joint carer, the rule is read in the normal way.

Deciding who is the child's primary carer isn't solely based on the financial contribution made.

Direct relative

41.53 The law doesn't define 'direct relative' but it probably means parent, grandparent, etc. DWP guidance (ADM C1832) states it doesn't include grandparent, but the law doesn't say this.

Being in education

41.54 Nursery education doesn't count but any education received that 'is equivalent to' compulsory education (such as a reception class) does (ADM para C1835). It doesn't matter that the child started their education after the EEA national parent finished work – only that the child lived with that parent during a time when they were a worker (ADM para C1833.2).

Self-sufficient persons

41.55 If you are an EEA national who entered the UK or settled here on the basis that you were self-sufficient (i.e. you had your own resources (VP v SSWP) you have the right to reside if you

(a) have enough resources not to be an 'unreasonable burden' on the benefits system and

(b) have comprehensive sickness insurance (para 41.59).

41.51 EEA 16(5),(8),(10)
Zambrano v Office national de l'emploi [2010] ECJ C-34/09

41.52 EEA 16(8)-(11); SI 2020/1309, sch 4 para 4(j)

41.53 EEA 16(8)(a)

41.54 EEA 16(7)(a)

41.55 EEA 4(1)(c),(3), 6(1) – 'qualified person', 14(1)
VP v SSWP (JSA) [2014] UKUT 32 (AAC)

41.56 The fact that your income is so low that you qualify for UC does not automatically mean you are not self-sufficient (although in most cases you will be) and the DWP has discretion to decide otherwise given your circumstances (ADM C1729.2). The fact that you have been able to manage without claiming UC until now is a relevant consideration in deciding whether you are an 'unreasonable burden' as is the length of time you are likely to be claiming (HBGM para C4.123). For example, if your funds have been temporarily disrupted the decision maker may decide you are self-sufficient.

Students

41.57 You have the right to reside as a student if:

(a) you are currently studying on a course in the UK

(b) you signed a declaration at the beginning of the course that you were able to support yourself without social assistance (which means UC and any legacy benefit)

(c) the declaration was true at the time it was signed and for the foreseeable future and

(d) you have comprehensive sickness insurance for the UK (para 41.59).

41.58 In practice, this means you are unlikely to get benefit as an EEA student unless your circumstances have changed since your course started (e.g. your funds have been disrupted). But you must also meet the other student conditions (table 3.1).

Comprehensive sickness insurance

41.59 The requirement for comprehensive sickness insurance is met if you were registered for NHS treatment (VI v HMRC). If you weren't registered, you are still likely to satisfy this condition if you receive a retirement or invalidity pension from an EEA member state (ADM C1730).

41.56 EEA 4(4)(b)

41.57 EEA 4(1)(d),(3), 6(1) – 'qualified person', 14(1)

41.58 EEA 4(4)(b)

41.59 VI v Commissioners for HMRC [2021] EUECJ C-247/20, overturning Ahmad v Home Secretary [2014] EWCA Civ 988

Chapter 42 **HB subsidy**

HB and CTR summary

42.1 This chapter describes the subsidy and grants councils get from the government for administering HB and CTR. For the separate rules about grants towards discretionary housing payments, see paras 31.20-23.

HB payments and administration

42.2 The DWP pays councils:

(a) an annual amount of subsidy towards the HB they pay (para 42.5) and

(b) an annual grant towards administration costs (staffing, accommodation etc).

The administration grant is augmented by one-off grants in years in which councils have new burdens placed on them, for example relating to welfare reforms, statistics and anti-fraud measures.

CTR payments and administration

42.3 Government support towards CTR payments and administration is included in the central government grant to councils and no amount is specified.

Subsidy claims, payments and overpayments

42.4 HB subsidy is calculated for each financial year and paid in instalments with a final balancing payment after the year ends. Councils have to claim on time, provide the information and evidence required, and have their final claim certified or assured by their auditor by 30 November following the end of the year. The DWP can recover overpaid subsidy (R (Isle of Anglesey County Council) v SSWP, R (LB Lambeth) v SSWP).

42.2 SSAA 140A, 140B(2),(4)

42.3 SSAA 140B(4A); HB(SO) 12(1)(b), sch 1; SI 2023/1040
www.gov.uk/government/publications/final-local-government-finance-report-2023-to-2024 (para 4.25)

42.4 SSAA 140C; HB(SO) 2-10
R (Isle of Anglesey County Council) v SSWP [2003] EWHC 2518 Admin
R (LB Lambeth) v SSWP [2005] EWHC 637 Admin

HB subsidy

42.5 The general rule is that the DWP pays subsidy equal to 100% of all 'correctly paid' HB paid in the year. This includes rebates, allowances and payments on account. It also includes payments made in the year for an earlier year (but each amount of HB can only get subsidy once). Exceptions are given in the rest of this chapter.

Subsidy and decision-making

42.6 When councils make decisions about HB, they have to apply HB law fairly, objectively and impartially. If a decision requires the council to use its judgment, it mustn't allow the subsidy rules to affect this. But if a decision allows the council to use its discretion, it may take its own financial position (including the subsidy rules) into account (R v Brent LBC HBRB ex parte Connery).

Subsidy law and guidance

42.7 The legal framework for HB subsidy is in sections 140A-140G of the Social Security Administration Act 1992, and the details are in the Income-related Benefits (Subsidy to Authorities) Order 1998, SI 1998 No. 562. DWP guidance is in the regularly updated HB Subsidy Guidance Manual; HB subsidy claims – local authority best practice guide; and the 'S' series of circulars [www].

Overpayments of HB

Overpayment subsidy categories

42.8 For subsidy purposes, HB overpayments fall into the categories shown in table 42.1. The categories qualify for different rates of subsidy, and councils decide which category applies to each overpayment.

42.9 The rules about which HB overpayments are recoverable don't always correspond to the subsidy categories. In broad terms, HB overpayments are recoverable unless they were due to official error or delay and the claimant or payee couldn't reasonably have realised they were being overpaid (paras 36.10-12).

42.5 SSAA 140B(1)-(3); HB(SO) 11(2) – 'qualifying expenditure', 13(1)(a),(b)

42.6 R v Brent LBC ex parte Connery (1989) 22 HLR 40, [1990] 2 All ER 353 (QBD)

42.7 www.gov.uk/government/collections/housing-benefit-for-local-authorities-subsidy-circulars

Table 42.1 **Overpayments subsidy categories**

Subsidy category	Amount of subsidy
(a) Departmental error overpayments	100%
(b) Authority error or delay overpayments	100%, 40% or nil
(c) Claimant or third party error overpayments	40%
(d) Fraudulent overpayments	40%
(e) Overpayments resulting from a court decisions	40%
(f) Payment on account overpayments	100%
(g) Duplicate payment overpayments	25%
(h) Technical overpayments	Nil
(i) Any other overpayments	40%

Departmental error overpayments

42.10 A departmental error overpayment means one caused by a mistake of fact or law (whether in the form of an act or omission):

(a) by the DWP or HMRC or someone providing services to them or

(b) in a decision of a First-tier or Upper Tribunal.

It doesn't include an overpayment to which the claimant, someone acting on their behalf, or the payee materially contributed.

42.11 Subsidy is 100% of:

(a) the total departmental error overpayments in the year

(b) minus the total departmental error overpayments recovered in the year (whether they were overpaid in the year or in a previous year).

This means the council doesn't qualify for subsidy towards amounts it recovers.

Authority error or delay overpayments

42.12 An authority error or delay overpayment means one caused by:

(a) a mistake of fact or law (whether in the form of an act or omission) by the council or

(b) a delay by the council in making a decision about a change of circumstances (so long as the delay wasn't caused by waiting for further information or evidence).

It doesn't include an overpayment to which the claimant, someone acting on their behalf, or the payee materially contributed.

T42.1 HB(SO) 11(2), 13(1), 18(1)-(3), 19(1)(e)-(i)

42.10 HB(SO) 18(4)

42.11 HB(SO) 18(1)(b)(i)

42.12 HB(SO) 18(6),(6ZA)

42.13 Subsidy depends on the total authority error or delay overpayments in the year, calculated as a percentage of the total HB paid in the year (HB that qualifies for 100% subsidy). If this percentage is:

(a) not more than 0.48% (the lower threshold), 100% subsidy is paid on all authority error or delay overpayments in the year

(b) more than 0.48% but not more than 0.54% (the higher threshold), 40% subsidy is paid on all these overpayments

(c) more than 0.54%, no subsidy is paid on any of these overpayments.

In cases (a) and (b), the council qualifies for this subsidy even towards amounts it recovers.

Example: Subsidy for authority error or delay overpayments

A council's annual expenditure on correctly paid HB is £10,000,000. So its lower threshold is £48,000 and its higher threshold is £54,000 for that year (para 42.13). If the total authority error or delay overpayments in that year are:

- £45,000, the council gets subsidy of 100% of this, which is £45,000
- £50,000, the council gets subsidy of 40% of this, which is £20,000
- £55,000, the council gets no subsidy for this.

Claimant or third party error overpayments

42.14 A claimant or third party error overpayment means one caused by the claimant, someone acting on their behalf, or their landlord/agent (whether or not the HB is paid to them) failing to provide required information or evidence. Subsidy is 40% of the total of these overpayments in the year. The council qualifies for this subsidy even towards amounts it recovers.

Fraudulent overpayments

42.15 A fraudulent overpayment means one where the claimant has been found guilty of an offence, made an admission under caution, or agreed to pay a penalty as an alternative to prosecution. Subsidy is 40% in these cases.

Overpayments resulting from a court decision

42.16 An overpayment can be caused by a court interpreting the law differently from the DWP, HMRC, a tribunal or the council. Subsidy is 40% in these cases.

42.13 HB(SO) 18(1)(e),(6A)

42.14 HB(SO) 18(1)(b)(iii)(d),(2),(4A)

42.15 HB(SO) 18(5),(5A)

42.16 HB(SO) 18(1)(b)(iii),(4)

Payment on account overpayments

42.17 A payment on account overpayment means one caused when a payment on account is greater than the amount of HB a claimant qualifies for (para 34.54). Subsidy is 100% of:

(a) the total payment on account overpayments in the year

(b) minus the total payment on account overpayments recovered in the year (whether they were overpaid in the year or in a previous year).

Duplicate payment overpayments

42.18 A duplicate payment overpayment means one caused when a duplicate payment of HB is issued because the first one was (or was alleged to have been) lost, stolen or not received, but the first one is then cashed. Subsidy is 25% of:

(a) the total duplicate payment overpayments in the year

(b) minus the total duplicate payments recovered in the year (whether they were issued in the year or in a previous year).

Technical overpayments

42.19 A technical overpayment means one caused because a council tenant's liability for rent ends, but HB has already been credited to their rent account for a period after that. No subsidy is paid on these overpayments.

Other HB subsidy rules

Exempt accommodation

42.20 Exempt accommodation is a specific kind of supported accommodation and is defined in table 13.1(a). Paras 42.21-22 explain how the council can receive reduced subsidy if it refers the claimant's rent to the rent officer (para 13.25). However, no referral is made (and so the council gets full subsidy) if:

(a) in most cases, the landlord is a registered housing association (para 12.26) or

(b) the claimant has a registered rent or similar old tenancy (para 12.45).

Exempt accommodation: general subsidy rule

42.21 When a referral is made to the rent officer, there is a subsidy limit equal to:

(a) the claim-related rent (CRR) (table 12.4(d))

(b) minus the standard amount for meals if the claimant's rent includes them (table 15.5).

Except as in para 42.22, no subsidy is paid on the HB attributable to the excess (i.e. any amount attributable to the council agreeing to an eligible rent above the subsidy limit).

42.17 HB(SO) 18(1)(f),(7B)

42.18 HB(SO) 18(1)(a)

42.19 HB(SO) 18(7),(7A)

42.20 HB(SO) 16(1),(2), sch 4 para 3

42.21 HB(SO) 13(1)(b), 16(1), sch 4 paras 7, 17 – 'ineligible amounts'

Additional subsidy when the claimant's rent is protected

42.22 If one of the protections in para 10.18 applies, 60% subsidy is paid on the excess described above. If the claimant's HB is less than their eligible rent (e.g. because of the taper) the weekly HB is attributed first to the excess (and gets 60% subsidy), then to the remainder (and gets 100% subsidy).

Examples: Subsidy for exempt accommodation

1. Claimant on full HB

Kai lives in exempt accommodation and is on UC and HB. His landlord charges £330 pw, and the rent officer gives the council a claim-related rent of £300 pw. The council decides Kai's eligible rent is £330 pw because he has limited capability for work and is therefore a protected occupier (para 10.28). Because he is on UC, he gets HB of £330 pw, which exceeds the rent officer's figure by £30 pw.

- The eligible rent is £30 above the claim-related rent, so the first £30 of the HB award (HB attributable to the excess) gets reduced subsidy paid at 60% — £18.00
- £300 of the award remains (HB not attributable to the excess), and so gets subsidy paid at 100% — £300.00
- Total subsidy is therefore — £318.00

2. Claimant on partial HB

Kai gets a part-time job. His eligible rent is still £330 pw (and still exceeds the rent officer's figure by £30.00 pw) but his HB reduces to £270 per week.

- 60% subsidy is paid on HB attributable to the £30 excess — £18.00
- 100% subsidy is paid on the HB not attributable to the excess — £240.00
- Total subsidy is therefore — £258.00

Temporary accommodation

42.23 Temporary accommodation means accommodation provided by a council for people who are homeless or threatened with homelessness and is defined in para 42.24.

42.24 The accommodation can be any of the following types.

(a) 'board and lodging' means accommodation provided for a charge that includes some meals cooked or prepared and eaten on the premises or nearby, or accommodation in a hotel, guest house, lodging house or similar establishment. It excludes residential care homes (table 10.2) and hostels (para 12.28).

42.22 HB(SO) sch 4 paras 8, 10

42.23 HB(SO) 17(1)(a)-(c), 17A(1)(a)-(c), 17B(1)(a)-(c), 17C(1)(a)-(c)

42.24 HB(SO) 11(1) – 'board and lodging accommodation', 17(1)(b), 17A(1)(b), 17B(1)(b), 17C(1)(b)

(b) 'leased' – this means accommodation the landlord holds on a lease, but in the case of English councils, the lease must be for no longer than ten years and the accommodation must be held outside the council's Housing Revenue Account

(c) 'licenced' – this means accommodation the landlord holds other than as a lease such as a licence

(d) 'owned' – this means accommodation a registered housing association (not the council) owns.

42.25 Subsidy in these cases is limited as described in table 42.2. But if the accommodation also meets the definition of exempt accommodation, the rules in paras 42.20-22 apply instead. DWP guidance is in circular S1/2011.

Table 42.2 **Subsidy limits in temporary accommodation**

Weekly subsidy is limited to the maximum amount, or if lower the cap figure.

(a) Maximum amount

The January 2011 figure for one-bedroom self-contained accommodation if you live in:

- board and lodging
- licenced accommodation (non-self-contained)

90% of the January 2011 figure for accommodation of the appropriate size (para 42.26) if you live in:

- licenced accommodation (self-contained)
- leased accommodation
- accommodation owned by a registered housing association

(b) Cap figure

- £500 pw if you live in certain parts of London
- £375 pw if you live elsewhere

Notes

- January 2011 LHA figures for England and Wales are available in the National Archives [www]
- The £500 cap applies to the following BRMAs: Central London, Inner East London, Inner North London, Inner South East London, Inner South West London, Inner West London and Outer South West London.
- For subsidy purposes, accommodation is self-contained if you and your household have exclusive use of a kitchen, bathroom and toilet.

42.25 HB(SO) 17B(1)(d), 17C(1)(d)

T42.2 HB(SO) 13(1)(b), 17(2),(3), 17A(2),(3), 17B(2),(3), 17C(2),(3), sch 8
https://tinyurl.com/LHA-England-Jan-2011
https://tinyurl.com/LHA-Wales-2011

42.26 In the table, the 'appropriate size' depends on the number of rooms, counting bedrooms and living rooms, in the claimant's accommodation (not the size of their household). If their accommodation contains:

(a) one or two rooms, the appropriate size is one-bedroom self-contained accommodation

(b) three rooms, the appropriate size is a two-bedroom dwelling

(c) four rooms, the appropriate size is a three-bedroom dwelling

(d) five or six rooms, the appropriate size is a four-bedroom dwelling

(e) seven or more rooms, the appropriate size is a five-bedroom dwelling (in January 2011 there were LHA figures for five-bedroom dwellings).

Local schemes

42.27 Many councils run a local scheme that disregards war pensions in full (paras 21.24-25). In these cases:

(a) first calculate the council's annual subsidy, but including only the HB that would be awarded if it didn't run a local scheme

(b) then add an amount towards the local scheme – this equals:

- 75% of the additional HB awarded in the year as a result of the local scheme or
- if lower, 0.2% of the council's annual subsidy.

42.26 HB(SO) 17(3), 17A(3),(4), 17B(3), 17C(3),(4)

42.27 HB(SO) 12(1)(d),(4)

Appendix 1 **Legislation**

Universal Credit

Main primary legislation

The Welfare Reform Act 2012 (Part 1, Sections 96-97)

The Social Security Administration Act 1992 (Sections 71ZB-71ZH)

The Housing Act 1996 (Section 122)

Main secondary legislation

SI 2013/376	The Universal Credit Regulations 2013
SI 2013/380	The Universal Credit, Personal independence Payment, Jobseeker's Allowance and Employment and Support Allowance (Claims and Payments) Regulations 2013
SI 2013/381	The Universal Credit, Personal Independence Payment, Jobseeker's Allowance and Employment and Support Allowance (Decisions and Appeals) Regulations 2013
SI 2013/382	The Rent Officers (Universal Credit Functions) Order 2013
SI 2013/383	The Social Security (Payments on Account of Benefit) Regulations 2013
SI 2013/384	The Social Security (Overpayments and Recovery) Regulations 2013

Recent amending regulations: UC

SI 2024/536	The Universal Credit (Administrative Earnings Threshold) (Amendment) (No 2) Regulations 2024

State Pension Credit

Main primary legislation

The State Pension Credit Act 2002

The Social Security Administration Act 1992 (Section 71)

Main secondary legislation

SI 2002/1792	The State Pension Credit Regulations 2002
SI 1987/1968	The Social Security (Claims and Payments) Regulations 1987
SI 1999/991	The Social Security and Child Support (Decisions and Appeals) Regulations 1999
SI 1988/664	The Social Security (Payments on account, Overpayments and Recovery) Regulations 1988

Housing Benefit

Main primary legislation

The Social Security Contributions and Benefits Act 1992 (Sections 130, 130A, 134-137)

The Social Security Administration Act 1992 (Sections 75, 122C-122E, 134, 139A-140G)

The Housing Act 1996 (Section 122)

The Child Support, Pensions and Social Security Act 2000 (Sections 68, 71 and schedule 7)

The Welfare Reform Act (Sections 96-97)

Main secondary legislation

SI 2006/213	The Housing Benefit Regulations 2006
SI 2006/214	The Housing Benefit (Persons who have attained the qualifying age for state pension credit) Regulations 2006
SI 2006/217	The Housing Benefit and Council Tax Benefit (Consequential Provisions) Regulations 2006
SI 1997/1984	The Rent Officers (Housing Benefit Functions) Order
SI 1997/1995	The Rent Officers (Housing Benefit Functions) (Scotland) Order
SI 1998/562	The Income-related Benefits (Subsidy to Authorities) Order 1998
SI 2001/1002	The Housing Benefit and Council Tax Benefit (Decisions and Appeals) Regulations

Recent amending regulations: HB

SI 2024/1092	The Income-related Benefits (Subsidy to Authorities) Amendment Order 2024

Support for Mortgage Interest

Main primary legislation

The Welfare Reform and Work Act 2016 (Sections 18-21)

Main secondary legislation

SI 2017/725	The Loans for Mortgage Interest Regulations 2017

Discretionary Housing Payments

Main primary legislation

The Child Support, Pensions and Social Security Act 2000 (Sections 69, 70)

The Social Security (Scotland) Act 2018, Part 5 (Sections 88-93)

Main secondary legislation

SI 2001/1167	The Discretionary Financial Assistance Regulations

Common provisions (UC, SPC, SMI, HB)

Main primary legislation

The Social Security Administration Act 1992 (Sections 1, 5, 115-115D)

The Social Security Act 1998 (Part 1)

The Immigration and Asylum Act 1999 (Section 115)

Tribunals, Courts and Enforcement Act 2007 (Part 1, Chapters 1-2)

The Welfare Reform Act 2012 (Sections 33-36, 130-133)

Main secondary legislation

SI 2000/636	The Social Security (Immigration and Asylum) Consequential Amendments Regulations 2000
SI 2008/2685	The Tribunal Procedure (First-tier Tribunal) (Social Entitlement Chamber) Rules 2008
SI 2008/2698	The Tribunal Procedure (Upper Tribunal) Rules 2008
SI 2012/1483	Social Security (Information-sharing in relation to Welfare Services etc) Regulations 2012
SI 2014/1230	The Universal Credit (Transitional Provisions) Regulations 2014

Recent amending regulations: common provisions

SI 2024/604	The Welfare Reform Act 2012 (Commencement No. 31 and Savings and Transitional Provisions) (Amendment) Order 2024
SI 2024/611	The Social Security (State Pension Age Claimants: Closure of Tax Credits) (Amendment) Regulations 2024
SI 2024/919	The Social Security (Scotland) Act 2018 (Disability Assistance) (Consequential Amendments) Order 2024
SI 2024/964	The Social Security (Infected Blood Capital Disregard) (Amendment) Regulations 2024
SI 2025/3	The Social Security (Miscellaneous Amendments) Regulations 2025
SI 2025/5	The Rent Officers (Housing Benefit and Universal Credit Functions) (Modification) Order 2025
SI 20025/44	The Social Security (Income and Capital Disregards) (Amendment) Regulations 2025
SI 2025/227	The Social Security (Scotland) Act 2018 (Disability Assistance) (Consequential Amendments) Order 2025
SI 2025/295	The Social Security Benefits Up-Rating Order 2025

Council Tax Rebates

Main primary legislation

The Local Government Finance Act 1992 (Sections 13A, 80, Schedules 1A, 1B)

Main secondary legislation England

SI 2012/2885	The Council Tax Reduction Schemes (Prescribed Requirements) (England) Regulations 2012
SI 2012/2886	The Council Tax Reduction Schemes (Default Scheme) (England) Regulations 2012
SI 2013/501	Council Tax Reduction Schemes (Detection of Fraud and Enforcement) (England) Regulations 2013
SI 2009/2269	Valuation Tribunal for England (Council Tax and Rating Appeals) (Procedure) Regulations 2009
SI 2013/465	The Valuation Tribunal for England (Council Tax and Rating Appeals) (Procedure) (Amendment) Regulations 2013

Recent amending secondary legislation England: council tax and CTR

SI 2024/1007	The Council Tax (Prescribed Classes of Dwellings and Consequential Amendments) (England) Regulations 2024
SI 2025/39	The Council Tax Reduction Schemes (Prescribed Requirements) (England) (Amendment) Regulations 2025

Main secondary legislation Scotland

SSI 2021/249	The Council Tax Reduction (Scotland) Regulations 2021
SSI 2012/319	The Council Tax Reduction (State Pension Credit) (Scotland) Regulations 2012
SSI 2013/87	Council Tax (Information-sharing in relation to Council Tax Reduction) (Scotland) Regulations 2013
SSI 2022/364	The First-tier Tribunal for Scotland Local Taxation Chamber (Rules of Procedure) Regulations 2022

Recent amending secondary legislation Scotland: council tax and CTR

SSI 2024/230	The Council Tax Reduction (Scotland) Amendment (No. 2) Regulations 2024
SSI 2024/310	The Council Tax Reduction (Scotland) Amendment (No. 3) Regulations 2024
SSI 2024/311	The Disability Assistance (Scottish Adult Disability Living Allowance) (Consequential Amendment, Revocation and Saving Provision) Regulations 2024
SSI 2025/24	The Council Tax Reduction (Scotland) Amendment Regulations 2025

Main secondary legislation Wales

SI 2013/3029	The Council Tax Reduction Schemes and Prescribed Requirements (Wales) Regulations 2013
SI 2013/3035	The Council Tax Reduction Schemes (Default Scheme) (Wales) Regulations 2013
SI 2013/588	Council Tax Reduction Schemes (Detection of Fraud and Enforcement) (Wales) Regulations 2013
SI 2010/713	The Valuation Tribunal for Wales Regulations 2010
SI 2013/547	The Valuation Tribunal for Wales (Wales) (Amendment) Regulations 2013

Recent amending secondary legislation Wales: council tax and CTR

SI 2024/998	The Local Government Finance (Consequential and Miscellaneous Amendments and Revocations) (Secondary Legislation) (Wales) Regulations 2024
SI 2025/59	The Council Tax Reduction Schemes (Prescribed Requirements and Default Scheme) (Wales) (Amendment) Regulations 2025

Appendix 2 **Selected weekly benefit rates from April 2025**

Universal credit

Standard allowance

single under 25	£316.98
single aged 25 or over	£400.14
couple both under 25	£497.55
couple at least one aged 25 or over	£628.10

Child element

higher rate	£339.00
lower rate	£292.81

Disabled child addition

higher rate	£495.87
lower rate	£158.76

Work capability elements

LCW element	£158.76
LCWRA element	£423.27
Carer element	£201.68

Childcare costs element

maximum for one child	£1031.88
maximum for two or more children	£1768.94

State pension credit

Standard allowance

single person	£227.10
couple	£346.60
polygamous spouse	£119.50

Child allowance

higher rate	£78.10
lower rate	£67.42

Disabled child addition

higher rate	£114.12
lower rate	£36.54

Carer addition

claimant/partner/each	£46.40

Severe disability addition

single rate	£82.90
double rate	£165.80

Savings credit threshold

single	£198.27
couple	£314.34

Savings credit maximum

single	£17.30
couple	£19.36

Housing benefit

Personal allowances

Single person		
new pension age rate		£227.10
old pension age rate		£244.40
working age rate		£92.05
lower rate		£72.90
Couple		
new pension age rate		£346.60
old pension age rate		£366.00
working age rate		£144.65
lower rate		£110.15
Polygamous spouse	new pension age rate	£119.50
	old pension age rate	£121.60
	working age/lower rate	£52.60
Child or young person	usually up to two amounts	£84.66
Additional amounts: any age		
Disabled child premium each child/young person		£81.37
Enhanced disability premium (child)	each child/young person	£32.75

Family premium	old HB cases	£19.48
Carer premium	claimant/partner/each	£46.40
Severe disability premium	single rate	£82.90
	double rate	£165.80
Additional amounts: working age only		
Disability premium	single person	£43.20
	couple	£61.65
Enhanced disability premium (adult)	single person	£21.20
	couple	£30.25
Support component	single person/couple	£48.50
WRA component	single person/couple	£36.55

Other benefits

Attendance allowance

Higher rate	£110.40
Lower rate	£73.90

Bereavement benefits

Widowed parent's allowance (standard rate)	£150.90
Bereavement allowance (standard rate)	£150.90
Bereavement support payment (higher rate)	£80.77
Bereavement support payment (lower rate)	£23.08

Child benefit

Eldest/only child	£26.05
Each other child	£17.25

Carer's allowance

Claimant	£83.30

Disability living allowance

Care component	
Highest rate	£110.40
Middle rate	£73.90
Lowest rate	£29.20
Mobility component	
Higher rate	£77.05
Lower rate	£29.20

Employment and support allowance (new style)

Under 25	£72.90
25 or over	£92.05
Work-related component	£36.55
Support component	£48.50
Guardian's allowance	£22.10

Industrial injuries disablement benefit

20% disabled	£45.06
For each further 10% disability up to 100%	£22.53
100% disabled	£225.30

Jobseeker's allowance (new style)

Single under 25	£72.90
Single over 25	£92.05

Maternity and paternity pay and allowance

Statutory maternity, paternity and adoption pay	£187.18
Maternity allowance	£187.18

Personal independence payment

Daily living component	
Enhanced	£110.40
Standard	£73.90
Mobility component	
Enhanced	£77.05
Standard	£29.20

Severe disablement allowance

Basic rate	£100.05
Age-related addition	
Higher rate	£14.95
Middle rate and lower rate	£8.30

State pension

New state pension (full rate)	£230.25
Old state pension single (basic rate)	£176.45
Old state pension spouse or civil partner's insurance (basic pension)	£105.70

Statutory sick pay

Standard rate	£118.75

Appendix 3: **Equivalent footnote references for Scotland and Wales**

Table A: council tax

This table shows the equivalent footnote references in chapter 27 for the law on council tax in Scotland and Wales. 'Not Scotland' means there is no equivalent law in Scotland. For abbreviations see the key to footnotes in appendix 4.

	Wales	Scotland
28.2	LGFA 1(1),(2)(b)	LGFA 70
28.3	LGFA 5(1A),(3)	LGFA 74(1),(2); SSI 2016/368
28.4	See text	LGFA 72
28.5-6	See text	LGFA 99(1) – definition – 'resident'
T28.1	LGFA 5(1A),(3),36(1)	LGFA 74(1),(2),93(1); SSI 2016/368
28.11	See text	LGFA 75(2)(a)-(e)
28.13	See text	LGFA 75(4), sch 1 paras 2, 4
28.14	See text	LGFA 75(1),(2)(a)-(e)
28.15	See text	LGFA 75(3),(4), 77
28.16	See text	LGFA 75(3),(4)
28.17	LGFA 8, The Council Tax (Liability for Owners) Regulations 1992, No 551	LGFA 76, The Council Tax (Liability of Owners) (Scotland) Regulations 1992, No 1331
28.18	Table 27.2 Class C as amended by SI 1993/151 and SI 1995/620	SI 1992/1331, sch para 3 as substituted by SSI 2003/137
T28.2(a)-(g)	LGFA 8(1),(3),(6); The Council Tax (Liability for Owners) Regulations 1992, No 551, reg 2, Classes A to F	LGFA 76(1)-(3), The Council Tax (Liability of Owners) (Scotland) Regulations 1992, No 1331, sch paras 1-7
T28.2(a)	Class C substituted by SI 1993/151, amended by SI 1995/620 reg 2	para 3 substituted by SSI 2003/137
T28.2(b),(c)	Class A substituted by SI 2004/2920	para 1
T28.2(d)	Class E amended by SI 1995/620 reg 3	para 5
T28.2(e)	Class B	para 2
T28.2(f)	Class D	para 4
T28.2(g)	Class F added by SI 2000/1024	para 7 added by SI 2000/715
T28.2(h)	LGFA 6(1),(2)(f)	LGFA 75(1),(2)(f)(iii)
28.20	Table 27.2 Class A; definition 'hostel', in DDO 6 as substituted by SI 2004/2921 art 4	LGFA sch 1 para 8, definition of 'hostel' repealed by Regulation of Care (Scotland) Act 2001, sch 3 para 18
28.21	LGFA 11(2), 12, 12A, 12B, The Council Tax (Exceptions to Higher Amounts) (Wales) Regulations 2015, No 2068; 2019/1458; 2023/253	Local Government in Scotland Act 2003, s33; The Council Tax (Variation for Unoccupied Dwellings) (Scotland) Regulations 2013, No 45, regs 2-4
T28.3	The Council Tax (Exempt Dwellings) Order 1992, SI 1992/558, reg 3, Classes A to X	The Council Tax (Exempt Dwellings) (Scotland) Order 1997, No 728, reg 3, sch 1 paras 1-25

T28.3(a)	Class N substituted by SI 1993/150, amended by SI 1995/619, SI 2004/2865; Class U substituted by SI 1999/536; Class S added by SI 1995/619; Class X added by SI 2019/432; amended by 2022/722	sch 1 paras 10, 18, 23; SI 1999/757; SSI 2018/45; SSI 2022/124
T28.3(b)	Class K substituted by SI 1993/150	sch 1 paras 11-12; SI 1998/561
T28.3(c)	Class M amended by SI 1993/150 and SI 1994/539	sch 1 para 16
T28.3(d)	Class I substituted by SI 2004/2921	sch 1 para 5
T28.3(e)	Class B, amended by SI 1994/539; SI 2003/673, regs 3, 4	sch 1 para 3
T28.3(f)	Class A substituted by SI 2000/1025; Class C substituted by SI 1993/150	sch 1 paras 2, 4; SSI 1999/140; SSI 2012/339
T28.3(g)	Class H	sch 1 para 9
T28.3(h)	Class Q added by SI 1993/150, amended by SI 1994/539	sch 1 para 21
T28.3(i)	Class L	sch 1 para 13
T28.3(j)	Class G	sch 1 para 7
T28.3(k)	Class O amended by SI 1992/2941	sch 1 para 17
T28.3(l)	Class P added by SI 1992/2941	sch 1 para 22
T28.3(m)	Class V added by SI1997/656, definition of dependent relative in class amended by SI 1998/291	Not Scotland
T28.3(n)	Class R added by SI 1994/539	Not Scotland
T28.3(o)	Class T added SI 1995/619	Not Scotland
T28.3(p)	Class W added by SI 1997/656, definition of dependent relative in class amended by SI 1998/291	Not Scotland
T28.3 (notes)	—	sch 1 paras 15, 26-29; SSI 2022/124; SSI 2022/272; SSI 2023/36
28.22	LGFA 4, 11, 13, 13A	LGFA 72, 79, 80
28.23	LGFA 4(1)-(2)	LGFA 72(1),(6)
28.24	LGFA 13(1),(4),(6),(7); The Council Tax (Reductions for Disabilities) Regulations 1992 No 554, reg 4 as amended by SI 1999/1004	The Council Tax (Reductions for Disabilities) (Scotland) Regulations 1992 No 1335, reg 4 as amended by SI 1999/756
28.25	The Council Tax (Reductions for Disabilities) Regulations 1992 No 554, reg 3(1),(3)	The Council Tax (Reductions for Disabilities) (Scotland) Regulations 1992 No 1335, reg 3(1),(3)
28.26	LGFA 11(1)-(3),12	LGFA 79(3); The Council Tax (Variation for Unoccupied Dwellings) (Scotland) Regulations 2013, No 45, reg 2
T28.4(a)-(m)	LGFA 11(5), sch 1	LGFA 79(5), sch 1
T28.4(a)	LGFA sch 1 paras 4, 5, 11; DDO art 4, sch 1 paras 2-7; DDR reg 5, class C; SI 2019/431	LGFA sch 1 paras 4, 5, 11; SI 1992/1409, reg 3, sch para 3; SSI 2003/176 art 6, 7; SSI 2011/5; SSI 2014/37
T28.4(b)	LGFA sch 1 para 2, DDO art 3; SI 2013/638; SI 2013/1048	LGFA sch 1 para 2; SSI 2003/176 art 4; SSI 2008/1879 reg 39; SSI 2013/65; SSI 2013/137 reg 14; SSI 2013/142 reg 8; SSI 2022/31 reg 9; SSI 2024/141 reg 7; SSI 2024/311 reg 10
T28.4(c)	LGFA sch 1 para 3	LGFA sch 1 para 3
T28.4(d)	LGFA sch 1 para 11; DDR reg 5, class G; SI 2019/431	LGFA sch 1 para 11; SI 1992/1409 reg 3, sch para 6; SSI 2018/39
T28.4(e)	LGFA sch 1 para 4; SI 2003/673 art 3	LGFA sch 1 para 4; SSI 2003/176 art 8

	Wales	Scotland
T28.4(f)	LGFA sch 1 para 4; DDO art 4, sch 1 para 1; SI 2007/580	LGFA sch 1 para 4; SSI 2003/176 art 5; SSI 2007/214
T28.4(g)	LGFA sch 1 para 9; DDR reg 2, sch paras 3, 4; SI 2013/639; SI 2013/1049	LGFA sch 1 para 9; SI 1992/1409 reg 2(3); SSI 2013/65; SSI 2013/142 reg 2; SSI 2022/31 reg 2; SSI 2024/141 reg 3; SSI 2024/311 reg 3
T28.4(h)	LGFA sch 1 para 9; DDR reg 2, sch paras 1, 2; SI 2007/581	LGFA sch 1 para 9; SI 1992/1409 reg 2(2); SSI 2007/213 reg 2
T28.4(i)	LGFA sch 1 para 10	LGFA sch 1 para 10
T28.4(j)	LGFA sch 1 paras 6, 7; DDO 6(b); SI 2004/2921 art 4	LGFA sch 1 para 8, as amended by Regulation of Care (Scotland) Act 2001, sch 3 para 18
T28.4(k)	LGFA sch 1 para 1; DDO arts 2,5; SI 2009/2054, sch 1 para 13; SI 2004/2921 art 4	LGFA sch 1 para 1; SSI 2003/176 art 3; SI 2009/2054, sch 1 para 23
T28.4(l)	LGFA sch 1 para 11; DDR reg 5, Class B; SI 2019/431	LGFA sch 1 para 11; SI 1992/1409 reg 3, sch para 2
T28.4(m)	LGFA sch 1 para 11; DDR reg 5, Class E; SI 2019/431	LGFA sch 1 para 11; SI 1992/1409 reg 3, sch para 1
T28.4(n)	LGFA sch 1 para 11; DDR reg 5, Class A, D, F; SI 2019/431	LGFA sch 1 para 11; SI 1992/1409 reg 3, sch para 1
T28.4(o)	LGFA sch 1 para 11; DDR reg 5 Class H; SI 2022/722; 2023/154 reg 2	LGFA sch 1 para 11; SI 1992/1409 reg 3, sch paras 7,8; SSI 2022/125 reg 2; SSI 2023/38 reg 29
28.27-30	LGFA 11(1)-(3)	LGFA 79(1)-(3)
28.31	See text	CT(A&E)S 10, 15
28.32	See text	LGFA 71
28.33	See text	LGFA 81, 82
28.34	See text	CT(A&E)S 7, 12
28.35	See text	See text

Table B: council tax rebates

This table shows the equivalent footnote references in chapters 18, 21-24 and 29 for the law on council tax rebates in Scotland and Wales. 'Not Wales' / 'Not Scotland' means there is no equivalent law for that country. For abbreviations see key to footnotes in appendix 4.

T18.1	CTRW(PR) 2(3),(4),(6), 23(f), 25(f), sch 1 para 7, sch 6 paras 3, 9, sch 7 para 14, sch 8 paras 8, 9, sch 10 paras 8, 9; CTRW(DS) 2(3),(4),(6), 14(f), 16(f), 26, 32, 34, sch 6 para 14, sch 7 paras 8, 9, sch 9 paras 8, 9	CTRSW 4(1) – 'qualifying income related benefit',(5),(6), 13(11), 79(1); CTRSP 2(9), 24, 47(1)
18.8	CTRW(PR) 4, 5, sch 1 para 1(1)(a),(2), sch 2 para 1, sch 6 paras 1(1)(a), 2, (3), sch 7 paras 1, 2; CTRW(DS) 4, 5, 23(1)(a),(2), 24(1)(a), 25, 26, sch 2 paras 1, sch 3 paras 1, 2	CTRSW 5, 35(a), sch 1 para 1; CTRSP 8, 20(a)
18.9	CTRW(PR) sch 2 para 1(1),(2); CTRW(DS) sch 2 para 1(1),(2)	CTRSW sch 1 para 1; CTRSP sch 1 para 2
18.10	CTRW(PR) sch 2 para 1(3),(4); CTRW(DS) sch 2 para 1(3),(4)	CTRSW 5, sch 1 para 1; CTRSP 8, sch 1 para 2
18.11	CTRW(PR) 33, sch 7 para 1(1)(a),(b),(2),(3), 2; CTRW(DS) 24, sch 3 para 1(1)(a),(b),(2),(3), 2	CTRSW sch 1 para 1
18.12	CTRW(PR) sch 7 para 1(1)(c); CTRW(DS) sch 3 para 1(1)(c)	CTRSW sch 1 para 1
18.13	CTRW(PR) sch 1 para 1(1)(b), sch 2 para 2, sch 6 para 1(1)(b), sch 7 para 3; CTRW(DS) 23(1)(b), 24(1)(b), sch 2 para 2, sch 3 para 3	CTRSW 35(c), sch 1 paras 3, 4, 4A-4C; CTRSP 20(d), sch 1 para 9
18.14	CTRW(PR) sch 2 para 8, sch 7 para 13; CTRW(DS) sch 2 para 8, sch 3 para 13	CTRSW sch 1 paras 3, 4, 4A-4C; CTRSP sch 1 para 8(1)
18.15	CTRW(PR) sch 2 para 7, sch 7 para 12; CTRW(DS) sch 2 para 7, sch 3 para 12	CTRSW sch 1 paras 3, 4, 4A-4C; CTRSP sch 1 para 8(1)
18.16	CTRW(PR) sch 2 paras 7(2), 8(c), sch 7 paras 12(2), 13(c); CTRW(DS) sch 2 paras 7(2), 8(c), sch 3 paras 12(2), 13(c)	CTRSW sch 1 paras 3, 4B; CTRSW sch 1 para 8(2)
18.17	CTRW(PR) SI 2015/44 reg 31	CTRSW 35(g), 98; CTRSP 20(e); SSI 2016/81 reg 2
18.18	CTRW(PR) sch 2 para 9, sch 7 para 14; CTRW(DS) sch 2 para 9, sch 3 para 14	CTRSW sch 1 paras 5, 6; CTRSP sch 1 para 8(1)
18.19	CTRW(PR) sch 2 paras 9(4), 11, sch 3 paras 14(1), 16; CTRW(DS) sch 2 paras 9(4), 11, sch 3 paras 14(1), 16	CTRSW sch 1 para 6; CTRSP sch 1 paras 10(4), 12
18.20	CTRW(PR) sch 2 para 6(1),(2), sch 7 para 11(1),(2); CTRW(DS) sch 2 para 6(1),(2), sch 3 para 11(1),(2)	CTRSW sch 1 para 13(1),(2); CTRSP sch 1 para 7(1),(2)
18.21	CTRW(PR) sch 2 paras 6(3)-(5), 12(1), sch 7 paras 11(3), 17(2); CTRW(DS) sch 2 paras 6(3)-(5), 12(1), sch 3 paras 11(3), 17(2)	CTRSW sch 1 paras 13(3), 17; CTRSP sch 1 paras 7(3)-(5), 13(1)
18.22	CTRW(PR) 2(1), sch 2 para 6(2)(a),(b), sch 7 para 11(2)(a),(b); CTRW(DS) 2(1), sch 2 para 6(2)(a),(b), sch 3 para 11(2)(a),(b)	CTRSW 4(1), sch 1 para 13(2)(a),(b); CTRSP 2(1), sch 1 para 7(2)(a),(b)

	Wales	Scotland
18.23	CTRW(PR) sch 2 para 6(4)-(7), sch 7 para 11(4),(5); CTRW(DS) sch 2 para 6(4)-(7), sch 3 para 11(4),(5)	CTRSW sch 1 para 13(4),(5); CTRSP sch 1 para 7(4)-(7)
18.24	CTRW(PR) sch 2 paras 6(8), 11, sch 7 paras 11(6),(7), 16; CTRW(DS) sch 2 paras 6(8), 11, sch 3 paras 11(6),(7), 16	CTRSW sch 1 paras 13(6),(7), 16; CTRSP sch 1 paras 7(8), 12
18.25	CTRW(PR) 3, sch 6 para 1(1)(d)-(f); CTRW(DS) 3, 24(d)-(f)	CTRSW 3, 35(d)-(f)
18.26	CTRW(PR) sch 7 paras 9, 10(8); CTRW(DS) sch 3 paras 9, 10(8)	CTRSW sch 1 paras 11, 12(8),(9)
18.27	CTRW(PR) sch 7 para 17(1); CTRW(DS) sch 3 para 17(1)	CTRSW sch 1 para 17
18.28	CTRW(PR) sch 7 para 10(1)(a),(2); CTRW(DS) sch 3 para 10(1)(a),(2)	CTRSW sch 1 para 12(1)(a),(2)
18.29	CTRW(PR) sch 7 para 12(1); CTRW(DS) sch 3 para 12(1)	CTRSW sch 1 para 14(1)
18.30	CTRW(PR) sch 7 para 17(5); CTRW(DS) sch 3 para 17(5)	CTRSW sch 1 para 17
18.31-32	CTRW(PR) sch 7 paras 18, 19, 22; CTRW(DS) sch 3 paras 18, 19, 22	CTRSW sch 1 paras 18, 19, 22
T18.3(a)	CTRW(PR) sch 2 paras 6(7), 7(1), s ch 7 paras 10(1), 11(5), 12(1),(3), 17(2); CTRW(DS) sch 2 paras 6(7), 7(1), sch 3 paras 10(1), 11(5), 12(1),(3), 17(2)	CTRSW sch 1 paras 12(1), 13(5), 14(1),(2), 17; CTRSP sch 1 paras 7(7), 8(1)
T18.3(b)	CTRW(PR) sch 2 paras 7(1)(a),(b), 8(a), sch 7 paras 12(1)(b), 13(a); CTRW(DS) sch 2 paras 7(1), 8(a), sch 3 paras 12(1), 13	CTRSW sch 1 paras 3, 4B, 14(1)(b),(2)(b); CTRSP sch 1 paras 8(1), 9(a)
T18.3(c)	CTRW(PR) sch 2 para 9(2)(b), sch 7 para 14(2),(4); CTRW(DS) sch 2 para 9(2), sch 3 para 14(2),(4)	CTRSW sch 1 para 5(6)(b),(8)(b); CTRSP sch 1 para 10(2)(b)
T18.3(d)	CTRW(PR) sch 2 para 9(2)(b), sch 7 para 14(2),(4); CTRW(DS) sch 2 para 9(2), sch 3 para 14(2),(4)	CTRSW sch 1 para 5(6)(b),(8)(b); CTRSP sch 1 para 10(2)(b)
21.2	CTRW(PR) 23(f), 25(f), 27, 30(1); CTRW(DS) 14(f), 16(f), 18, 21(1)	CTRSW 13(1),(6), 14(1),(5), 66; CTRSP 14(1),(5), 14A(1),(5), 40
21.3	CTRW(PR) sch 1 para 5(1),(2), sch 6 para 7(1),(2), sch 9 para 25; CTRW(DS) 30(1),(2), sch 7 para 25	CTRSW 36, sch 3 para 17; CTRSP 21(1),(3)
21.4	CTRW(PR) sch 1 para 5, sch 6 para 7; CTRW(DS) 30	CTRSW 5(2), 36(1); CTRSP 21(1),(2)
21.8	CTRSW 43, 44(1), 47(1),(2)	
21.9	CTRW(PR) sch 1 para 24(1), sch 6 paras 10(1), 11(1), 12(1), 20(1); CTRW(DS) 44(1), 45(1), 46(1), 54(1)	CTRSW 38(1),(2), 39(1), 40(1), 41(1)
21.10	CTRW(PR) sch 1 para 10(1)(b)-(x), sch 6 para 17(1),(2); CTRW(DS) 36(1)(b)-(x), 51(1),(2)	CTRSW 57(1)(a)-(r); CTRSP 27(1)(b)-(x)
21.11	CTRW(PR) sch 1 para 11(13), sch 9 para 4; CTRW(DS) 37(13), sch 7 para 4	CTRSP 31(12)
T21.1(a)-(s)		
T21.1(t)	CTRW(PR) sch 9 para 15; CTRW(DS) sch 7 para 15	CTRSW 57(1)
T21.1(v)	CTRW(PR) sch 1 paras 12(2)(f), 17(3), sch 6 para 14(2)(d), sch 9 paras 5, 6; CTRW(DS) 38(2)(f), 43(3), 48(2)(d), sch 7 paras 5, 6	CTRSW 46(2), 49(3)(b), 57(1); CTRSP 32(2)(f), 39(3)

T21.1(w)	CTRW(PR) sch 9 para 44; CTRW(DS) sch 7 para 44	CTRSW 57(1); CTRSP 27(1)
T21.1(x) i	CTRW(PR) sch 9 paras 46-48; CTRW(DS) sch 7 paras 46-48	CTRSW 57(1); CTRSP 27(1)
T21.1(y)	CTRW(PR) sch 9 para 28; CTRW(DS) sch 7 para 28	CTRSW 50(2)(l),(3)(e), 57(1); CTRSP 32(1)(g),(3)
21.13	Not Wales	CTRSW 57(1)(b)(iv),(iva); CTRSP 27(1)(j)(iiia),(iiib),(xxi)-(xxv)
21.14	CTRW(PR) sch 1 paras 10(2), 11(7), sch 6 paras 12(2), 17(3),(4); CTRW(DS) 36(2), 37(7), 46(2), 50(3),(4)	CTRSW 41(2), 57(1)(b); CTRSP 27(3)
T21.2(a)	CTRW(PR) sch 1 para 8(2)(a); CTRW(DS) 33(2)(a)	CTRSP 25(2)(a)
T21.2(b)-(h)	CTRW(PR) sch 1 para 10(1)(j), sch 6 para 17(1); CTRW(DS) 36(1)(j), 51(1)	CTRSW 57(1)(a),(b); CTRSP 27(1)(j)
T21.2(i)	CTRW(PR) sch 4 paras 7, 8, sch 9 para 21; CTRW(DS) sch 5 paras 7, 8, sch 7 para 21	CTRSW 57(1)(b)(v),(vi),(4); CTRSP sch 3 paras 6, 7
T21.2(j)	CTRW(PR) sch 1 para 10(1)(k), sch 6 para 17(1); CTRW(DS) 36(1)(k), 51(1)	CTRSW 57(1)(c),(e); CTRSP 27(1)(k)
T21.2(k)	CTRW(PR) sch 1 para 10(1)(j)(i)-(v), sch 9 paras 11, 14; CTRW(DS) 36(1)(j)(i)-(v), sch 7 paras 11, 14	CTRSW 57(1)(b); CTRSP 27(1)(j)(ii)-(vi)
T21.2(l)	CTRW(PR) sch 1 para 10(1)(j)(vi),(vii), sch 9 paras 52, 66; CTRW(DS) 36(1)(j)(vi),(vii), sch 7 paras 52, 66	CTRSW 57(1)(b); CTRSP 27(1)(j)(vii)-(viii)
T21.2(m)	CTRW(PR) sch 1 paras 7, 10(1)(j)(xi),(xx), sch 6 paras 3, 9, sch 9 para 42; CTRW(DS) 26, 32, 34, 36(1)(j)(xi),(xx), 37, sch 7 para 42	CTRSW 57(1)(b),(p),(2)(d); CTRSP 24, 27(1)(j)(xiii),(xxvi)
T21.2(n)	CTRW(PR) sch 9 paras 8, 9; CTRW(DS) sch 7 paras 8, 9	CTRSW 57(1)(b); CTRSP 27(1)(j)
T21.2(o)	Not Wales	CTRSW 57(1)(b)(iva); CTRSP 27(1)(j),(xxi)-(xxv)
T21.2(p)	CTRW(PR) sch 1 para 16(1)(j)(xiii), sch 9 para 67; CTRW(DS) 39(1)(j)(xiii), sch 7 para 67	CTRSW 57(1)(b); CTRSP 27(1)(j)(xva)
T21.2(q)	CTRW(PR) sch 1 para 10(1)(j), sch 6 para 17(1); CTRW(DS) 36(1)(j), 51(1)	CTRSW 57(1)(b); CTRSP 27(1)(b)
21.18	CTRW(PR) 2(1), sch 1 para 10(1)(j)(iii)-(v), sch 4 para 2, sch 9 para 14; CTRW(DS) 2(1), 36(1)(j)(iii)-(v), sch 5 para 2, sch 8 para 14	CTRSW 4(1), 57(1)(b)(ix); CTRSP 2(1), 27(1)(j)(ii)-(v)
21.19	CTRW(PR) sch 1 para 8(1),(2); CTRW(DS) 33(1),(2)	CTRSP 25(1),(2)
21.20	CTRW(PR) sch 1 paras 10(1)(c),(d),(t),(x), 12(2)(c); CTRW(DS) 36(1)(c),(d),(t),(x), 38(2)(c), 48(2)(c), 51(1)	CTRSW 57(1)(a),(j),(n),(2)(d), 58; CTRSP 2(1), 27(1)(c),(d),(t),(x)
21.22	CTRW(PR) sch 1 para 16(2),(3),(11A)-(11D), sch 5 paras 27, 27A; CTRW(DS) 42(2),(3),(11A)-(11D), sch 8 paras 27, 27A	CTRSW 65(3),(4); CTRSP 38(2),(3),(9A),(9B), sch 4 para 30A
21.23	CTRW(PR) sch 1 para 16, sch 6 para 19(2)(c); CTRW(DS) 42, 53(2)(c)	CTRSW 65(3),(4); CTRSP 38
21.24	CTRW(PR) 2(1); CTRW(DS) 2(1)	CTRSW 4(1); CTRSP 2(1)
21.25	LGFA sch 1B para 3(7); CTRW(PR) sch 1 paras 10(1)(e)-(h),(l),(m), sch 4 paras 1-6, sch 9 paras 13, 14, 20, 54-56; CTRW(DS) 2(1)2(1), 36(1)(e)-(h),(l),(m), sch 5 paras 1-6, sch 7 paras 13, 14, 20, 54-56	CTRSW 57(1); CTRSP 27(1)(e),(h),(l),(m), sch 3 paras 1-5

21.26	CTRW(PR) sch 1 para 10(1)(o), sch 9 para 50; CTRW(DS) 2(1)36(1)(o), sch 7 para 50	CTRSW 57(1)(d); CTRSP 27(1)(o)
21.27	CTRW(PR) sch 1 para 10(1)(o), sch 4 para 20, sch 9 para 49; CTRW(DS) 2(1)36(1)(o), sch 5 para 20, sch 7 para 49	CTRSW 57(6); CTRSP 27(1)(o), sch 3 para 19
21.28	CTRW(PR) sch 1 para 10(1), sch 9 paras 30-34, 59; CTRW(DS) 36(1), sch 7 paras 30-34, 59	CTRSW 57(1); CTRSP 27(1)
21.29	CTRW(PR) sch 1 para 10(1)(p),(v), sch 4 paras 9, 10, sch 9 paras 26, 27; CTRW(DS) 36(1)(p),(v), sch 5 paras 9, 10, sch 7 paras 26, 27	CTRSW 57(1); CTRSP 27(1)(p),(v), sch 3 paras 8, 9
21.30	CTRW(PR) sch 1 paras 10(1)(i), 11(12), sch 9 para 22; CTRW(DS) 36(1)(i), 37(12), sch 7 para 22	CTRSW 57(1); CTRSP 27(1)(i), 31(11)
21.31	CTRW(PR) sch 9 paras 18, 61, sch 10 paras 39, 52; CTRW(DS) sch 7 paras 18, 61, sch 9 paras 39, 52	CTRSW 51(6)(b), 57(1)(g),(h),(2)(b)
21.32	CTRW(PR) sch 1 para 10(1), sch 11 para 1(1); CTRW(DS) 36(1), 70(1)	CTRSW 57(1)(f), 59(1),(6); CTRSP 27(1)
21.33	Not Wales	CTRSW 44(1), 62
21.34	CTRW(PR) sch 11 paras 4(3), 9(2),(5); CTRW(DS) 73(3), 78(2),(5)	CTRSW 59, 60, 61
21.35	CTRW(PR) sch 11 para 8; CTRW(DS) 77	CTRSW 57(1)(f), 59
T21.3(a)	CTRW(PR) sch 11 paras 1(1), 4(1),(6), 9(1), 10; CTRW(DS) 70(1), 73(1),(6), 78(1), 79	CTRSW 59(2),(5), 60(2),(3), 62
T21.3(b)	CTRW(PR) sch 9 para 16, sch 10 para 53, sch 11 paras 4(2),(3), 10, 11; CTRW(DS) 73(2),(3), 79, 80, sch 7 para 16, sch 9 para 53	CTRSW 59(4), 61, 62
T21.3 Note:	CTRW(PR) sch 11 paras 1(1), 4(7), 9(3),(4); CTRW(DS) 70(1), 73(7), 78(3),(4)	CTRSW 60(1)-(3)
21.36	CTRW(PR) sch 1 para 10(1), sch 9 para 35; CTRW(DS) 36(1), sch 7 para 35	CTRSW 57(1)(i); CTRSP 27(1)
21.37	CTRW(PR) sch 4 paras 14, 15, sch 6 para 18(5), sch 9 para 19(1)(d),(e); CTRW(DS) 52(5), sch 5 paras 14, 15, sch 7 para 19(1)(d),(e)	CTRSW 57(1)(j),(k), 74; CTRSP sch 3 paras 13, 14
21.38	CTRW(PR) sch 4 para 12, sch 9 para 19(1)(c); CTRW(DS) sch 5 para 12, sch 7 para 19(1)(c)	CTRSW 57(1)(k), 74; CTRSP sch 3 para 11
21.39	CTRW(PR) sch 1 paras 10(1)(d), 11(12), sch 4 paras 14, 15, sch 5 para 31, sch 6 para 18(2), sch 9 para 19(1)(d); CTRW(DS) 36(1)(d), 37(12), 52(2), sch 4 paras 14, 15, sch 7 para 19(1)(d), sch 8 para 31	CTRSW 57(1)(j); CTRSP 27(1)(d), 31(11), sch 3 paras 13, 14
21.40	CTRW(PR) sch 1 para 10(1)(w),(5); CTRW(DS) 36(1)(w),(5)	CTRSW 57(1); CTRSP 27(1)(w),(6)
21.41	CTRW(PR) sch 1 para 10(1), sch 9 para 19(1)(a),(b); CTRW(DS) 36(1), sch 7 para 19(1)(a),(b)	CTRSW 57(1); CTRSP 27(1)
21.42	CTRW(PR) sch 1 para 10(1), sch 9 paras 37, 64, 65; CTRW(DS) 36(1), sch 7 paras 37, 64, 65	CTRSW 57(1); CTRSP 27(1)
21.43	CTRW(PR) sch 1 para 10(1), sch 5 paras 14, 16, 28B, sch 9 para 41, sch 10 paras 29, 38, 57, 64; CTRW(DS) 36(1), sch 7 para 41, sch 8 paras 14, 16, 28B, sch 9 para 29, 38, 57, 64	CTRSW 57(1)(k), 75; CTRSP 27(1), sch 4 paras 14, 16, 30C

21.44	CTRW(PR) sch 1 paras 10(1)(q),(r), 11(5),(6),(9),(10), sch 6 para 16(3),(4); CTRW(DS) 36(1)(q),(r), 37(5),(6),(9),(10), 50(3),(4)	CTRSW 51(2),(5)-(8); CTRSP 27(1)(q),(r), 31(4),(5),(8),(9)
21.45	CTRW(PR) sch 1 para 16, sch 6 para 19(2); CTRW(DS) 42, 53(2)	CTRSW 65; CTRSP 38
22.1	CTRW(PR) 2(1), sch paras 12(1), 15(1), sch 6 paras 14(1), 16(1); CTRW(DS) 2(1), 38(1), 41(1), 48(1), 50(1)	CTRSW 4(1), 45, 49(2), 50(2), 51(1); CTRSP 32(1), 35(1)
22.2	CTRW(PR) 2(1); CTRW(DS) 2(1)	CTRSW 4(1); CTRSP 2(1)
22.3	CTRW(PR) sch 1 para 5(1),(2), sch 6 para 7(1),(2); CTRW(DS) 30(1),(2)	CTRSW 36(1); CTRSP 21(1)
22.4	CTRW(PR) sch para 13(1),(2), sch 6 para 15(1)-(3); CTRW(DS) 39(1),(2), 49(1)-(3)	CTRSW 49(2),(6), 50(3); CTRSP 33(1),(2)
T22.1(a)	CTRW(PR) sch 1 para 12(1)(a)-(k), sch 6 para 14(1)(a)-(l); CTRW(DS) 38(1)(a)-(k), 48(1)(a)-(l)	CTRSW 49(2),(4), 50(2)(a)-(l); CTRSP 32(1)(a)-(k)
T22.1(b)	CTRW(PR) sch 1 para 13(1),(2), sch 6 para 15(2),(3); CTRW(DS) 39(1),(2), 49(2),(3)	CTRSW 49(6), 50(3),(4); CTRSP 33(1),(2)
T22.1(c)	CTRW(PR) sch 1 para 12(1)(b),(2), sch 6 paras 14(1)(b),(2), 27(2), sch 8 paras 1, 2, 9; CTRW(DS) 38(1)(b),(2), 48(1)(b),(2), 49(2), 61(2), sch 6 paras 1, 2, 9	CTRSW 49(2),(5),(6), 50(2)(b),(3)(e)-(i), sch 3 paras 1, 2, 9; CTRSP 32(1)(b),(2)
22.5	CTRW(PR) 6 para 19(6),(7); CTRW(DS) 53(6),(7)	CTRSW 55(5),(6)
22.6	Not Wales	CTRSW 55(1),(2)
22.7	CTRW(DS) 39(1), 41(1), 45(1), 51(1), 54(1)	CTRSW 47(3); CTRSP 27(1), 32(1), 45(1)
22.8	Not Wales	CTRSW 47(1),(2)
22.9-11	Not Wales	CTRSW 47(2)
22.12	Not Wales	CTRSW 44(1), 47(1)
22.13-14	Not Wales	CTRSW 47(2), 48
22.18	CTRW(PR) sch 1 para 11(3A),(4A), sch 6 para 10A; CTRW(DS) 37(3A),(4A), 44A	CTRSW 34(12); CTRSP 59(9)
22.19	CTRW(PR) sch 1 para 11(1)-(3); CTRW(DS) 37(1)-(3)	CTRSP 31(1),(2)
22.20	CTRW(PR) sch 6 para 10(1),(2); CTRW(DS) 44(1),(2)	CTRSW 39(1),(2), 42(2), 43
22.21	CTRW(PR) sch 1 para 40(7),(8), sch 6 para 46(7),(8); CTRW(DS) 105(7),(8)	CTRSW 34(11),(12); CTRSP 59(8),(9)
22.22	CTRW(PR) sch 13 paras 5(4), 7(1),(2); CTRW(DS) 111(4), 113(1),(2)	CTRSW 27(1), 31(1); CTRSP 66(1), 69(1)
22.23	CTRW(PR) sch 1 para 11(3A),(4A), sch 6 para 10A; CTRW(DS) 37(3A),(4A), 44A	CTRSW 44(2); CTRSP 31
22.24-26	Not Wales	CTRSW 4(1) – 'award of universal credit', 48
T22.2	Not Wales	CTRSW 48
22.27	CTRW(PR) sch 1 para 11(9), sch 6 paras 15(2), 24(2); CTRW(DS) 37(9), 49(2), 58(2)	CTRSW 49(6)(d), 50(3)(i), 51(2) 'step 6',(8); CTRSP 31(8)
22.30	CTRW(PR) sch 1 paras 11(9), 18(1),(c), sch 3, sch 6 paras 15(2), 20(1),(c), 24(2), sch 8; CTRW(DS) 37(9), 49(2), 54(1)(c), 58(2), sch 4, sch 6	CTRSW 49(6)(d), 50(3)(i), 51(2) 'step 6',(8), sch 3; CTRSP 28(1)(c), 31(8), sch 2
T22.4(a)	CTRW(PR) sch 3 para 6, sch 8 para 12; CTRW(DS) sch 4 para 6, sch 6 para 12	CTRSW sch 3 para 12; CTRSP sch 2 para 6
T22.4(b)	CTRW(PR) sch 3 para 2, sch 8 para 5; CTRW(DS) sch 4 para 2, sch 6 para 5	CTRSW sch 3 para 5; CTRSP sch 2 para 2

T22.4(c)	CTRW(PR) sch 3 para 5, sch 8 para 4; CTRW(DS) sch 4 para 5, sch 6 para 4	CTRSW sch 3 para 4; CTRSP sch 2 para 5
T22.4(d)	CTRW(PR) sch 3 para 4, sch 8 paras 6, 7; CTRW(DS) sch 4 para 4, sch 6 paras 6, 7	CTRSW sch 3 paras 6, 7; CTRSP sch 2 para 4
T22.4(e)	CTRW(PR) sch 8 paras 9, 10; CTRW(DS) sch 6 paras 9, 10	CTRSW sch 3 paras 9, 10
T22.4(f)	CTRW(PR) sch 3 para 8, sch 8 paras 10, 11; CTRW(DS) sch 4 para 8, sch 6 paras 10, 11	CTRSW sch 3 paras 10, 11; CTRSP sch 2 para 8
T22.5(a)	CTRW(PR) sch 1 para 19(8), sch 6 para 21(8); CTRW(DS) 55(8)	CTRSW 77(9); CTRSP 29(8)
T22.5(b)	CTRW(PR) sch 1 para 19(6), sch 6 para 21(6); CTRW(DS) 55(6)	CTRSW 77(7); CTRSP 29(6)
T22.5(c)	CTRW(PR) sch 1 para 19(1)(a), sch 6 para 21(1)(a); CTRW(DS) 55(1)(a)	CTRSW 77(2)(a); CTRSP 29(1)(a)
T22.5(d)	CTRW(PR) sch 1 para 19(1)(b),(c),(11), sch 6 para 21(1)(b),(c),(11); CTRW(DS) 55(1)(b),(c),(11)	CTRSW 77(2)(b),(c),(12); CTRSP 29(1)(b),(c),(11)
T22.5(e)	CTRW(PR) sch 1 para 18(1)(c),(3), sch 6 para 20(1)(c),(3); CTRW(DS) 4(1)(c),(3)	CTRSW 38(2)(c), 42(2)(c); CTRSP 28(1)(c),(3)
T22.6	CTRW(PR) sch 3 para 10, sch 8 para 18; CTRW(DS) sch 4 para 10, sch 6 para 18	CTRSW sch 3 para 15; CTRSP sch 2 para 10
23.1	CTRW(PR) 2(1), sch 1 para 15(1), sch 6 para 16(1); CTRW(DS) 2(1), 41(1), 50(1)	CTRSW 4(1), 51(1),(2),(6); CTRSP 35(1)
23.2	CTRW(PR) sch 1 para 5(1),(2), sch 6 para 7(1),(2); CTRW(DS) 30(1),(2)	CTRSW 36(1); CTRSP 21(1)
23.3	CTRW(PR) sch 1 paras 23, 24, sch 6 paras 24, 25; CTRW(DS) 58, 59	CTRSW 51; CTRSP 36, 37
T23.1(a)	CTRW(PR) sch 1 paras 11(10), 15(1), sch 6 paras 11(2), 16(1),(3); CTRW(DS) 37(10), 41(1), 45(2), 50(1),(3)	CTRSW 40(2), 43, 51(2),(5),(7),(8); CTRSP 31(9), 35(1)
T23.1(b)	CTRW(PR) sch 1 paras 11(9),(10), 23(1),(2), sch 6 para 24(1)-(3); CTRW(DS) 37(9),(10), 58(1)-(3)	CTRSW 51(2),(5),(9); SSI 2013/303 regs 37, 38; CTRSP 31(8),(9), 36(1),(2)
T23.1(note)	CTRW(PR) sch 1 paras 15(1), 23(5),(7)(b), sch 6 paras 16(1), 24(6),(8)(b); CTRW(DS) 41(1), 50,(1), 58(6),(8)(b)	CTRSW 51(2)-(4),(9), 53(2)-(4), SSI 2013/303 reg 37(6),(8); CTRSP 35(1), 36(5),(7)(b)
23.4	CTRW(PR) sch 1 para 24, sch 6 para 25; CTRW(DS) 59	CTRSW 51(2),(9), SSI 2013/303 reg 38; CTRSP 37
23.5	CTRW(PR) sch 6 para 19(6)-(9); CTRW(DS) 56(6)-(9)	CTRSW 55(5),(6)
23.6	CTRW(PR) sch 1 para 23(2)(a),(7)(a), sch 6 para 24(3)(a),(8)(a); CTRW(DS) 58(3)(a),(8)(a)	CTRSW 51(9), 53(1); SSI 2013/303 reg 37(3)(a),(8)(a); CTRSP 36(2)(a),(7)(a)
T23.2(a)	CTRW(PR) sch 1 para 23(3),(5),(7)(b), sch 6 para 24(4),(6),(8)(b); CTRW(DS) 58(4),(6),(8)(b)	CTRSW 51(9), 53(1); SSI 2013/303 reg 37(4),(6),(8)(b); CTRSP 36(3),(5),(7)(b)
T23.2(b)	CTRW(PR) sch 1 para 23(4), sch 6 para 24(5); CTRW(DS) 58(5)	CTRSW 51(9), 53(3); SSI 2013/303 reg 37(5); CTRSP 36(4)
23.7	Not Wales	CTRSW 52
23.8	Not Wales	CTRSW 53
23.9	Not Wales	CTRSW 54(2)
23.10	Not Wales	CTRSW 54(3)
23.11	Not Wales	CTRSW 54(4)
23.12	CTRW(PR) sch 1 para 24(4)(b), sch 6 para 25(4)(b); CTRW(DS) 59(4)(b)	CTRSW 51(9); SSI 2013/303 reg 38(3)(b); CTRSP 37(3)(b)

23.13	Not Wales	CTRSW 44, 47(1)
23.14	Not Wales	CTRSW 47(1),(2), 51(2)
23.15	Not Wales	CTRSW 47(1), 51(2) step 1
23.17	Not Wales	CTRSW 47(2)
23.18	CTRW(PR) sch 1 para 14(1), sch 6 para 11(1); CTRW(DS) 40(1), 45(1)	CTRSW 40(1); CTRSP 34(1)
23.20	CTRW(PR) sch 13 para 5(4); CTRW(DS) 113(4)	CTRSW 31(1); CTRSP 66(1)
23.21	Not Wales	CTRSW 56(1),(4)
23.22	Not Wales	CTRSW 56(1)
23.23	Not Wales	CTRSW 56(1)(b),(2)
23.24	Not Wales	CTRSW 56(4)
23.25	Not Wales	CTRSW 56(2),(4)
24.2	CTRW(PR) 27, 30; CTRW(DS) 18, 21	CTRSW 13(1), 14(1)(c), 66; CTRSP 40
24.3	CTRW(PR) sch 1 para 31, sch 6 para 33; CTRW(DS) 68, 69	CTRSW 63; CTRSP 27(2)
T24.1	CTRW(PR) 27, 30, sch 1 para 31, sch 6 para 33; CTRW(DS) 18, 21, 68, 69	CTRSW 13(1), 14(1), 63, 66; CTRSP 27(2), 40
24.5	CTRW(PR) sch 1 para 5, 9, 25, sch 6 para 7, 9, 26; CTRW(DS) 30, 34, 35, 60	CTRSW 36, 67; CTRSP 21, 26, 41
24.6	CTRW(PR) sch 1 para 26, sch 6 para 28; CTRW(DS) 62	CTRSW 70(1); CTRSP 42
24.7	CTRW(PR) sch 1 para 30, sch 6 para 32; CTRW(DS) 67	CTRSW 68; CTRSP 46
24.8	CTRW(PR) sch 1 paras 11(12), 25(1), sch 5 paras 5, 30, sch 6 para 26(1), sch 10 paras 10, 37; CTRW(DS) 37(12), 60(1), sch 8 paras 5, 30, sch 9 paras 10, 37	CTRSW 63(3), 67(1), sch 4 para 7; CTRSP 31(11), 41(1), sch 4 paras 5, 32
24.9	CTRW(PR) sch 1 para 11(12), sch 5 paras 17, 32, sch 10 paras 17, 18; CTRW(DS) 37(12), sch 8 paras 17, 32, sch 9 paras 17, 18	CTRSW 74; CTRSP 31(11), sch 4 paras 17, 34
24.11	CTRW(PR) sch 6 para 18, sch 10 para 22; CTRW(DS) 52(1), sch 9 para 22	CTRSW 67(4)
24.12	CTRW(PR) sch 1 paras 11(12), 31, sch 4 paras 22, 23, sch 6 paras 27(5), 33; CTRW(DS) 37(12), 61(5), 68, 69, sch 5 paras 22, 23;	CTRSW 63(1),(3); CTRSP 27(2), 31(11), sch 3 paras 21, 22
24.13	CTRW(PR) sch 1 para 27, sch 5 para 23, sch 6 para 29, sch 10 para 28; CTRW(DS) 63, sch 8 para 23, sch 9 para 28;	CTRSW 70(2),(3); CTRSP 43, sch 4 para 23
24.14	CTRW(PR) sch 1 para 25(2), sch 5, sch 6 para 26(2), sch 10; CTRW(DS) 60(2), sch 8, sch 9;	CTRSW 69(1), 74, 75, 76, sch 4; CTRSP 41(2), sch 4
T24.2(a)	CTRE(PR) sch 5 para 26, sch 10 para 4; CTRE(DS) sch 8 para 26, sch 9 para 4	CTRSW sch 4 para 1; CTRSP sch 4 para 26
T24.2(b)	CTRE(PR) sch 5 para 4(a), sch 10 para 7(a); CTRE(DS) sch 8 para 4(a), sch 9 para 7(a)	CTRSW sch 4 para 2; CTRSP sch 4 para 4(a)
T24.2(c)	CTRE(PR) sch 5 para 4(b), sch 10 para 7(b); CTRE(DS) sch 8 para 4(b), sch 9 para 7(b)	CTRSW sch 4 para 3; CTRSP sch 4 para 4(b)
T24.2(d)	CTRE(PR) sch 5 para 6, sch 10 para 30; CTRE(DS) sch 8 para 6, sch 9 para 30	CTRSW sch 4 para 5(a); CTRSP sch 4 para 6
T24.2(e)	CTRE(PR) sch 5 para 7, sch 10 para 31; CTRE(DS) sch 8 para 7, sch 9 para 31	CTRSW sch 4 para 6; CTRSP sch 4 para 7
T24.2(f)	CTRE(PR) sch 5 paras 1-3, sch 10 paras 5, 32, 33; CTRE(DS) sch 8 paras 1-3, sch 9 paras 5, 32, 33	CTRSW sch 4 para 4; CTRSP sch 4 paras 1-3

T24.2(g)	CTRW(PR) sch 5 paras 18, 20(a), sch 10 paras 6, 14(b), 41(a); CTRW(DS) sch 8 paras 18, 20(a), sch 9 paras 6, 14(b), 41(a)	CTRSW sch 4 para 16; CTRSP sch 4 paras 18, 20(a)
T24.2(h)	CTRW(PR) sch 5 paras 18, 20(a), sch 10 para 14(a); CTRW(DS) sch 8 paras 18, 20(a), sch 9 para 14(a)	CTRSW sch 4 para 16; CTRSP sch 4 paras 18, 20(a)
T24.2(i)	CTRW(PR) sch 5 paras 17, 20(b), sch 10 para 13(b); CTRW(DS) sch 8 paras 17, 20(b), sch 9 para 13(b)	CTRSW sch 4 para 18; CTRSP sch 4 paras 17, 20(b)
T24.2(j)	CTRW(PR) sch 5 paras 9, 10, sch 10 para 11; CTRW(DS) sch 8 paras 9, 10, sch 9 para 11	CTRSW sch 4 para 9; CTRSP sch 4 paras 9, 10
T24.2(k)	CTRW(PR) sch 5 para 8, sch 10 para 15; CTRW(DS) sch 8 para 8, sch 9 para 15	CTRSW 67(2), 71(1),(2); CTRSP sch 4 para 8
T24.2(l)	CTRW(PR) sch 1 para 11(12), sch 5 paras 11, 12, 24, 31, sch 10 paras 16, 21, 35, 36; CTRW(DS) 37(12), sch 8 paras 11, 12, 24, 31, sch 9 paras 16, 21, 35, 36	CTRSW 67(3), 74(3), sch 4 paras 10, 11; CTRSP 31(11), sch 4 paras 11, 12, 24, 31
T24.2(m)	CTRW(PR) sch 5 paras 18, 19, sch 10 para 13(a); CTRW(DS) sch 8 paras 18, 19, sch 9 para 13(a)	CTRSW sch 4 para 17; CTRSP sch 4 paras 18, 19
T24.2(n)	CTRW(PR) sch 5 para 17, sch 6 para 18(5), sch 10 paras 17, 18, 48, 49; CTRW(DS) 52(5), sch 8 para 17, sch 9 paras 17, 18, 48, 49	CTRSW 74; CTRSP sch 4 para 17
T24.2(o)	CTRW(PR) sch 5 paras 18, 21, 22, sch 10 para 12; CTRW(DS) 52(5), sch 8 paras 18, 21, 22, sch 9 para 12	CTRSW sch 4 para 21; CTRSP sch 4 paras 18, 21, 22
T24.2(p)	CTRW(PR) sch 5 paras 8, 21(1)(e),(f),(2)(m), 27A, 28, 28C(1), 29B, 29C; sch 10 paras 12(1)(d),(h), 15, 23, 24, 25(b), 50, 59-62, 65; CTRW(DS) sch 8 paras 8, 21(1)(e), (f),(2)(m), 27A, 28, 28C(1), 29B, 29C, sch 9 paras 12(1)(d),(h), 15, 23, 24, 25(b), 50, 59-62, 65	CTRSW 67(2), sch 4 paras 20, 22, 23, 26, 35, 36, 40, 44; CTRSP sch 4 paras 8, 21(2)(n), 29, 30B, 30K
24.15	CTRW(PR) sch 1 para 28(1),(3),(5), sch 6 para 30(1),(5),(7); CTRW(DS) 64(1),(7),(9)	CTRSW 71(1),(2), 76(1),(2); CTRSP 44(1),(3),(5)
24.16	CTRW(PR) sch 1 para 28(1), sch 6 para 30(1); CTRW(DS) 64(1)	CTRSW 71(1); CTRSP 44(1)
24.18	CTRW(PR) sch 1 para 28(2); CTRW(DS) 64(2)	CTRSP 44(2)
24.19	CTRW(PR) sch 1 para 29, sch 6 para 31; CTRW(DS) 65, 66	CTRSW 72, 73; CTRSP 45
24.20	CTRW(PR) sch 1 para 28(3),(4), sch 6 para 30(5),(6); CTRW(DS) 64(7),(8)	CTRSW 76(1)-(3); CTRSP 44(3),(4)
T29.1	LGFA 13A(1)(c),(2), sch 1B paras 3(1)-(3), 4; CTRW(PR) 21-25; CTRW(DS) 13-16	°LGFA 80; CTRSW 13(1),(3)-(7), 14; CTRSP 14(1),(3)-(6), 14A
29.2	LGFA sch 1B para 3(7)(a)-(c); CTRW (PR) 22(a), 23(a), 24(a), 25(a); CTRW(DS) 13(a), 14(a), 15(a), 16(a)	LGFA 80(1); CTRSW 13(3)(a), 14(3)(a); CTRSP 14(3)(a), 14A(3)(a)
29.3	LGFA sch 1B para 3(7)(e); CTRW(PR) 9; CTRW(DS) 9	CTRSW 8; CTRSP 3
29.4	CTRW(PR) 2(1); CTRW(DS) 2(1) – 'qualifying age for state pension credit'	CTRSW 4(1) definition – 'pensionable age'; CTRSP 2(1)
T29.2	CTRW(PR) 3, 22(f), 23(g), 24(f), 25(g), sch 13 para 1; CTRW(DS) 3, 13(f), 14(g), 15(f), 16(g), 107(1)	CTRSW 3, 11, 13(3)(c), 14(3)(c); CTRSP 7, 12, 14(3)(c), 14A(3)(c), 61

29.5	LGFA 13A(4),(5), sch 1B paras 1-4; CTRW(PR) 11, 12, 14, 15, 32, 33	LGFA 80; CTRSW 13, 14; CTRSP 14, 14A
29.6	Not Wales	See text
29.7	See text	Not Scotland
29.8	LGFA 13A(1)(b),(4),(5), sch 1B paras 3-5; CTRW(PR) 3-10, 12, 14-18, 27-29	Not Scotland
29.9-12	Not Wales	Not Scotland
29.13	LGFA sch 1B para 3(5),(7)(a),(b),(e); CTRW(PR) 12(1), 14(b), 15(2),(3)	Not Scotland
29.14	See text	Not Scotland
29.15	LGFA sch 1B paras 3-5; CTRW(PR) 3-10, 27-31, 34(1)-(3)	Not Scotland
29.16	LGFA sch 1B paras 2, 6; CTRW(PR) 13, 17, 18	Not Scotland
29.17	Not Wales	Not Scotland
29.18	Not Wales	Not Scotland
29.19	LGFA sch 1B para 4(4),(5)	Not Scotland
29.20	LGFA 13A(1)(c),(6),(7)	Not Scotland
29.21	LGFA 13A(1)(c),(6), sch 1B para 4(1),(2)	Not Scotland
29.22	LGFA 13A(1)(c),(6); CTRW(PR) sch 12 para 11(2)	Not Scotland
29.23	Not Wales	Not Scotland
29.24	LGFA sch 1B para 3(1)(b); CTRW(PR) 21-31, sch 11 para 3(1),(2); CTRW(DS)13-22, 72(1),(2)	CTRSW 13(3)(b), 14(3)(b), 15-20, 66; CTRSP 14(3)(b), 14A(3)(b), 15-19, 40
29.25-54	See text	See text
30.2-11	See text	See text
30.12	CTRW(PR) sch 1 paras 2(1),(3)-(5), sch 6 paras 4(1),(3)-(5); CTRW(DS) 27(1),(3)-(5) CTRSW 79(1),(4);	CTRSP 47(1),(2)
30.13	CTRW(PR) 2(2), sch 1 paras 2(1), 4, sch 6 paras 4(1), 6; CTRW(DS) 2(2), 27(1), 29	CTRSW 4(7), 13(9)(b), 79(1); CTRSP 2(7), 14(8)(b), 47(1)
T30.1	See text	See text
30.15-34	See text	See text

Appendix 4 **Abbreviations and key to footnotes**

Abbreviations

The principal abbreviations used in the guide are given below.

AA	Attendance allowance
ADM	The DWP's Advice for decision making: staff guide
ADP	Adult disability payment
BORG	The DWP's Benefit overpayment recovery guide
CDP	Child disability payment
CTC	Child tax credit
CTR	Council tax rebate
DHP	Discretionary housing payment
DLA	Disability living allowance
DMG	The DWP's Decision makers' guide: staff guide
DWP	The Department for Work and Pensions
ESA	Employment and Support Allowance
ESA(IR)	Income-related employment and support allowance
HB	Housing benefit
HBGM	The DWP's Housing benefit and council tax benefit guidance manual
HBOG	The DWP's Housing benefit overpayments guide
HMRC	His Majesty's Revenue and Customs
IS	Income support
JSA	Jobseeker's allowance
LHA	Local housing allowance
MHCLG	The Ministry of Housing, Communities and Local Government
OG	The DWP's Universal credit operational guidance
PADP	Pension age disability payment
PIP	Personal independence payment
SADLA	Scottish adult disability living allowance
SDA	Severe disablement allowance
SMI	Support for mortgage interest
SPC	State pension credit
UC	Universal credit
UK	England, Scotland, Wales and Northern Ireland
WTC	Working tax credit

Key to footnotes: legislation

The abbreviations used for legislation referred to in the footnotes are given below.

art	Article number
CLCA	Children (Leaving Care) Act 2000
CLC(E)	The Children (Leaving Care) (England) Regulations 2001, SI No 2874
CLC(S)	The Children (Leaving Care) Social Security Benefits (Scotland) Regulations 2004, SI No 747
CLC(W)	The Children (Leaving Care) (Wales) Regulations 2001, SI No 2189
CSPSSA	The Child Support, Pensions and Social Security Act 2000
CT(A&E)	The Council Tax (Administration and Enforcement) Regulations 1992, SI No 613
CT(A&E)S	The Council Tax (Administration and Enforcement) (Scotland) Regulations 1992, SI No 1332
CT(ALA)S	The Council Tax (Alteration of Lists and Appeals) (Scotland) Regulations 1993, SI No 355
CT(DDO)	The Council Tax (Discount Disregards) Order 1992, SI 1992 No 548
CT(DDR)	The Council Tax (Additional Provisions for Discount Disregards) Regulations 1992, SI 1992 No 552
CT(ED)	The Council Tax (Exempt Dwellings) Order 1992, SI No 558
CT(LO)	The Council Tax (Liability of Owners) Regulations 1992, SI No 551
CT(RD)	The Council Tax (Reductions for Disabilities) Regulations 1992, SI No 554
CTRE(DS)	The Council Tax Reduction Schemes (Default Scheme) (England) Regulations 2012, SI No 2886
CTRE(PR)	The Council Tax Reduction Schemes (Prescribed Requirements) (England) Regulations 2012, SI No 2885
CTRSP	The Council Tax Reduction (State Pension Credit) (Scotland) Regulations 2012, SSI No 319
CTRSW	The Council Tax Reduction (Scotland) Regulations 2021, SSI No 249
CTRW(PR)	The Council Tax Reduction Scheme and Prescribed Requirements (Wales) Regulations 2013, SI No 3029
CTRW(DS)	The Council Tax Reduction Schemes (Default Scheme) (Wales) Regulations 2013, SI No 3035
DFA	The Discretionary Financial Assistance Regulations 2001, SI No 1167
EEA	The Immigration (European Economic Area) Regulations 2016, SI No 1052
FTPR	The Tribunal Procedure (First-tier Tribunal) (Social Entitlement Chamber) Rules 2008, SI No 2685
FTSLT	The First-tier Tribunal for Scotland Local Taxation Chamber (Rules of Procedure) Regulations 2022, SSI No 364

HB(CP)	The Housing Benefit and Council Tax Benefit (Consequential Provisions) Regulations 2006, SI No 217
HB(D&A)	The Housing Benefit and Council Tax Benefit (Decisions and Appeals) Regulations 2001, SI No 1002
HBP	The Housing Benefit (Persons who have attained the age for state pension credit) Regulations 2006, SI No 214
HB(ROO)	In England and Wales, The Rent Officers (Housing Benefit Functions) Order 1997, SI 1984; in Scotland, The Rent Officers (Housing Benefit Functions) (Scotland) Order 1997, SI 1995
HB(SO)	The Income Related Benefits (Subsidy to Authorities) Order 1998, SI No 562
HBW	The Housing Benefit Regulations 2006, SI No 213
IAA	The Immigration and Asylum Act 1999
LMI	The Loans for Mortgage Interest Regulations 2017, SI No 725
LGFA	The Local Government Finance Act 1992
OPR	The Social Security (Overpayments and Recovery) Regulations 2013, SI No 384
para	Paragraph number
PC	The State Pension Credit Regulations 2002, SI No 1792
reg	regulation
sch	Schedule
SI	Statutory Instrument
SPCA	The State Pension Credit Act 2002
SSA	The Social Security Act 1998
SSAA	The Social Security Administration Act 1992
SSA(Scot)	The Social Security (Scotland) Act 2018
SSCBA	The Social Security Contributions and Benefits Act 1992
SS(C&P)	The Social Security (Claims and Payments) Regulations 1987, SI No 1968
SS(D&A)	The Social Security and Child Support (Decisions and Appeals) Regulations 1999, SI No 991
SSFA	The Social Security Fraud Act 2001
SSI	Scottish Statutory Instrument
SS(Info WS)	The Social Security (Information-sharing in relation to Welfare Services etc.) Regulations 2012, SI No 1483
SS(LB)	The Social Security (Loss of Benefit) Regulations 2001, SI No 4022
SS(O&R)	The Social Security (Overpayments and Recovery) Regulations 2013, SI No 3844
SS(PAB)	The Social Security (Payments on Account of Benefit) Regulations 2013, SI No 383

SS(PAOR)	The Social Security (Payments on account, Overpayments and Recovery) Regulations 1988, SI No 664
TCEA	Tribunals, Courts and Enforcement Act 2007
TSA	Tribunals (Scotland) Act 2014
UC	The Universal Credit Regulations 2013, SI No 376
UC(C&P)	The Universal Credit, Personal Independence Payment, Jobseeker's Allowance and Employment and Support Allowance (Claims and Payments) Regulations 2013, SI No 380
UC(C&P)(Scot)	The Universal Credit (Claims and Payments) (Scotland) Regulations 2017, SSI No 227
UC(D&A)	The Universal Credit, Personal Independence Payment, Jobseeker's Allowance and Employment and Support Allowance (Decisions and Appeals) Regulations 2013, SI No 381
UC(ROO)	The Rent Officers (Universal Credit Functions) Order 2013, SI No 382
UCTP	Universal Credit (Transitional Provisions) Regulations 2014, SI No 1230
UTPR	The Tribunal Procedure (Upper Tribunal) Rules 2008, SI No 2698
VCCTR	The Valuation and Community Charge Tribunals Regulations 1989, No 439, as amended by SI 2009/2271
VTRE	The Valuation Tribunal for England (Council Tax and Rating Appeals) (Procedure) Regulations 2009, No 2269, as amended by SI 2013/465
VTRW	The Valuation Tribunal for Wales Regulations 2010, No 713, as amended by SI 2013/547
WRA	The Welfare Reform Act 2012
WRWA	The Welfare Reform and Work Act 2016

Key to footnotes: case law

The abbreviations used for case law referred to in the footnotes are given below.

AAC	Administrative Appeals Chamber
AACR	Administrative Appeals Chamber Reports, The Stationery Office (TSO)
AC	Appeal Cases, published by ICLR, London
All ER	All England Law Reports, published by Butterworths
BC	Borough Council
BMLR	Butterworths Medico-Legal Reports
CA	Court of Appeal for England and Wales
CC	City Council
Crim LR	Criminal Law Review, Sweet and Maxwell
CS	Court of Session, Scotland
CSIH	Court of Session, Inner House, Scotland
DC	District Council
ECJ	European Court of Justice
EHCR	European Court of Human Rights
EWCA Civ	England and Wales Court of Appeal (Civil Division)
EWHC Admin	England and Wales High Court (Administrative Court)
EWHC (QB)	England and Wales High Court (Queens Bench Division)
HBRB	Housing Benefit Review Board
HLR	Housing Law Reports, published by Sweet & Maxwell
ICLR	The Incorporated Council of Law Reporting for England and Wales
LB/LBC	London Borough/London Borough Council
MBC	Metropolitan Borough Council
NICom	Northern Ireland Commissioners Decisions
PNLR	Professional Negligence and Liability Reports, Sweet and Maxwell
PTSR	Public and Third Sector Law Reports, ICLR
QBD	High Court (England and Wales), Queens Bench Division
RA	Rating Appeals (Rating Publishers Ltd)
SLT	Scots Law Times, published by W. Green, Edinburgh
SSWP	Secretary of State for Work and Pensions
UKHL	UK House of Lords
UKSC	UK Supreme Court
UKUT	United Kingdom Upper Tribunal
WLR	Weekly Law Reports, published by ICLR
WLR(D)	Weekly Law Reports, daily case summaries, ICLR

Index

References in the index are to paragraph numbers (not page numbers), except that 'A' refers to appendices, 'T' refers to tables in the text and 'Ch' refers to a chapter.

C

D

E

F

M

N

O

P

R

V

W

Y